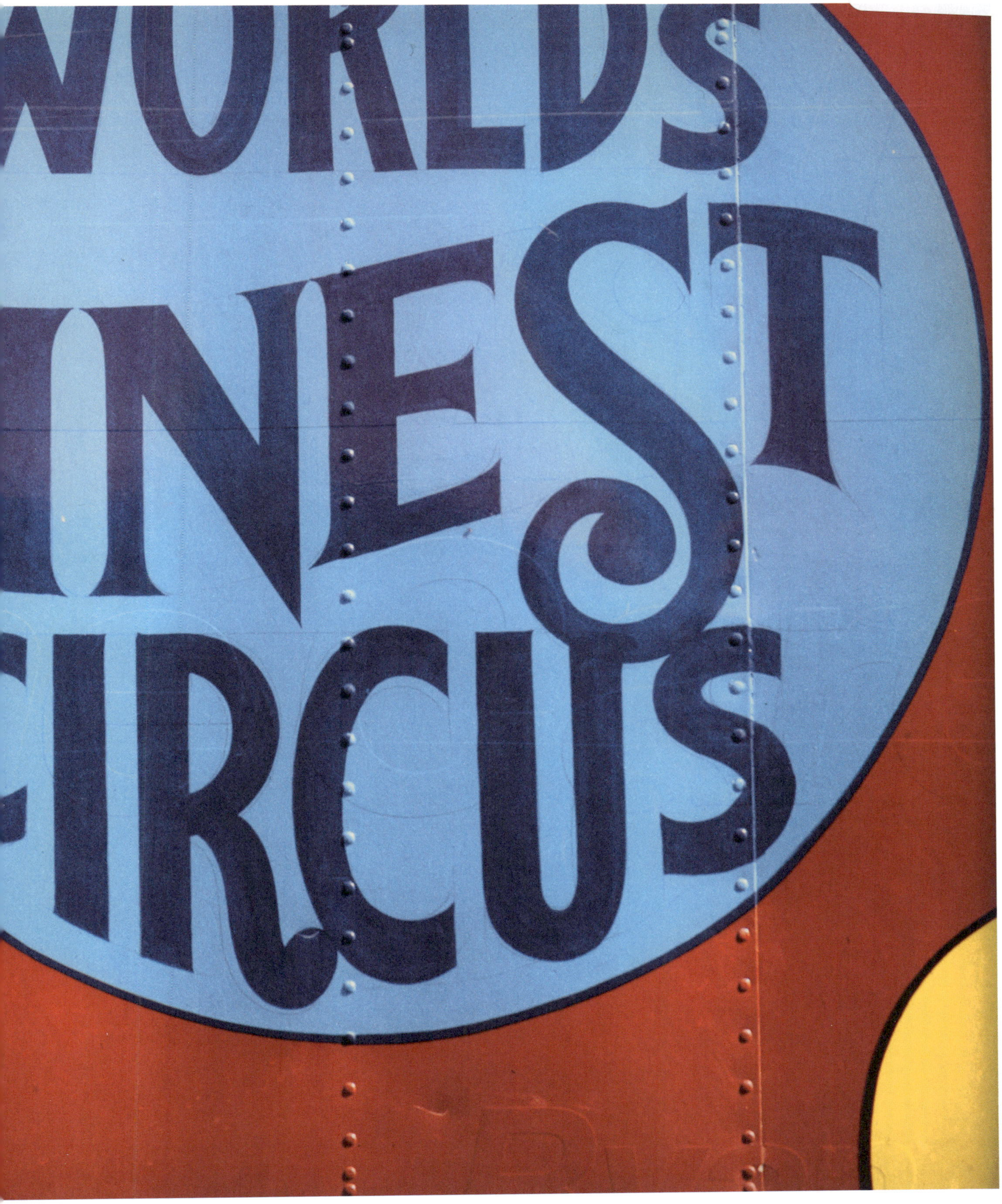
WORLDS
INEST
IRCUS

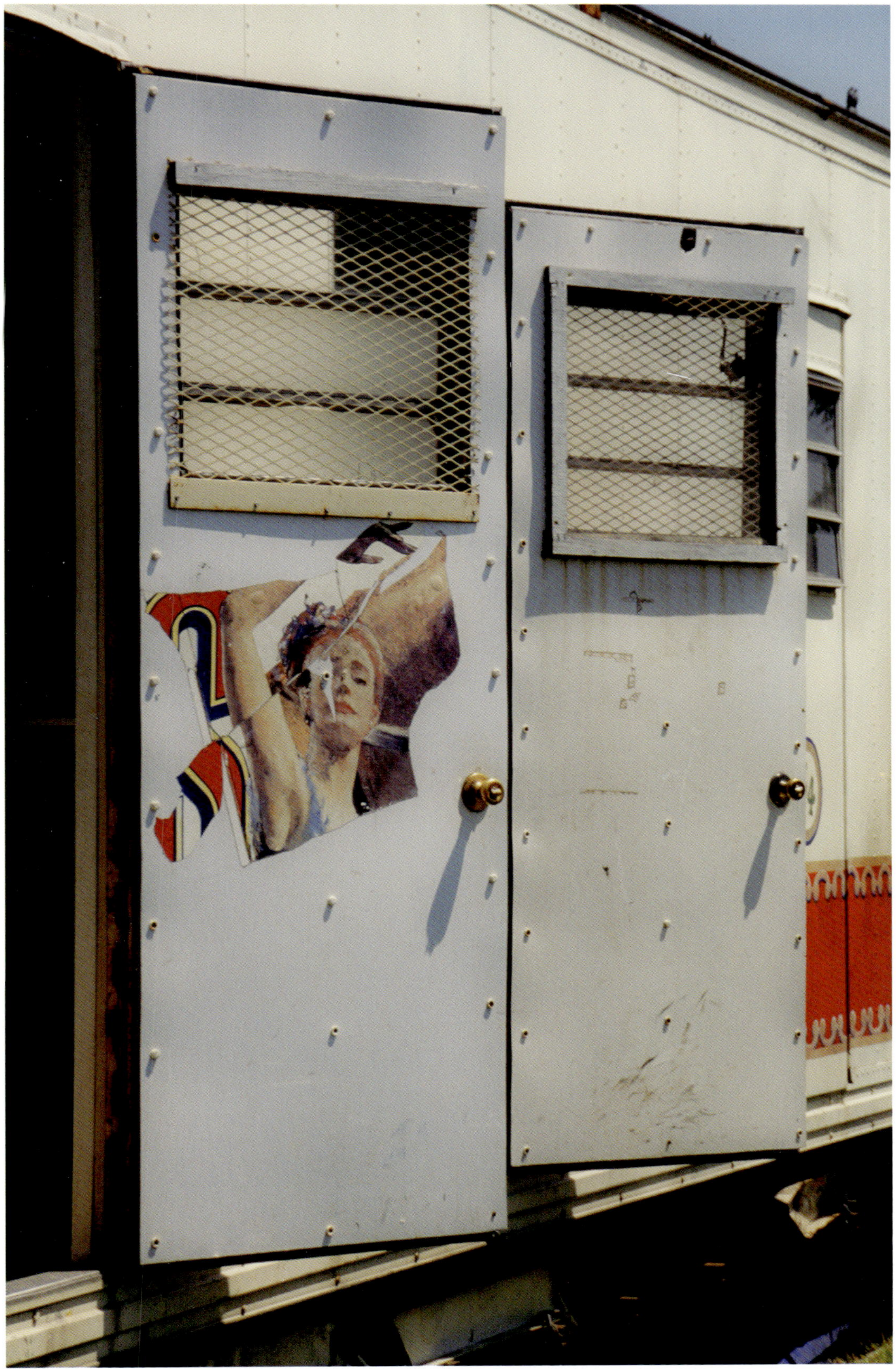

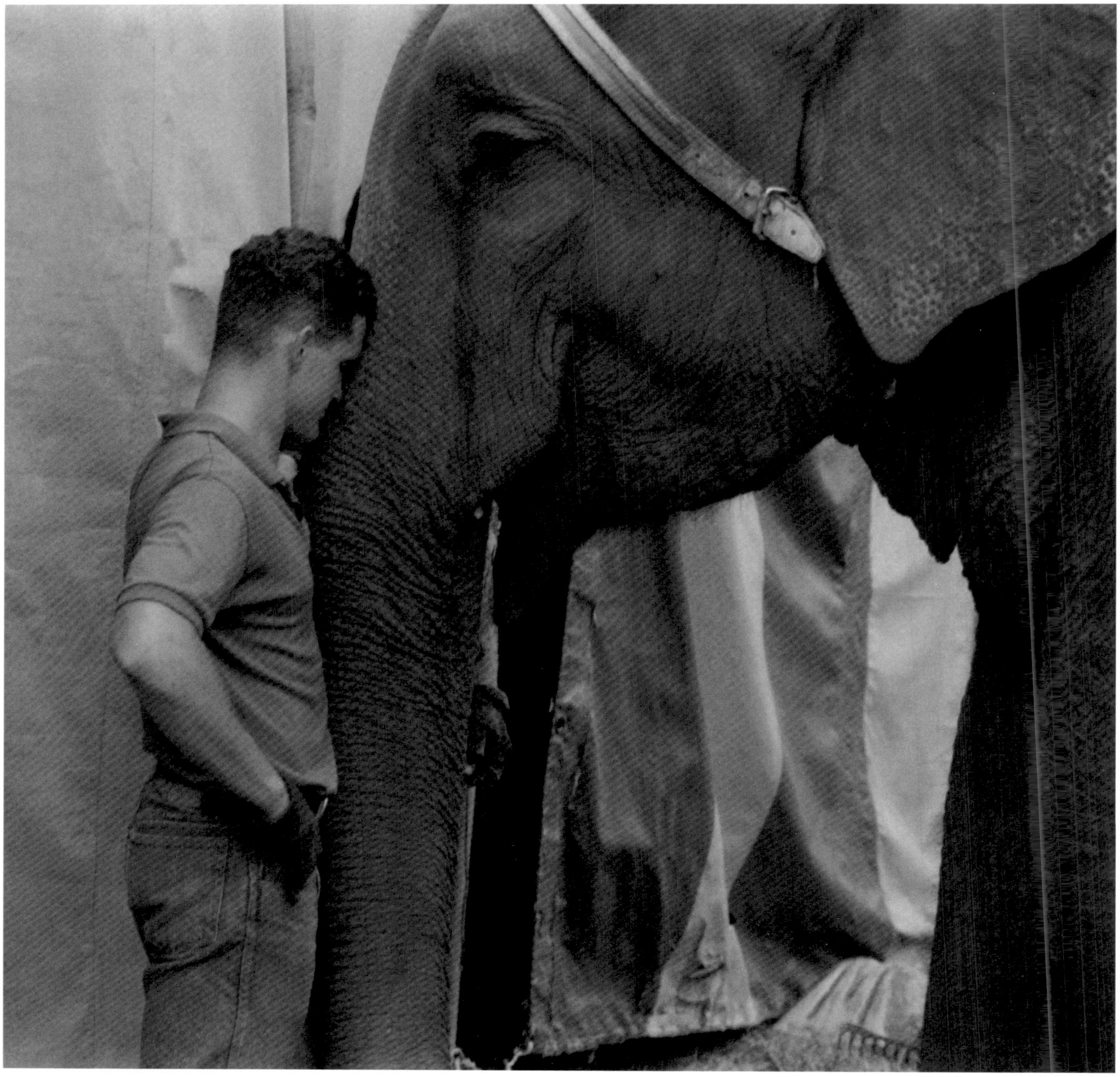

WHEN THE CIRCUS CAME TO TOWN!

An American Tradition in Photographs

★ PHOTOGRAPHS BY DAWN V. ROGALA ★

★ ★ ★ ★ ★

ESSAYS BY DAWN V. ROGALA, DAVID E. HABERSTICH,
AND SHANNON T. PERICH

Smithsonian
Scholarly Press

A Smithsonian Contribution to Knowledge

Published by
SMITHSONIAN INSTITUTION SCHOLARLY PRESS
P.O. Box 37012, MRC 957
Washington, D.C. 20013-7012
https://scholarlypress.si.edu

Library of Congress Cataloging-in-Publication Data
Names: Haberstich, David. | Perich, Shannon Thomas. | Rogala, Dawn V. Works. Selections. | National Museum of American History (U.S.). Archives Center.
Title: When the circus came to town! : an American tradition in photographs / photographs by Dawn V. Rogala ; essays by Dawn V. Rogala, David E. Haberstich, and Shannon T. Perich.
Other titles: When the circus came to town (2019)
Description: Washington, D.C. : Smithsonian Scholarly Press, 2019. | Includes bibliographical references and index.
Identifiers: LCCN 2019041942 | ISBN 9781944466336 (hardcover)
Subjects: LCSH: Circus—United States—Pictorial works. | Circus performers—Portraits. | Documentary photography—United States. | Rogala, Dawn V. | Circus—United States—Archival resources.
Classification: LCC GV1816 .W49 2019 | DDC 791.3022/2—dc23
LC record available at https://lccn.loc.gov/2019041942

Design and composition by Julie Allred, BW&A Books, Inc.
Printed in Canada

♾ The paper used in this publication meets the minimum requirements of the American National Standard for Permanence of Paper for Printed Library Materials Z39.48–1992.

Uncaptioned images:
front cover: detail from plate 174, Vidbel's Olde Tyme Circus, 1993
back cover: plate 163, Carson & Barnes Circus, 1995
front endsheet: Kelly Miller Circus, 1995
page i: plate 70, Big Apple Circus, 1995
page ii: detail from plate 59, Franzen Brothers Circus, 1994
back endsheet: Franzen Brothers Circus, 1996

Contents

Director's Note

At the Smithsonian Institution's National Museum of American History, we care for the many stories that make up the richness and complexity of American history. The museum is home to more than 1.8 million objects and more than three shelf-miles of archival collections. Our artifacts form a fascinating mosaic of American life and comprise the greatest single collection of American history in the world. We are honored to preserve and share this extraordinary national collection.

Scores of staff across many specialist teams care for our collections, and the stories they tell can reach across the museum, and beyond. Collecting, and the stewardship of collections, is an effort that crosses time. When the photographer Dawn Rogala first captured these images, she did not know that she was witness to a singular moment in American history, a time when the circus was still a thriving part of our cultural landscape. We are grateful to Dawn for choosing the museum as the repository of her archive and for telling her own story in the pages of this book. I hope that you are as entranced as I am by the fleeting world of the circus, presented as it traveled across the American landscape.

The mission of the National Museum of American History is to help people understand the past, make sense of the present, and shape a more informed future. As part of this calling, scholars across the museum work together to interpret our collections and the stories they tell. This book showcases two of our curators specializing in the history of photography, David Haberstich and Shannon Perich, who bring different but complementary perspectives to Rogala's circus images. Rooted in a deep respect for history balanced with modern inquiry and reevaluation, scholarship brings new life to our collections and their stories. In this book, we are pleased to present that important dialogue between collections and scholarship, and we are grateful to the Smithsonian Institution Scholarly Press for the support and efforts that made this publication a reality.

I hope that when you come to the museum, you will find a story that resonates with you, and that you will see yourself and your communities reflected in the exhibitions, collections, and programs in this incredible nation's history museum. As you watch the circus march by on these pages, we hope you feel inspired to photograph the world around you, and find new ways to connect past and future.

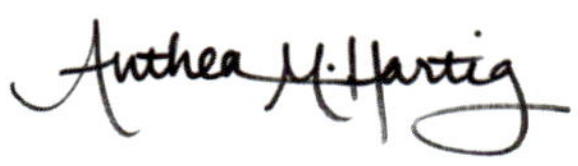

Anthea M. Hartig, Ph.D.
Elizabeth MacMillan Director
National Museum of American History

Introduction

From row upon row of workers and animals setting up a tent the size of a football field to the quiet of day-to-day life behind the pretty fence to the jostling crowds of the colorful preshow midway, the more than ten thousand images of the Dawn V. Rogala Circus Photographs and Papers Collection at the National Museum of American History (NMAH) bring us inside the fascinating world of the traveling circus.

The livelihoods, skills, and history of the circus are an important part of American culture. If you search the Smithsonian Institution's collections, references to the circus appear in paintings, sculpture, postage stamps, textile patterns, Little Golden Books for children, broadside posters and advertising, lapel pins, and even a birdcage shaped like a circus wagon. If you look in the finding aids that inventory and describe Smithsonian collections and archives, the term *circus* will lead you to a former astronaut who was a unicyclist in a circus, stories of Native Americans encountering African animals, and accounts of early attempts to mechanize the raising of circus tents.

Within this menagerie of cultural output that documents the circus, circus life, and the inspiration it provides are the photographic and material records of Dawn Rogala, now part of the NMAH. The Rogala Collection is the largest circus collection at the Smithsonian Institution, a documentary record in images, interviews, and ephemera that follows the photographer's travels with eleven tented shows as they crisscrossed the United States. Rogala left her job, purchased an RV, and spent most of the 1990s documenting this rapidly vanishing part of our national landscape. Over the course of this multiyear, self-directed project, Rogala amassed thousands of photographic negatives and prints; interviews and behind-the-scenes commentary from members of the circus community; and letters, documents, and other printed materials related to circus life. All of these materials, including hundreds of photographic contact sheets and proof prints, are now in the NMAH Archives Center, and a selected print portfolio of Rogala's images can be found in the museum's Photographic History Collection. This book presents a broad sampling from the Rogala Collection, with more than two hundred color and black-and-white images interspersed with interview excerpts that bring the American circus to life. Essays by NMAH photography curators David Haberstich (Archives Center) and Shannon Perich (Photographic History Collection) help place the images in the context of photography as history, as archive, and as art, while an essay by Rogala and a finding aid for the collection materials outline the scope of the project and the resulting documentary collection. A special note from National Museum of American History Director Anthea Hartig introduces this photographic journey into a rapidly vanishing part of American culture.

The photographs in this book focus on the people who create the magic of the circus—from midway artists to roustabouts, from performers and their families to the audiences who watch them each night. Rogala's work presents the highs and lows of circus life with a powerful combination of documentary pragmatism and empathy that conveys day-to-day details with a sense of wonder. Her rich black-and-white images follow light and shadow (and dust) from set up to rehearsal to performance, with color photography underscoring the drama of a red tent against a clear blue sky or the flash of sequins under the spotlight.

In her essay "Running Away with the Circus: A Photographer's Story," Rogala recalls how she was introduced to the world of the circus, how the project came about, and the people, adventures, and lessons learned from life in, around, and under the tent. Almost twenty years later, when Rogala was working as a paintings conservator at the Smithsonian's Museum Conservation Institute, the Smithsonian Institution featured Circus Arts as part of its 2017 Folklife Festival. The festival explored the role of circus in America and led to the donation of the Rogala Collection to the National Museum of American History. In this recollection of her experience as a young photographer, Rogala discusses learning her craft while living day-to-day in this remarkable world, and learning about human nature while viewing the world around her through the lens of the circus.

In "Step Right Up: The History of Work Photography and Circus Photographs in Context," David Haberstich—Curator of Photography at the NMAH's Archives Center—reviews the history of documentary photography with an emphasis on depictions of people and their work. Haberstich discusses such influential figures as Lewis Hine and his biting depiction of the horrors of child labor, and brings attention to important work by anonymous photographers who surveyed the lifestyles and labor of traveling societies and immigrant groups. Photographs in Archives Center collections are featured, from nineteenth-century stereographs of workers around the world—packaged in "armchair travel" sets—to portraits of twentieth- and twenty-first-century American labor by photographers including Eadweard Muybridge, Katherine Joseph, and Addison N. Scurlock. The essay discusses Rogala's circus photographs and how her images of circus workers, whether performers or manual laborers, fit into that history.

In the essay "Ladies and Gentlemen: Historical Parallels in Circus and Photography," Shannon Perich—Curator of the Photographic History Collection at the NMAH—explores the changing roles and relationships between photography and the circus. Striking examples of the public's ongoing fascination with circus and photography can be found throughout the NMAH's Photographic History Collection, as rapid advances in technology captured more than a century of traveling shows across the American landscape. This essay places Rogala's documentary photographs among a long history of circus photography, and explores the changing roles and relationships between photography and the American circus, which both matured in a growing industrialized economy that fostered new forms of entertainment and created a national culture built on shared experiences. Each section of the essay highlights photographic technologies from different periods as they relate to our exploration of American culture and identity.

This book closes with an Archives Center finding aid to the Rogala Collection, a listing of materials befitting a topic as rich and lively as circus life, including letters, notes, travel schedules, circus yearbooks, route arrows, and oral histories. A brief explanation of how to use a finding aid, both in the book and in the searchable finding aid online, is provided.

In its long history, the circus has touched the lives of millions, spurring imaginations, inspiring wonder, and giving livelihood to those willing to brave the intensity of itinerant life. Dynamism and a spirit of collaboration are at the heart of circus life, animate Rogala's archive, and are central to scholarship at the Smithsonian. The Smithsonian Institution comprises many museums, research centers, and collections; collaboration and scholarship helps us all to better understand our artifacts and archival collections. The authors hope that others will be inspired to study the Smithsonian's collections and to explore the Rogala Collection in their own studies of American culture.

David E. Haberstich
Curator of Photography, Archives Center
National Museum of American History

Shannon T. Perich
Curator, Photographic History Collection
National Museum of American History

Dawn V. Rogala
Conservator and Program Manager
Museum Conservation Institute

Why do people join? Sometimes it's the romance. . . . They see the excitement and the beauty of the product, and don't realize that behind it is an enormous amount of focus and work, which isn't romantic at all. It's only romantic in the other guy's eyes.

—Paul Binder, co-founder and artistic director, Big Apple Circus (1995)

I was born in the business. My dad was working in the Blackpool Tower circus. He came down to see me between shows. . . . So the first time I ever saw my dad, he was in makeup.

—Graham Polakovs, performer, Walker Bros. Circus (1995)

All people have to do is take the initiative, show that they can. Anybody on this lot, *anybody*, if they follow the right path and have the right focus, can get to be a boss.

—David LeBlanc, director of operations and tent boss, Big Apple Circus (1995)

PHOTOGRAPHS FROM THE DAWN V. ROGALA CIRCUS PHOTOGRAPHS AND PAPERS

If someone had said to me ten years ago: "Hey Reggie, someday you'll be in a ring with three to four elephants, with a little old stick in your hand, cueing them to do tricks," I would have told them to go jump off a bridge.

—Reginald "Reggie" Lindsey, Sr., exotic animal handler, Carson & Barnes Circus (1995)

The tent is really the star, and it will be as long as there are hardy, foolish people like we are, I guess, that are willing to put up with the hardships.

—Barbara Byrd, director and co-owner, Carson & Barnes Circus (1995)

Before there was television, there was circus. Before there was radio, there was circus. Before there were most theaters and zoos, there was circus. Before there was *anything*, there was circus.

—Al Calienes, performing company member, Big Apple Circus (1995)

★ ★ ★ ★ ★ ★ ★ ★ ★ ★

Personalities, characters, beliefs, moral scruples . . . all the things that make people people—all the people I thought I'd seen out there in the world—I've had a better look at them at the circus. They show up sooner or later. They do.

—Reginald "Reggie" Lindsey, Sr., exotic animal handler, Carson & Barnes Circus (1995)

★ ★ ★ ★ ★ ★ ★ ★ ★ ★

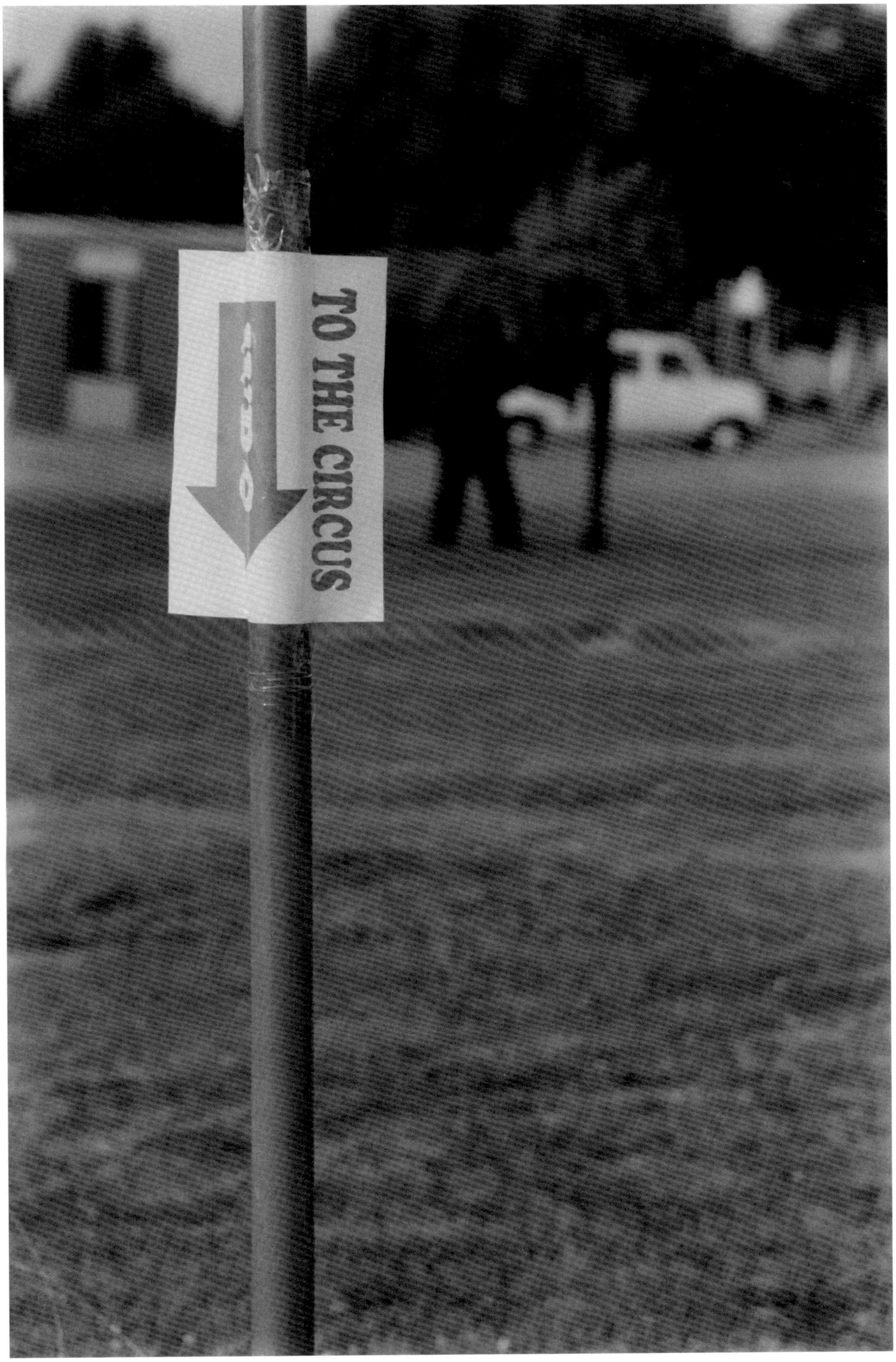

PLATE 1

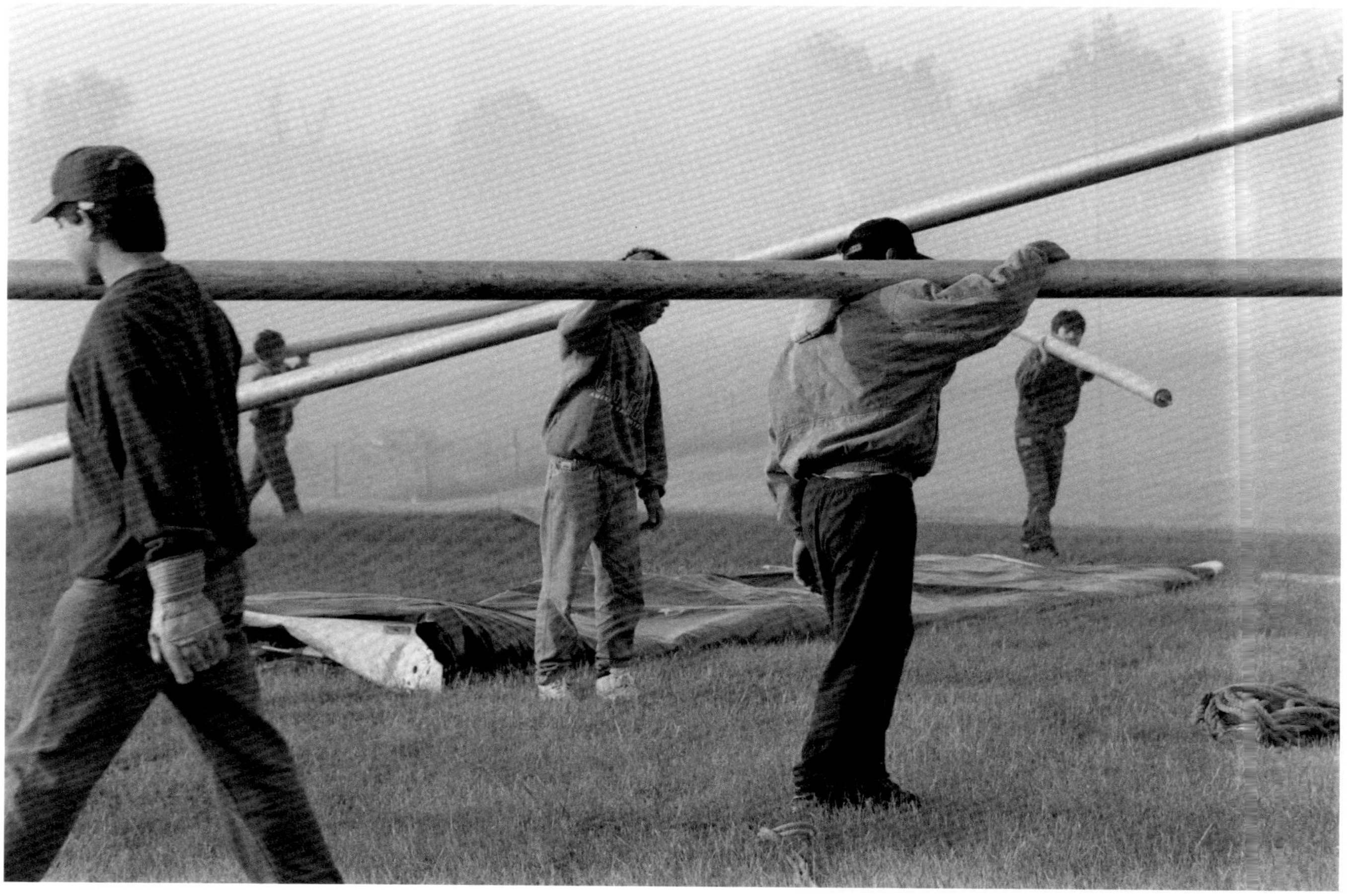

PLATE 2

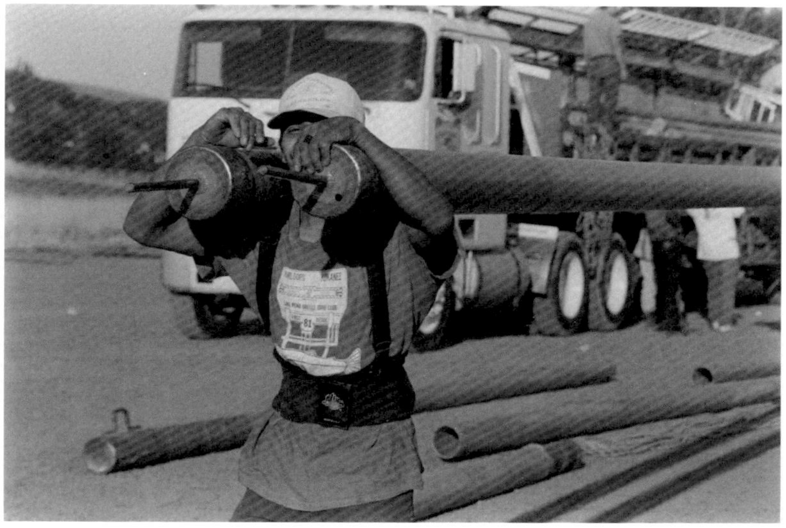

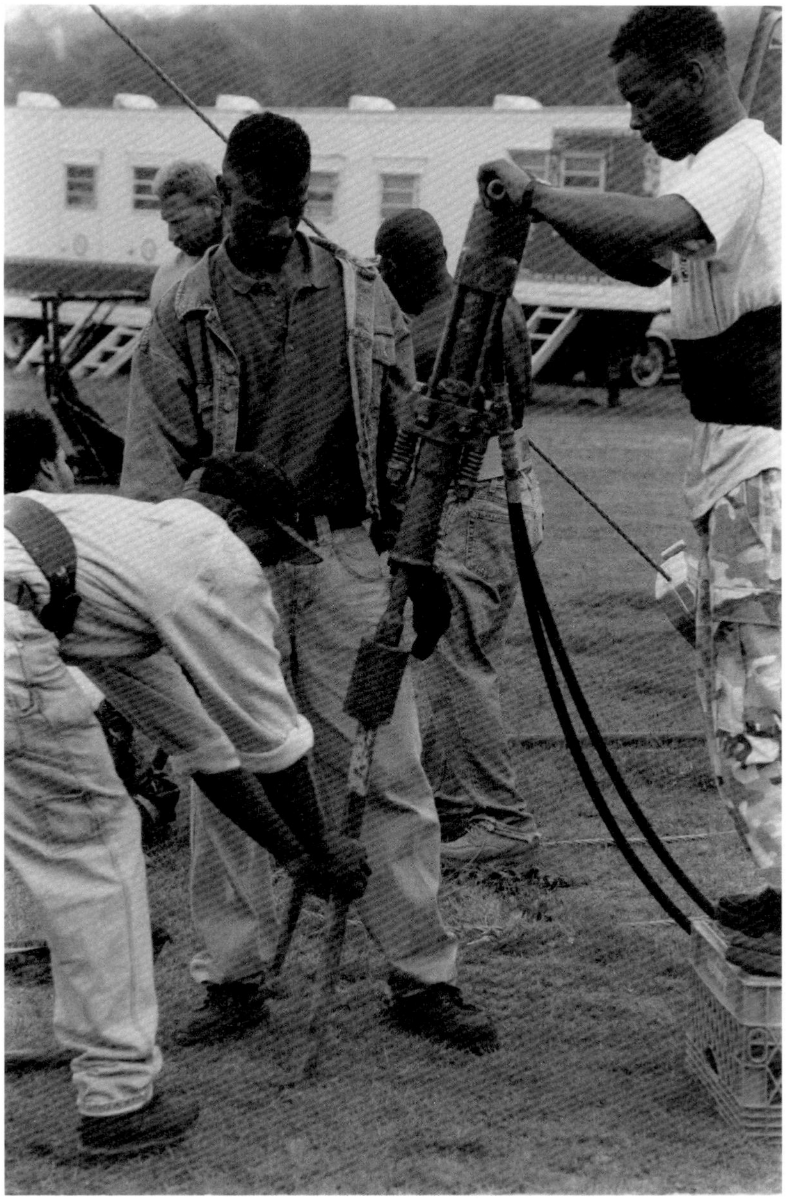

PLATES 3 & 4

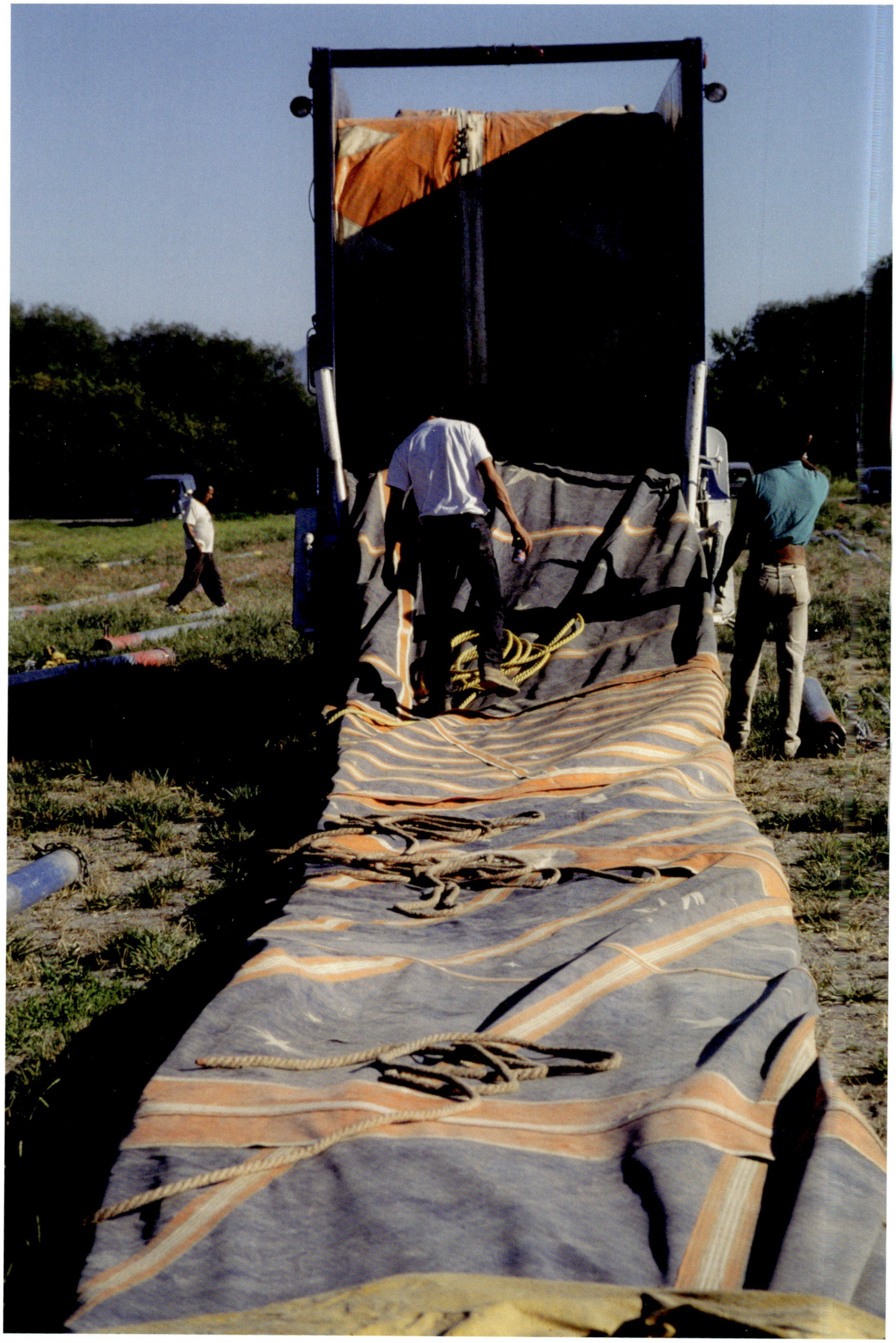

PLATE 5

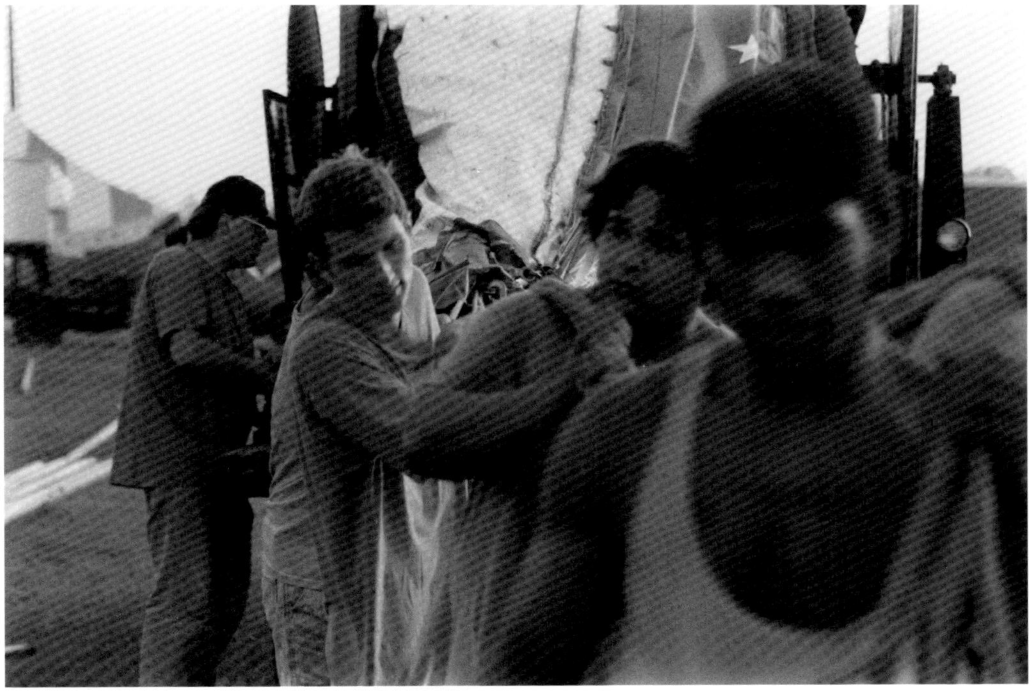

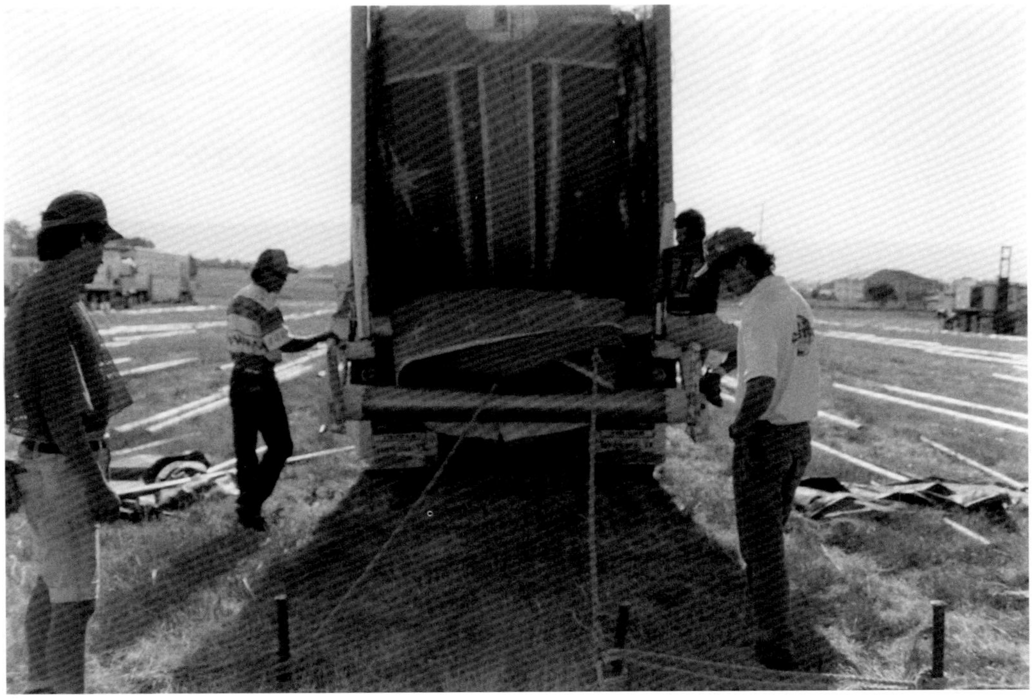

PLATES 6 & 7

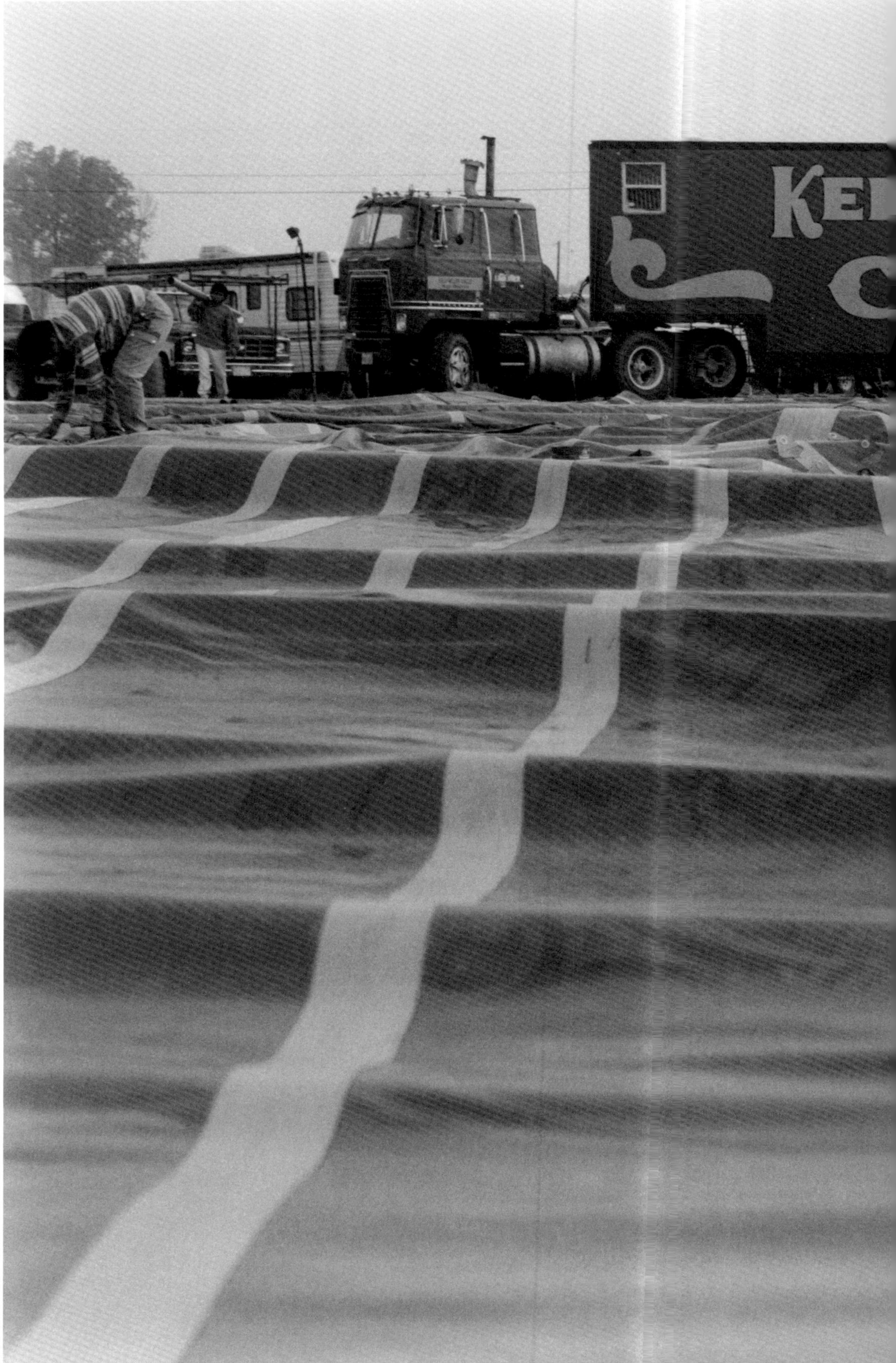

PLATE 8

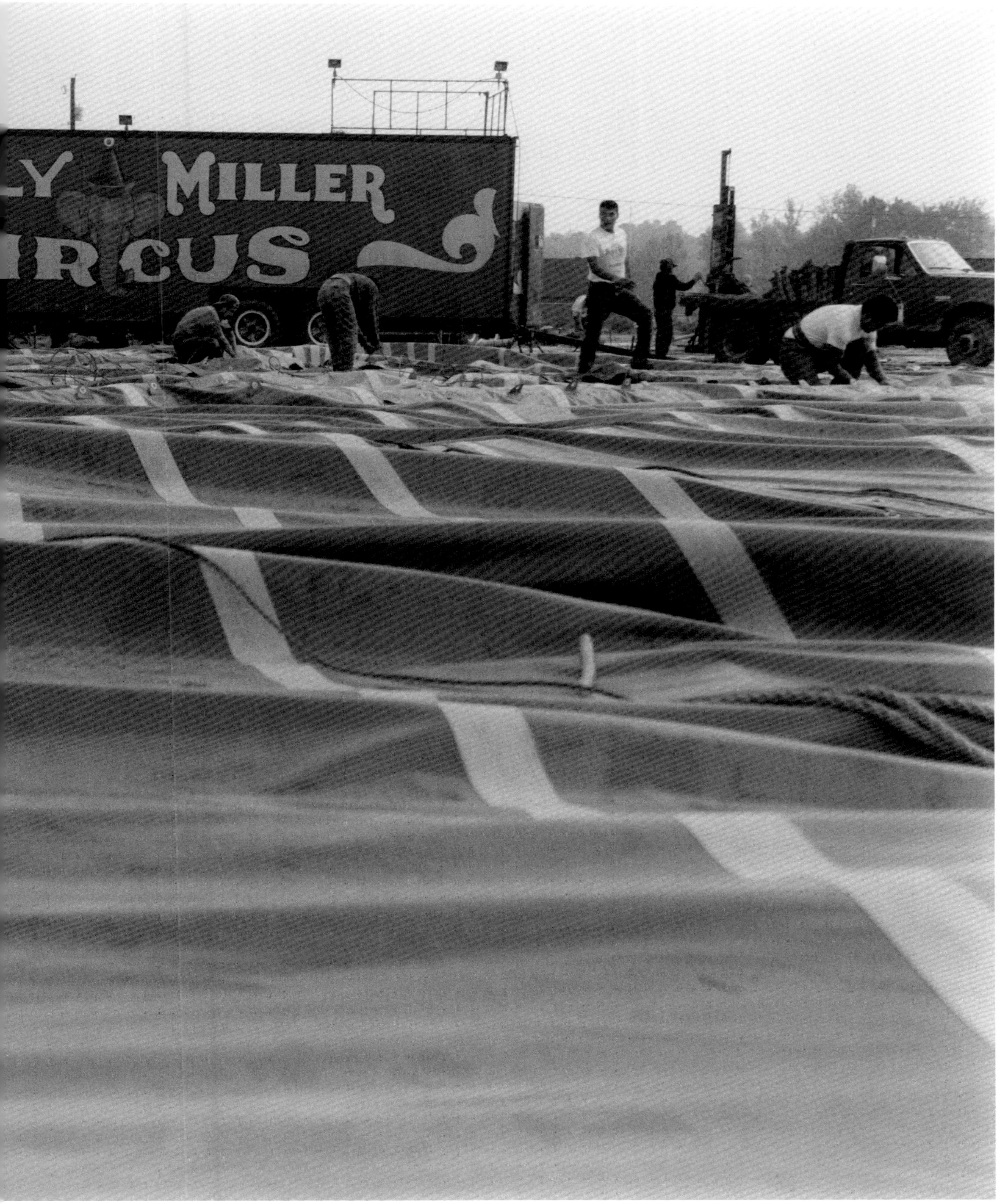
LY MILLER
IRCUS

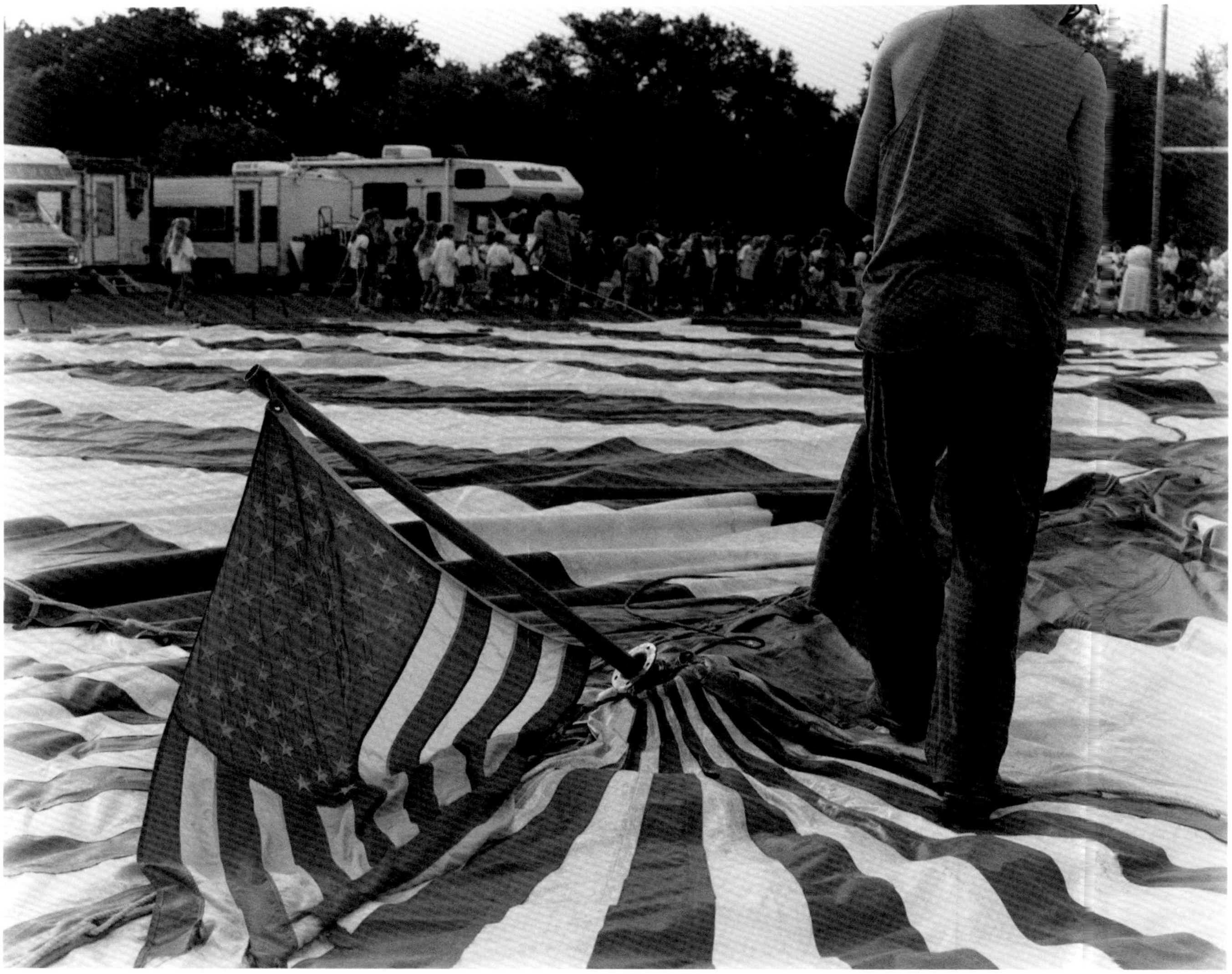

PLATE 9

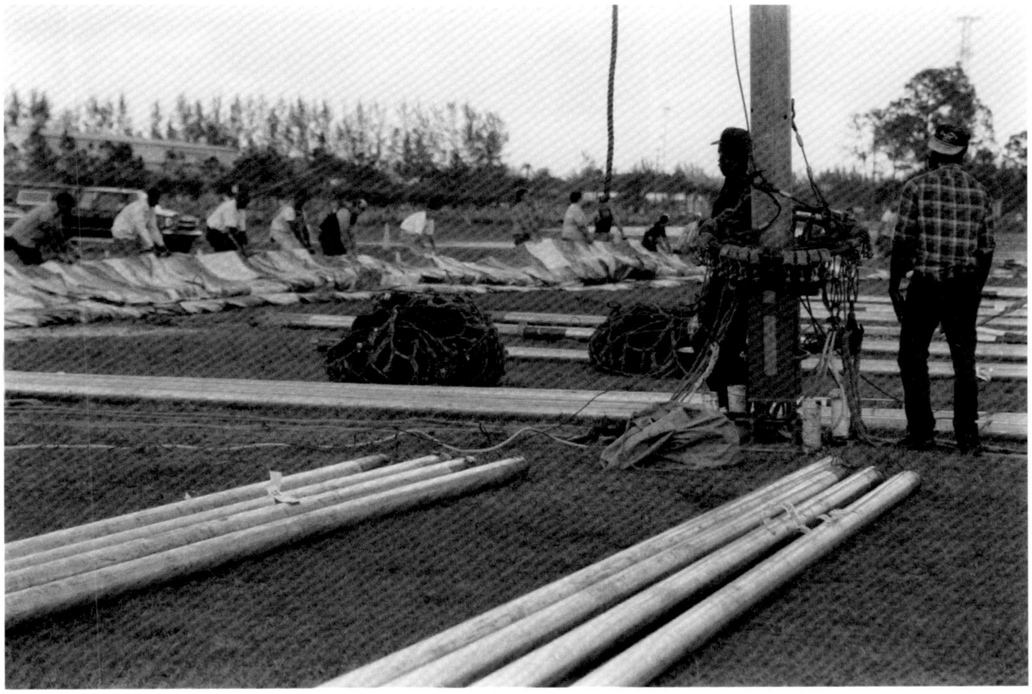

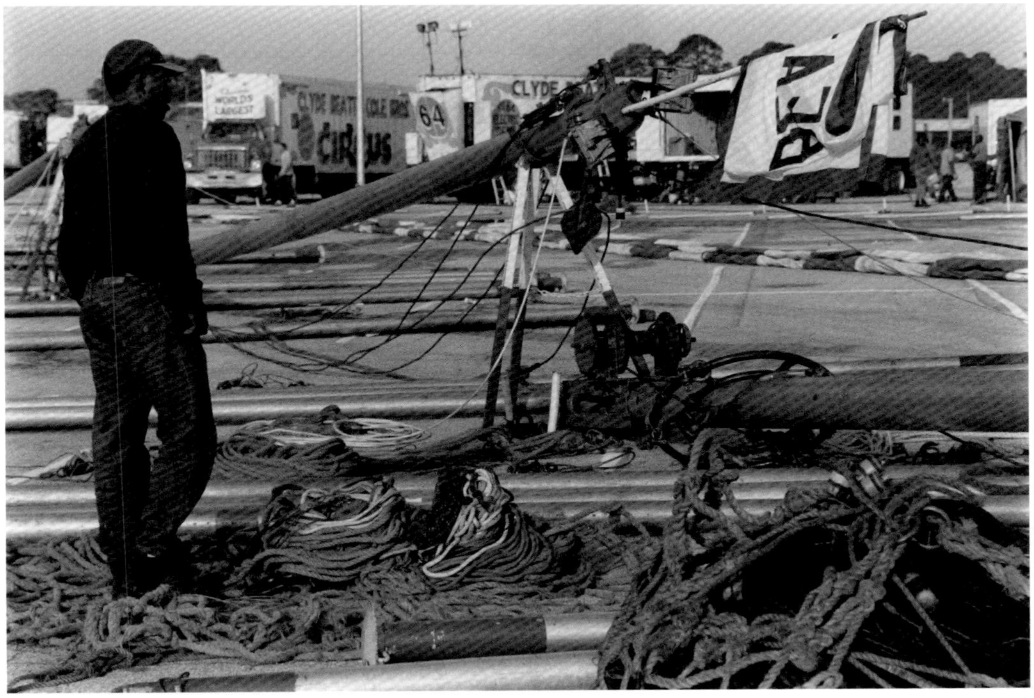

PLATES 10 & 11

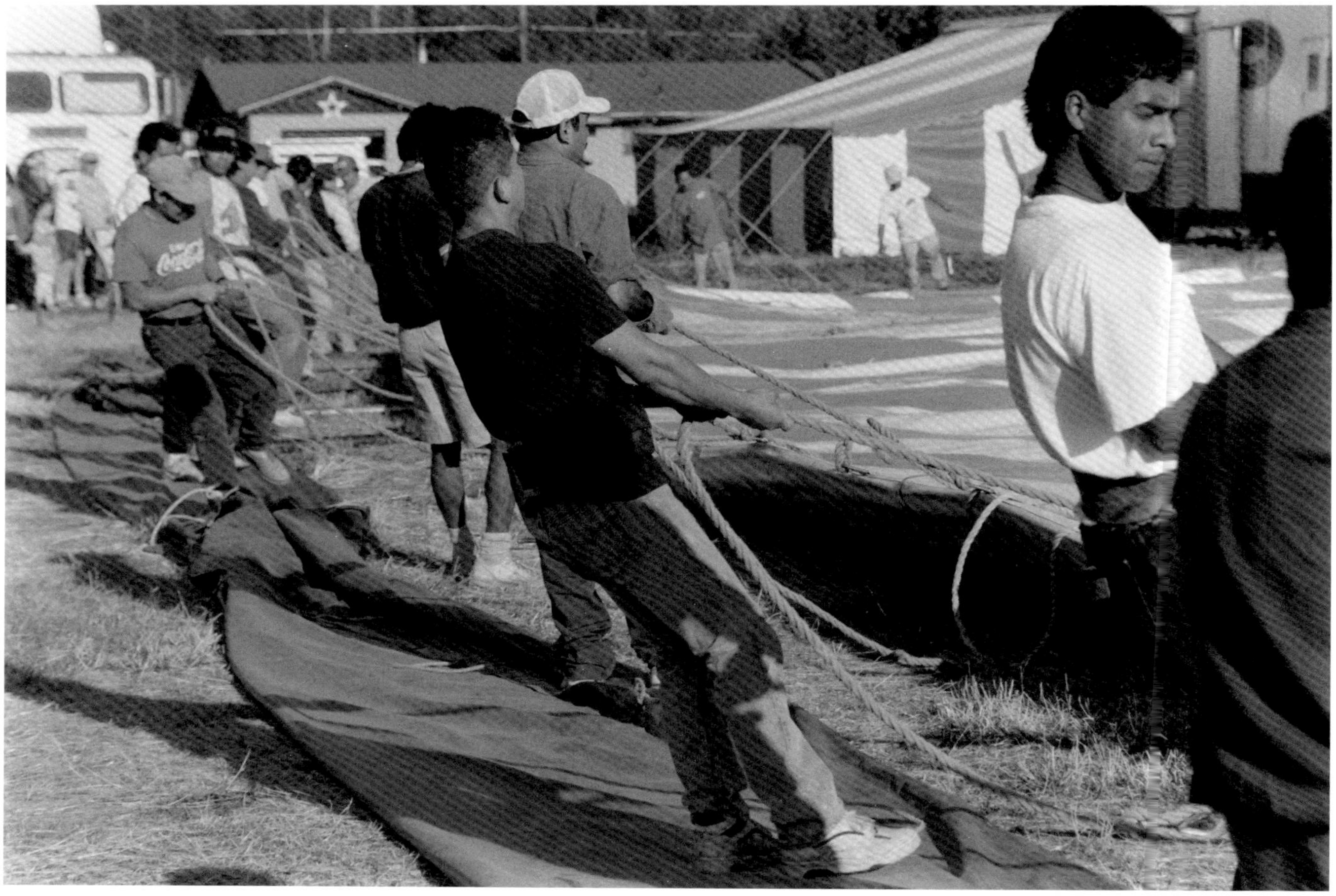

PLATE 12

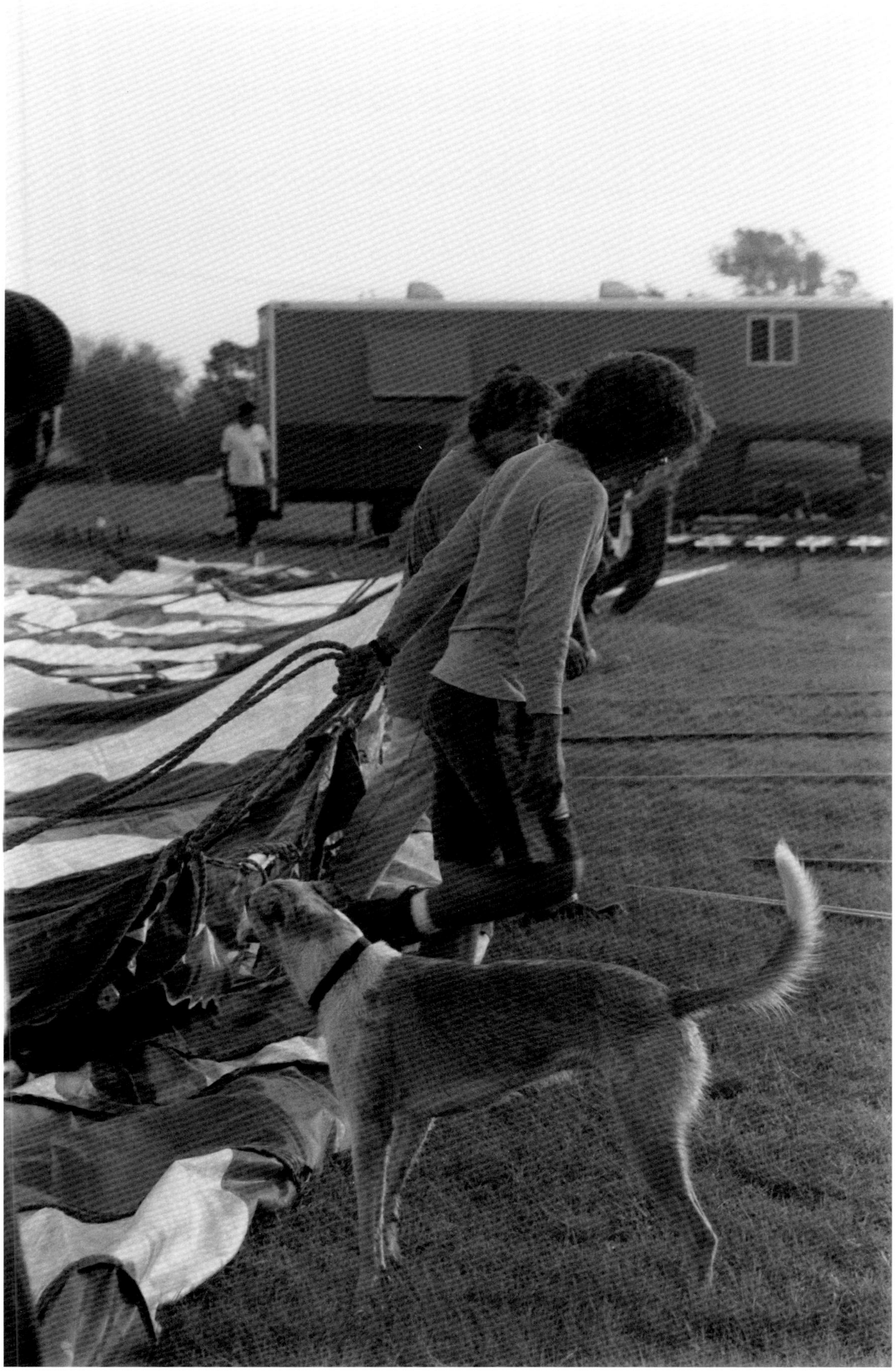

PLATE 13

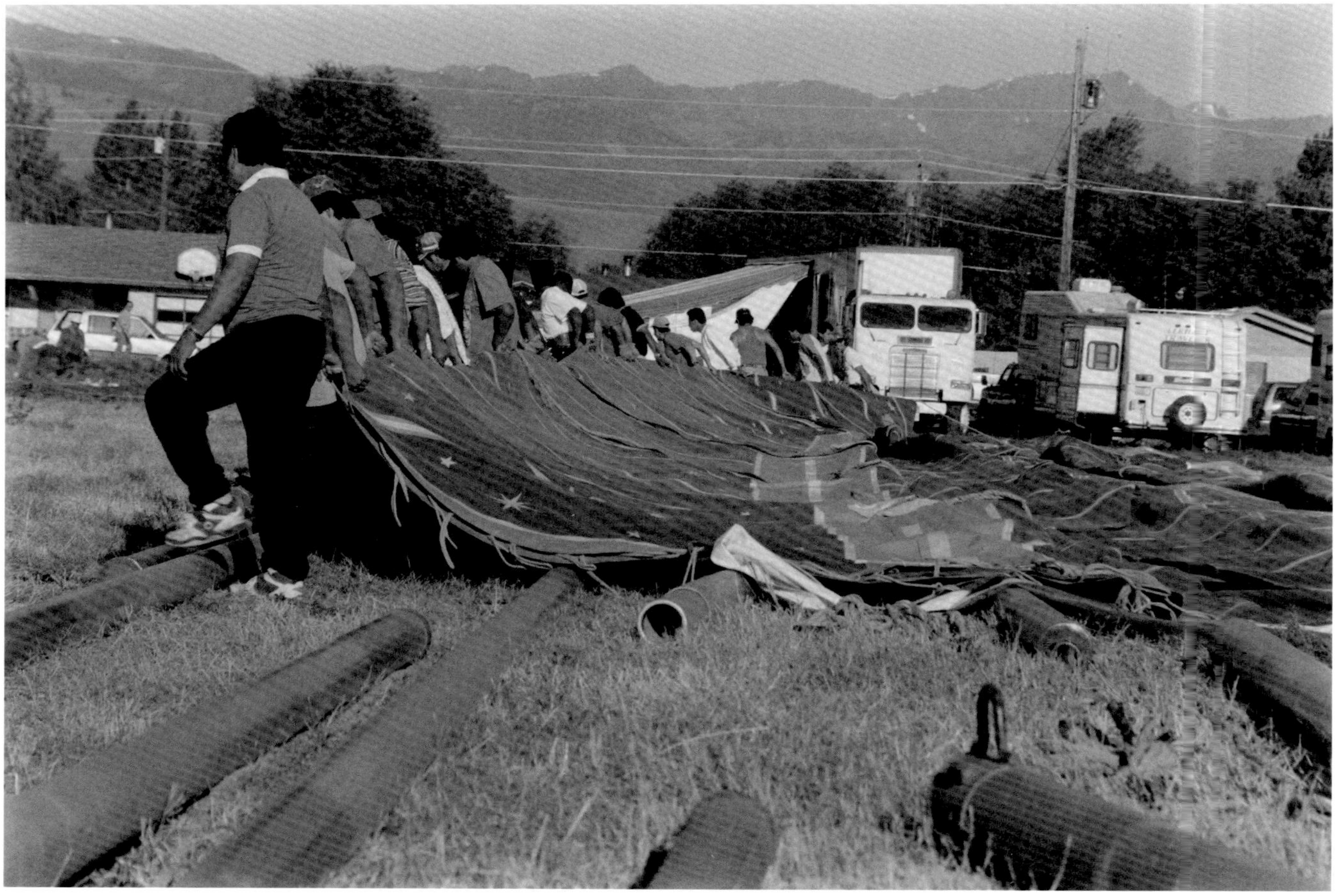

PLATE 14

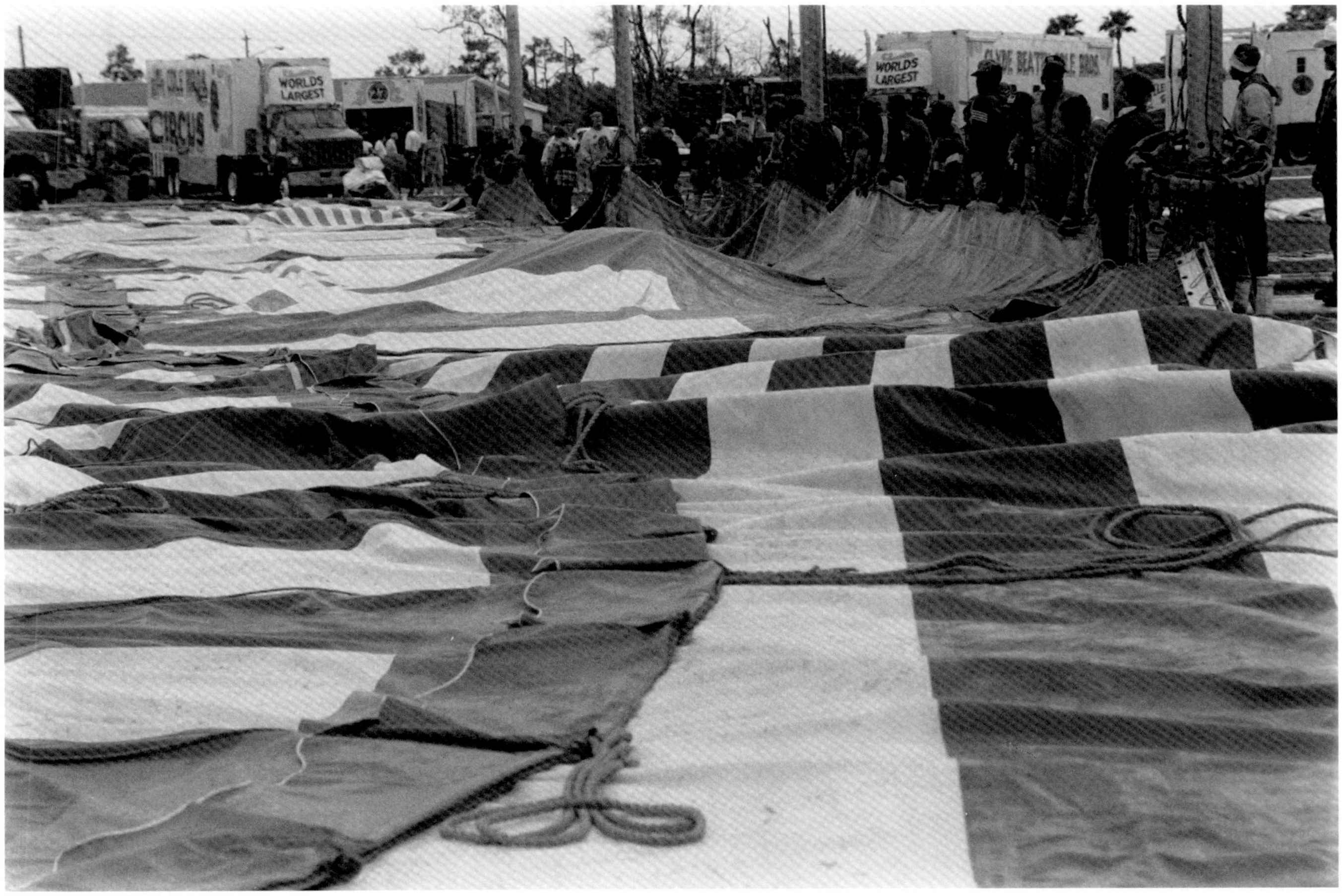

PLATE 15

★ ★ ★ ★ ★ ★ ★ ★ ★ ★

When I'm feeling bad, I go into the tent, and . . . it will make me feel at least a little bit better. I've pretty much decided that the tent is my personal deity, and that she is perfect.

—J. R. Lara, house crew, Big Apple Circus (1995)

★ ★ ★ ★ ★ ★ ★ ★ ★ ★

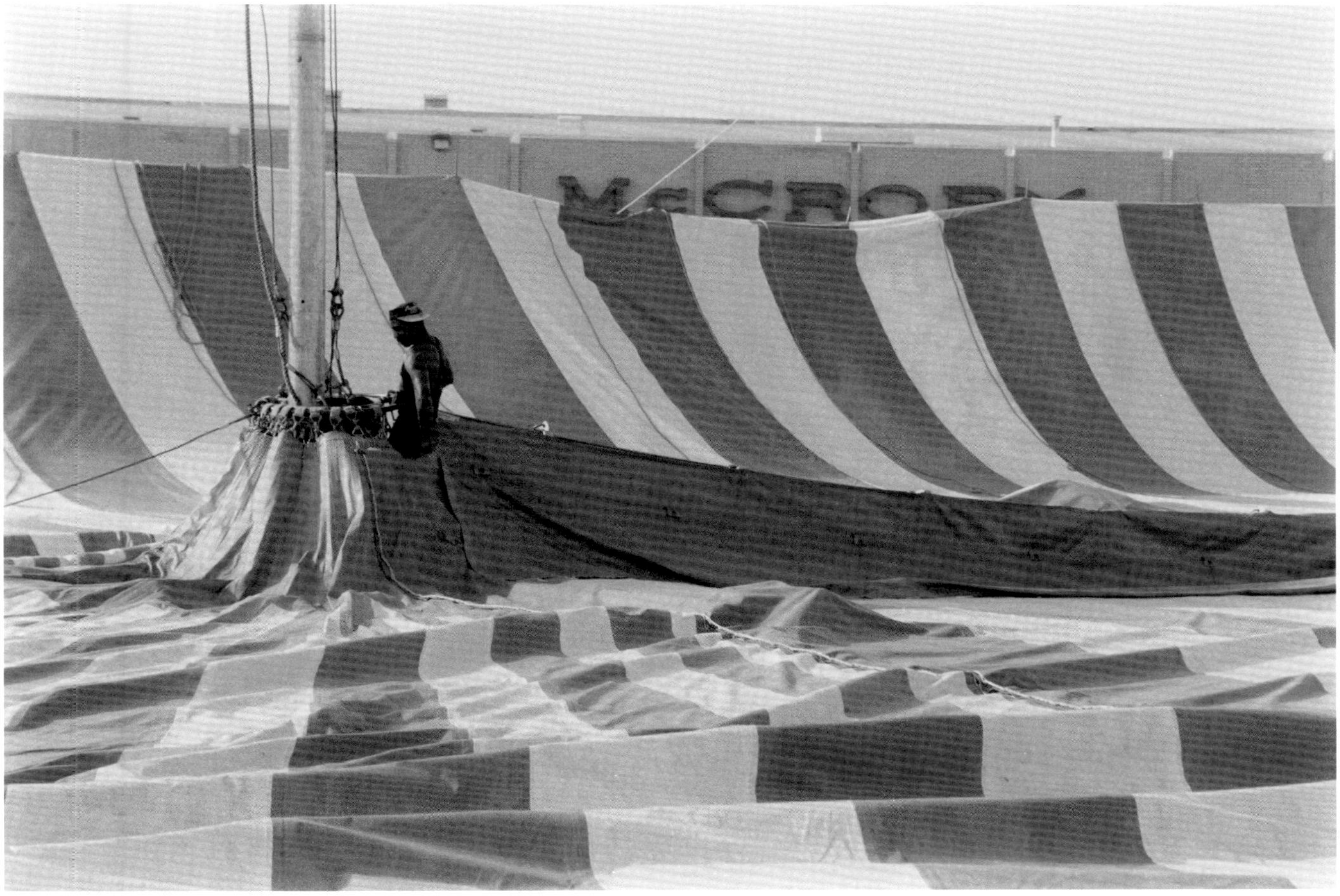

PLATE 16

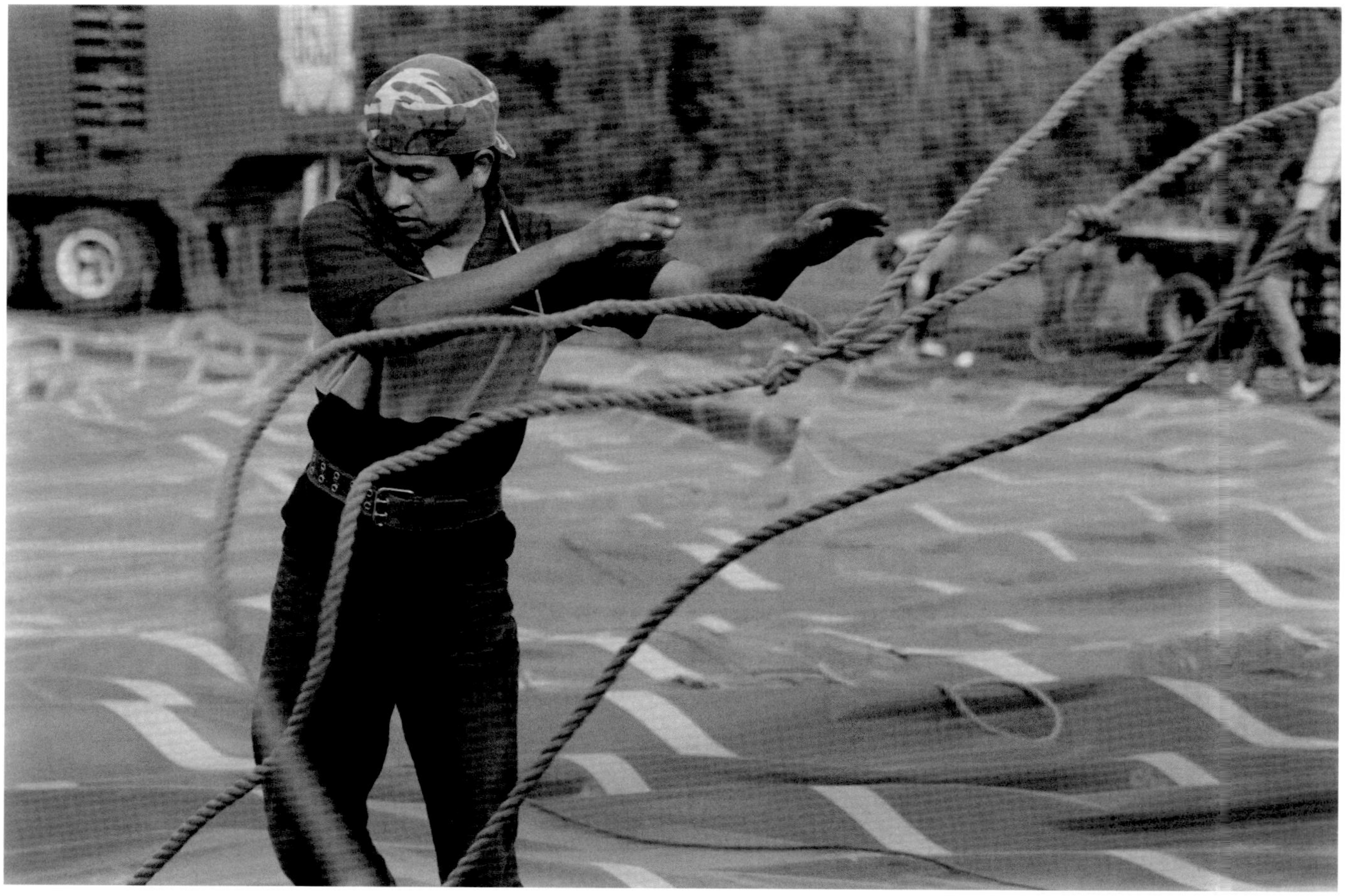

PLATE 17

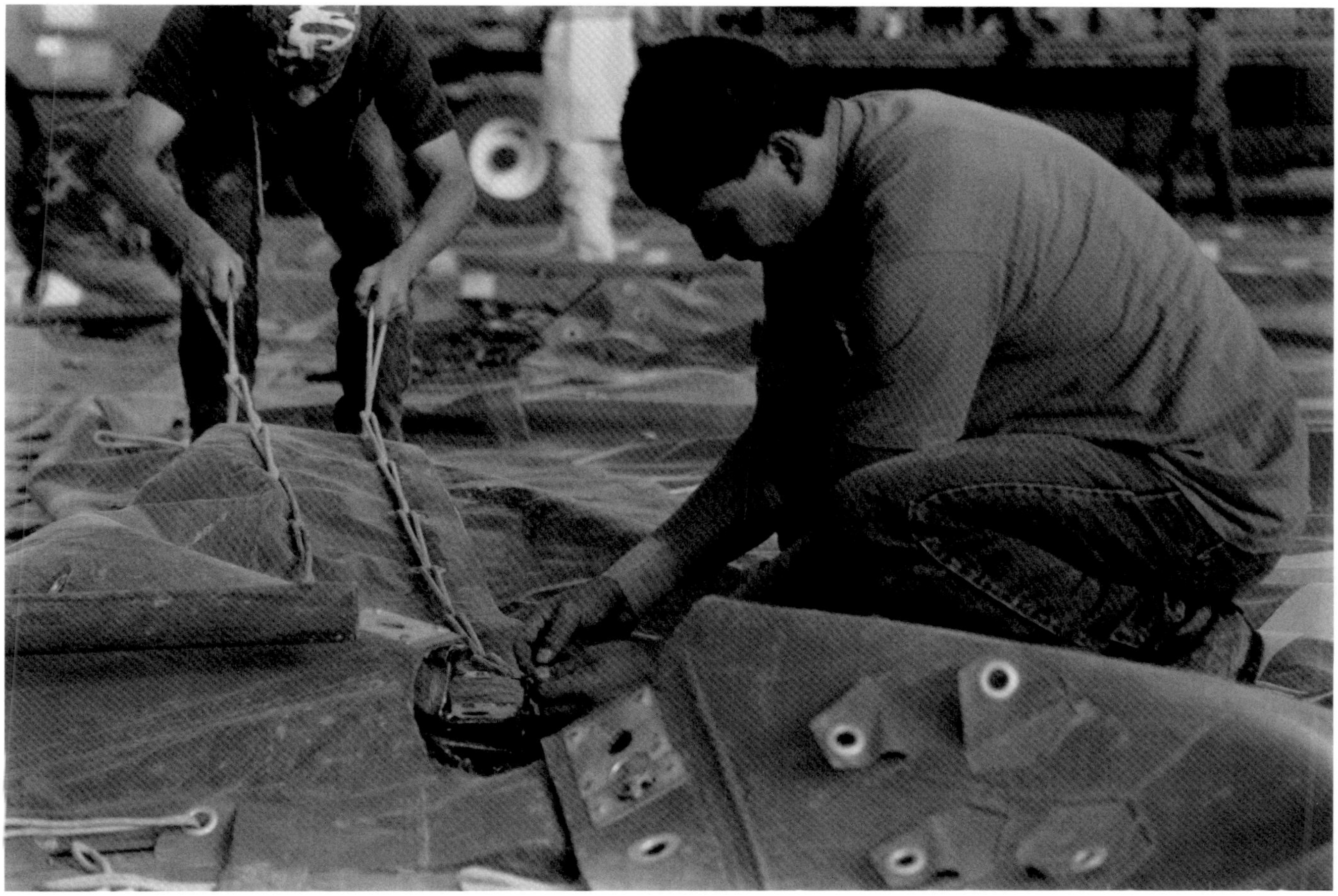

PLATE 18

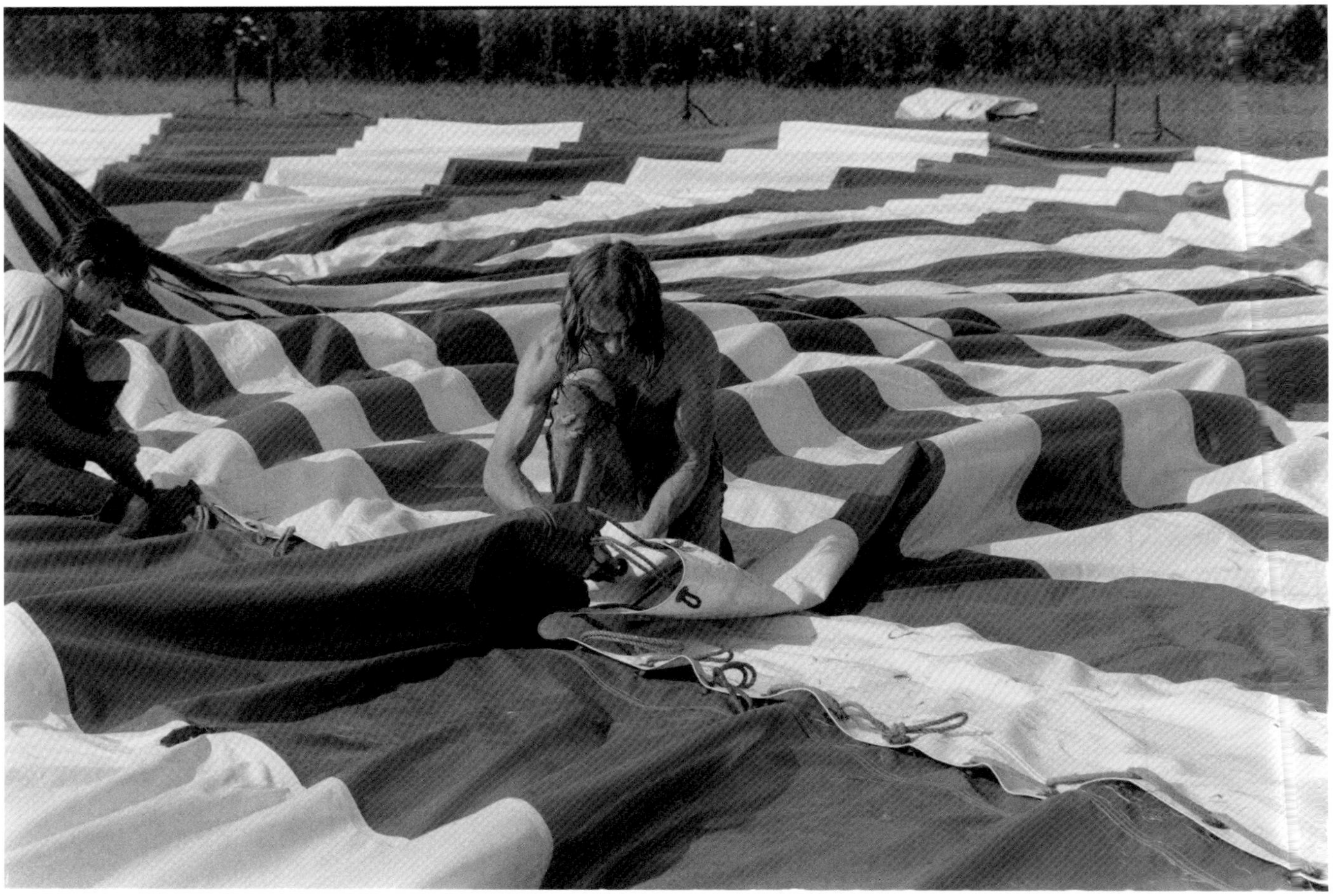

PLATE 19

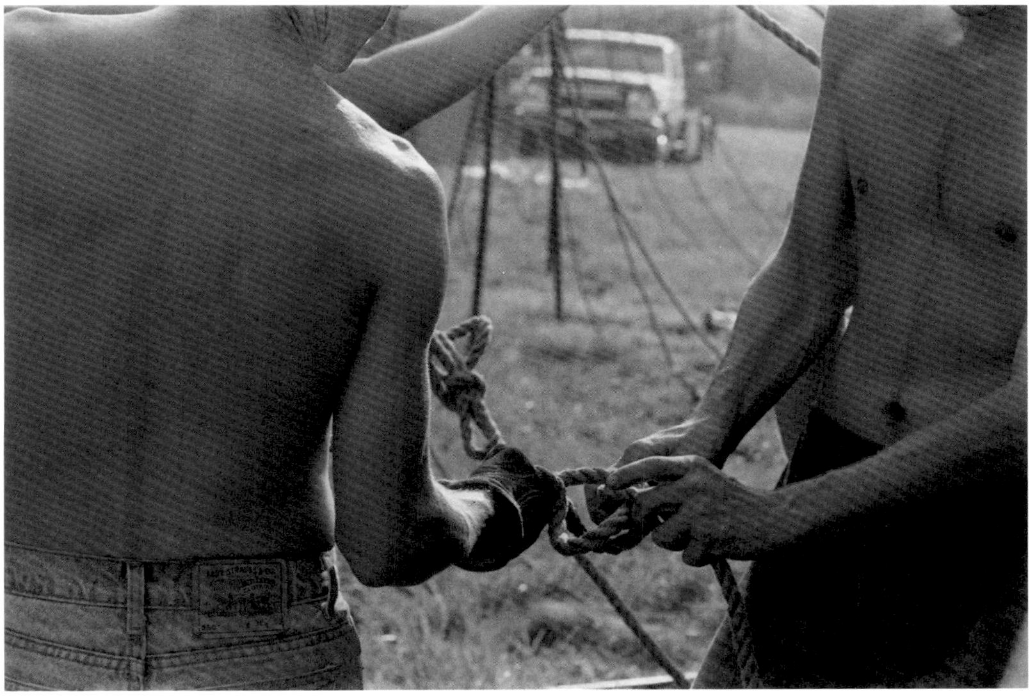

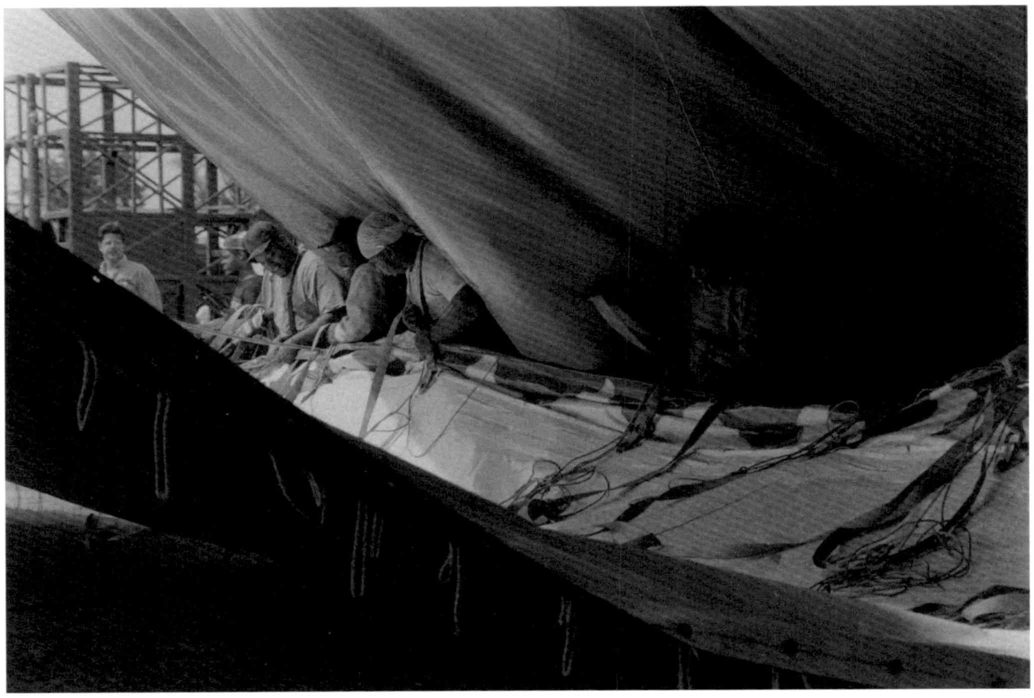

PLATES 20 & 21

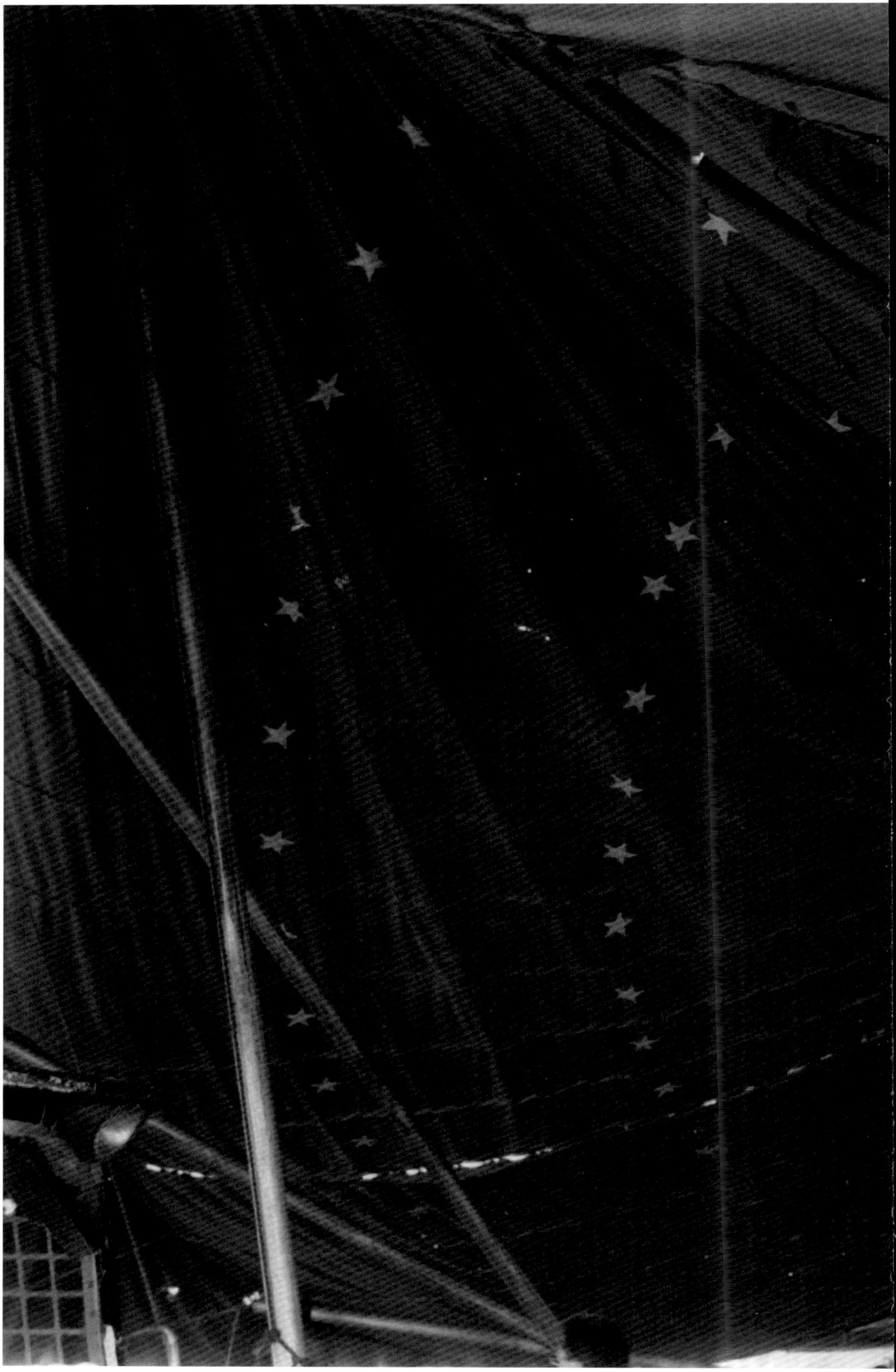

PLATE 22

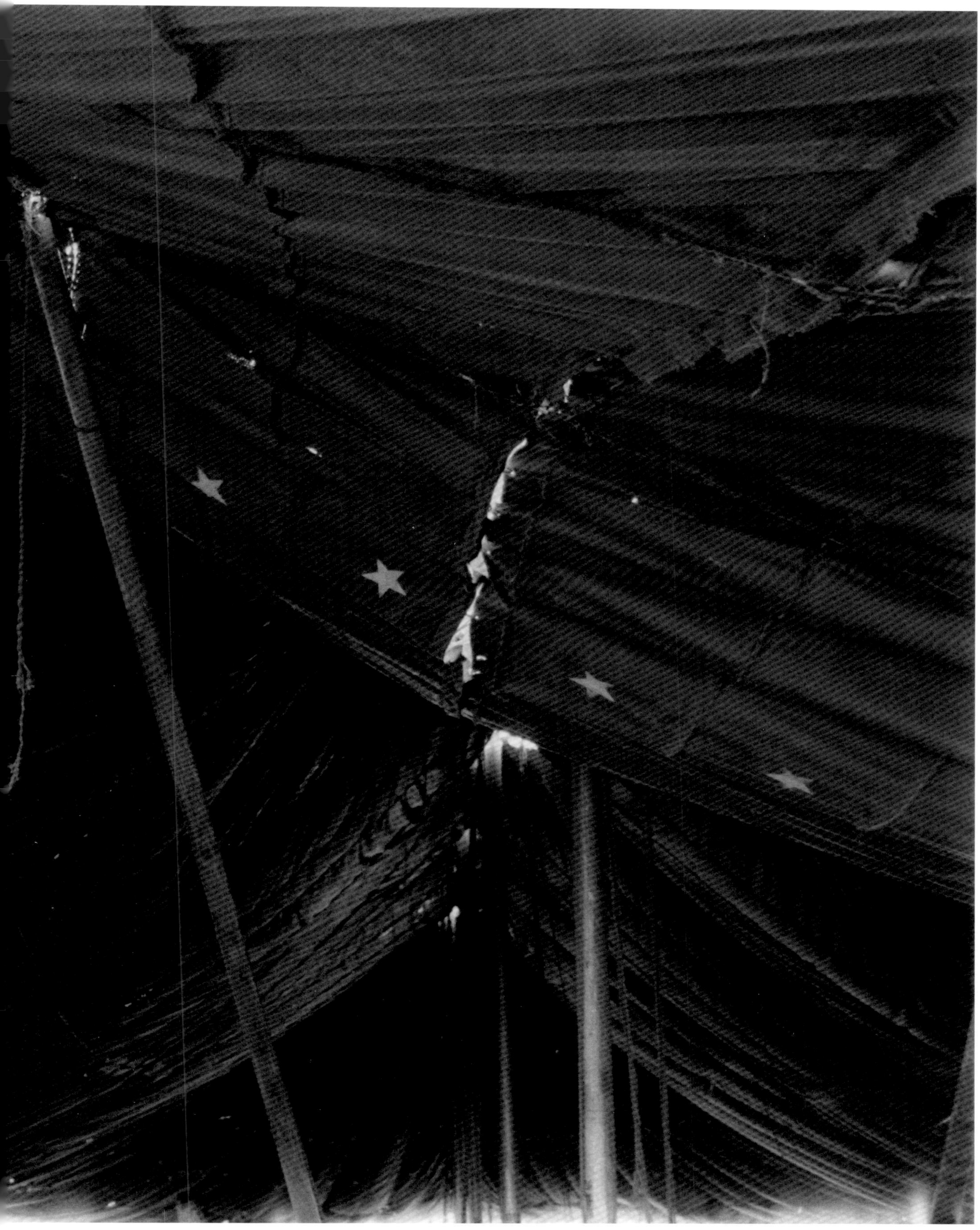

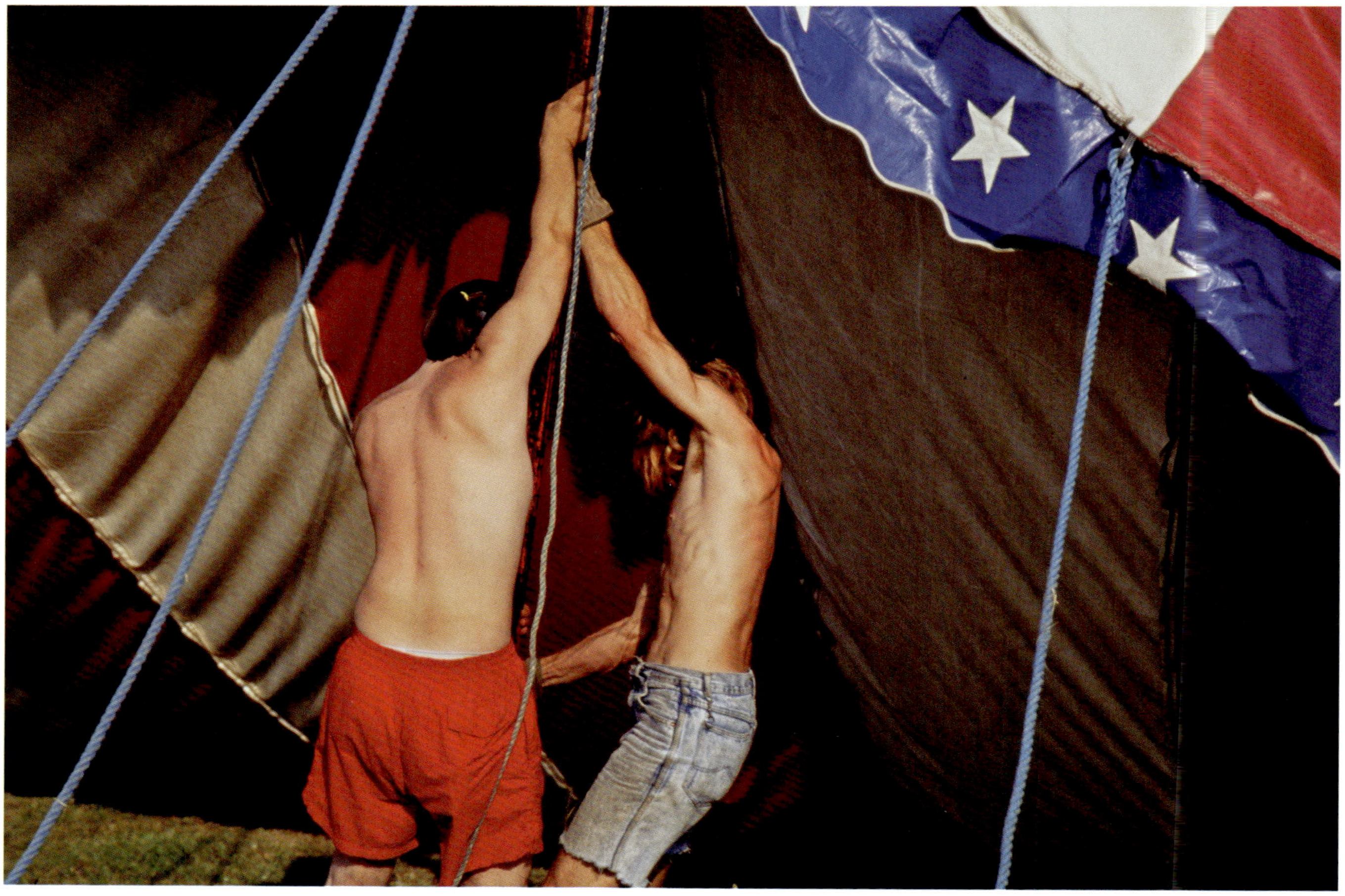

PLATE 23

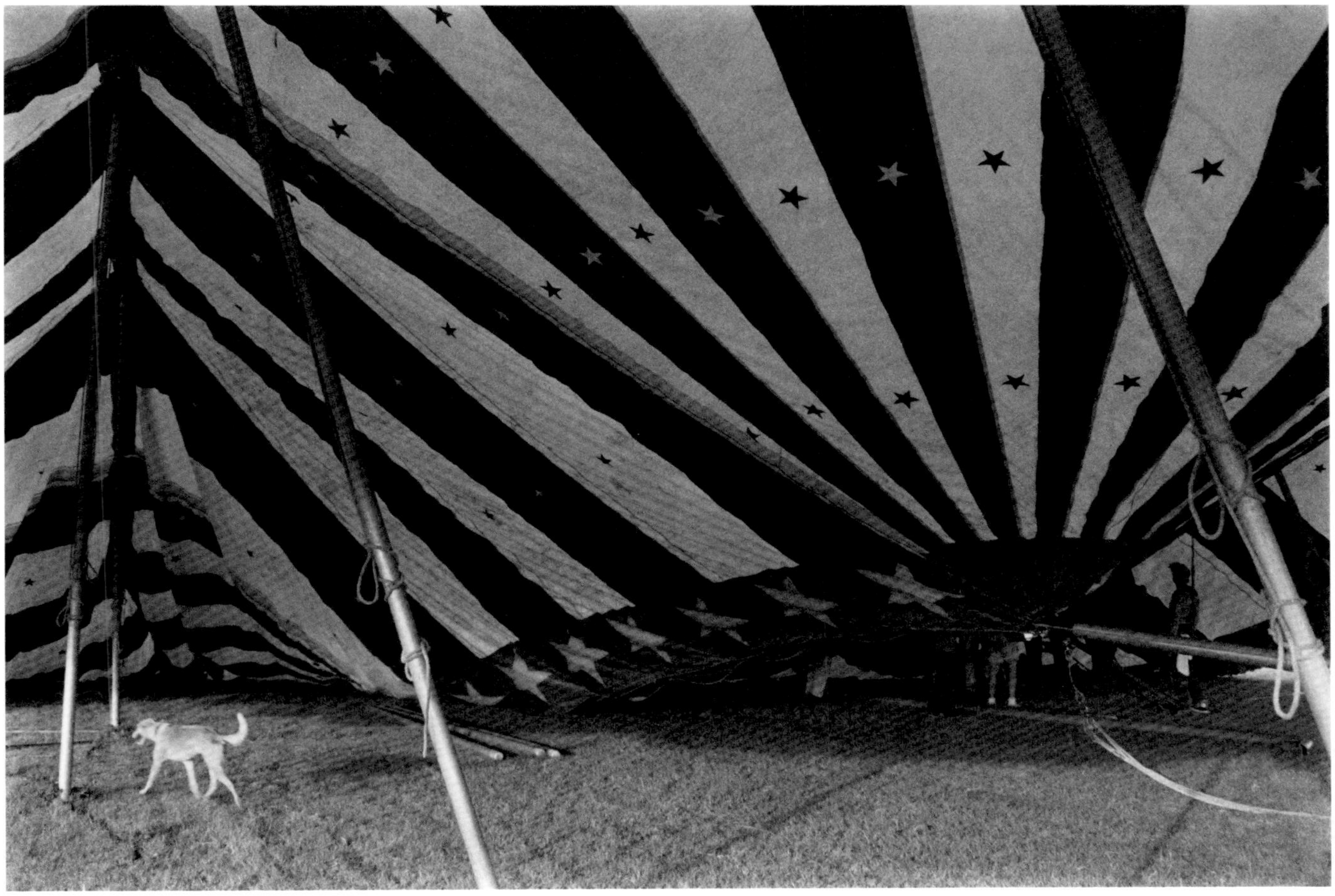

PLATE 24

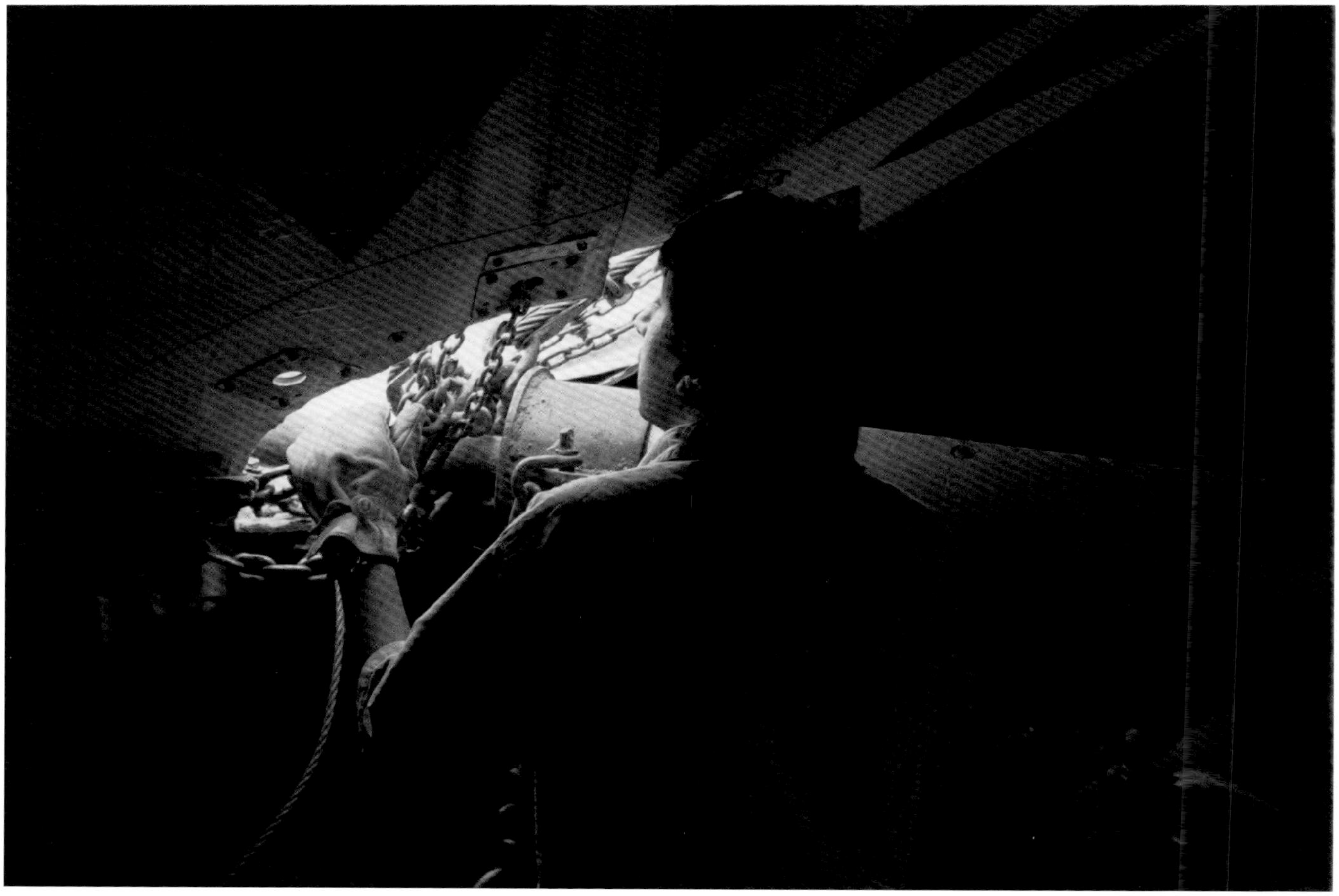

PLATE 25

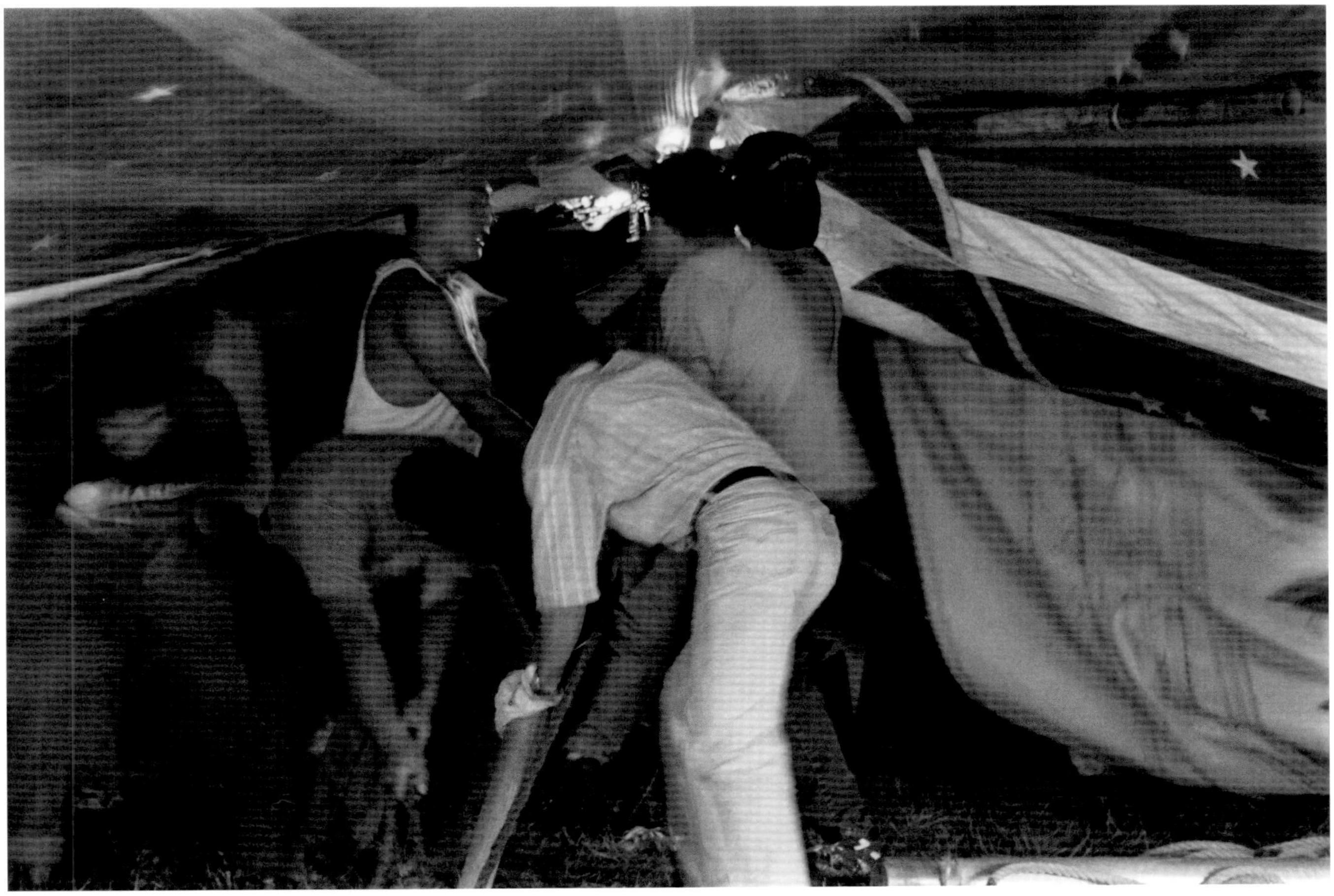

PLATE 26

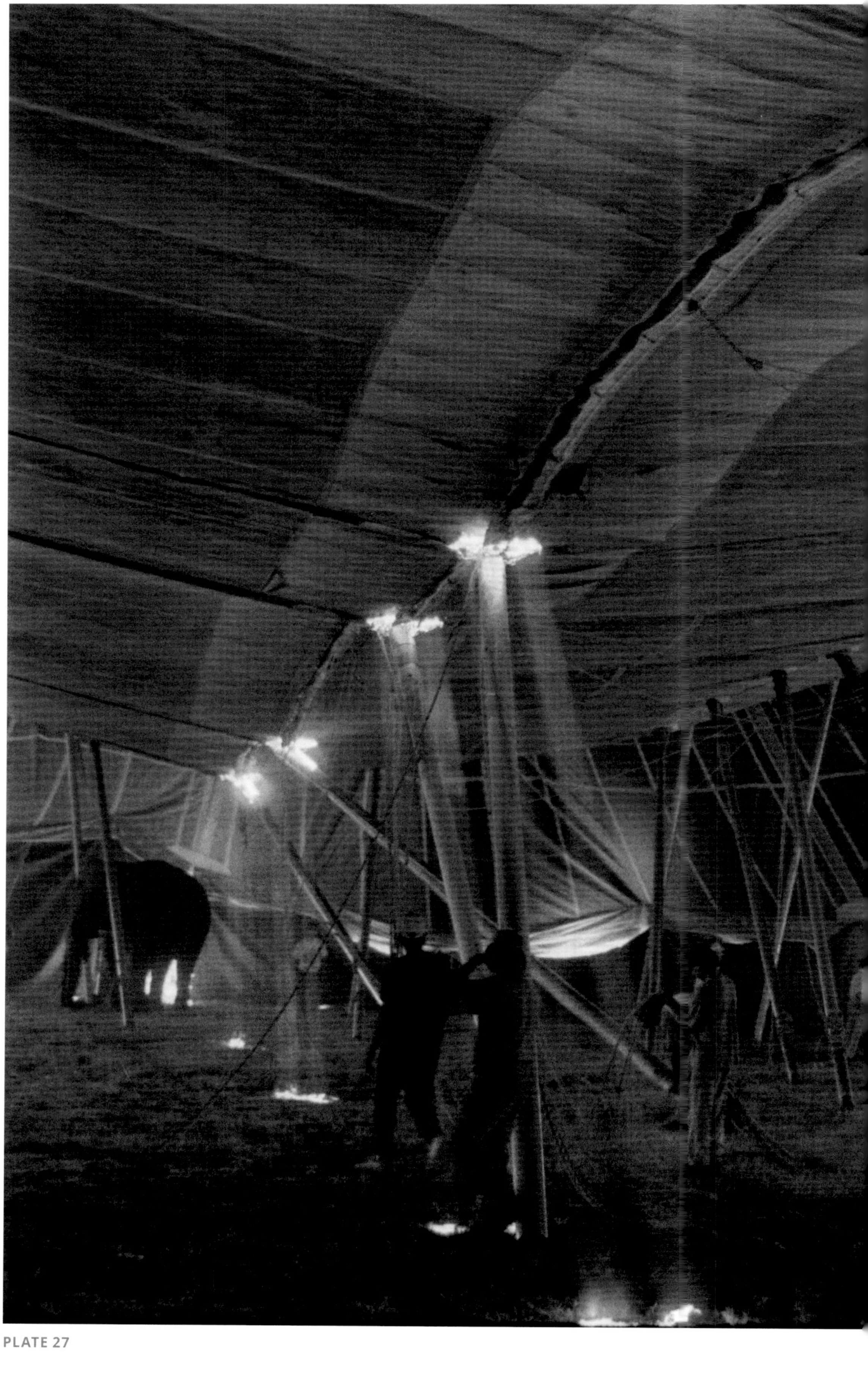

PLATE 27

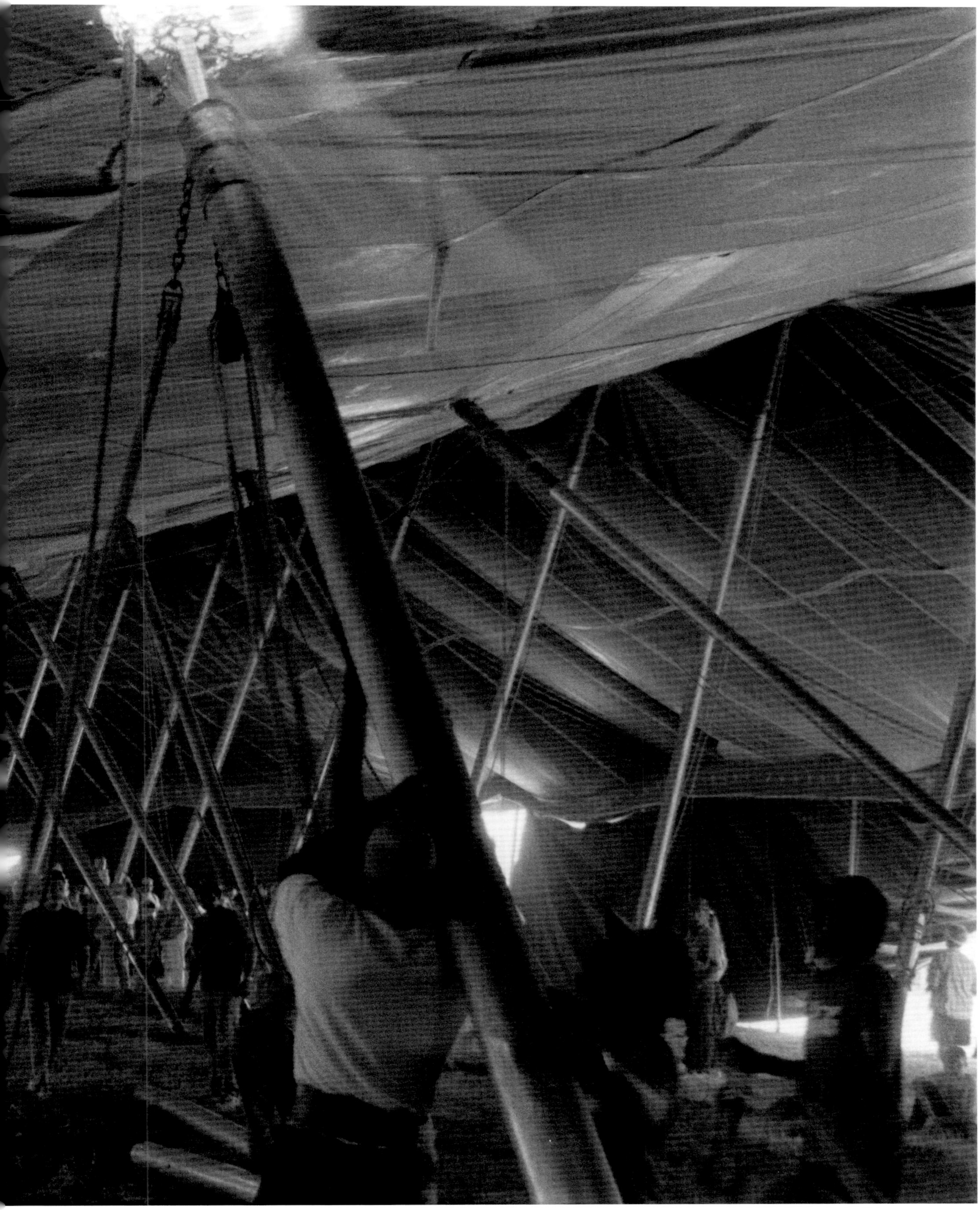

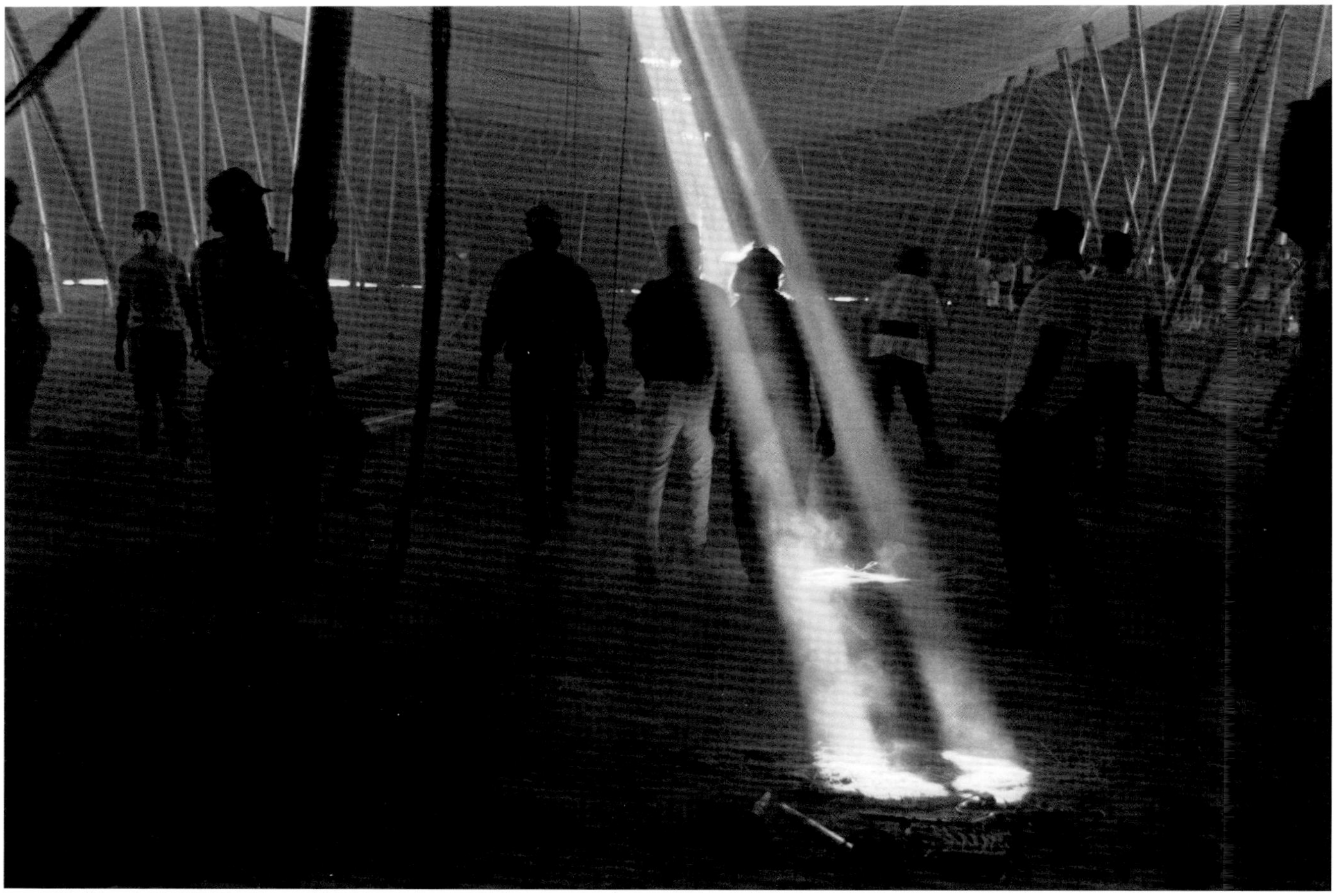

PLATE 28

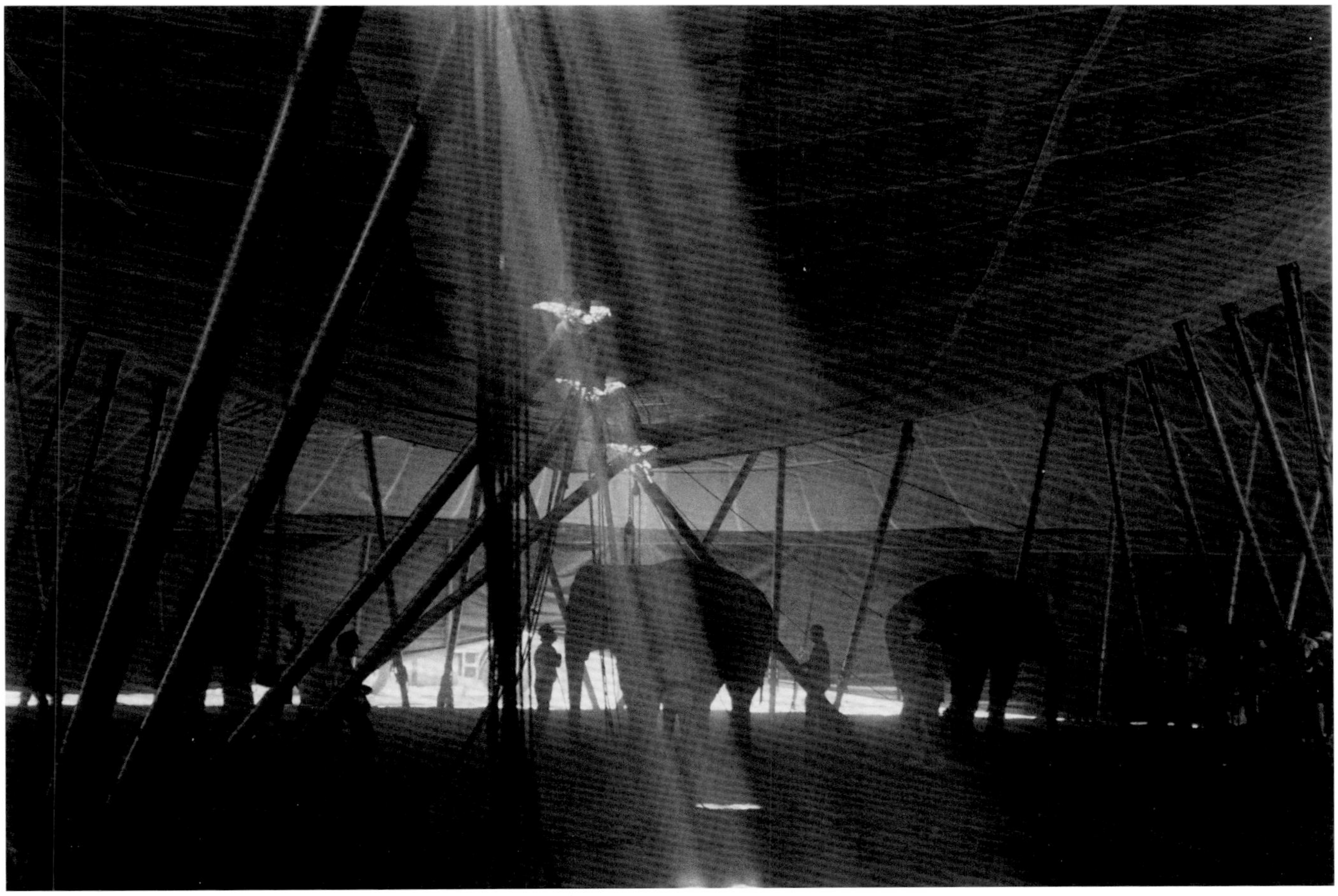

PLATE 29

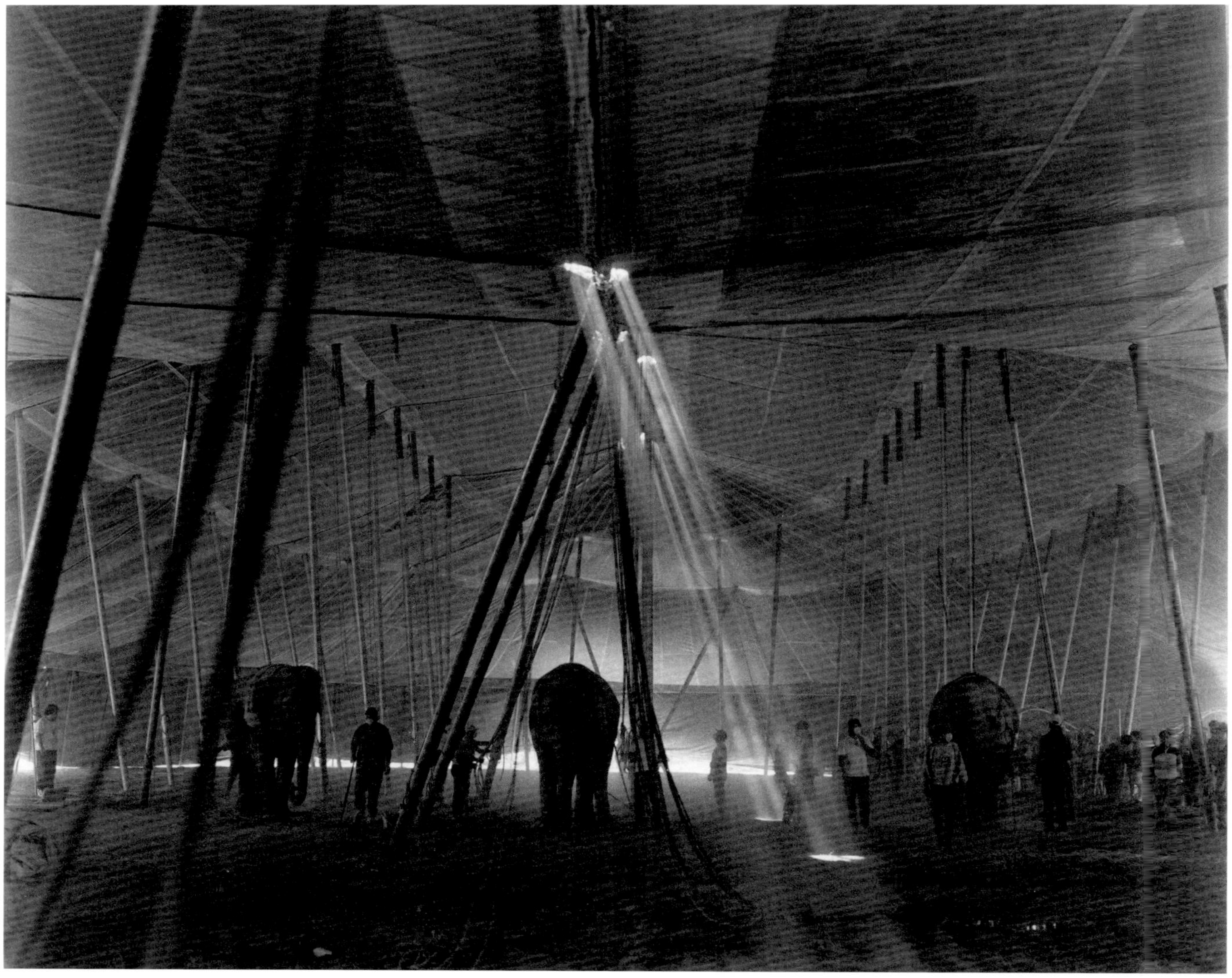

PLATE 30

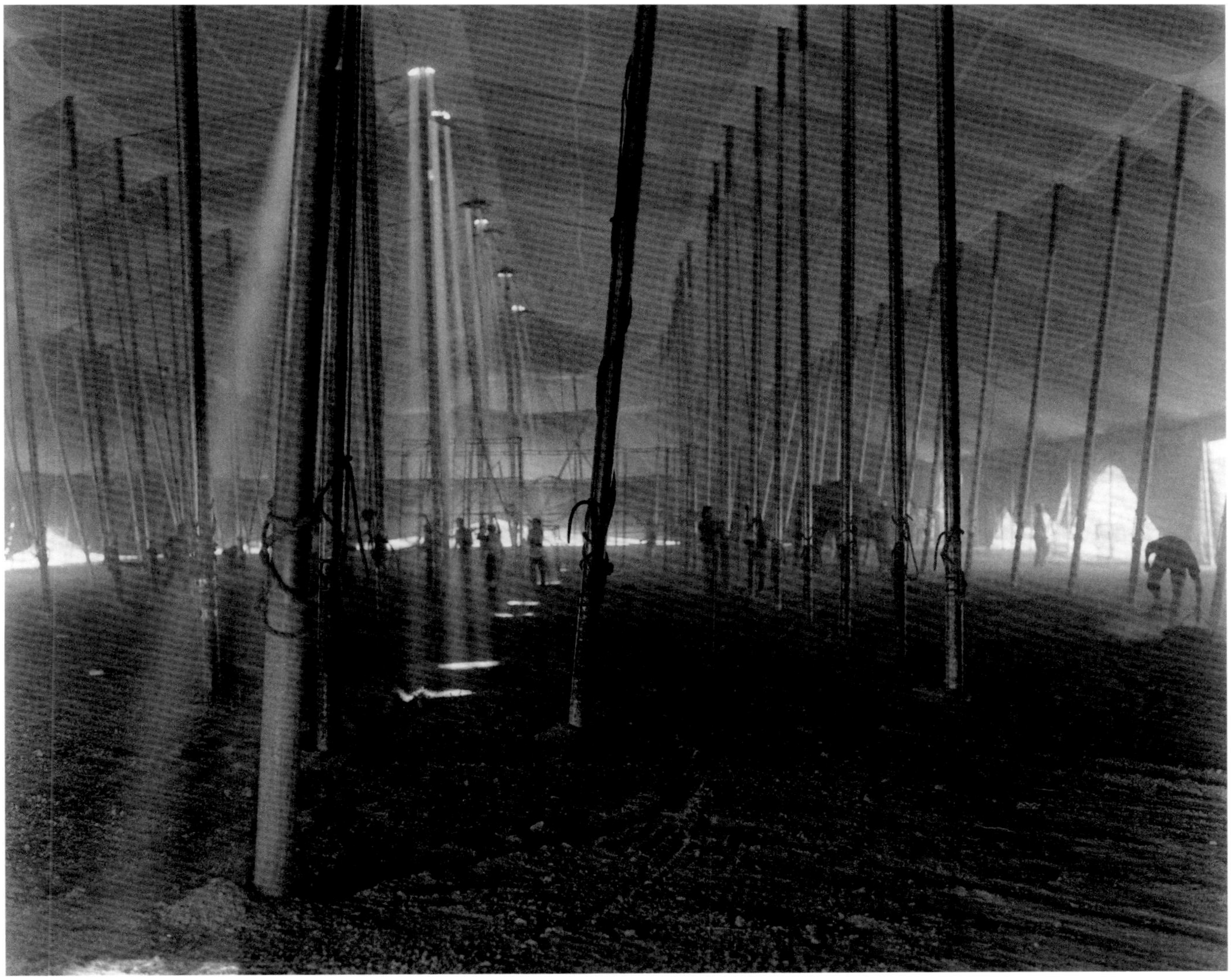

PLATE 31

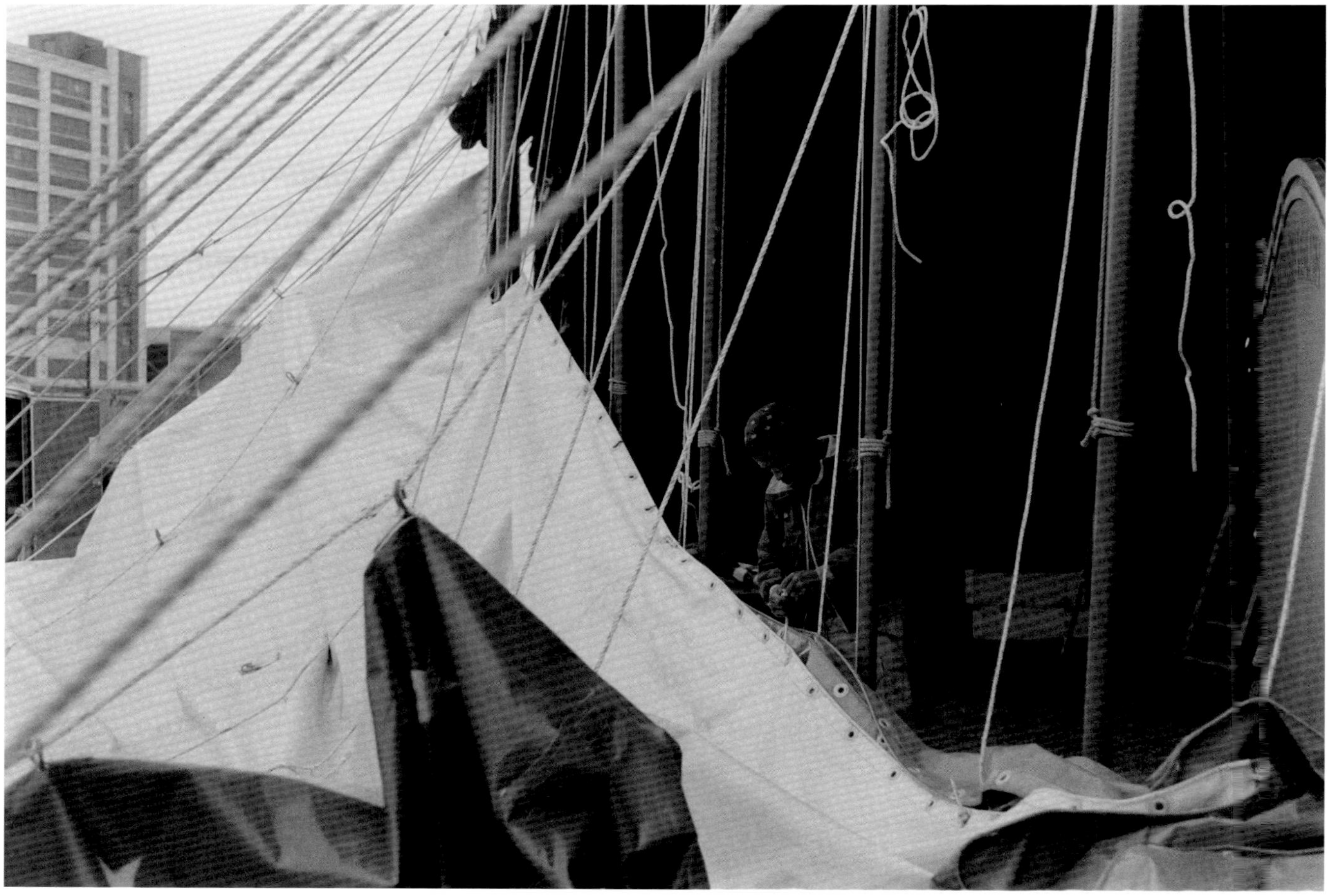

PLATE 32

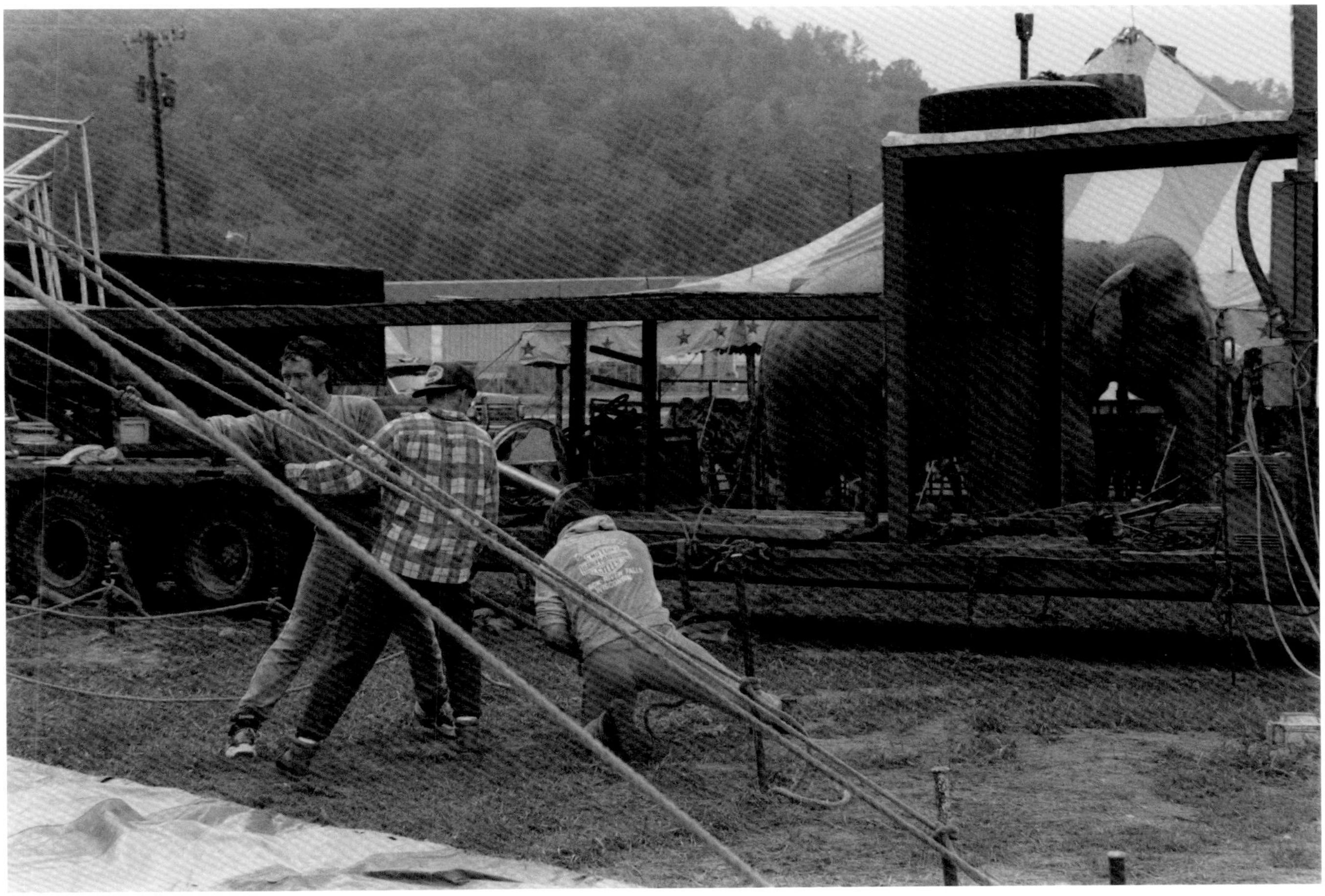

PLATE 33

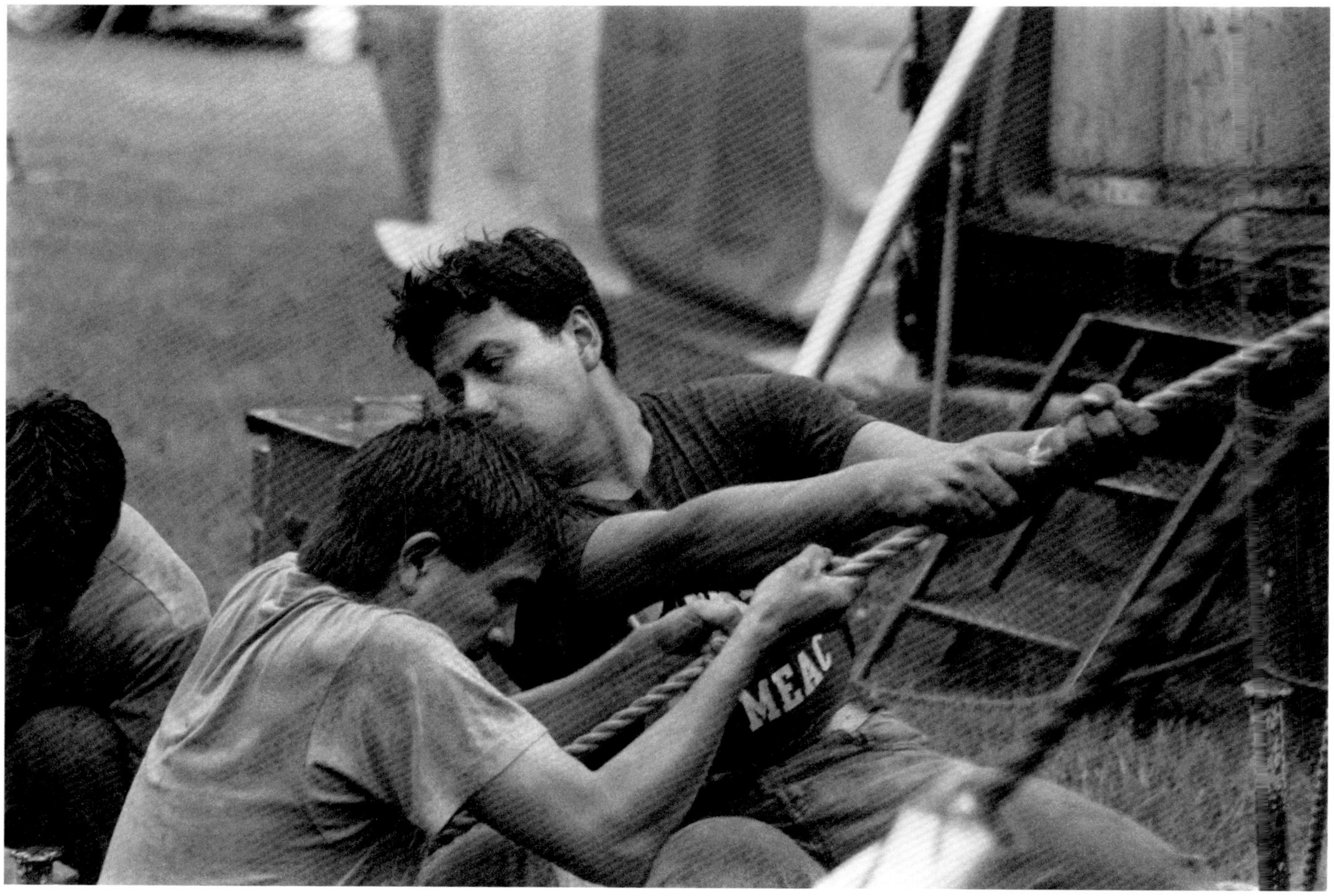

PLATE 34

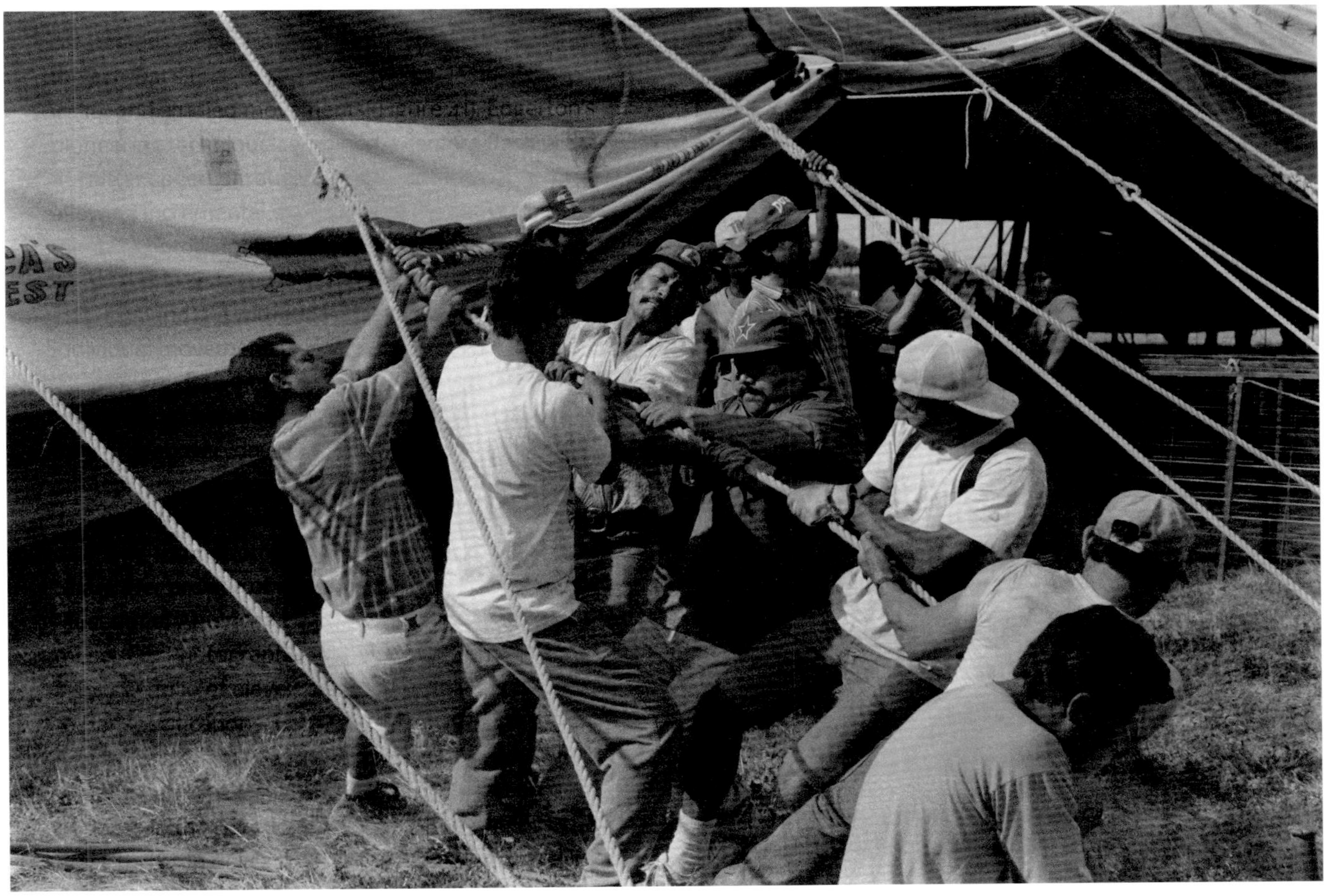

PLATE 35

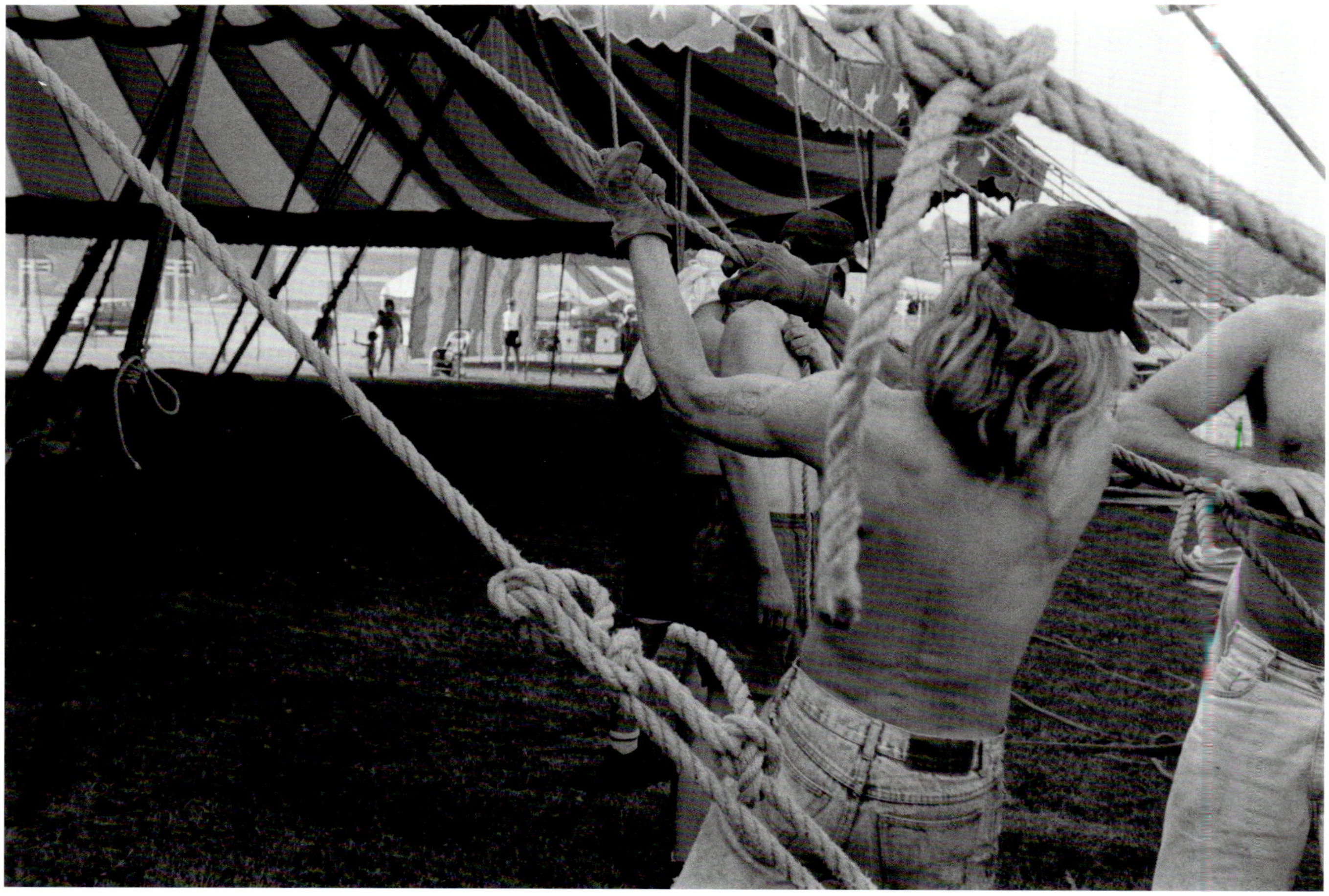

PLATE 36

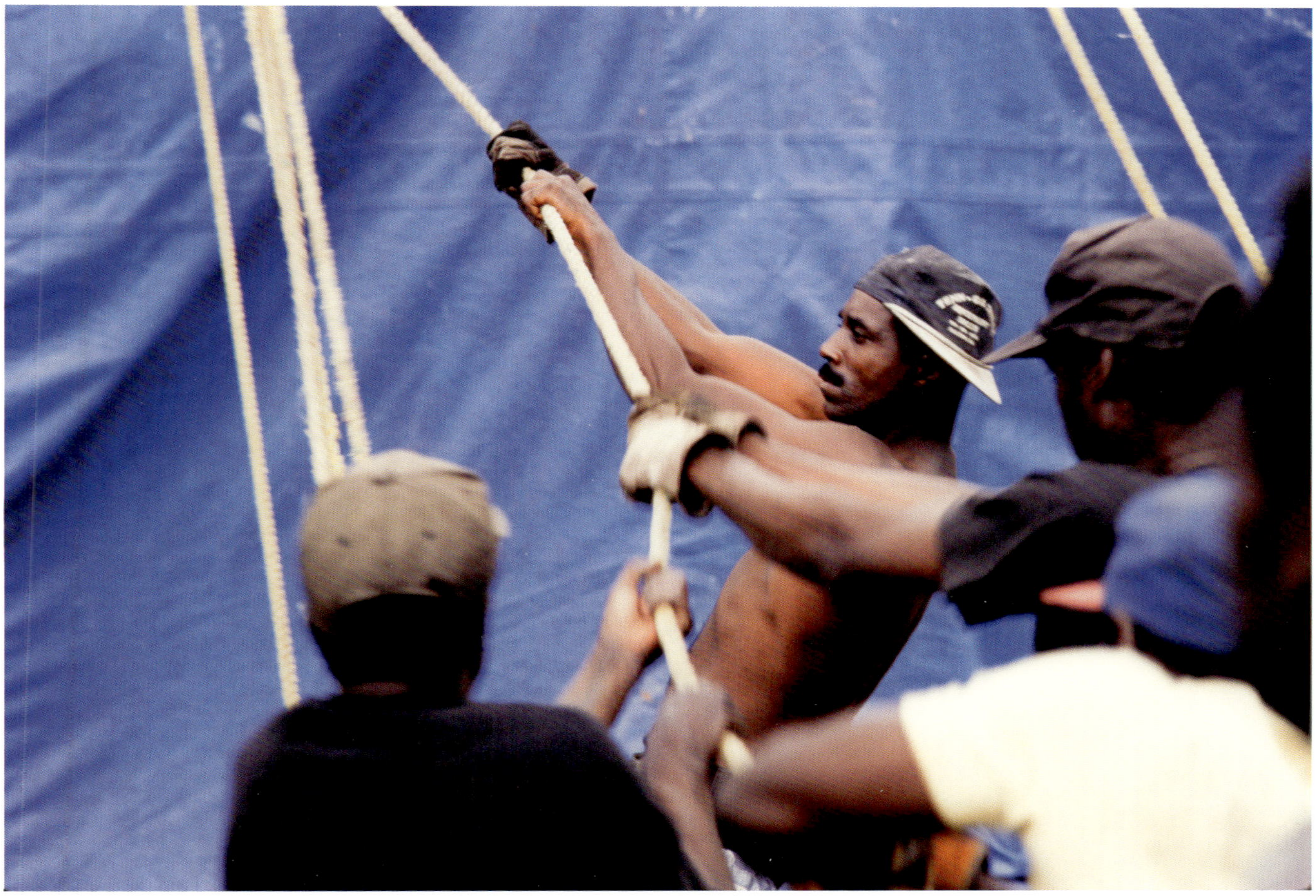

PLATE 37

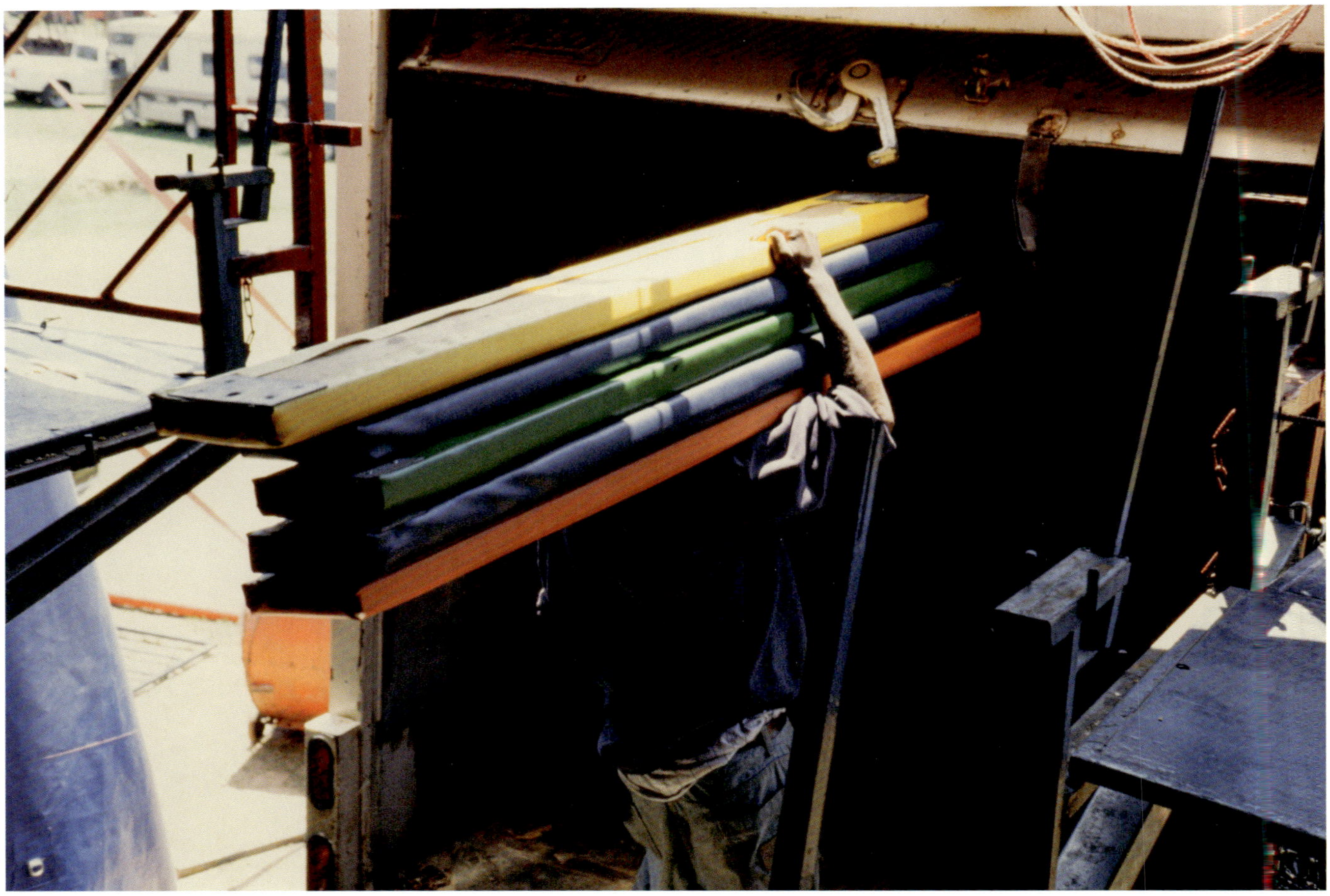

PLATE 38

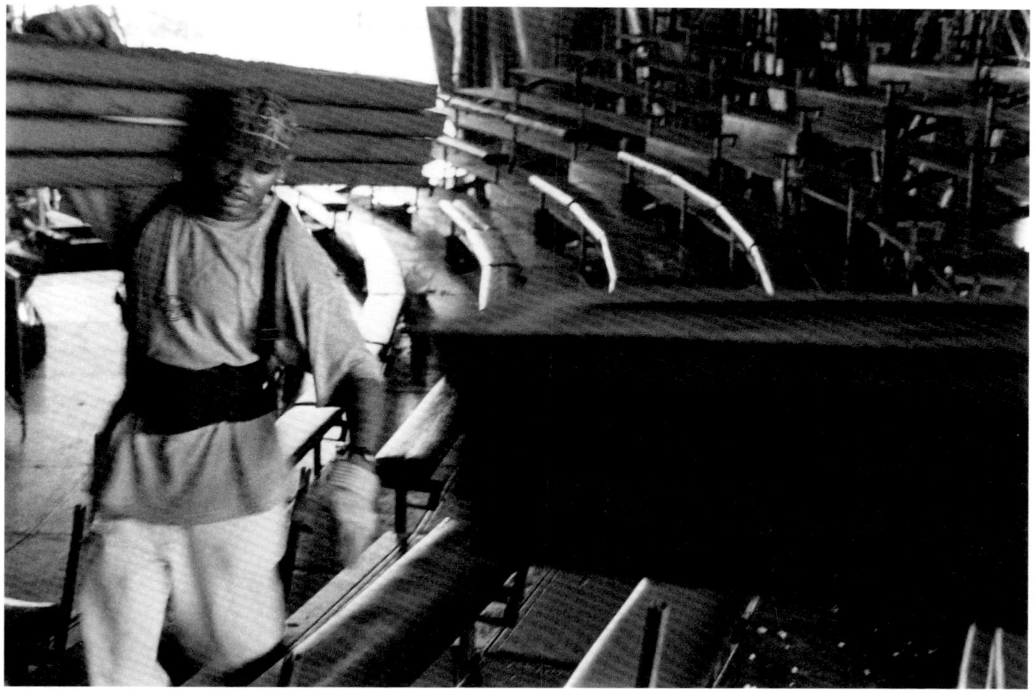

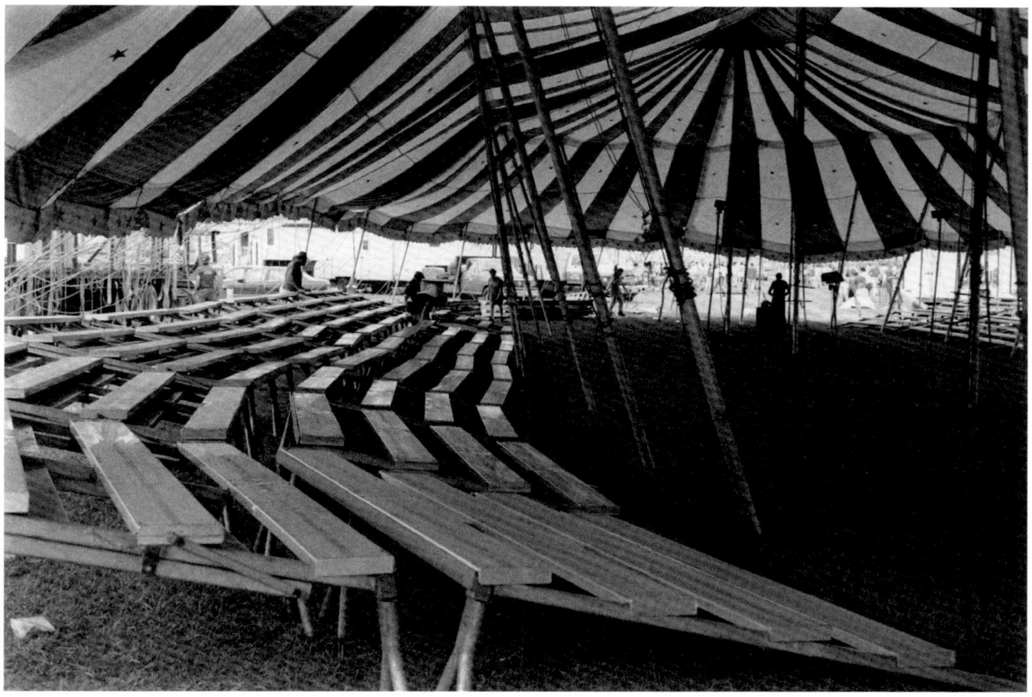

PLATES 39 & 40

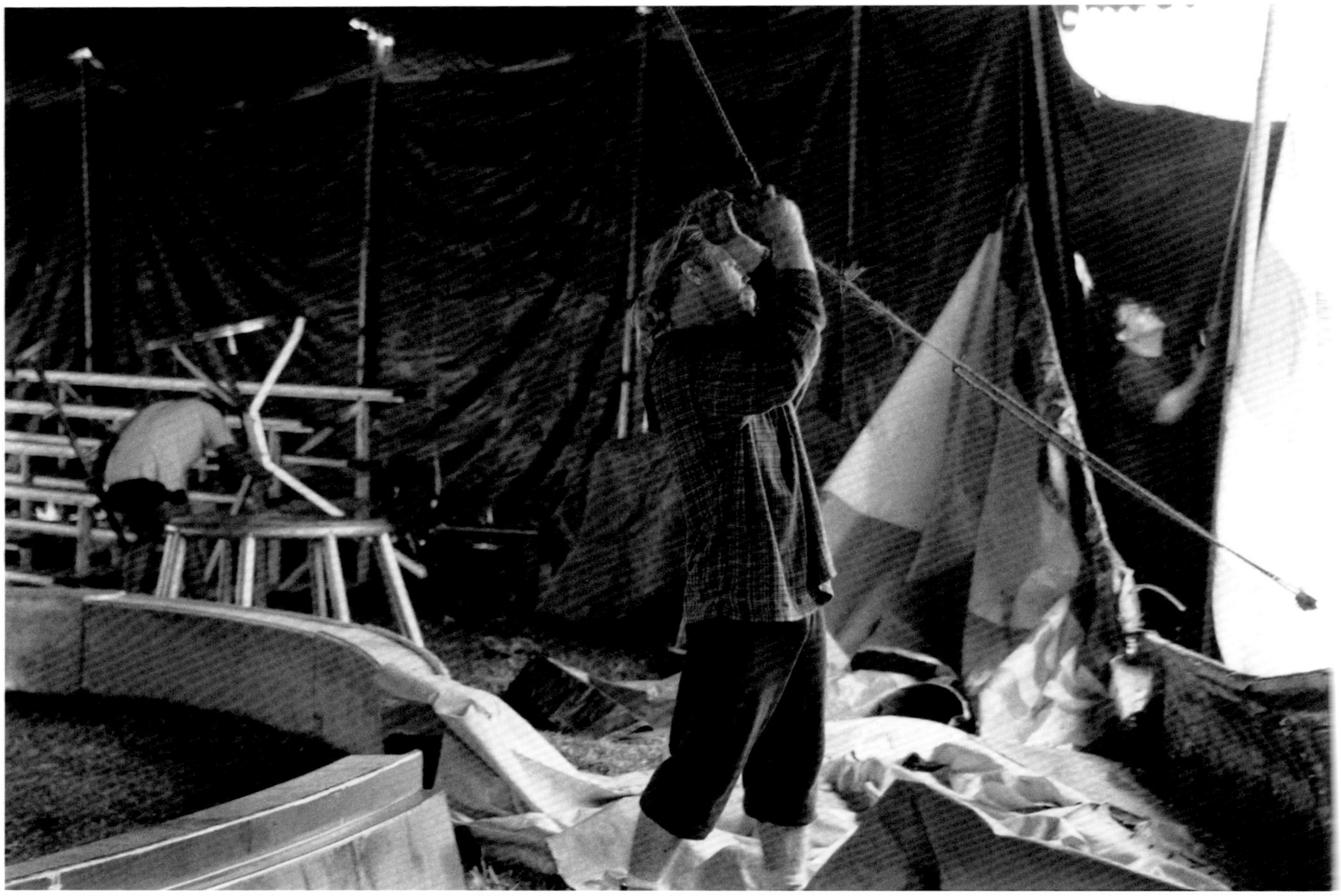

PLATE 41

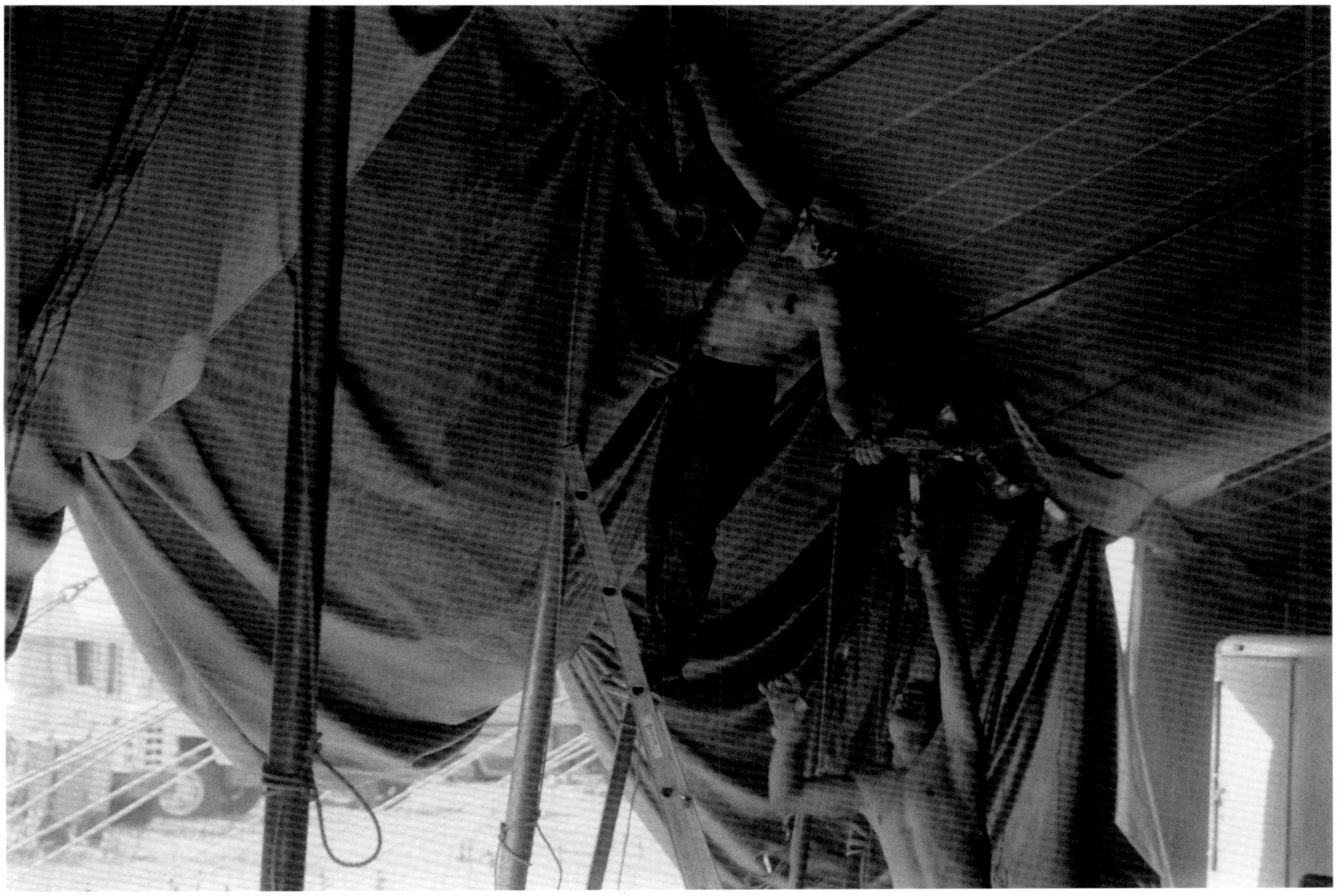

PLATE 42

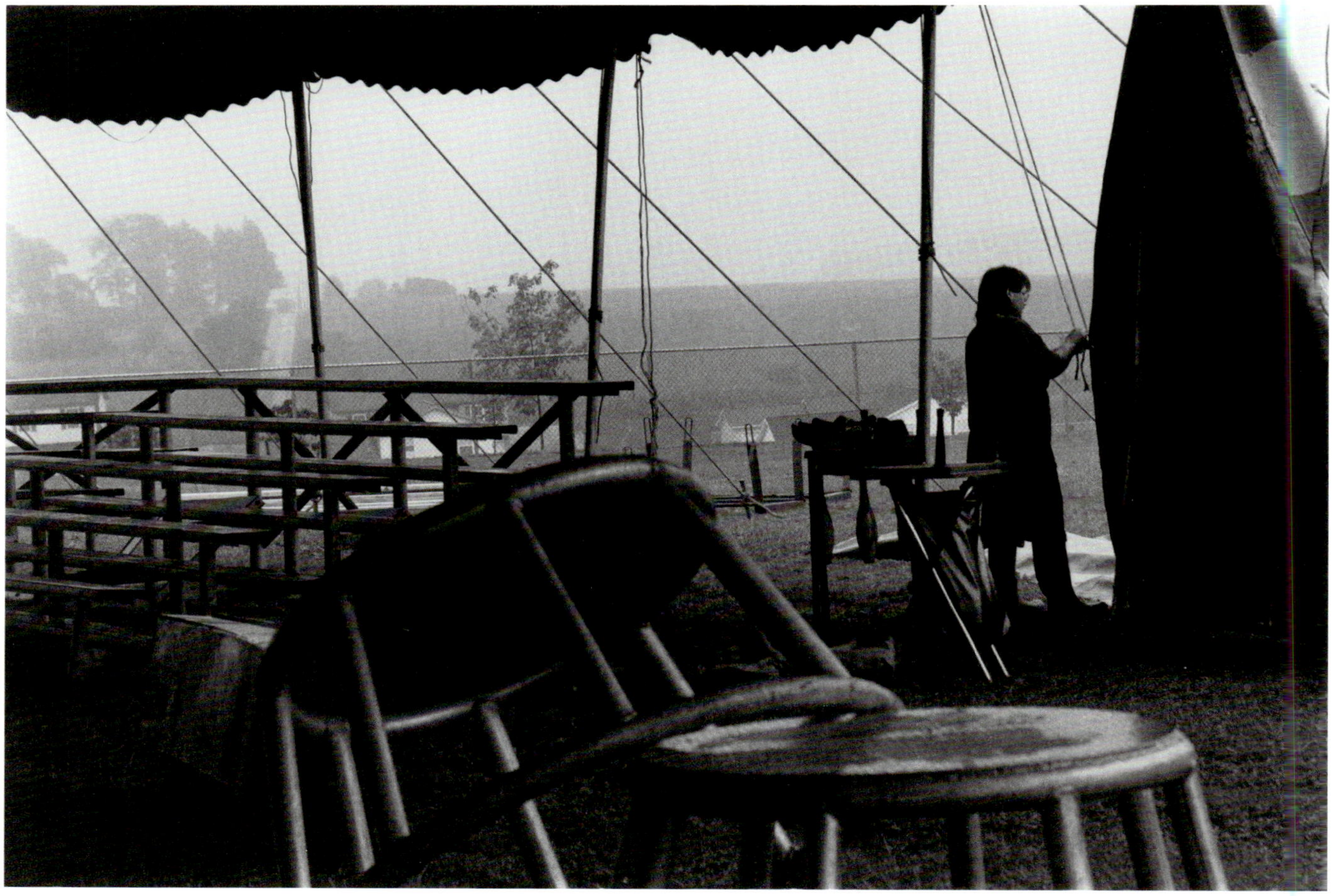

PLATE 43

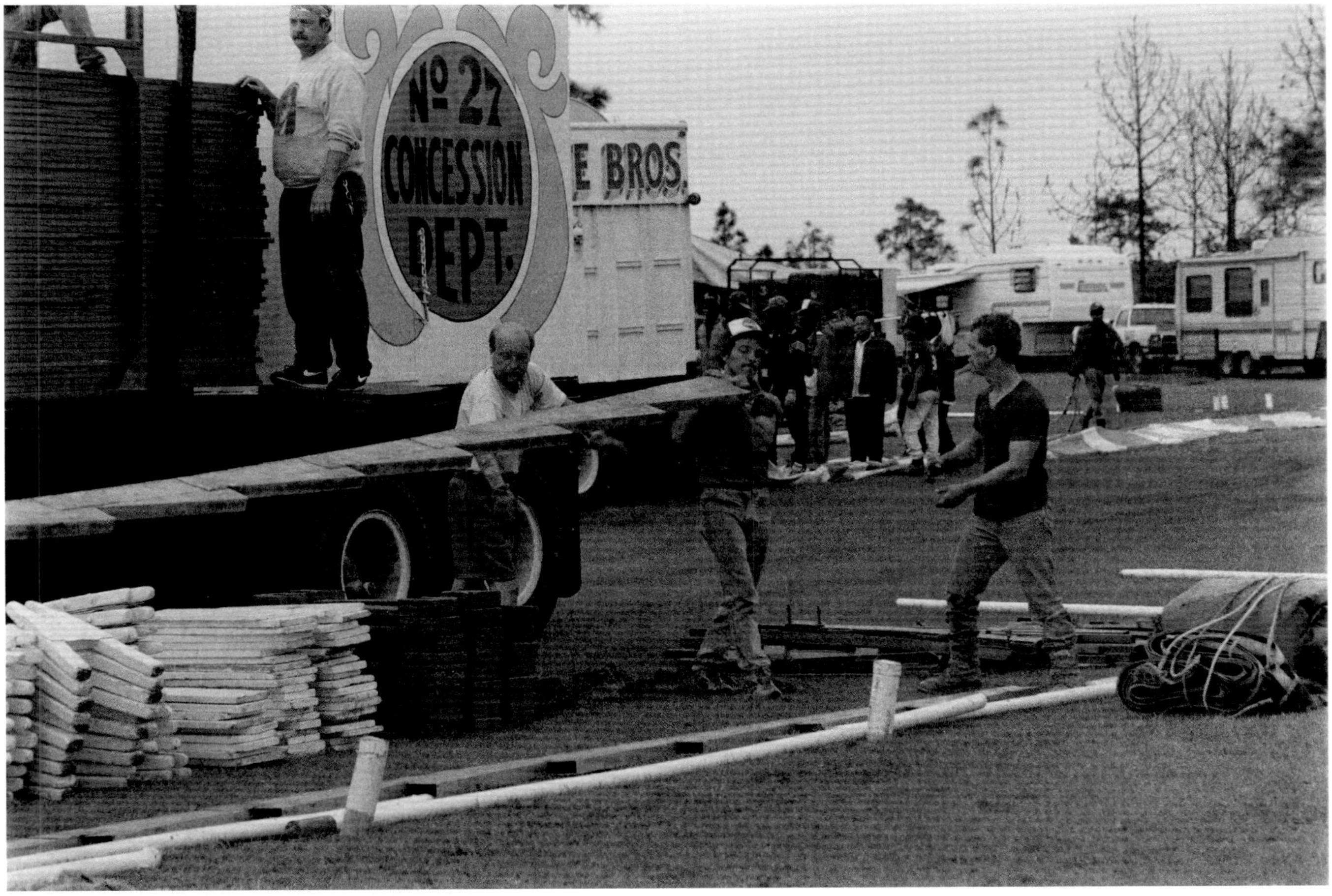

PLATE 44

★ ★ ★ ★ ★ ★ ★ ★ ★ ★ ★

Circus life is hard. There are no lazy people in the circus. You have to want to be in the circus or you will be miserable. Nothing is worse than having to work for a circus if you don't want to be there.

—Jimmy James, performance director and ringmaster, Clyde Beatty-Cole Bros. Circus (1995)

★ ★ ★ ★ ★ ★ ★ ★ ★ ★ ★

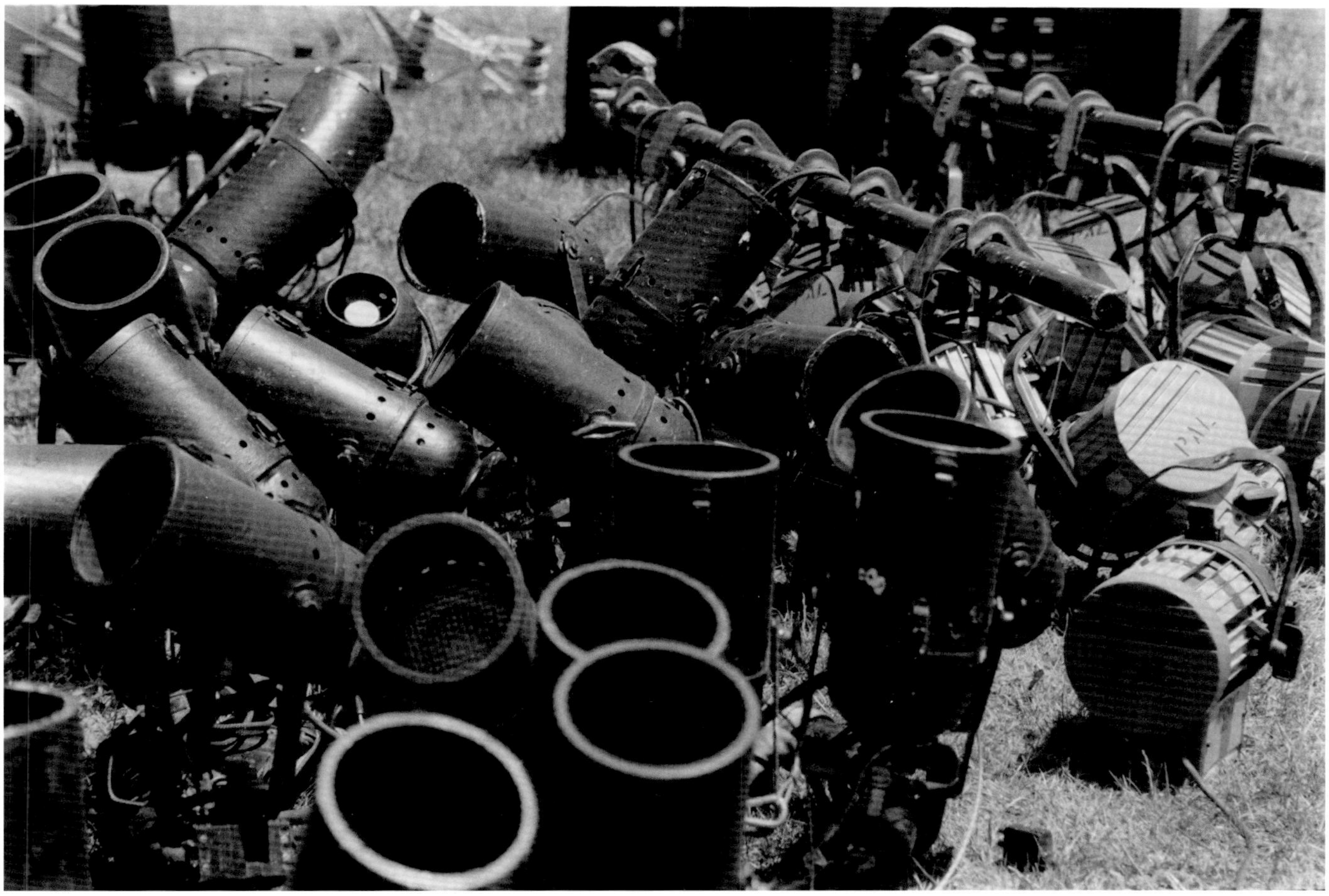

PLATE 45

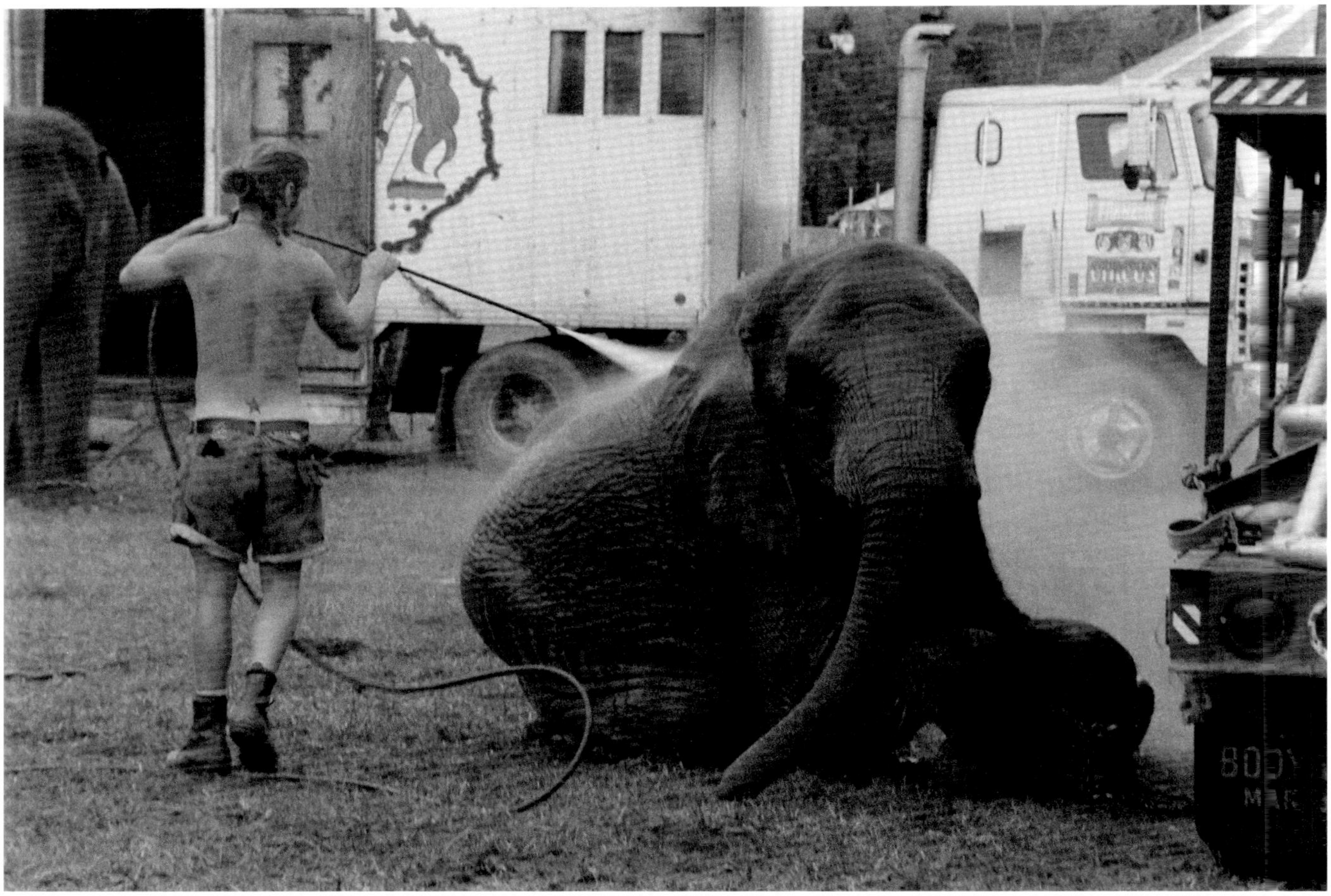

PLATE 46

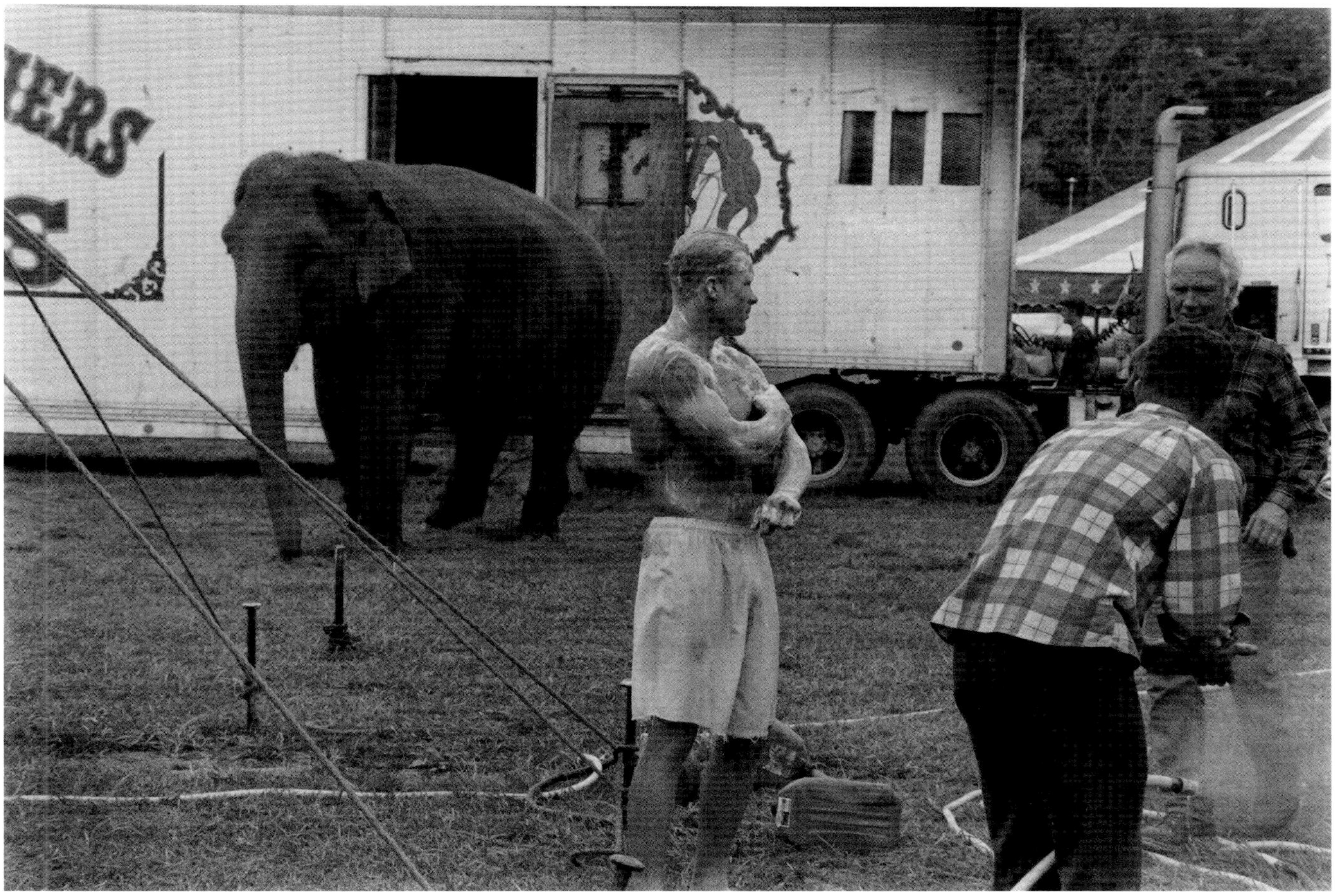

PLATE 47

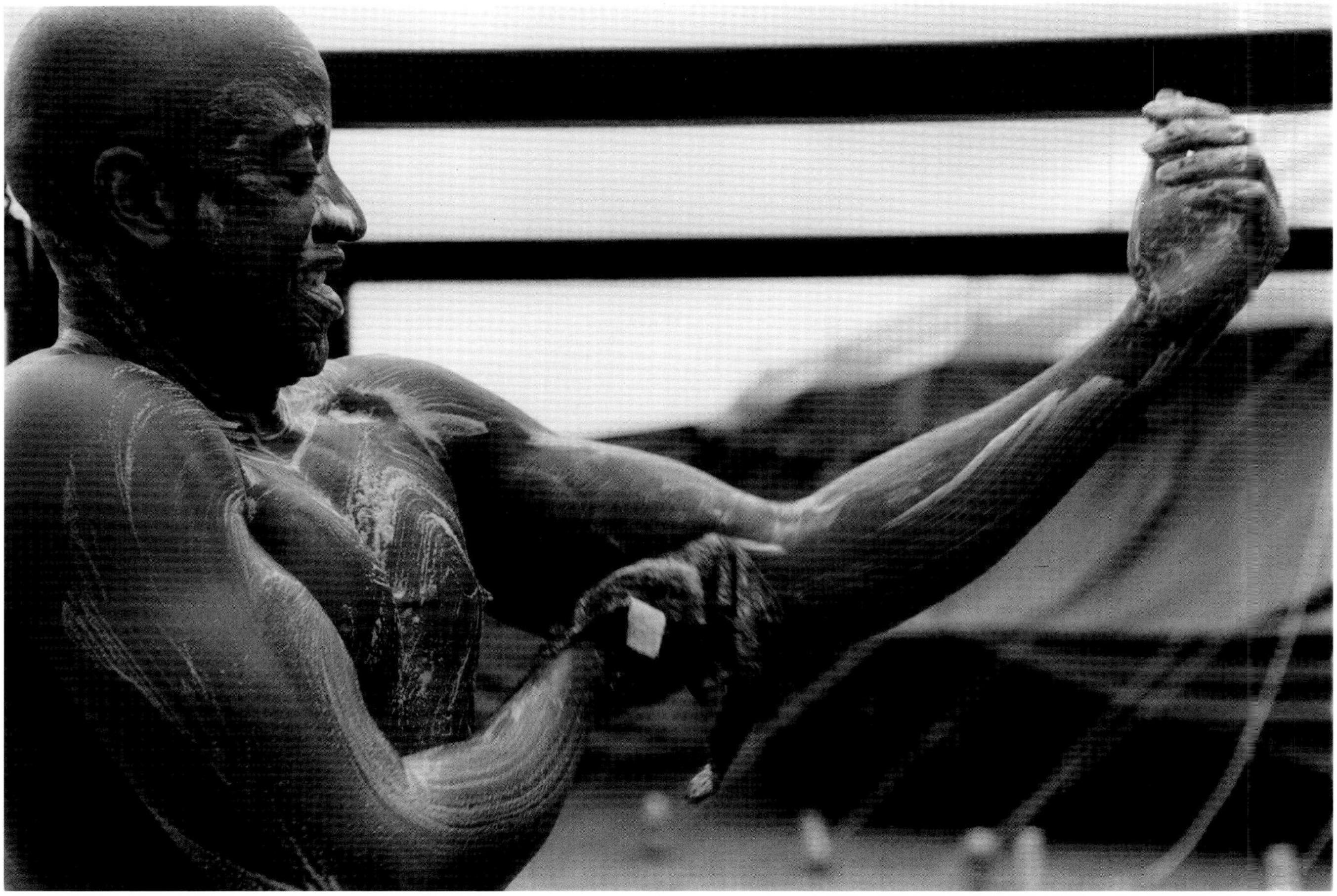

PLATE 48

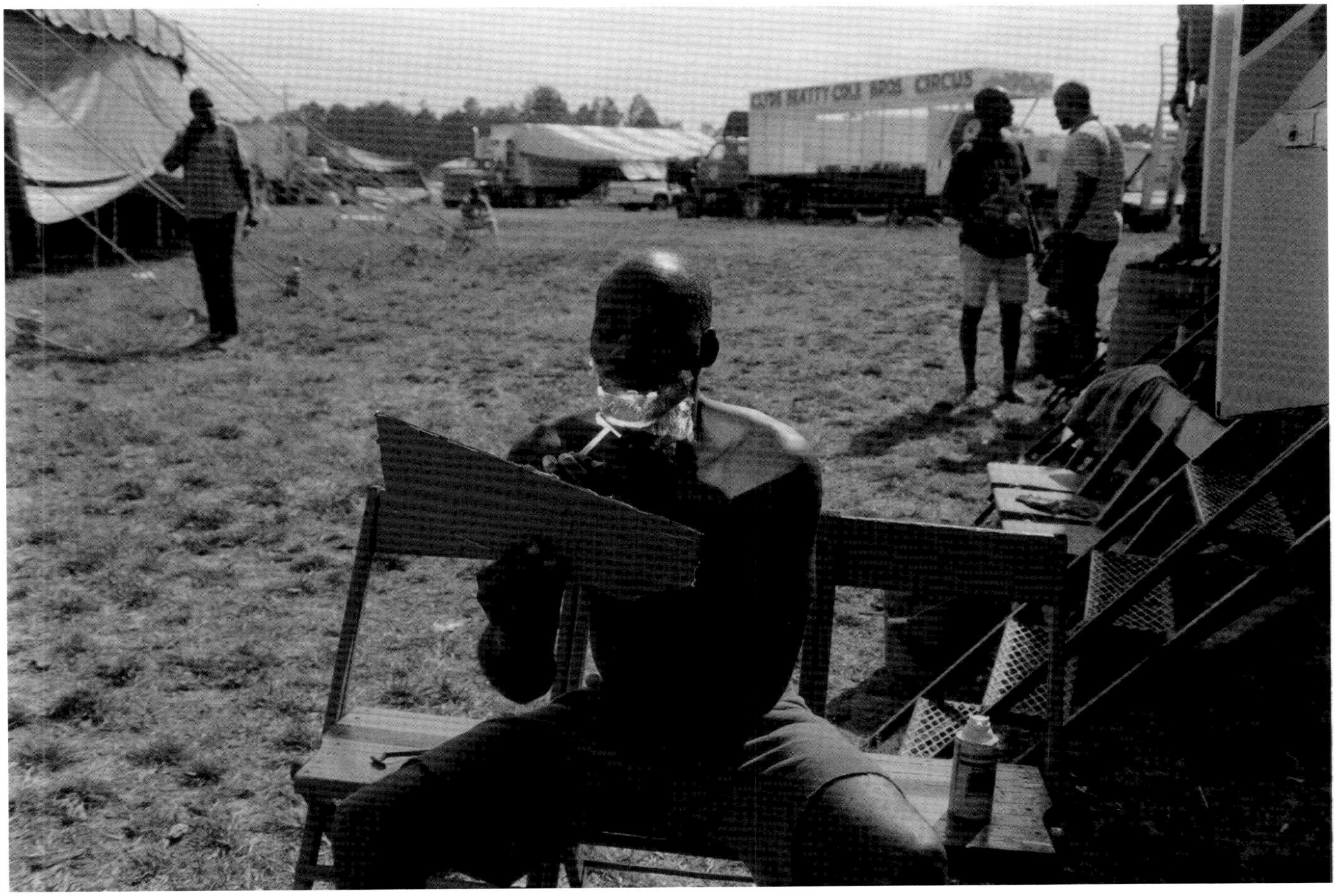

PLATE 49

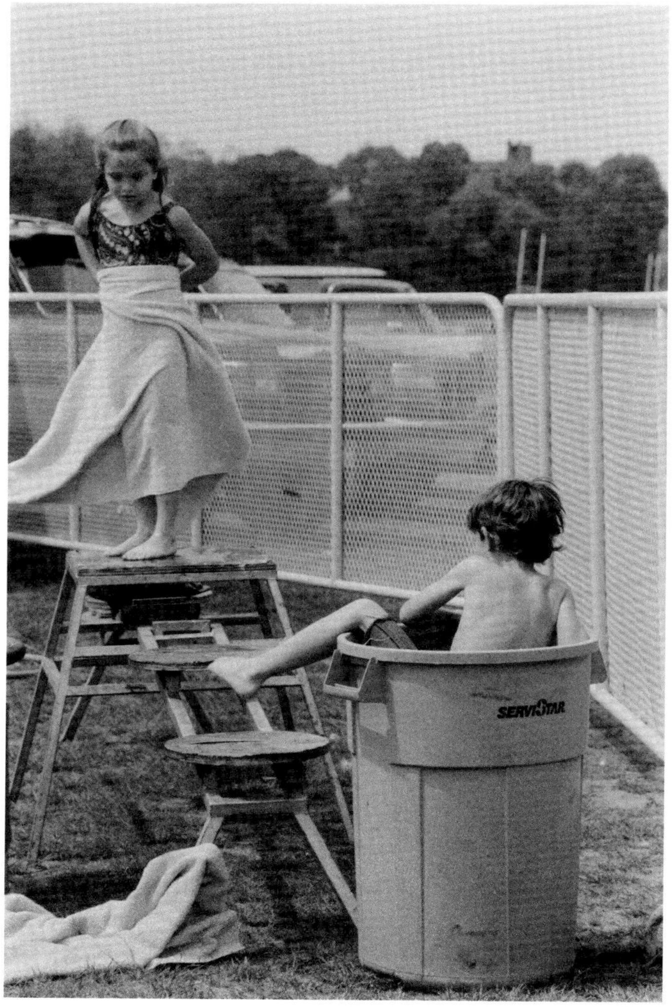

PLATE 50

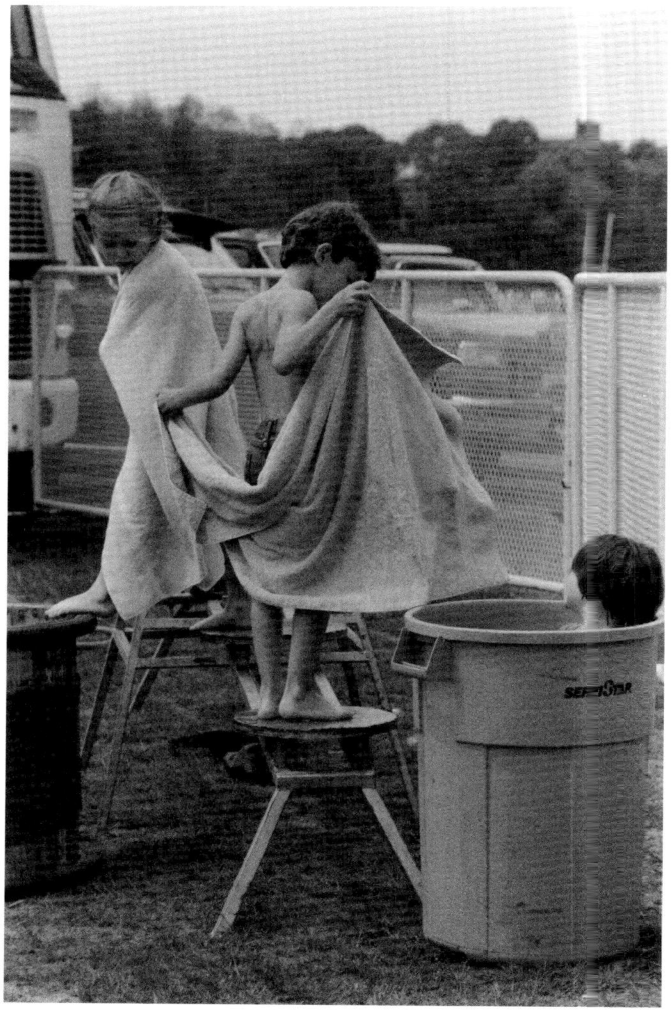

PLATE 51

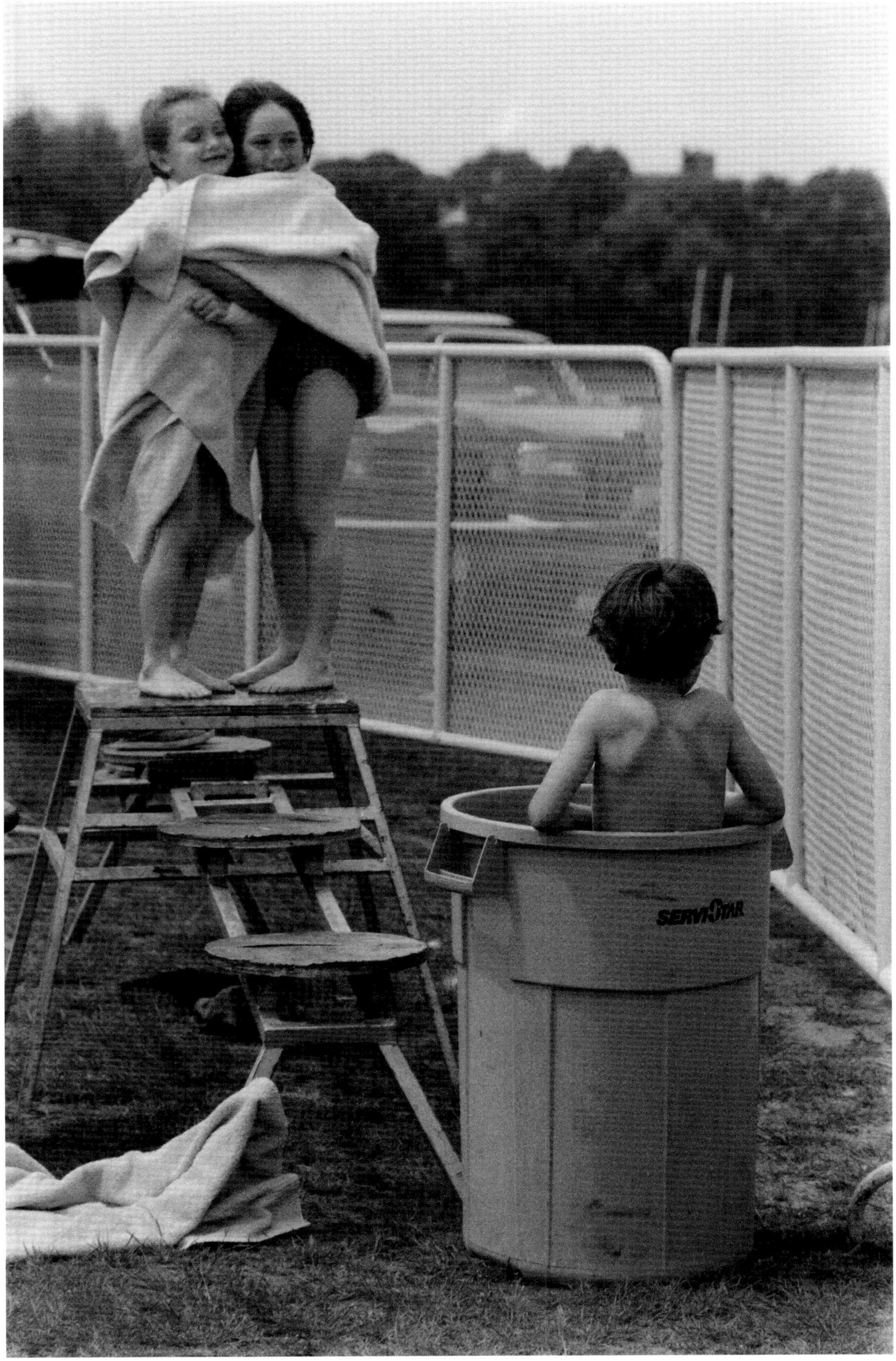

PLATE 52

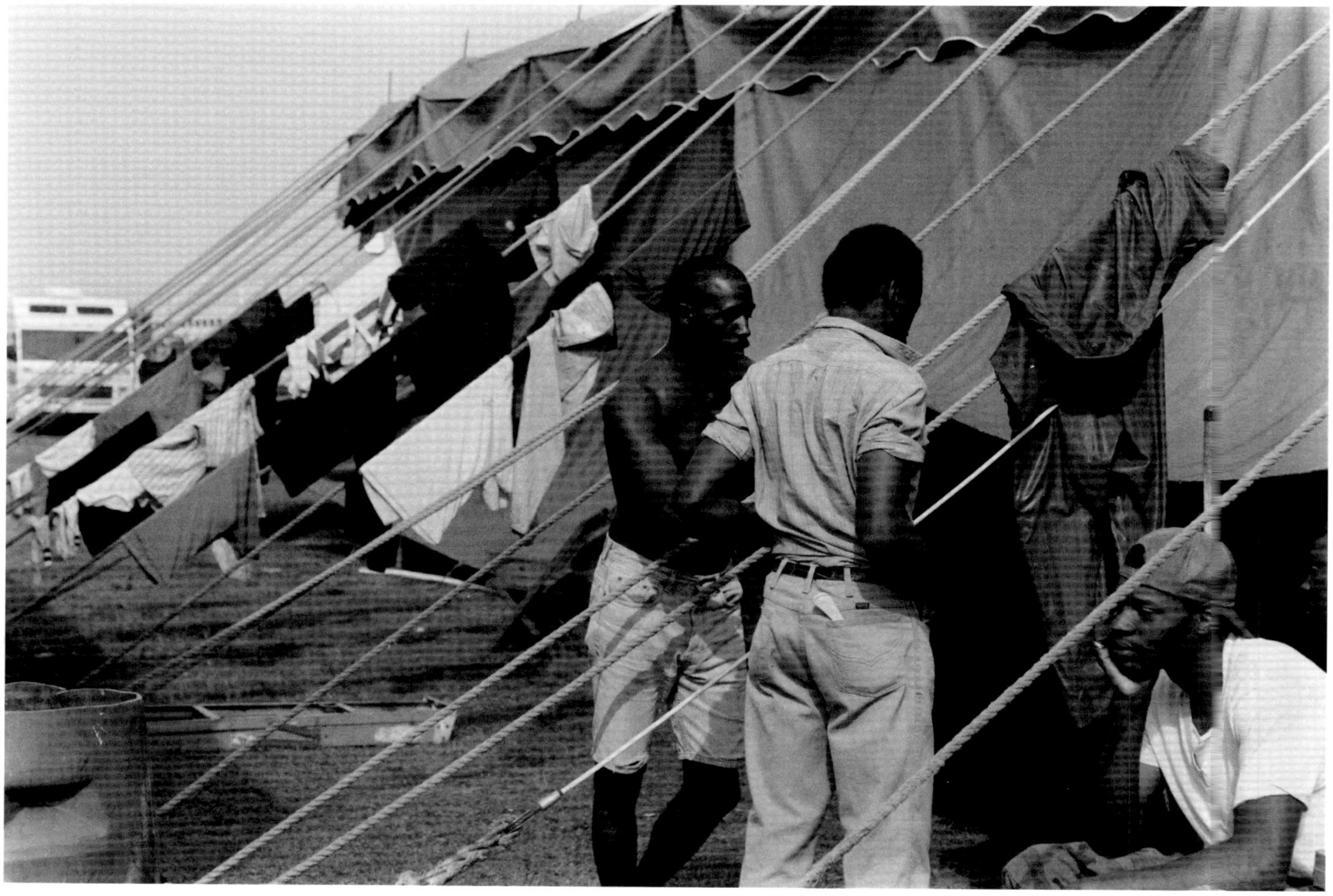

PLATE 53

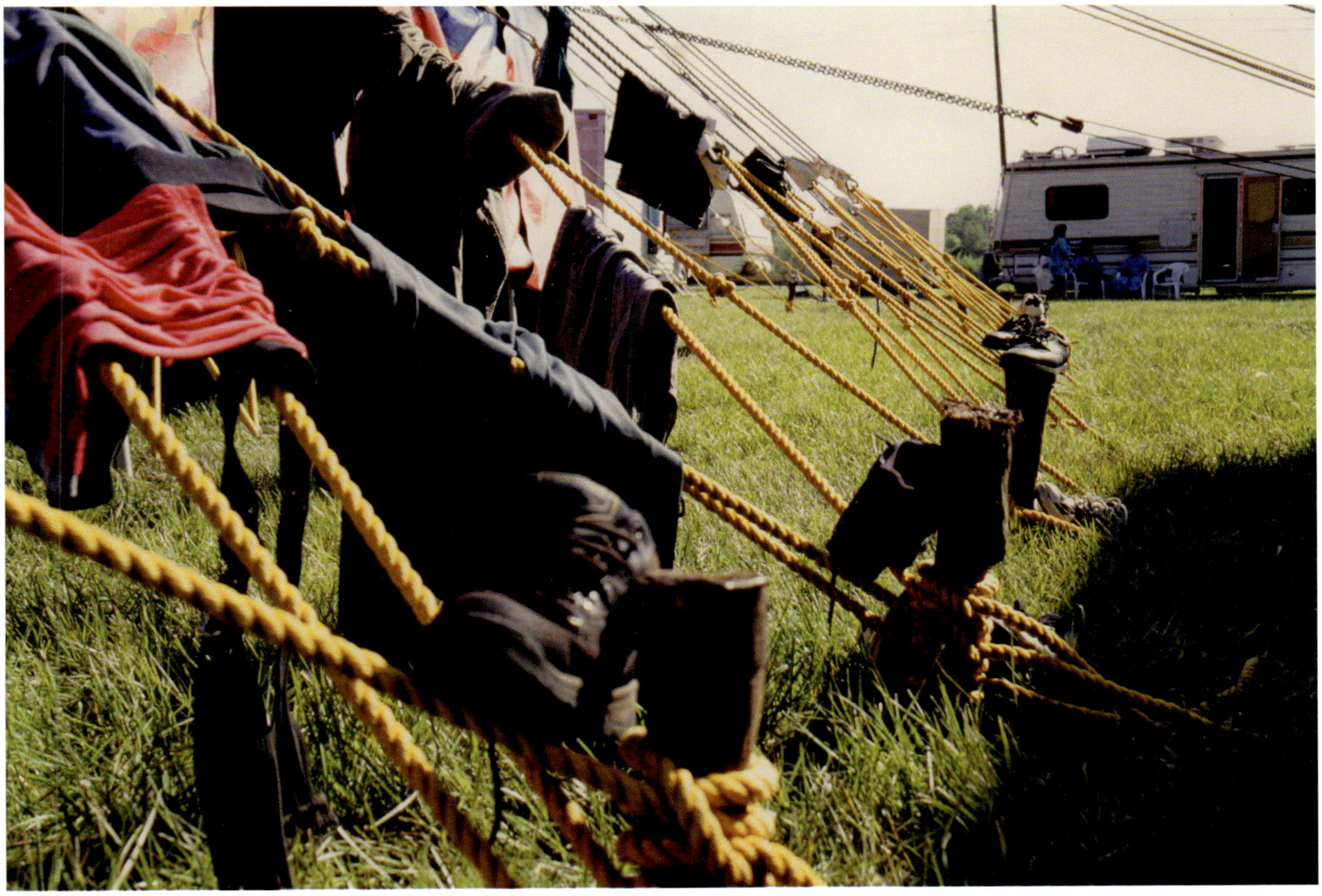

PLATE 54

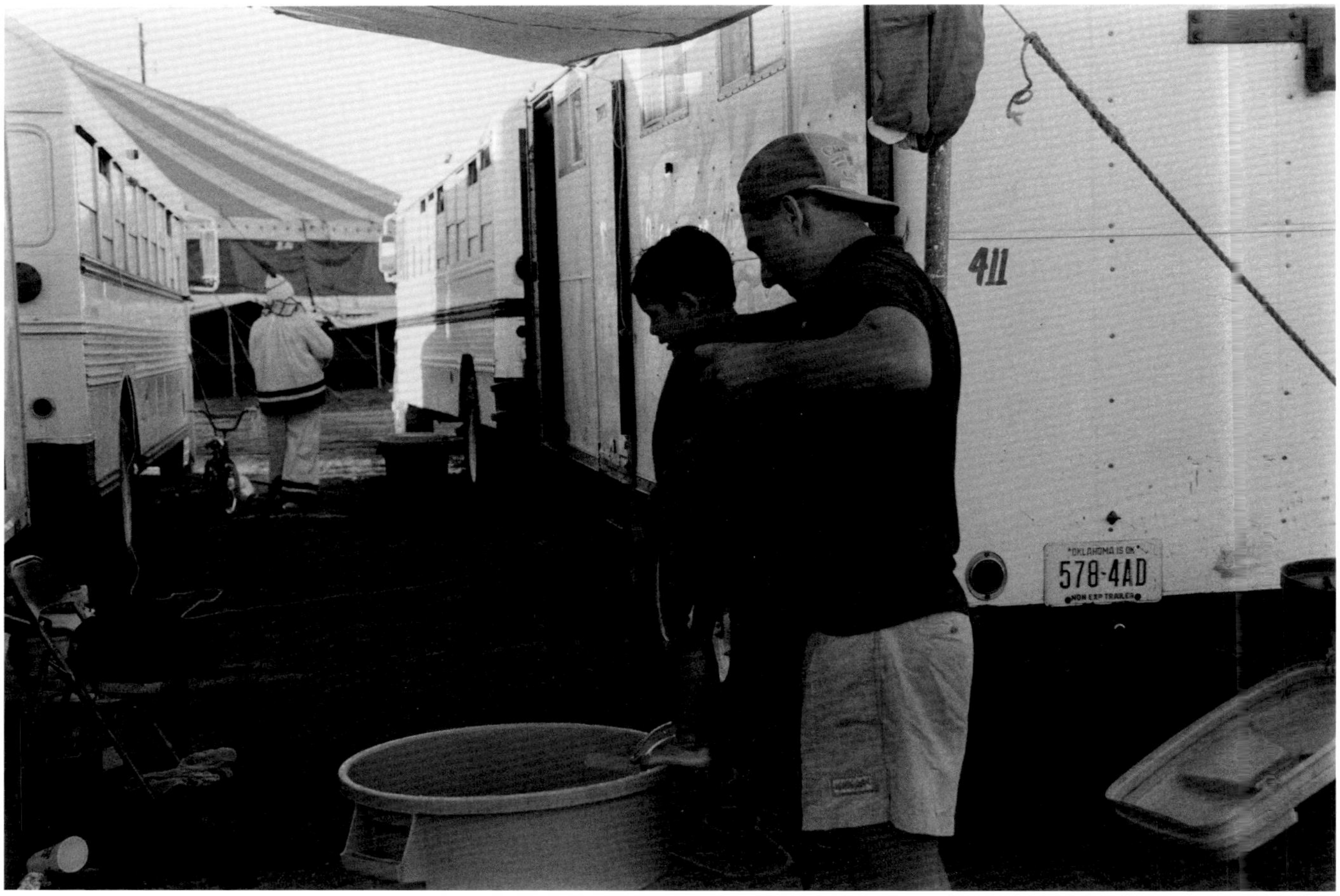

PLATE 55

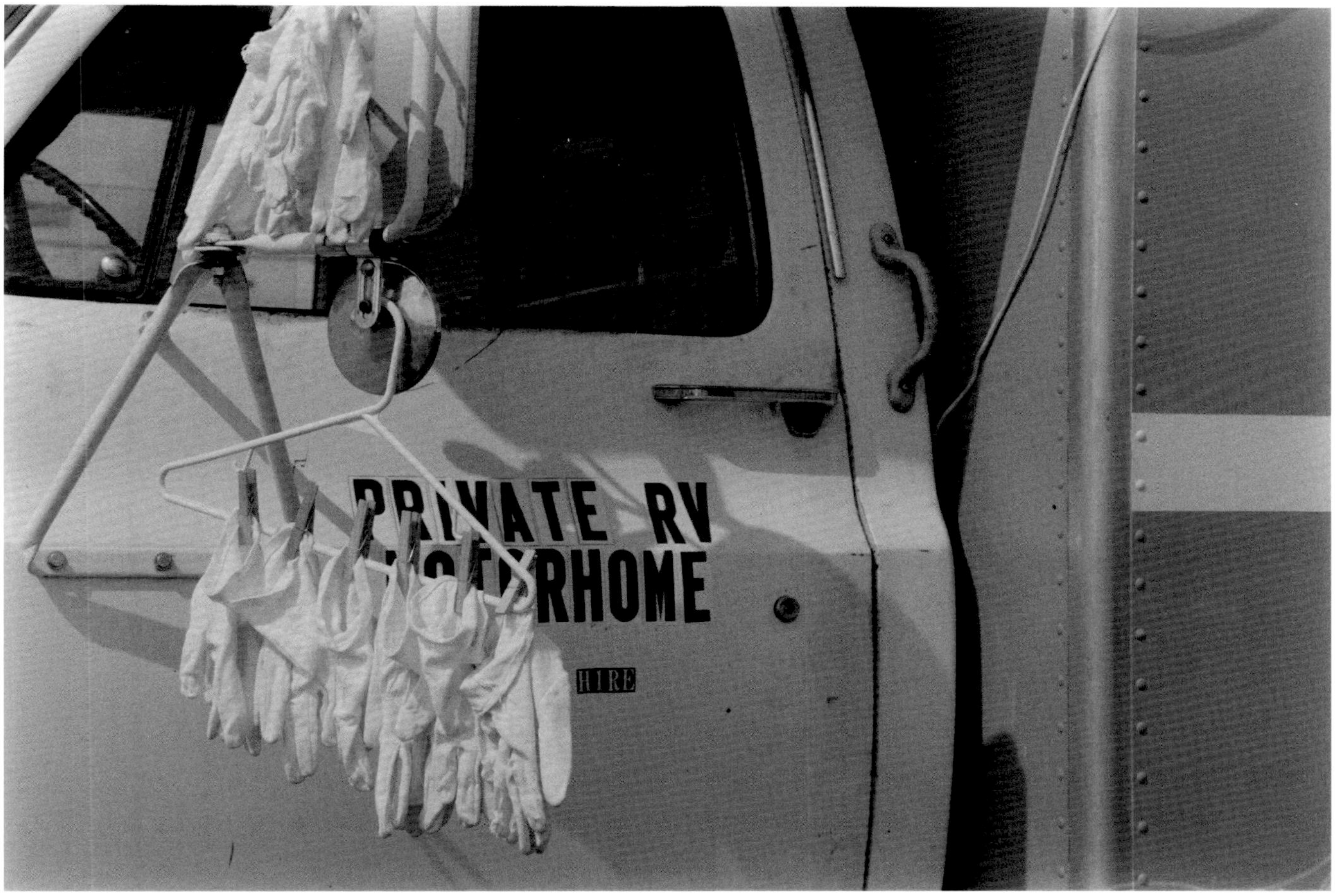

PLATE 56

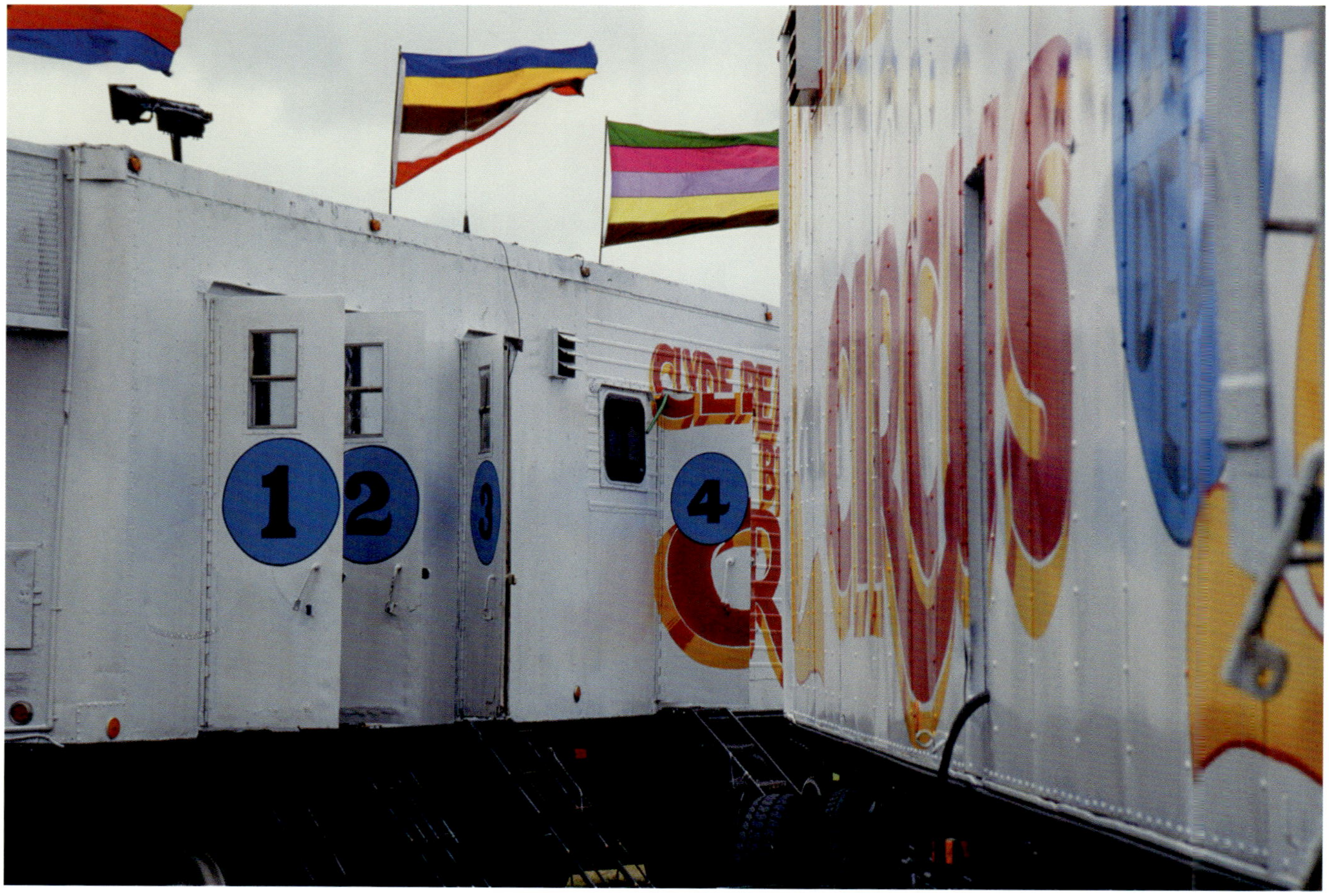

PLATE 57

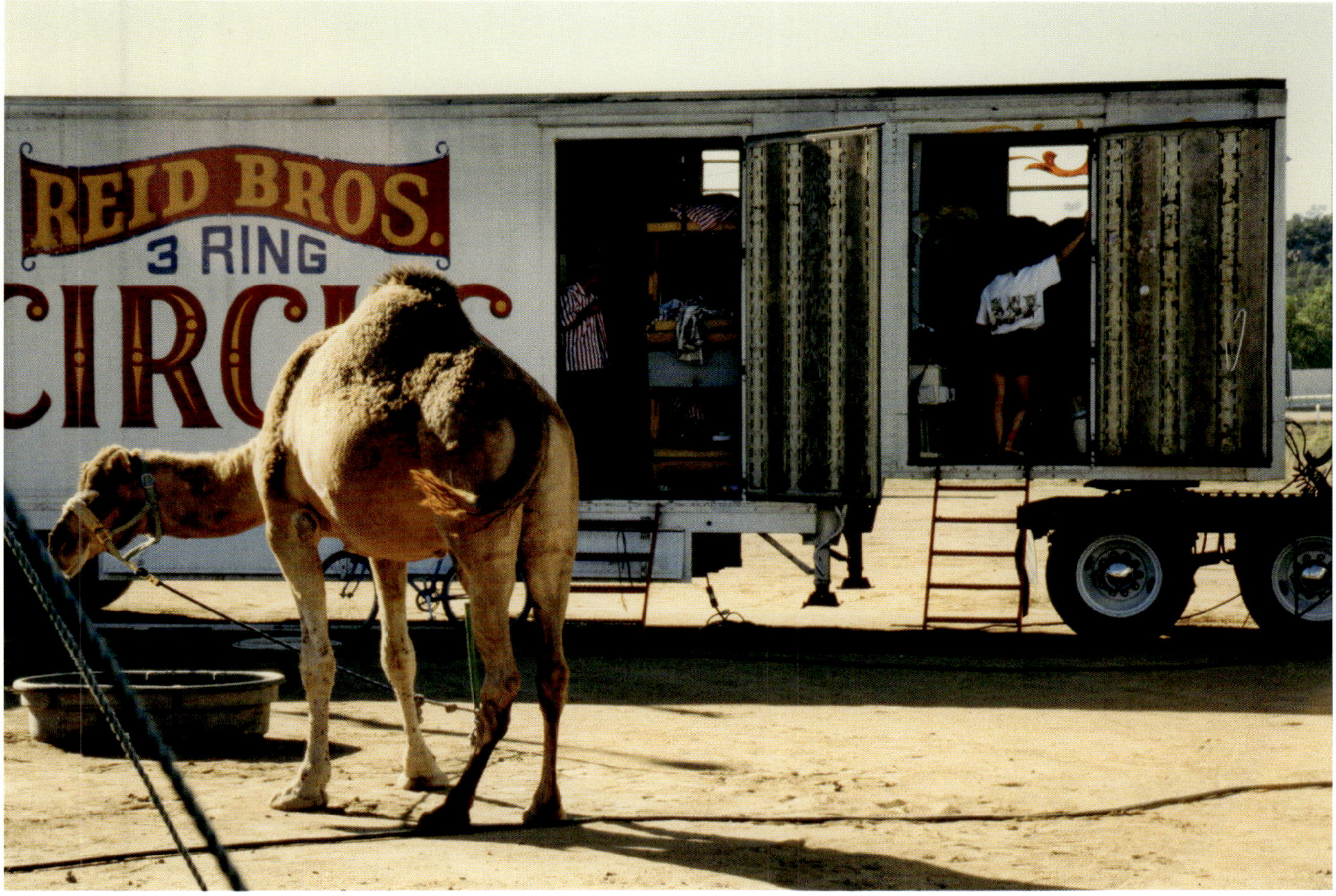

PLATE 58

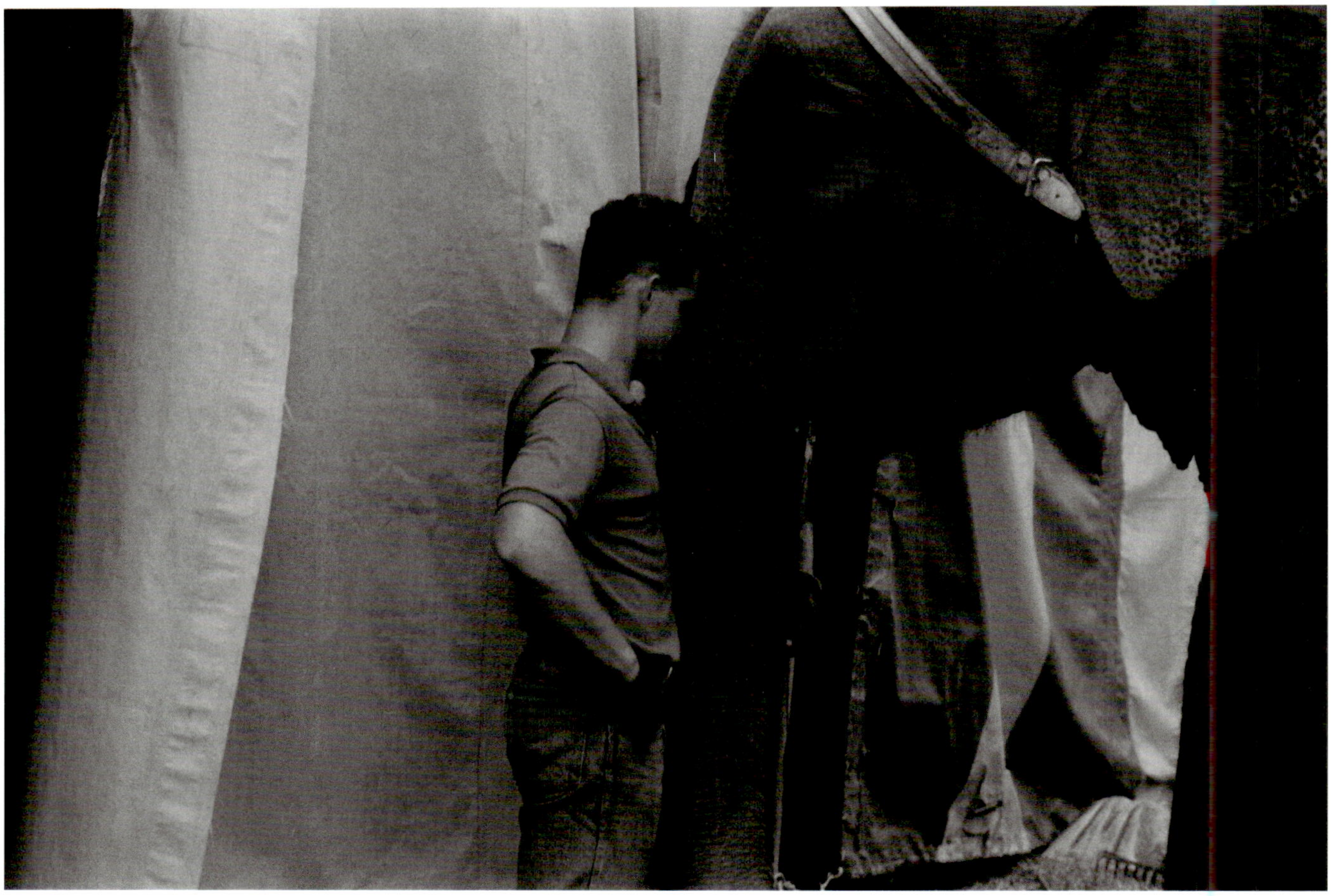

PLATE 59

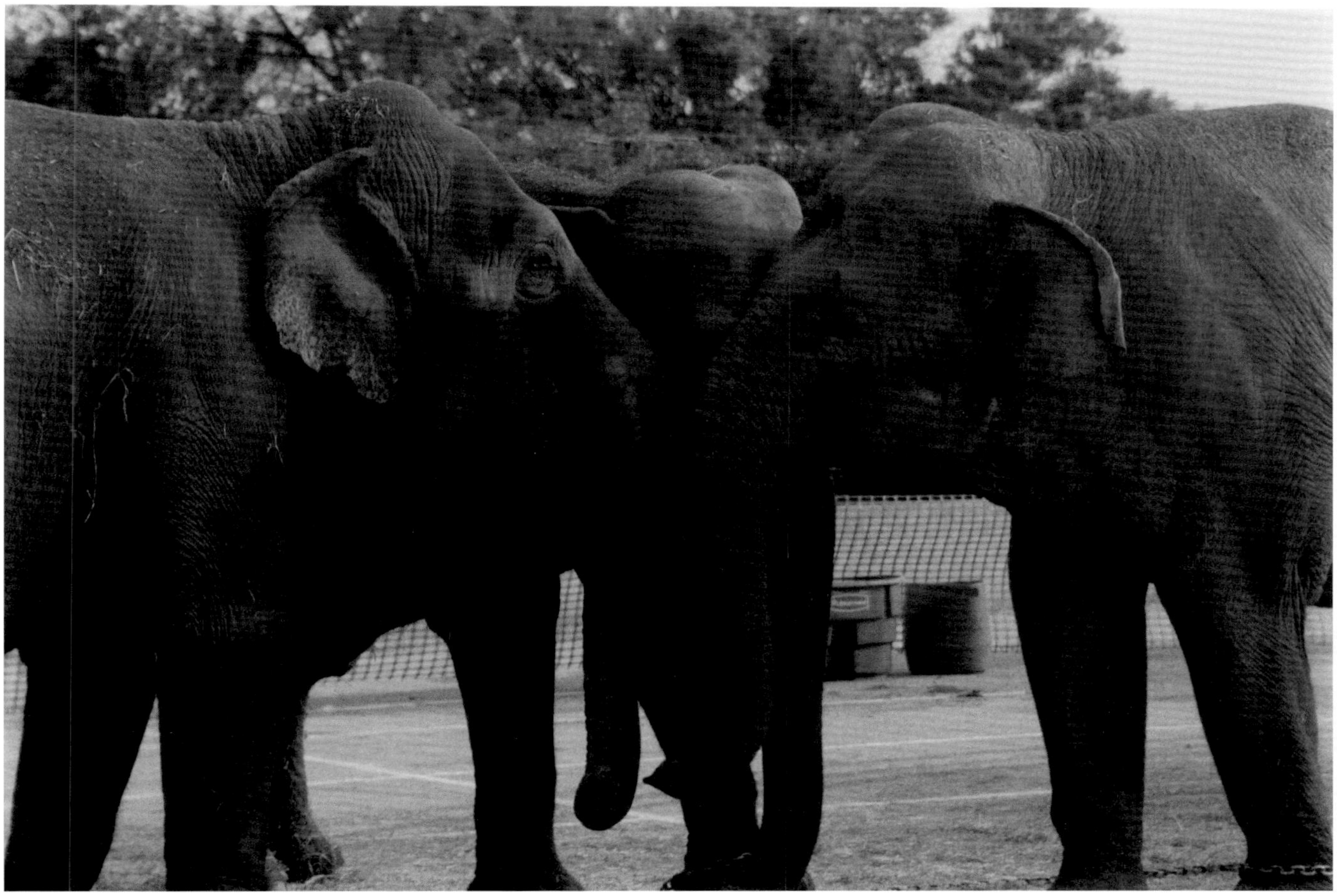

PLATE 60

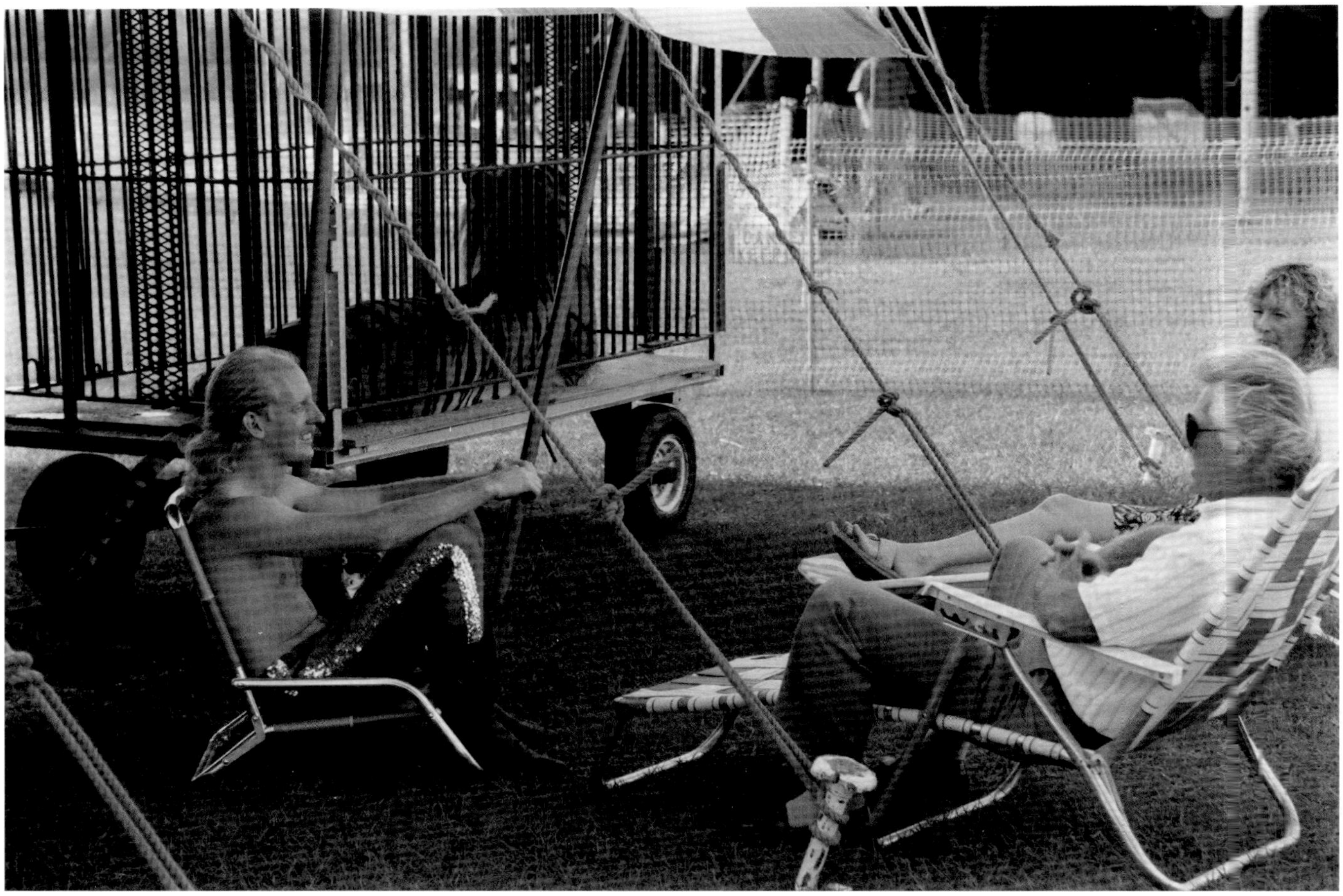

PLATE 61

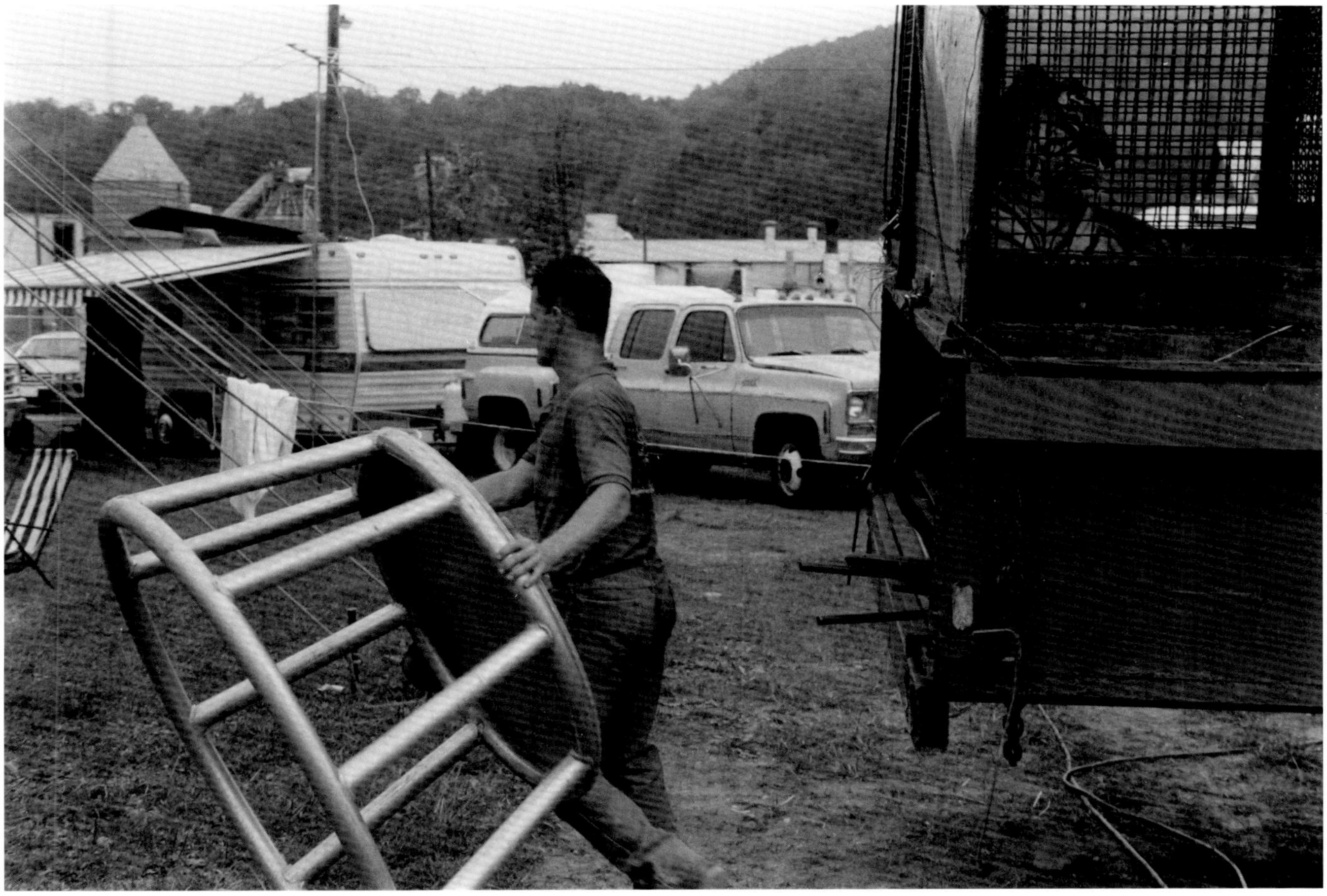

PLATE 62

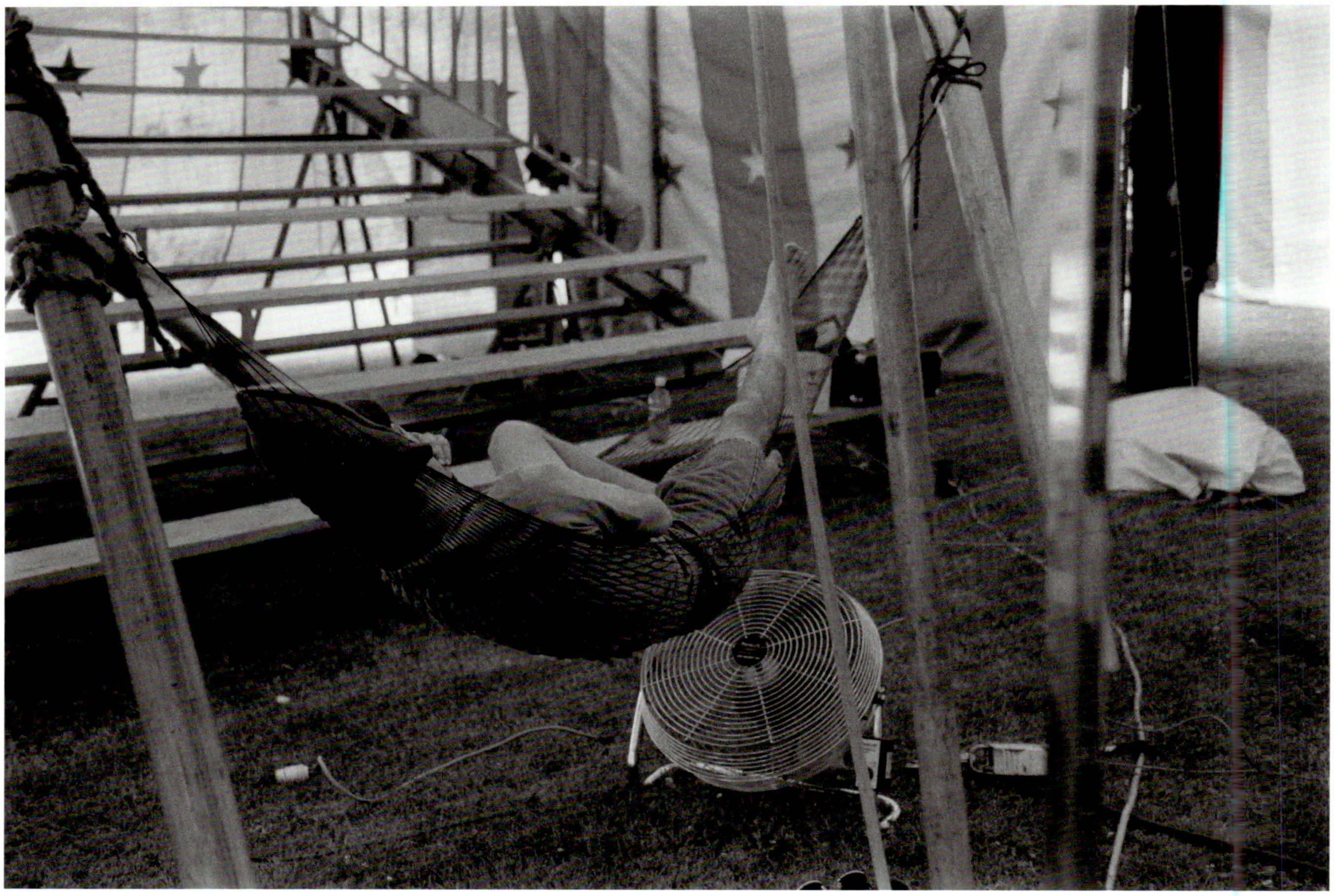

PLATE 63

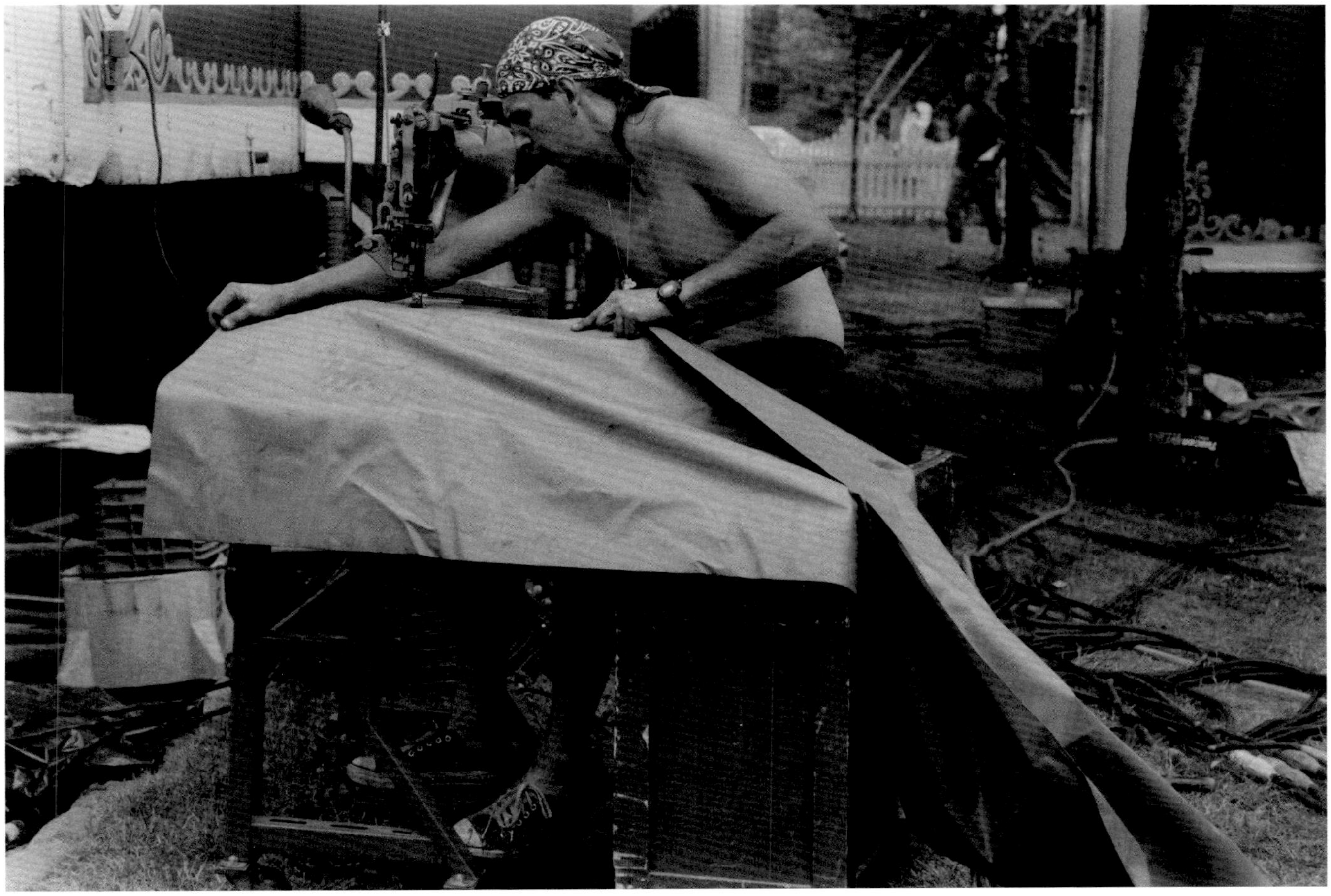

PLATE 64

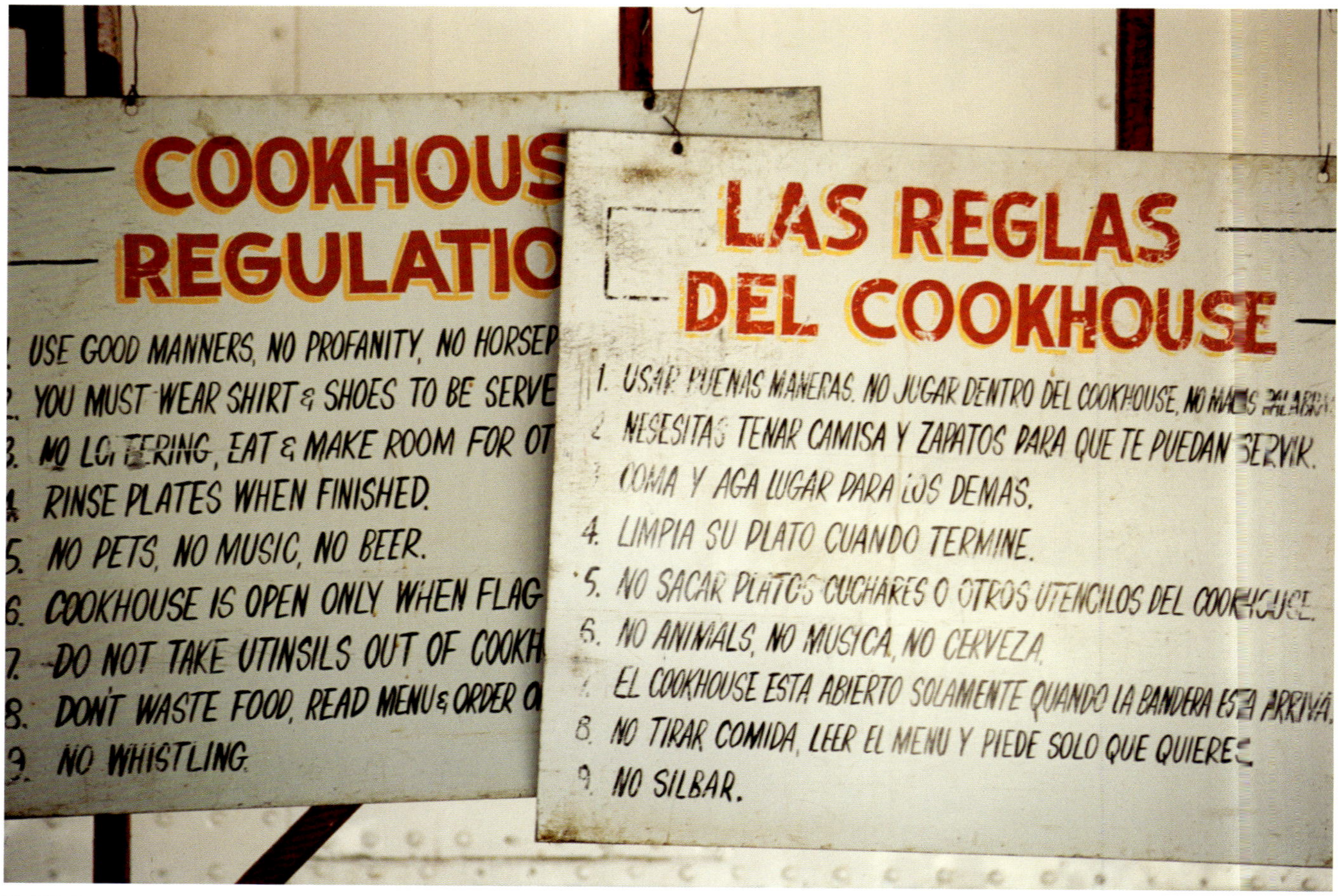
COOKHOUS
REGULATIO
1. USE GOOD MANNERS, NO PROFANITY, NO HORSEP
2. YOU MUST WEAR SHIRT & SHOES TO BE SERVE
3. NO LO TERING, EAT & MAKE ROOM FOR OT
4. RINSE PLATES WHEN FINISHED.
5. NO PETS, NO MUSIC, NO BEER.
6. COOKHOUSE IS OPEN ONLY WHEN FLAG
7. DO NOT TAKE UTINSILS OUT OF COOKH
8. DON'T WASTE FOOD, READ MENU & ORDER O
9. NO WHISTLING.
LAS REGLAS
DEL COOKHOUSE
1. USAR BUENAS MANERAS. NO JUGAR DENTRO DEL COOKHOUSE,
2. NESESITAS TENAR CAMISA Y ZAPATOS PARA QUE TE PUEDAN SERVIR.
3. COMA Y AGA LUGAR PARA LOS DEMAS.
4. LIMPIA SU PLATO CUANDO TERMINE.
5. NO SACAR PLATOS CUCHARES O OTROS UTENCILOS DEL COOKHOUSE.
6. NO ANIMALS, NO MUSICA, NO CERVEZA.
7. EL COOKHOUSE ESTA ABIERTO SOLAMENTE QUANDO LA BANDERA ESTA ARRIVA.
8. NO TIRAR COMIDA, LEER EL MENU Y PIEDE SOLO QUE QUIERES.
9. NO SILBAR.

PLATE 65

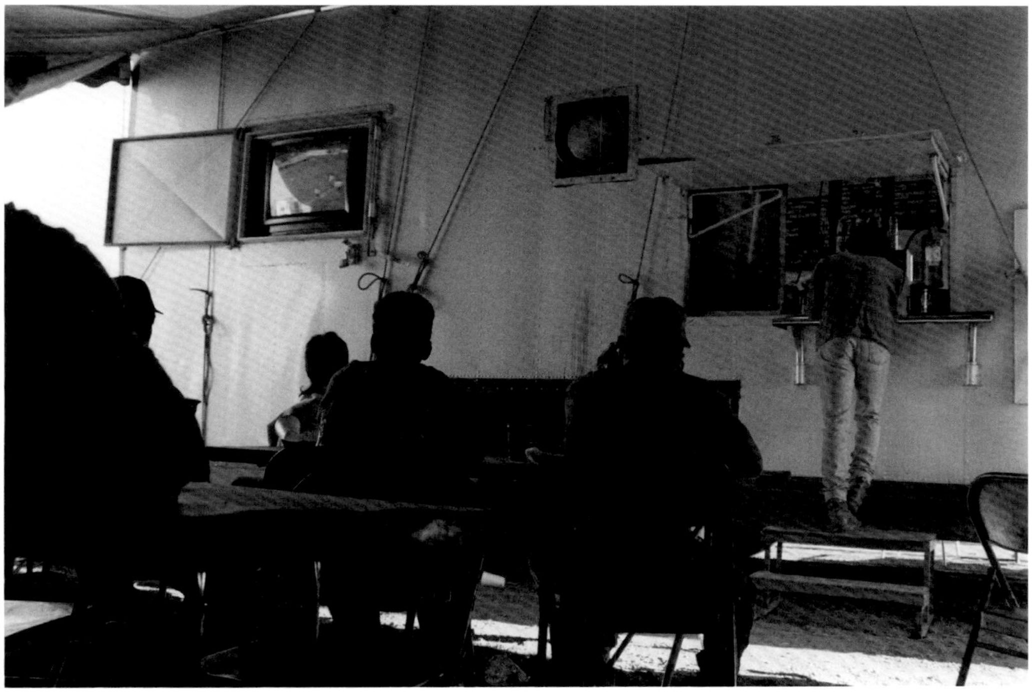

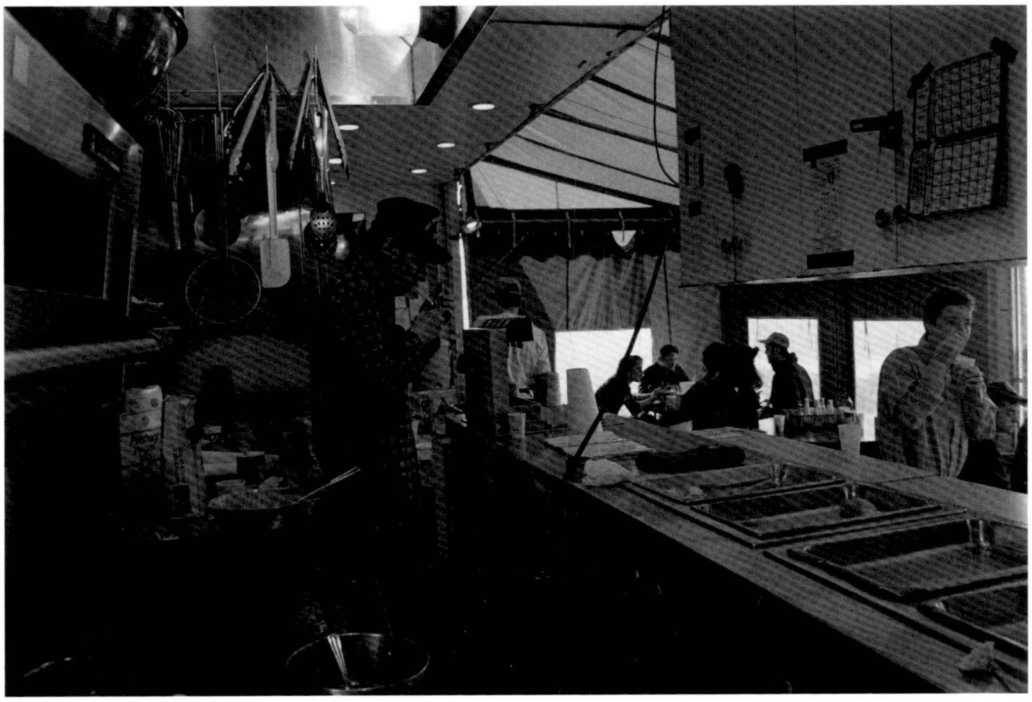

PLATES 66 & 67

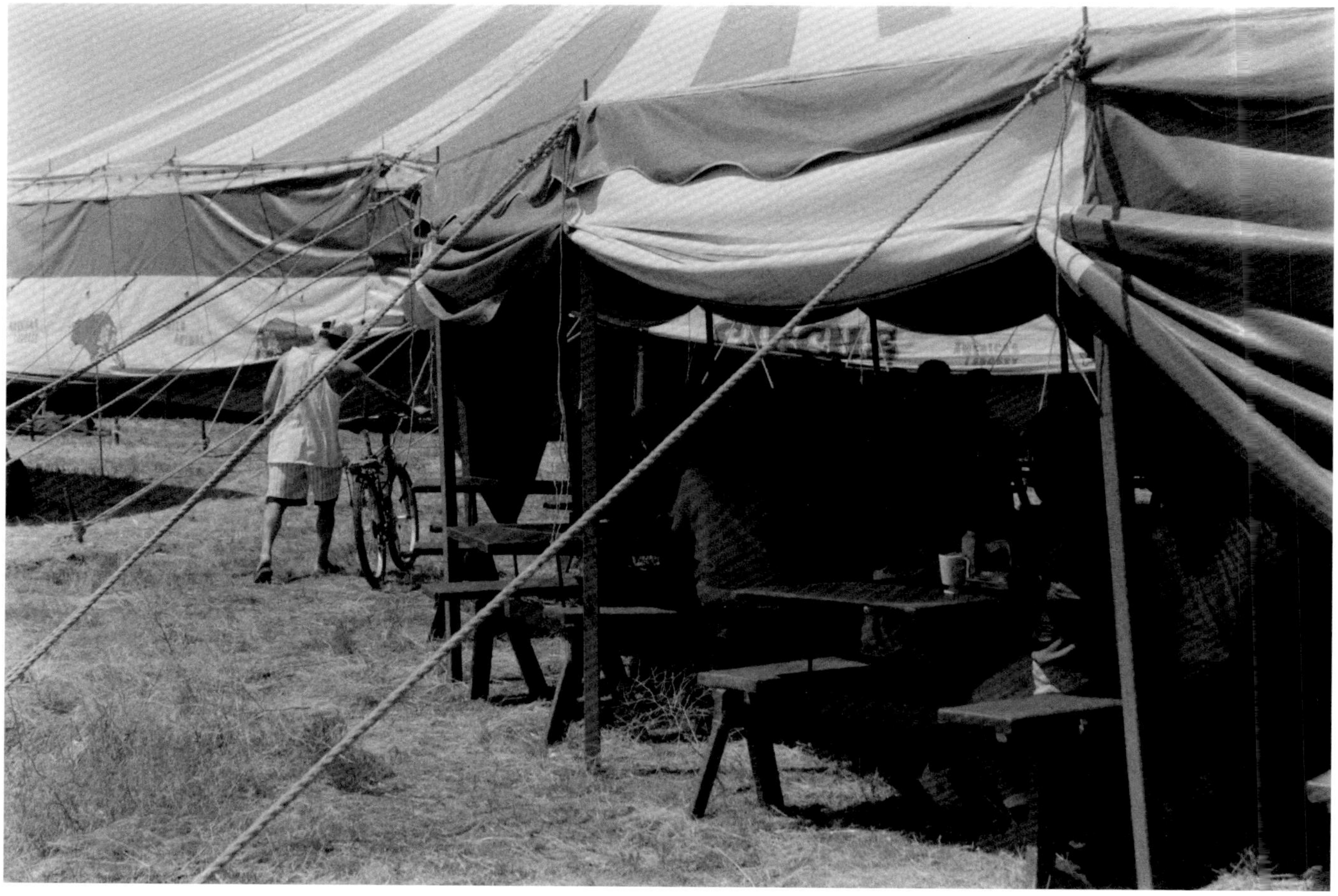

PLATE 68

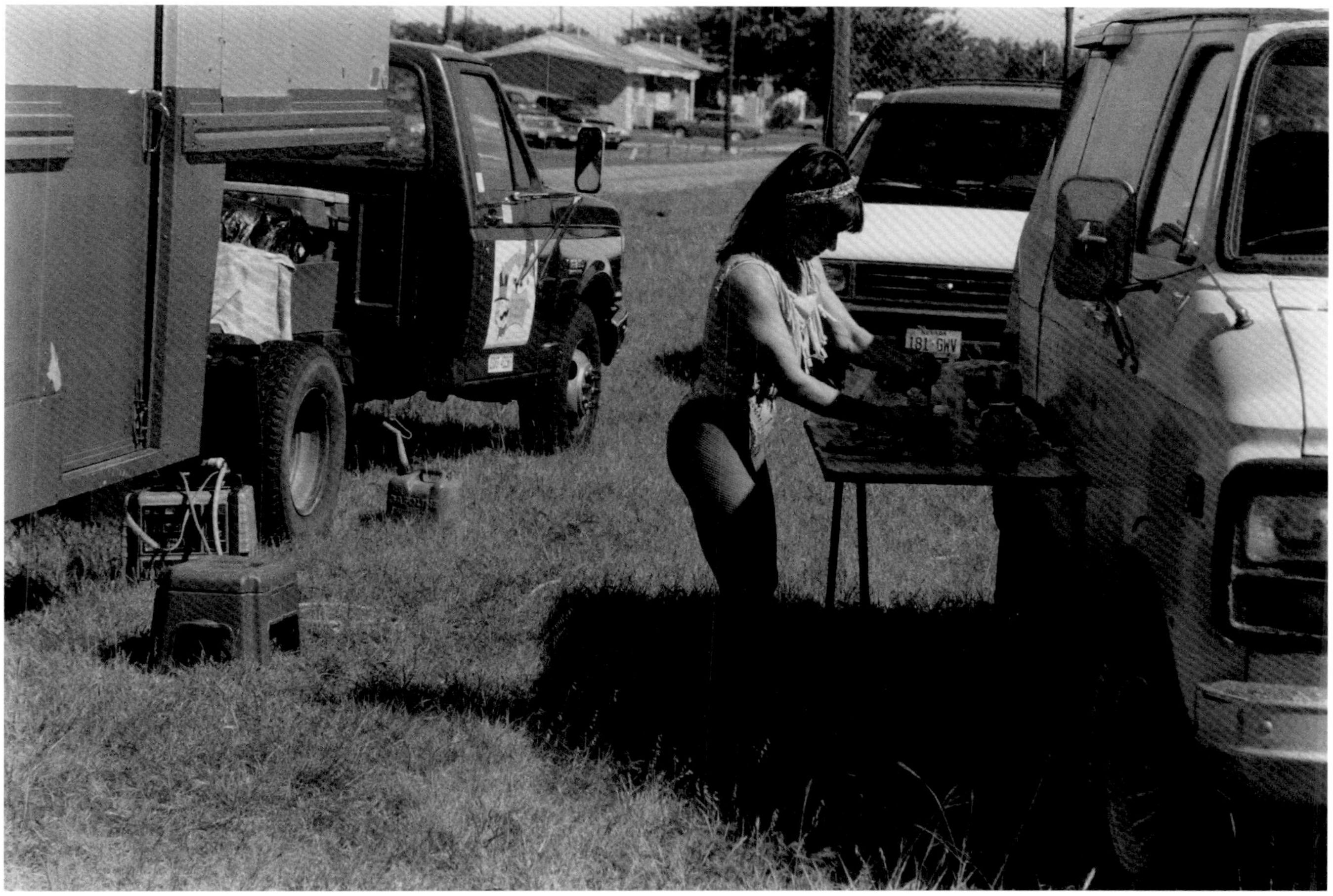

PLATE 69

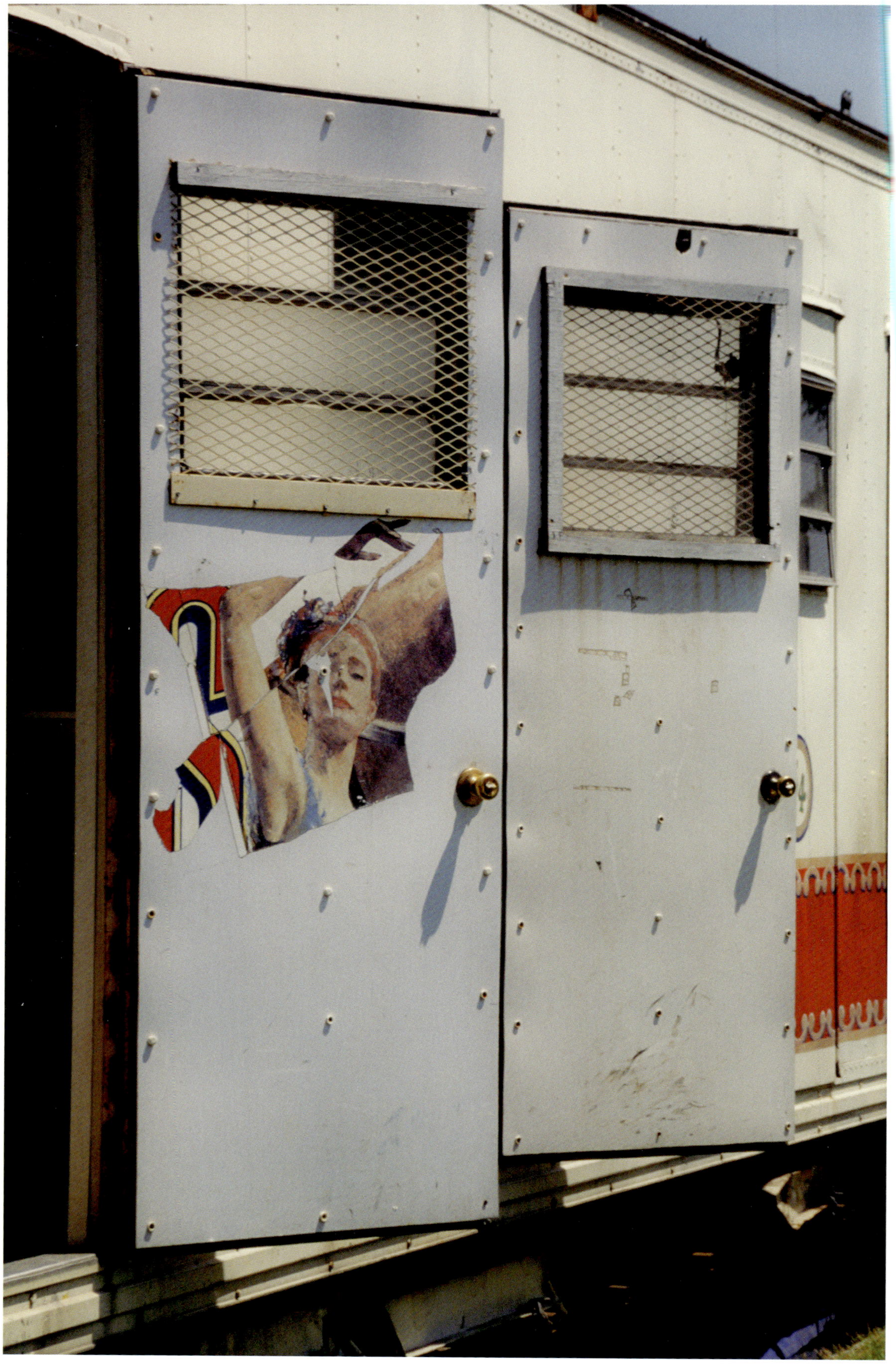

PLATE 70

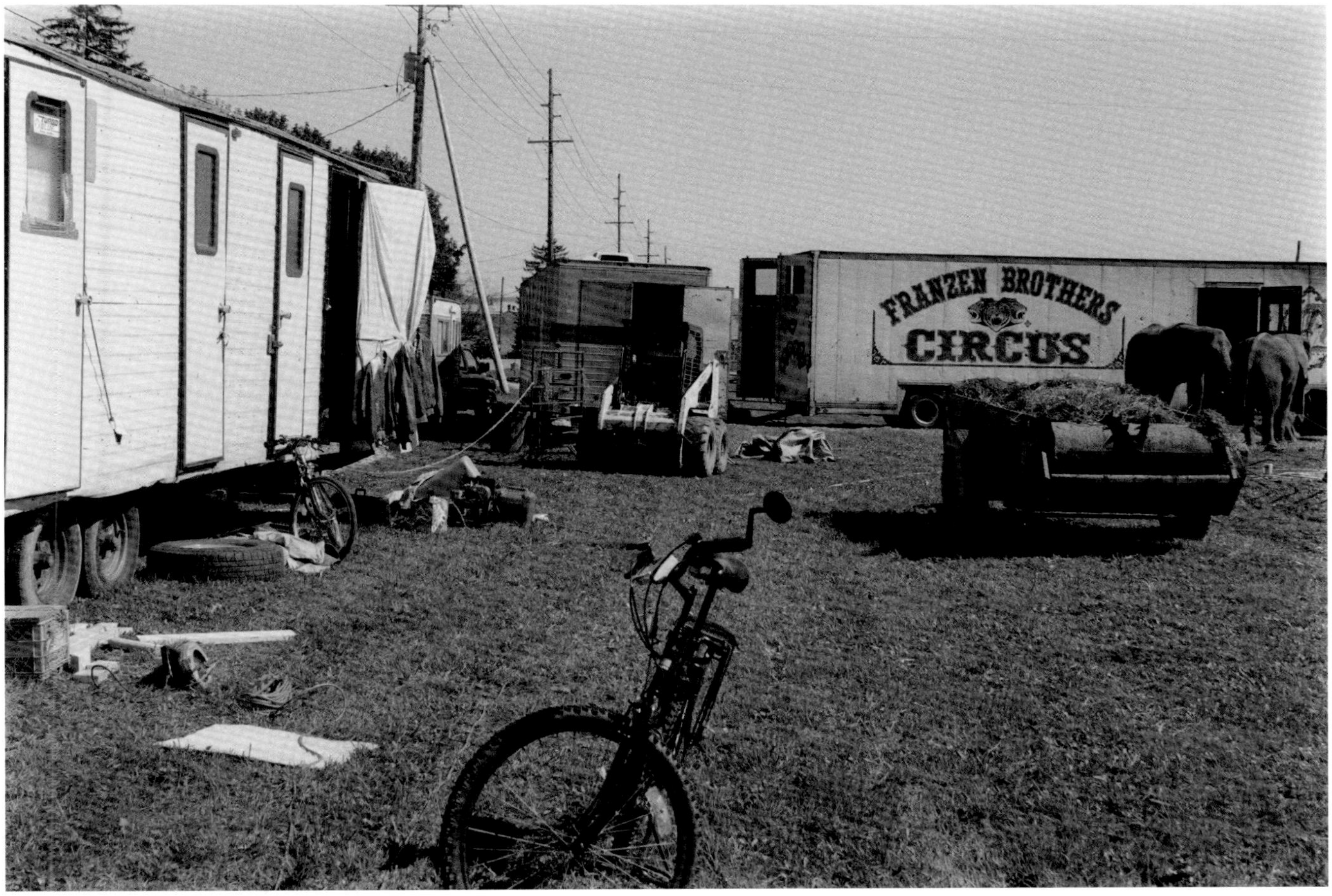

PLATE 71

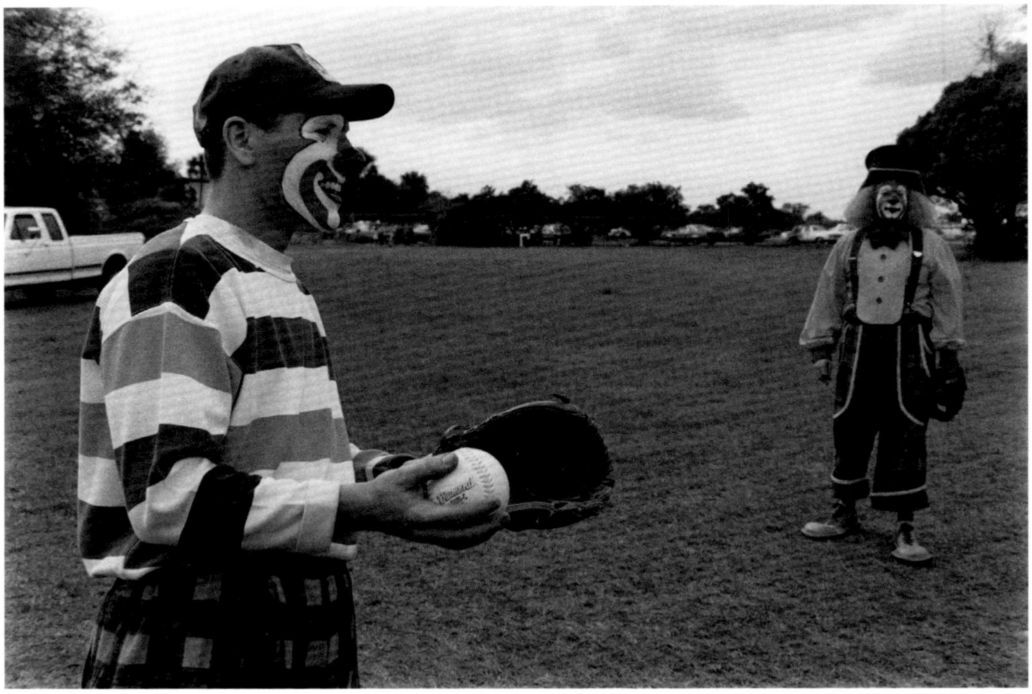

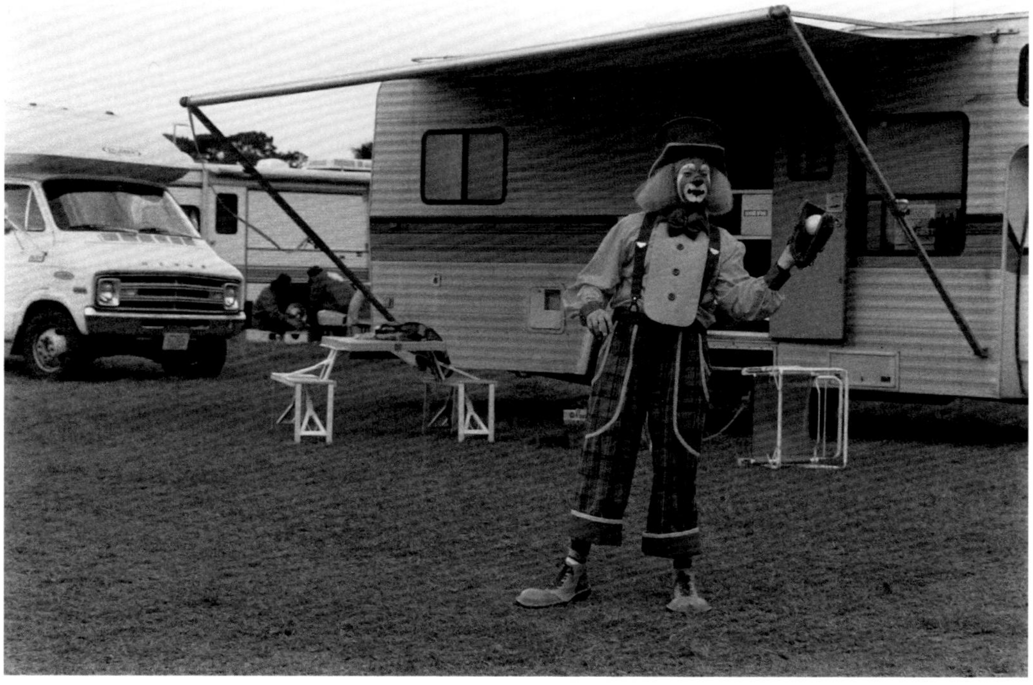

PLATES 72 & 73

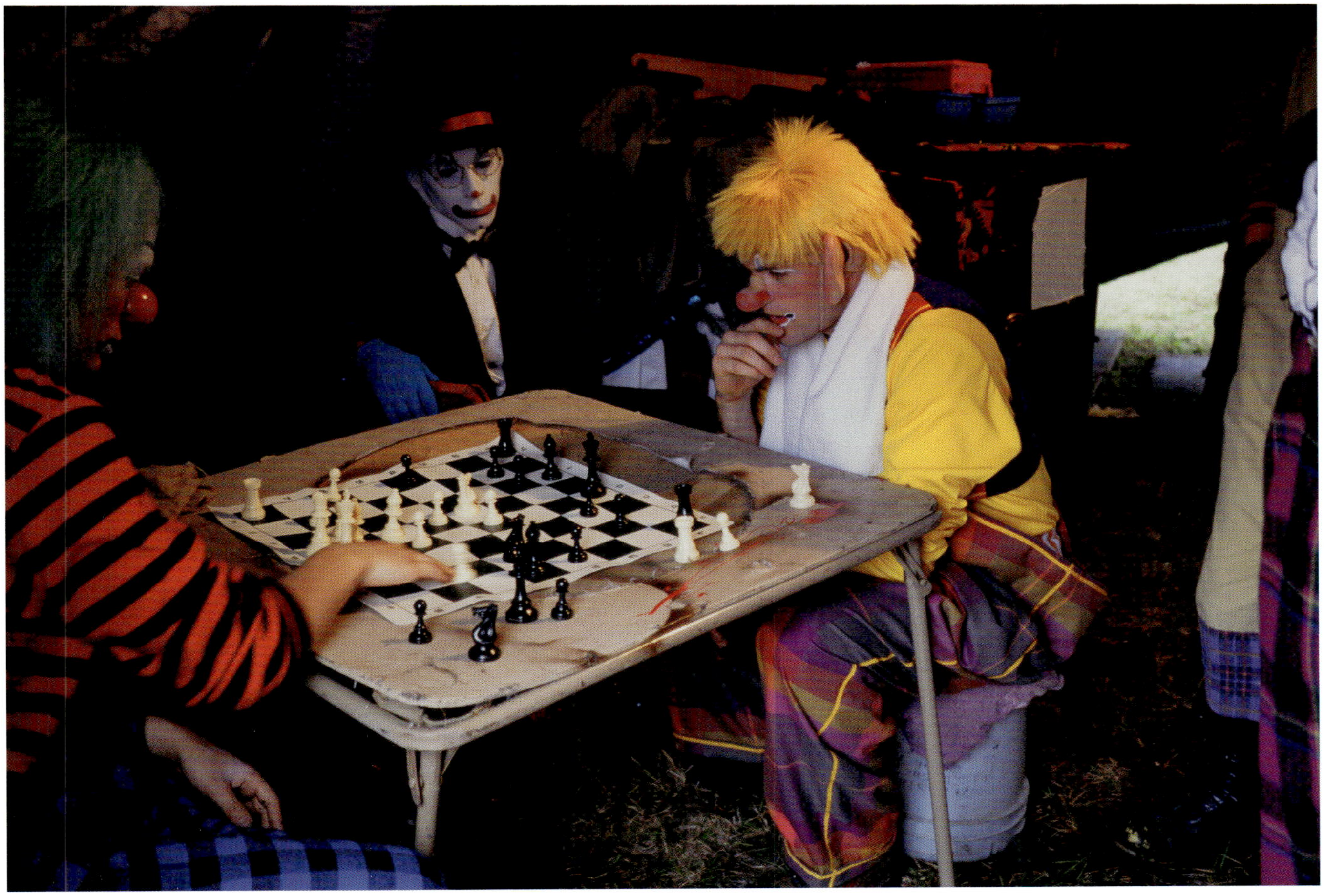

PLATE 74

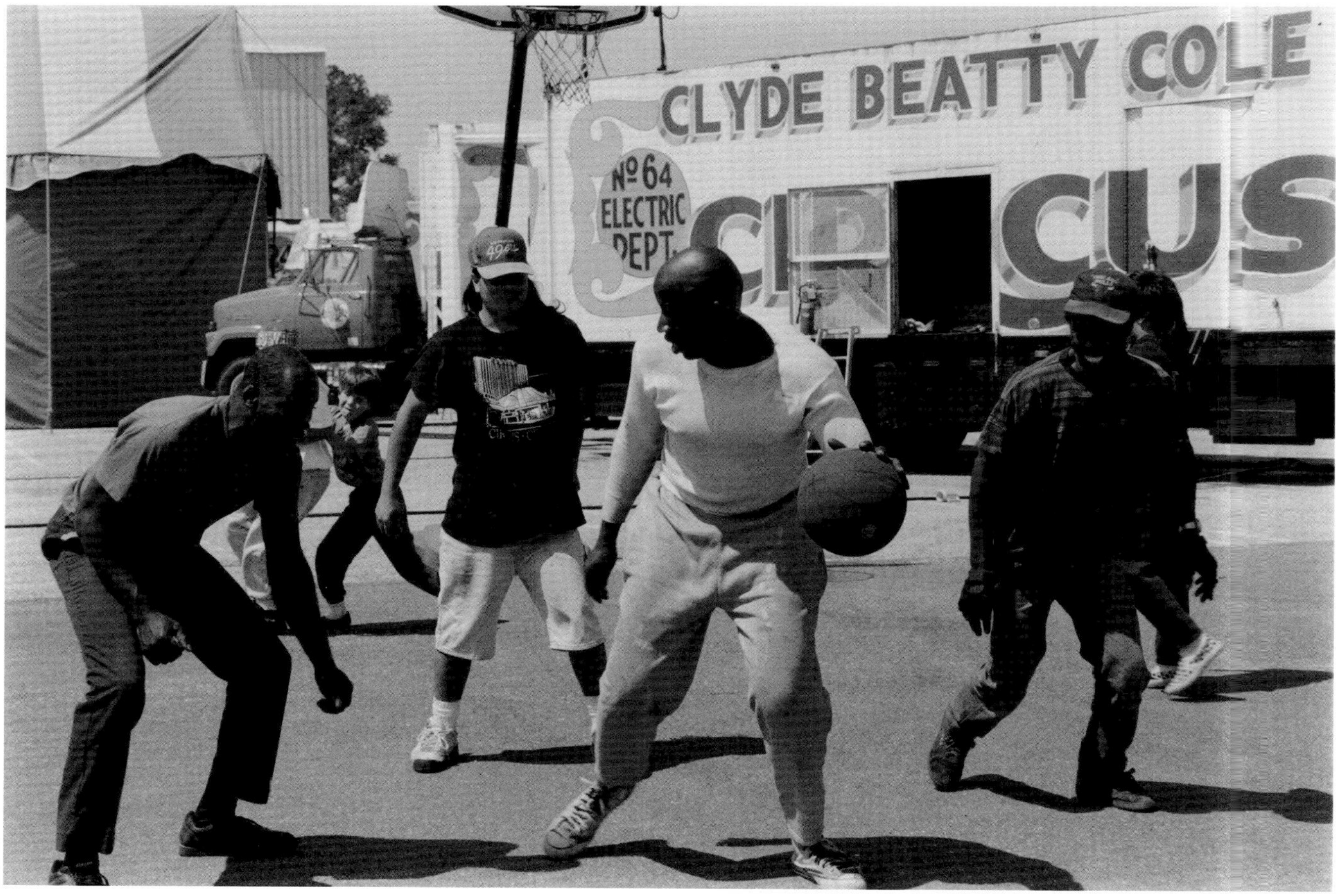

PLATE 75

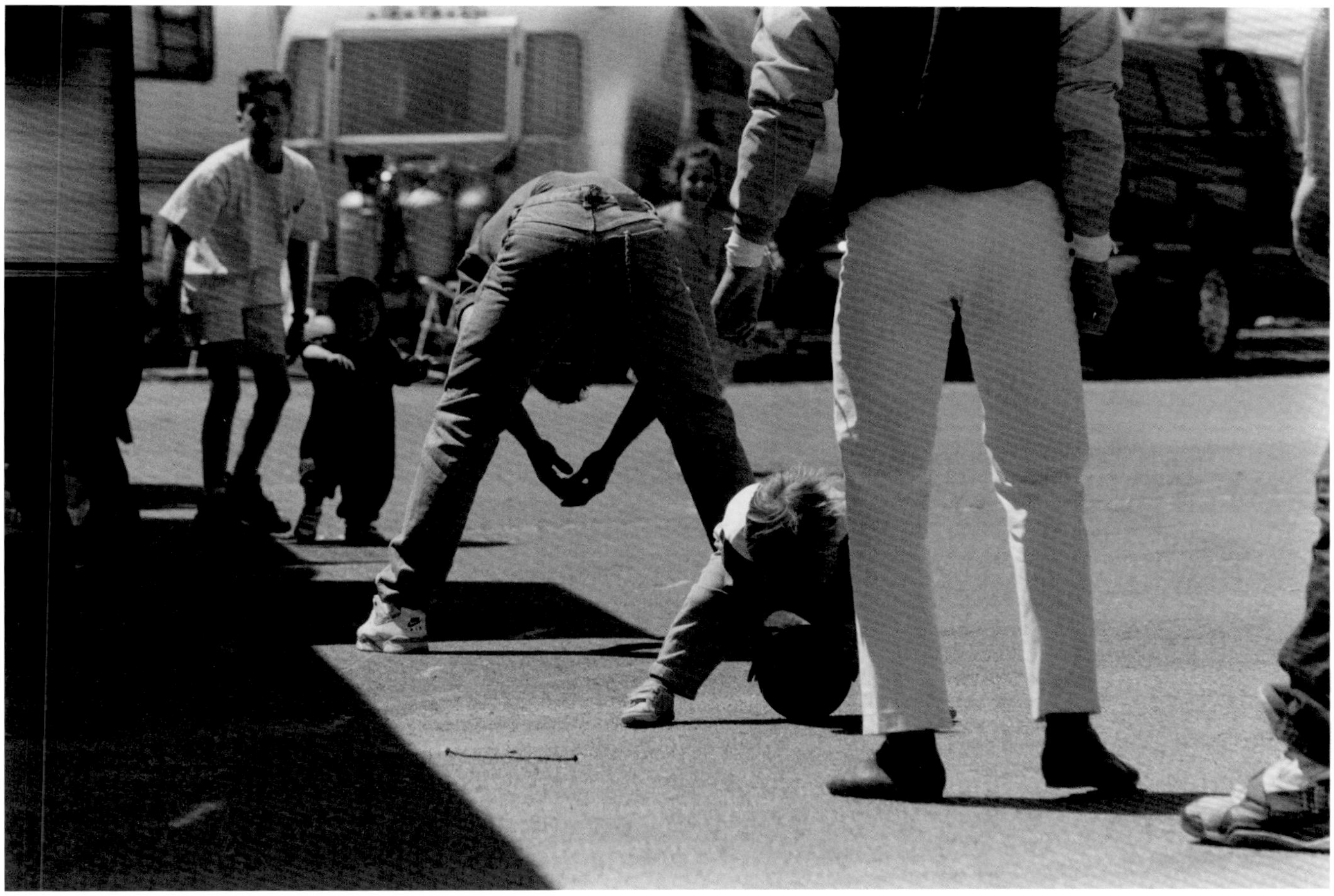

PLATE 76

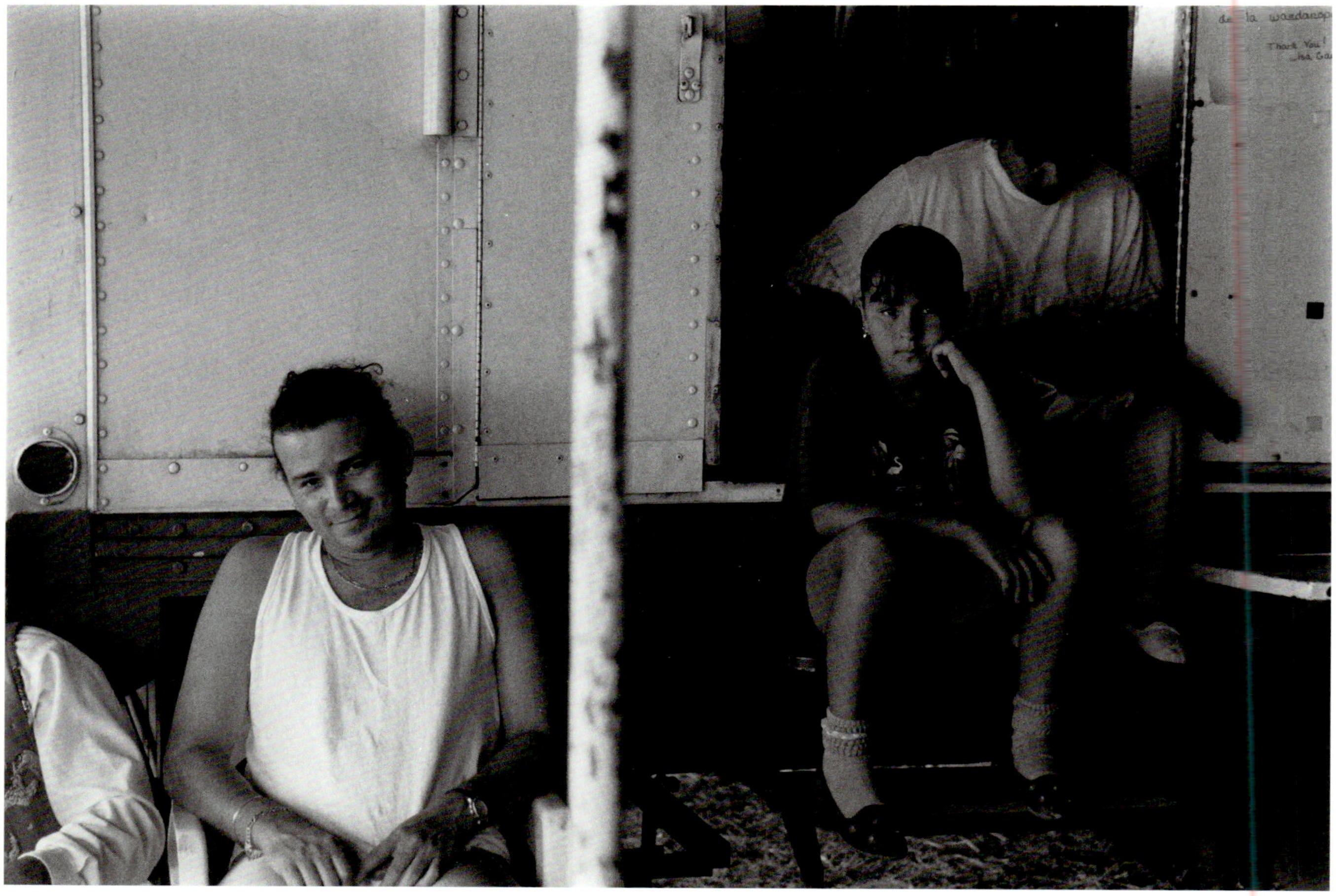

PLATE 77

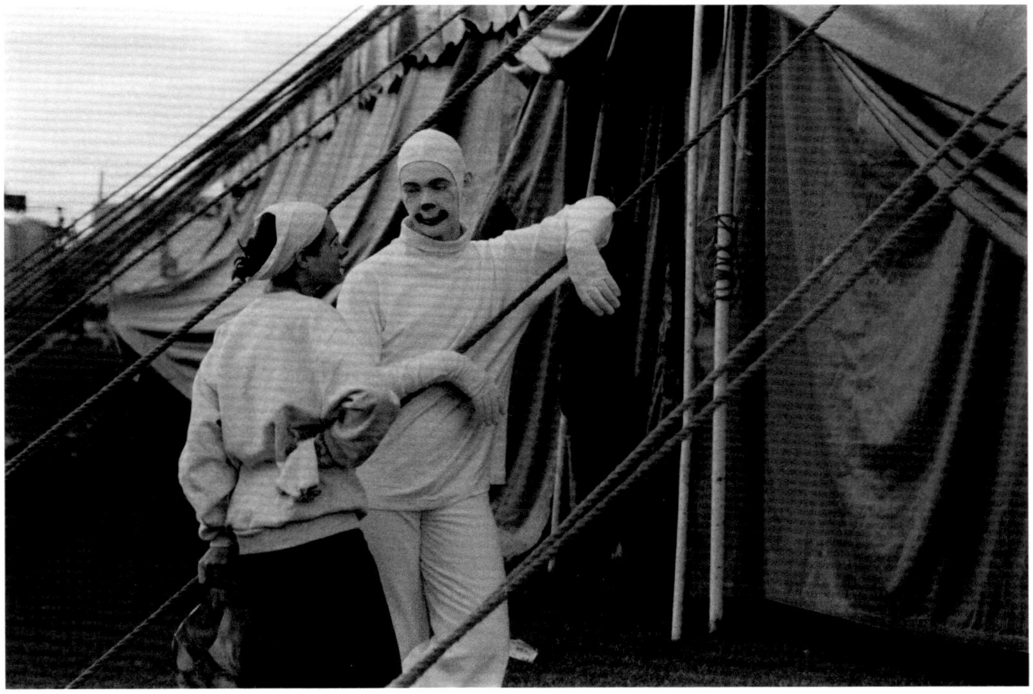

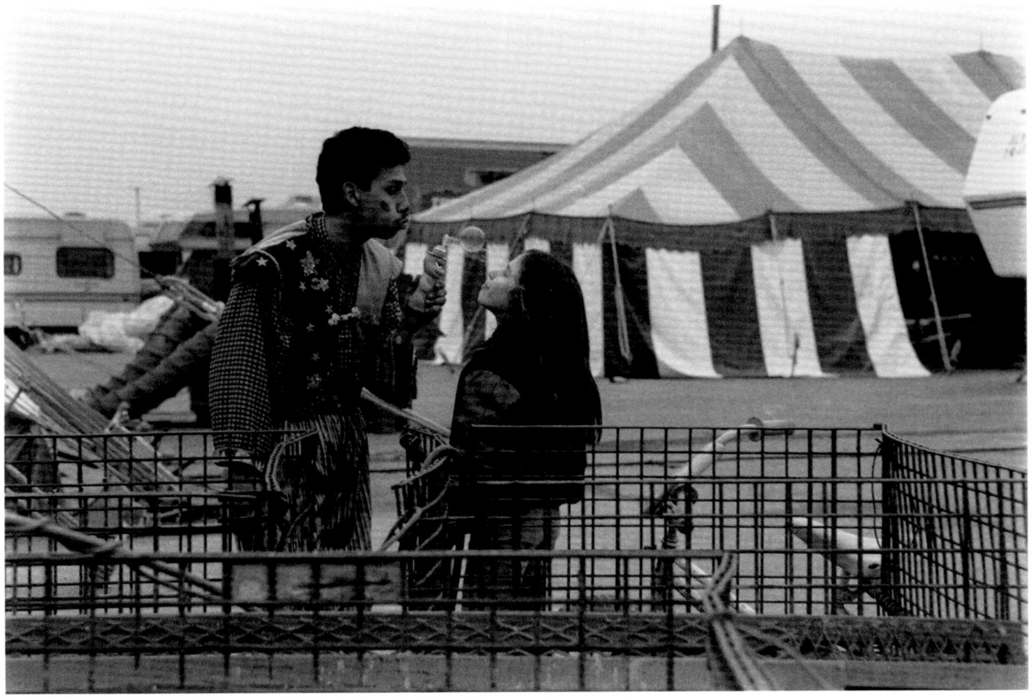

PLATES 78 & 79

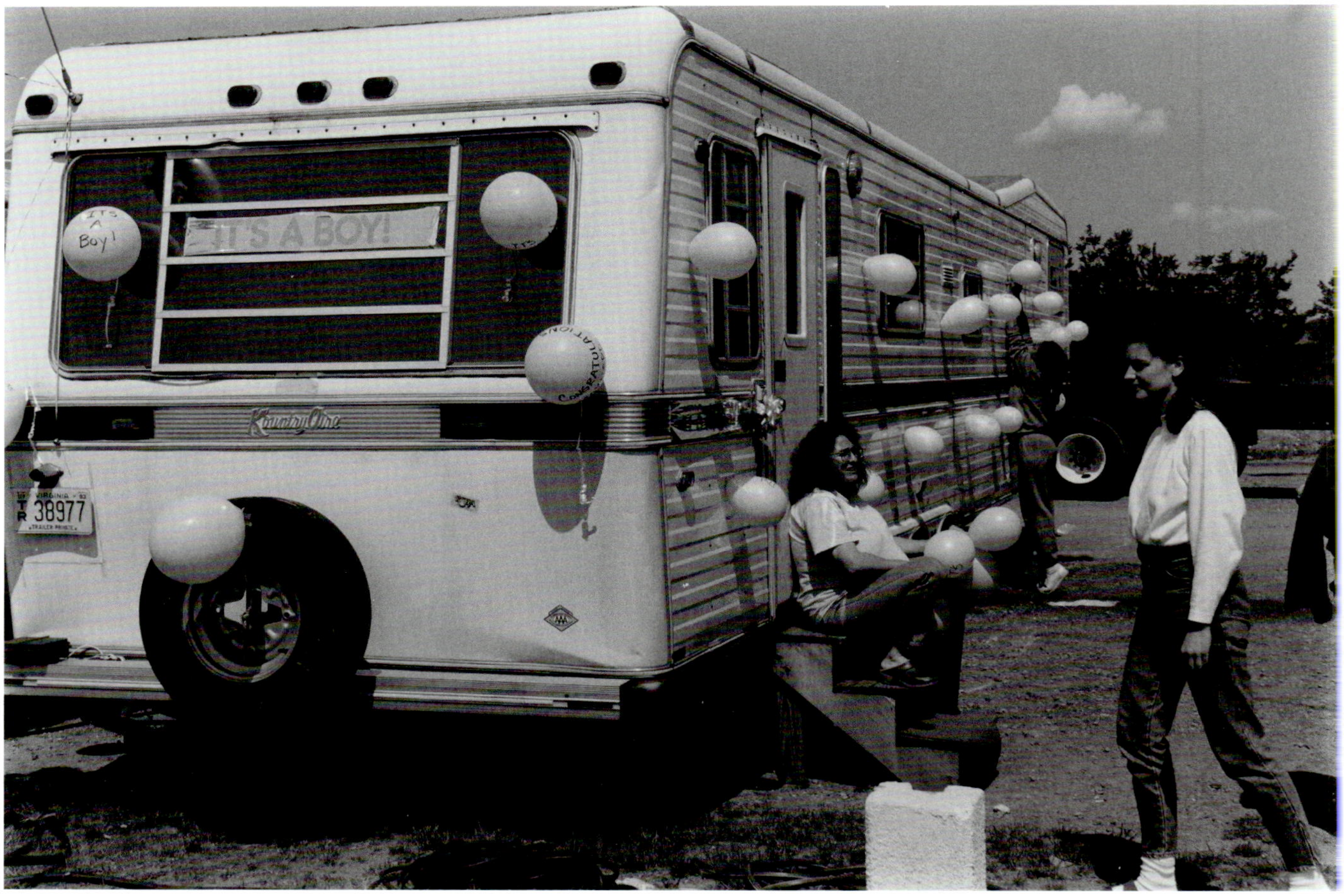

PLATE 80

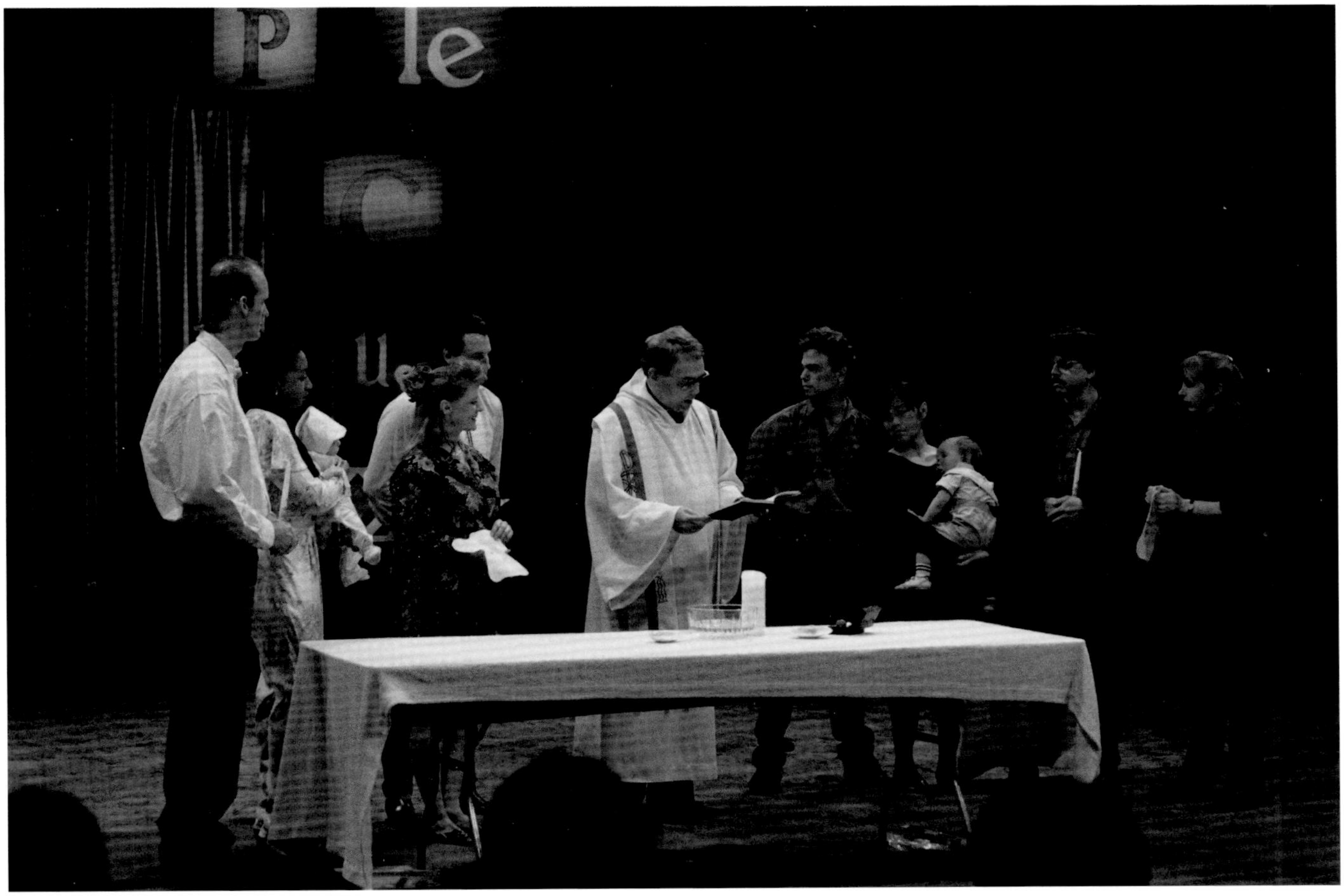

PLATE 81

★ ★ ★ ★ ★ ★ ★ ★ ★ ★ ★ ★ ★ ★

When I think of kids that I have known that have grown up in this business, they are terrific human beings. There's no street corner to hang out on. They grow up with family values. They don't miss anything really; they know what's going on in the world. Show kids . . . they're the hippest kids in the world.

—Jimmy James, performance director and ringmaster, Clyde Beatty-Cole Bros. Circus (1995)

★ ★ ★ ★ ★ ★ ★ ★ ★ ★ ★ ★ ★ ★

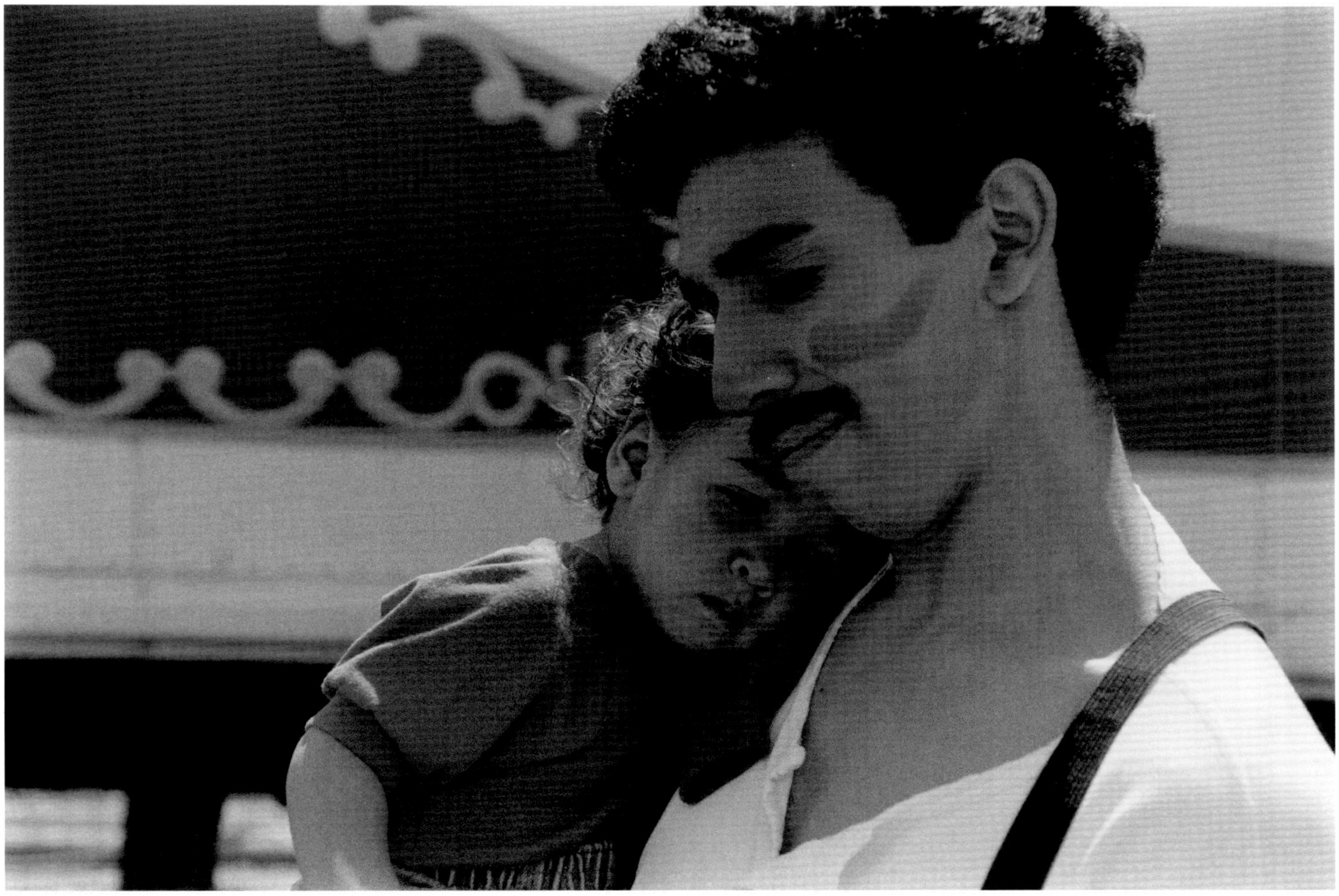

PLATE 82

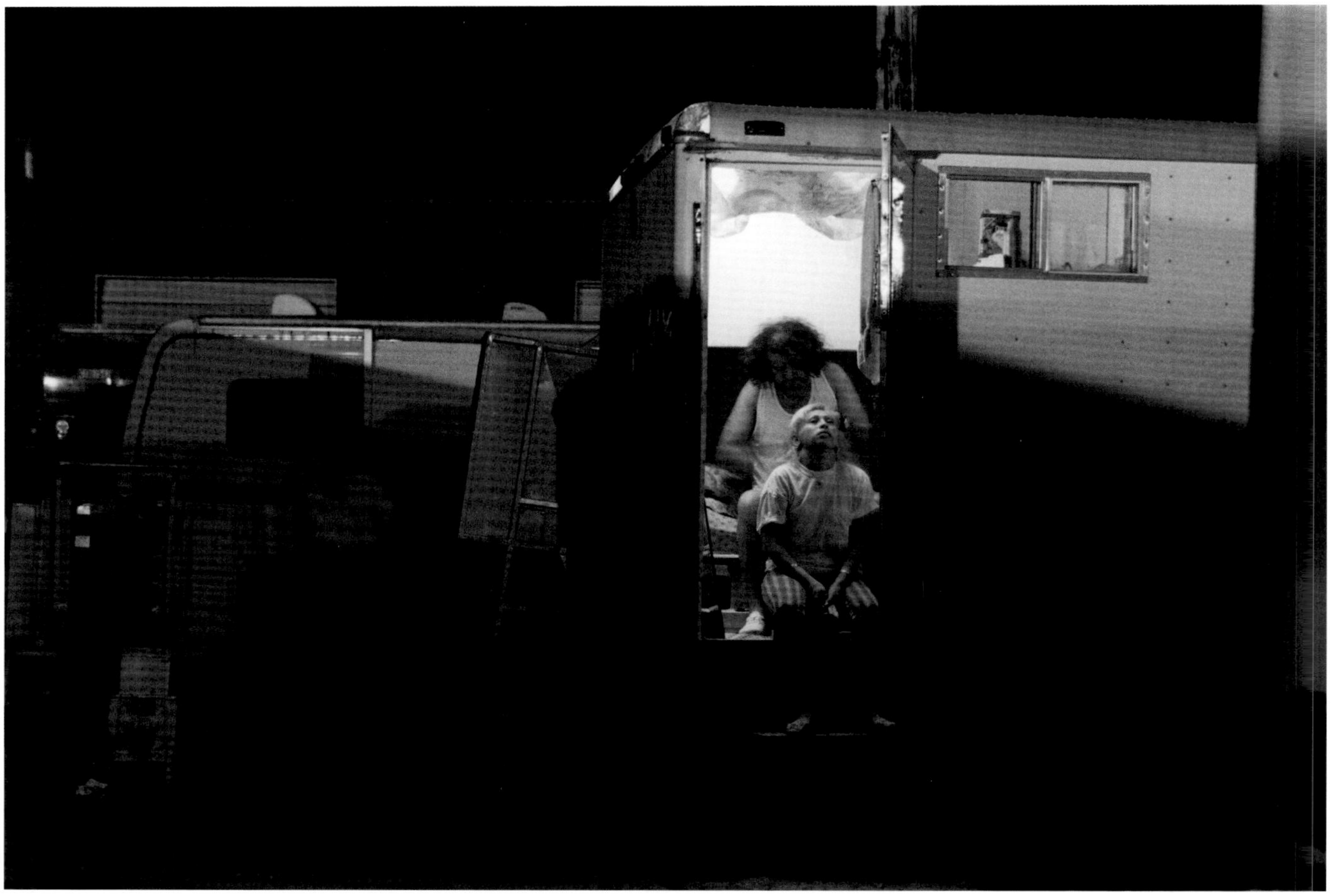

PLATE 83

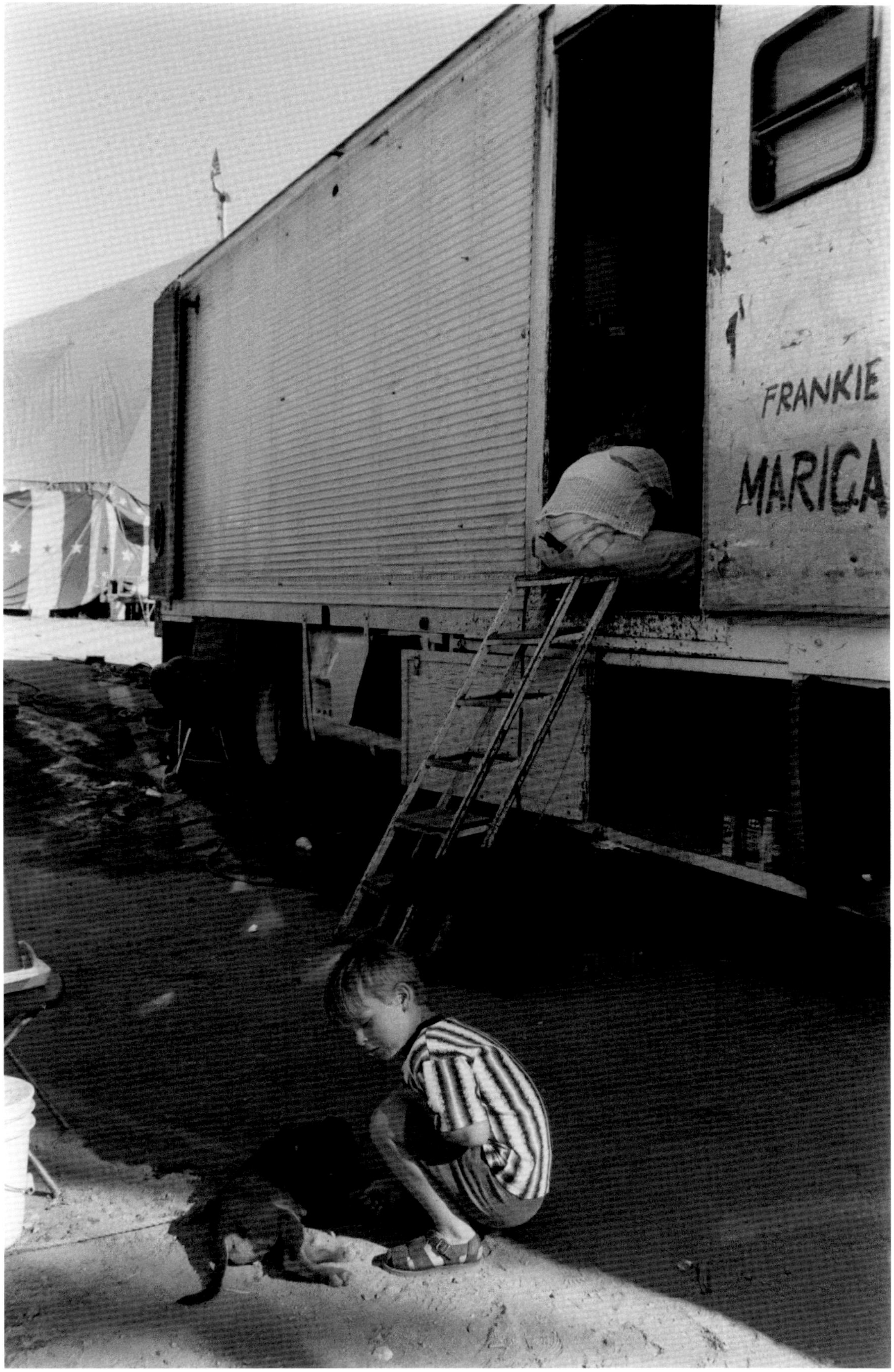

PLATE 84

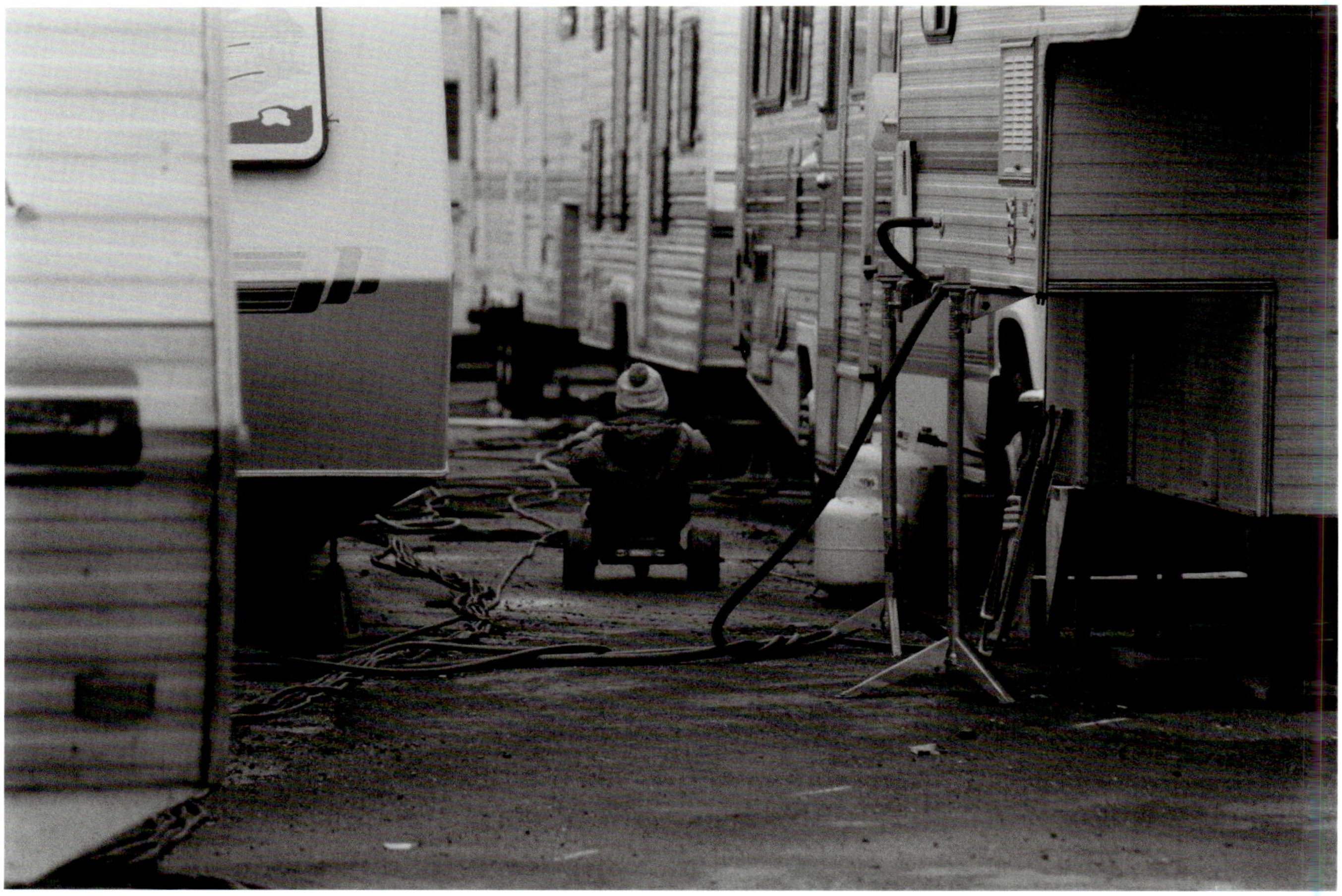

PLATE 85

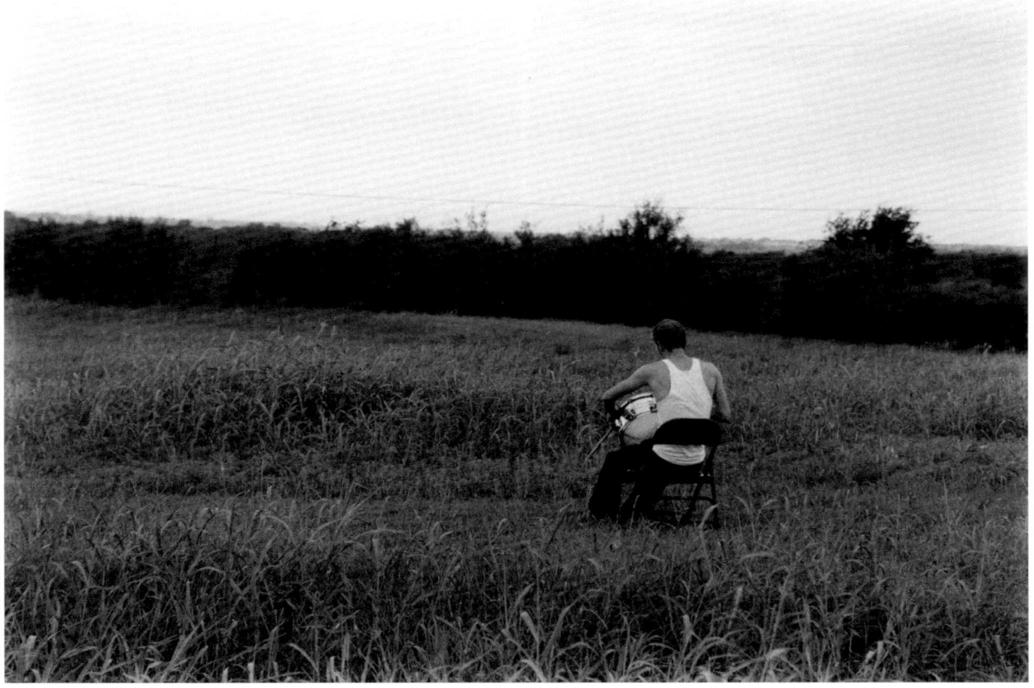

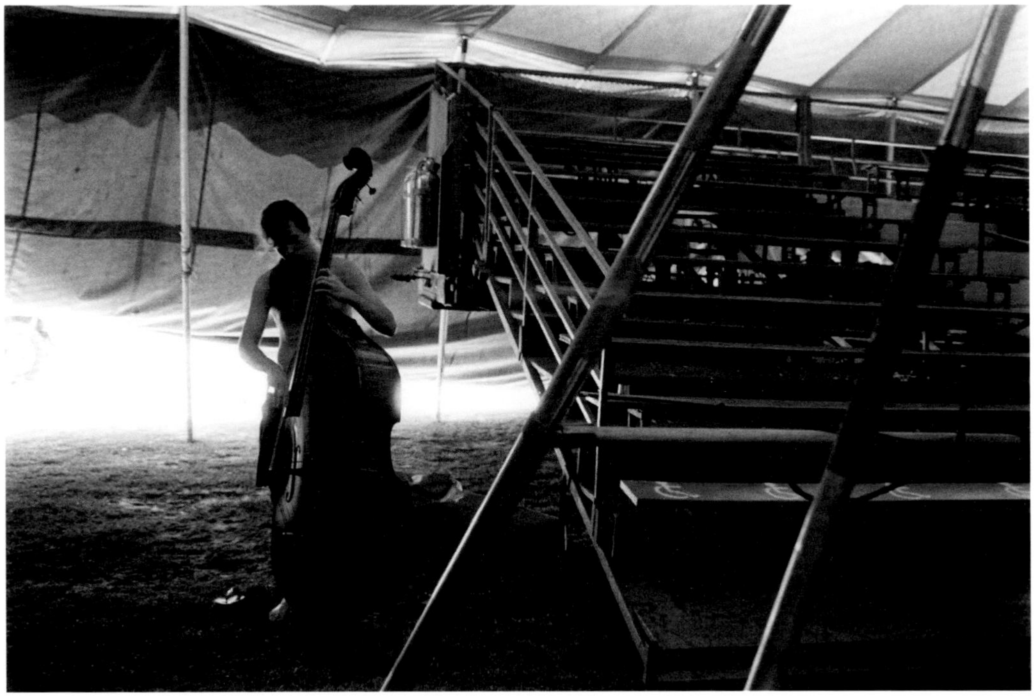

PLATES 86 & 87

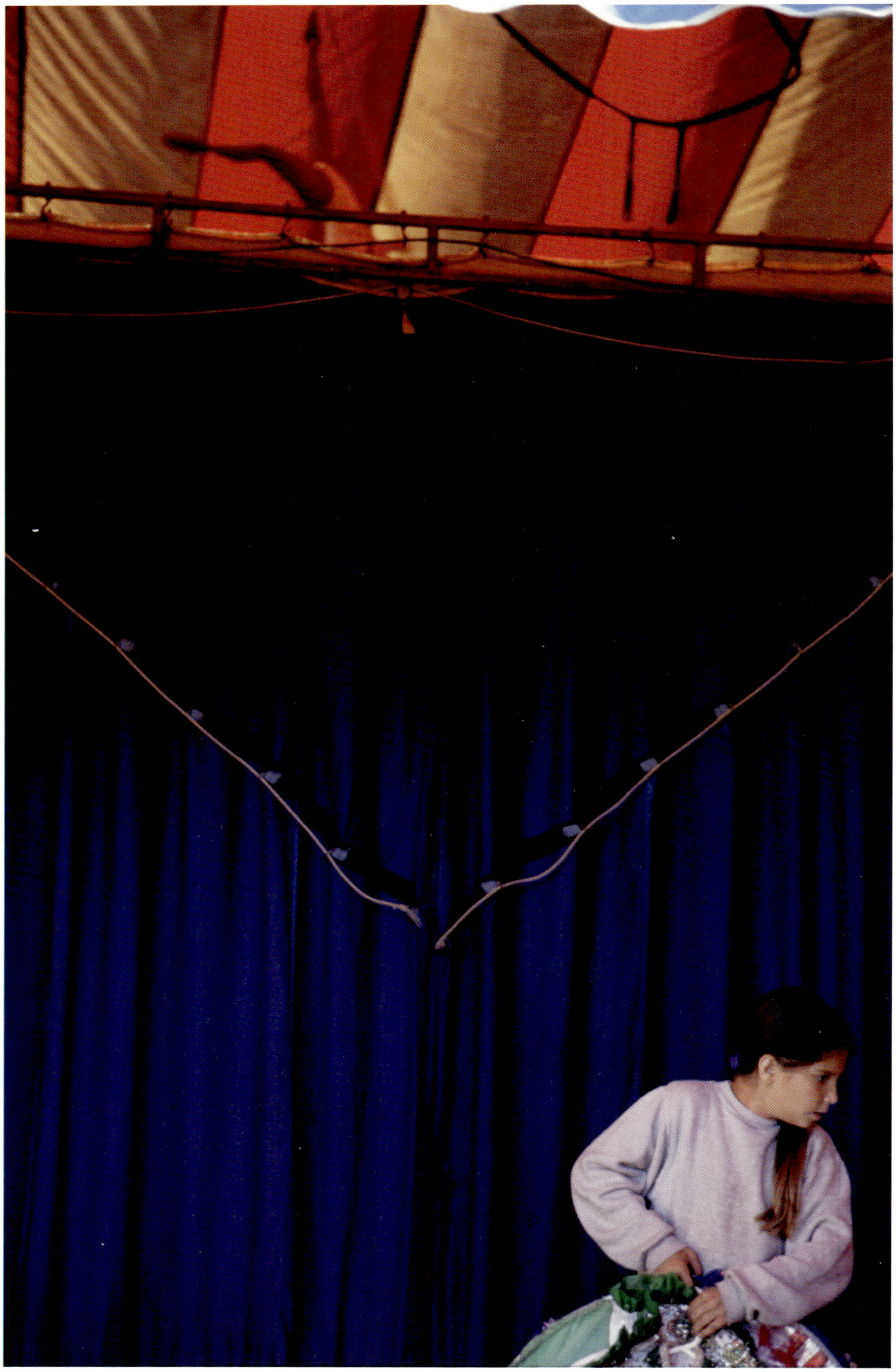

PLATE 88

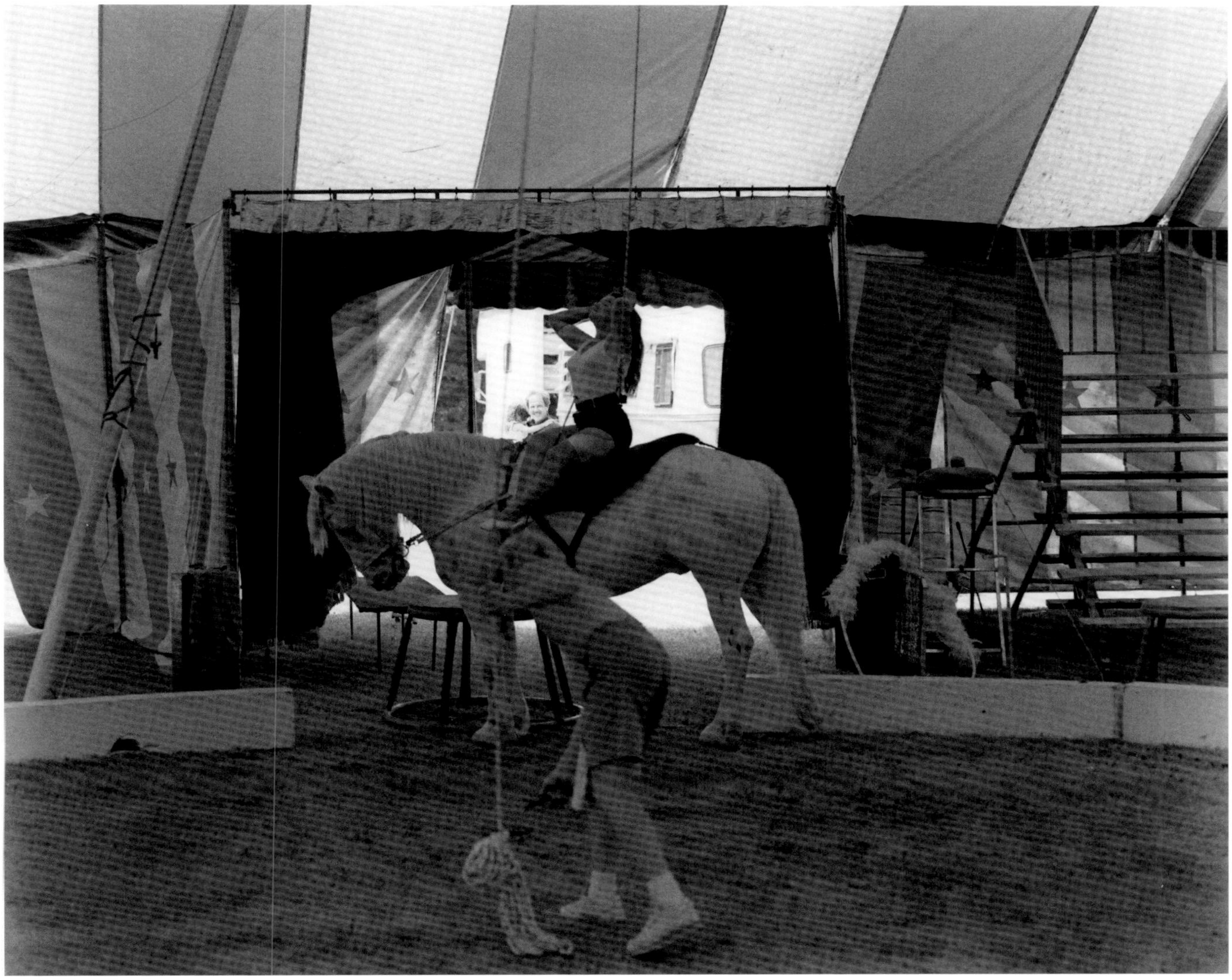

PLATE 89

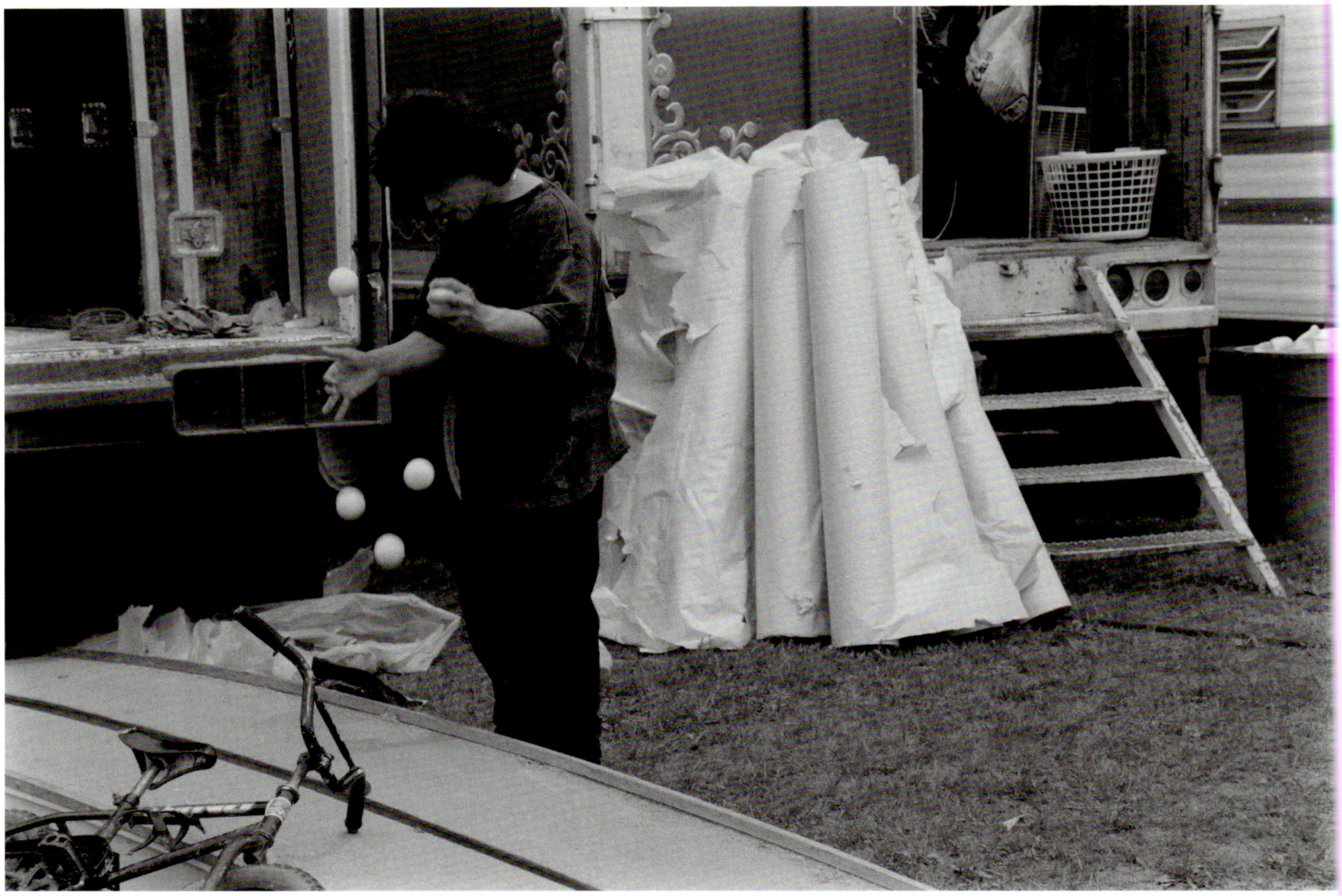

PLATE 90

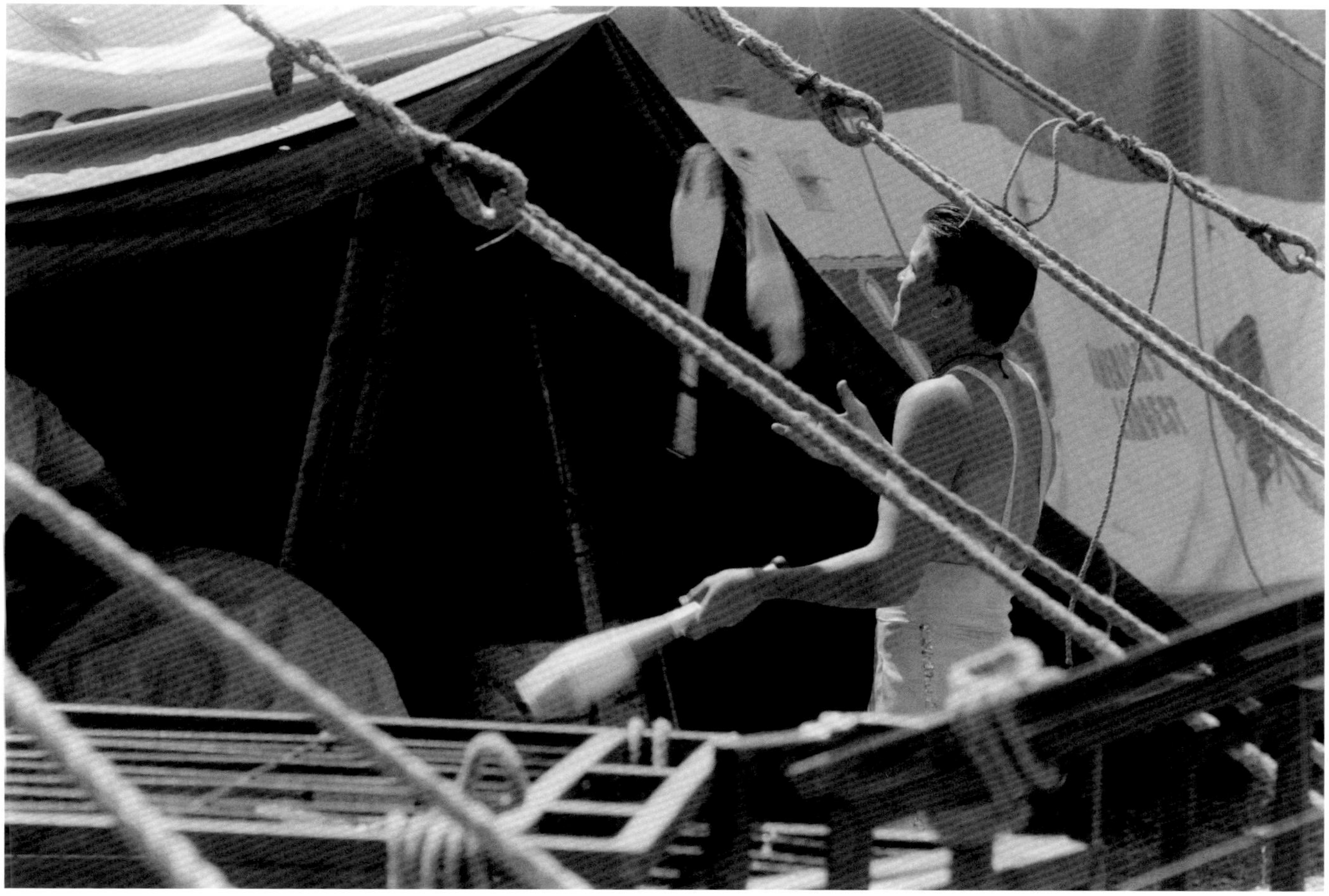

PLATE 91

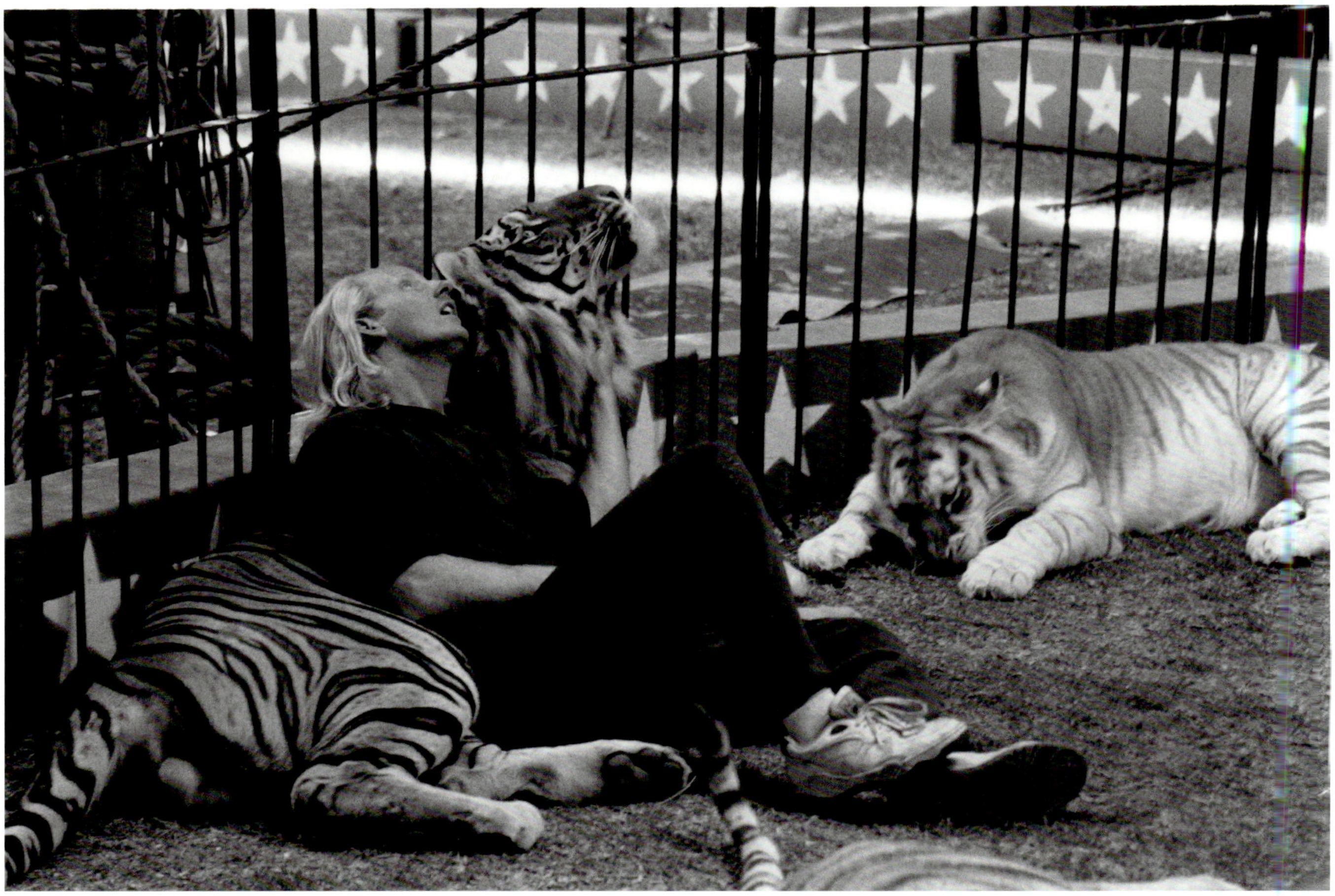

PLATE 92

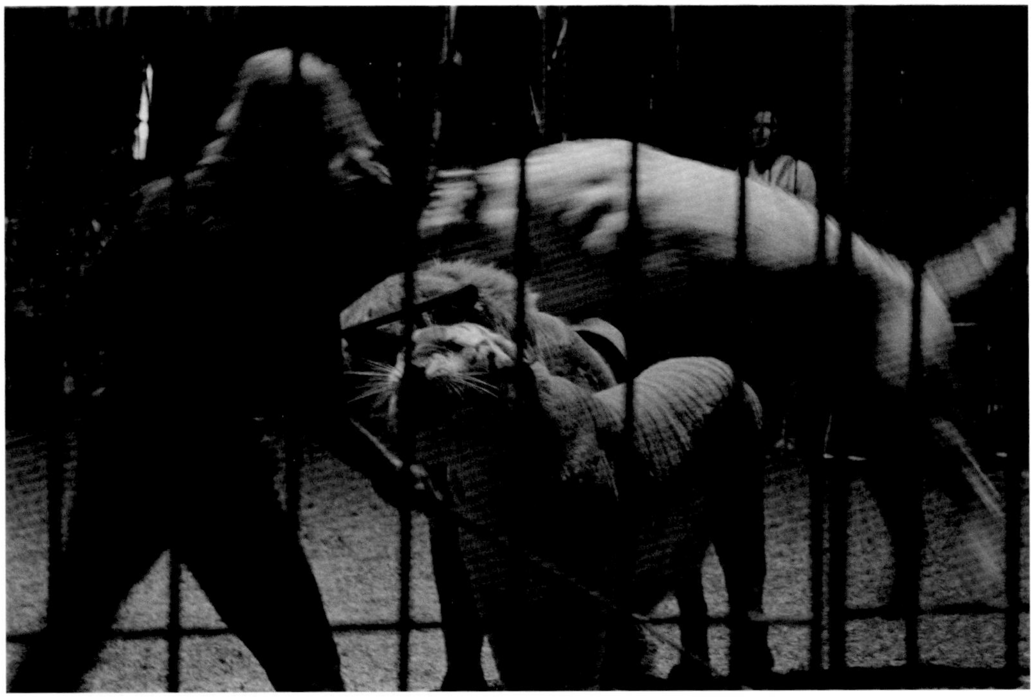

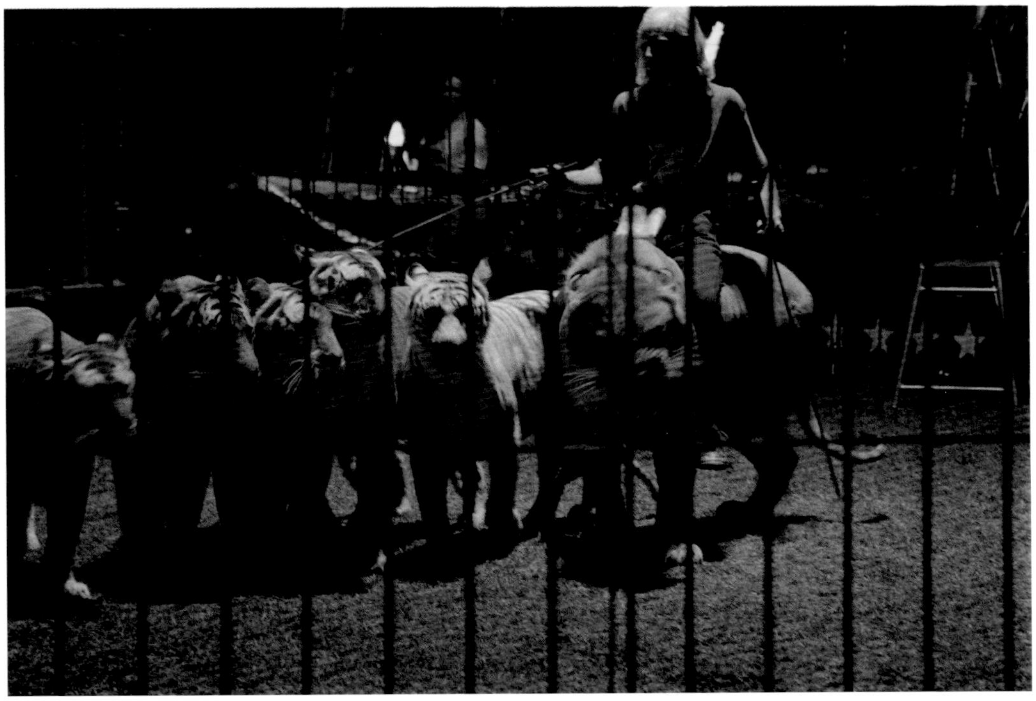

PLATES 93 & 94

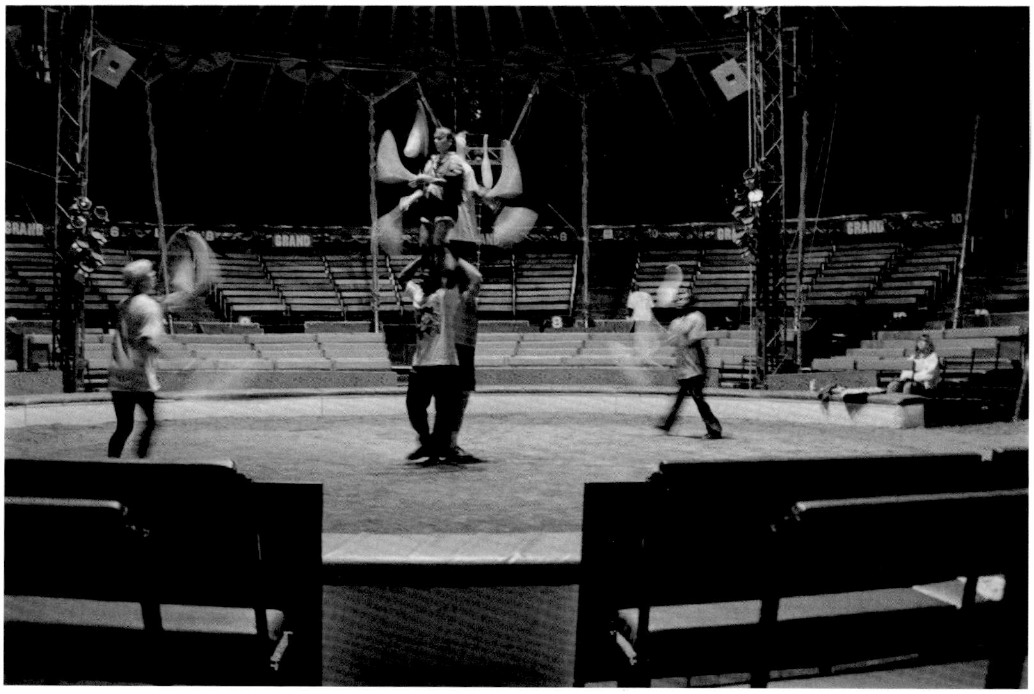

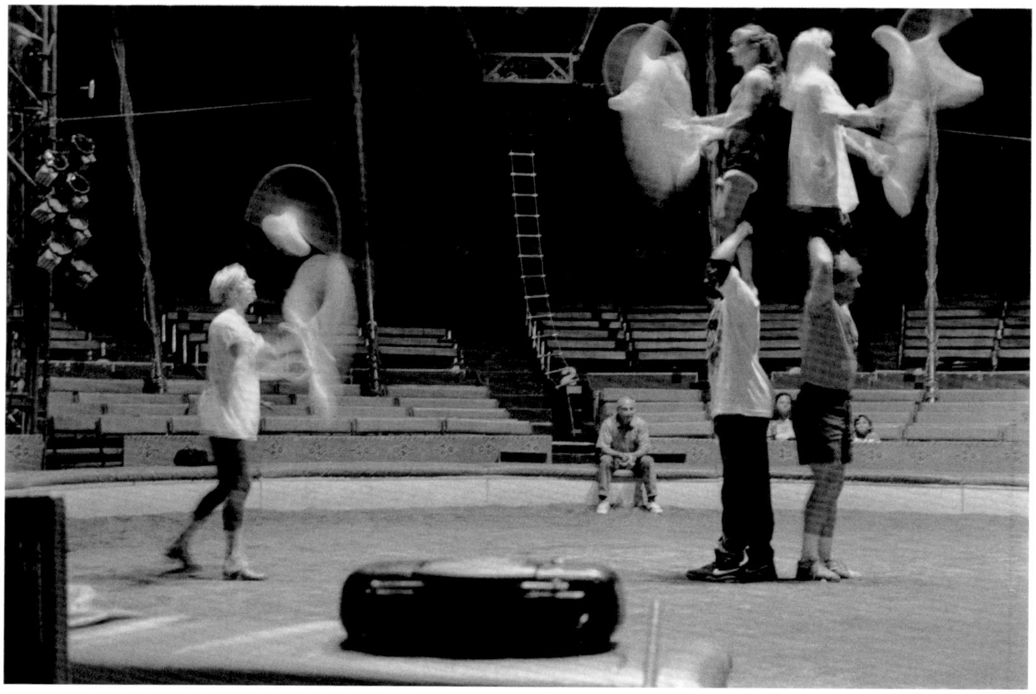

PLATES 95 & 96

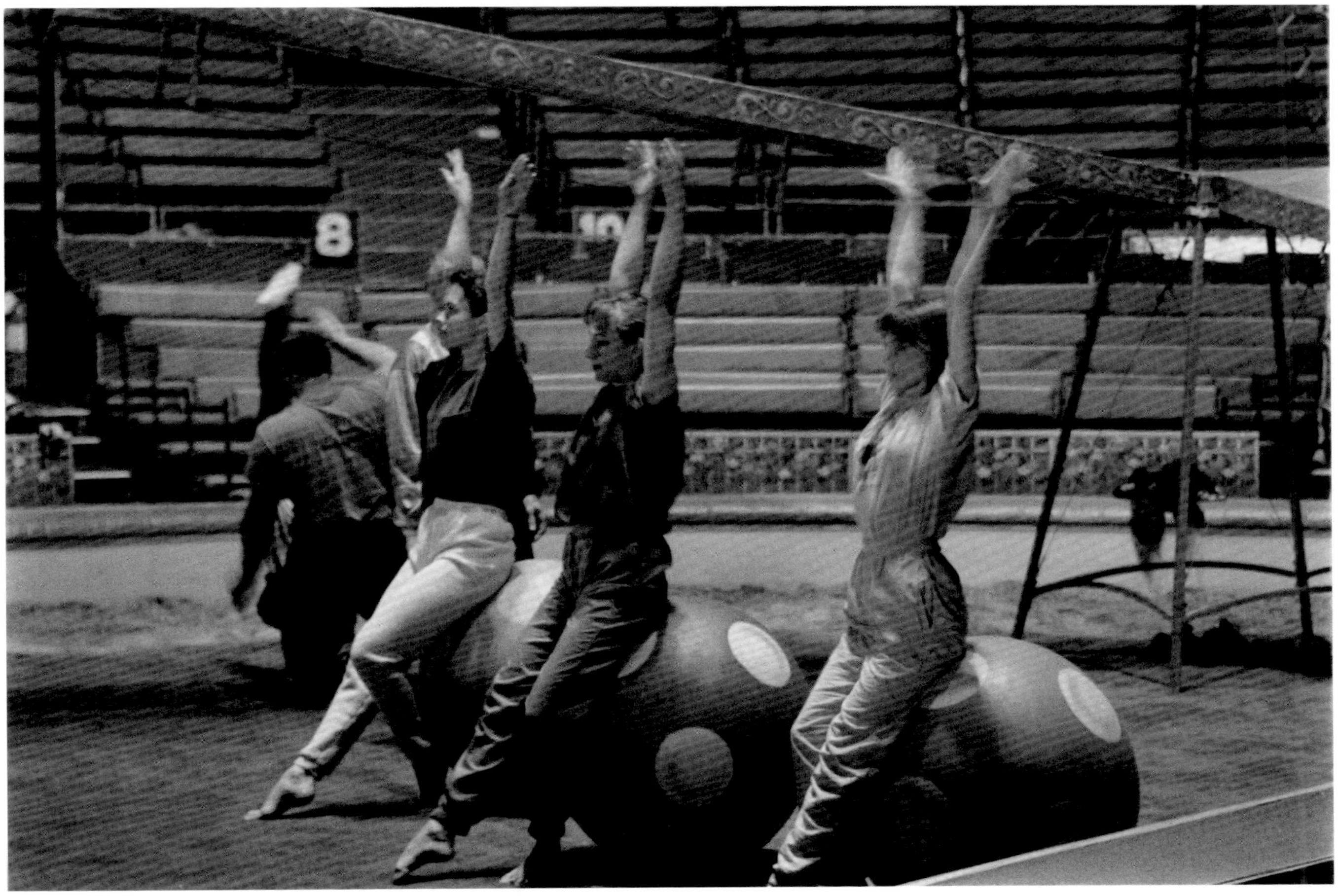

PLATE 97

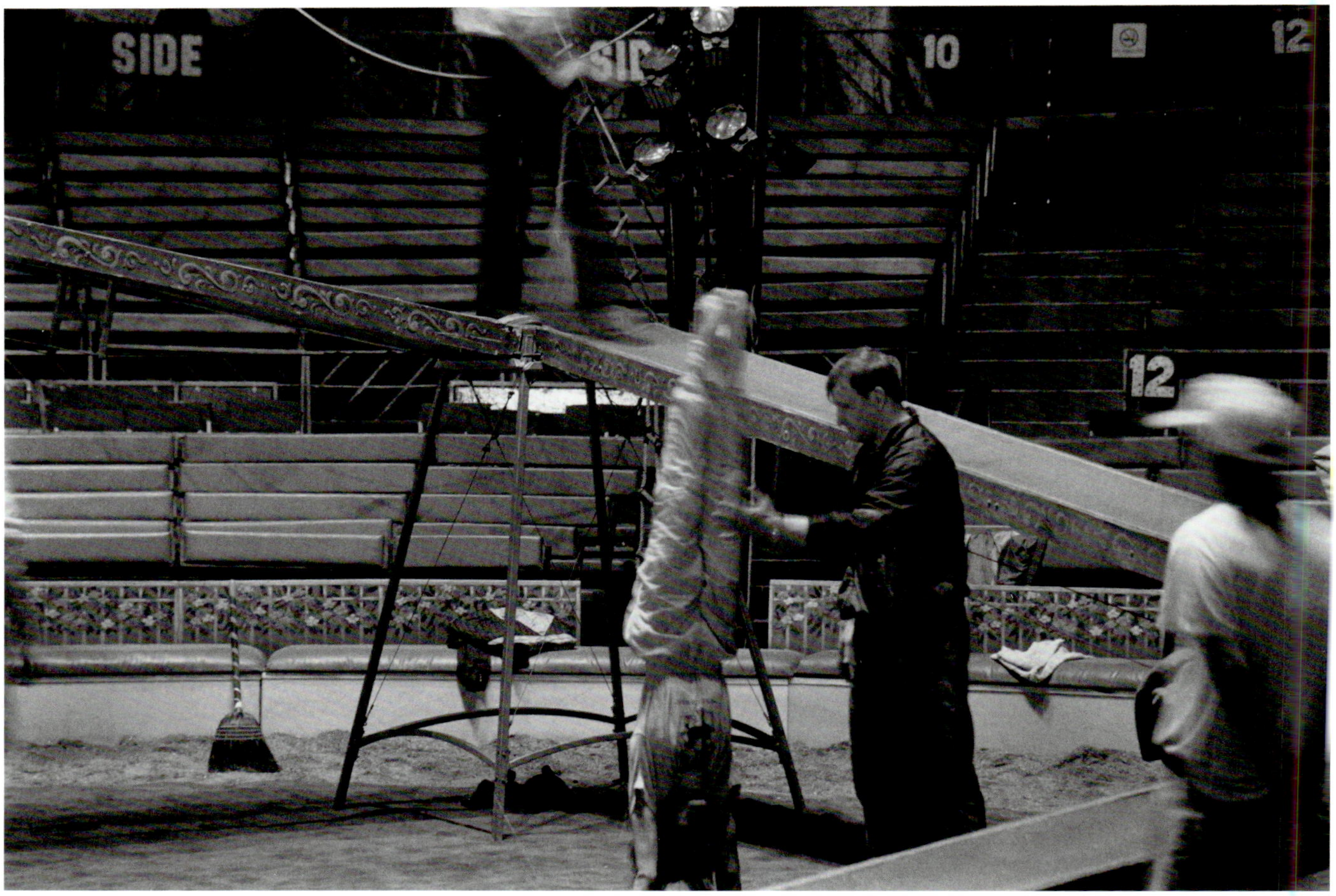

PLATE 98

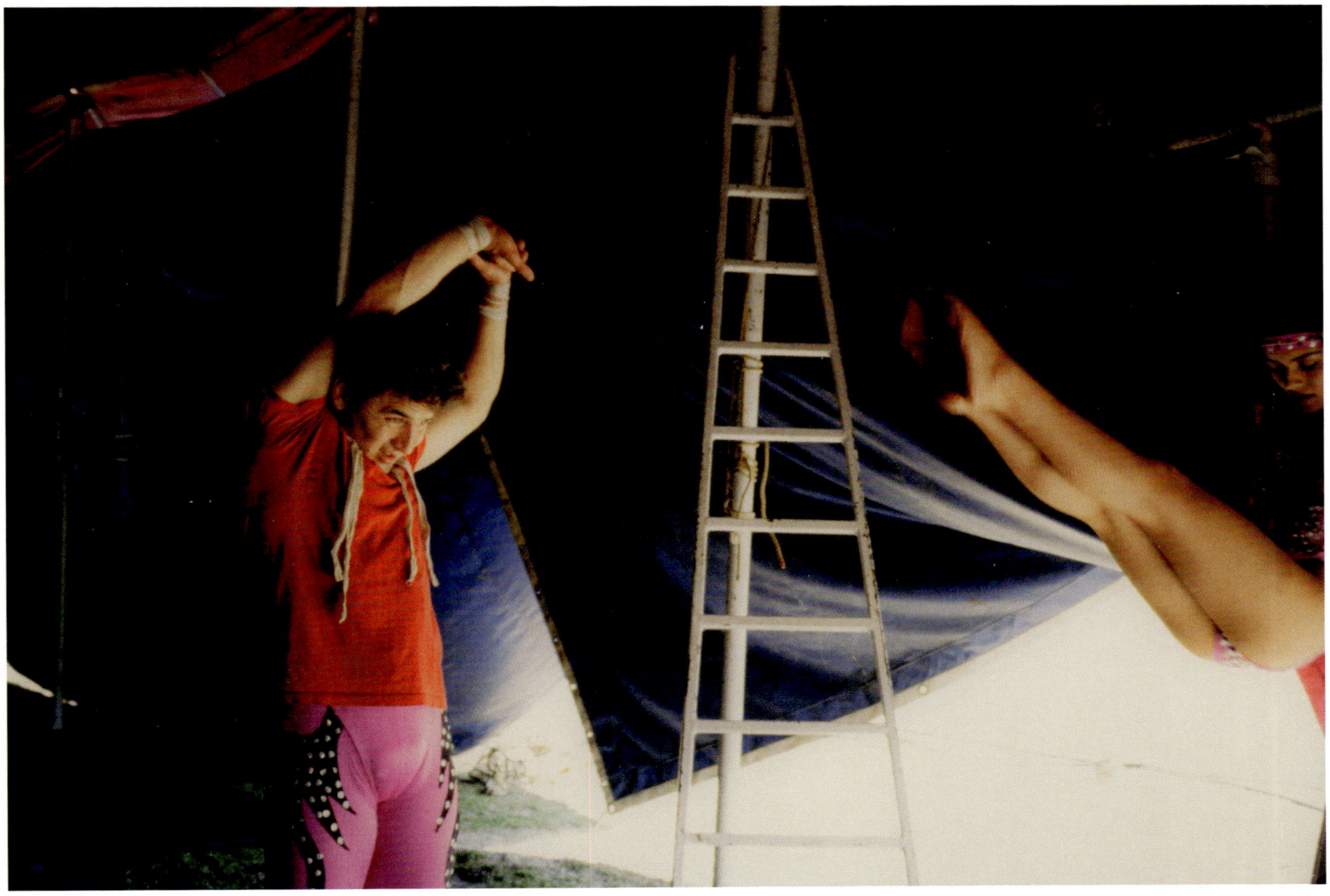

PLATE 99

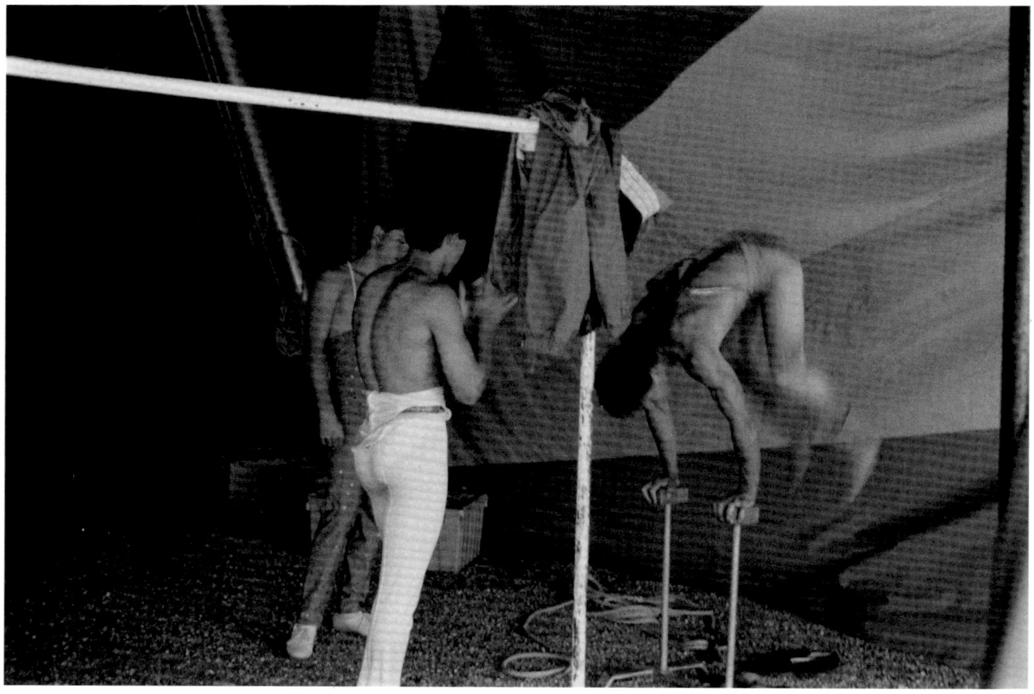

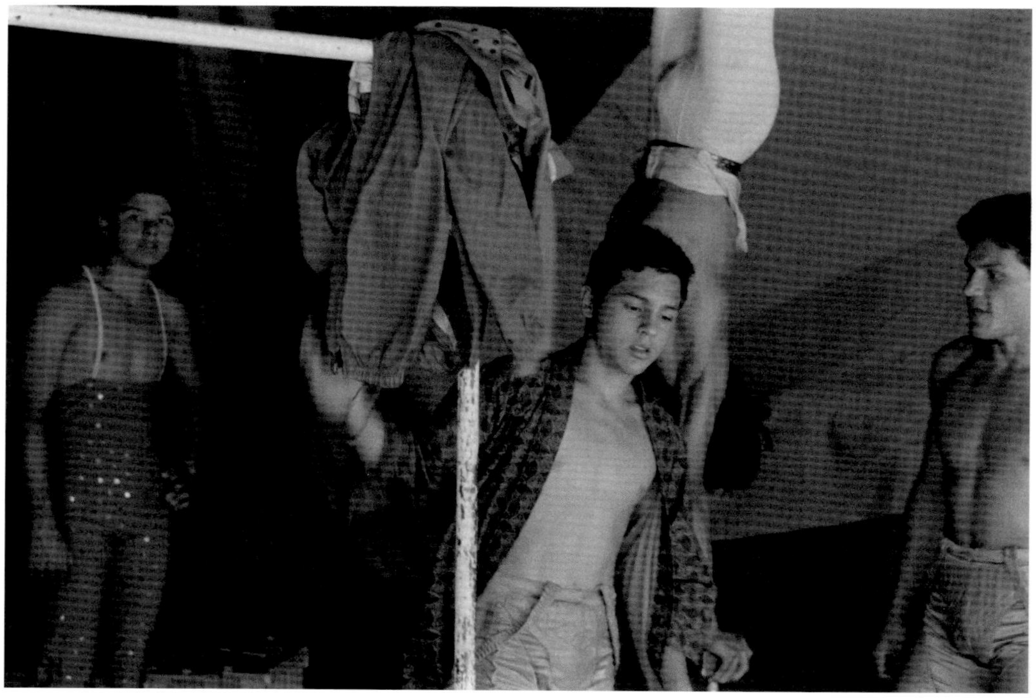

PLATES 100 & 101

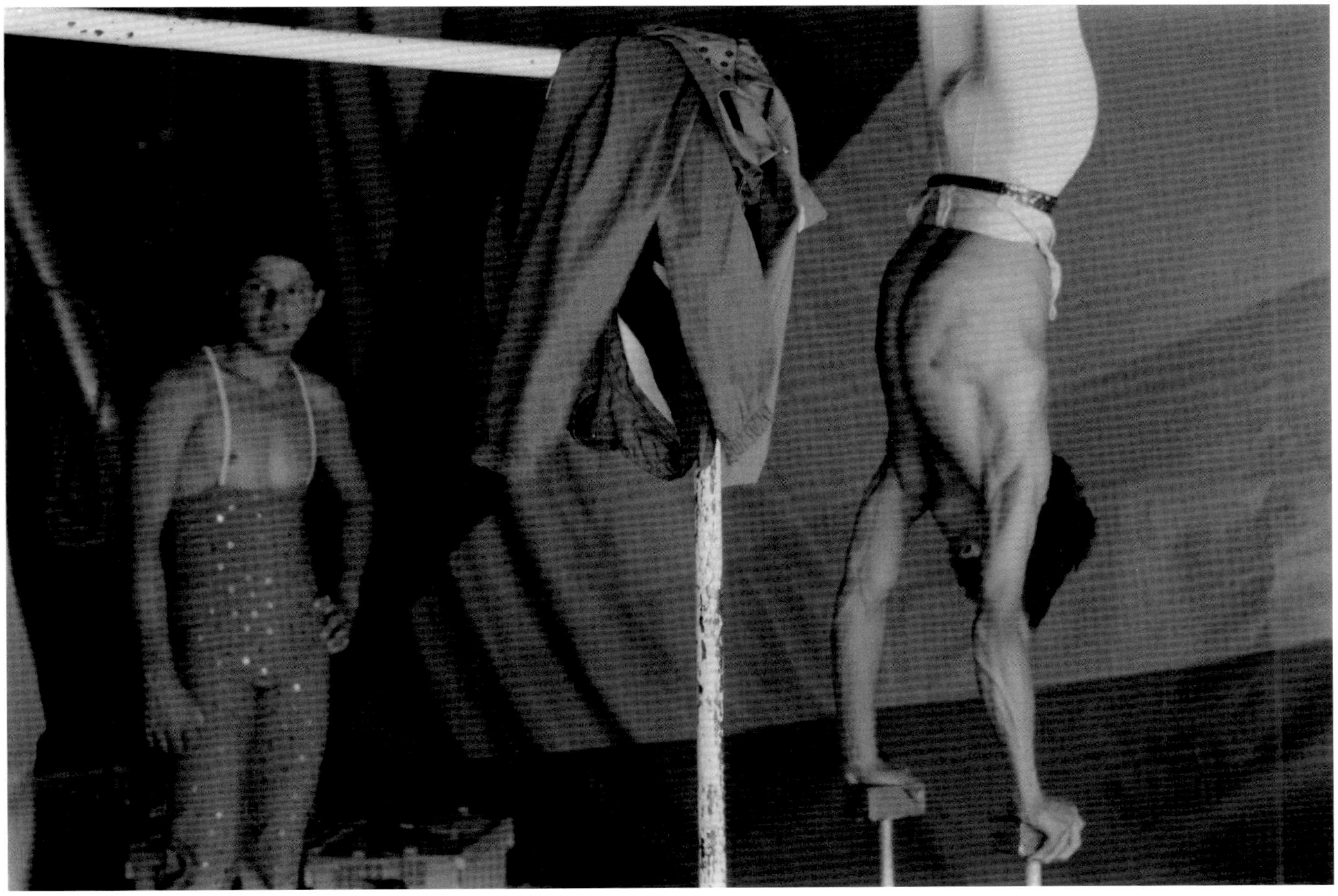

PLATE 102

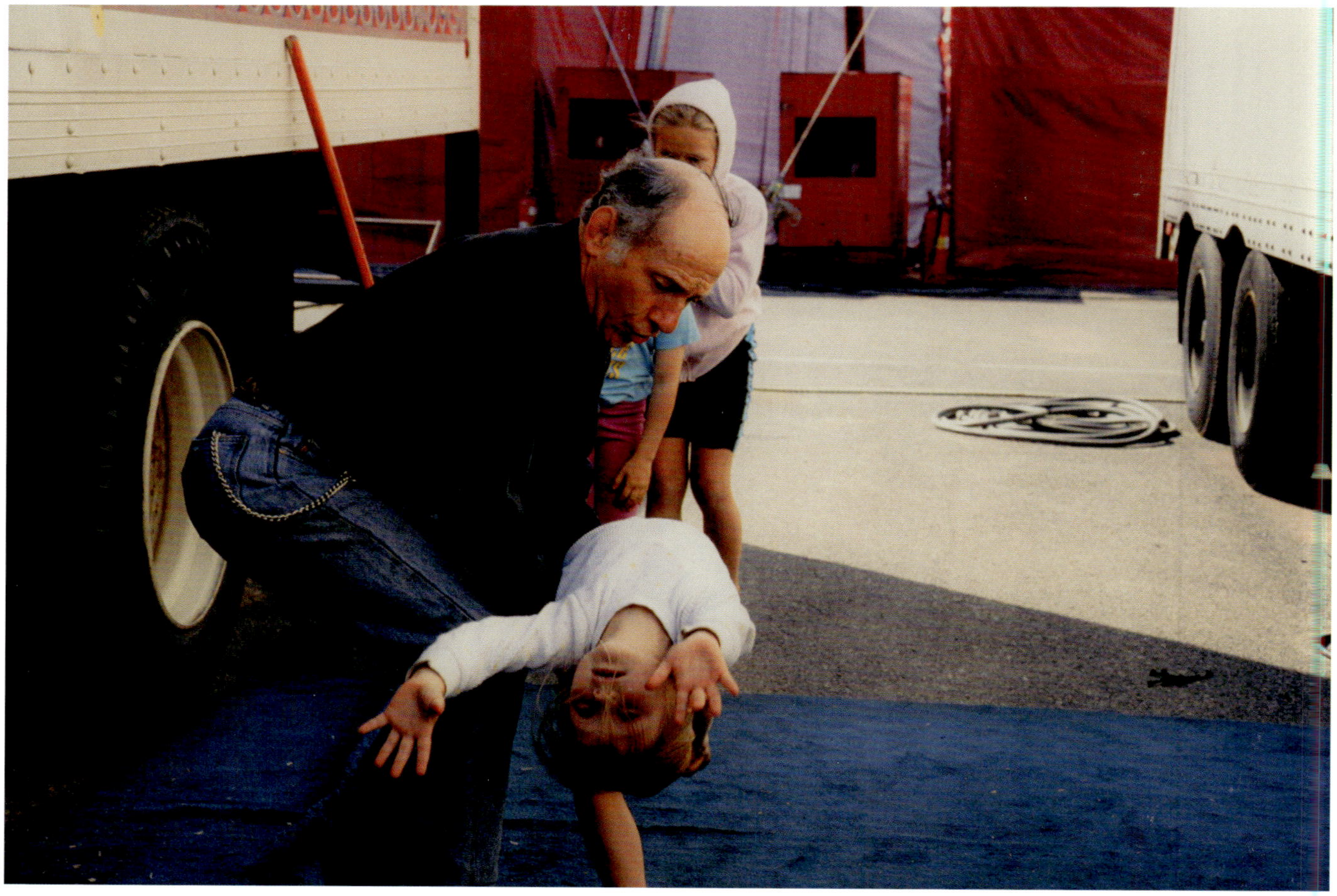

PLATE 103

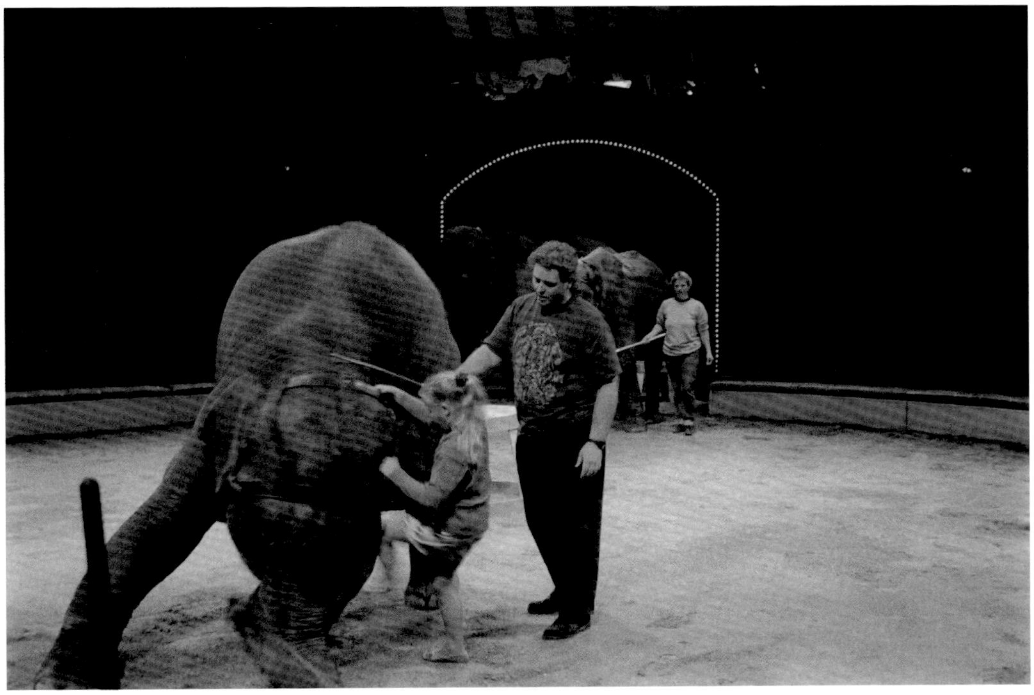

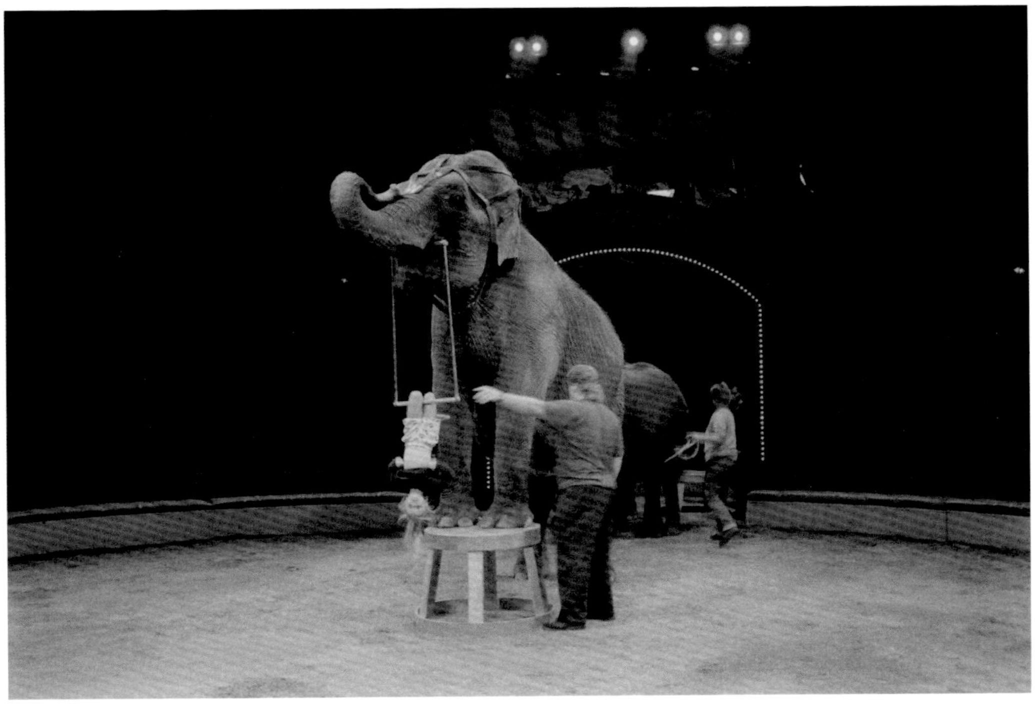

PLATES 104 & 105

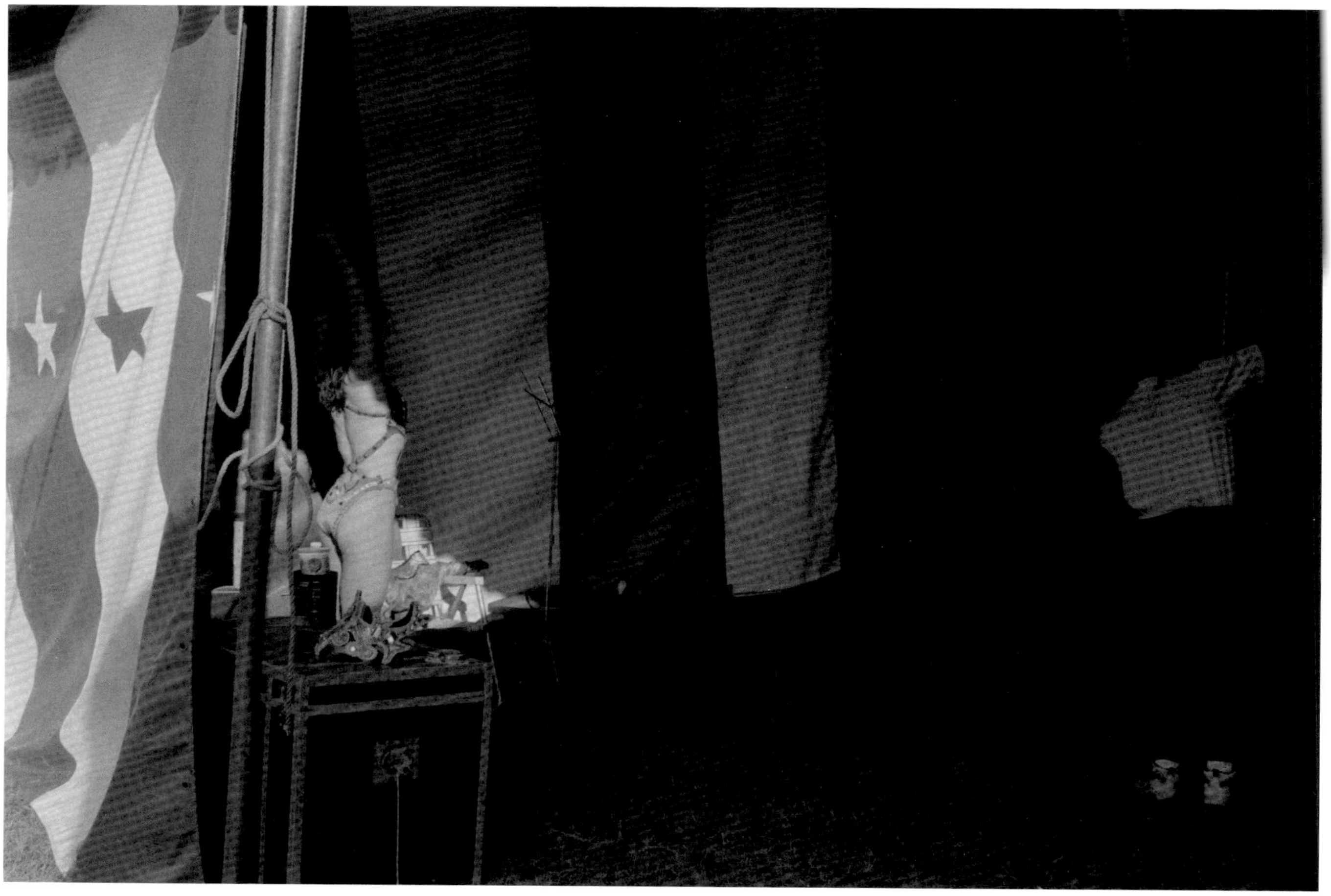

PLATE 106

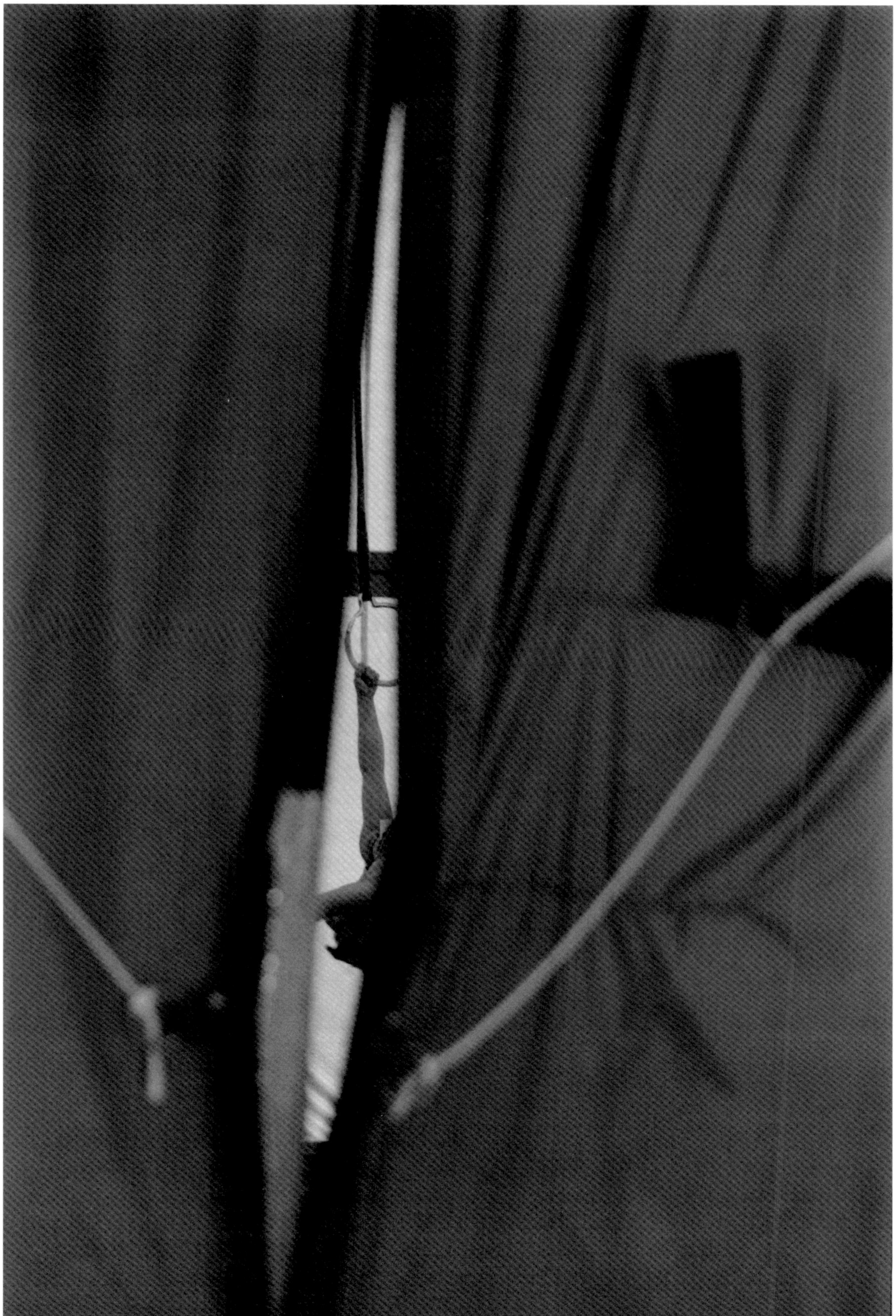

PLATE 107

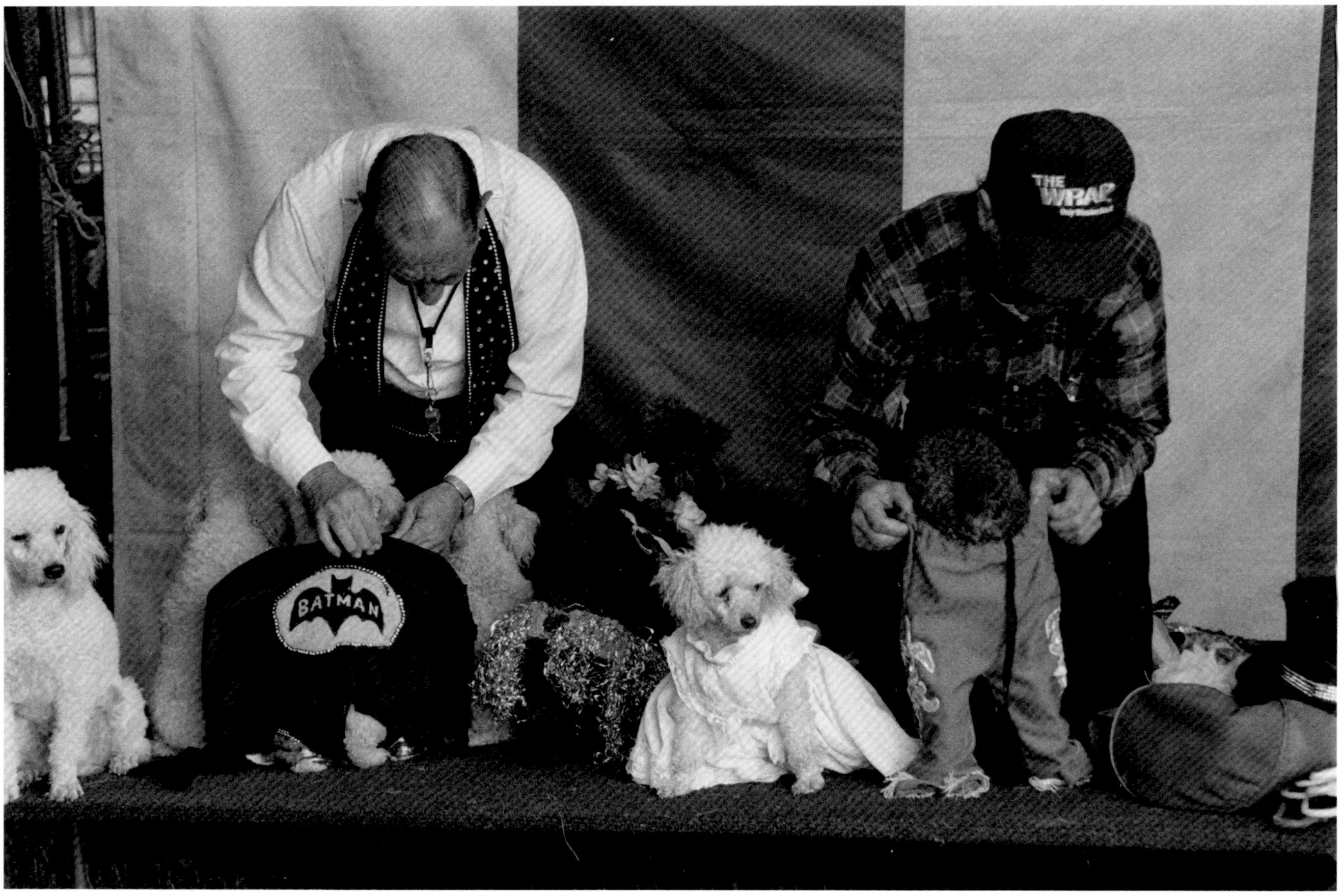

PLATE 108

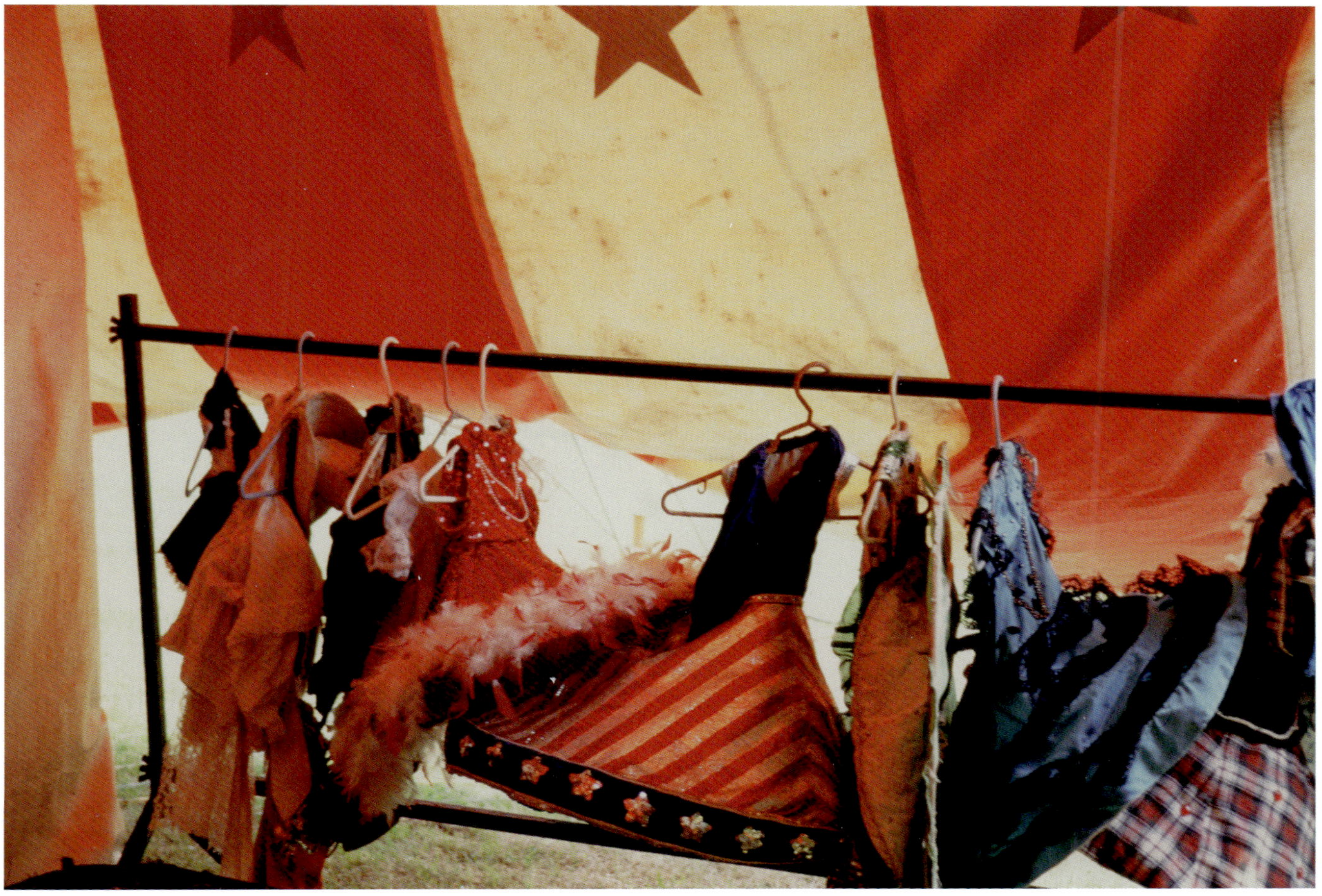

PLATE 109

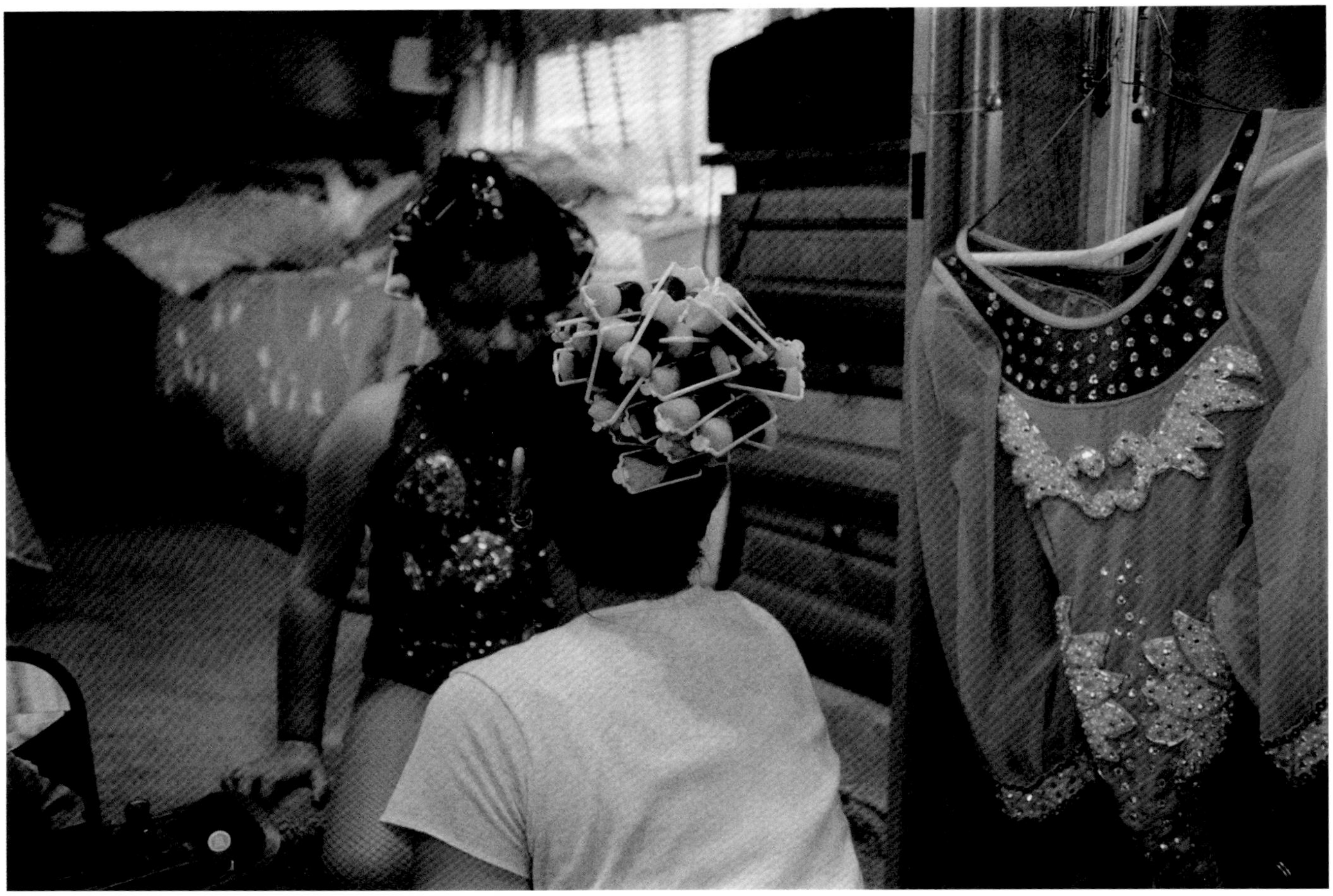

PLATE 110

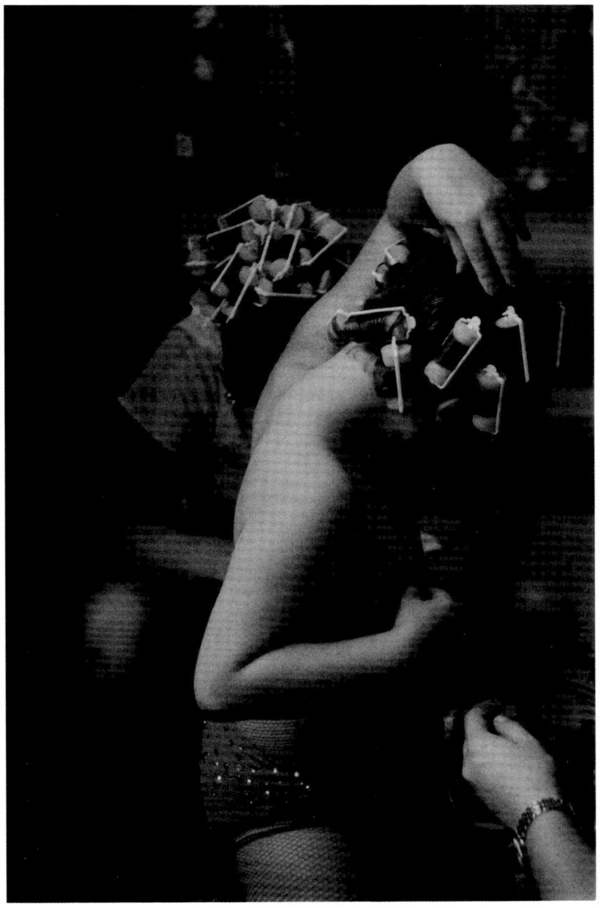

PLATE 111

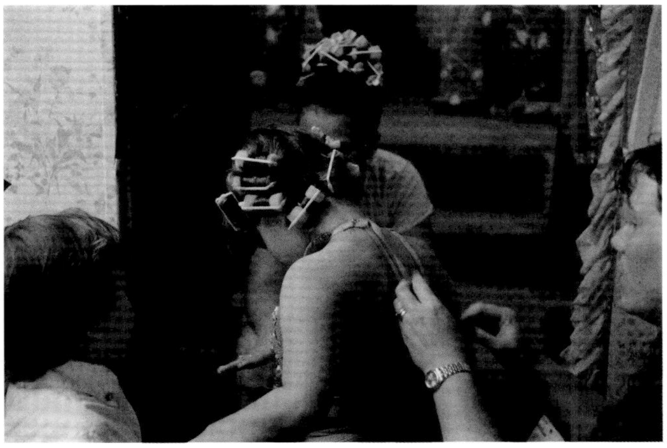

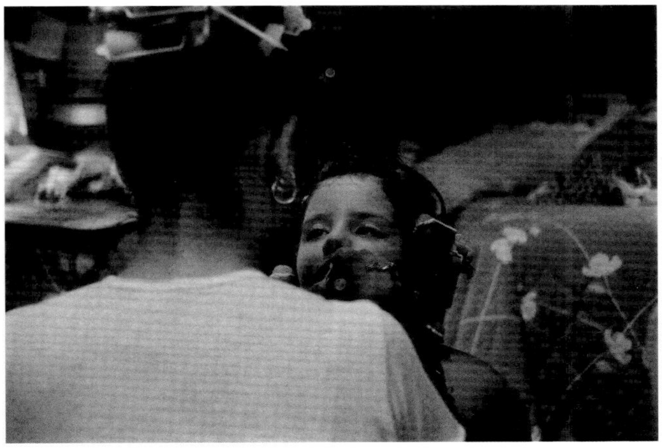

PLATES 112 & 113

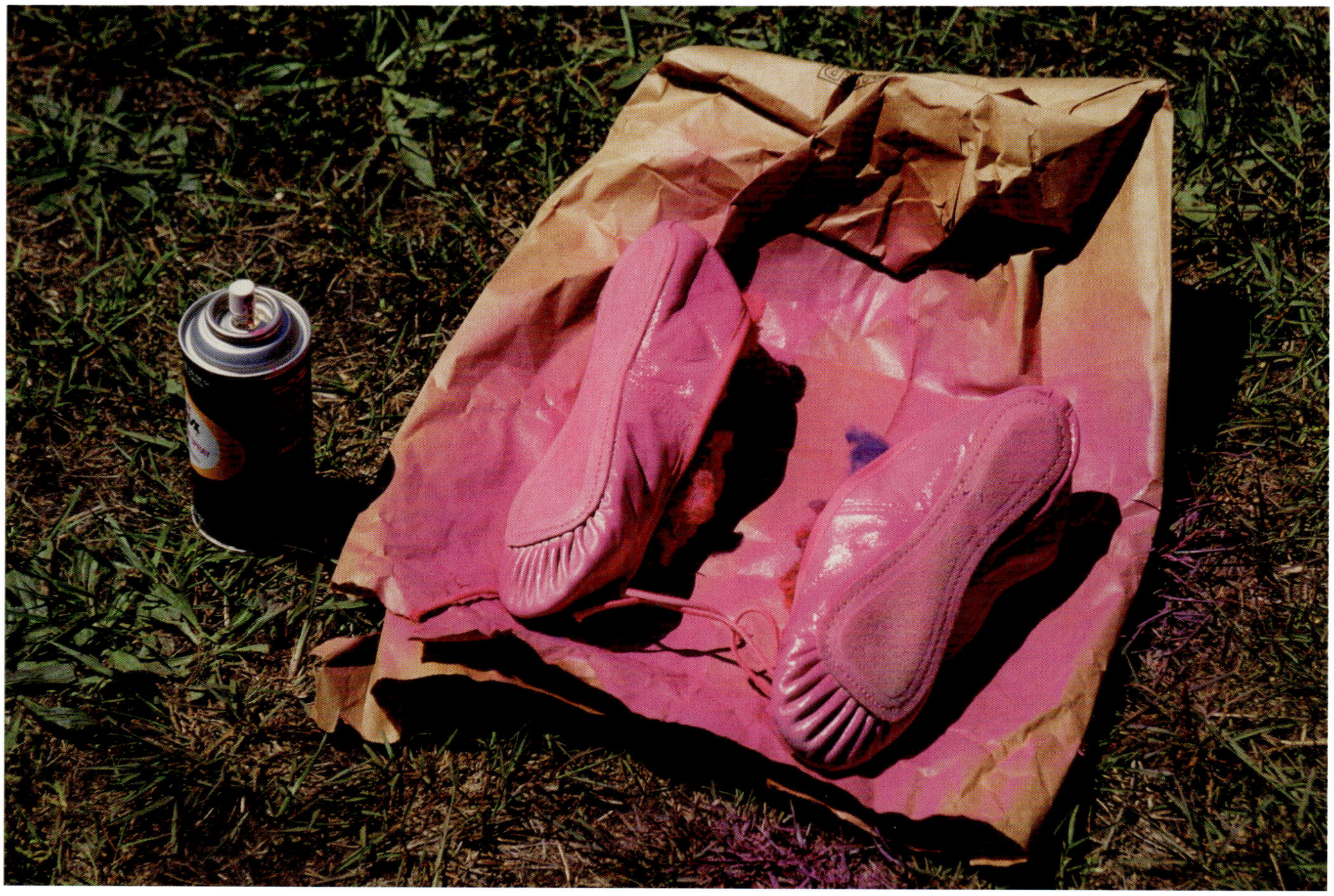

PLATE 114

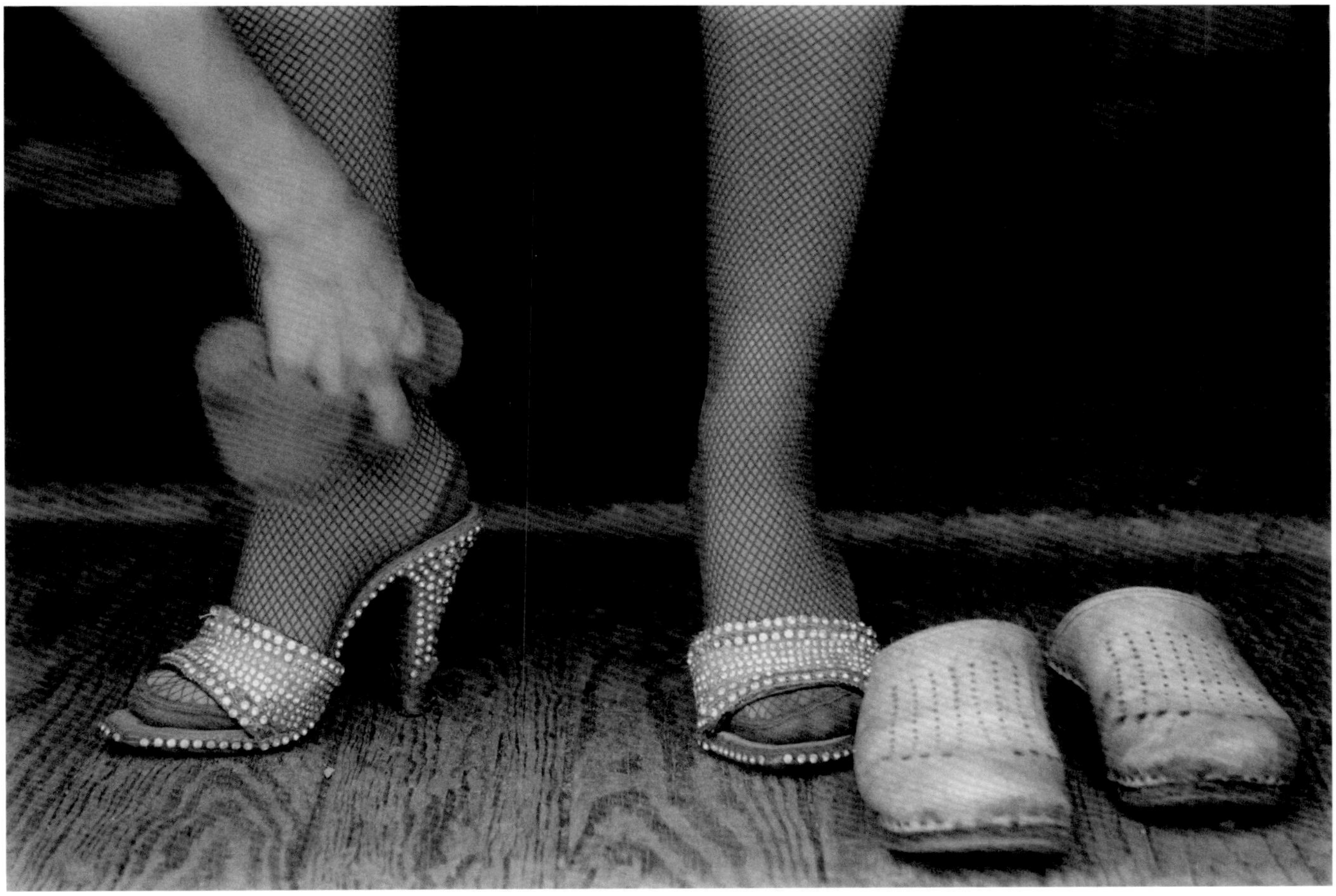

PLATE 115

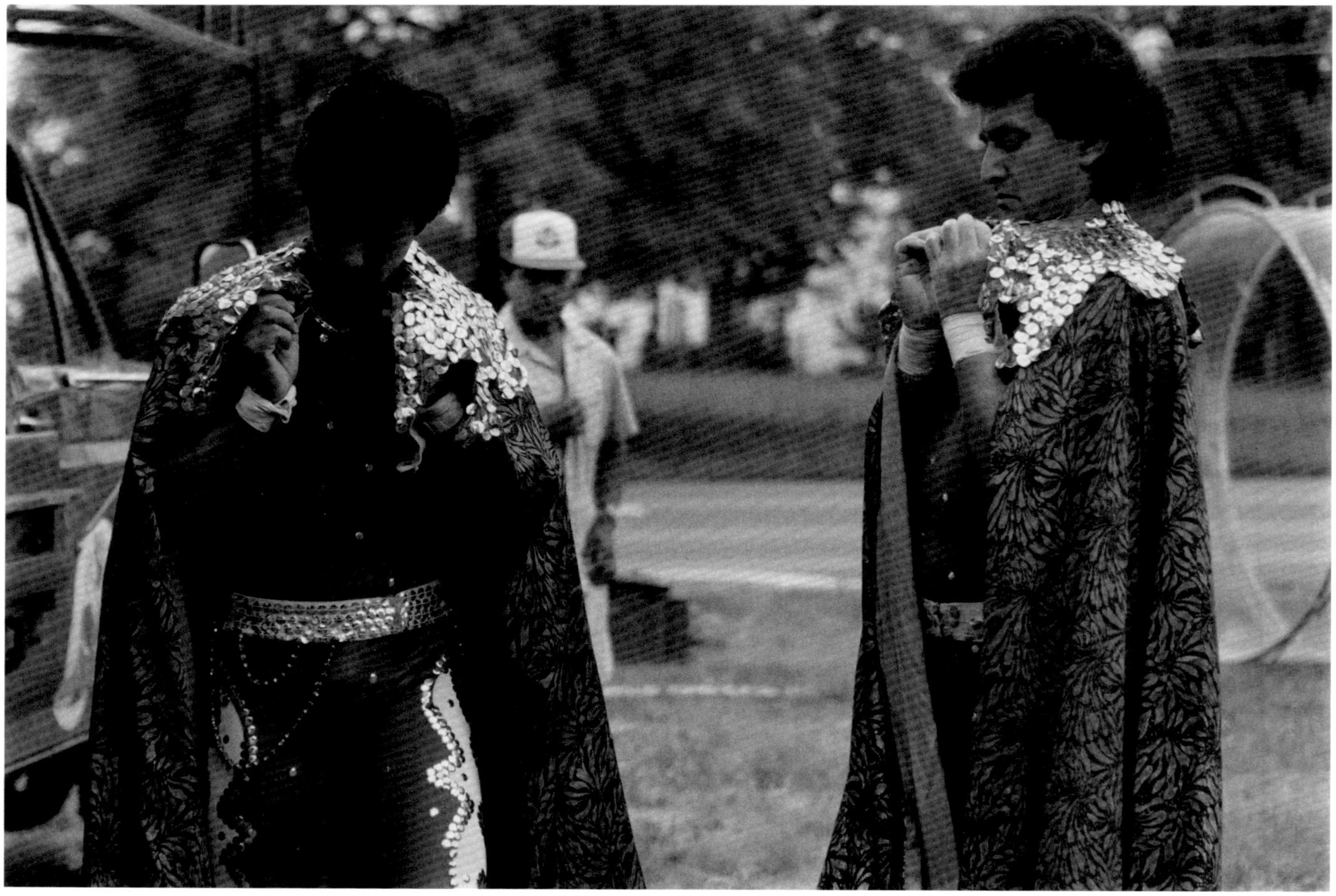

PLATE 116

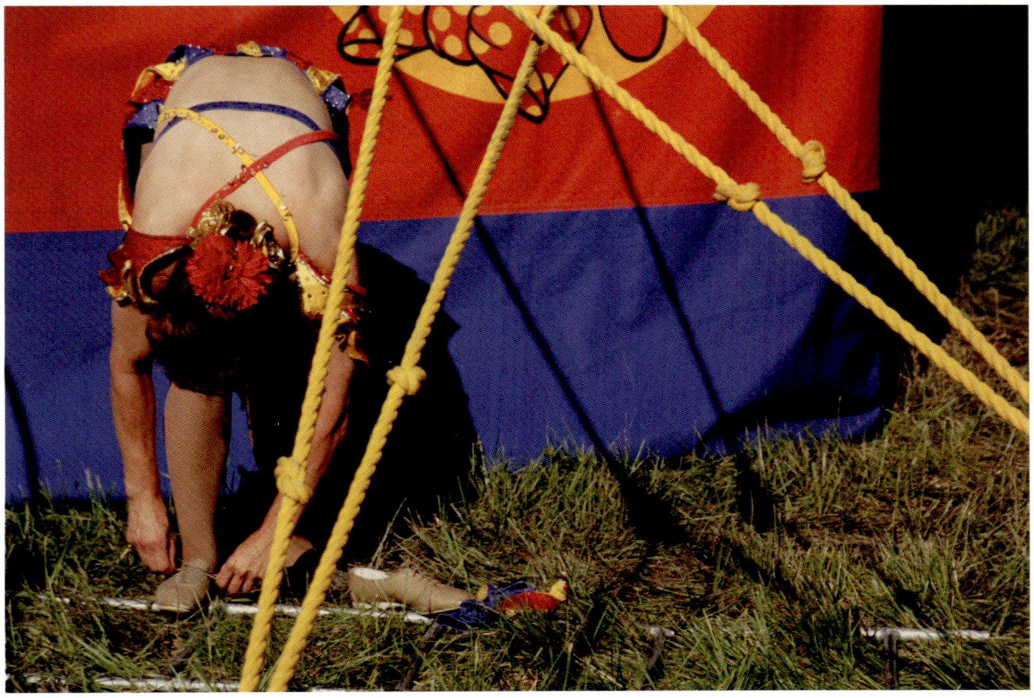

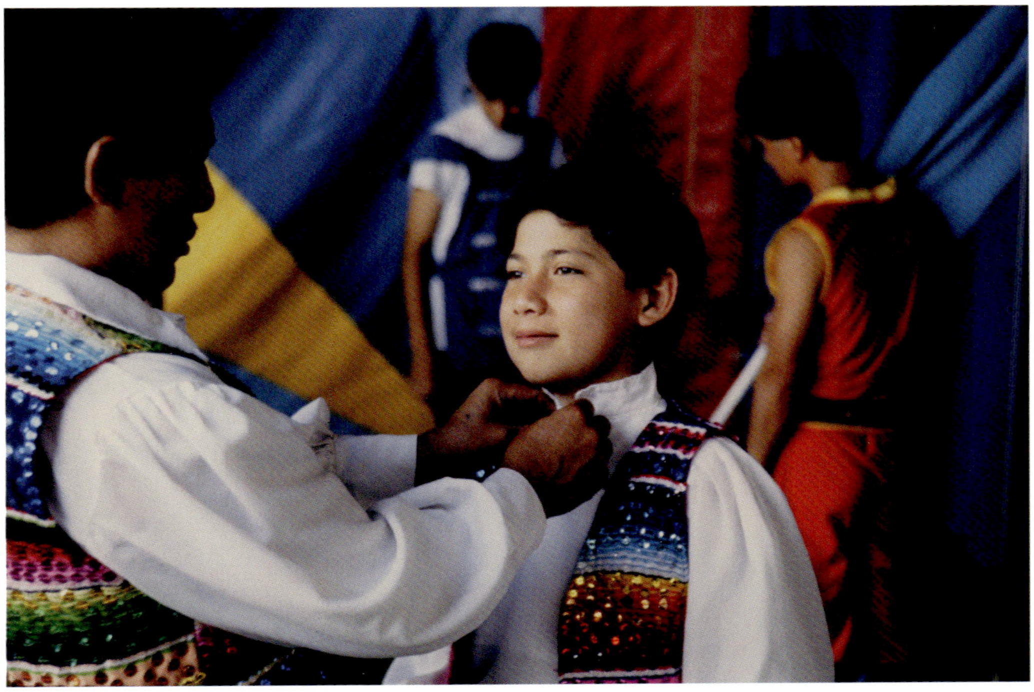

PLATES 117 & 118

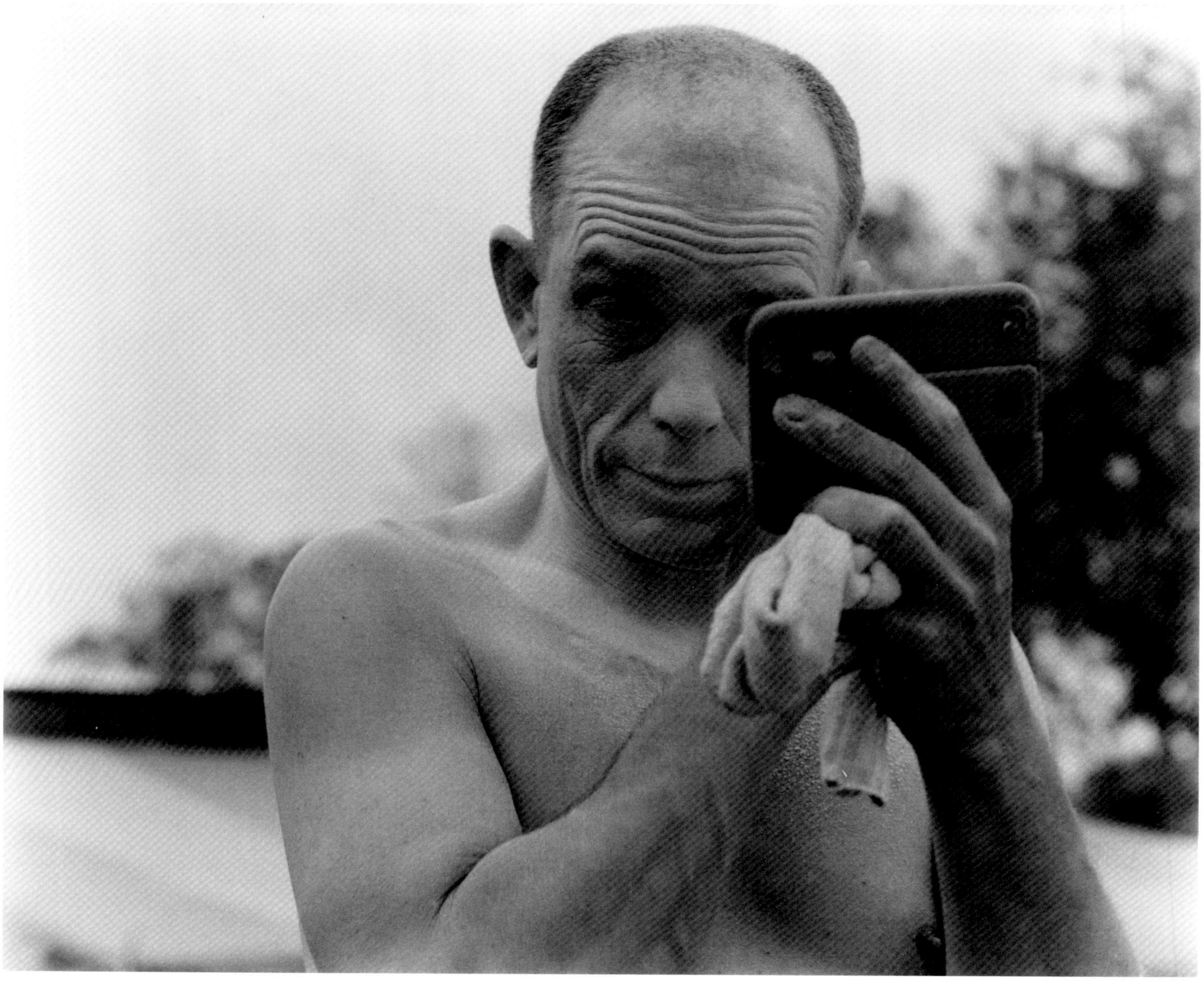

PLATE 119

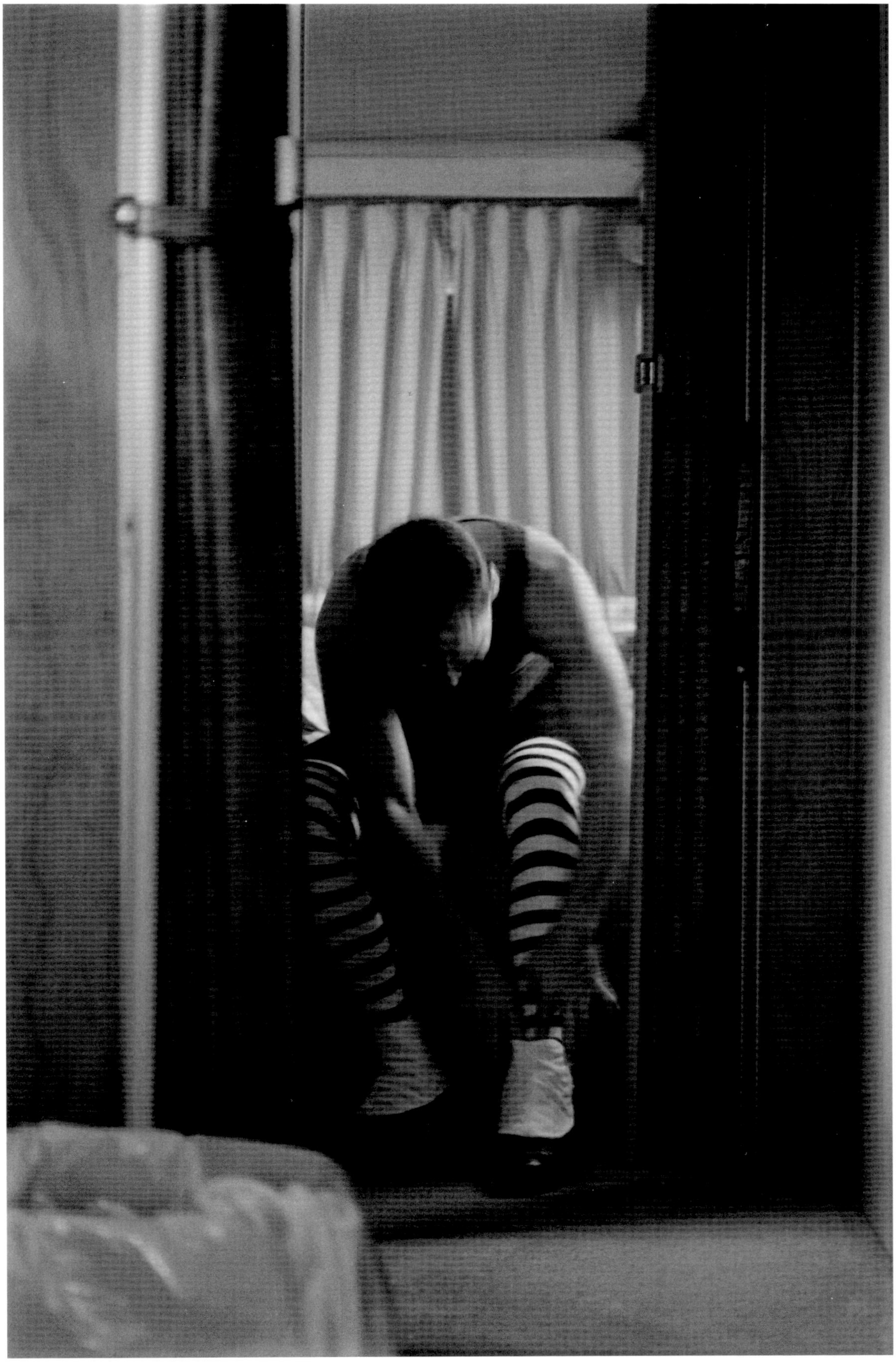

PLATE 120

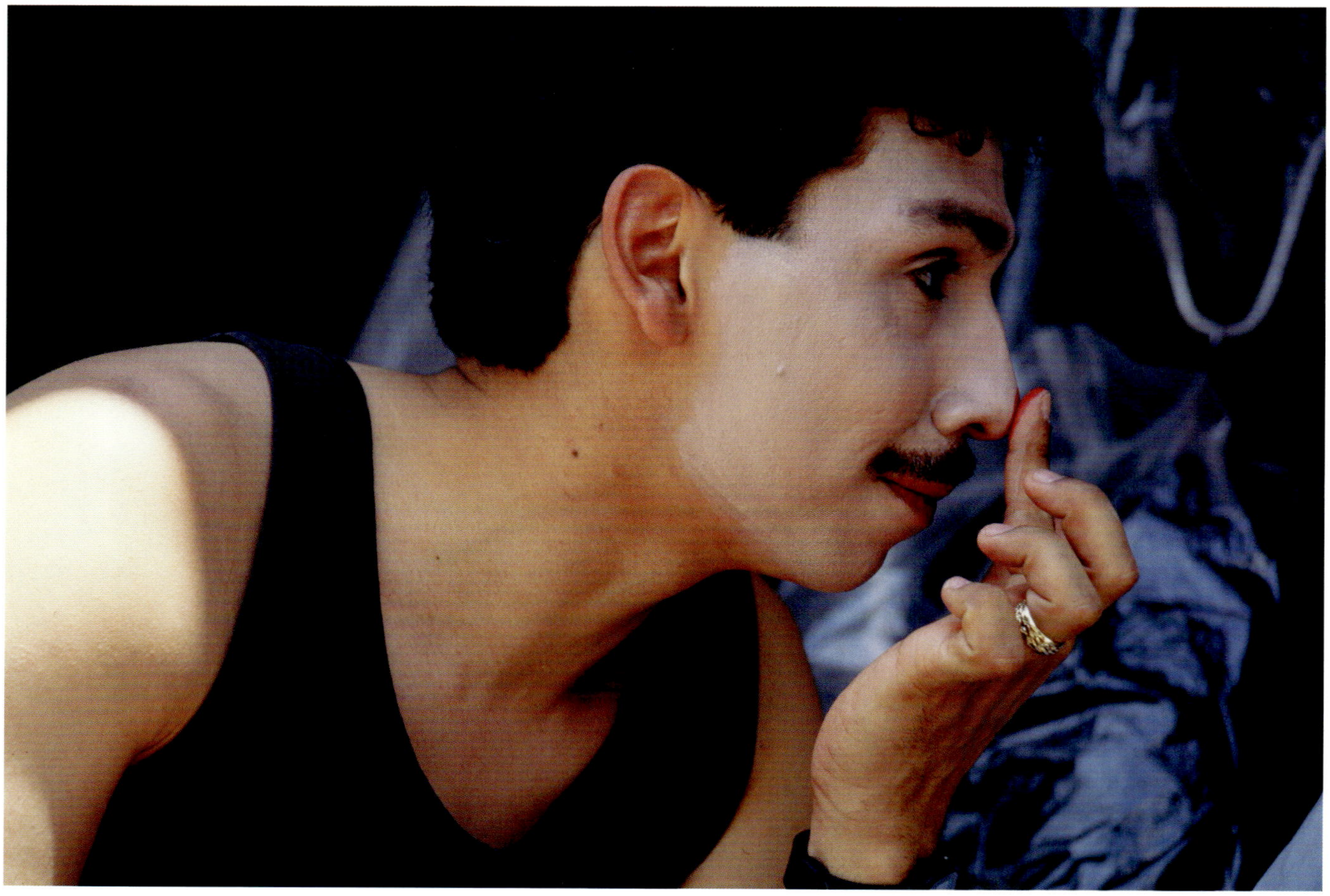

PLATE 121

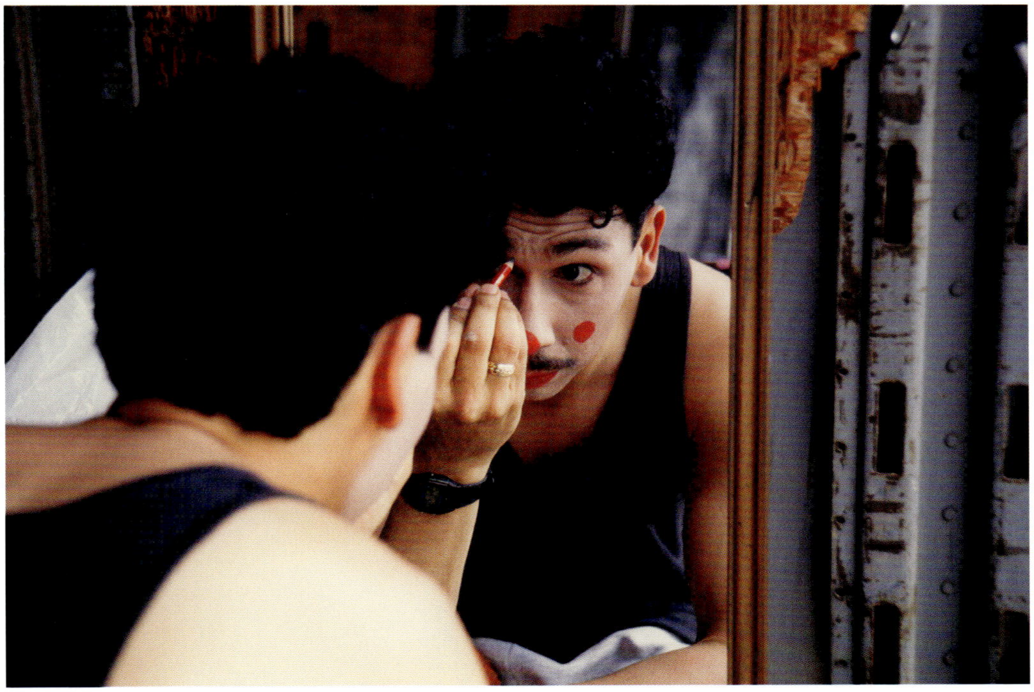

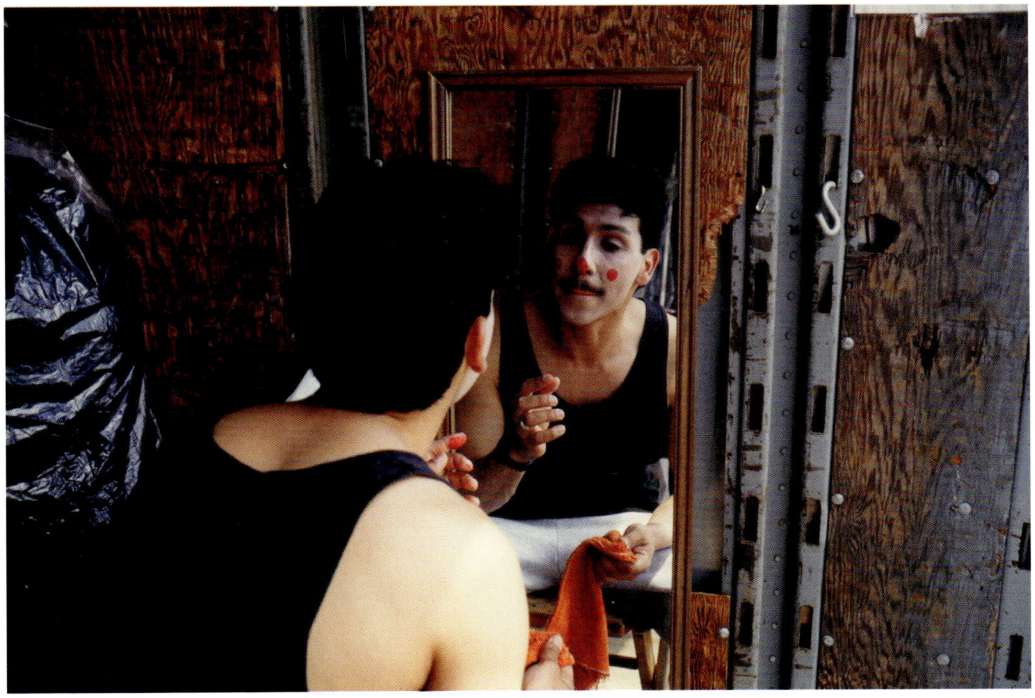

PLATES 122 & 123

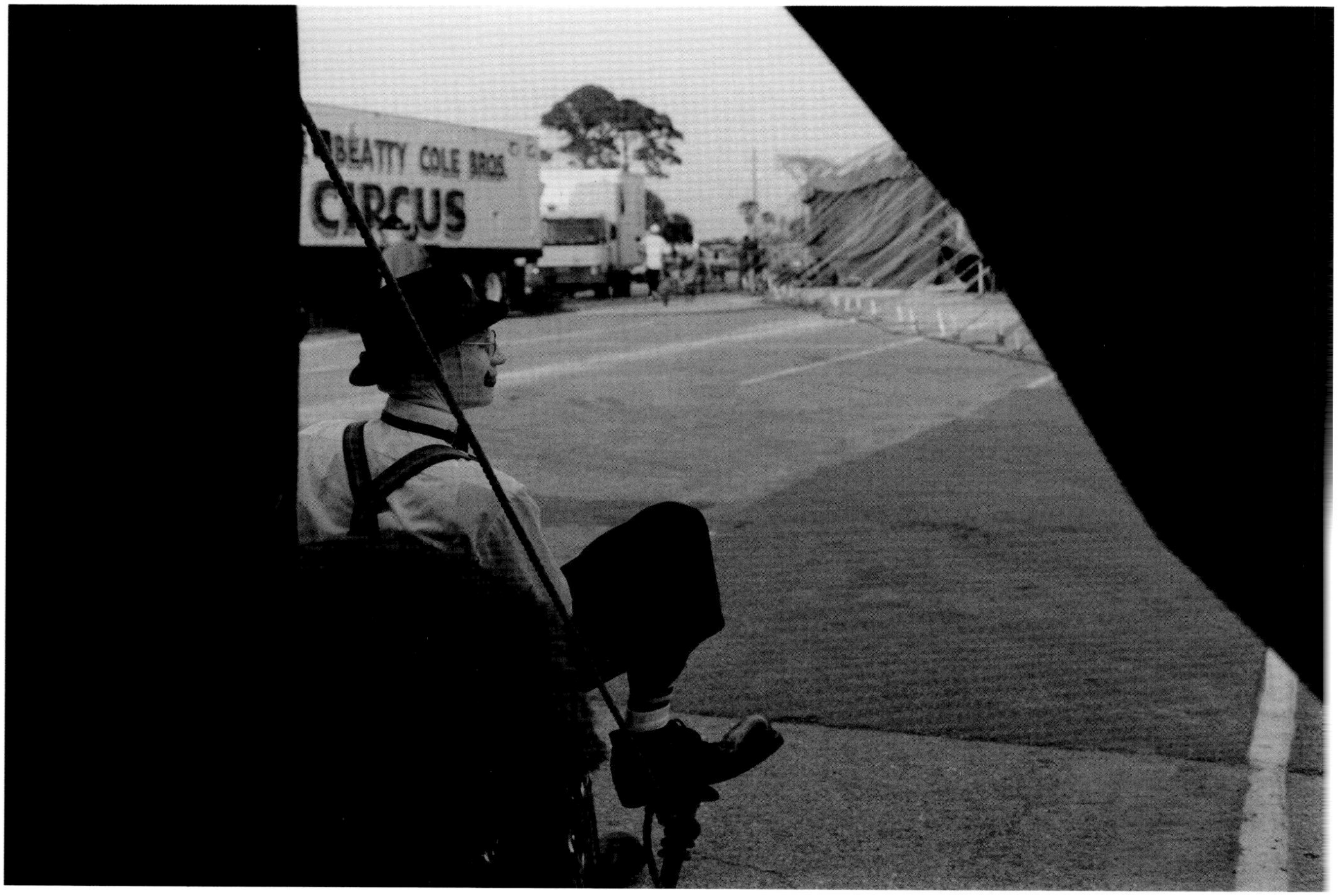

PLATE 124

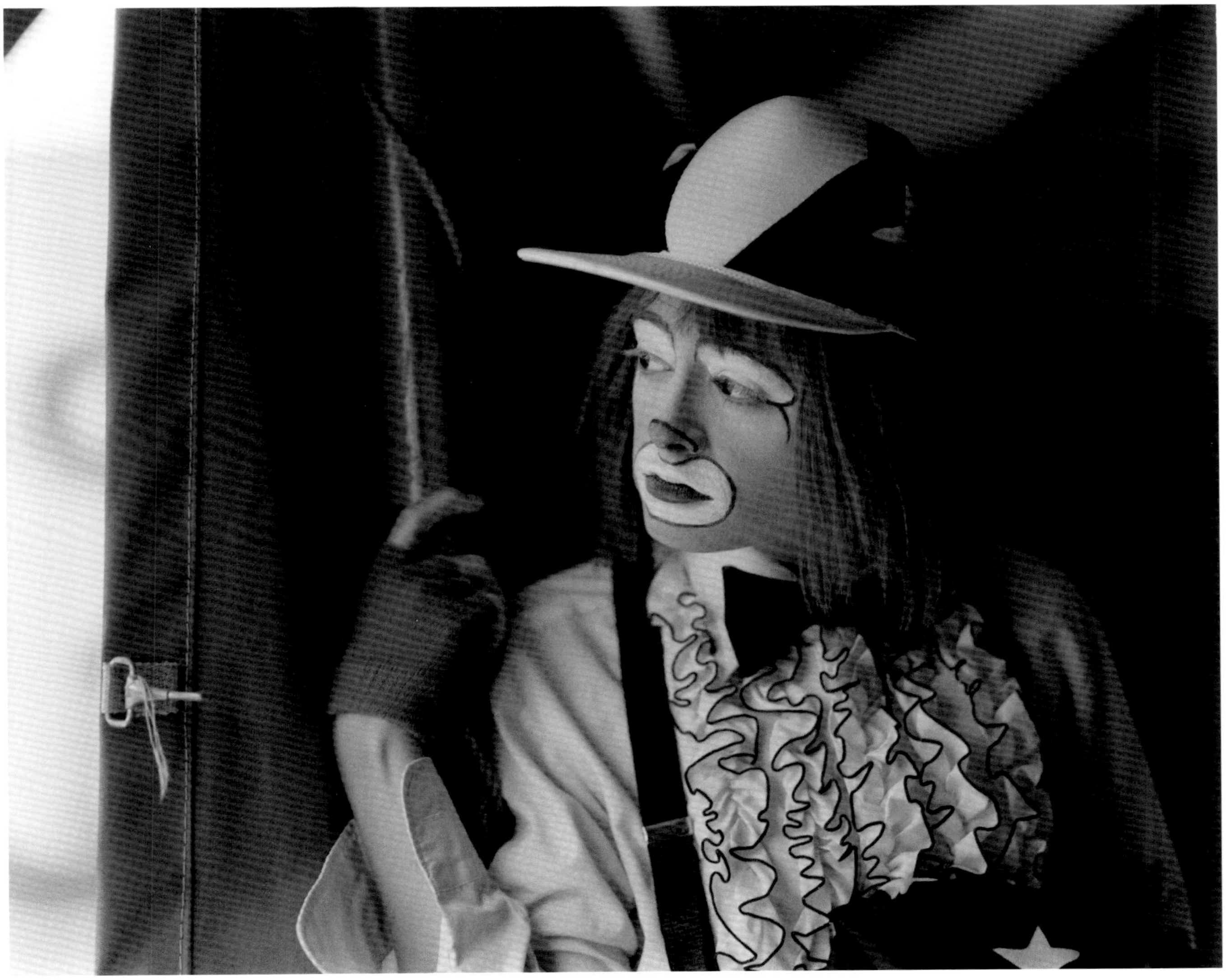

PLATE 125

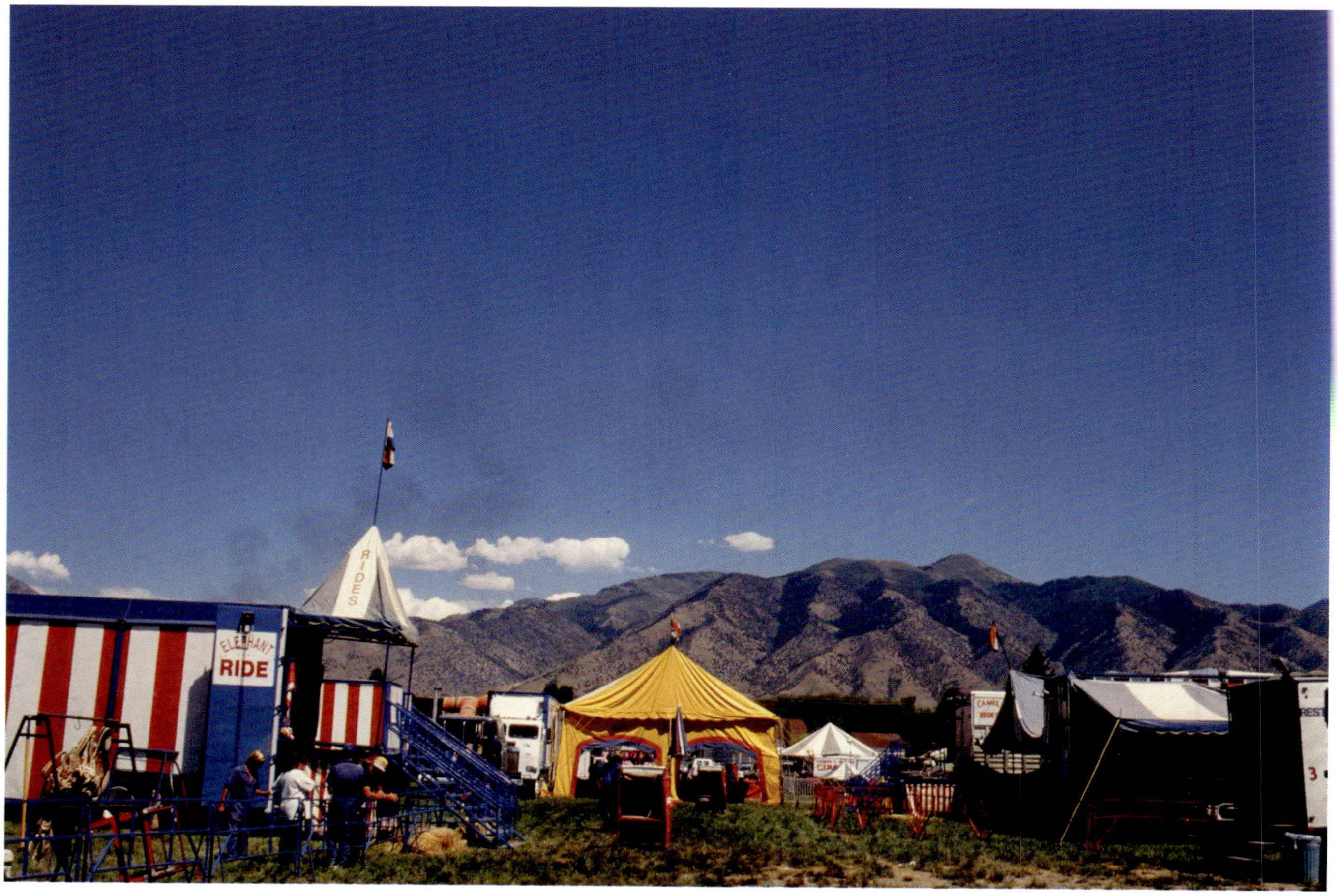

PLATE 126

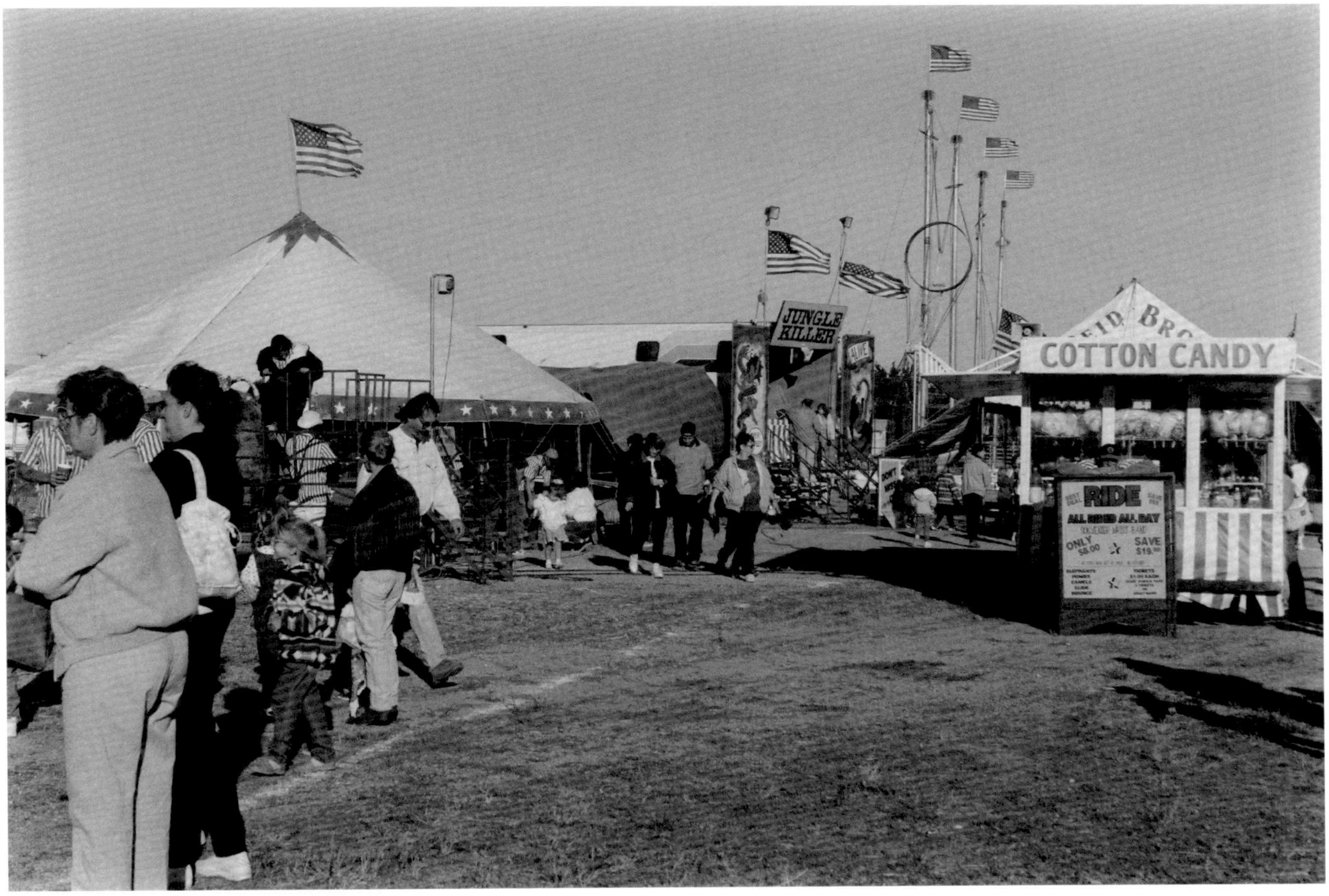
JUNGLE KILLER
COTTON CANDY
RIDE
ALL RIDES ALL DAY
ONLY $8.00
SAVE $19.00

PLATE 127

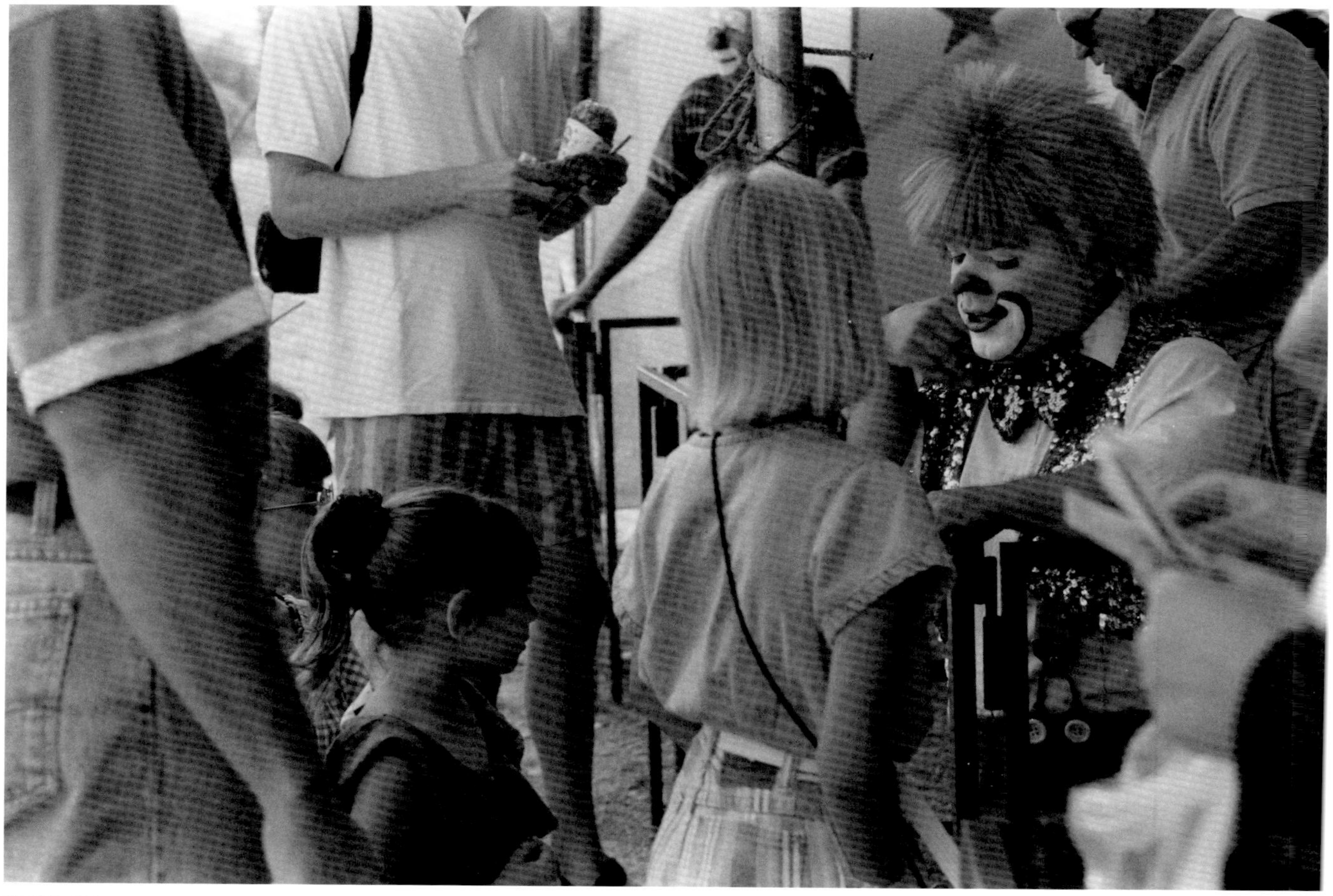

PLATE 128

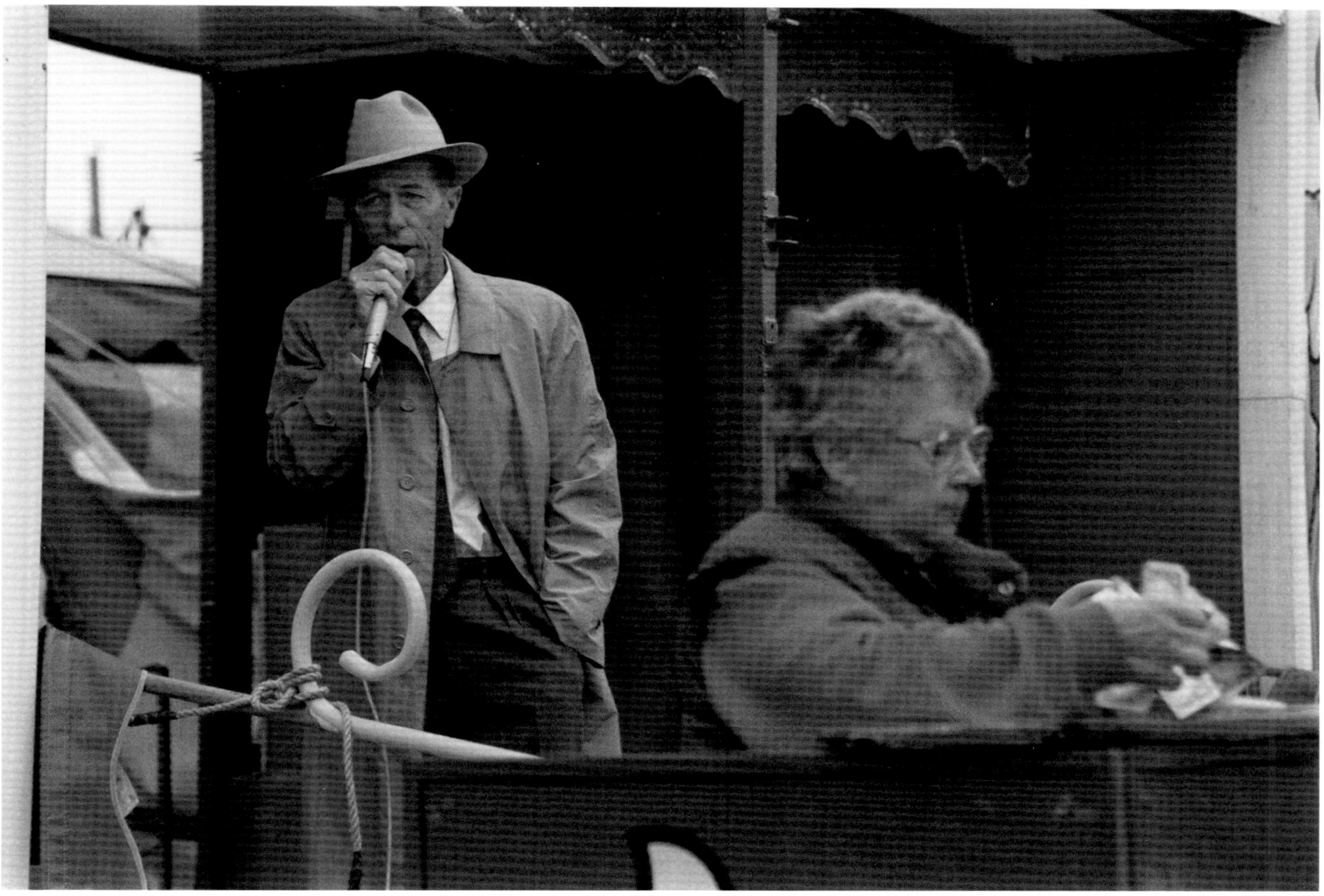

PLATE 129

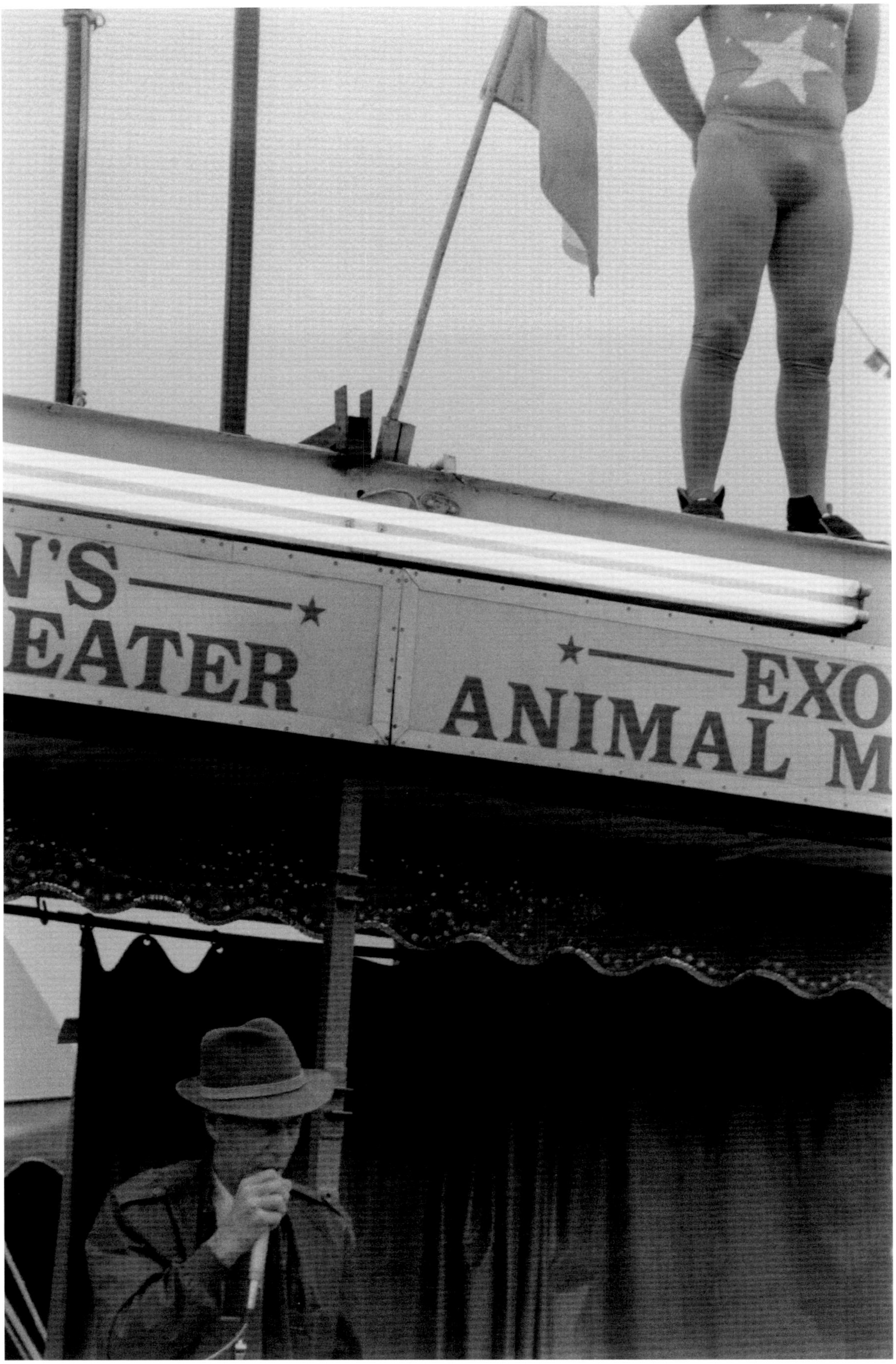

PLATE 130

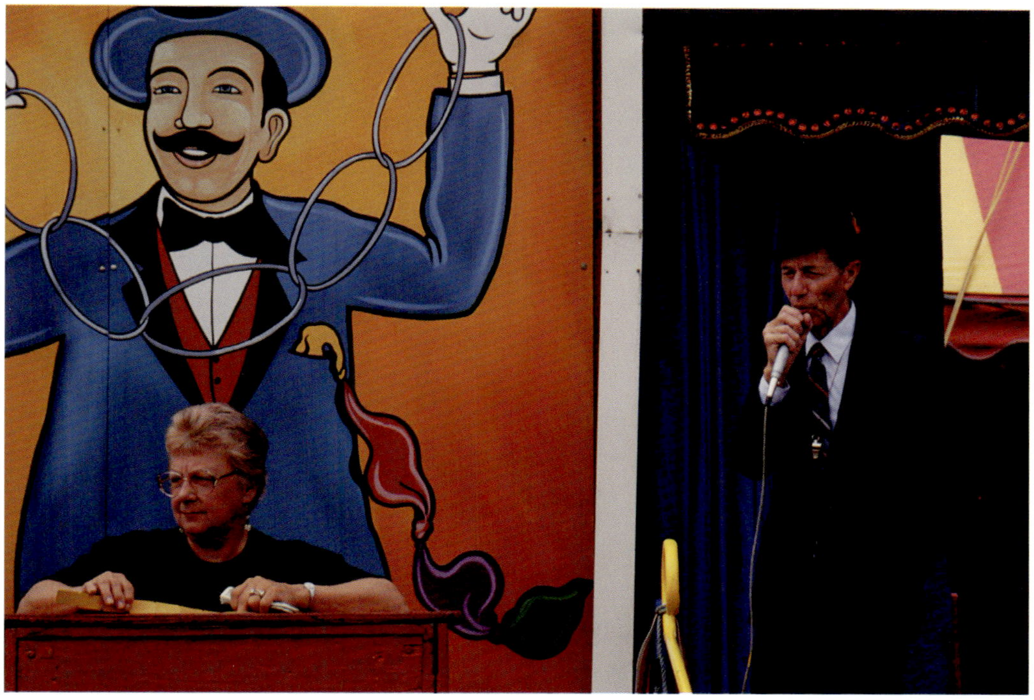

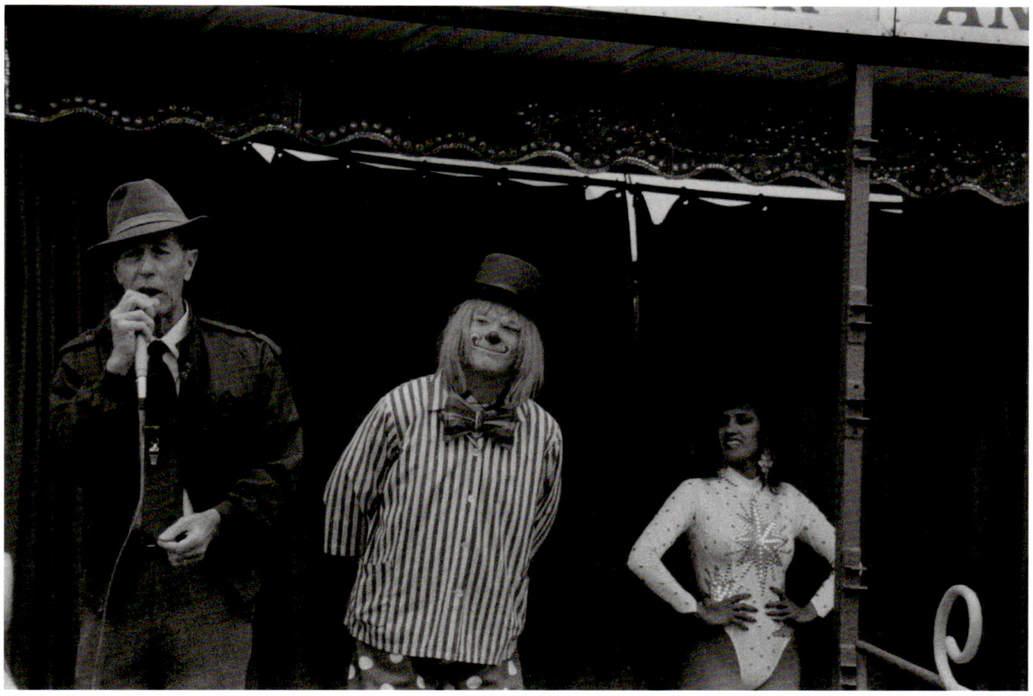

PLATES 131 & 132

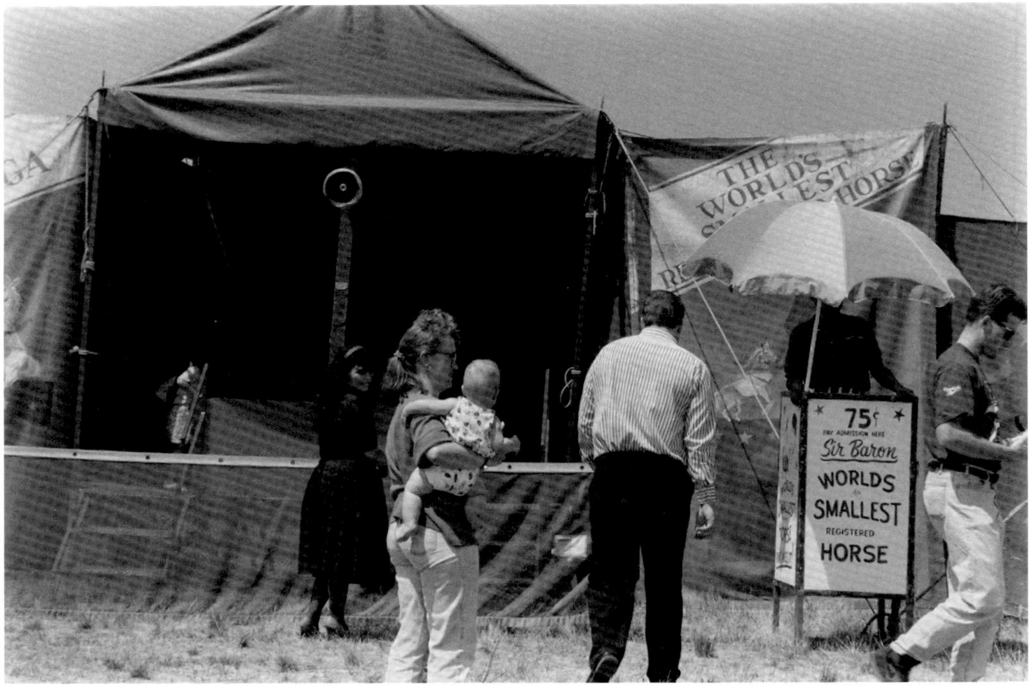

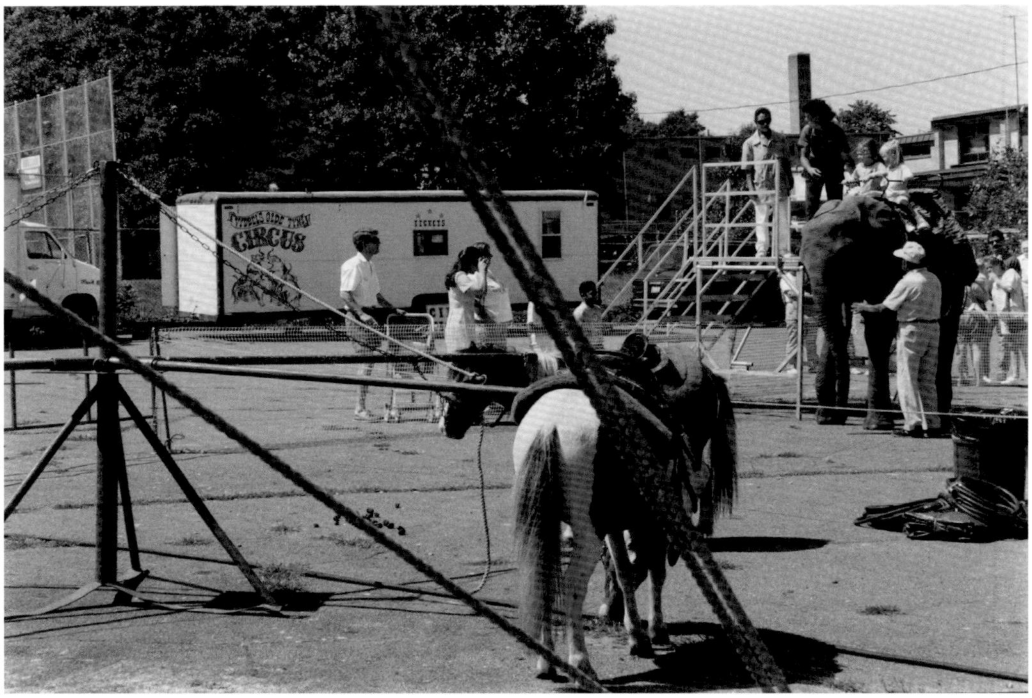

PLATES 133 & 134

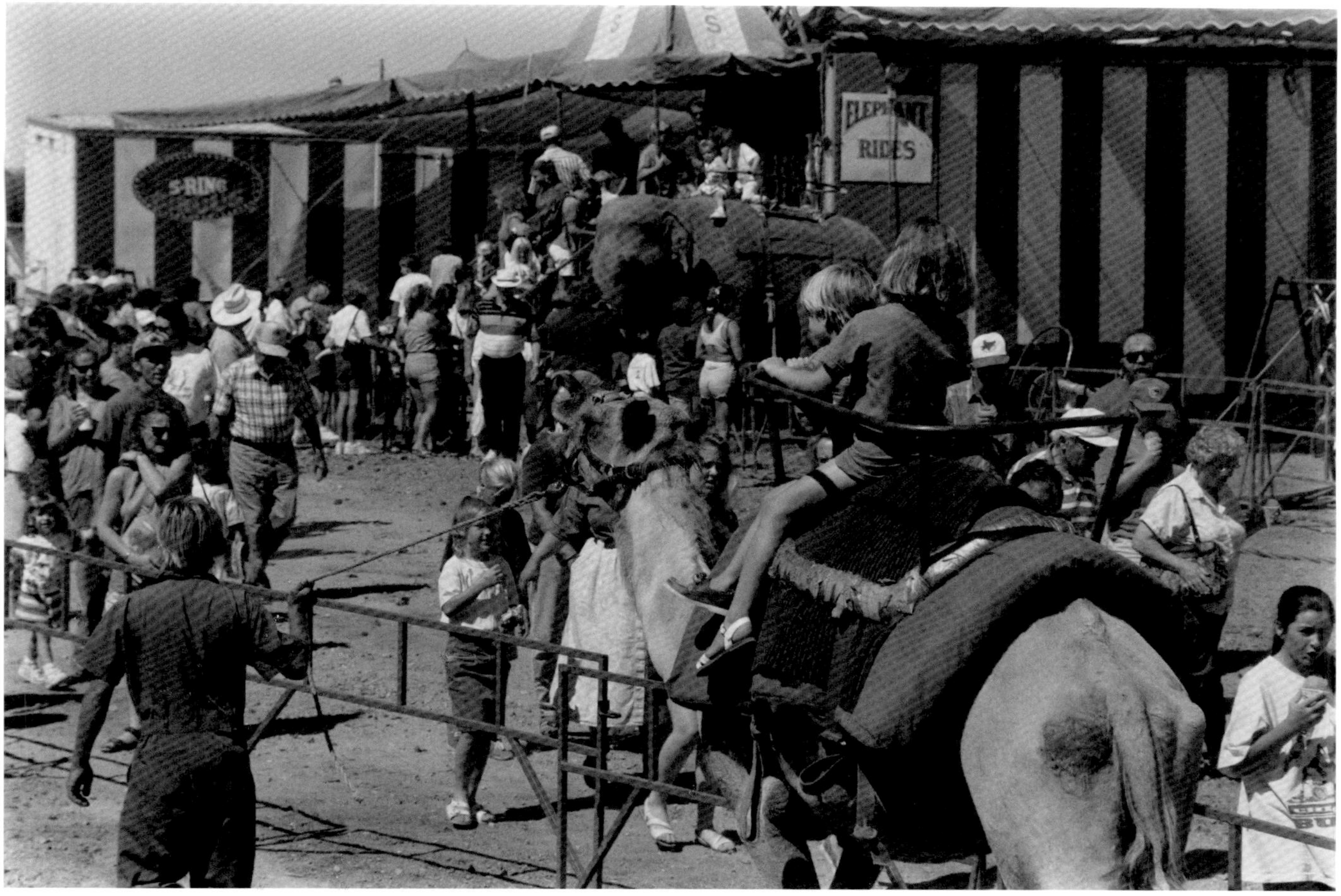

PLATE 135

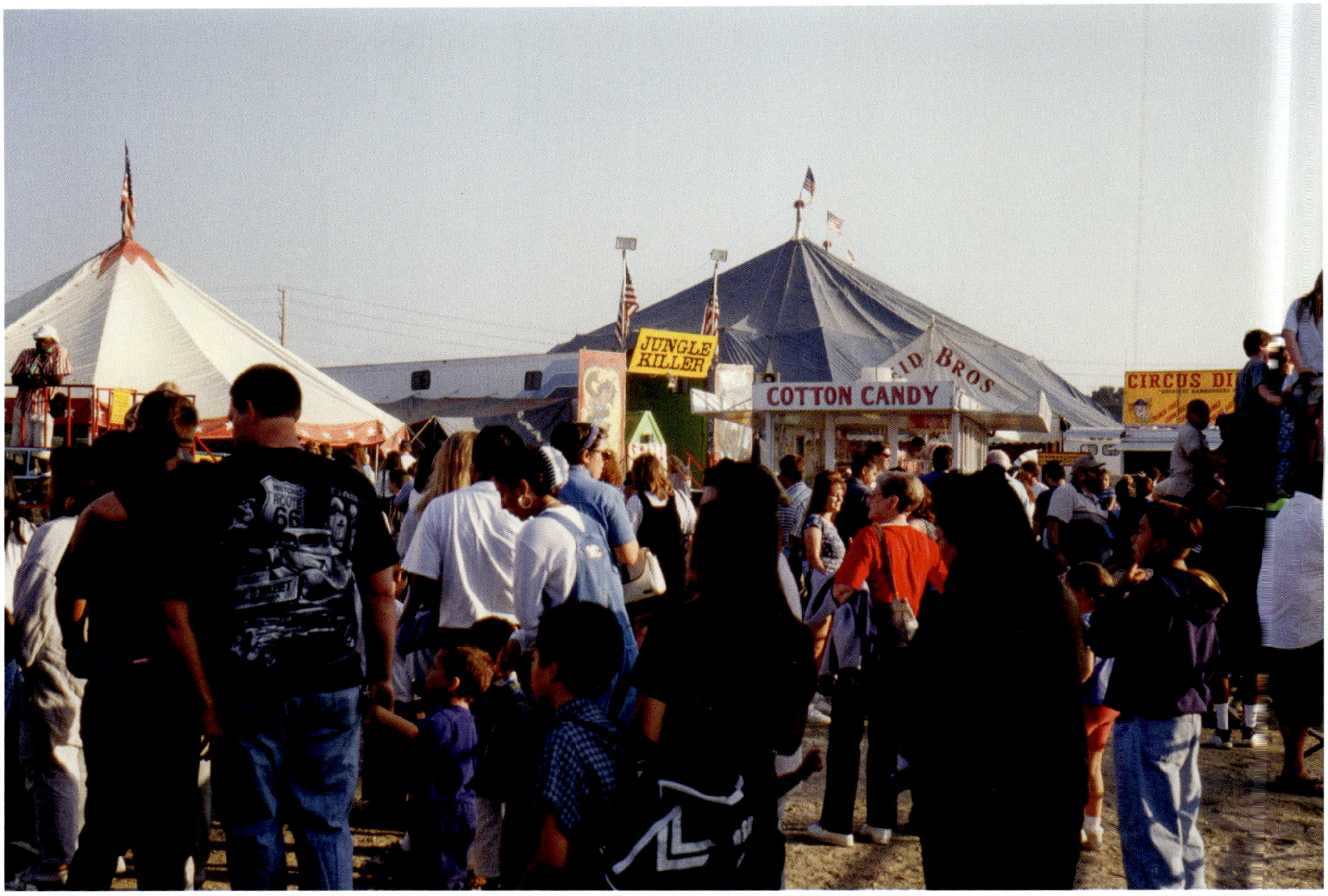

PLATE 136

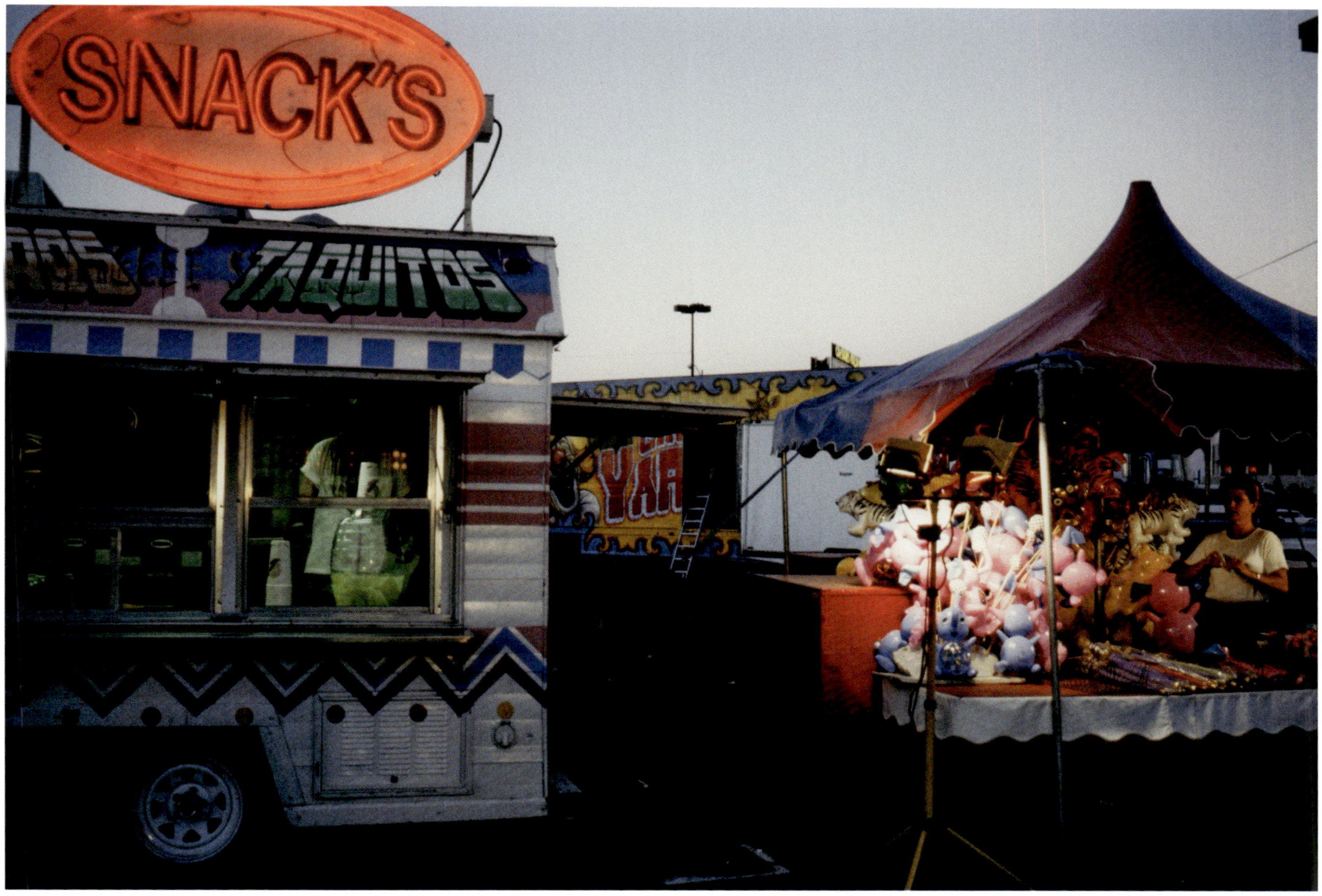

PLATE 137

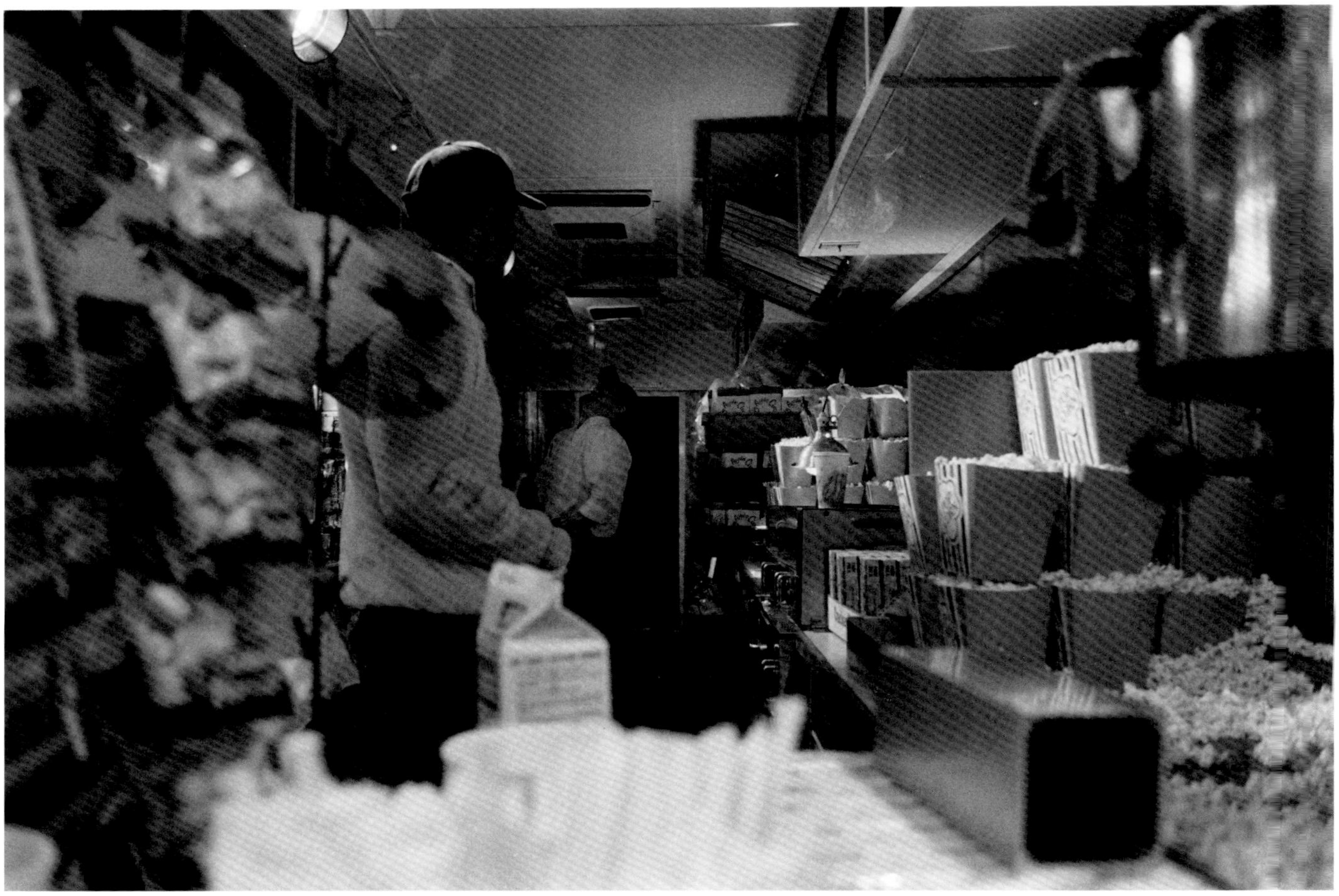

PLATE 138

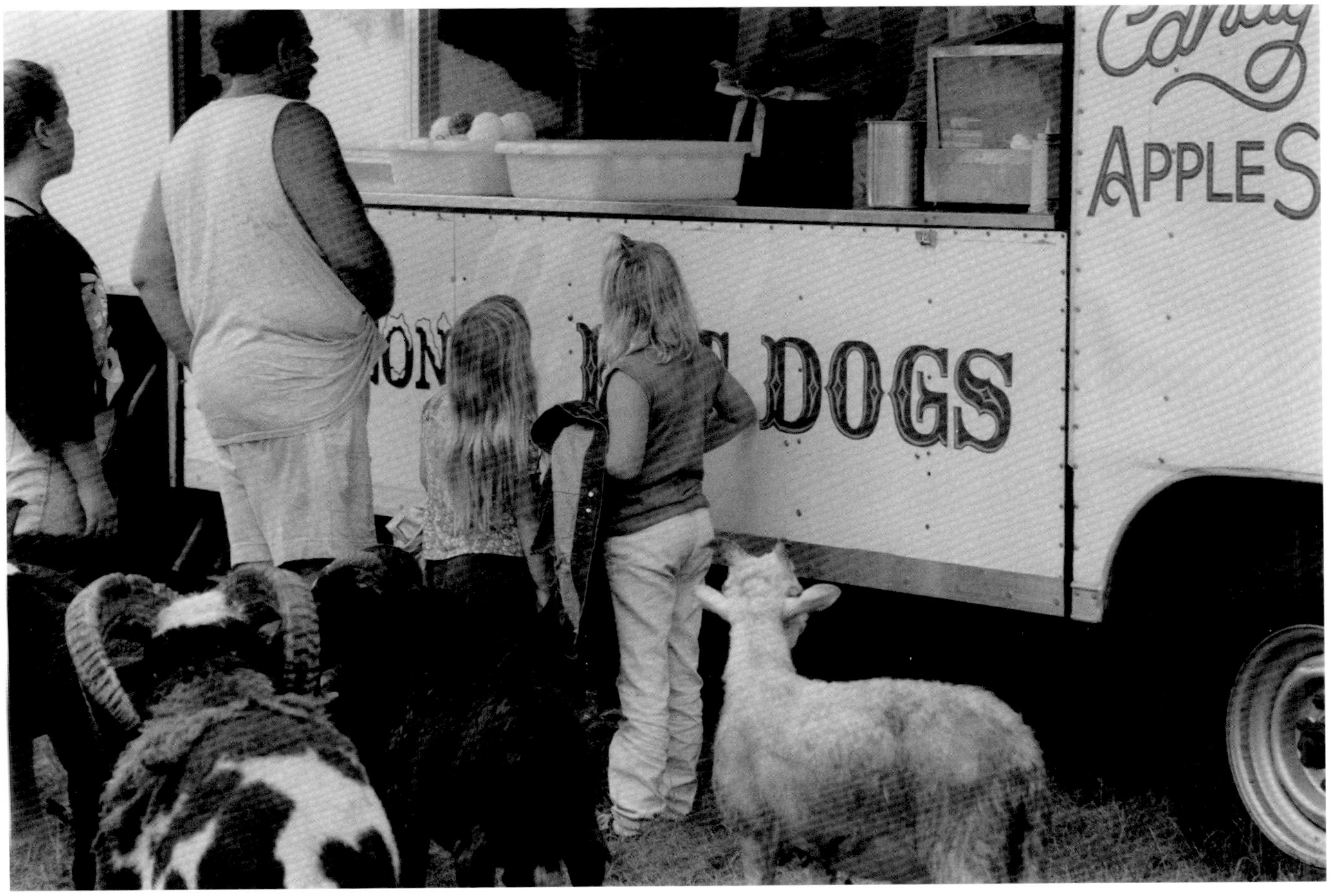

PLATE 139

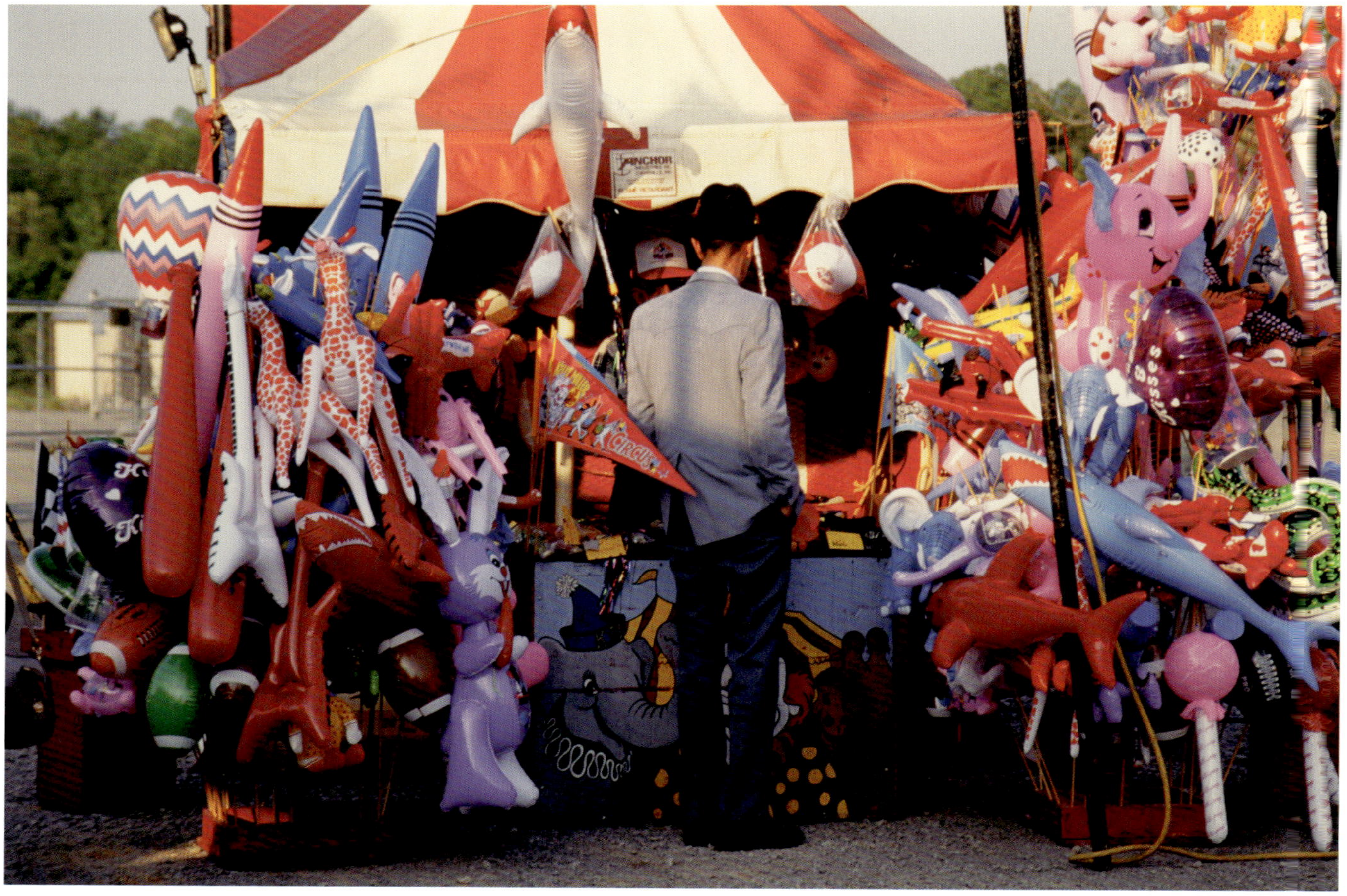

PLATE 140

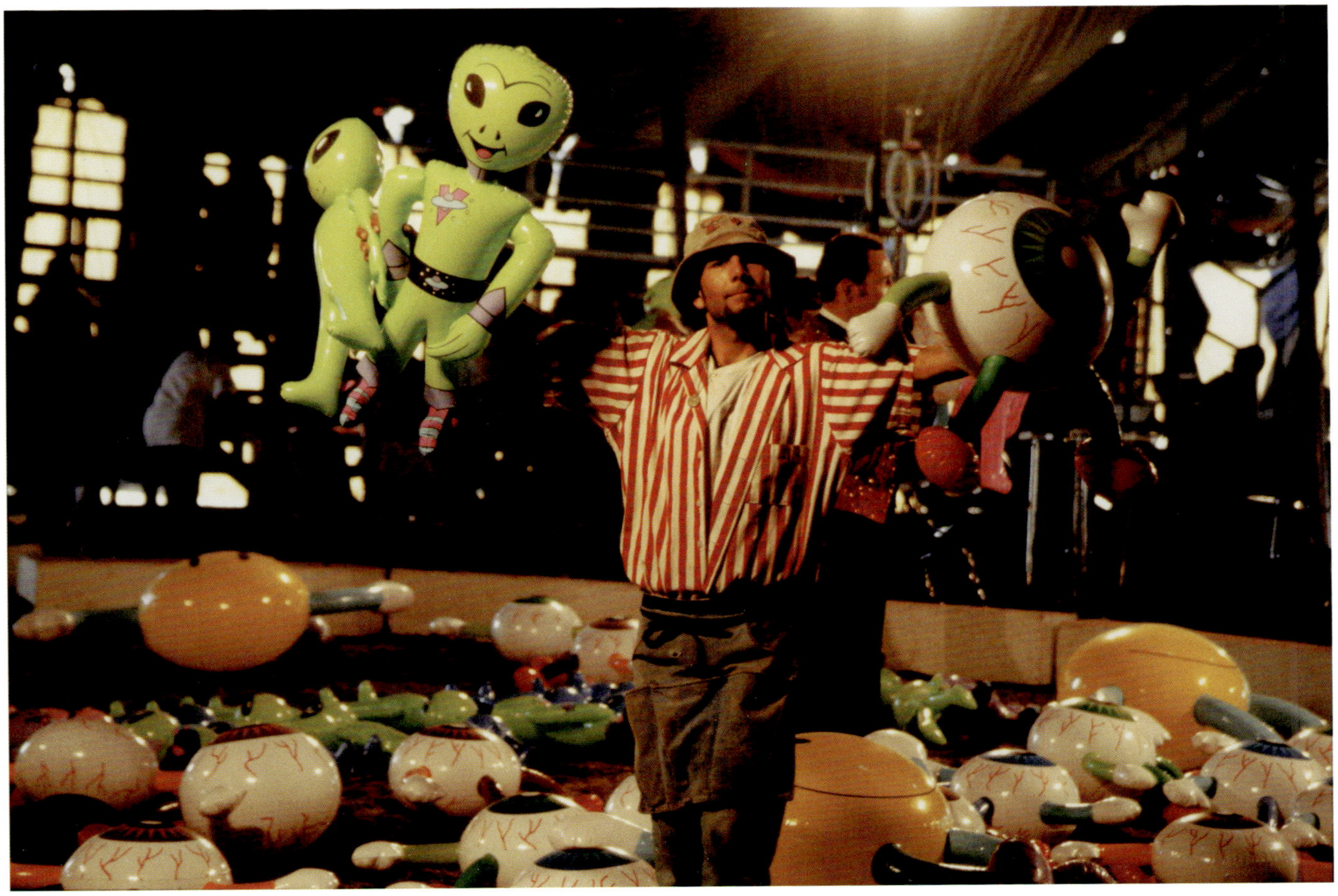

PLATE 141

★ ★ ★ ★ ★ ★ ★ ★ ★ ★ ★ ★ ★

I won't be part of hurting somebody's feelings to get a cheap laugh, when I can get a good laugh *not* doing that. Be a little more creative, a little more imaginative! If anybody should get humiliated, it should be *you. You* should be able to take a joke. Don't count on anyone else being able to take a joke.

—Al Calienes, performing company member, Big Apple Circus (1995)

★ ★ ★ ★ ★ ★ ★ ★ ★ ★ ★ ★ ★

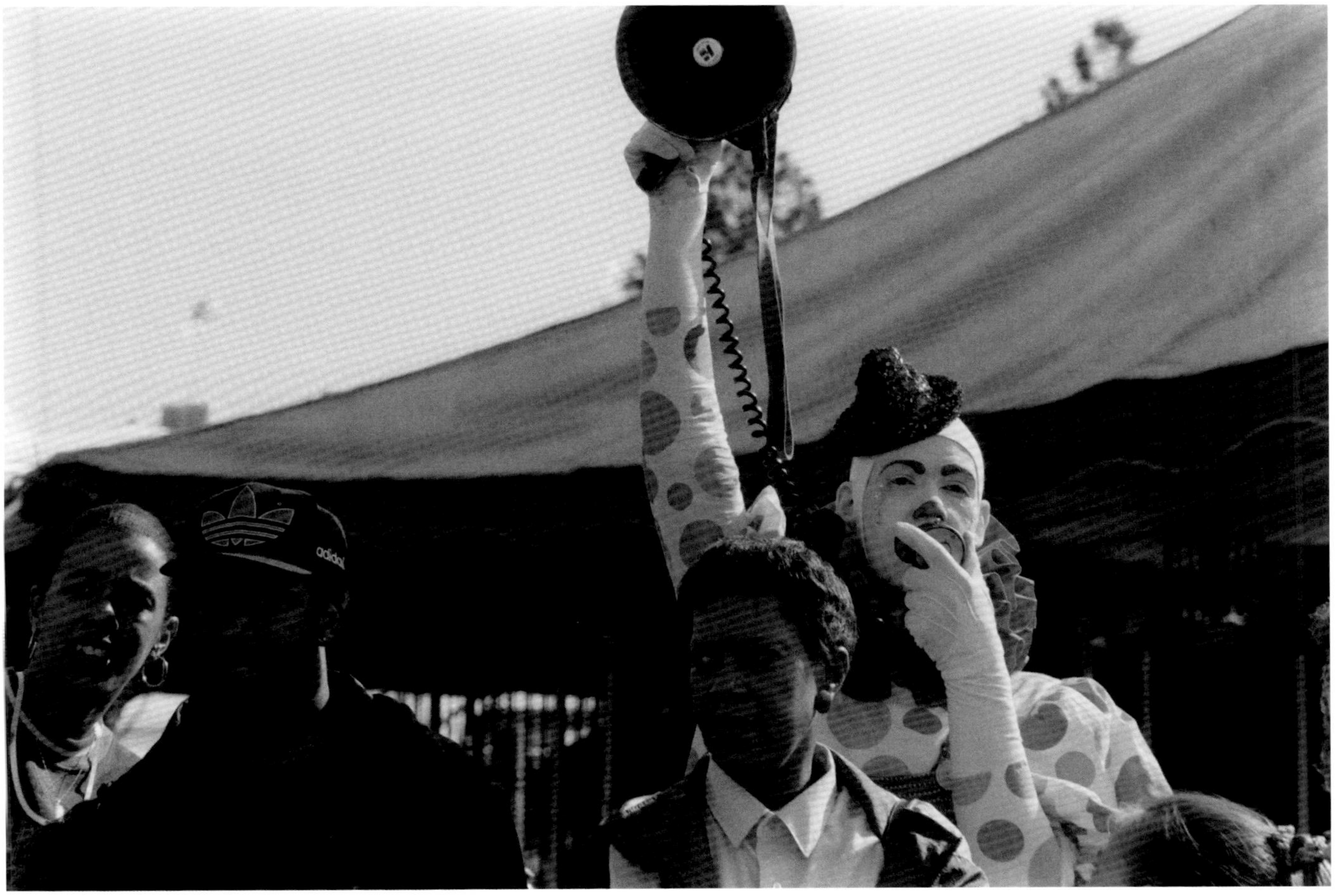

PLATE 142

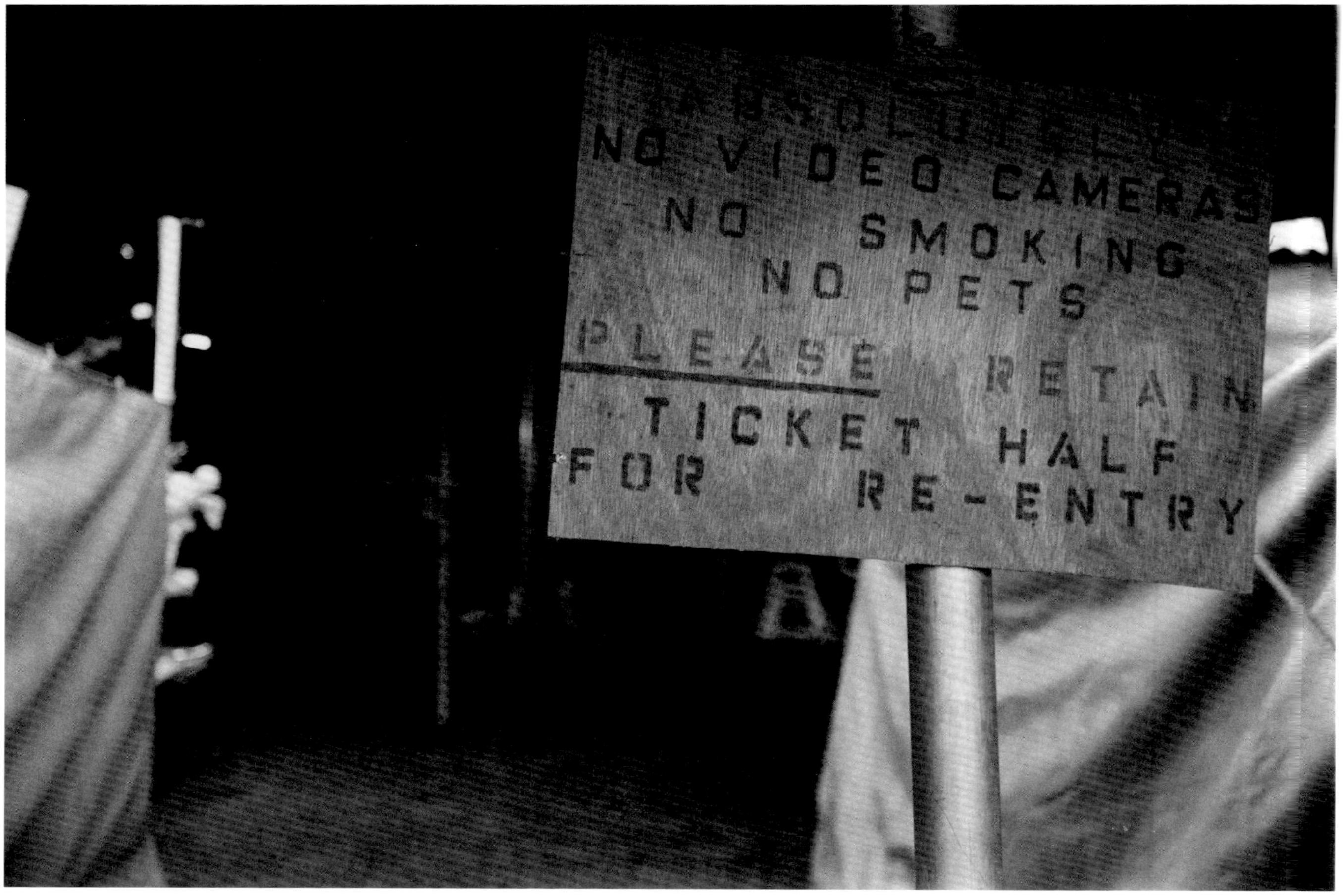
NO VIDEO CAMERAS
NO SMOKING
NO PETS
PLEASE RETAIN
TICKET HALF
FOR RE-ENTRY

PLATE 143

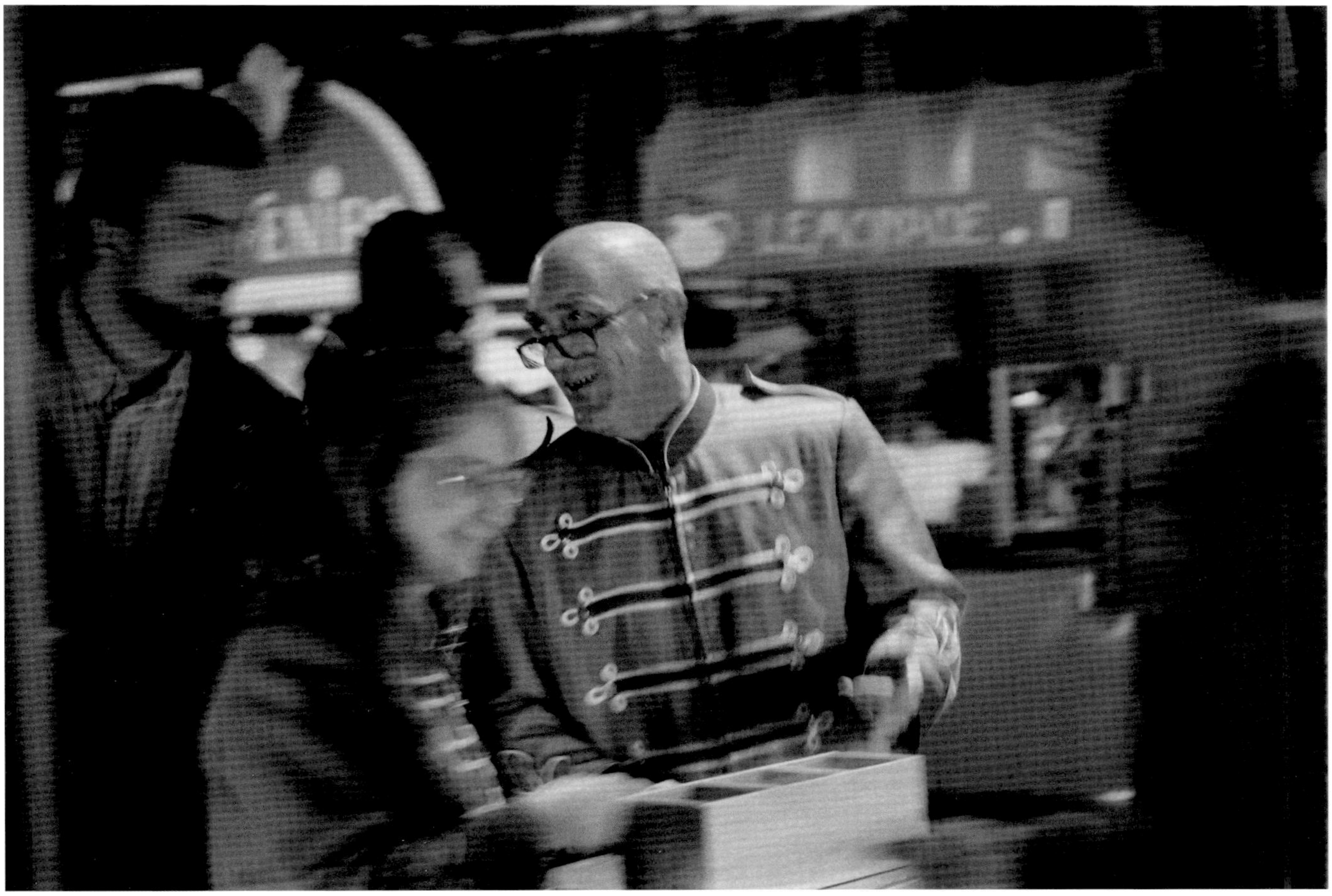

PLATE 144

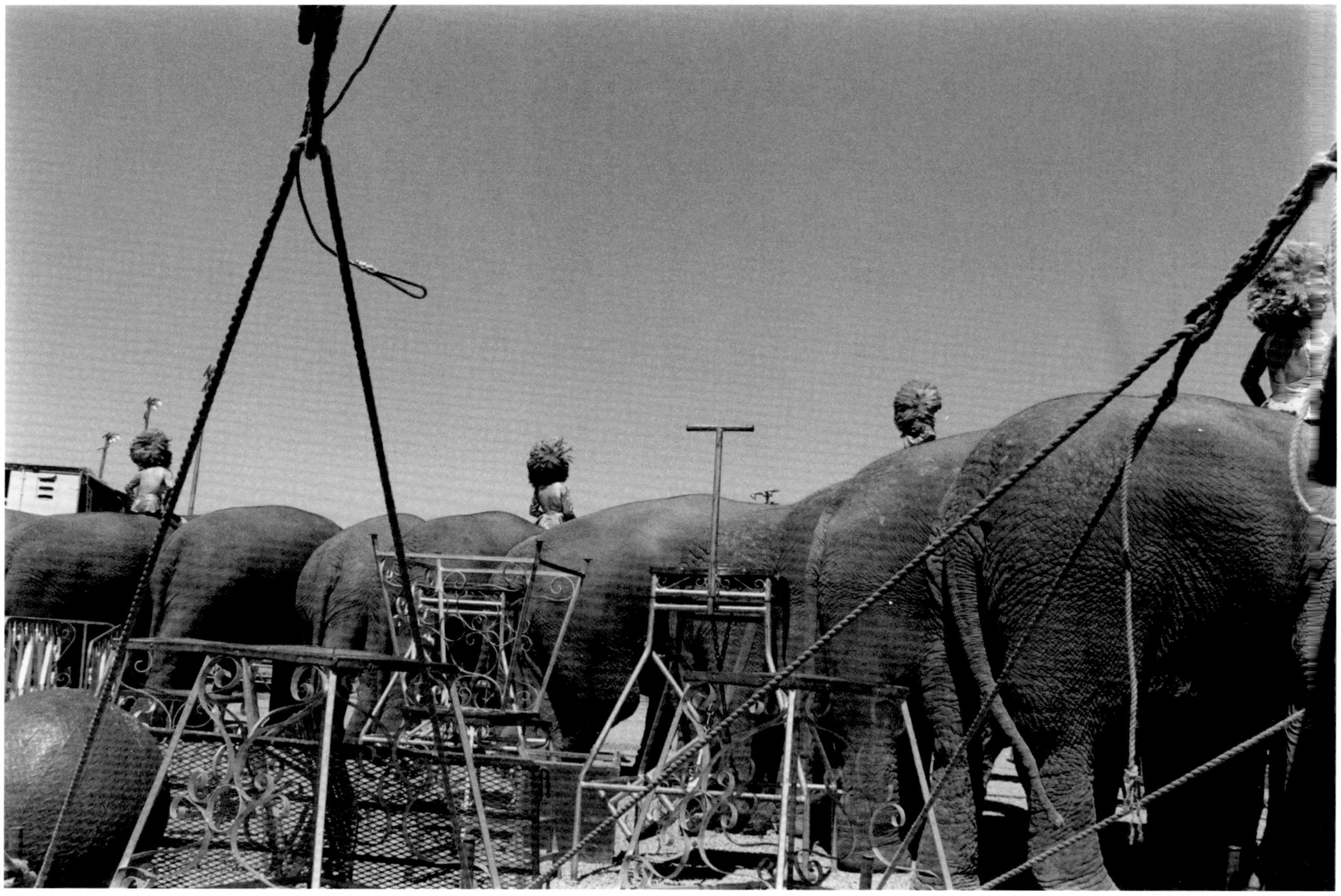

PLATE 145

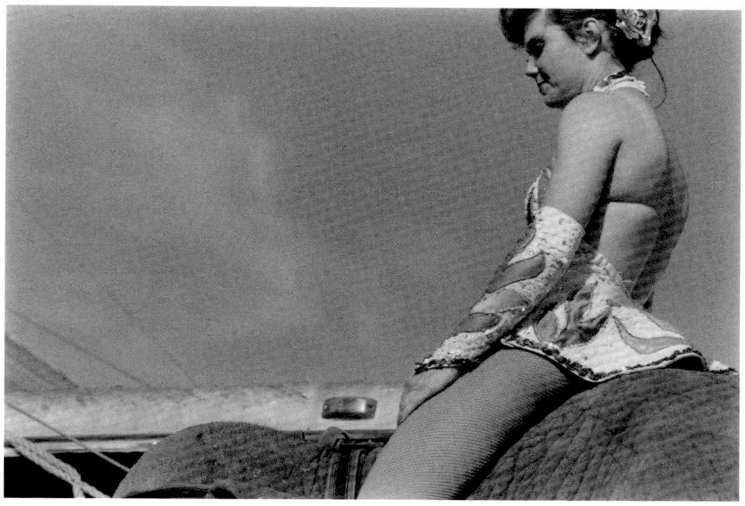

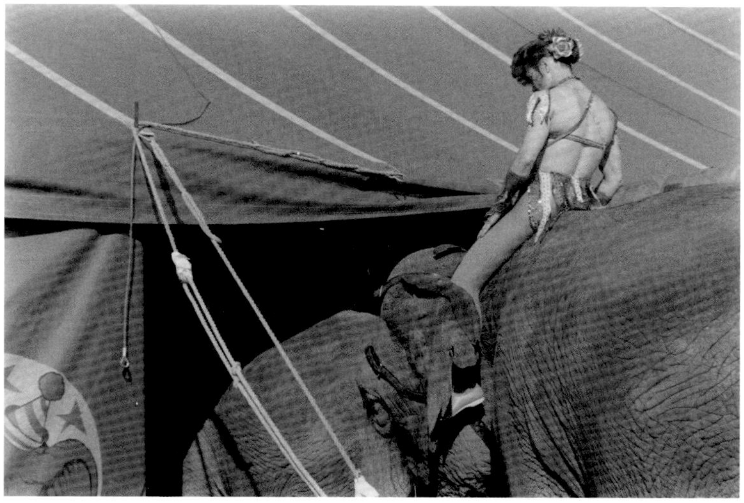

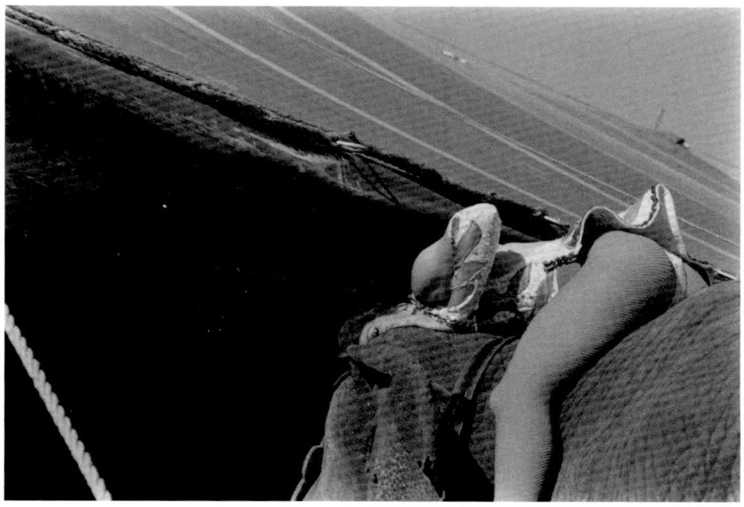

PLATES 146–148

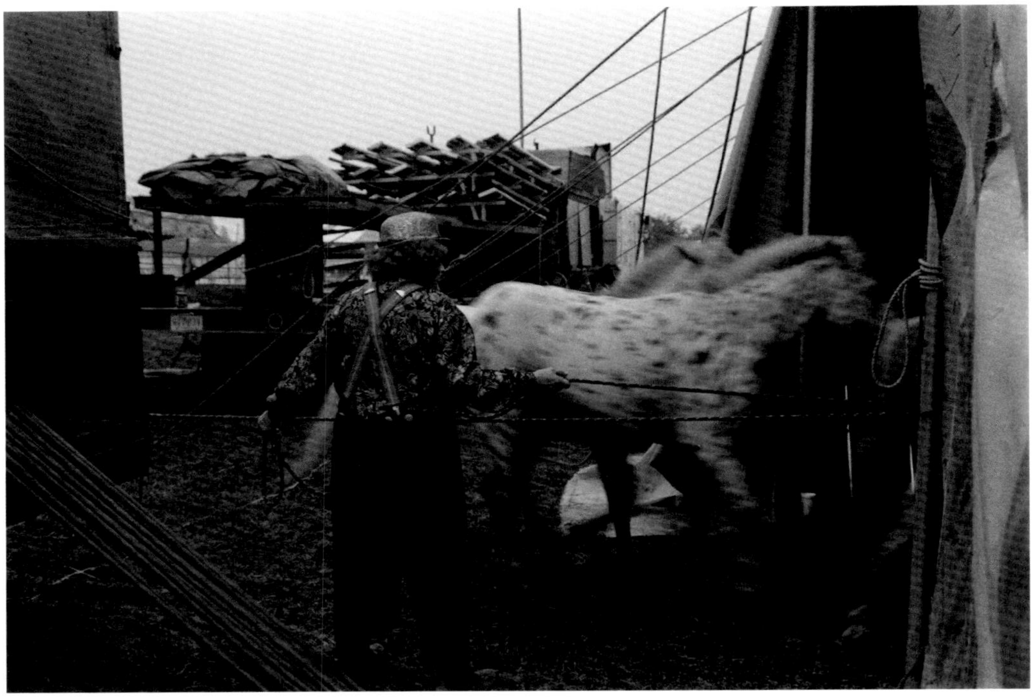

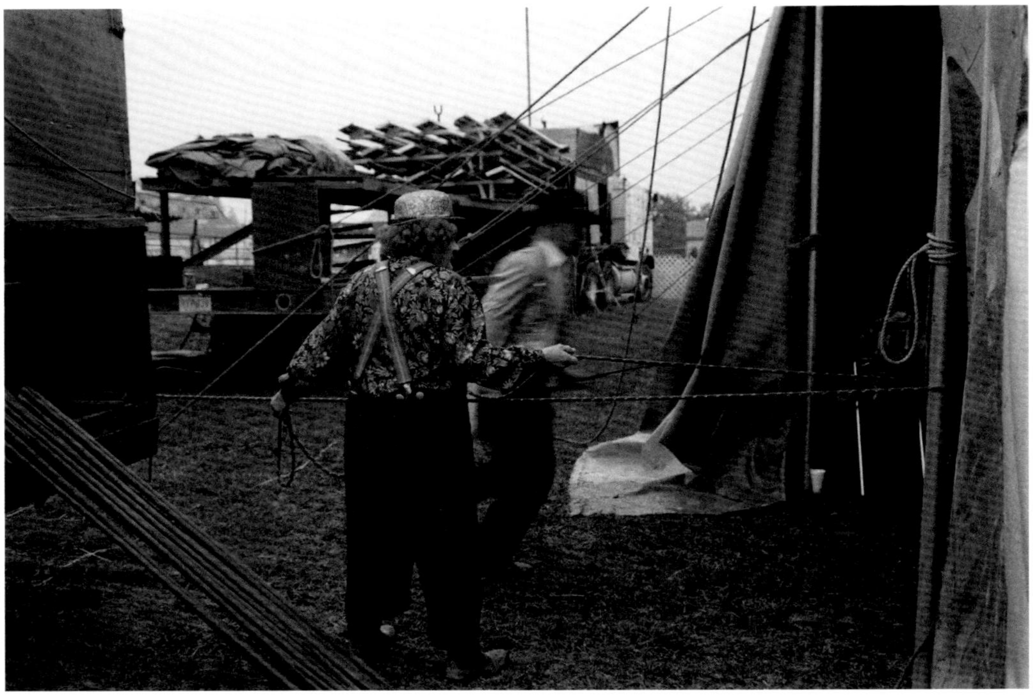

PLATES 149 & 150

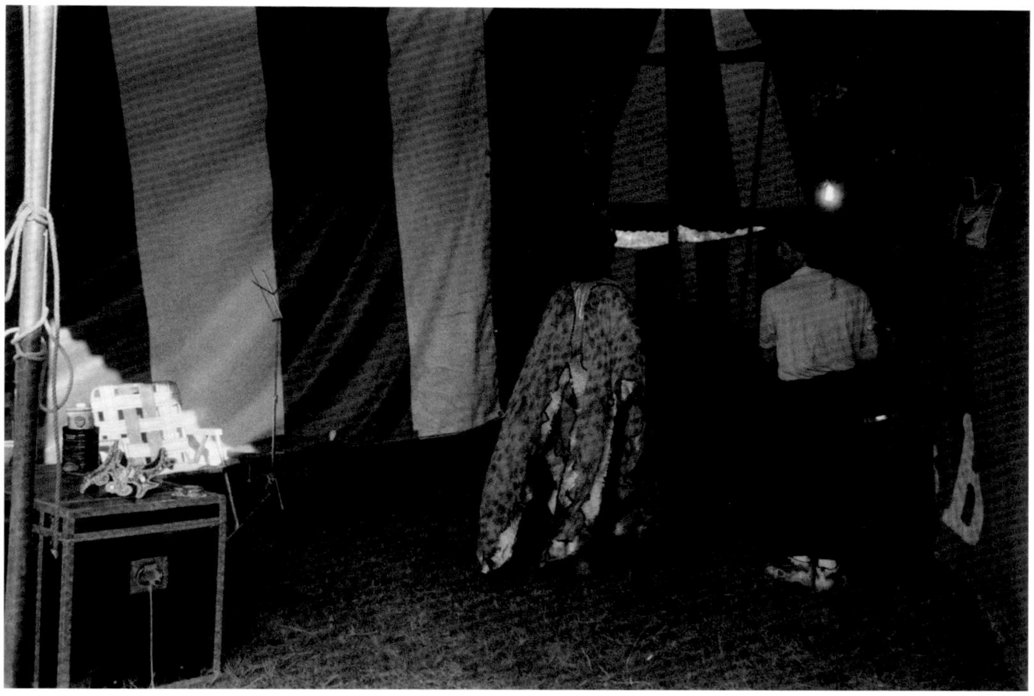

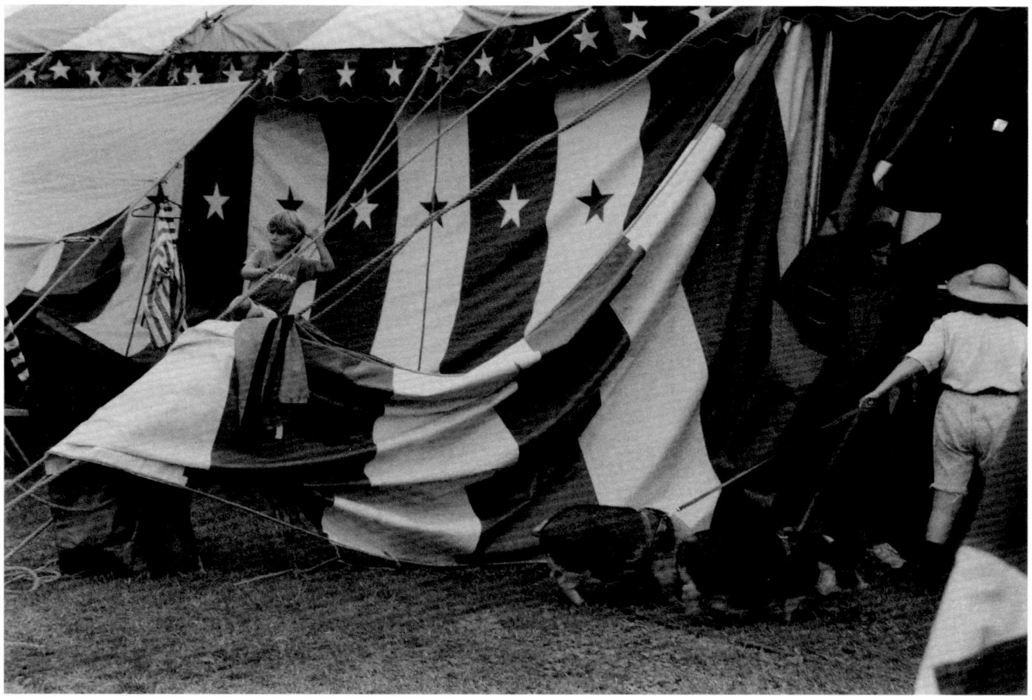

PLATES 151 & 152

This is how I gamble. I don't need to put quarters in a machine and wait to see what's going to happen. I don't need to pick a horse. I gamble by going on the road every year. The payoff is that you have a good season, you make some money; you get through it safely, healthy, and happy. Everything is fine. That's what you get if you win.

—Tim Tegge, performer, Clyde Beatty-Cole Bros. Circus (1995)

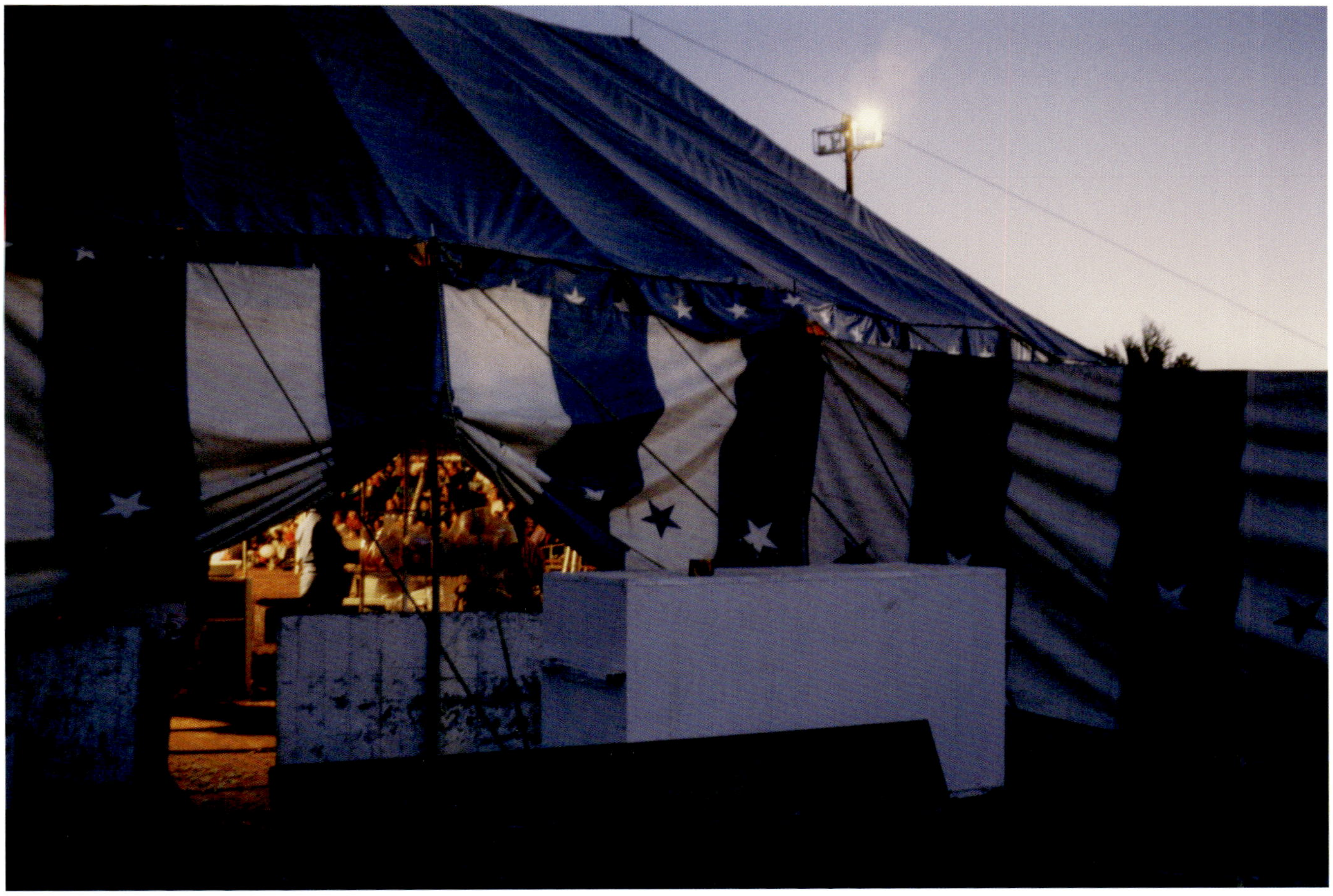

PLATE 153

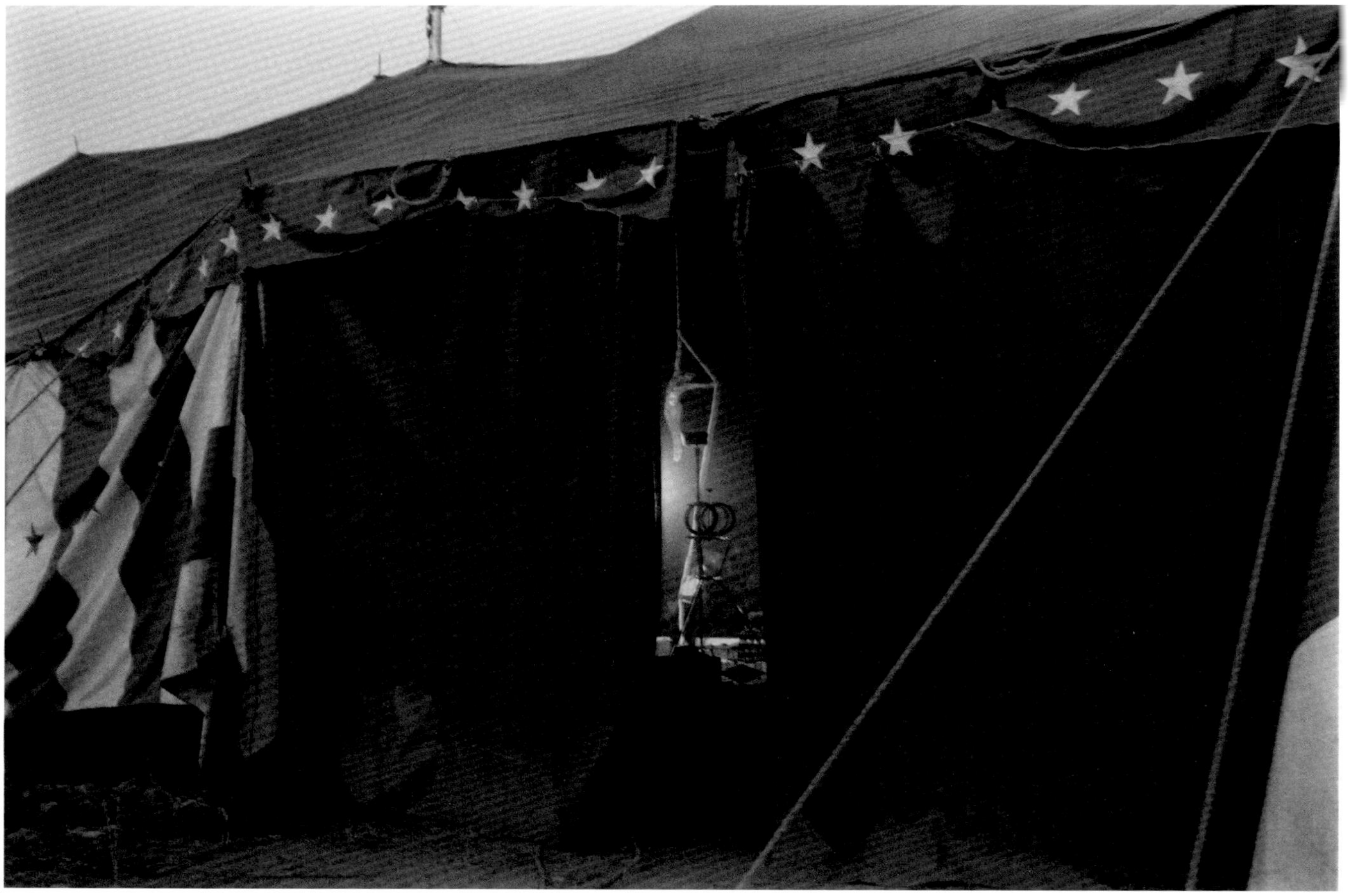

PLATE 154

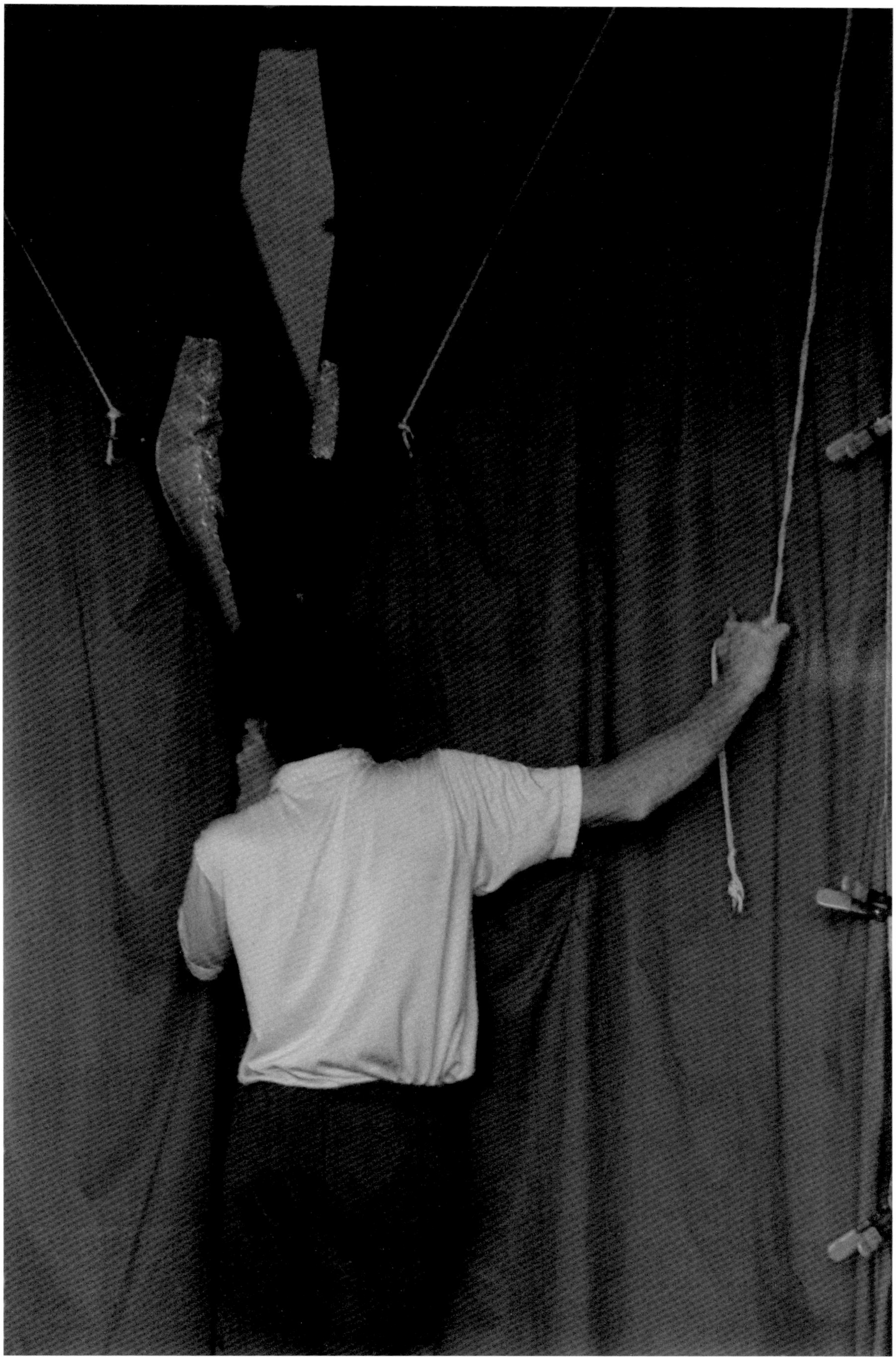

PLATE 155

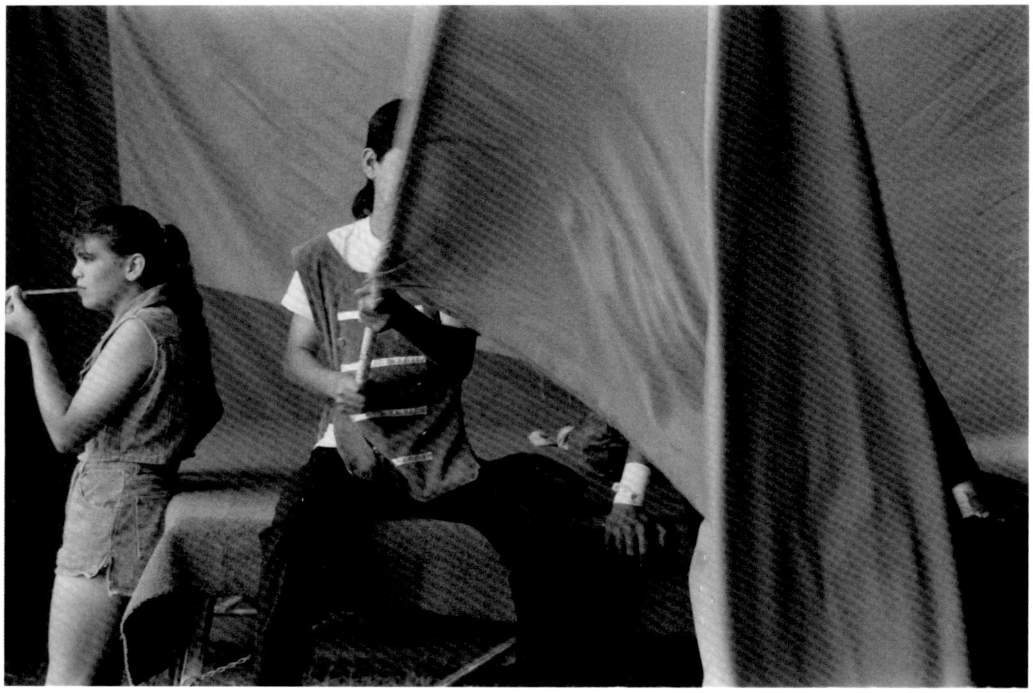

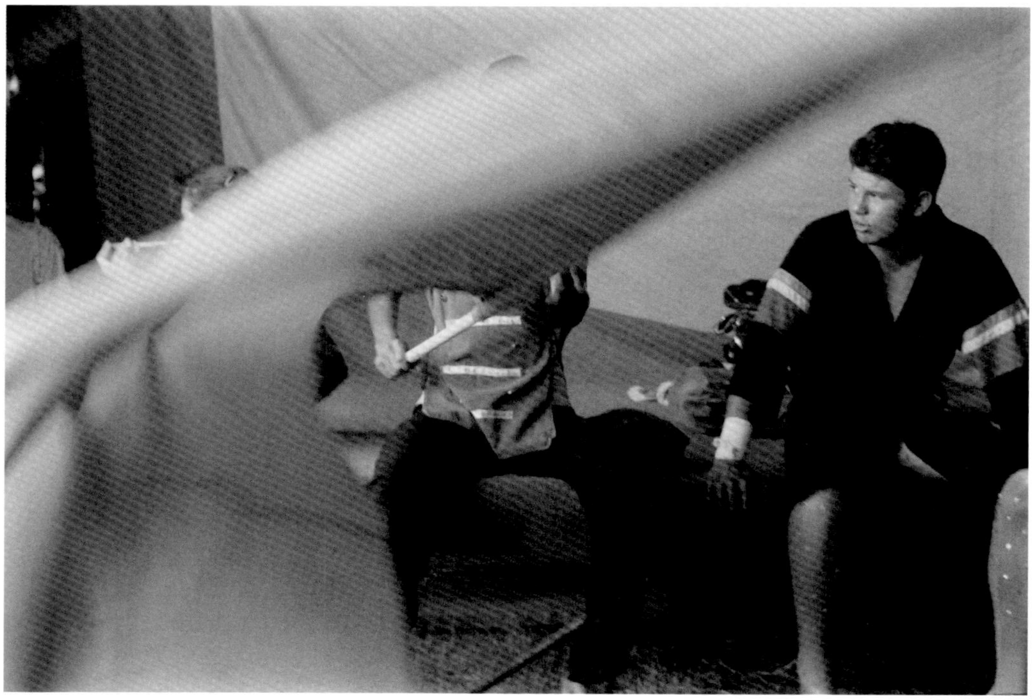

PLATES 156 & 157

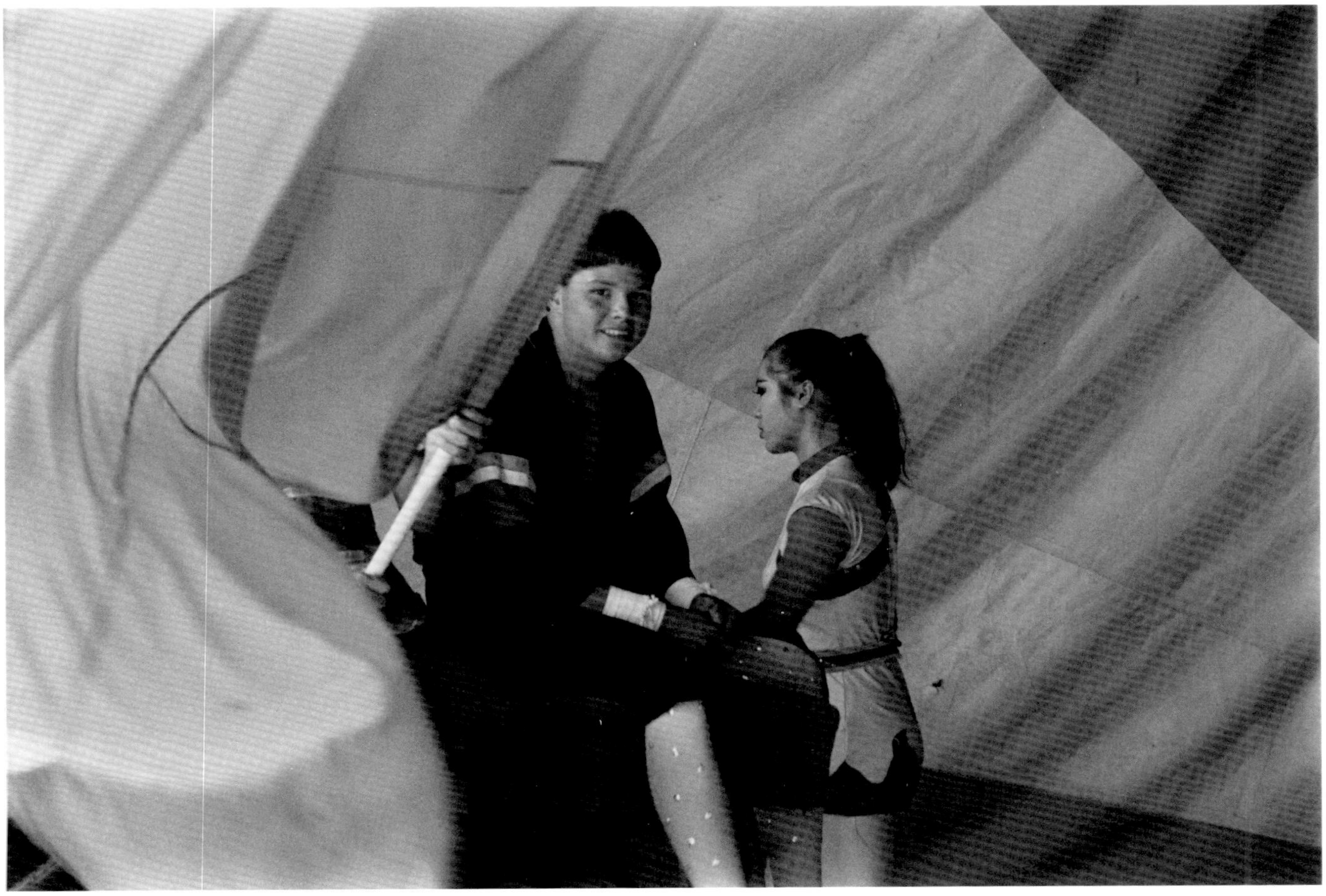

PLATE 158

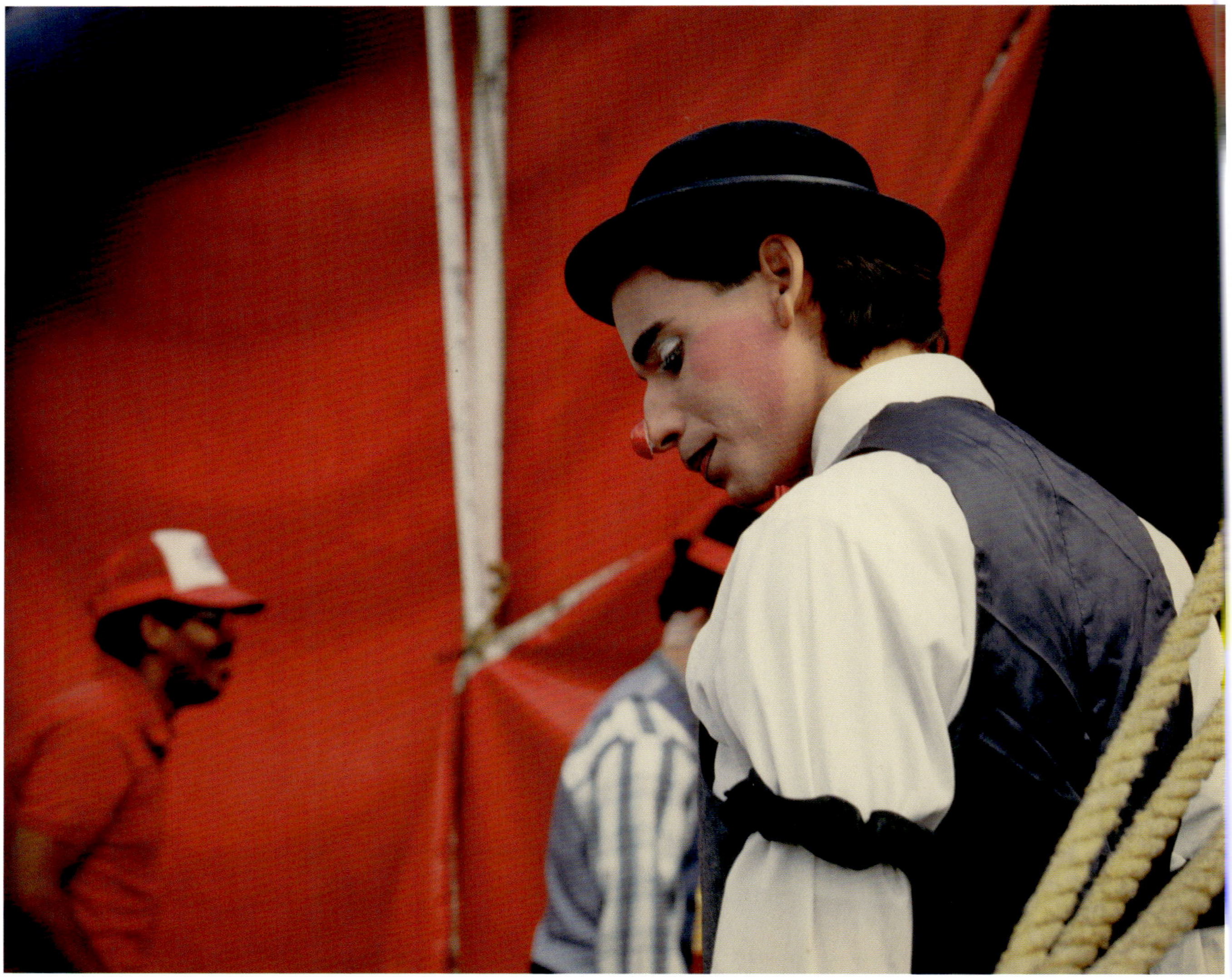

PLATE 159

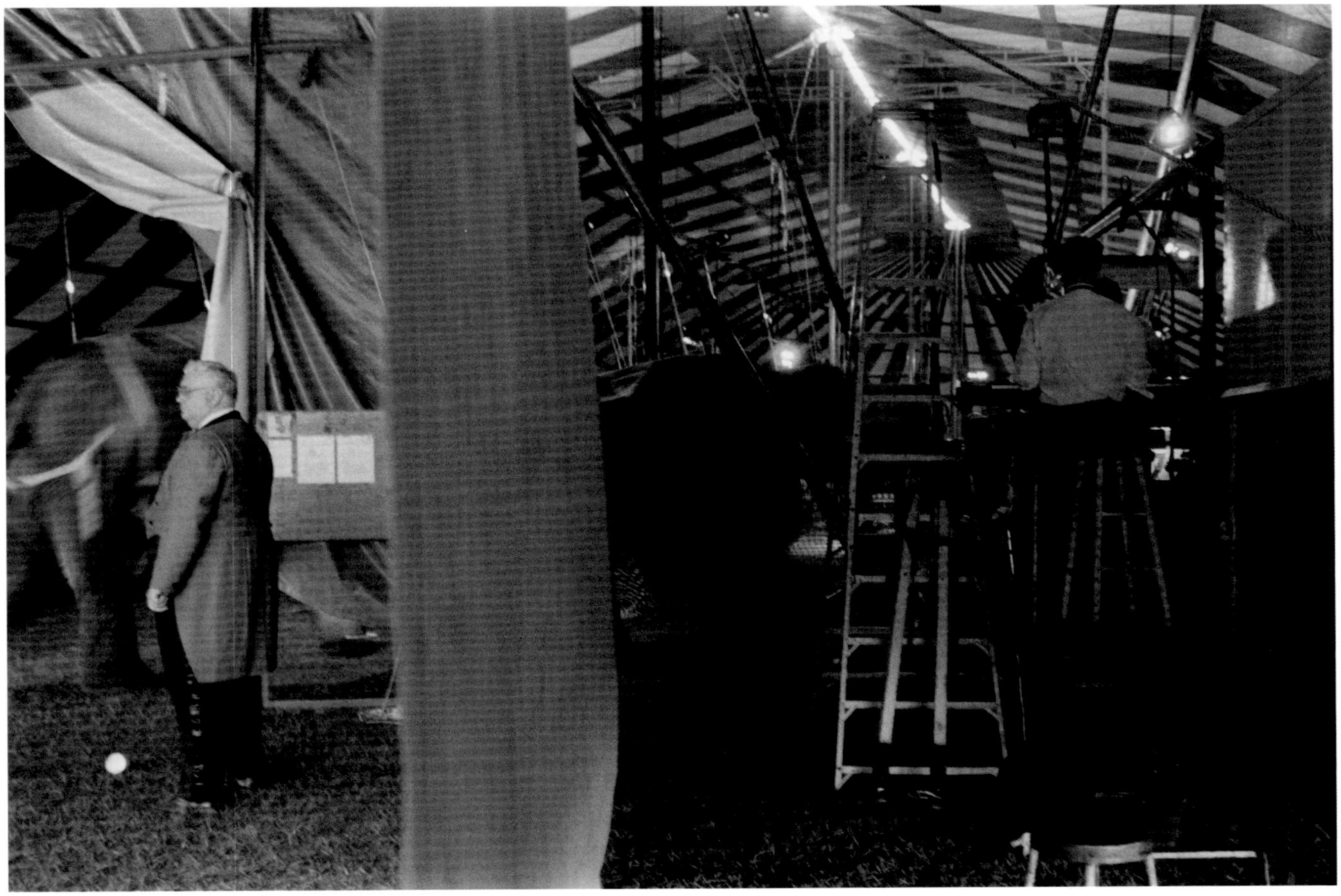

PLATE 160

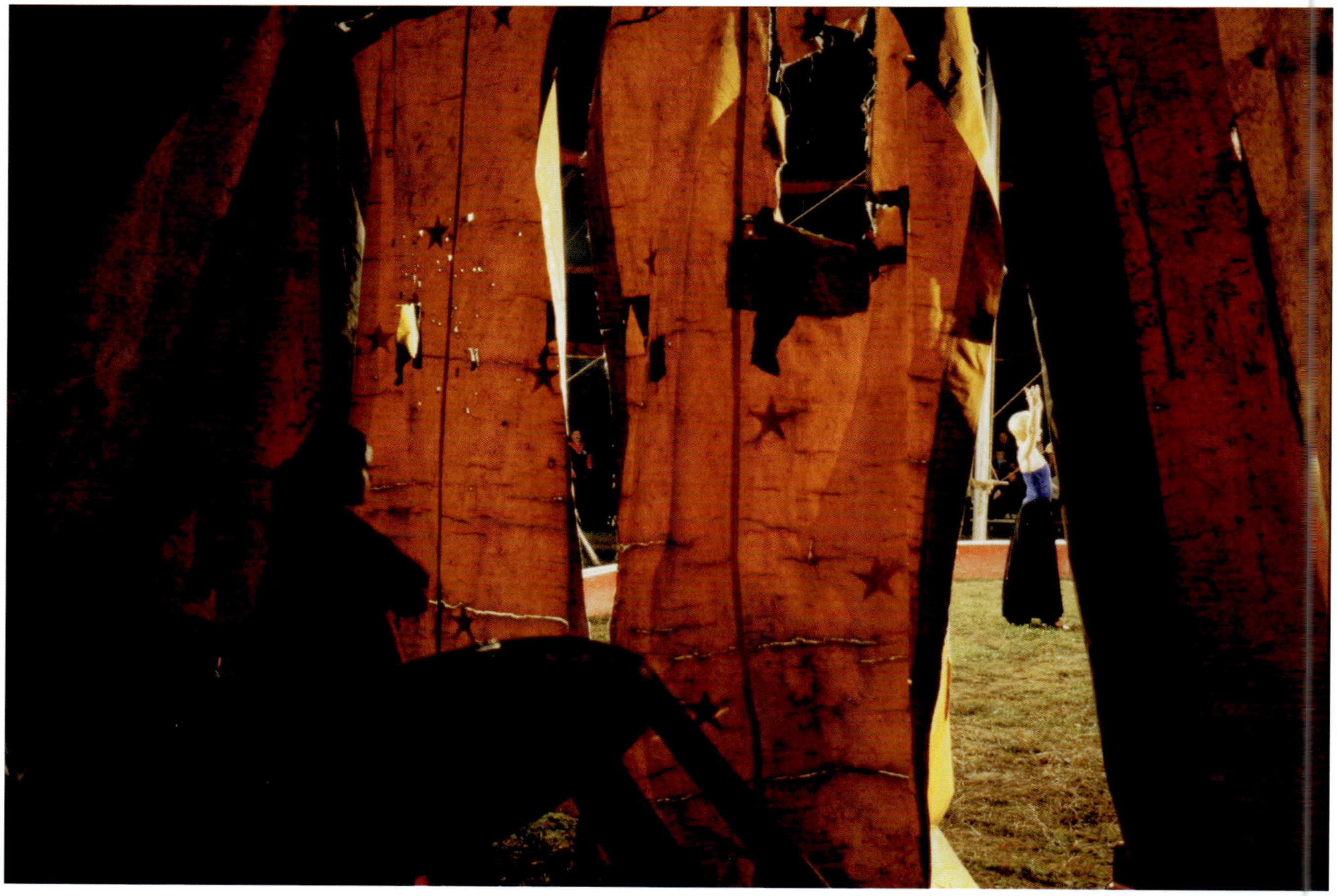

PLATE 161

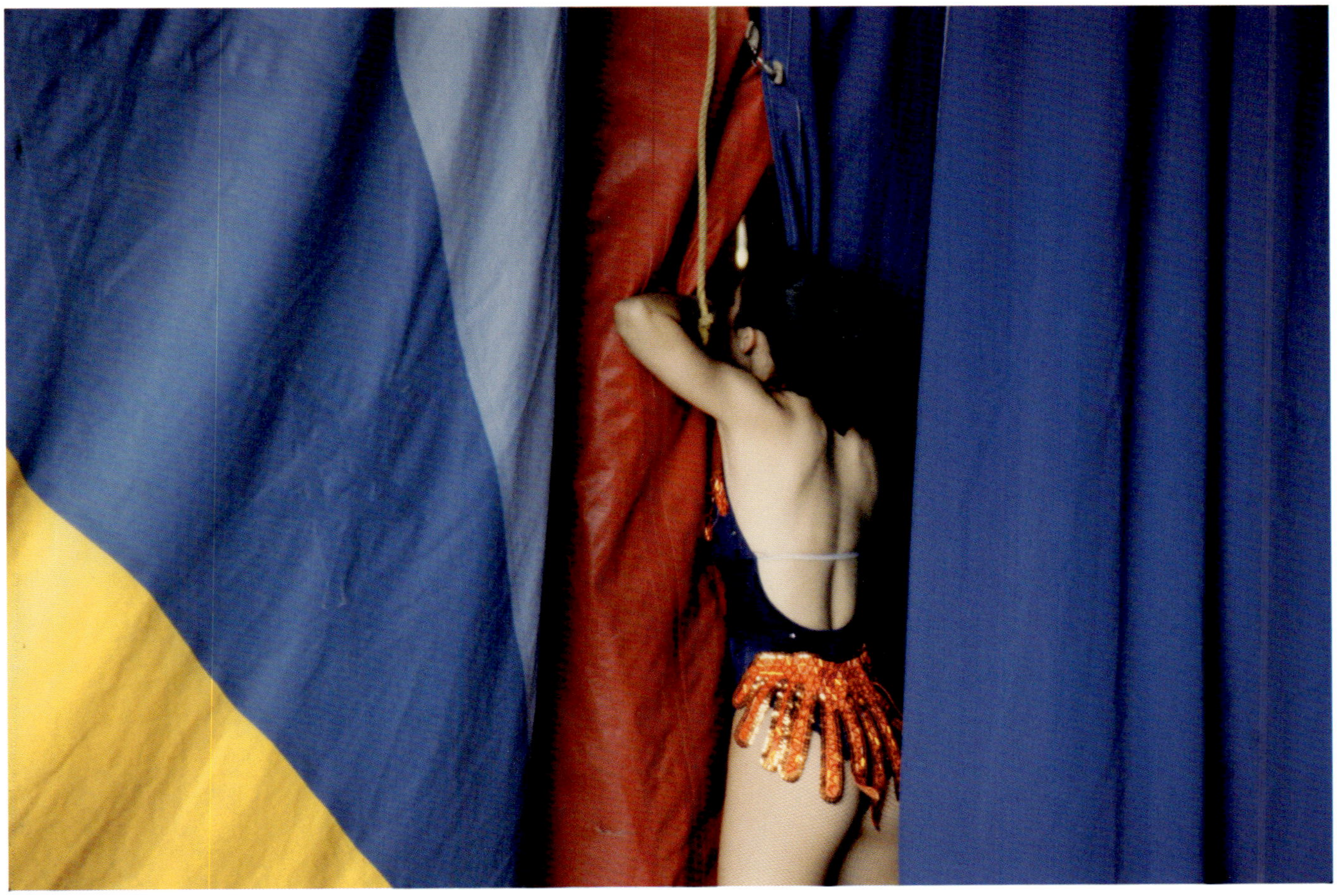

PLATE 162

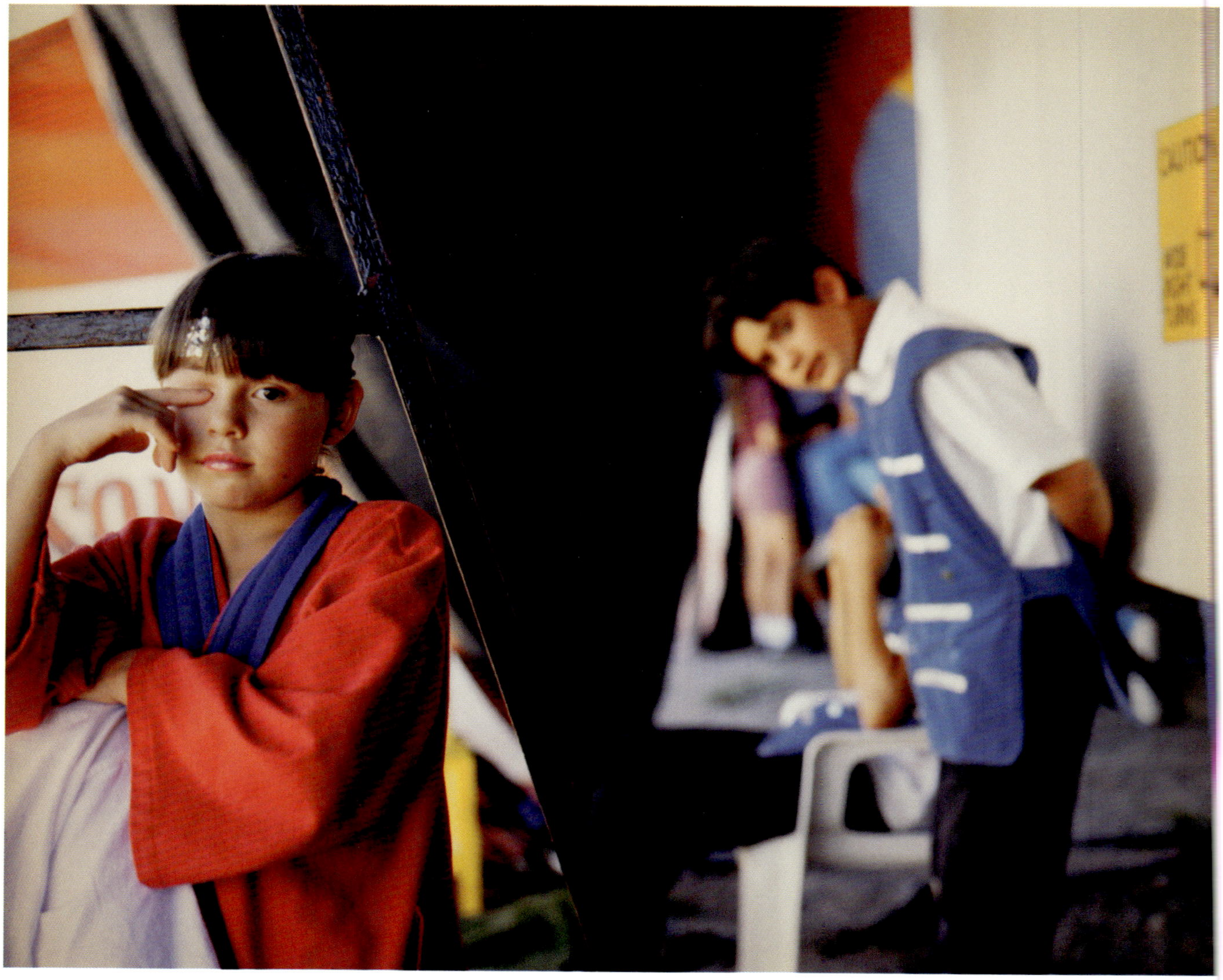

PLATE 163

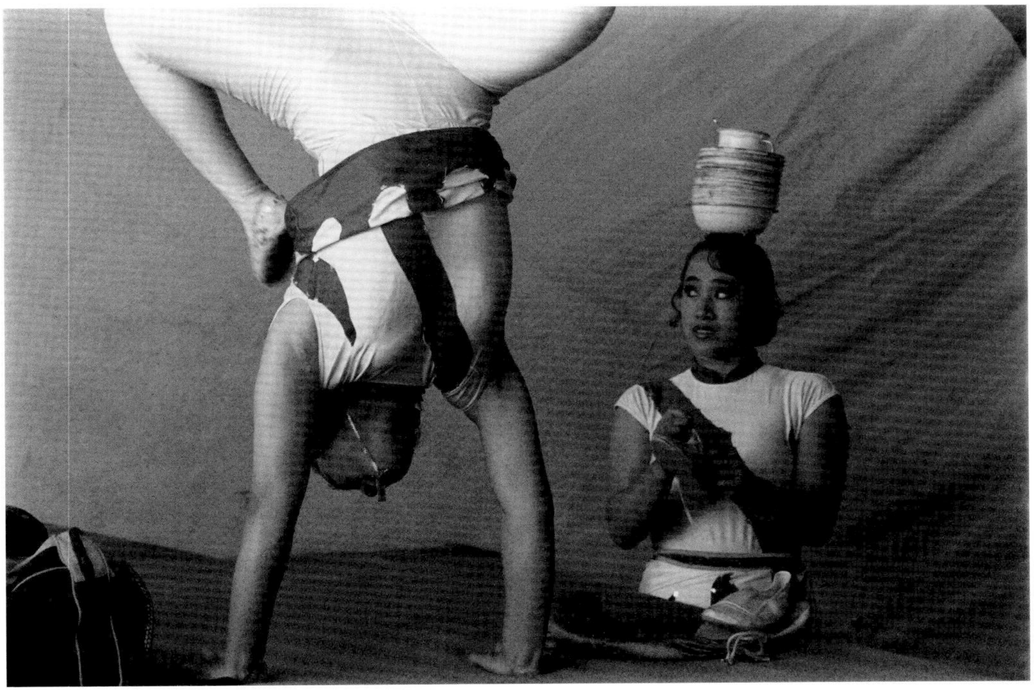

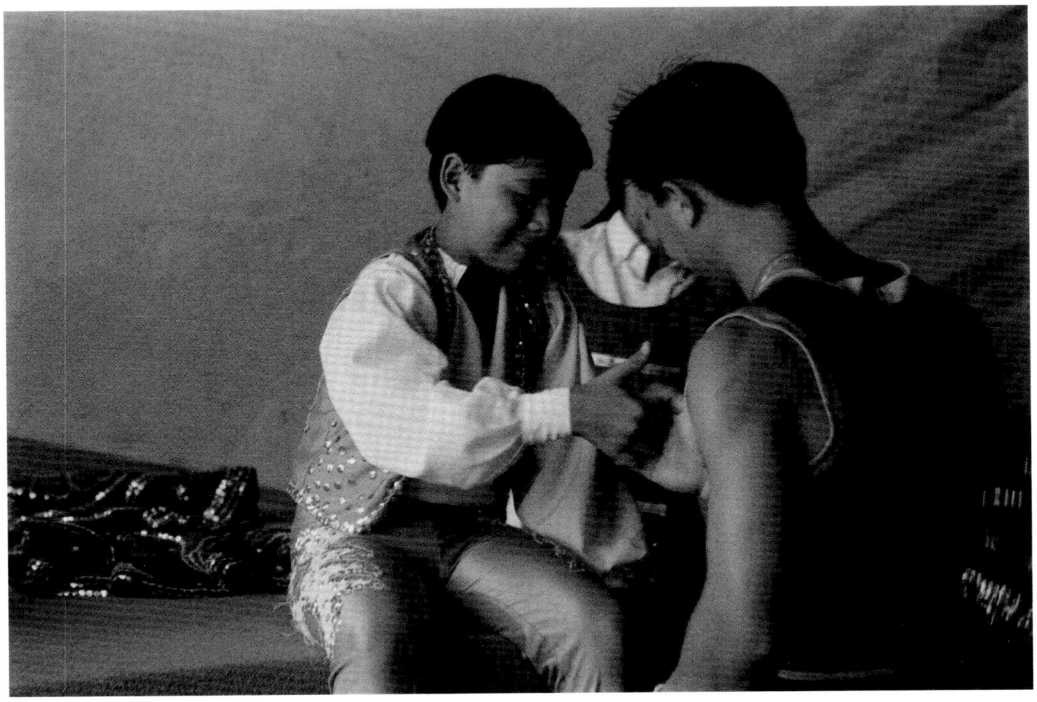

PLATES 164 & 165

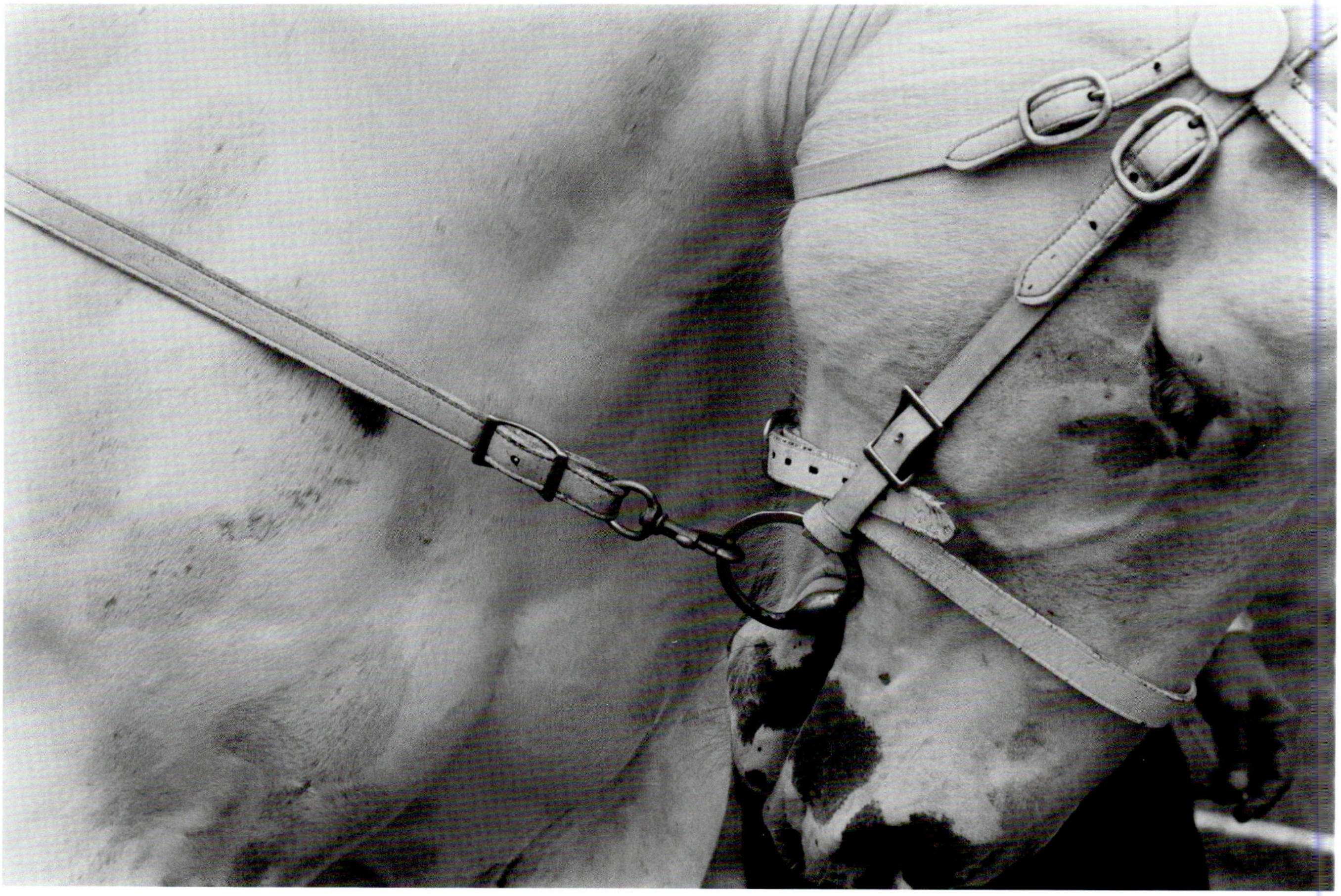

PLATE 166

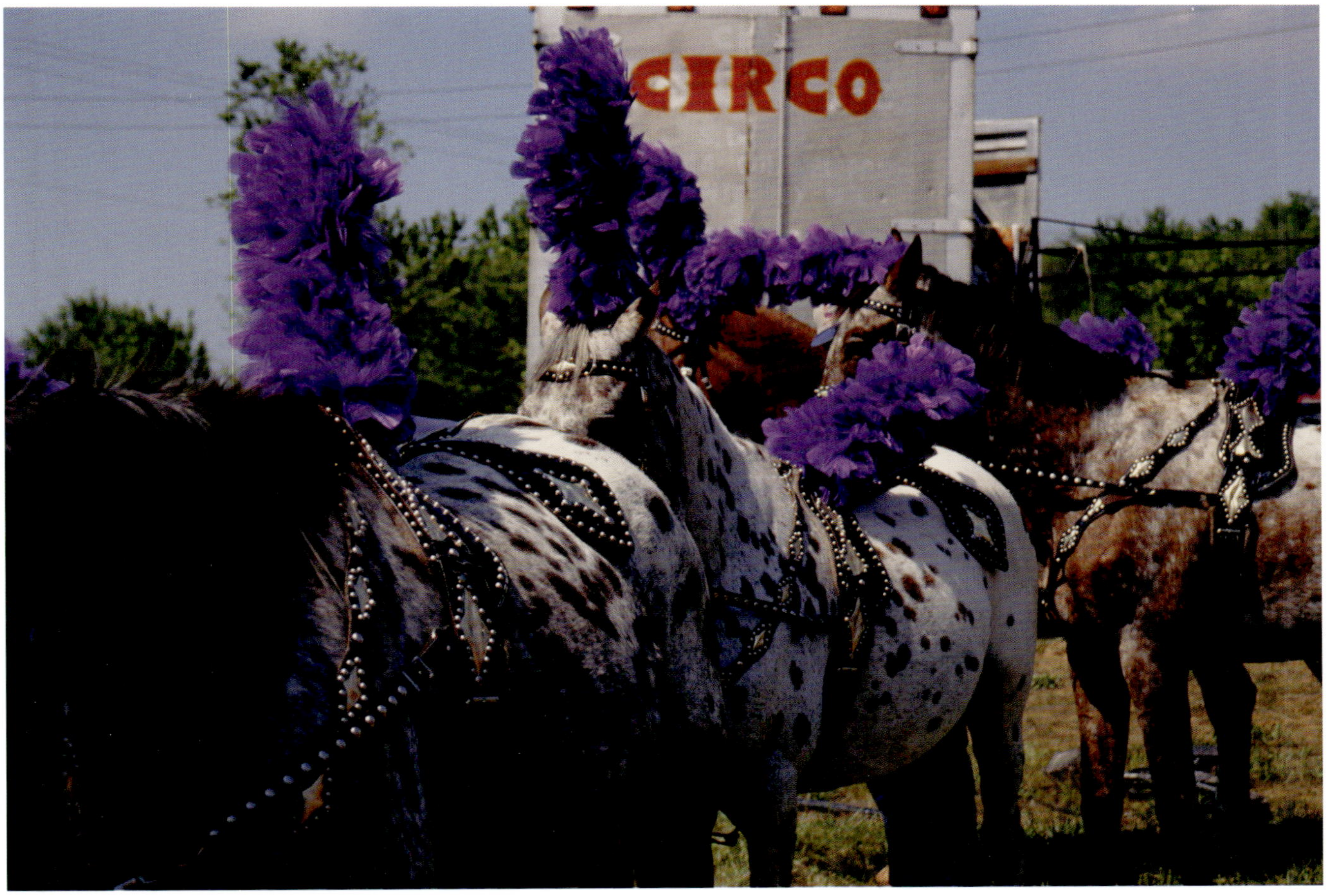

PLATE 167

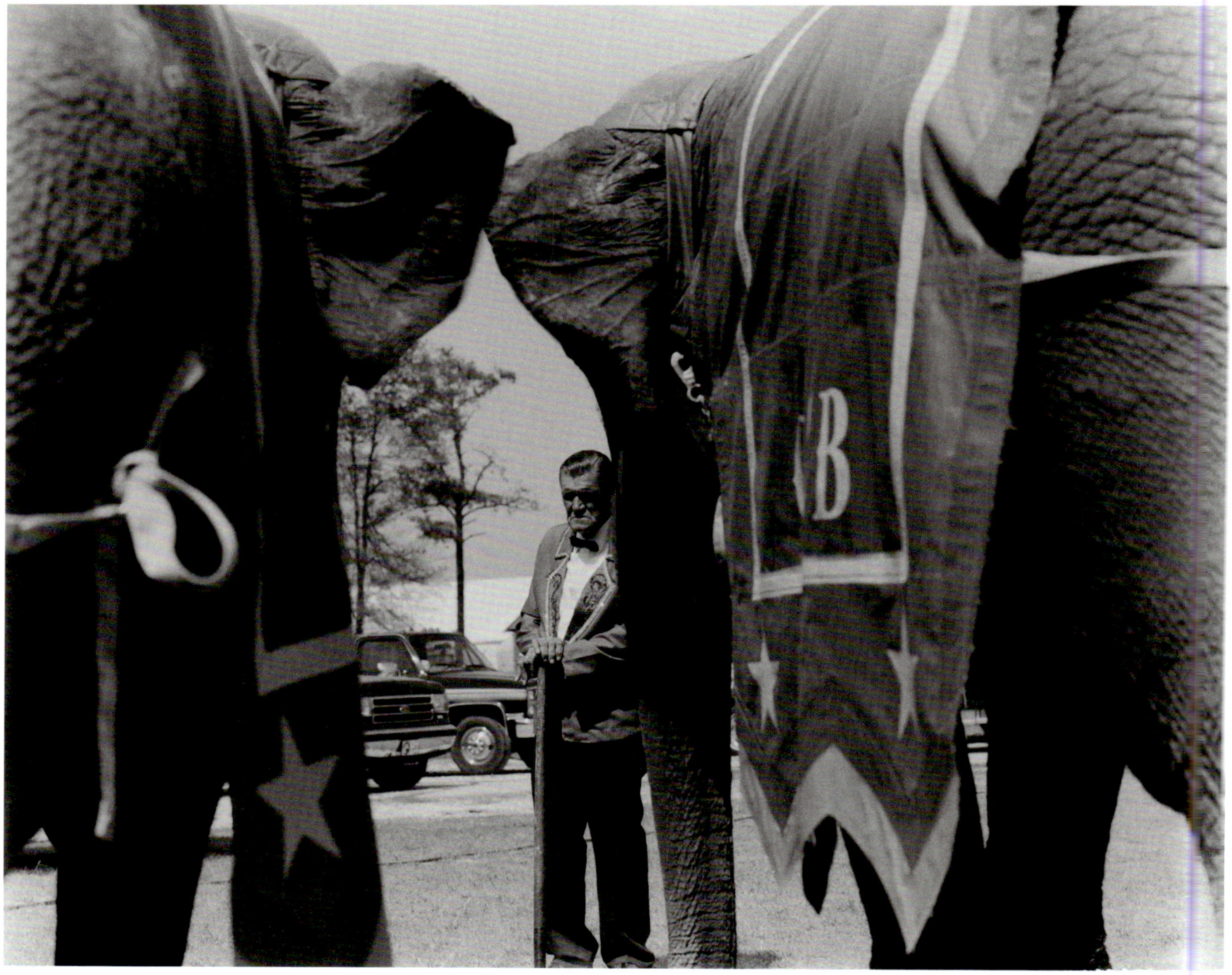

PLATE 168

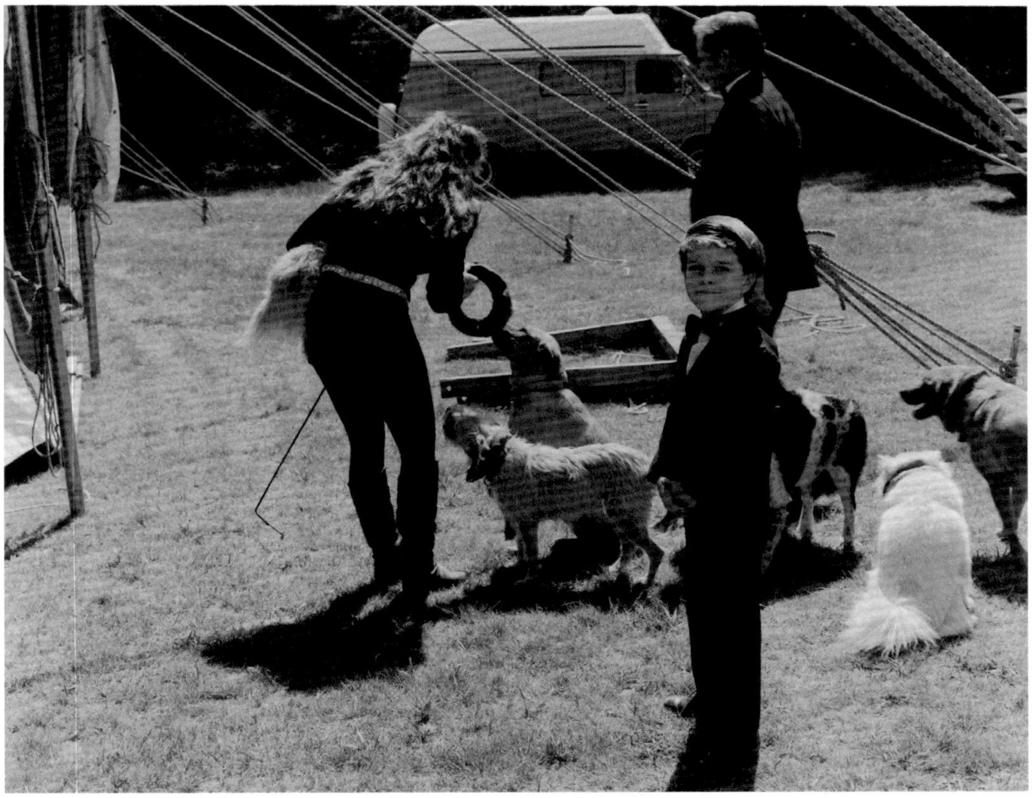

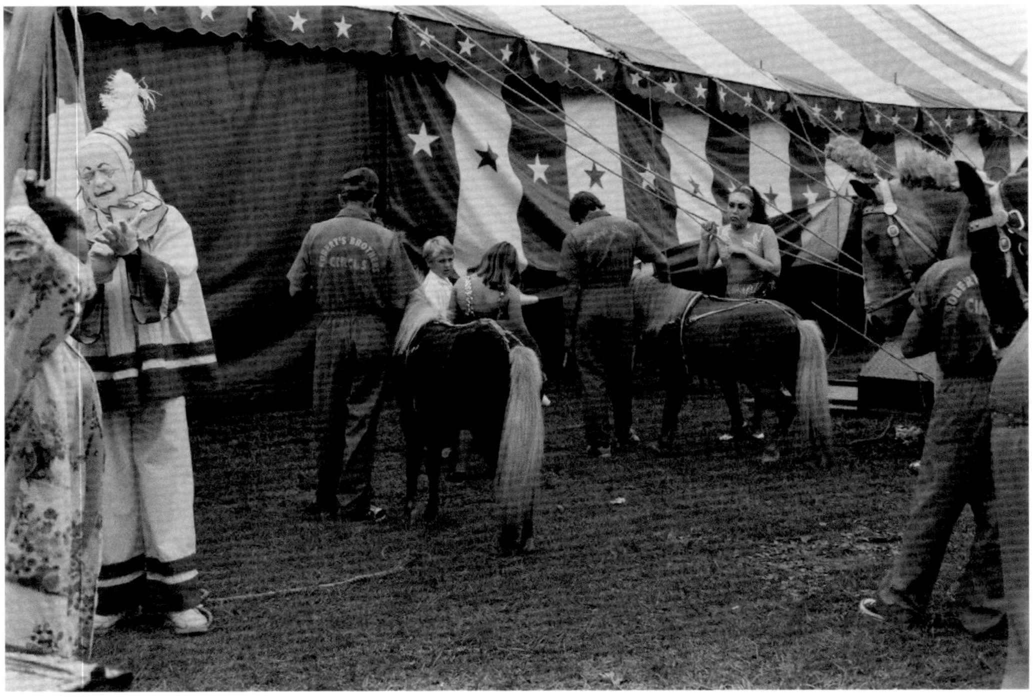

PLATES 169 & 170

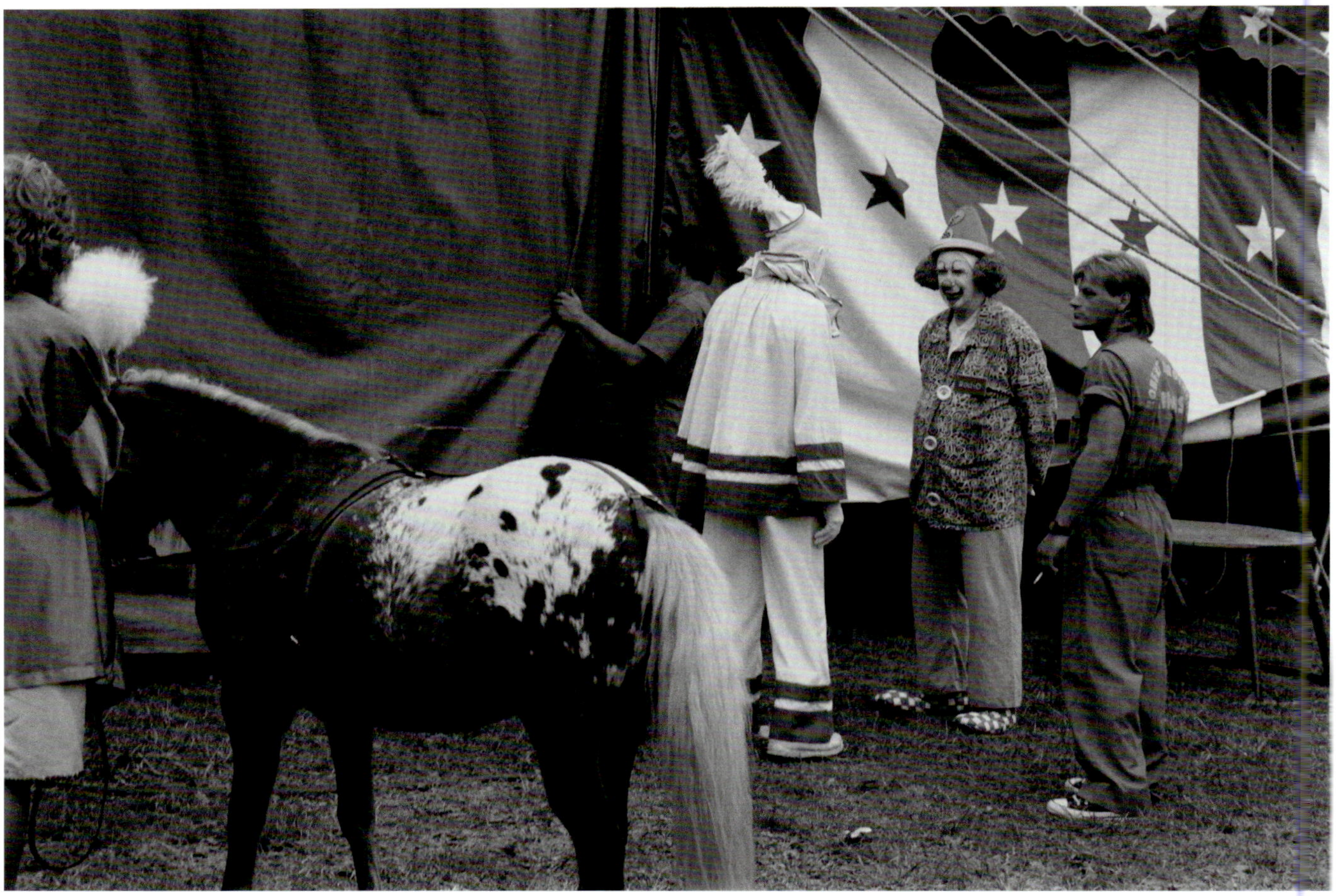

PLATE 171

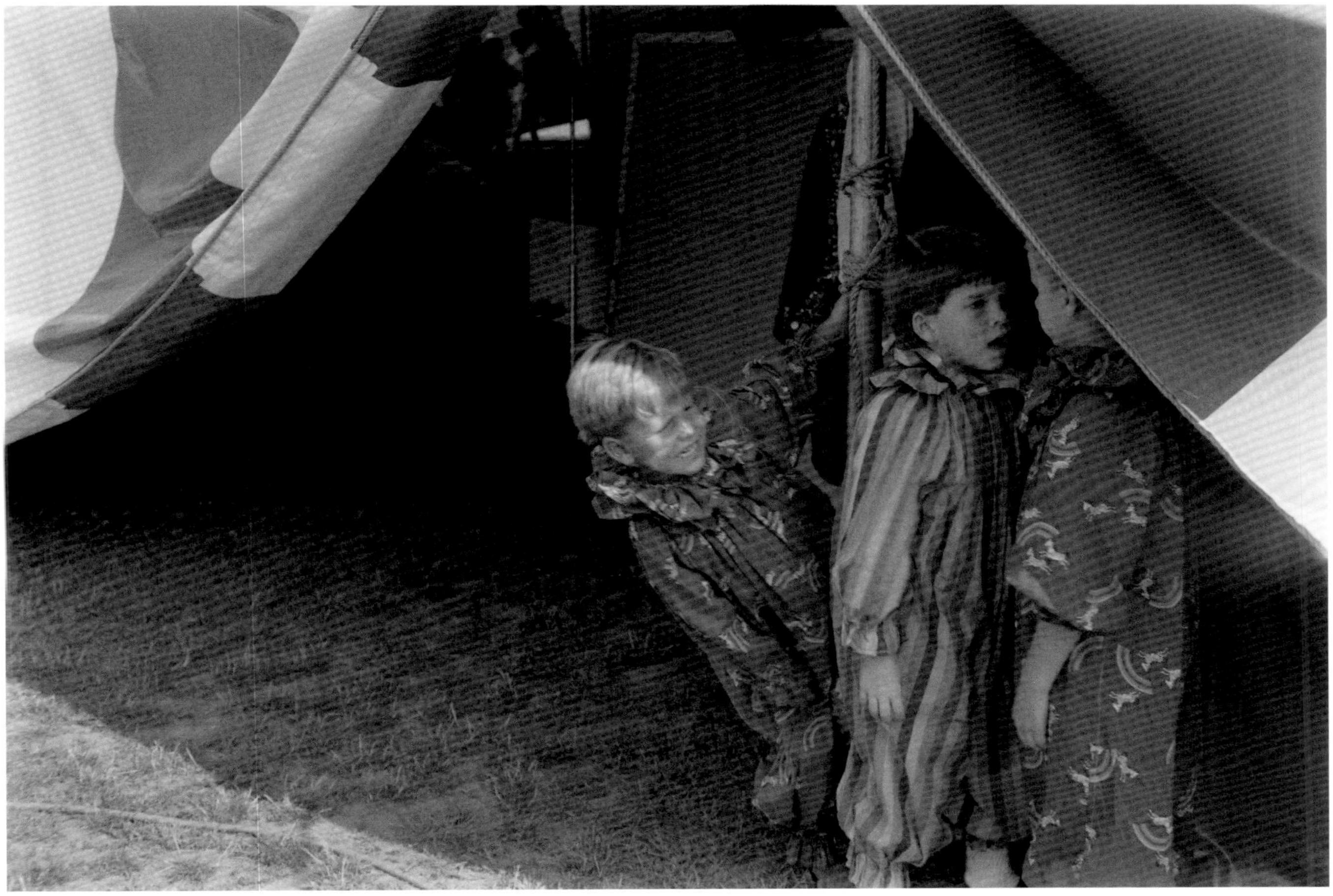

PLATE 172

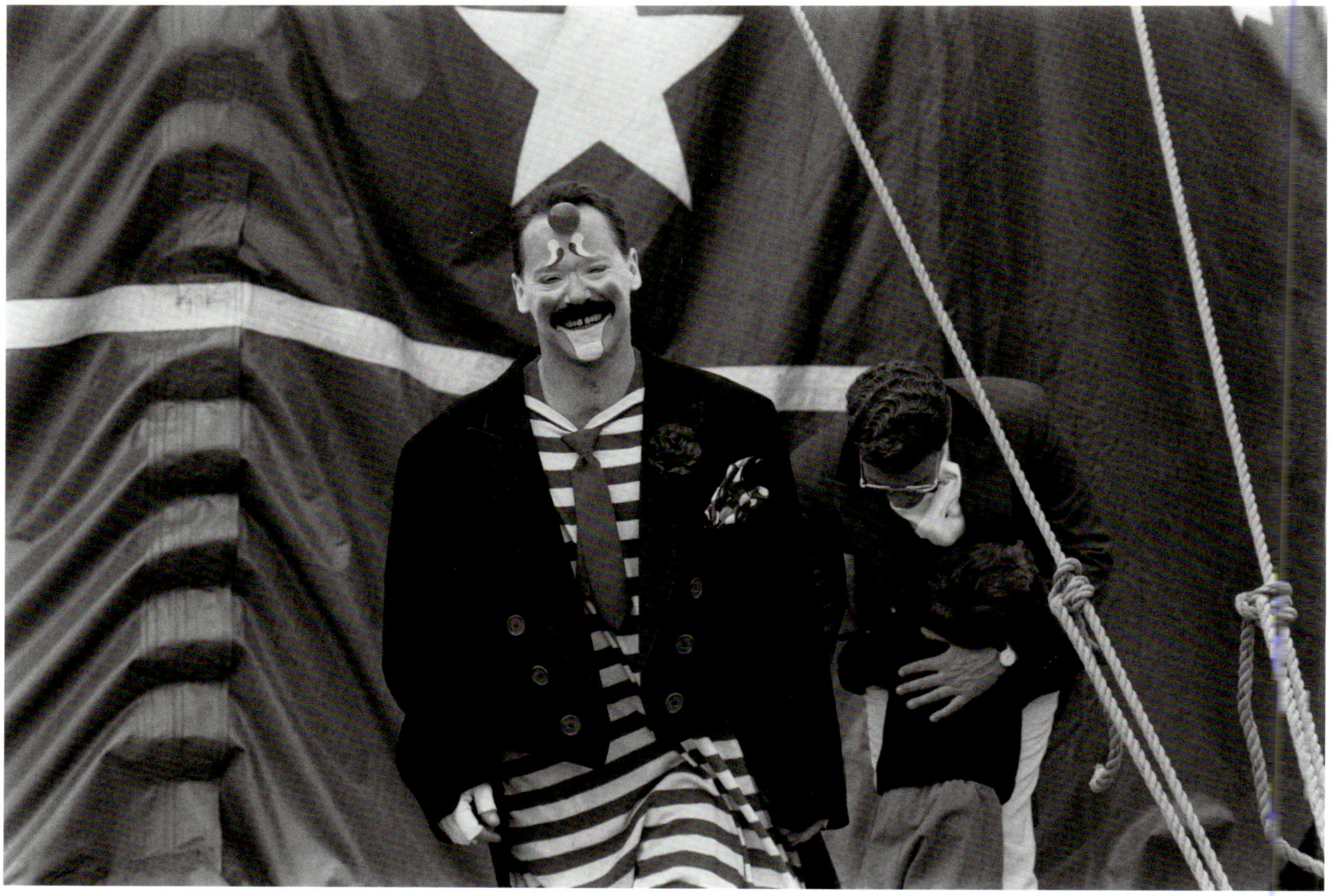

PLATE 173

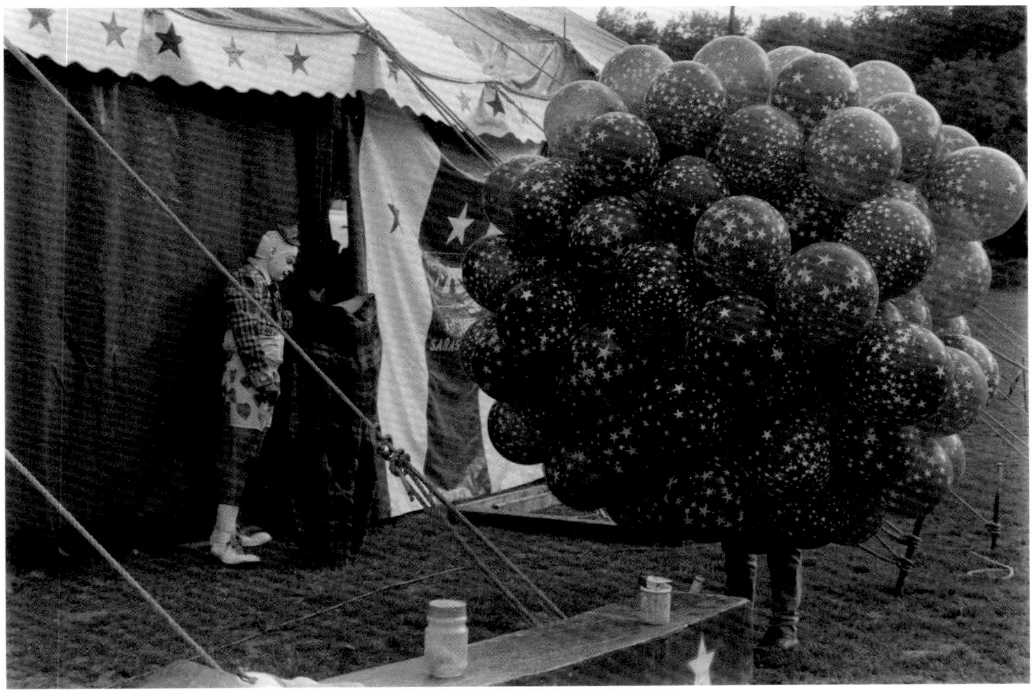

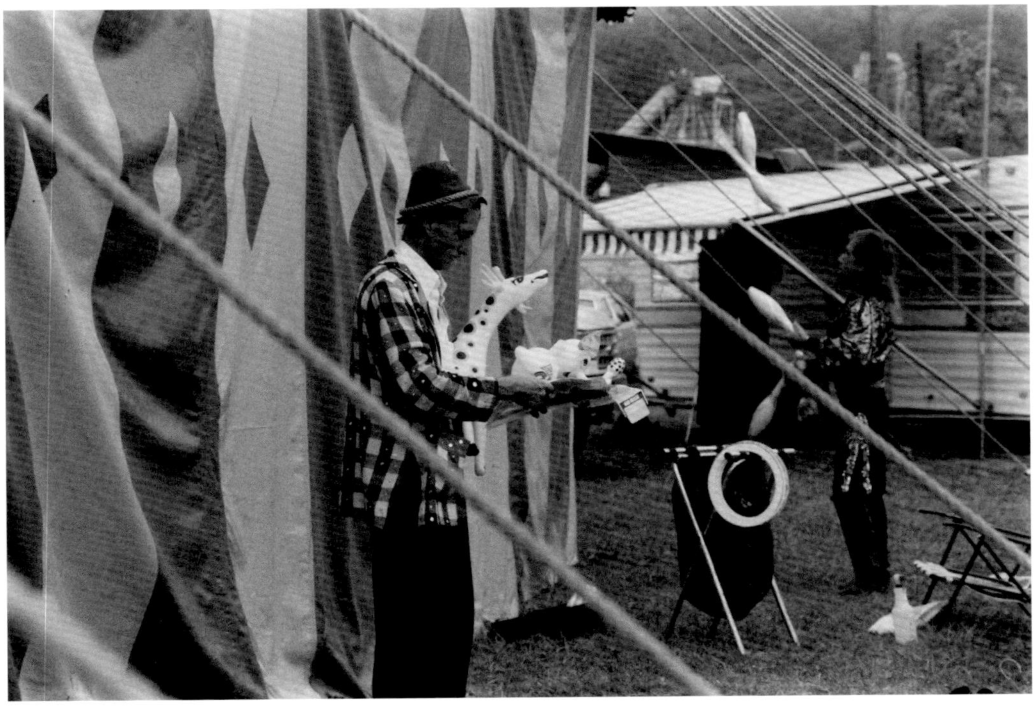

PLATES 174 & 175

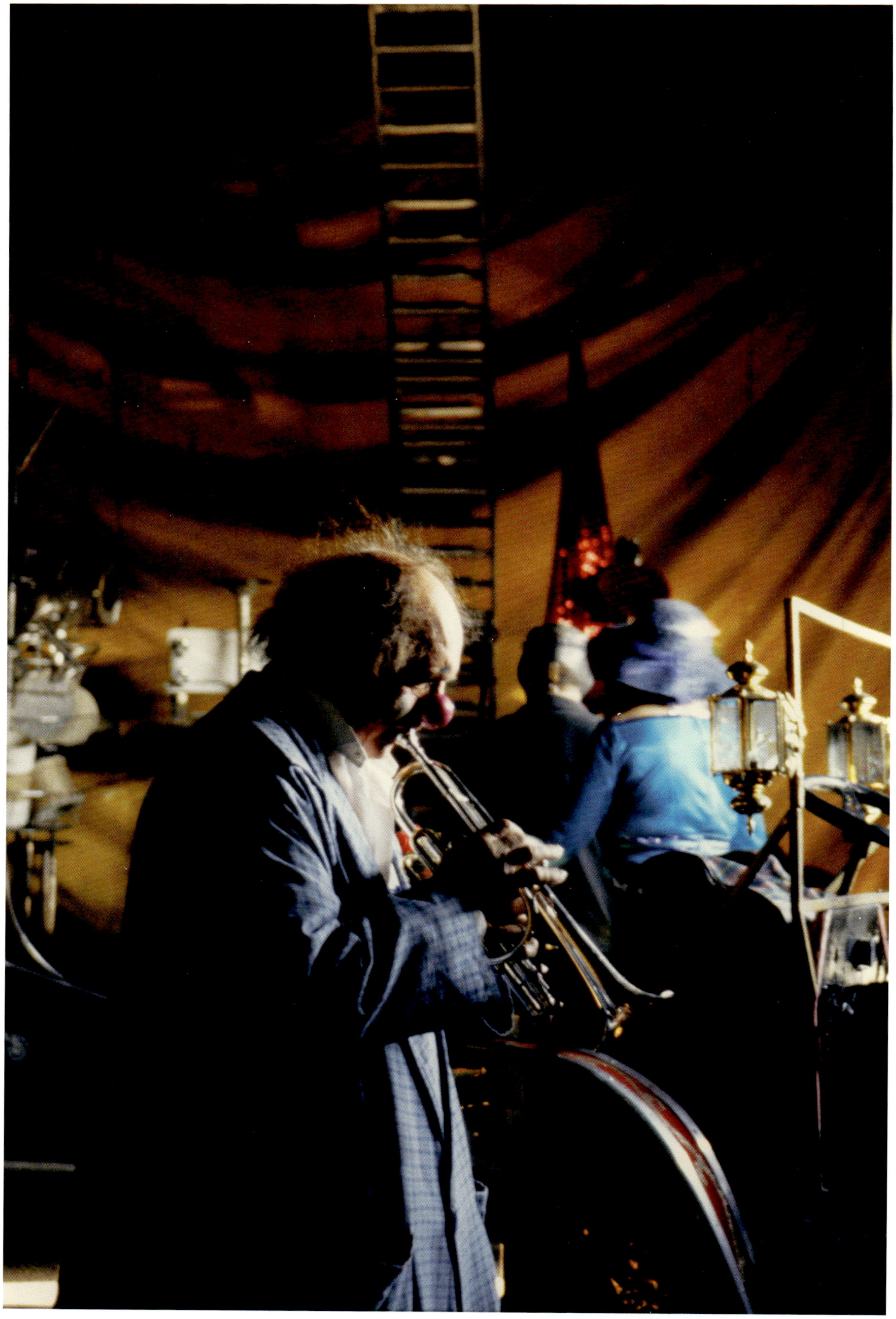

PLATE 176

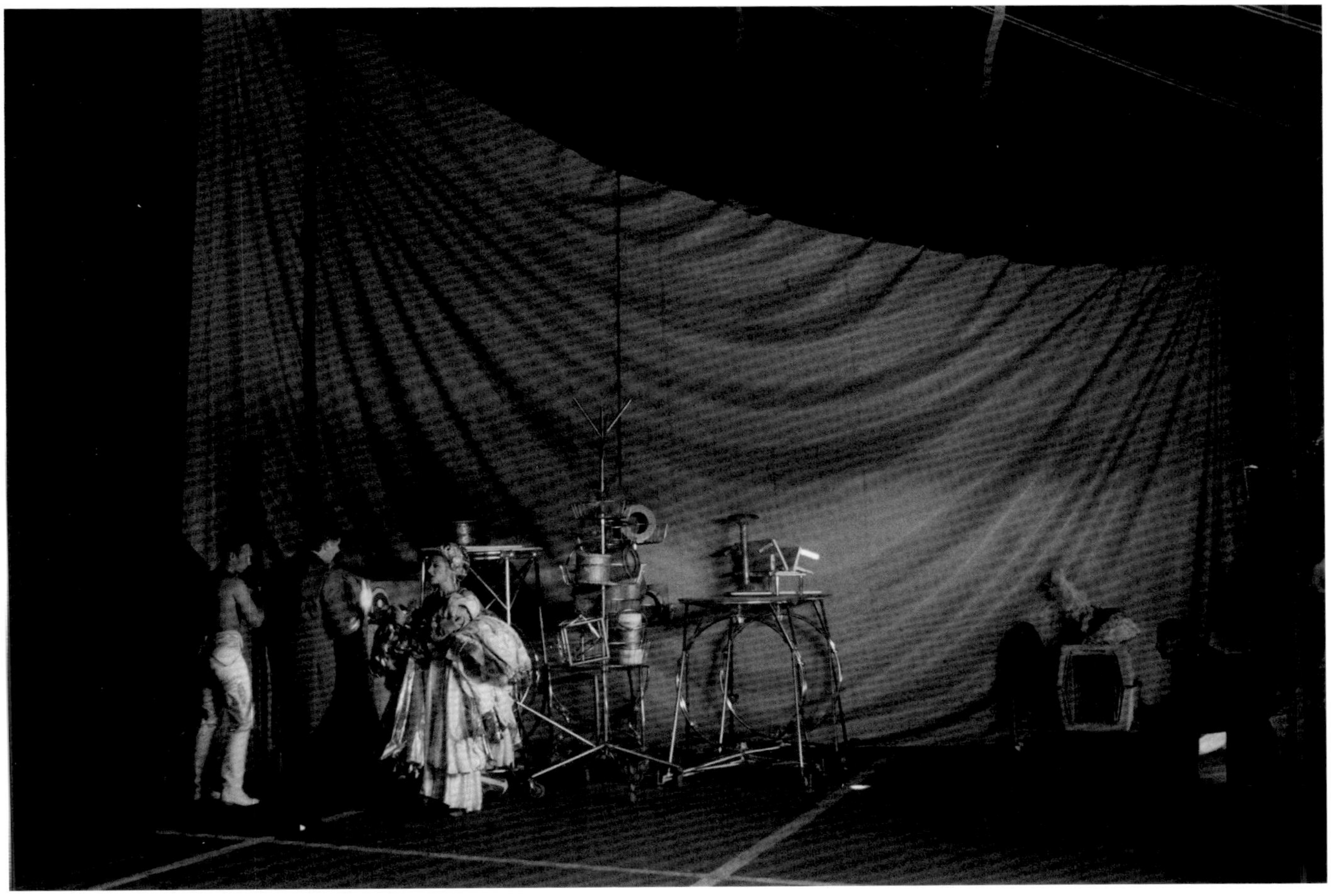

PLATE 177

★ ★ ★ ★ ★ ★ ★ ★ ★ ★

You've got to do something really amazing. You've got to use *all* your energy in the show, to make them look at you, and clap for a while.

—Eli Milcheva, performing company member, Big Apple Circus (1995)

★ ★ ★ ★ ★ ★ ★ ★ ★ ★

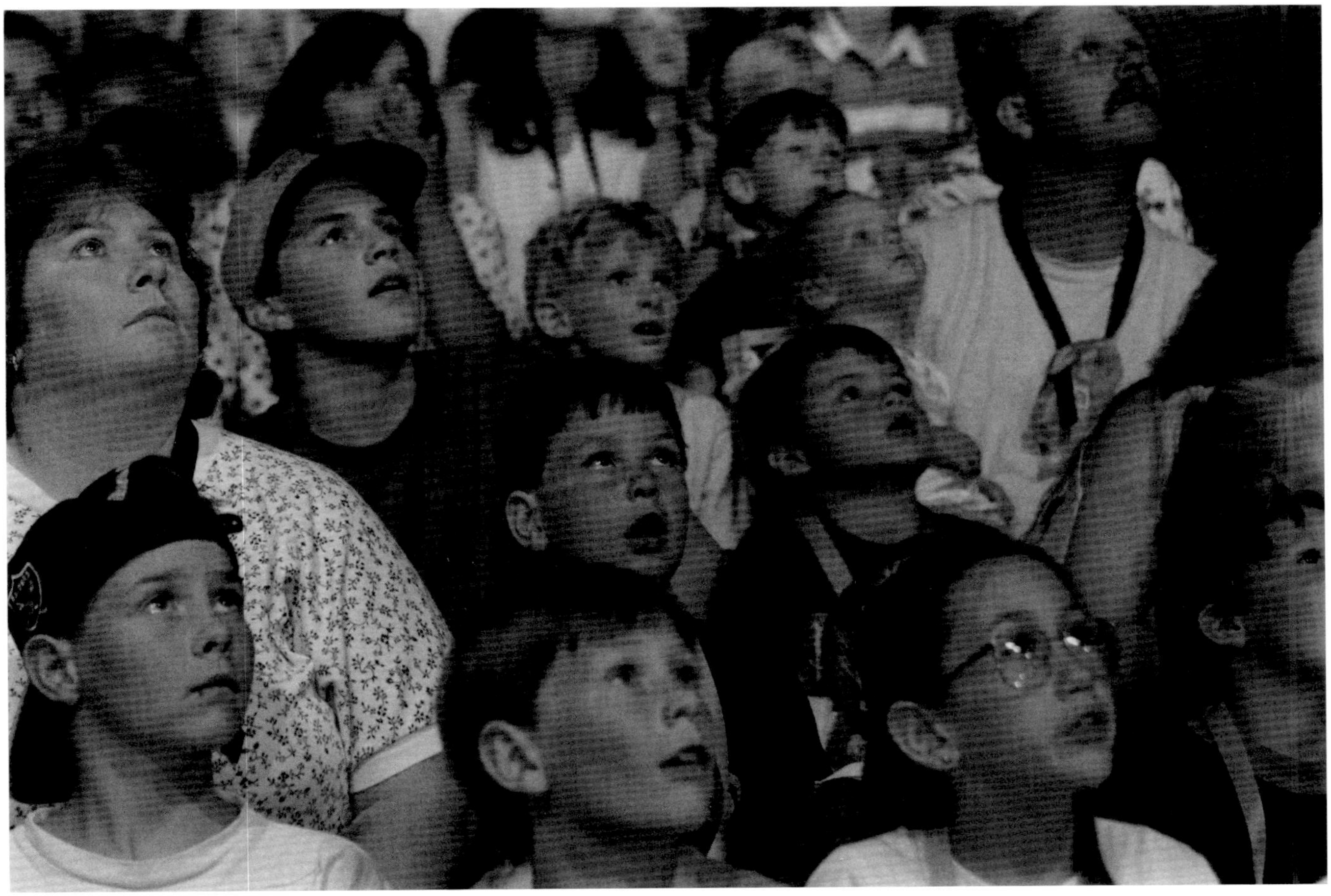

PLATE 178

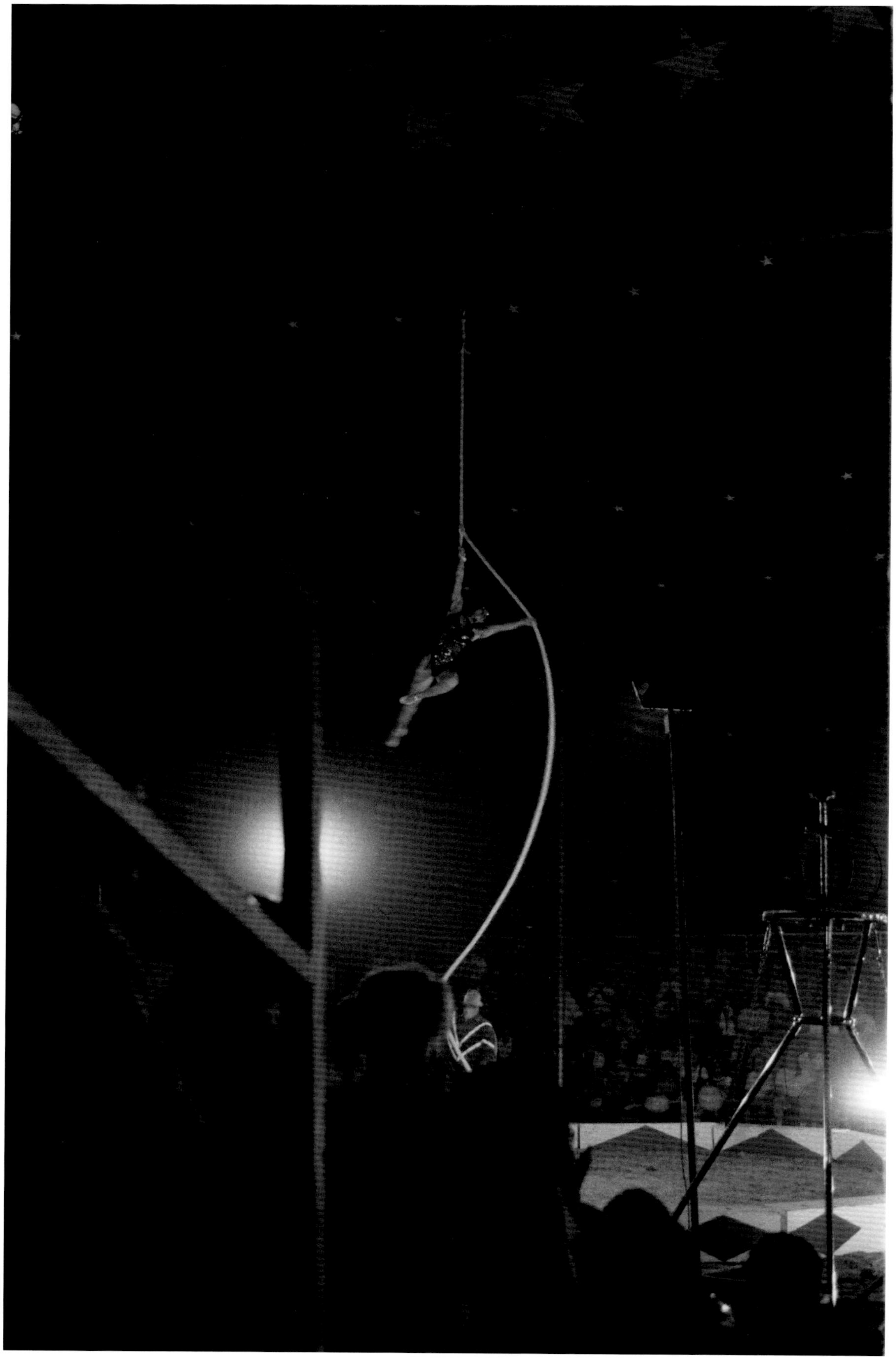

PLATE 179

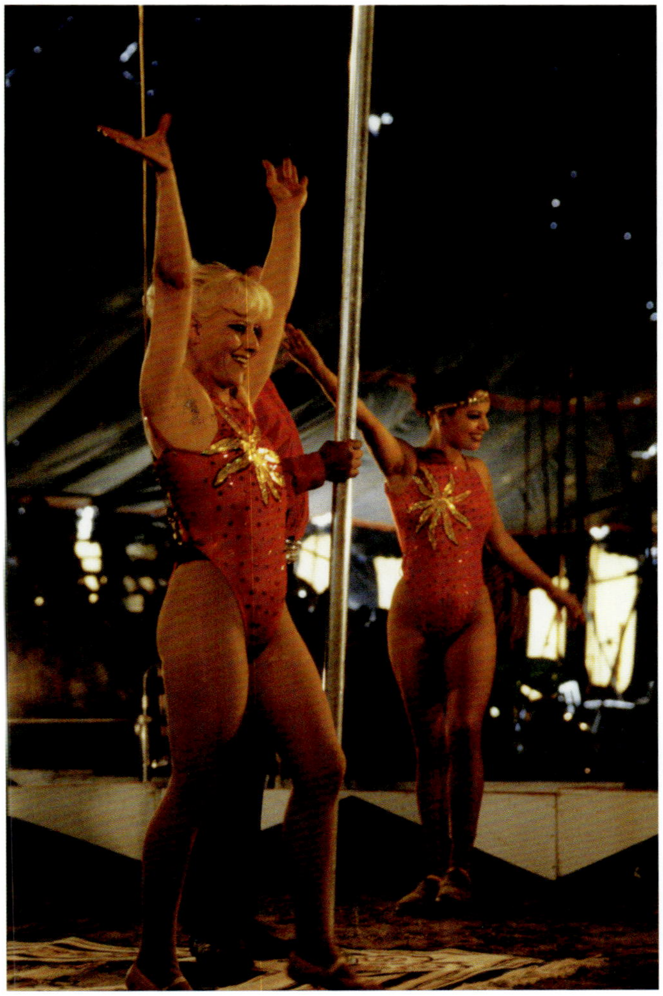

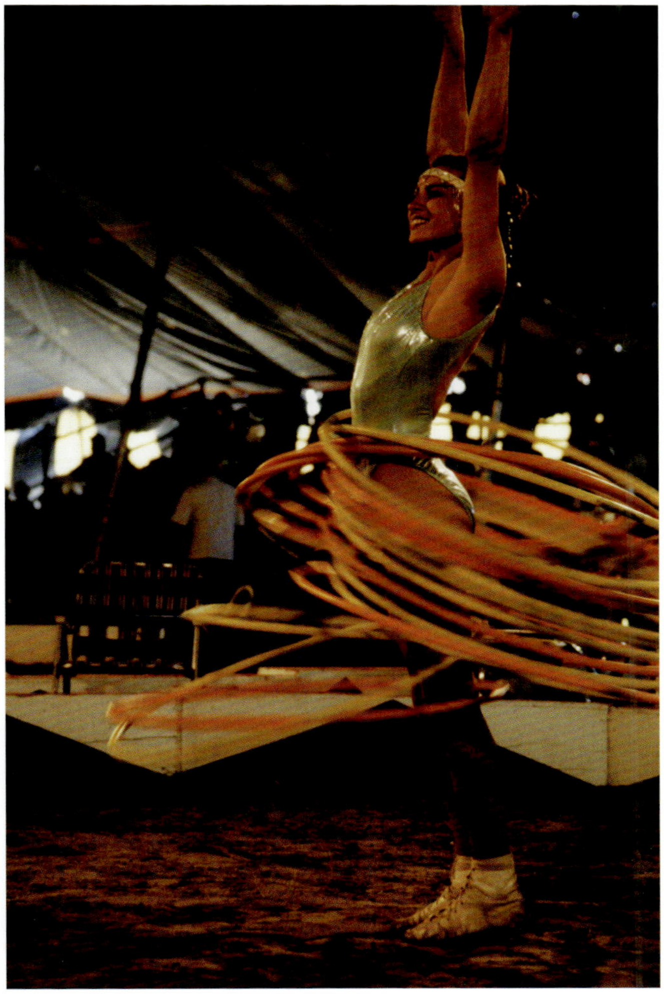

PLATES 180 & 181

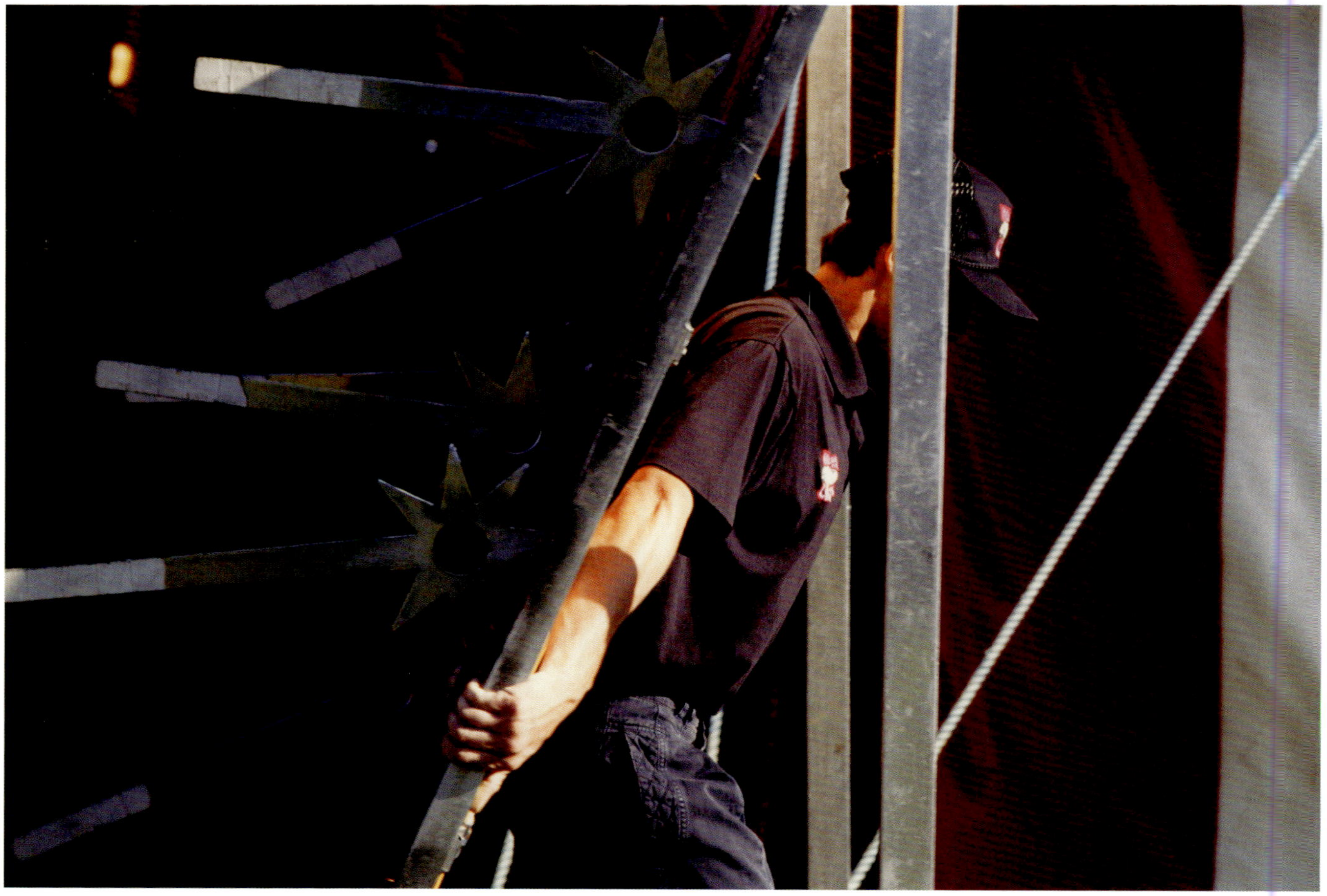

PLATE 182

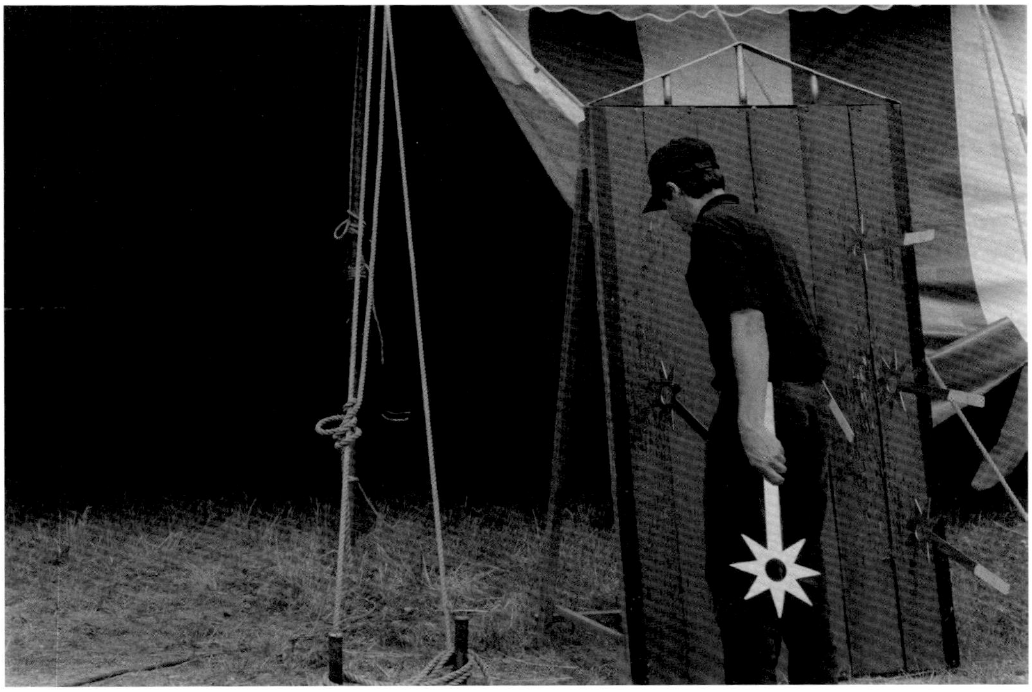

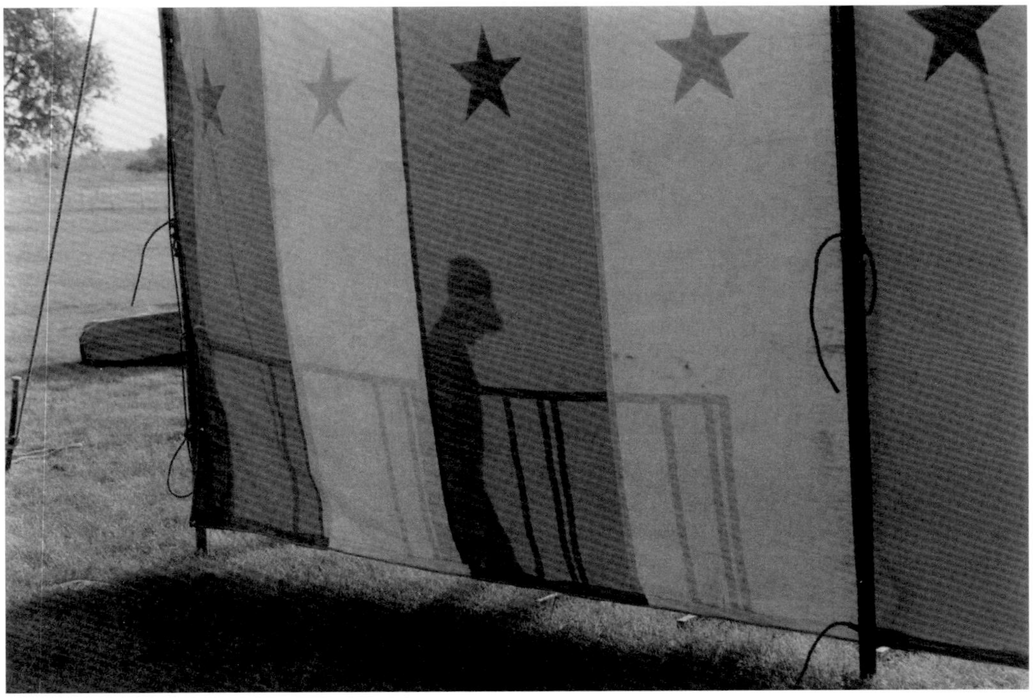

PLATES 183 & 184

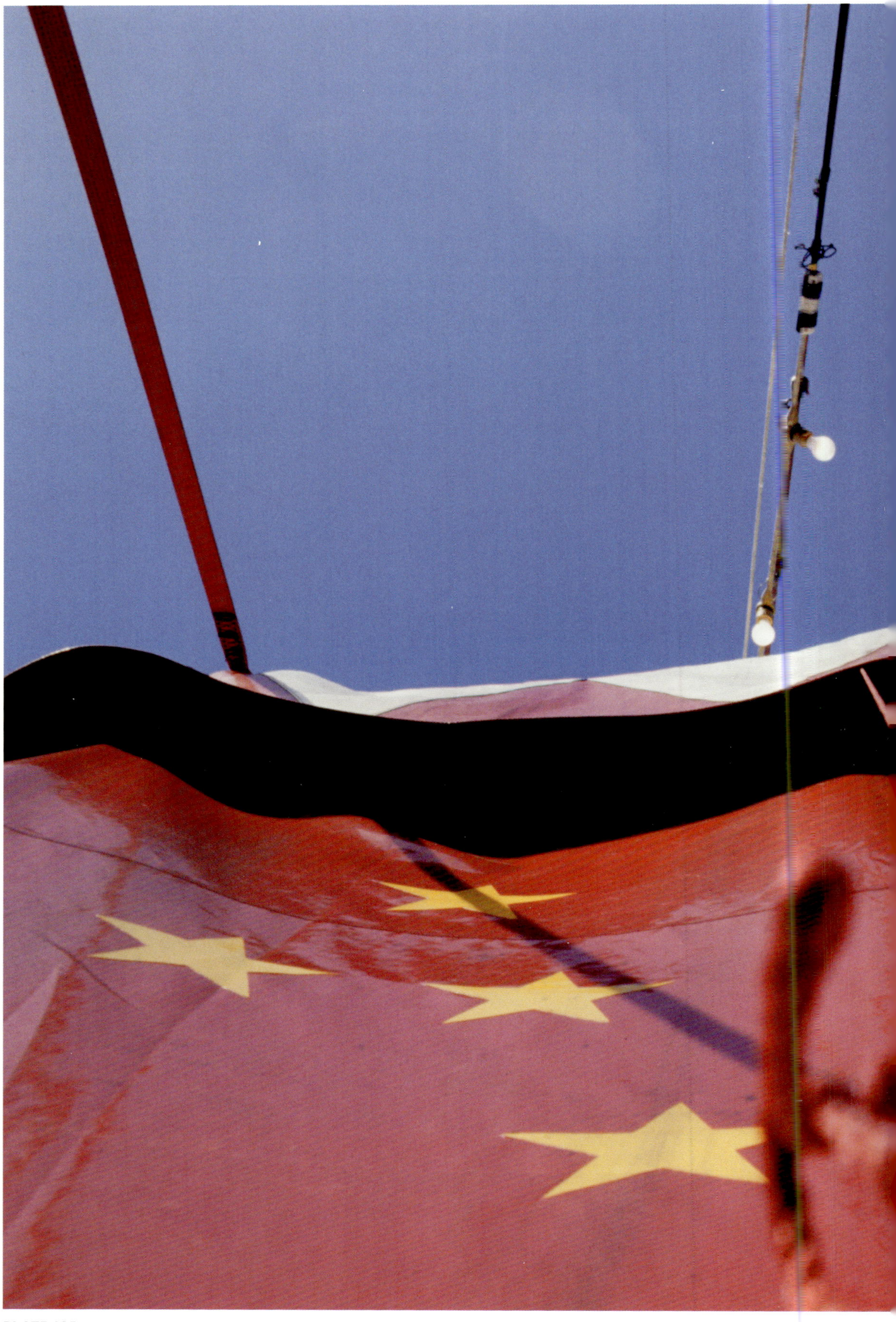

PLATE 185

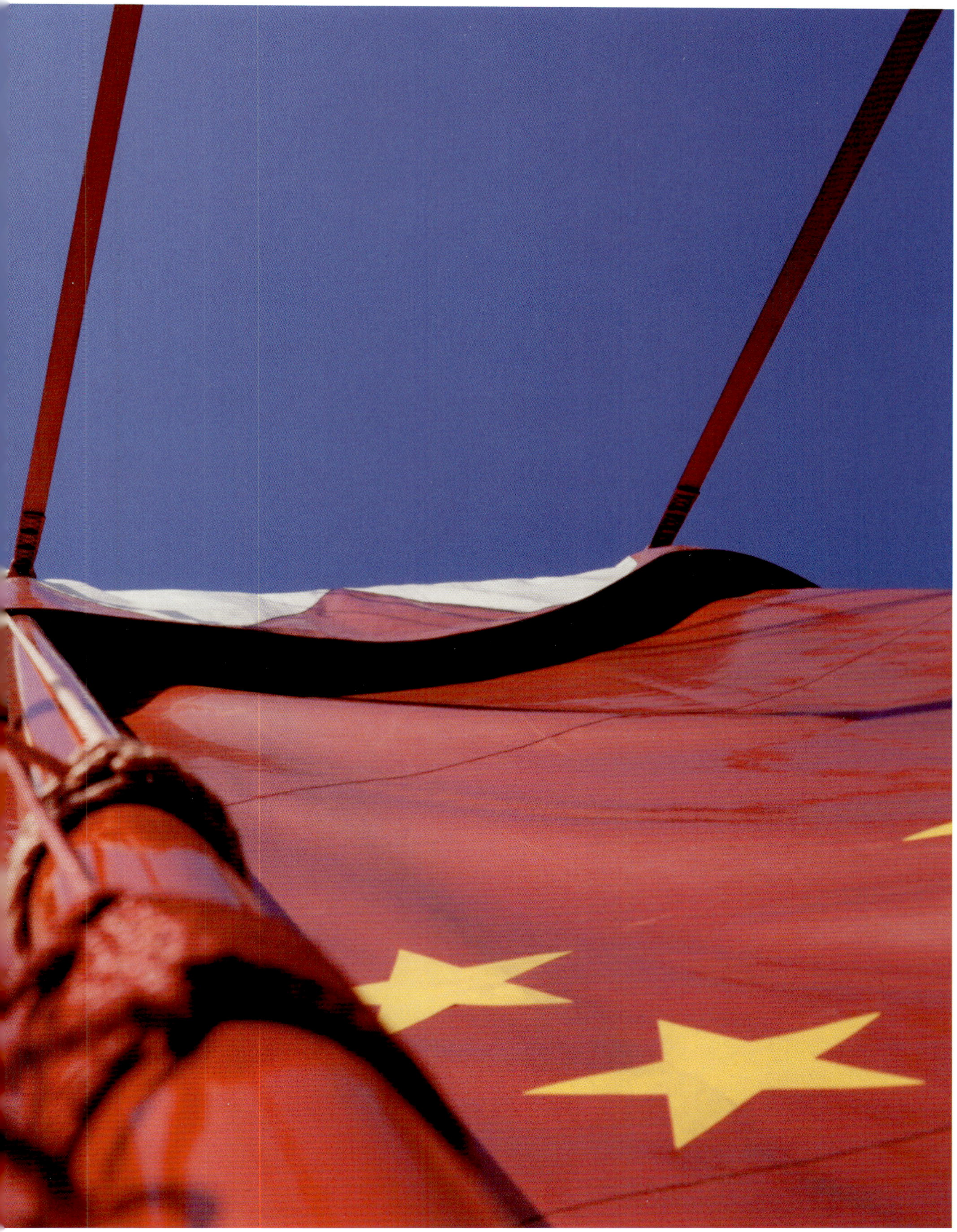

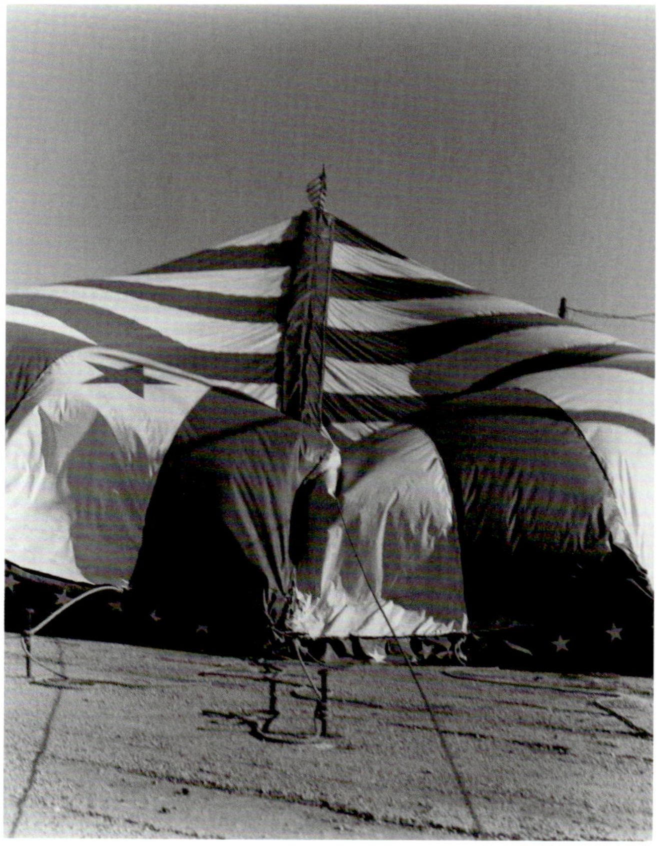

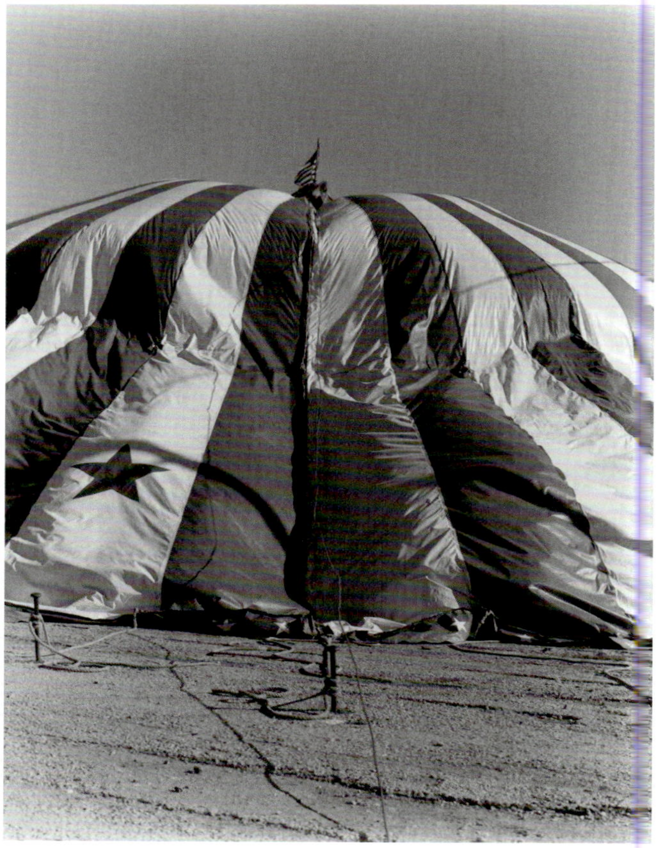

PLATES 186 & 187

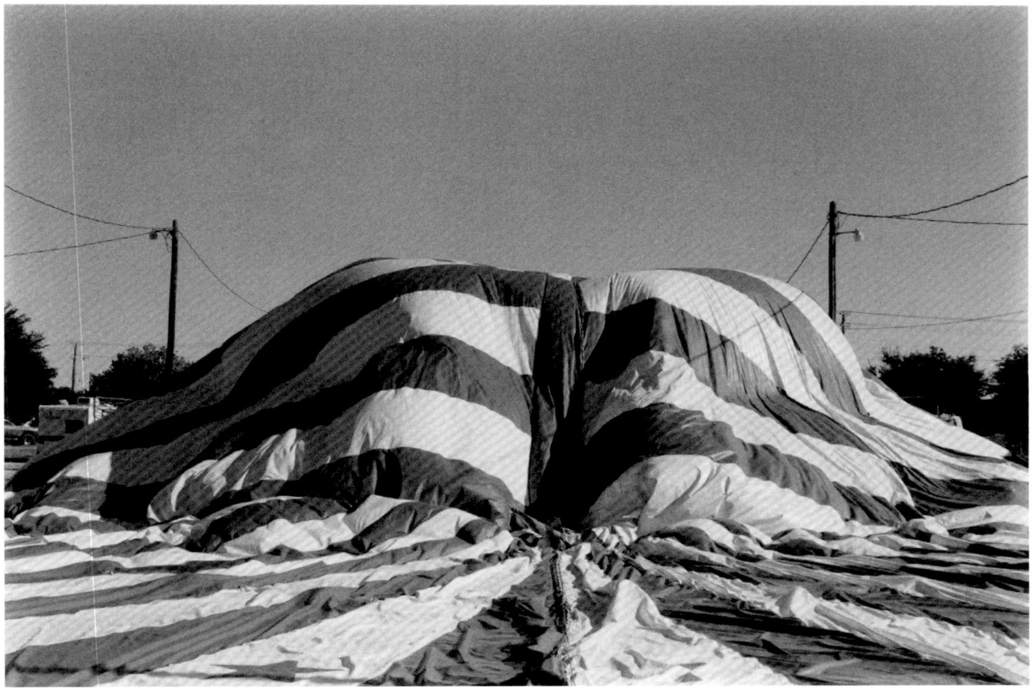

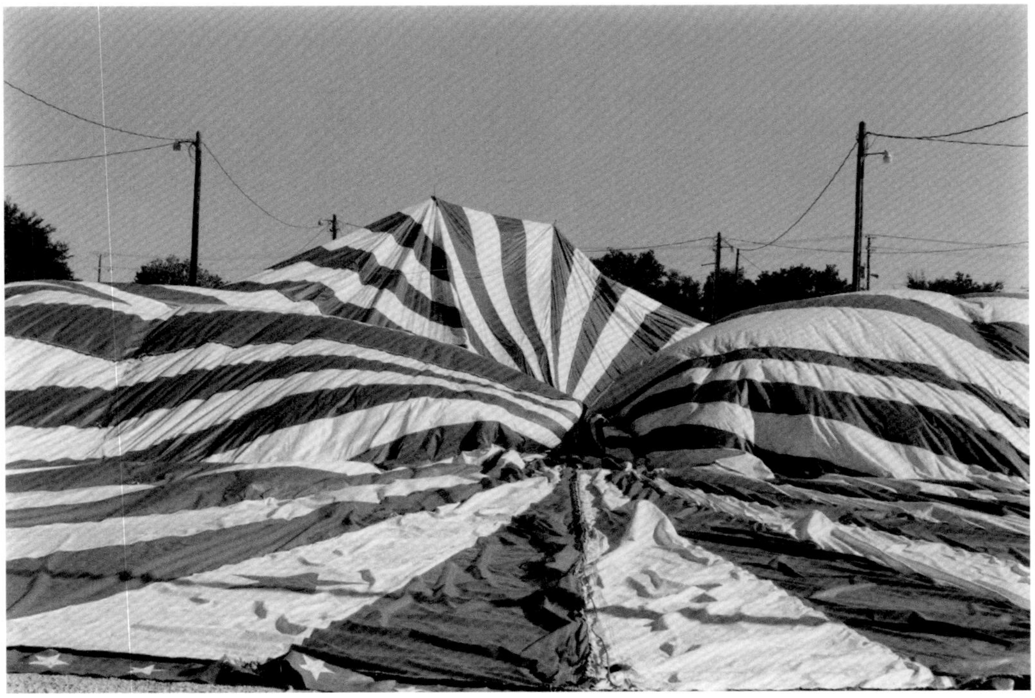

PLATES 188 & 189

★ ★ ★ ★ ★ ★ ★ ★ ★ ★ ★ ★ ★ ★ ★ ★ ★ ★

My wife's aunt was my stepmother, and her children are my wife's first cousins and my brothers and sisters . . . half-brothers and sisters. The Wheel of Destiny guys are my first cousins. The flying act guys are my brothers-in-law, and the other troupes are my wife's cousins.

The performance director is uncle to the bareback rider, and also uncle to the guys who do the Wheel of Destiny. The performance director's wife does the wardrobe. Her uncle is married to one of the bareback rider's aunts. And her sister is married to another one of the bareback rider's uncles, who is one of the performance director's brothers. That rider's brother is married to another rider's sister, and they have a kid. And those two riders are married and have a kid. That first rider's sister, who is also a rider, is the wardrobe lady's niece . . . and the wardrobe boss is married to the tent boss, who also owns the pie car. His cousins run the pie car, and one of them also drives the water truck. His daughter does the spec and a few other acts, and she's cousins with one of the bareback riders . . . by marriage. And they are related to the owners of the show. The wardrobe boss is also sister to the lot manager, and the mechanic, and their mother runs the souvenir stand—and she's a cousin of the owner's wife. The daughter of the founder is now the owner, and her daughters are also in the show, and . . .

—Armando Rosales, bareback rider, with Peter Coolidge and Megan Murray, midway and concessions and horses, Carson & Barnes Circus (1995)

★ ★ ★ ★ ★ ★ ★ ★ ★ ★ ★ ★ ★ ★ ★ ★ ★ ★

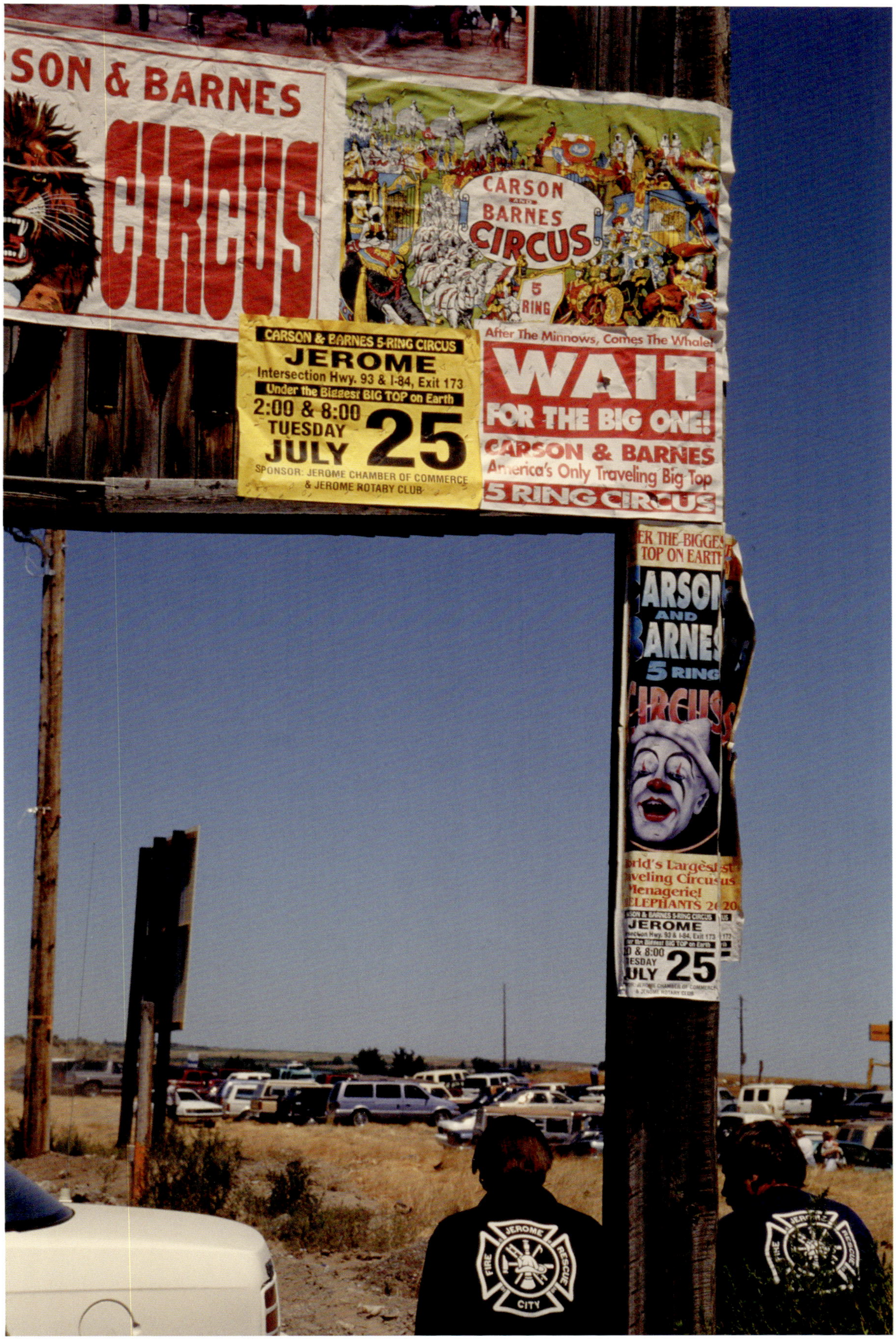
SON & BARNES
CIRCUS
CARSON AND BARNES CIRCUS
5 RING
CARSON & BARNES 5-RING CIRCUS
JEROME
Intersection Hwy. 93 & I-84, Exit 173
Under the Biggest BIG TOP on Earth
2:00 & 8:00
TUESDAY
JULY 25
SPONSOR: JEROME CHAMBER OF COMMERCE
& JEROME ROTARY CLUB
After The Minnows, Comes The Whale!
WAIT
FOR THE BIG ONE!
CARSON & BARNES
America's Only Traveling Big Top
5 RING CIRCUS
5 RING
JEROME
25
JEROME
FIRE
RESCUE
CITY

PLATE 190

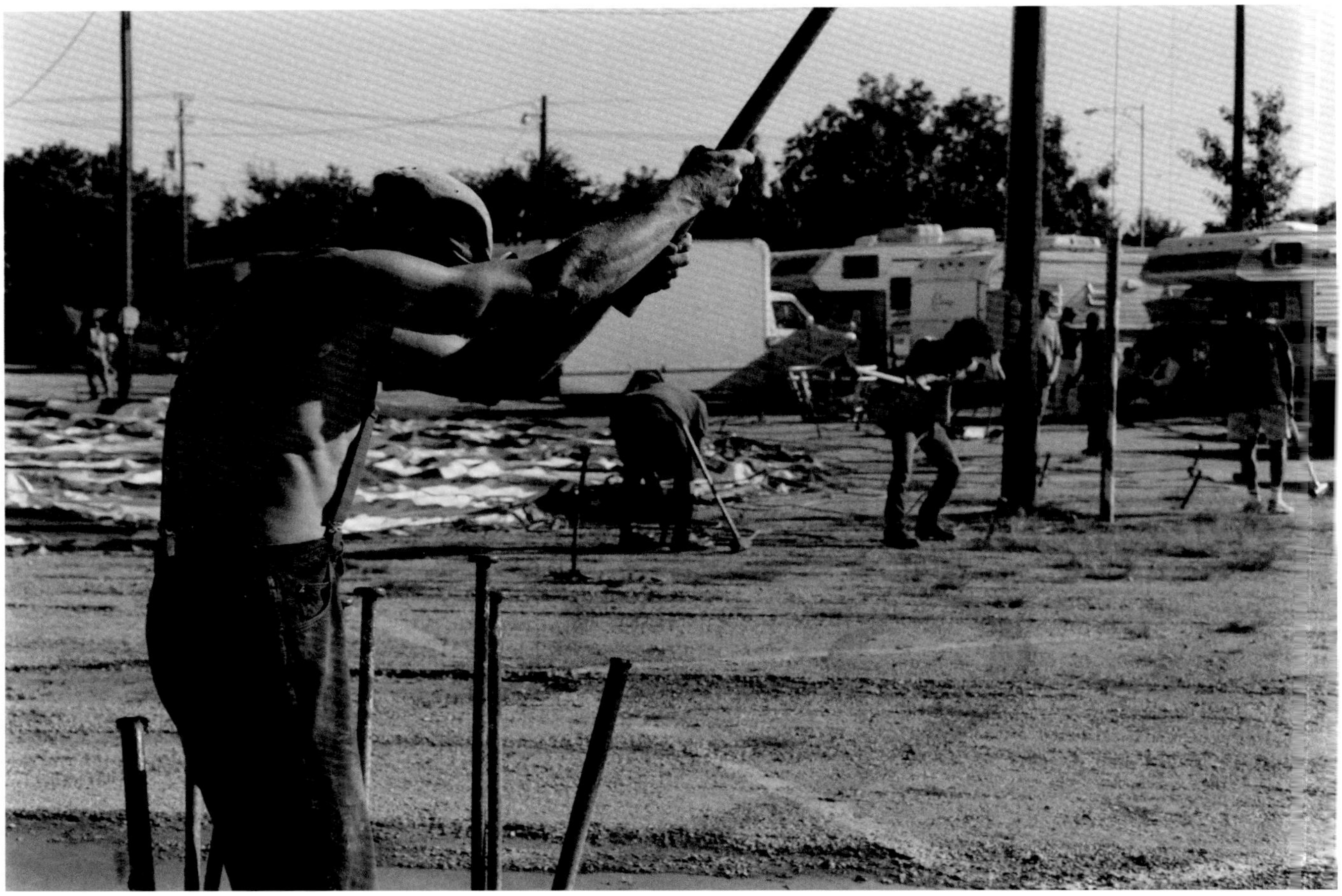

PLATE 191

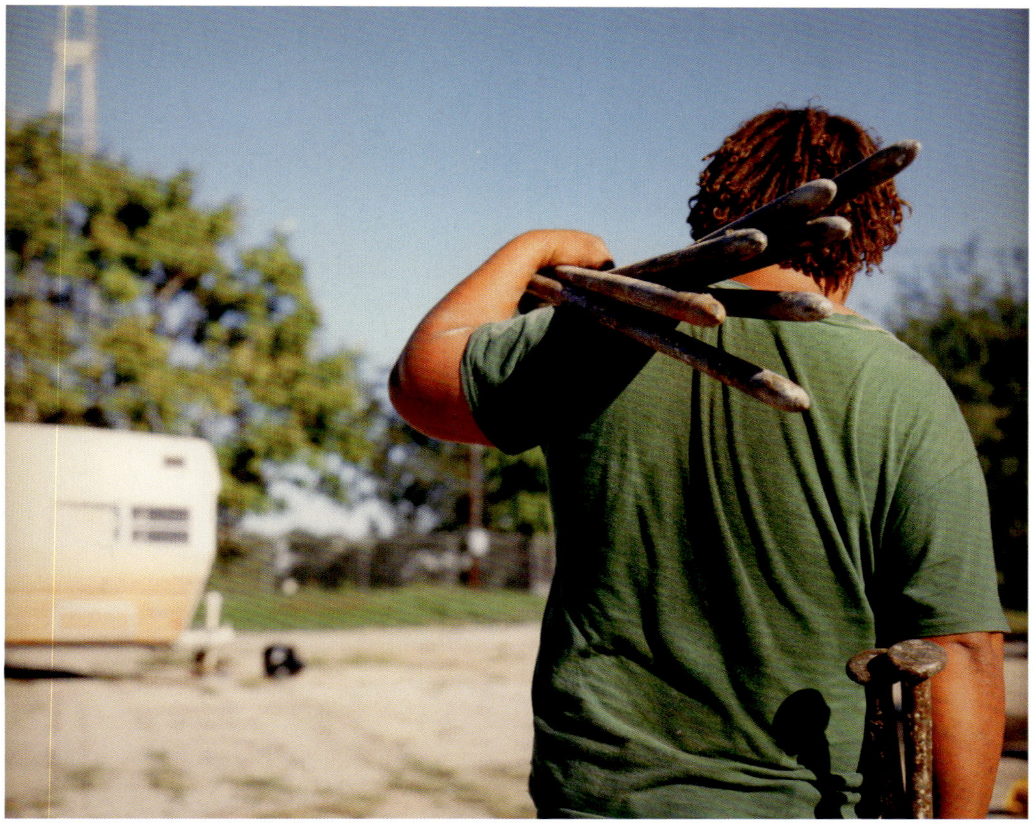

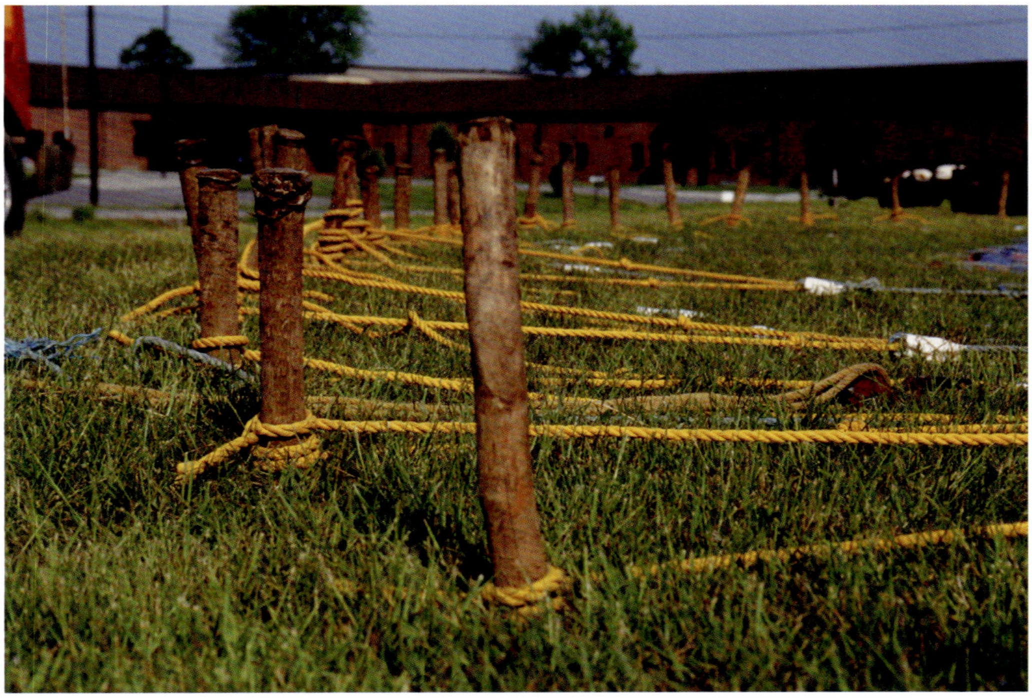

PLATES 192 & 193

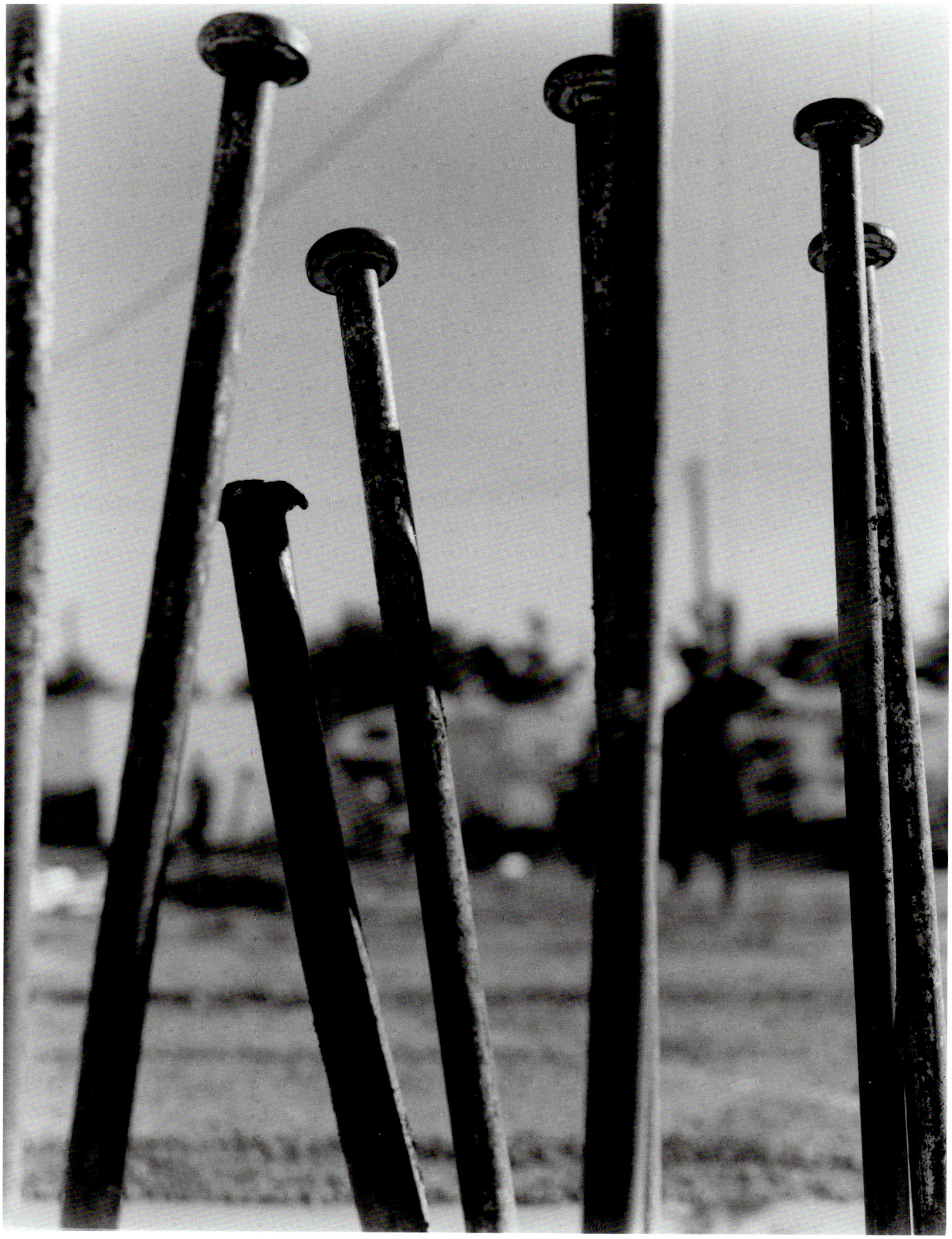

PLATE 194

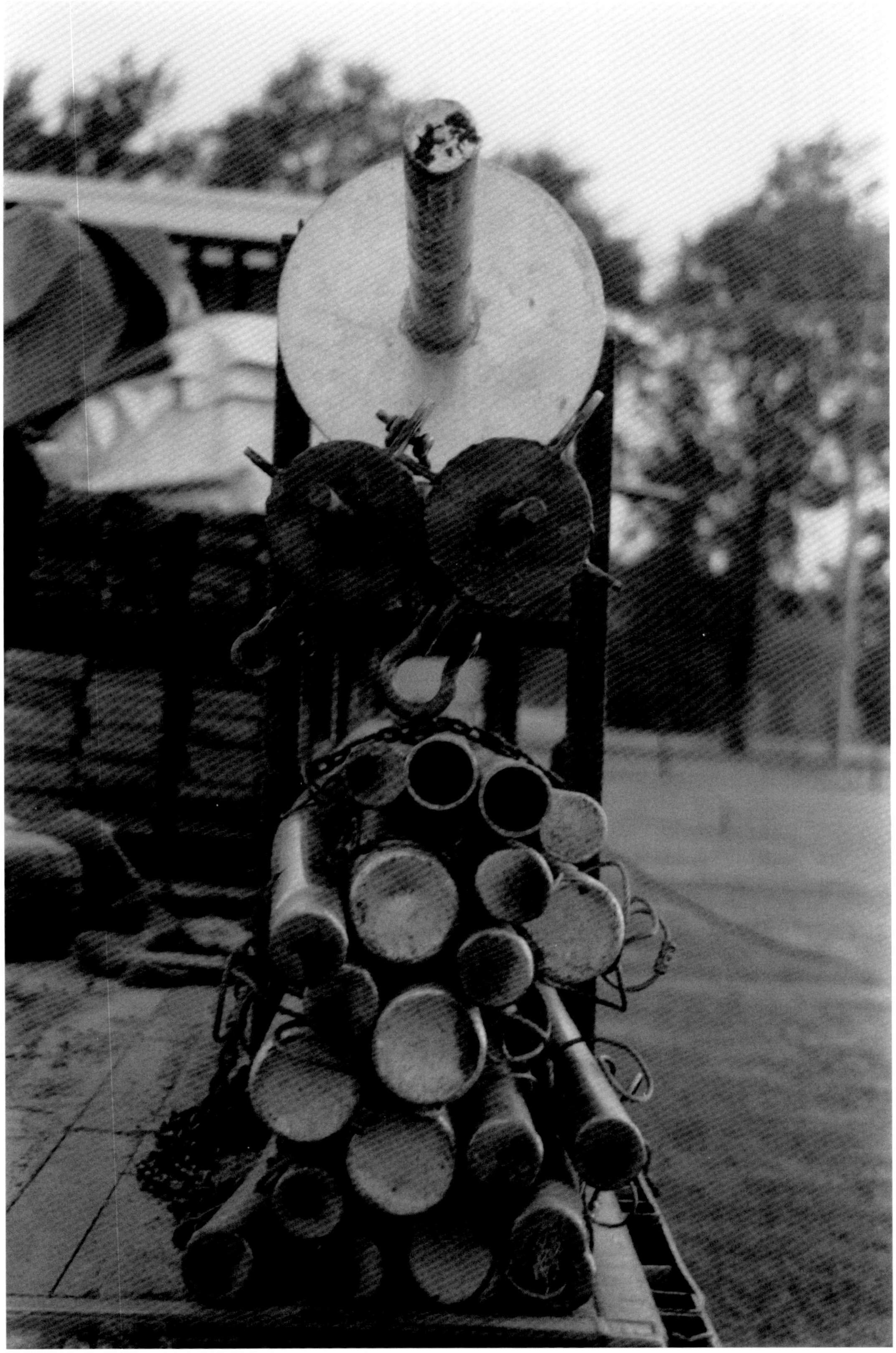

PLATE 195

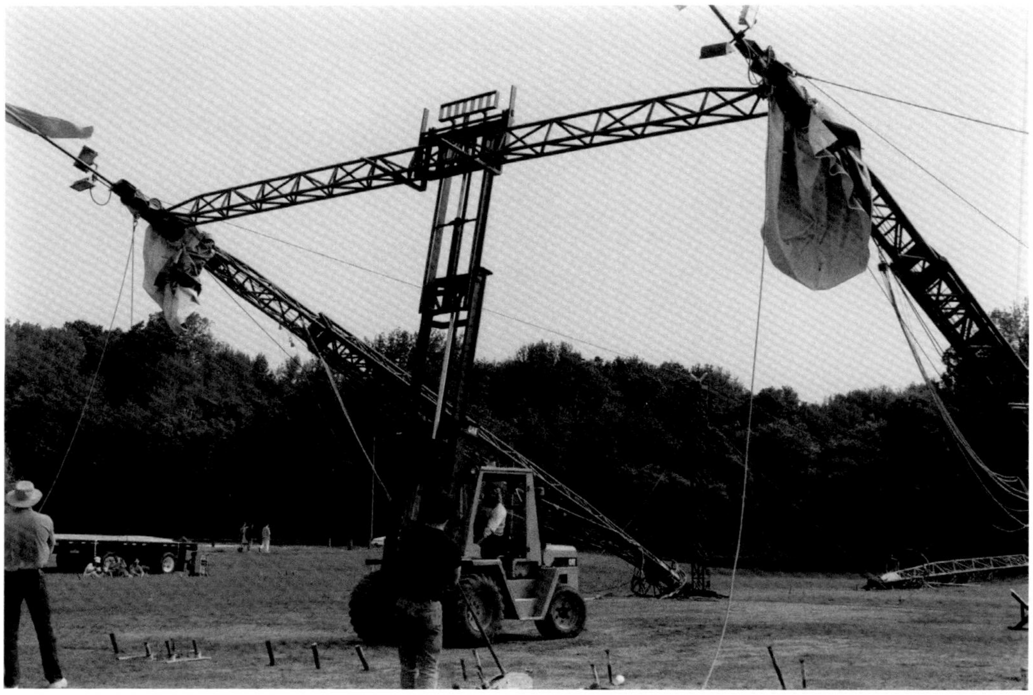

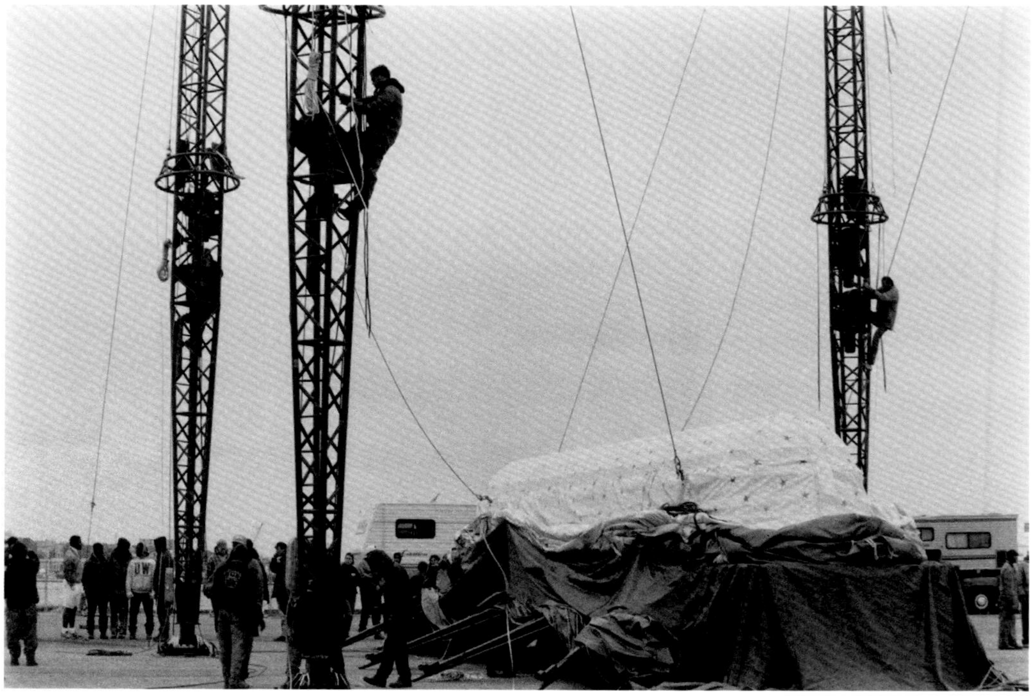

PLATES 196 & 197

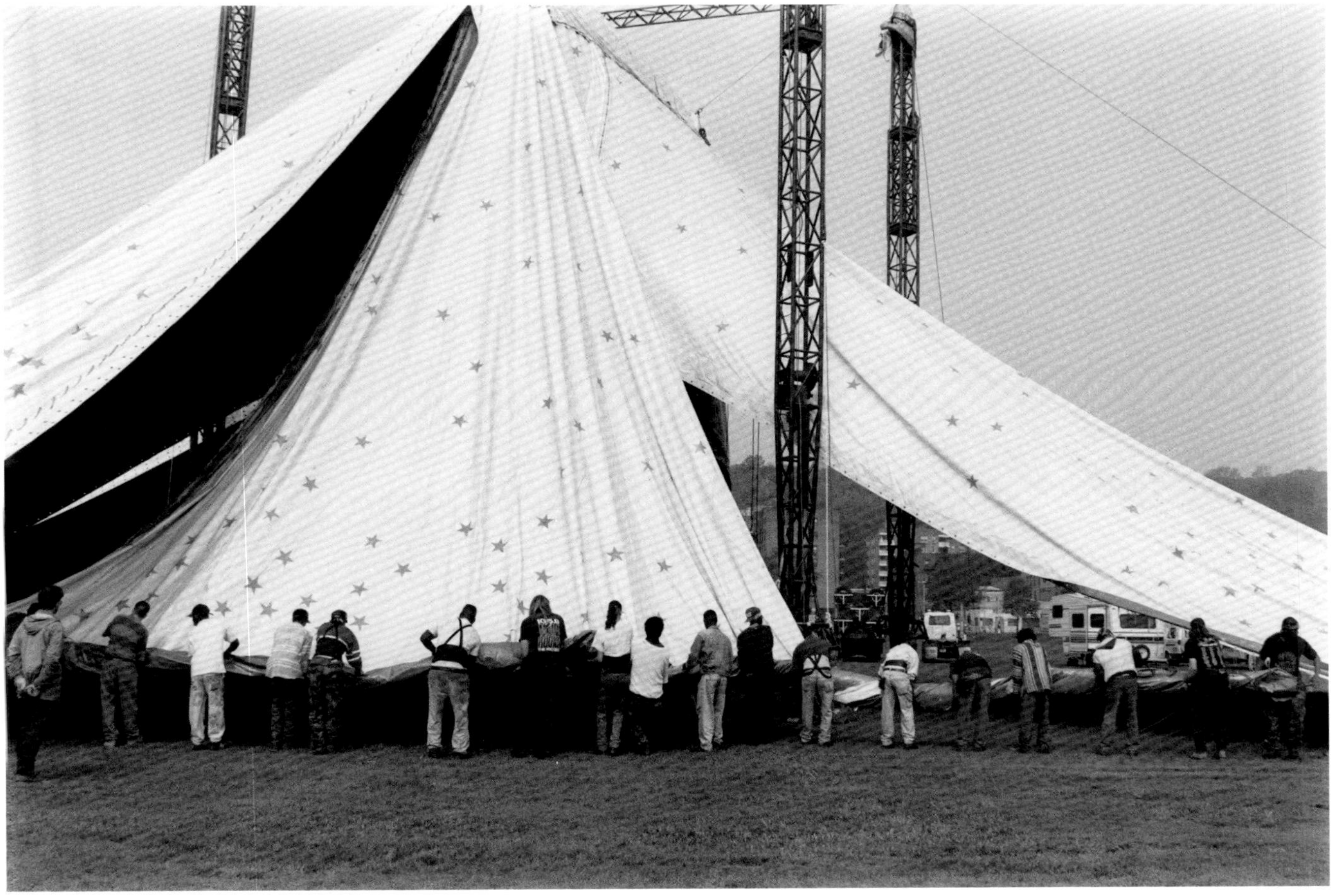

PLATE 198

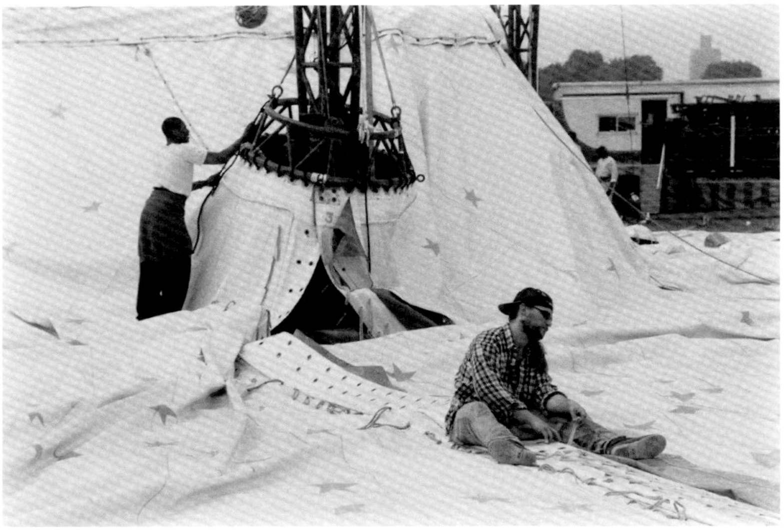

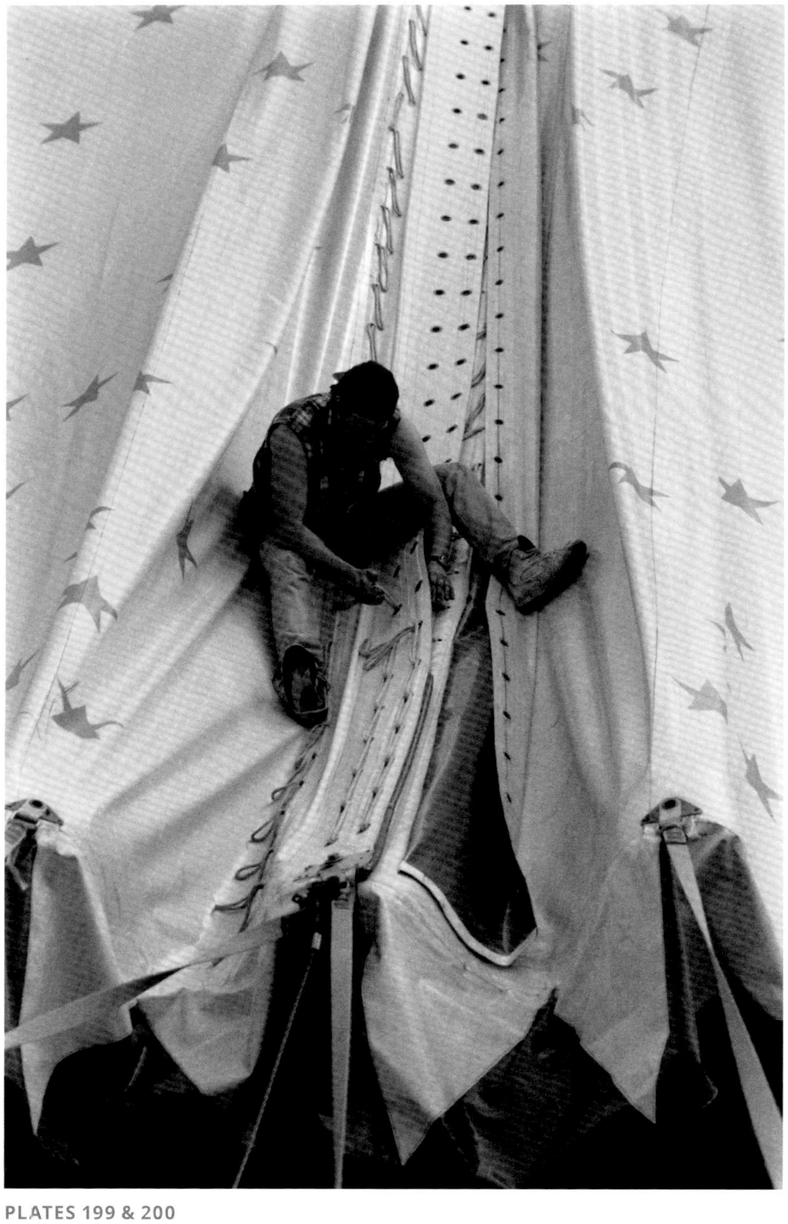

PLATES 199 & 200

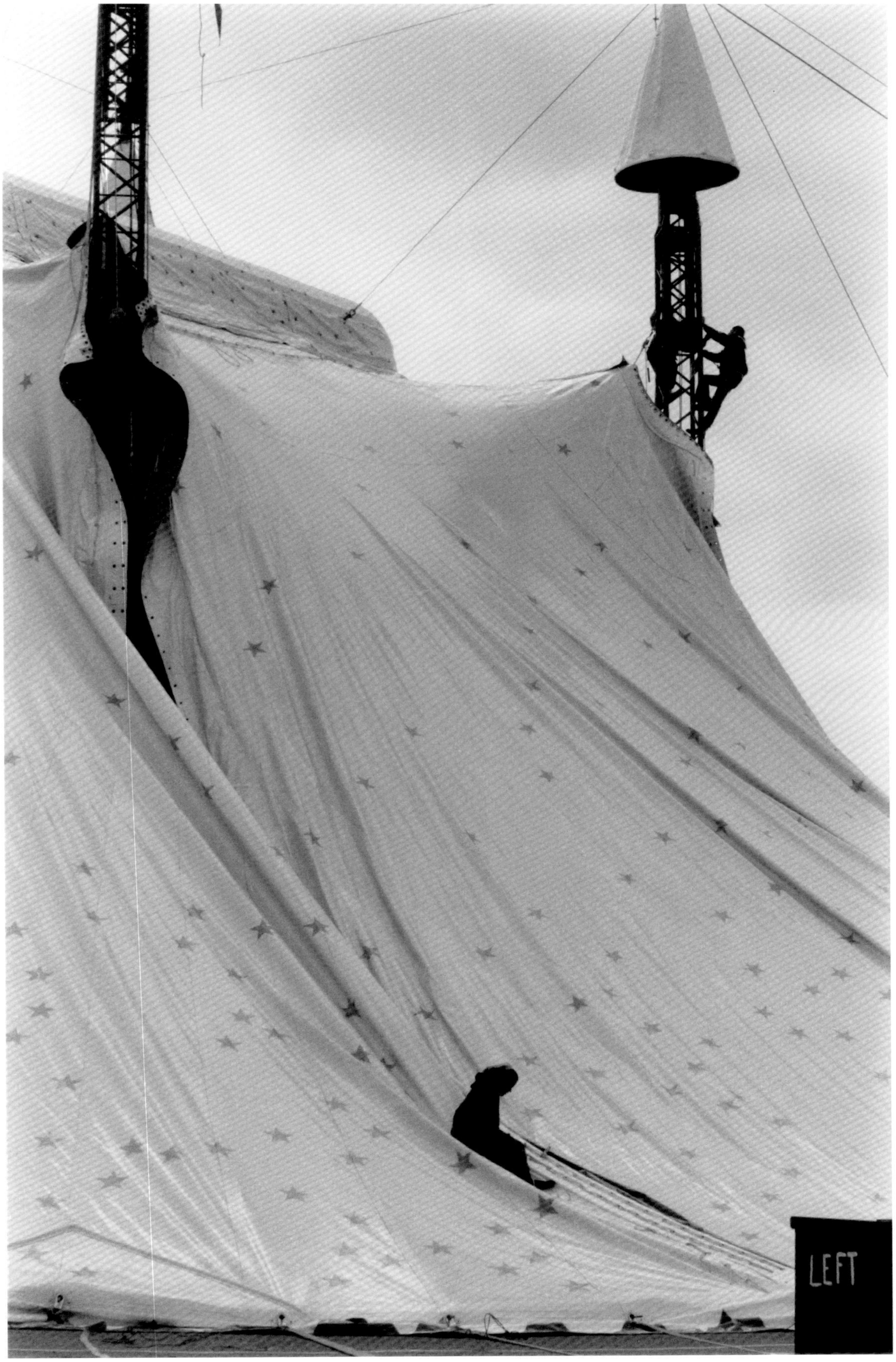

PLATE 201

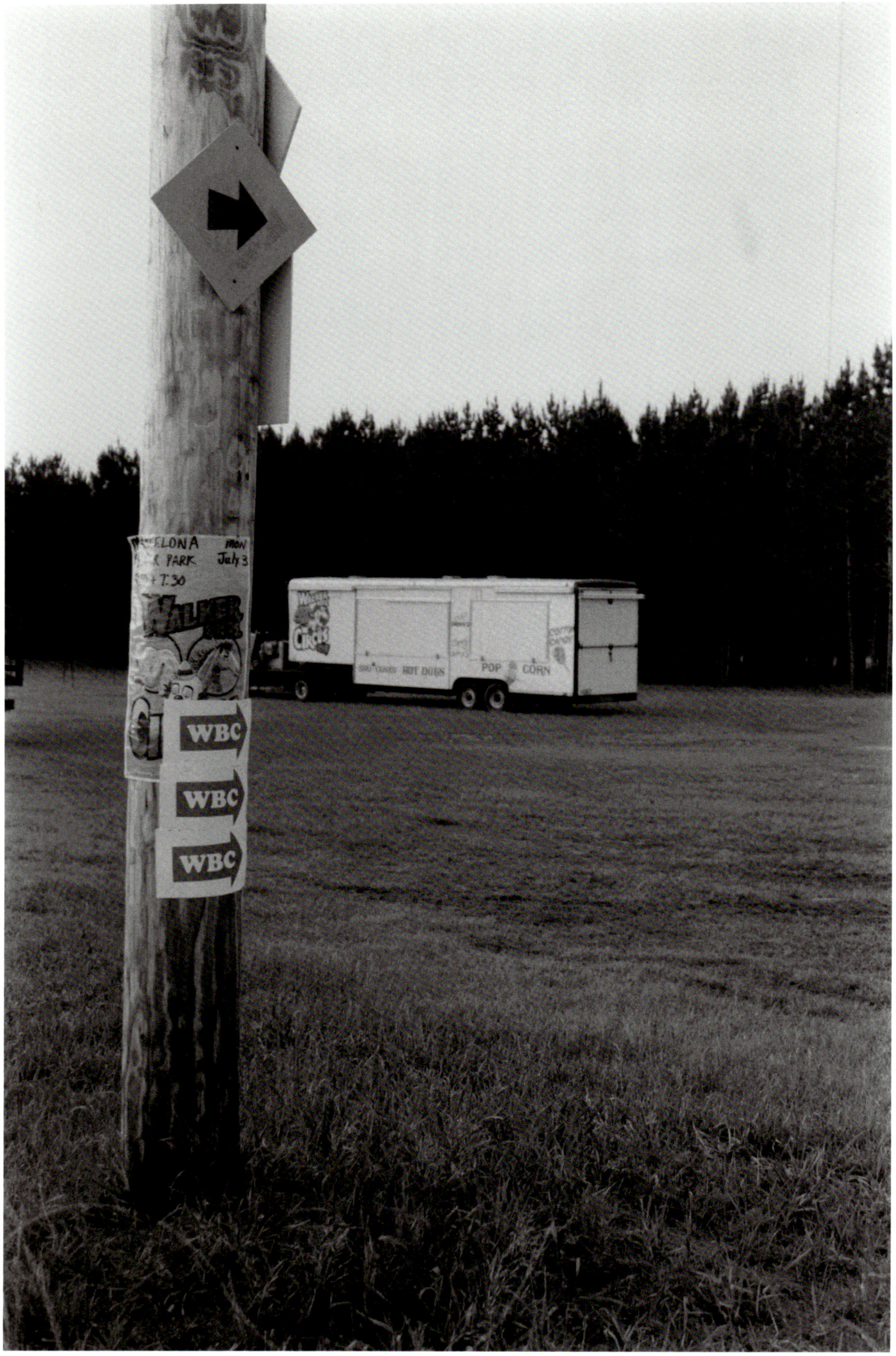

PLATE 202

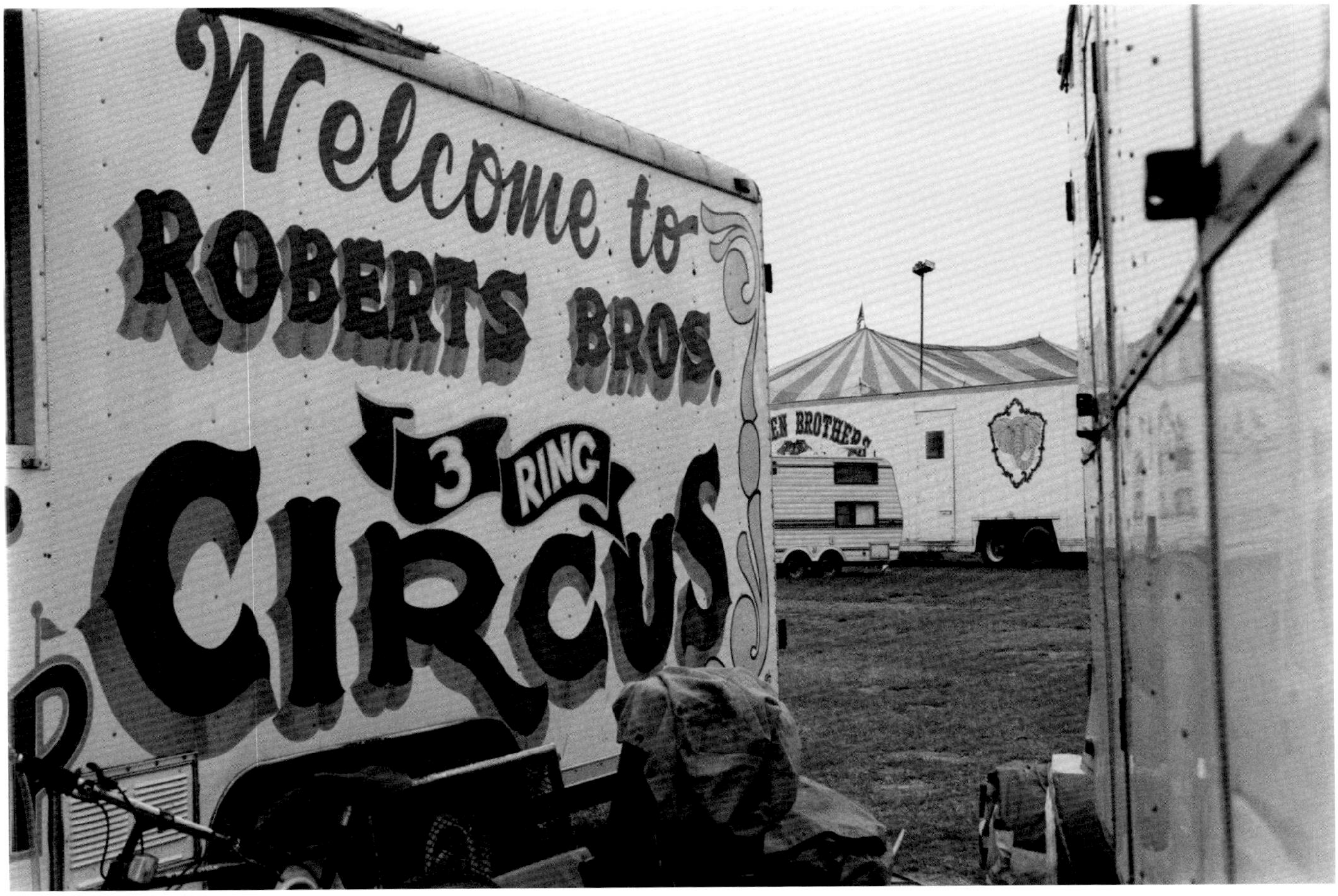

PLATE 203

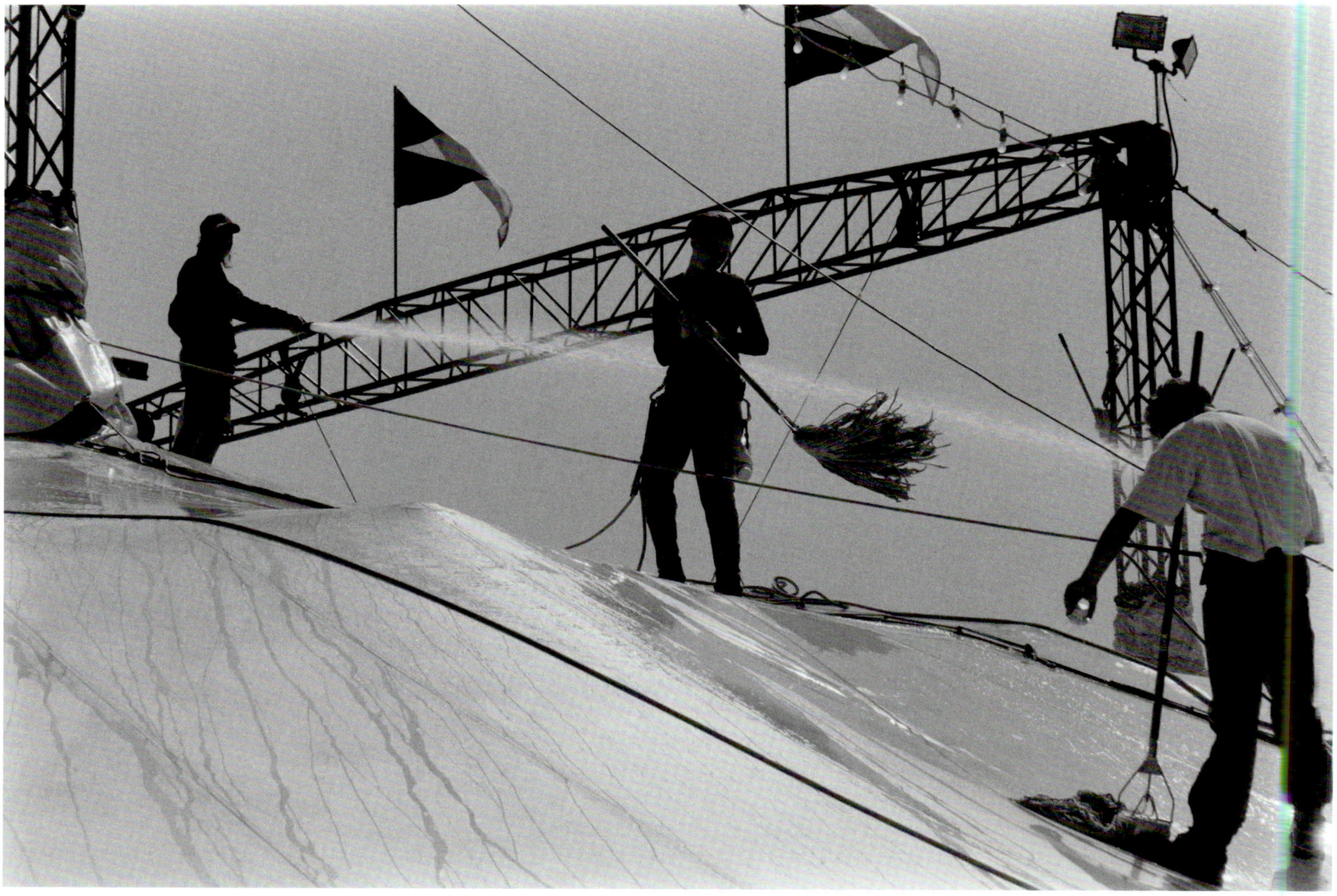

PLATE 204

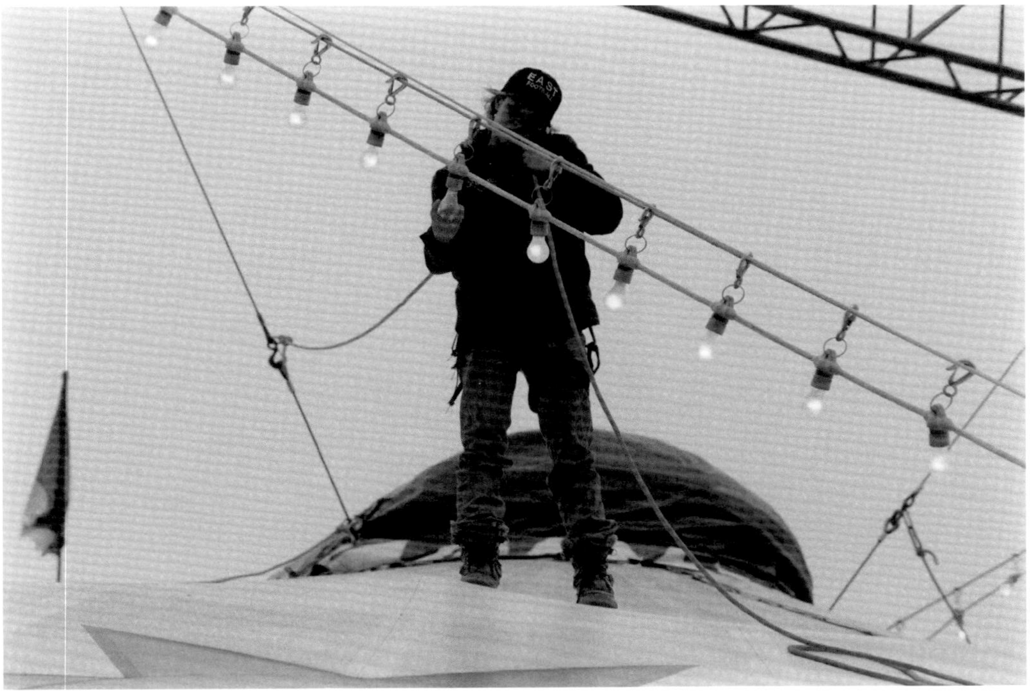

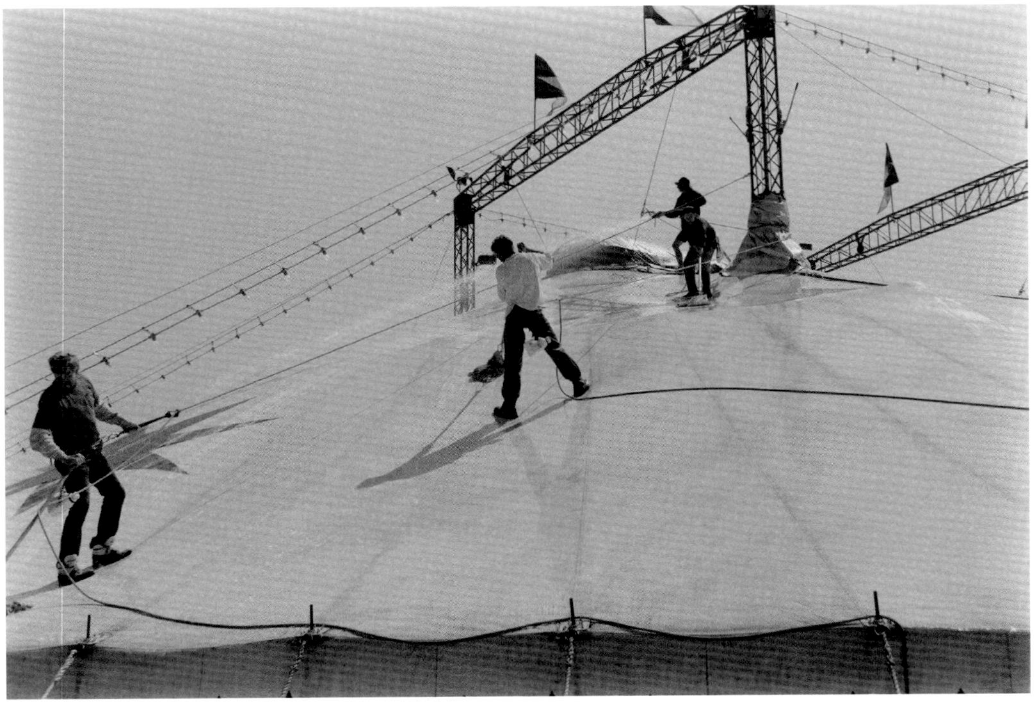

PLATES 205 & 206

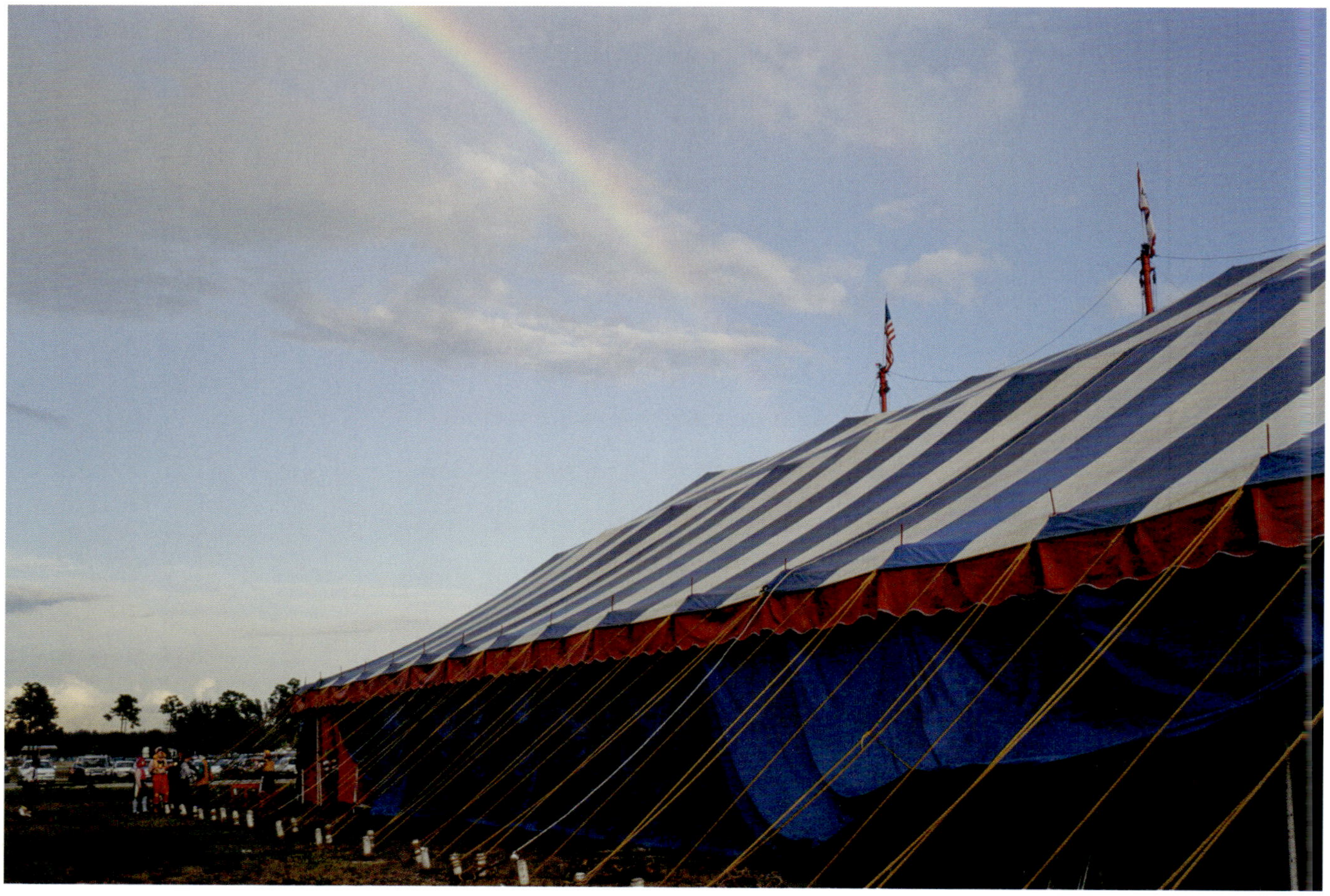

PLATE 207

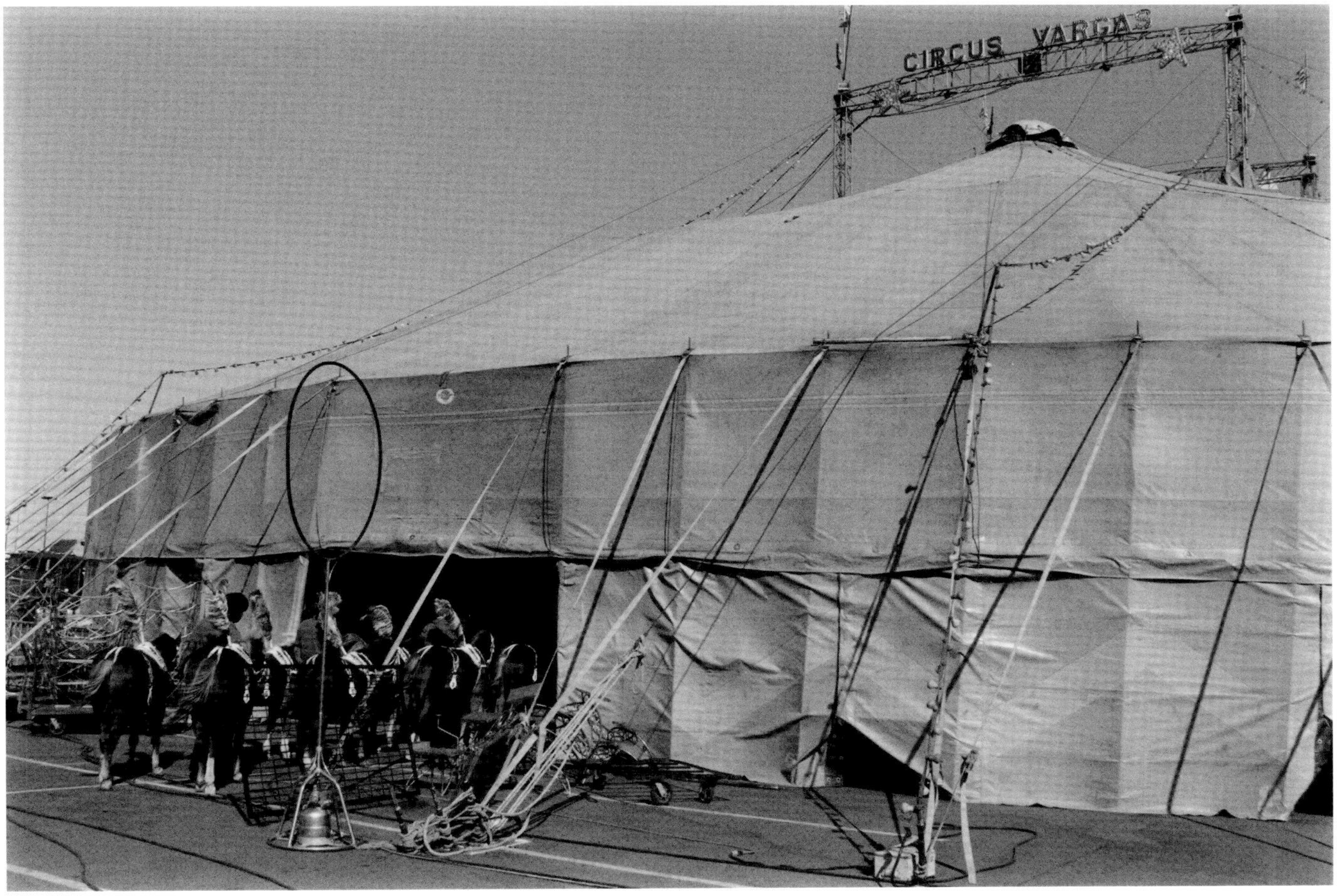

PLATE 208

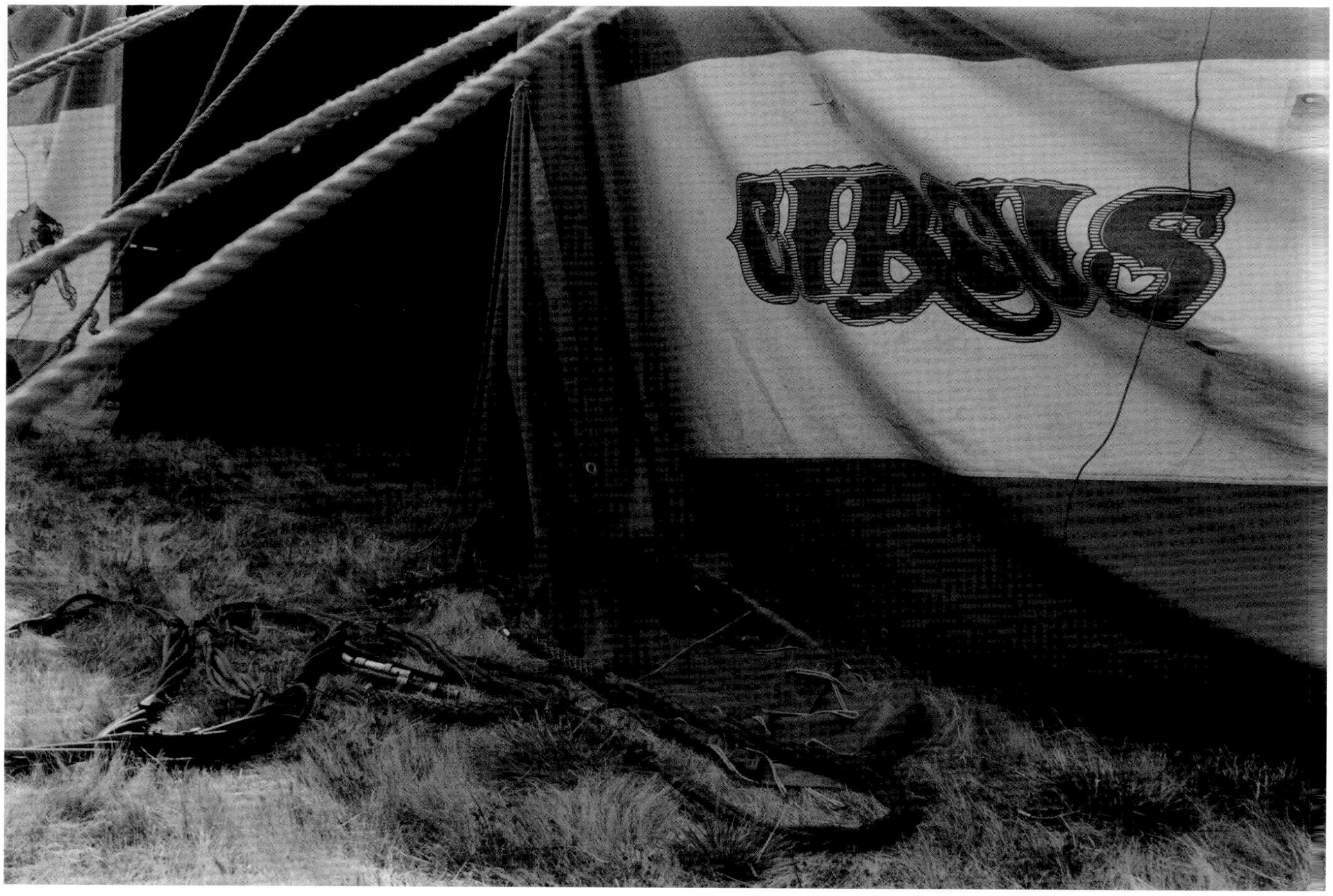

PLATE 209

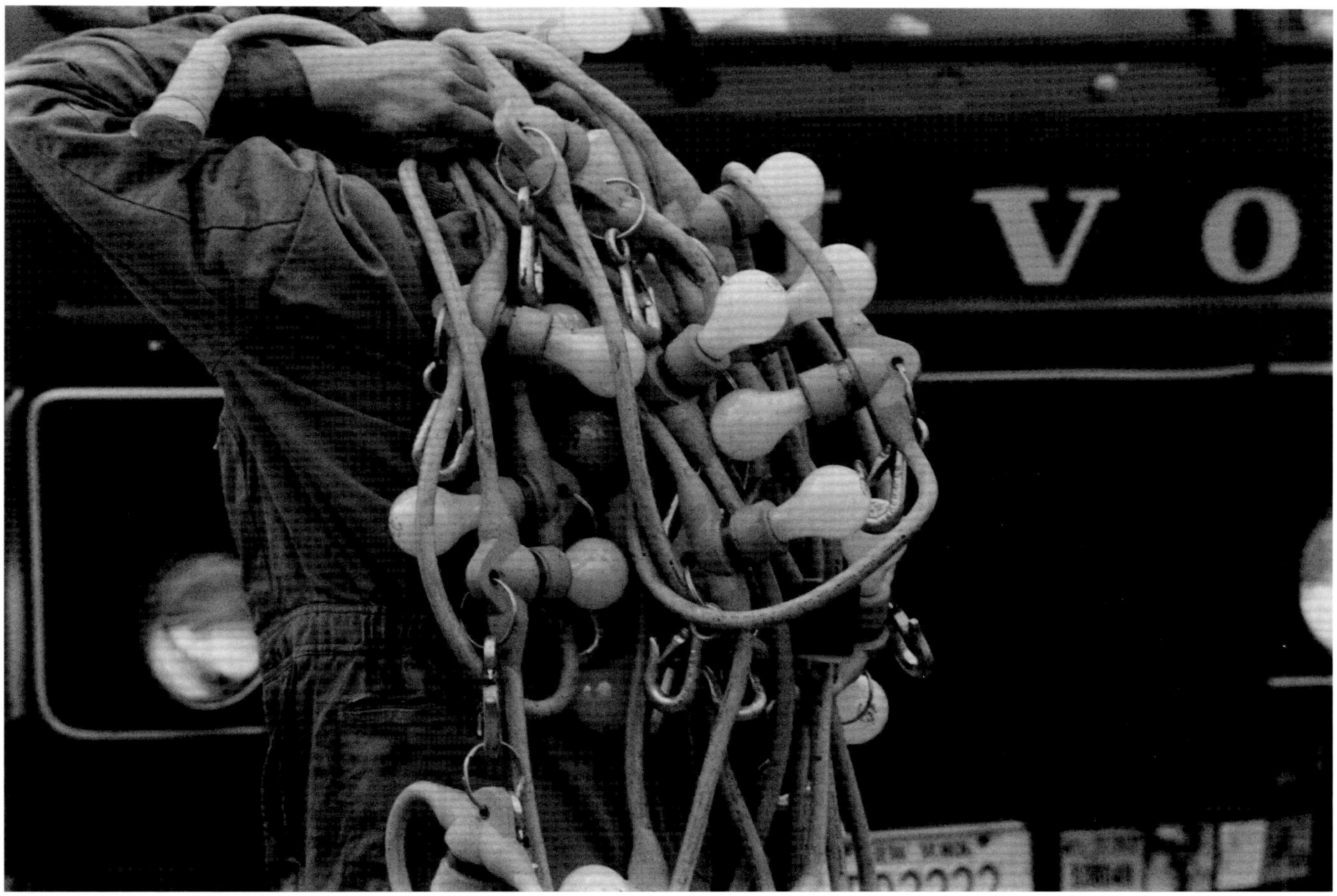

PLATE 210

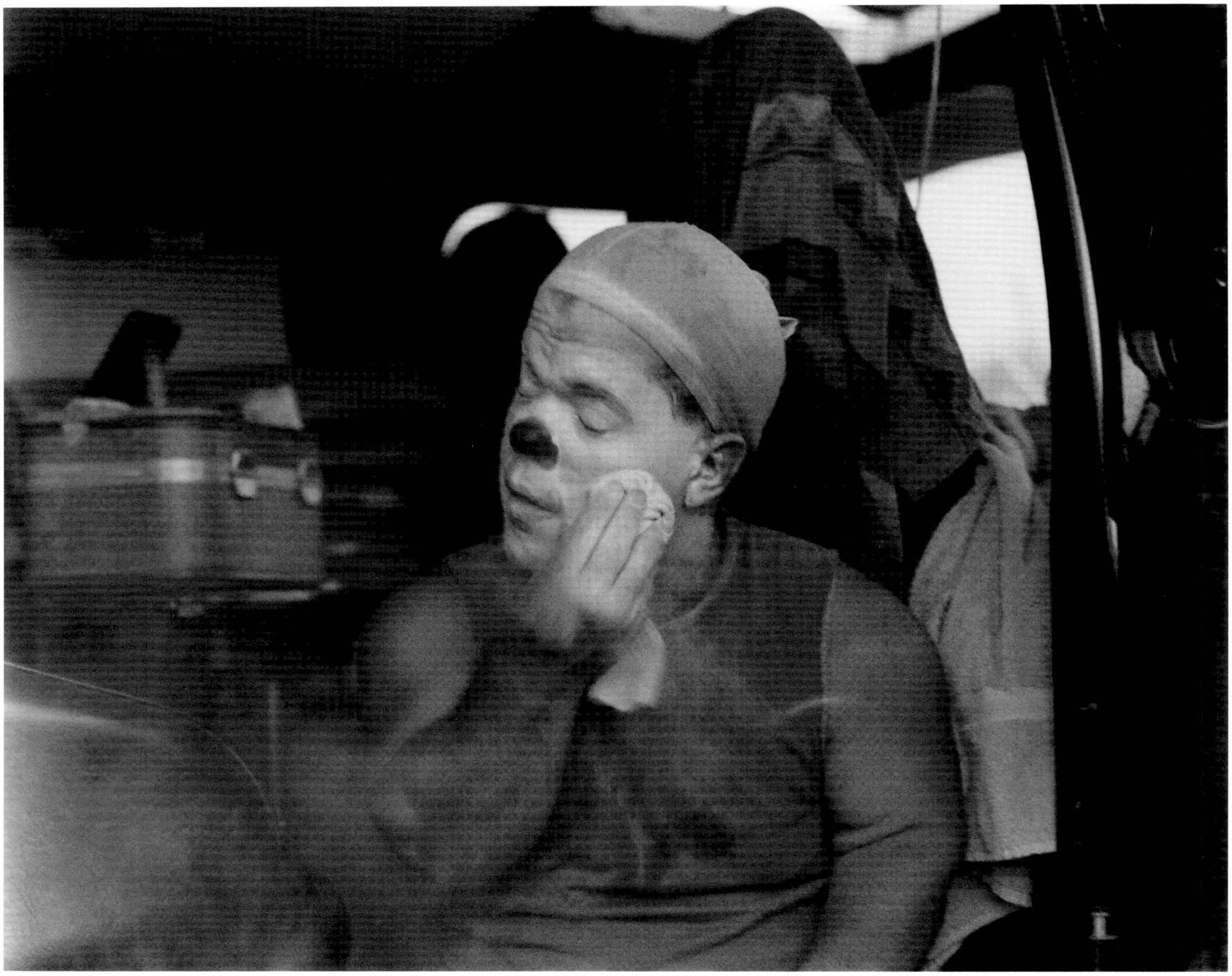

PLATE 211

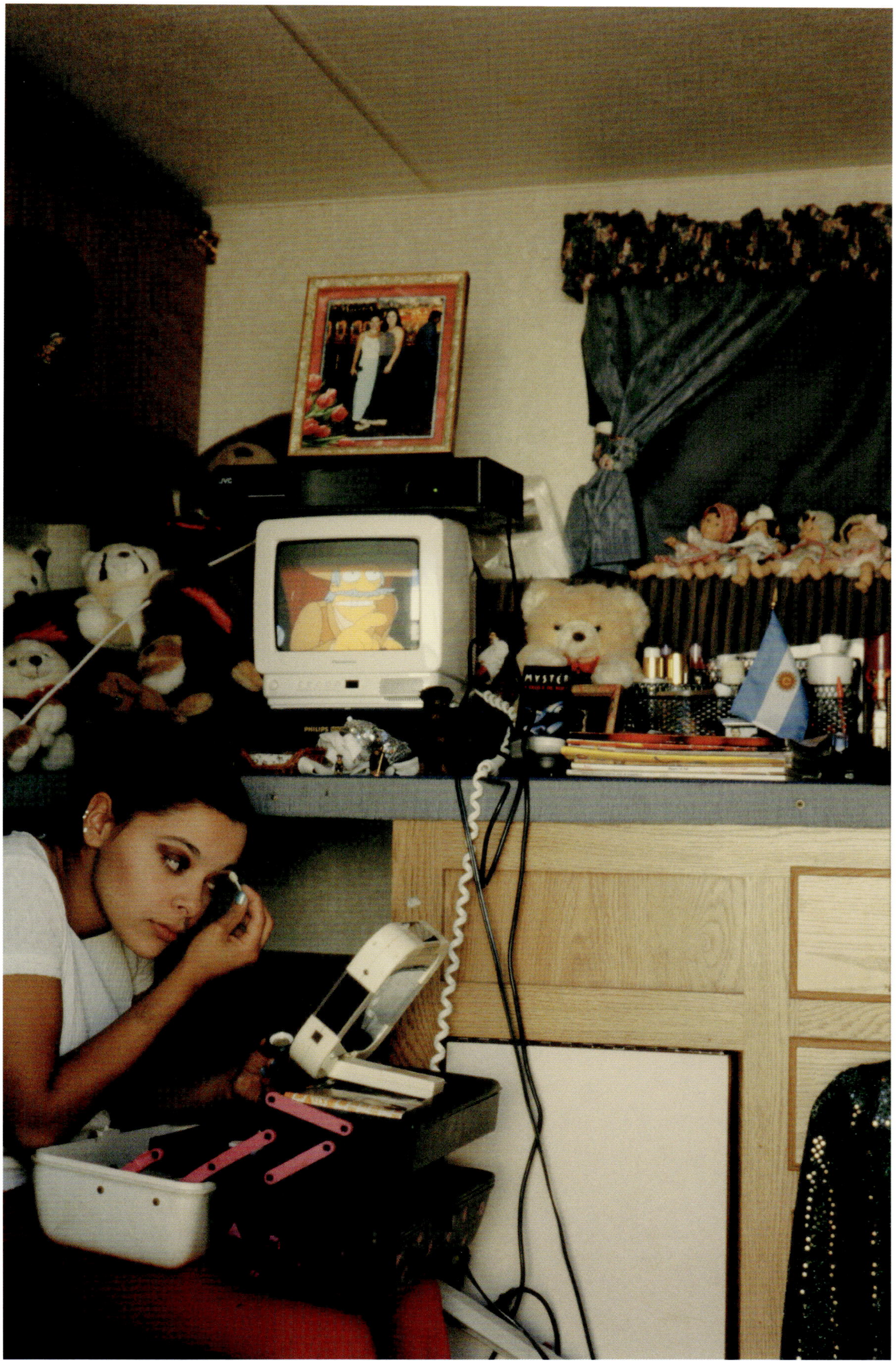

PLATE 212

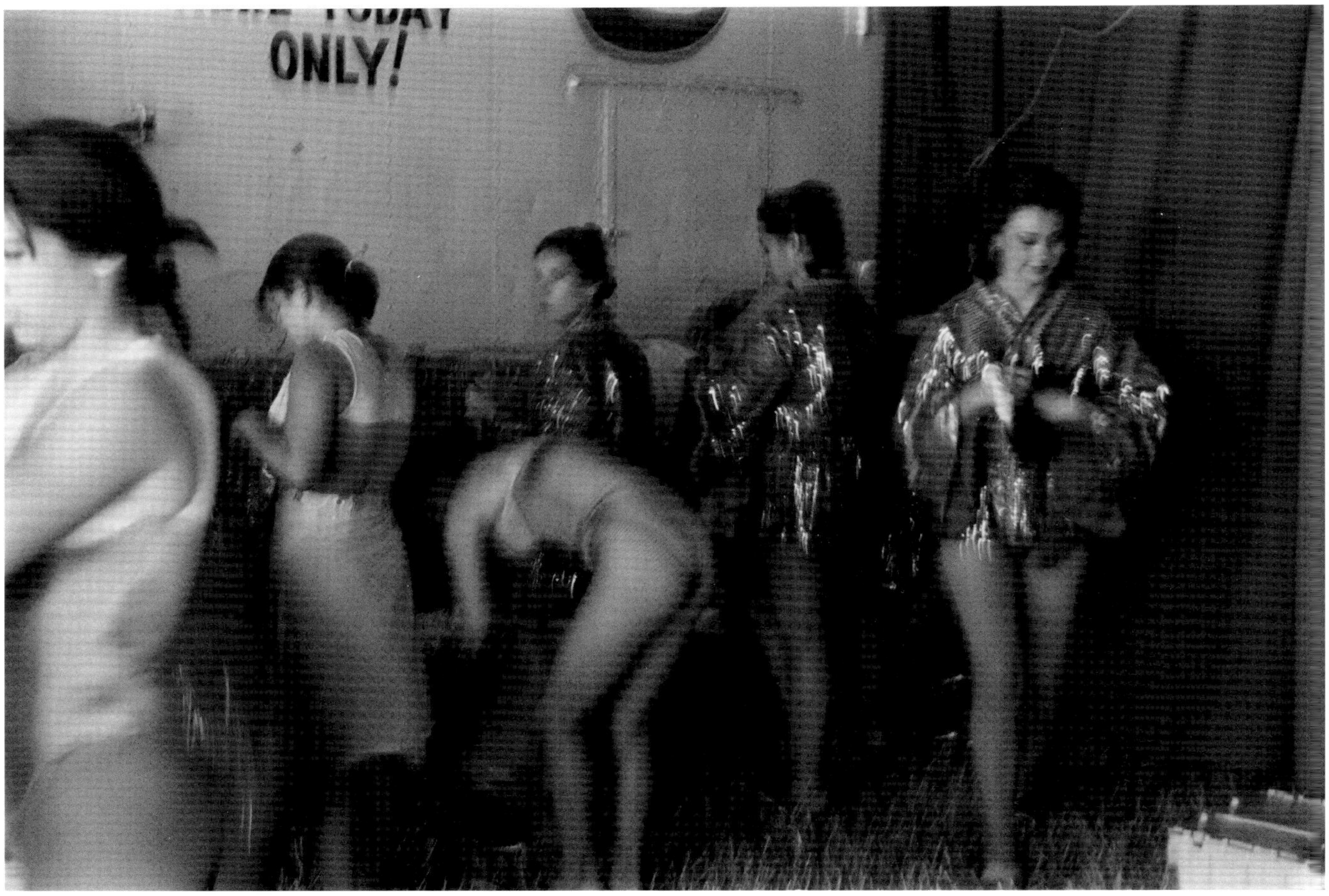

PLATE 213

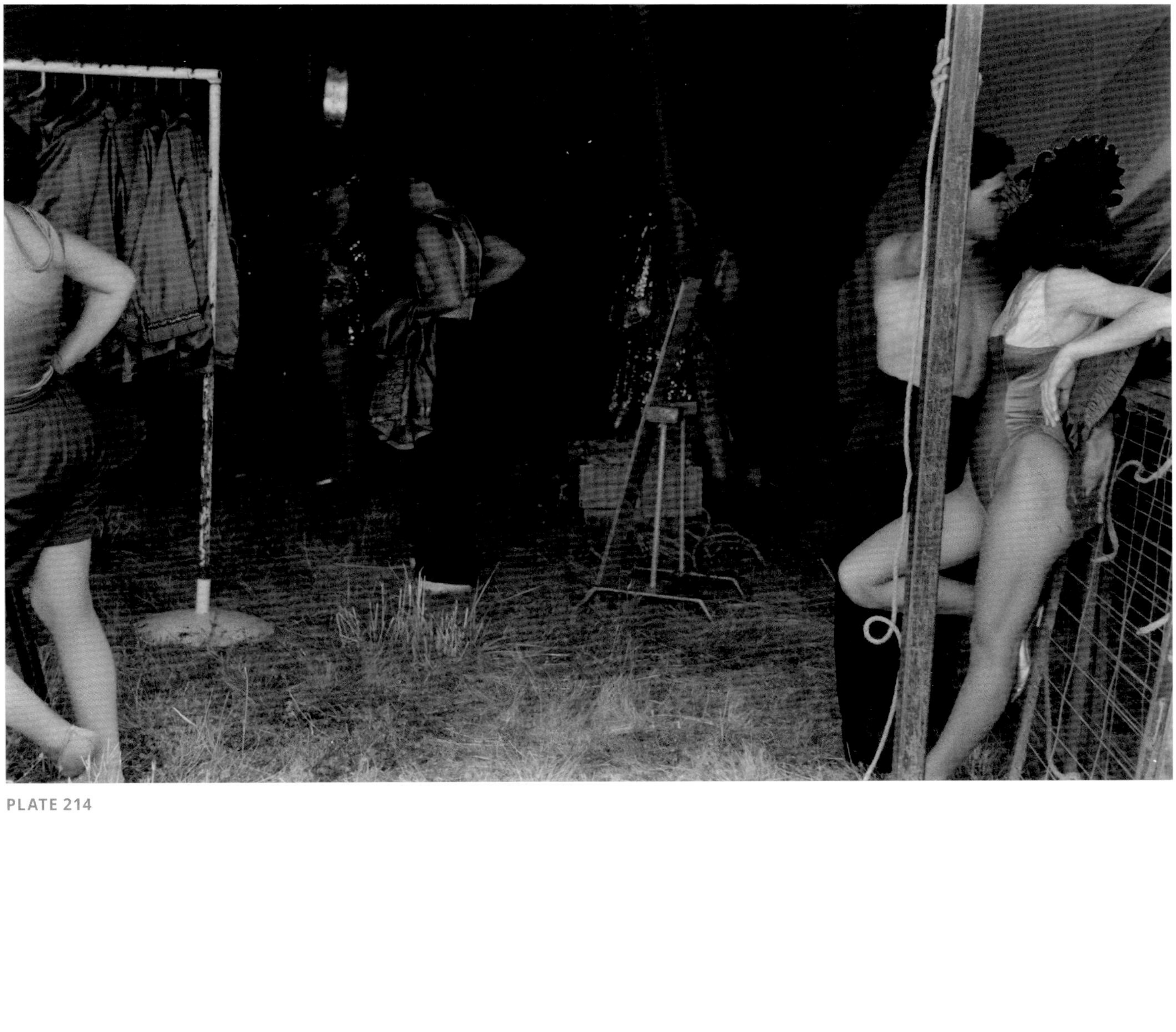
PLATE 214

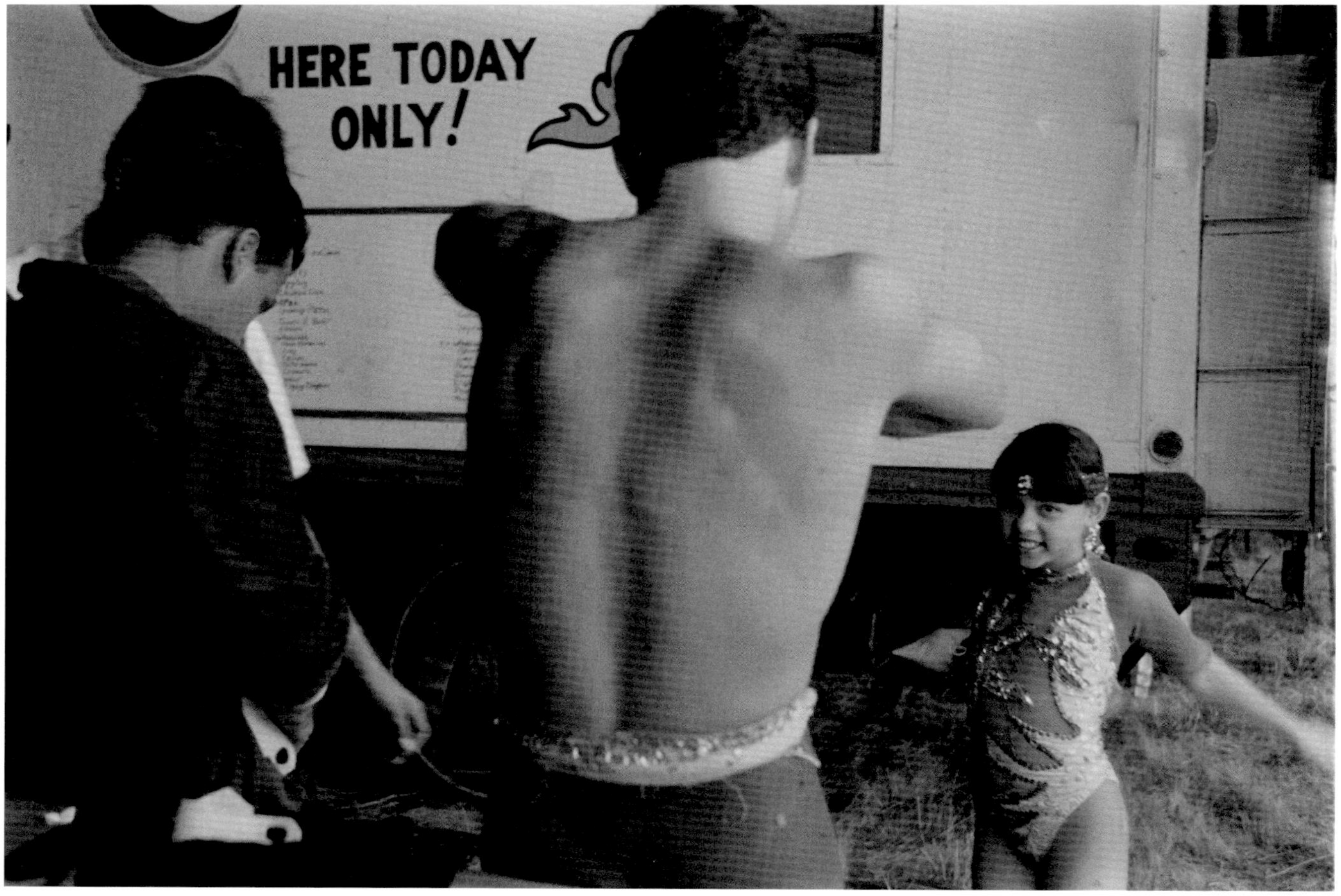

PLATE 215

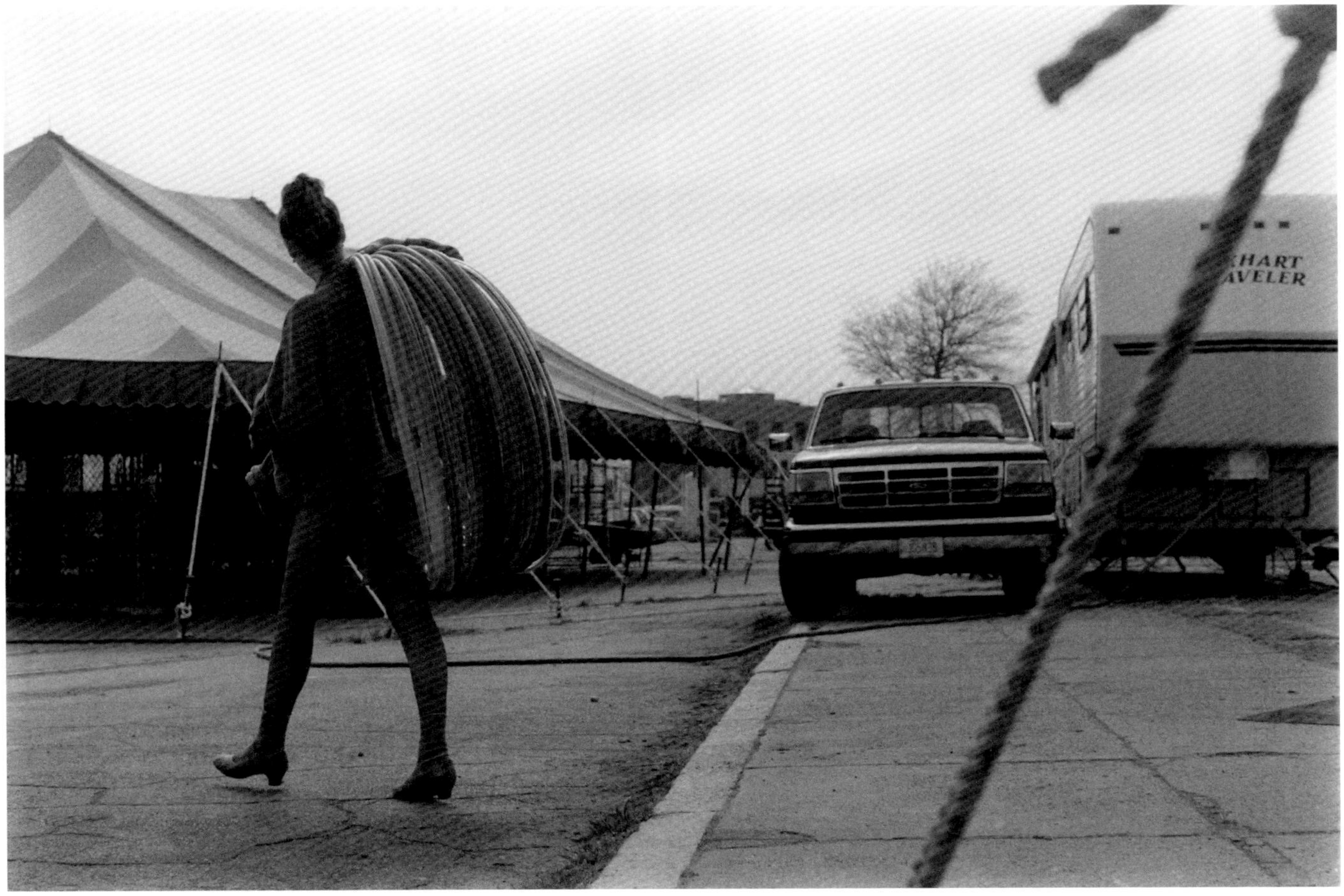

PLATE 216

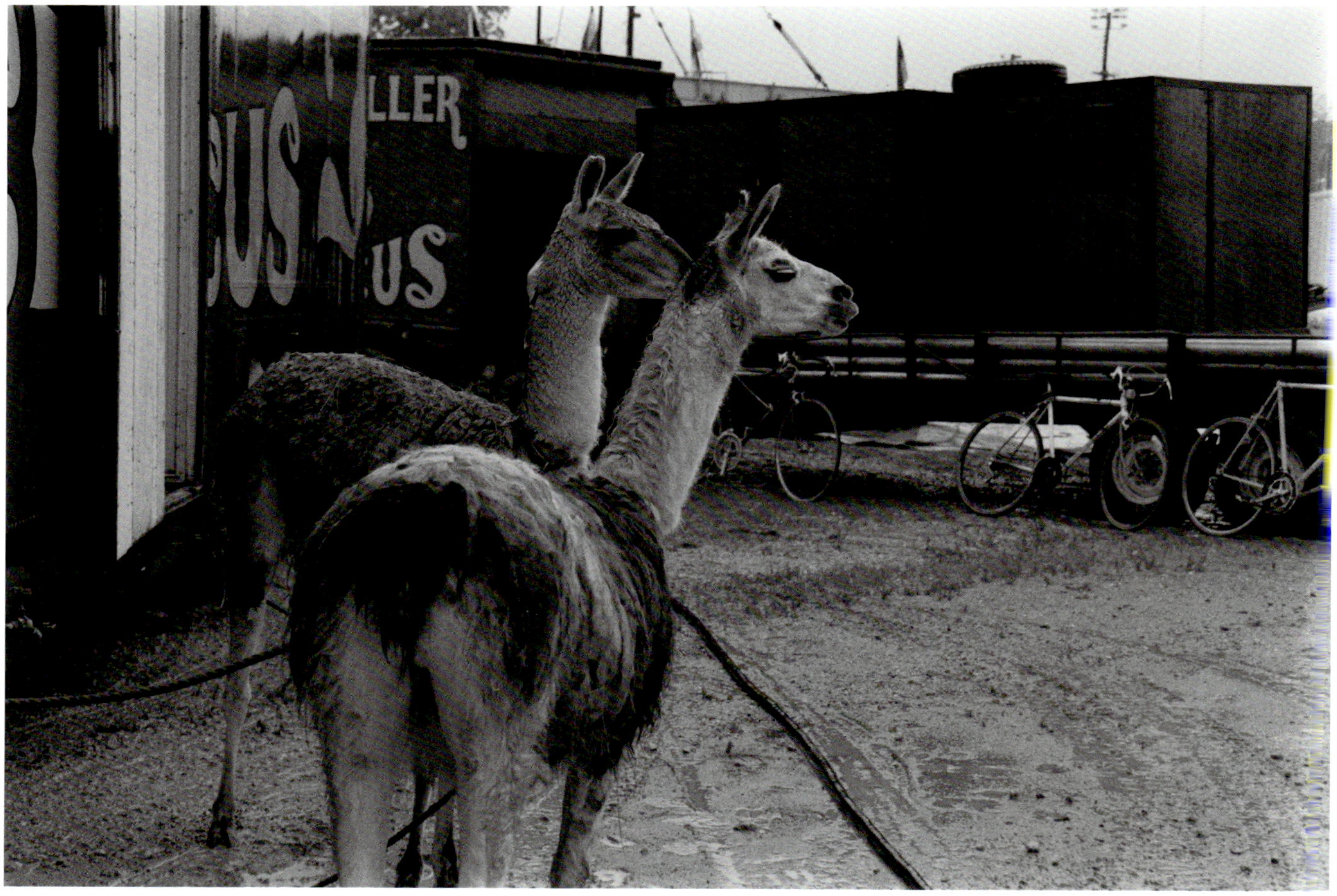

PLATE 217

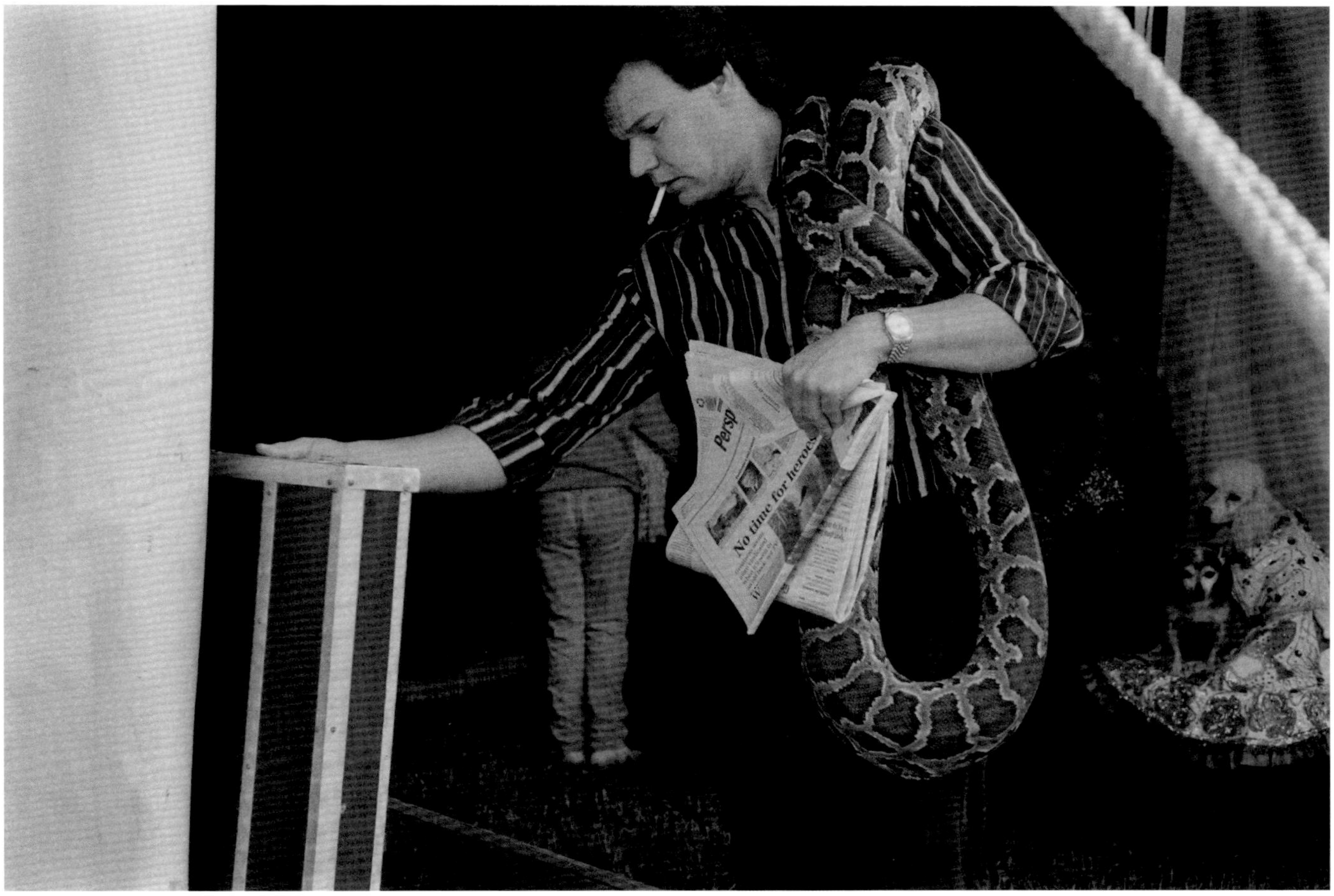

PLATE 218

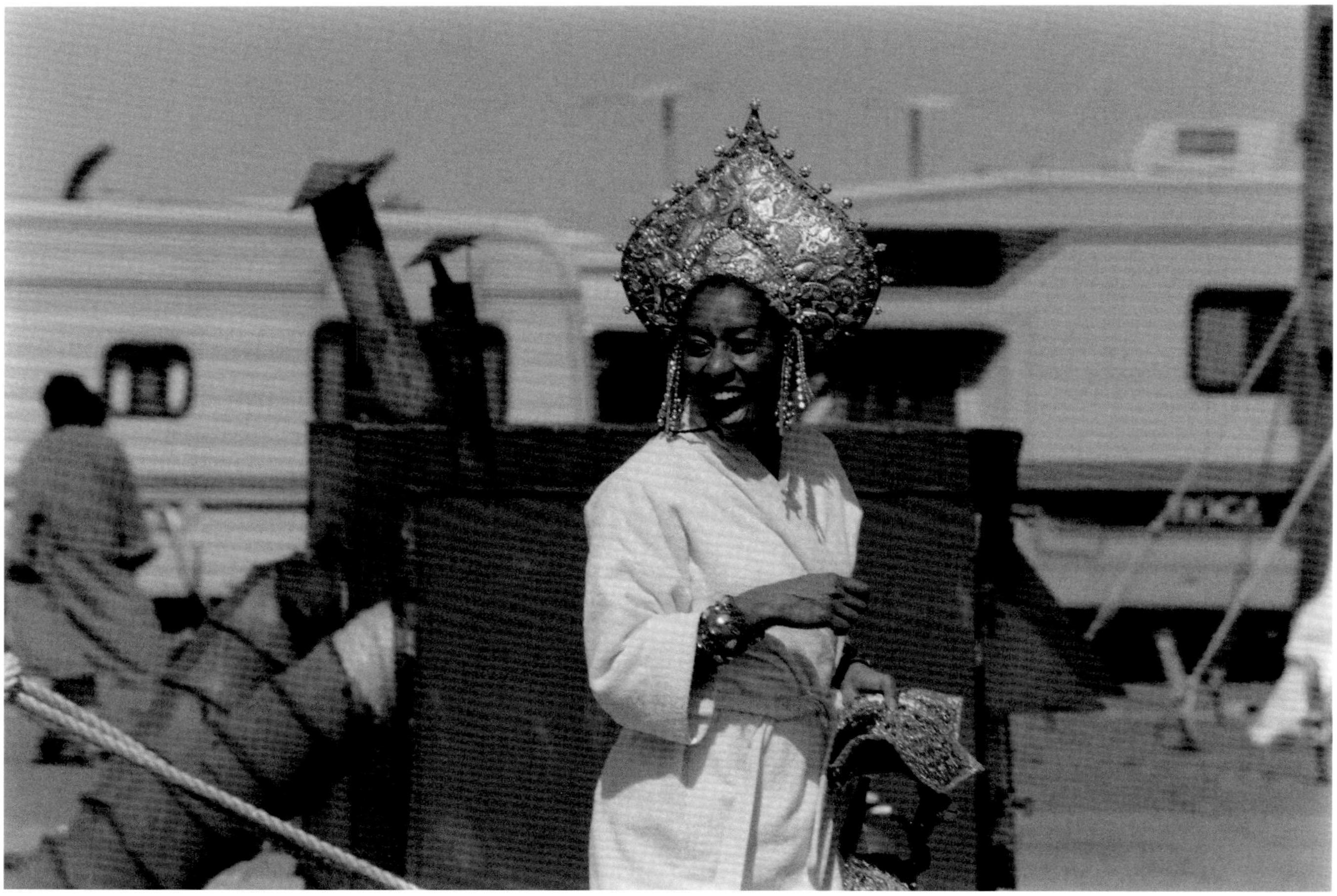

PLATE 219

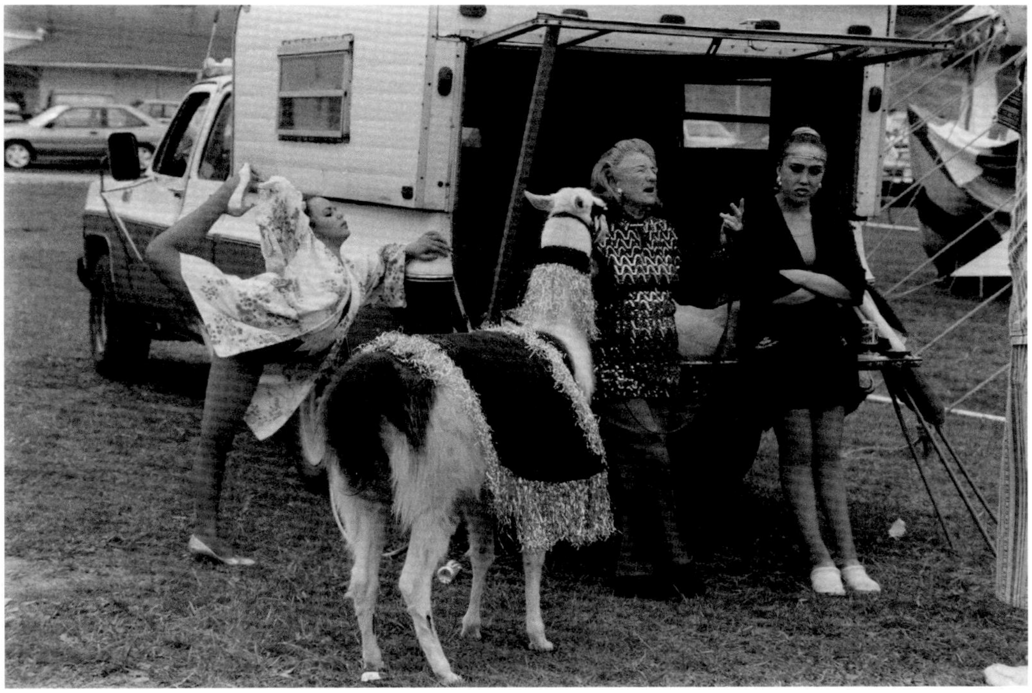

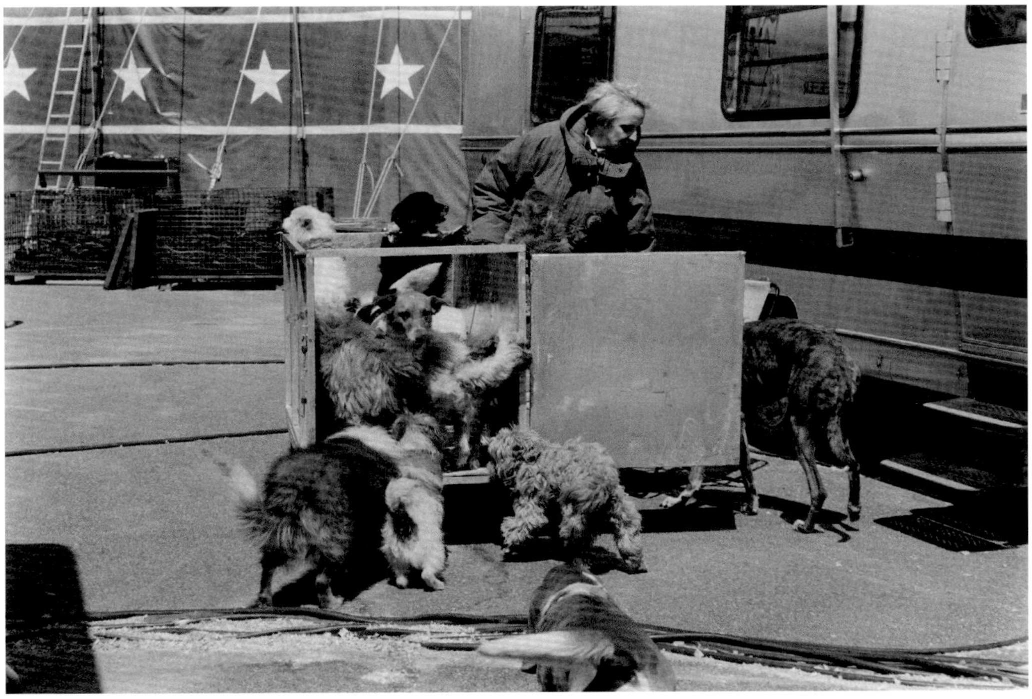

PLATES 220 & 221

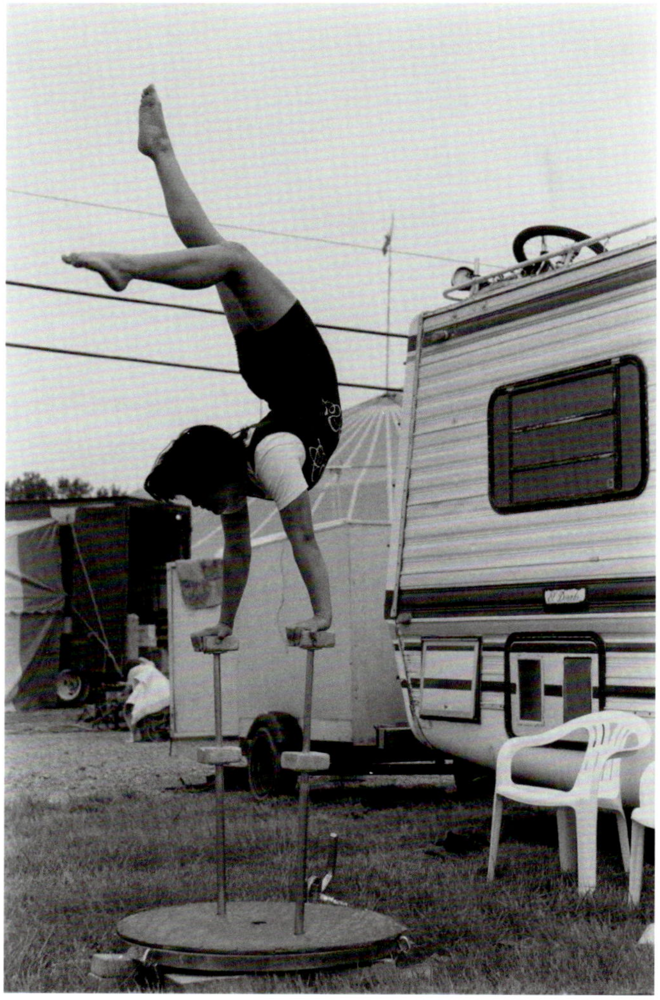

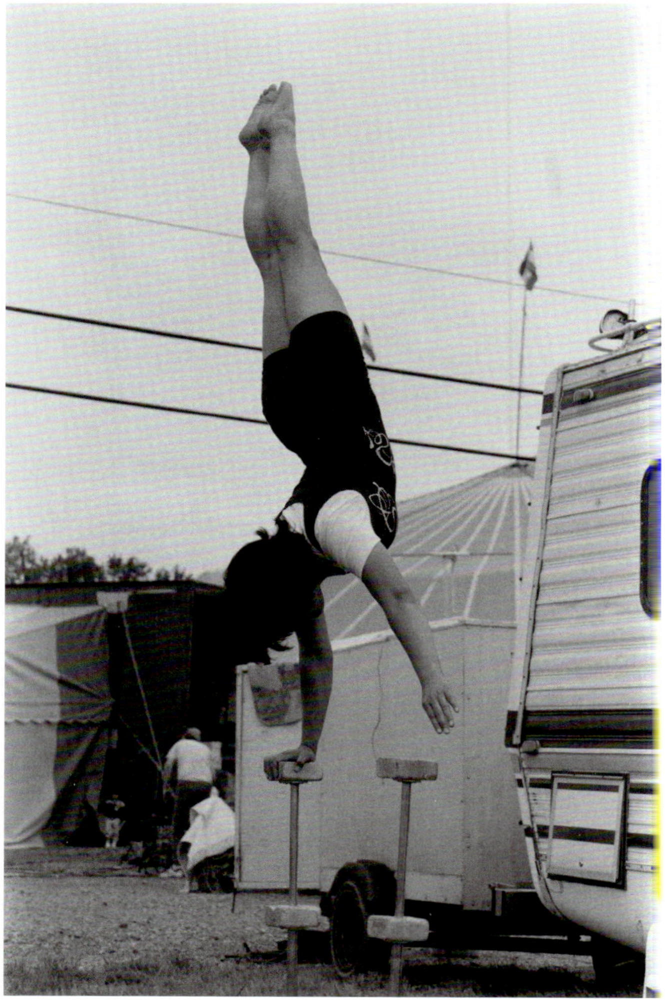

PLATES 222 & 223

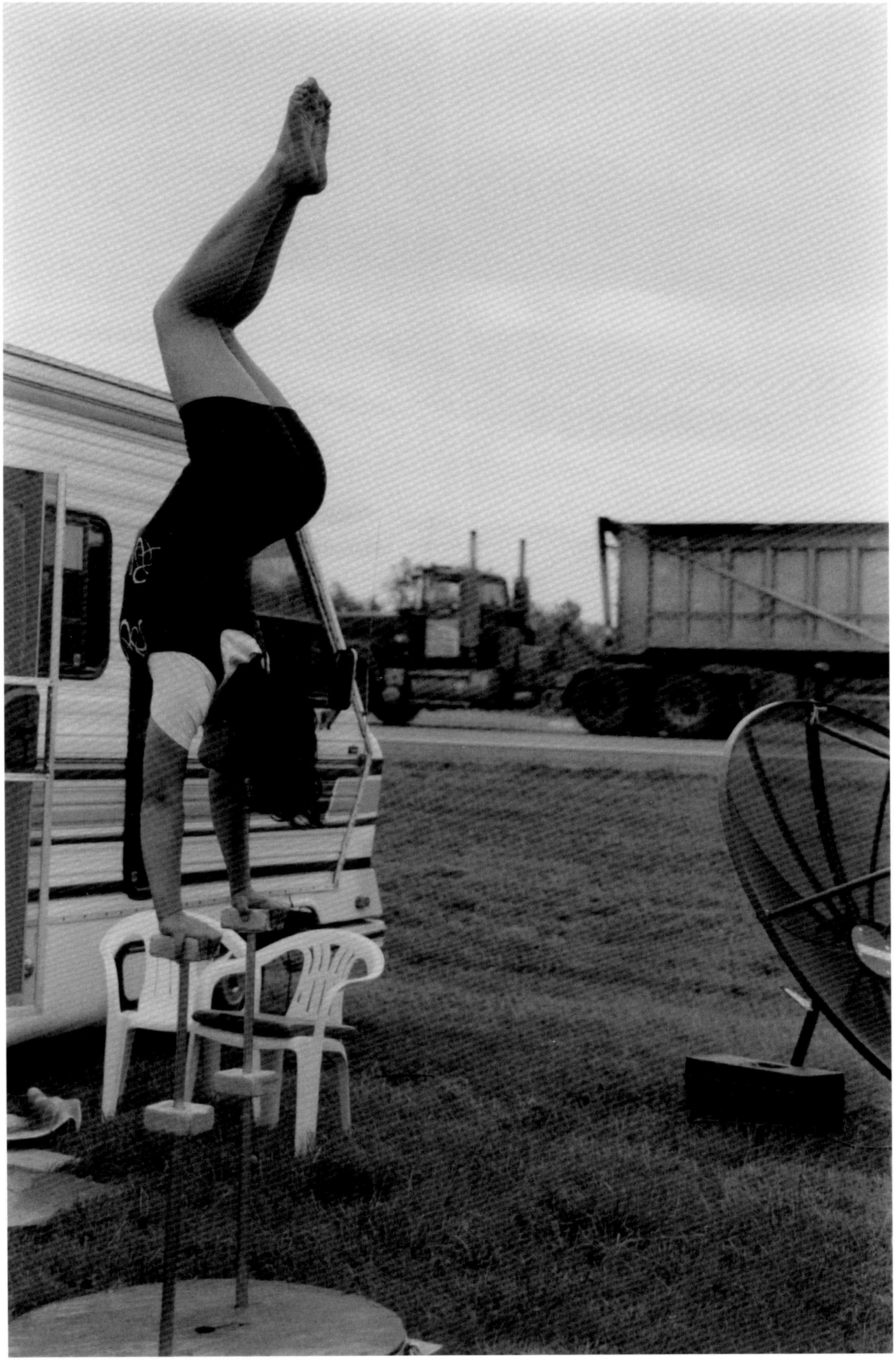

PLATE 224

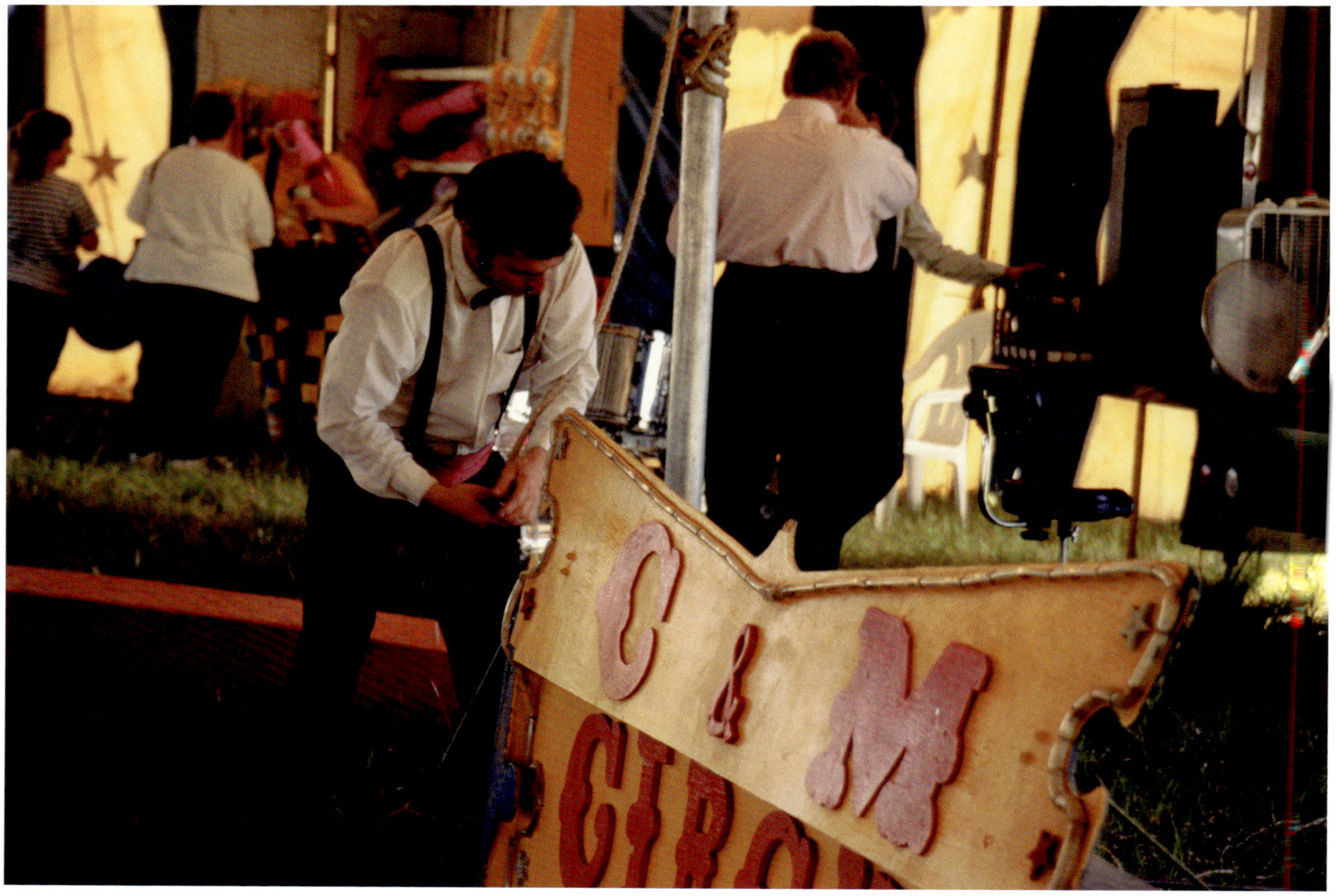

PLATE 225

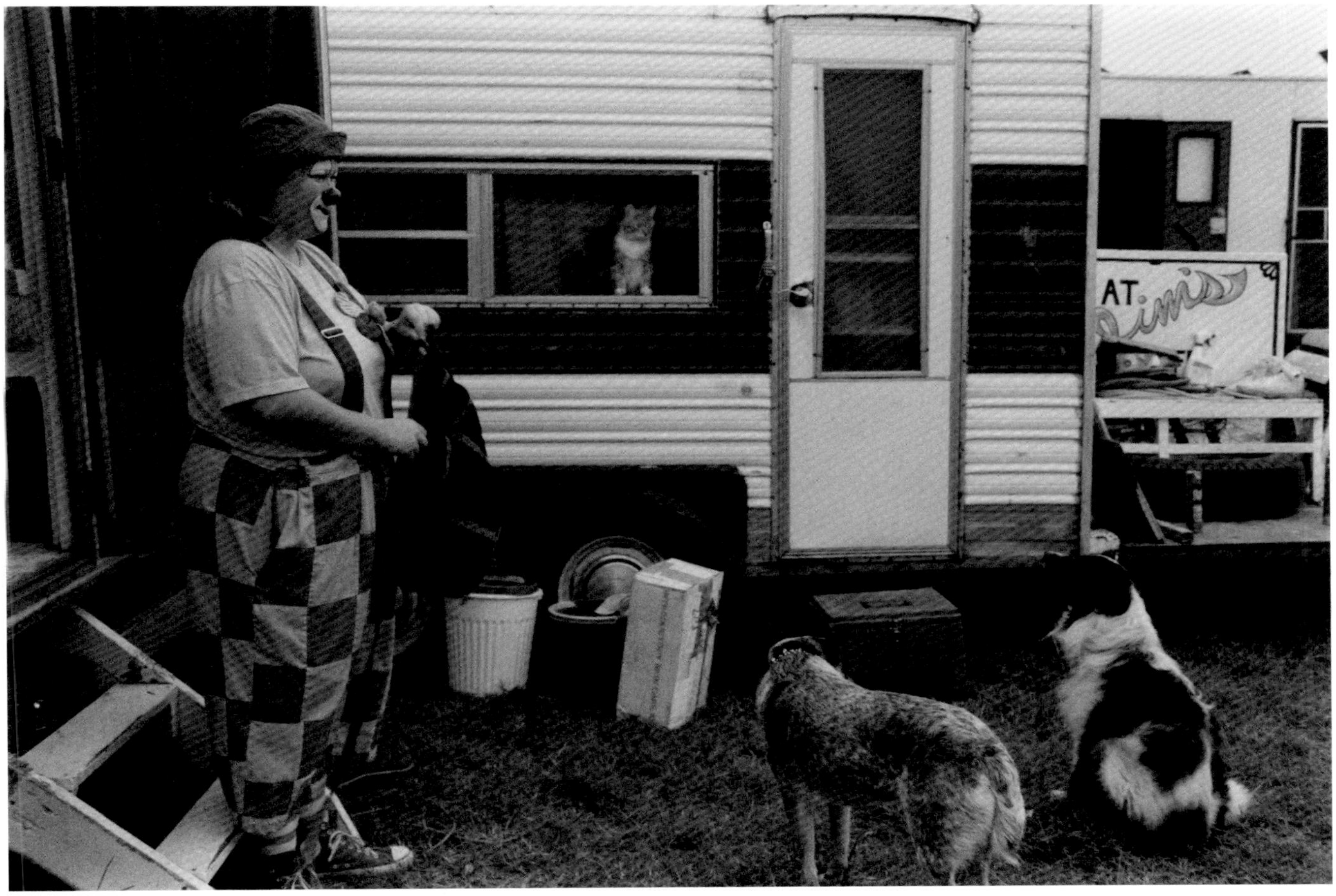

PLATE 226

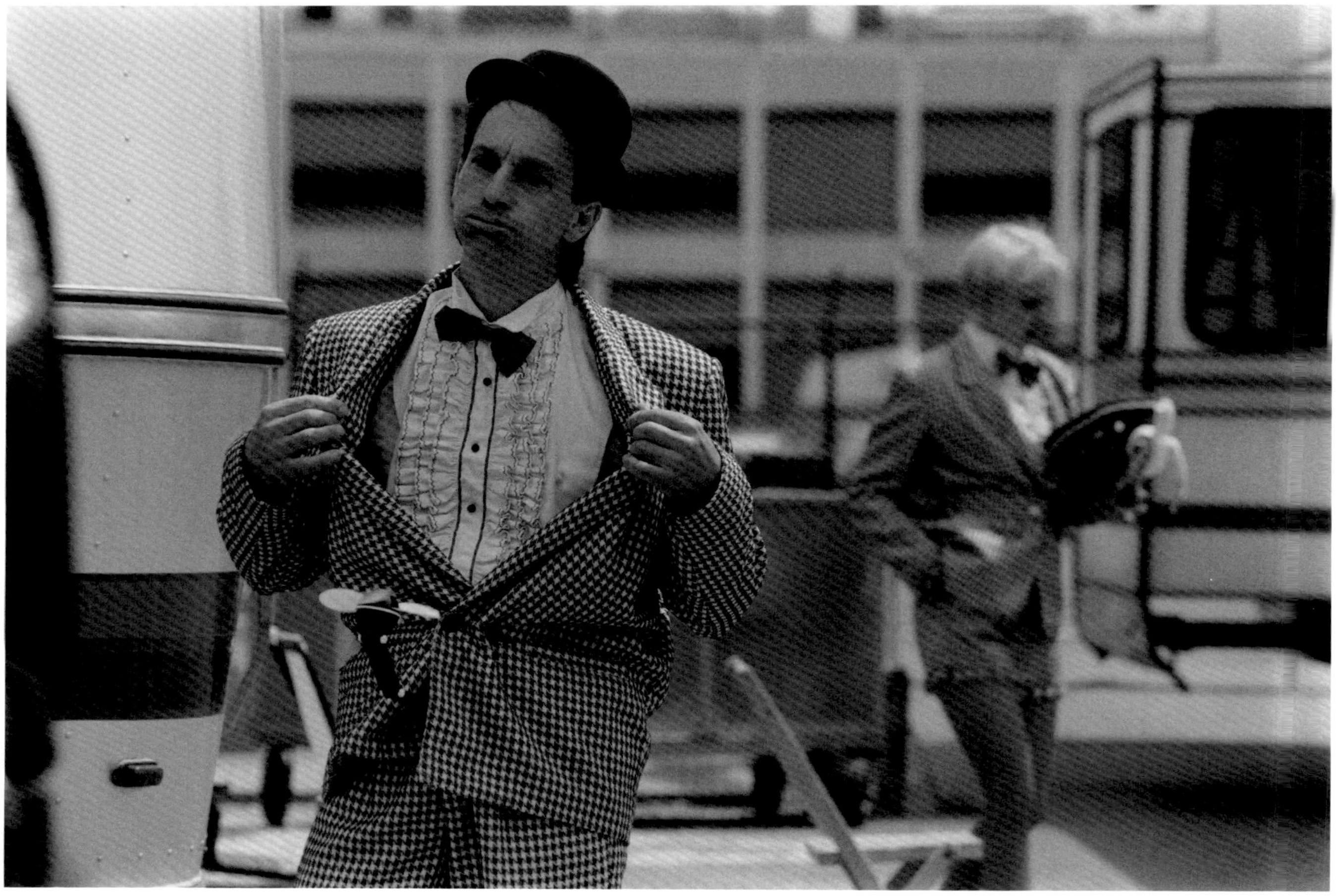

PLATE 227

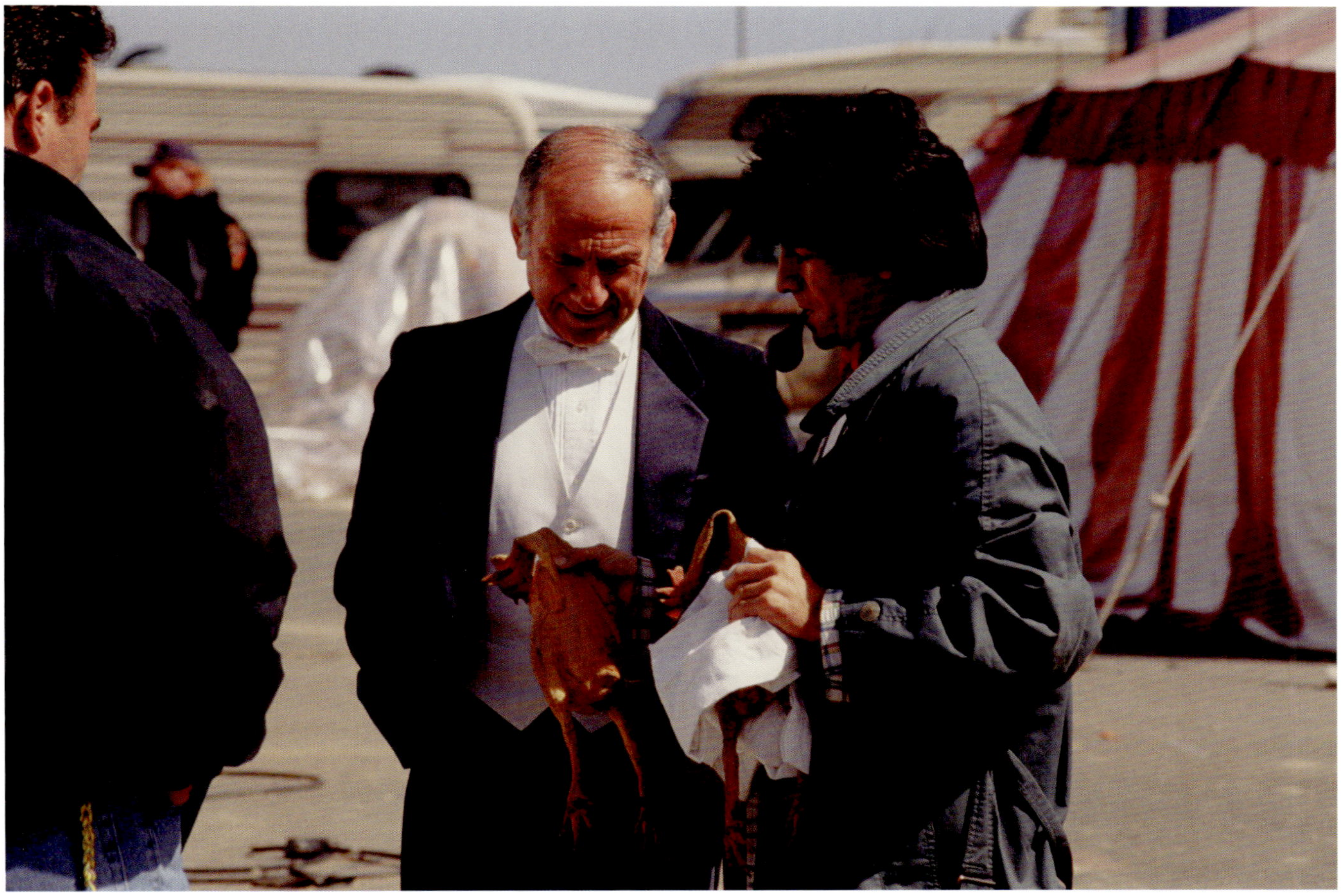

PLATE 228

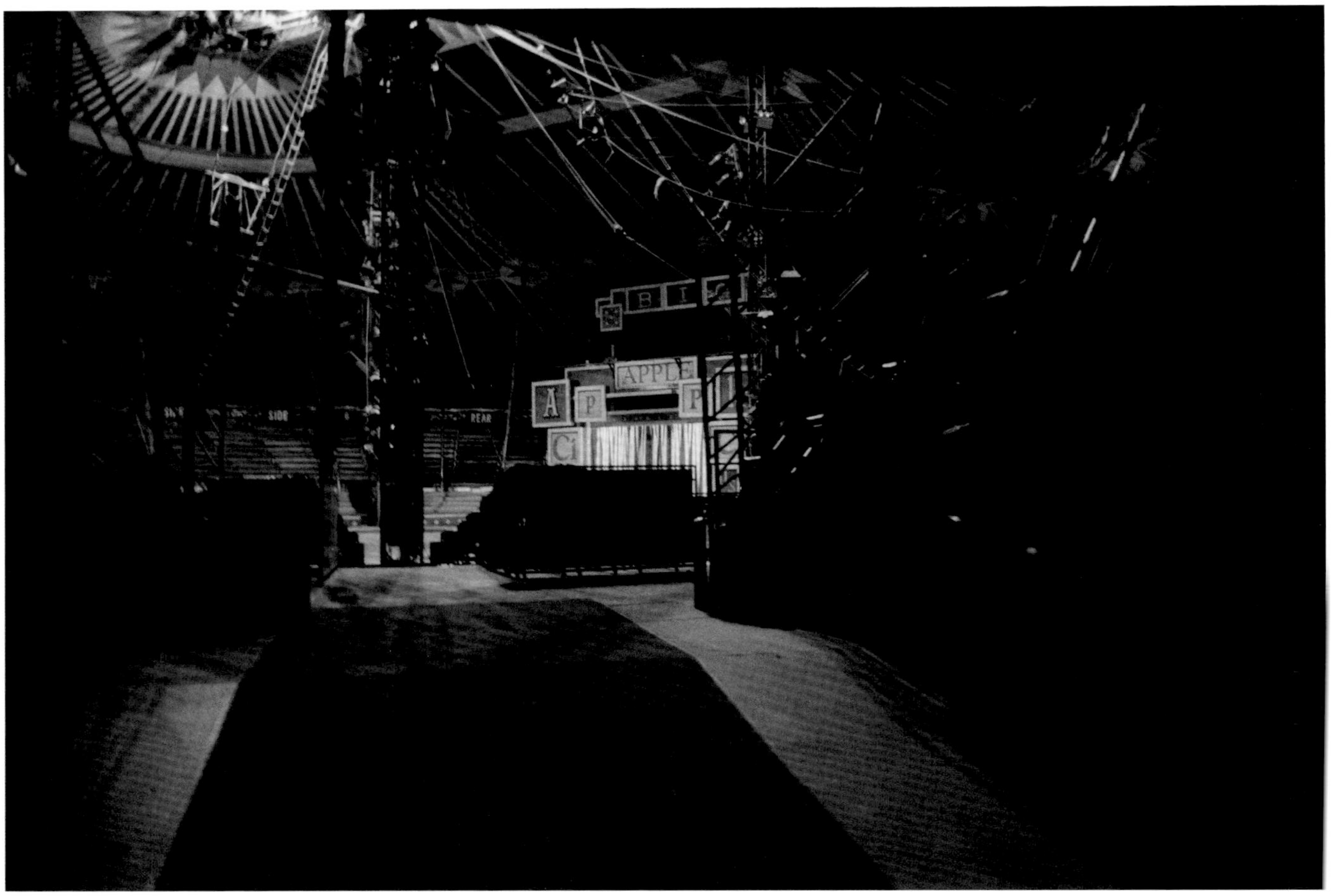

PLATE 229

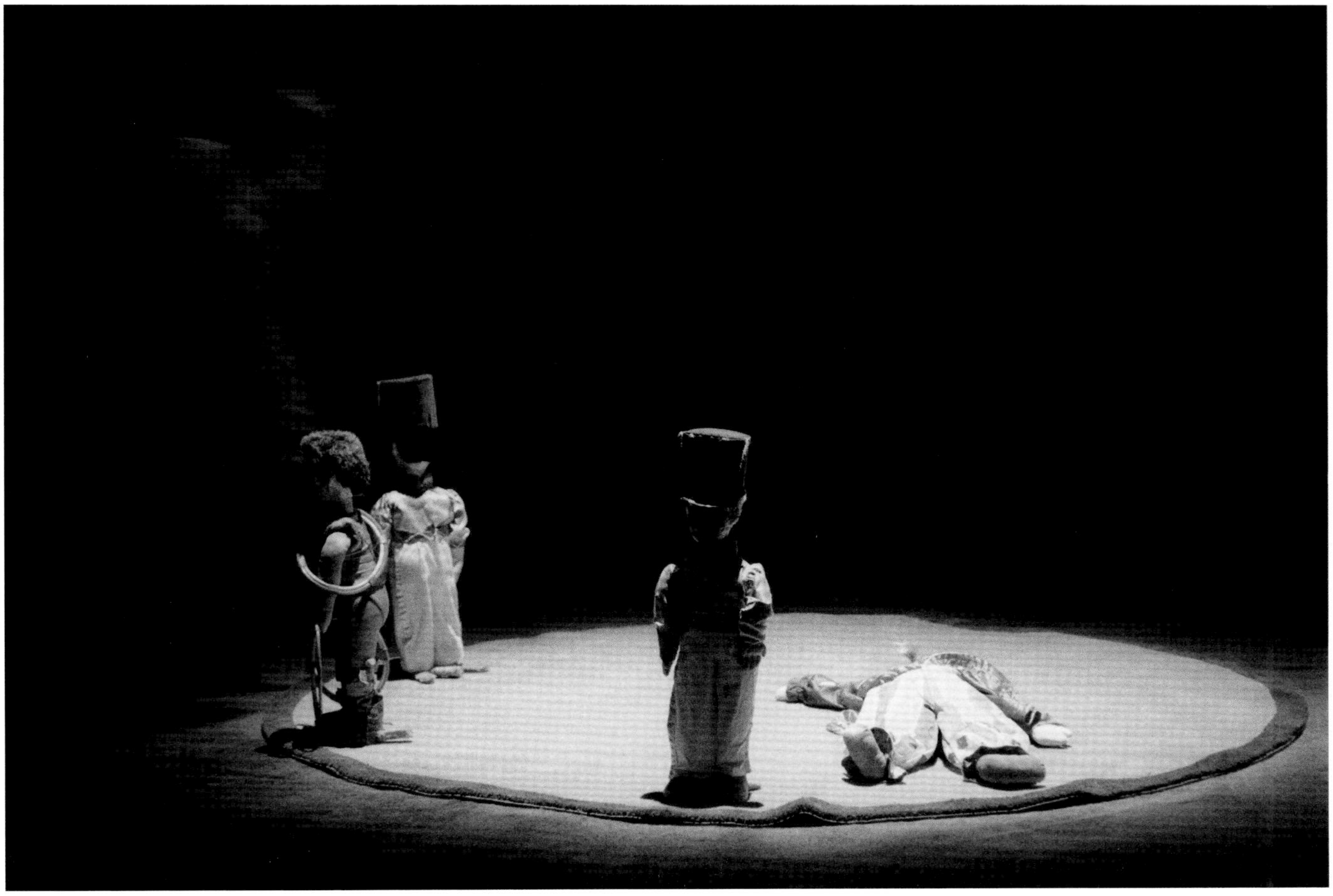

PLATE 230

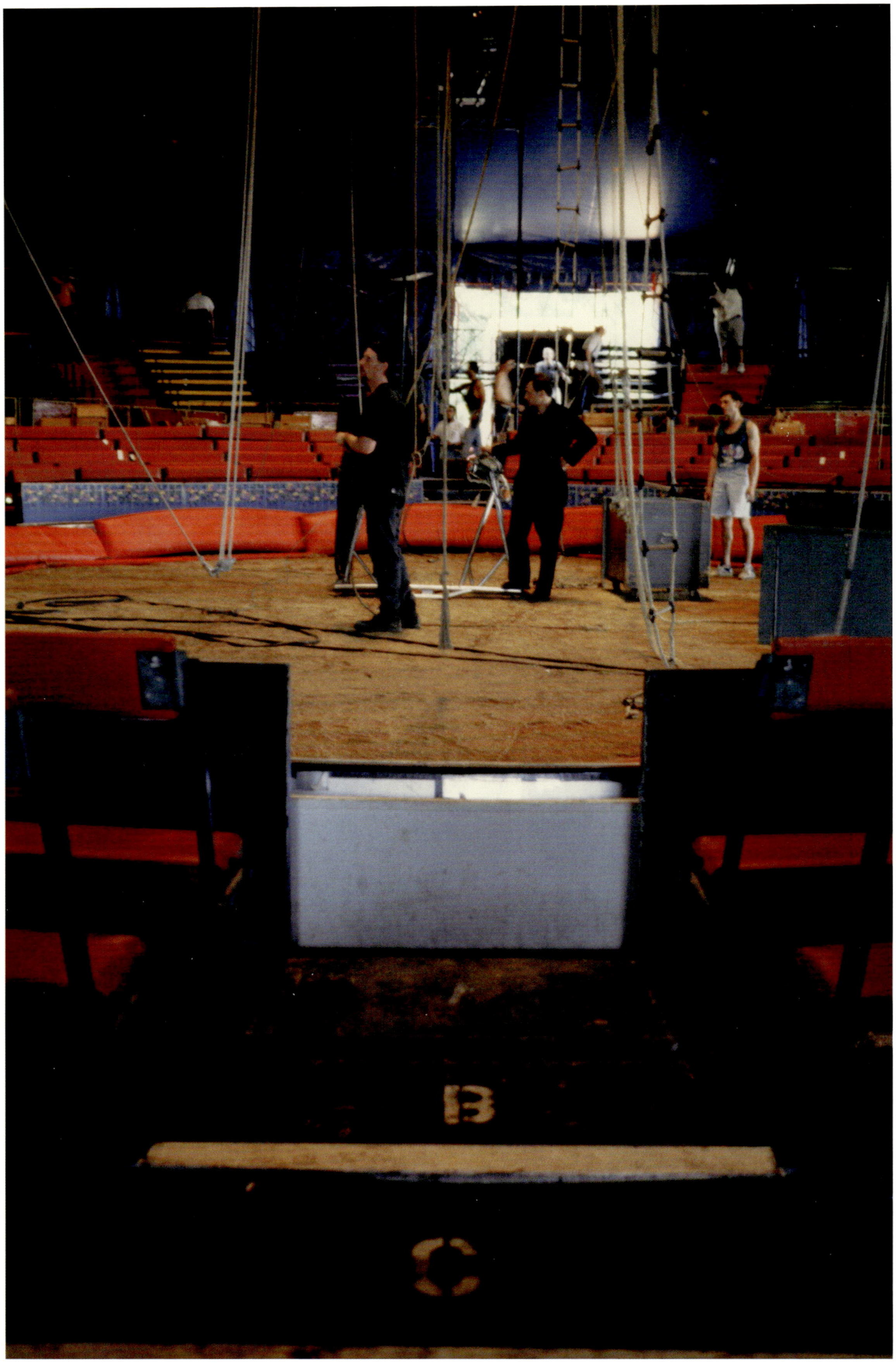

PLATE 231

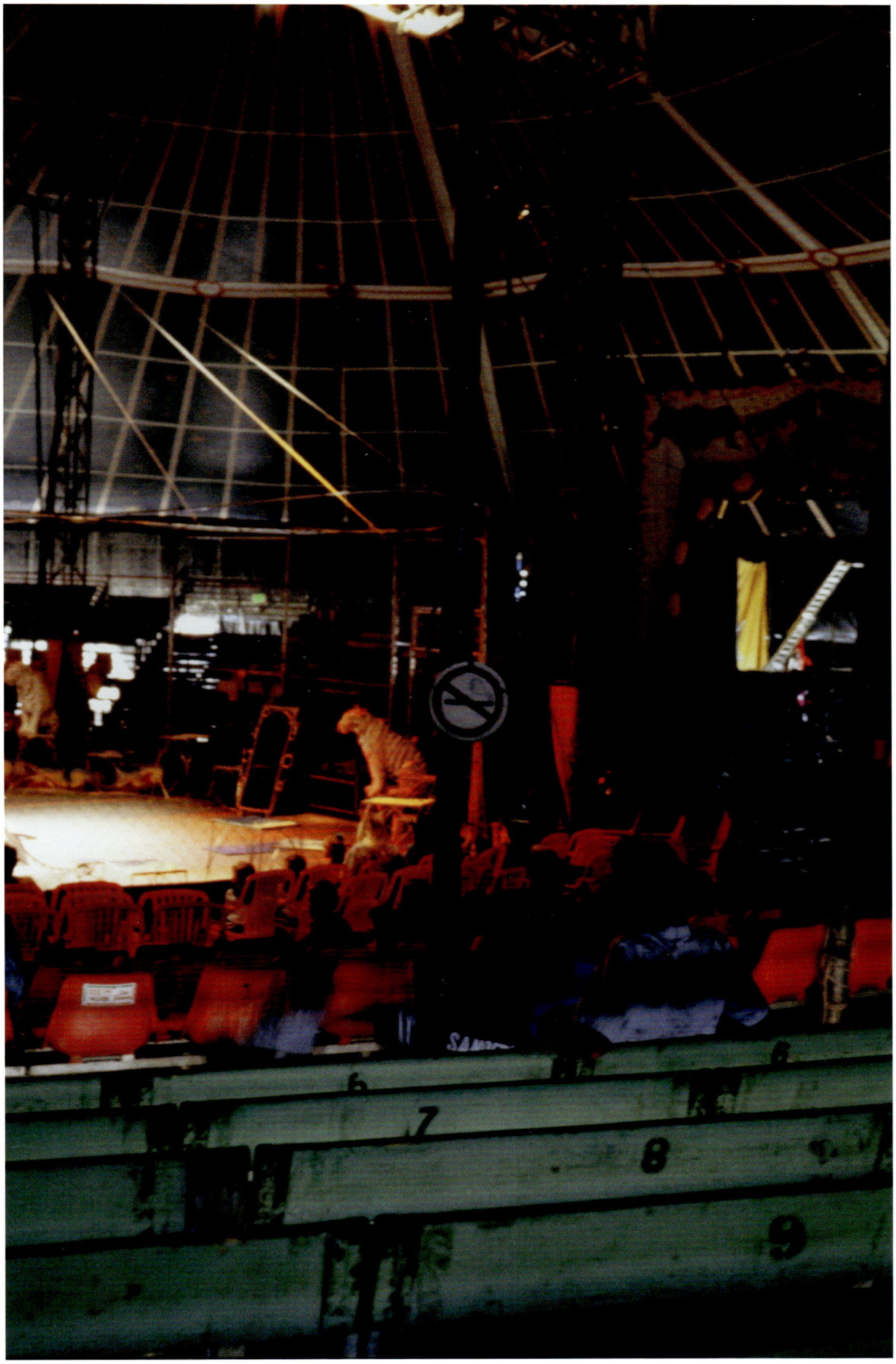

PLATE 232

We have more nationalities in this business than anybody else that I can think of, but we all have one thing in common: circus. Performers, workers, artistic directors, doesn't matter: we're here to give a show, to give the people a magical experience. The circus is in its own little realm, its own little bubble. We put the show up; the people come; they see the magic of it all—then they go away and say they had a great time.

—Guy Pickup, assistant tent manager, Big Apple Circus (1995)

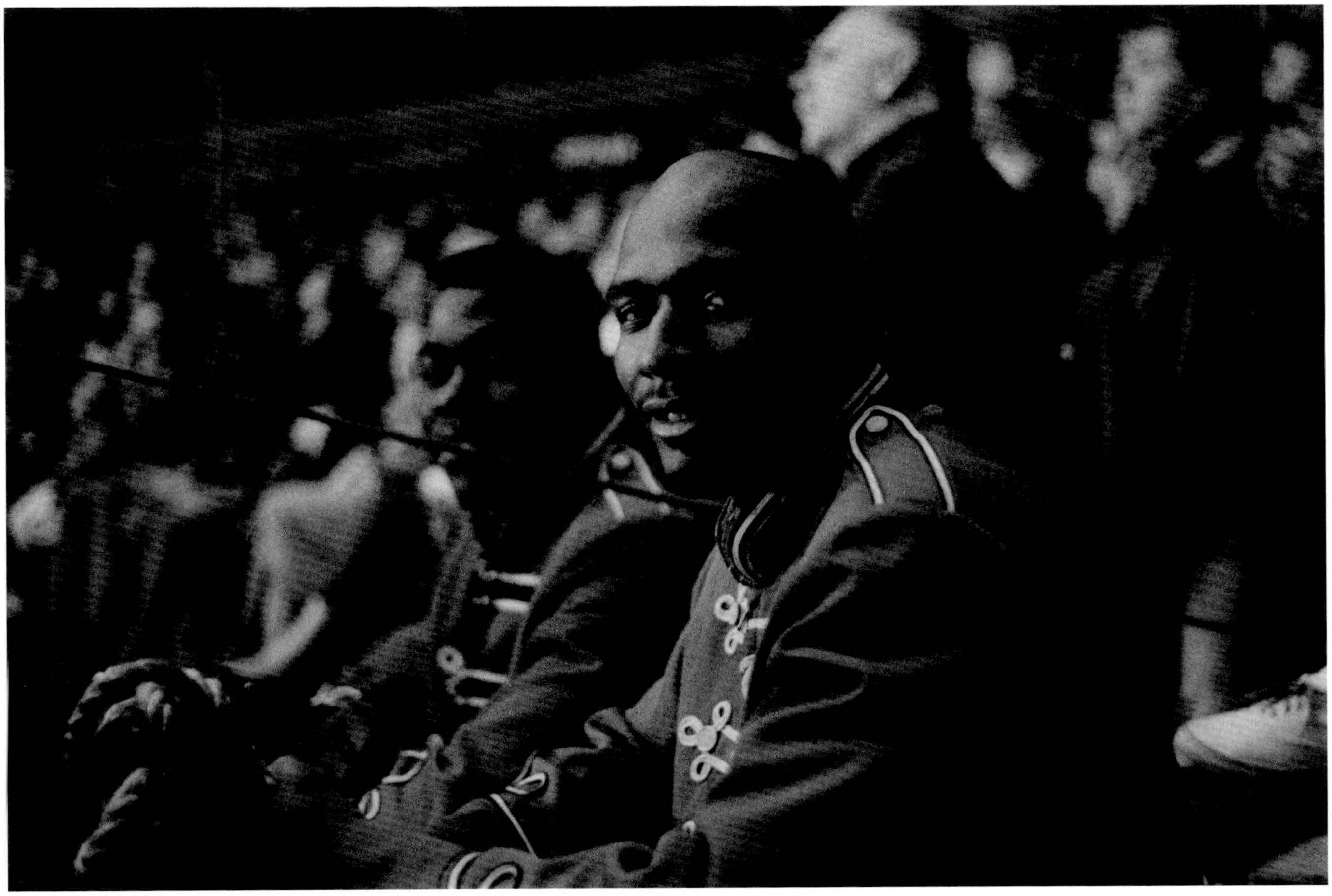

PLATE 233

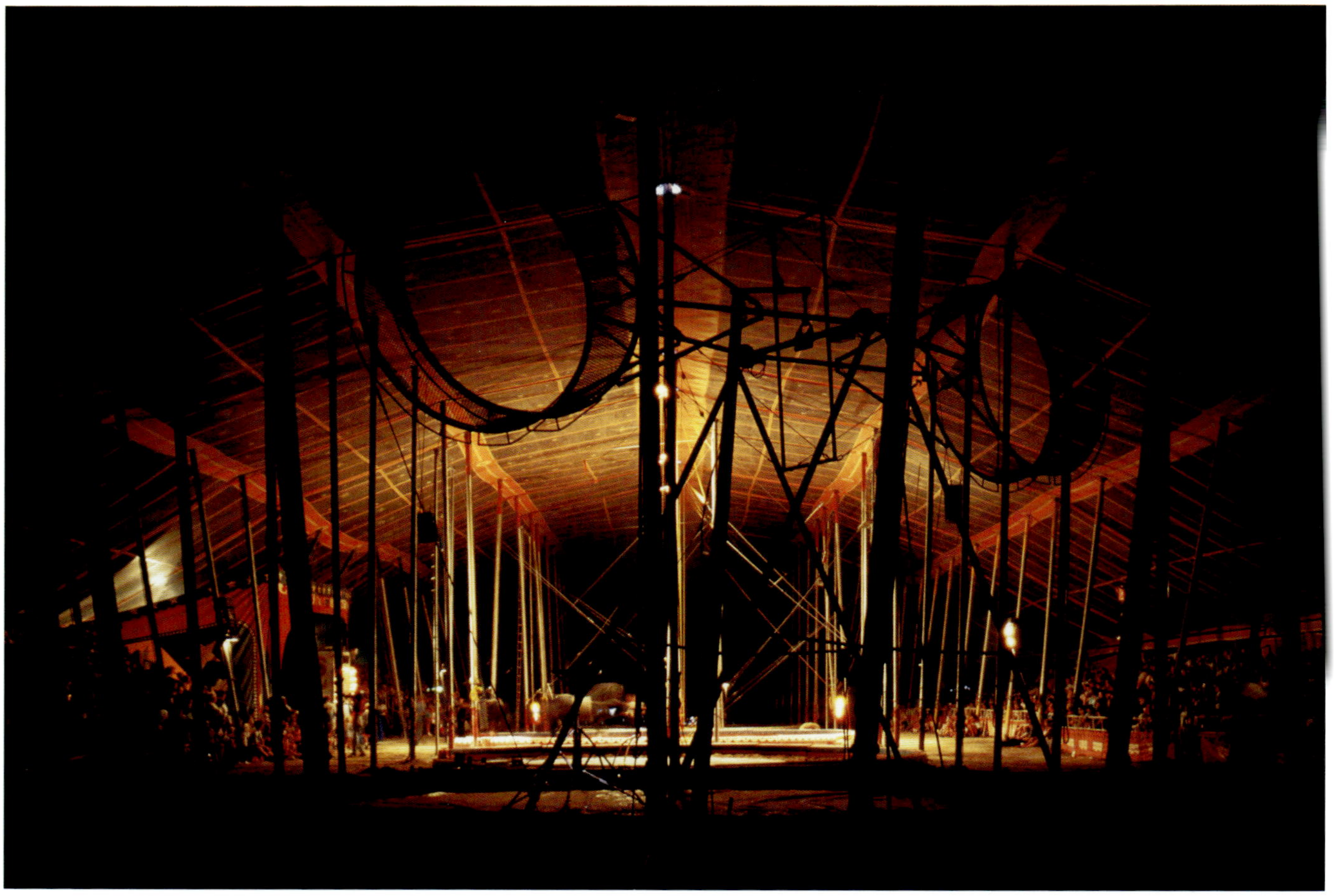

PLATE 234

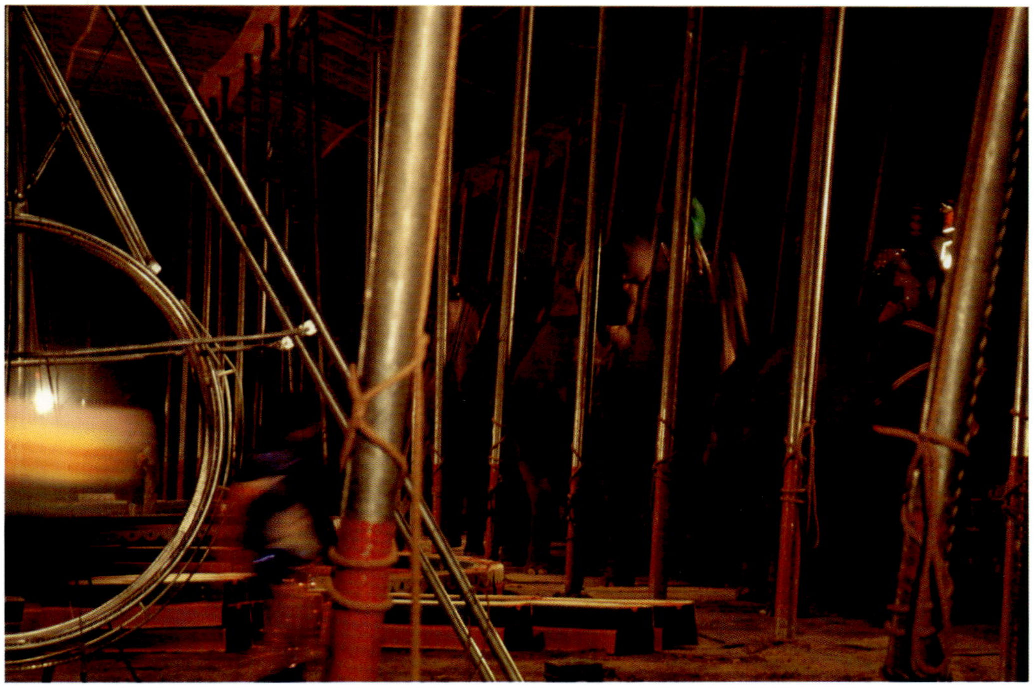

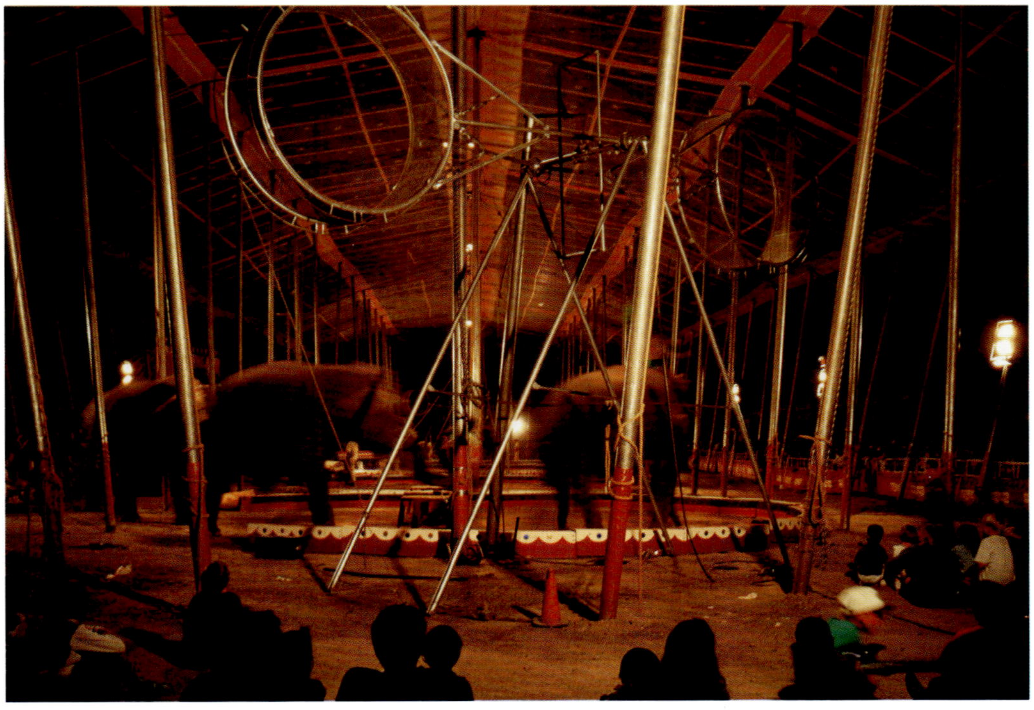

PLATES 235 & 236

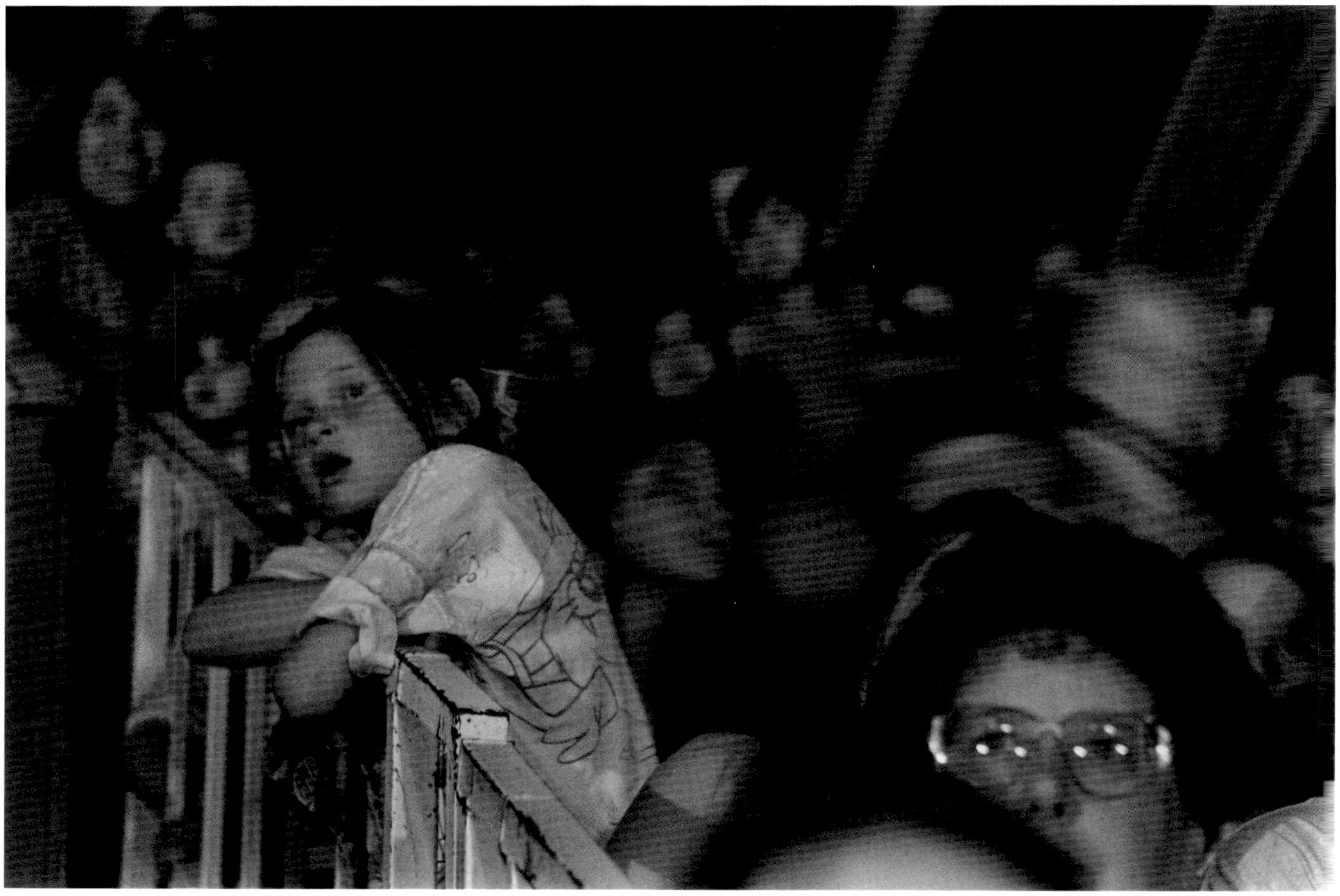

PLATE 237

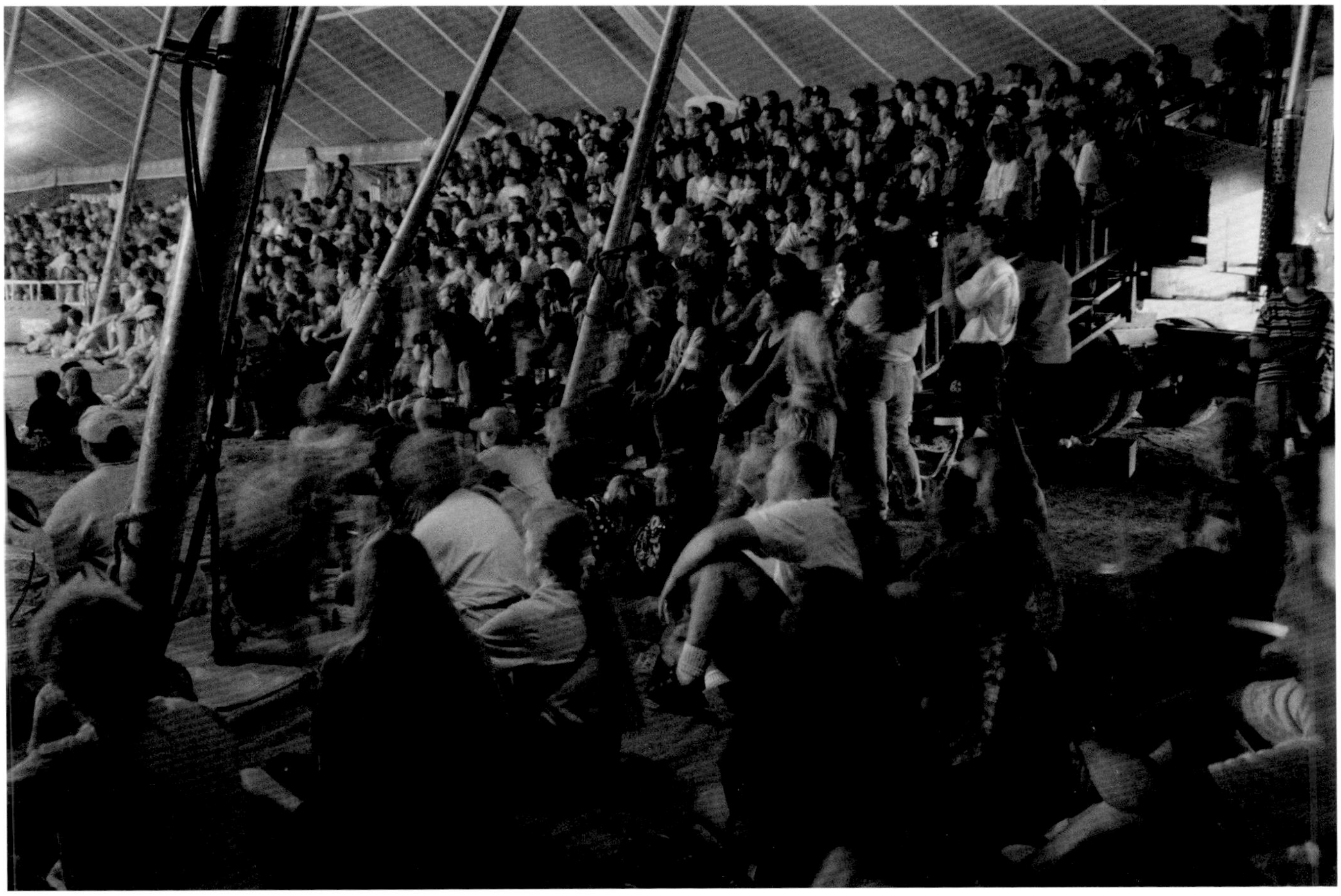

PLATE 238

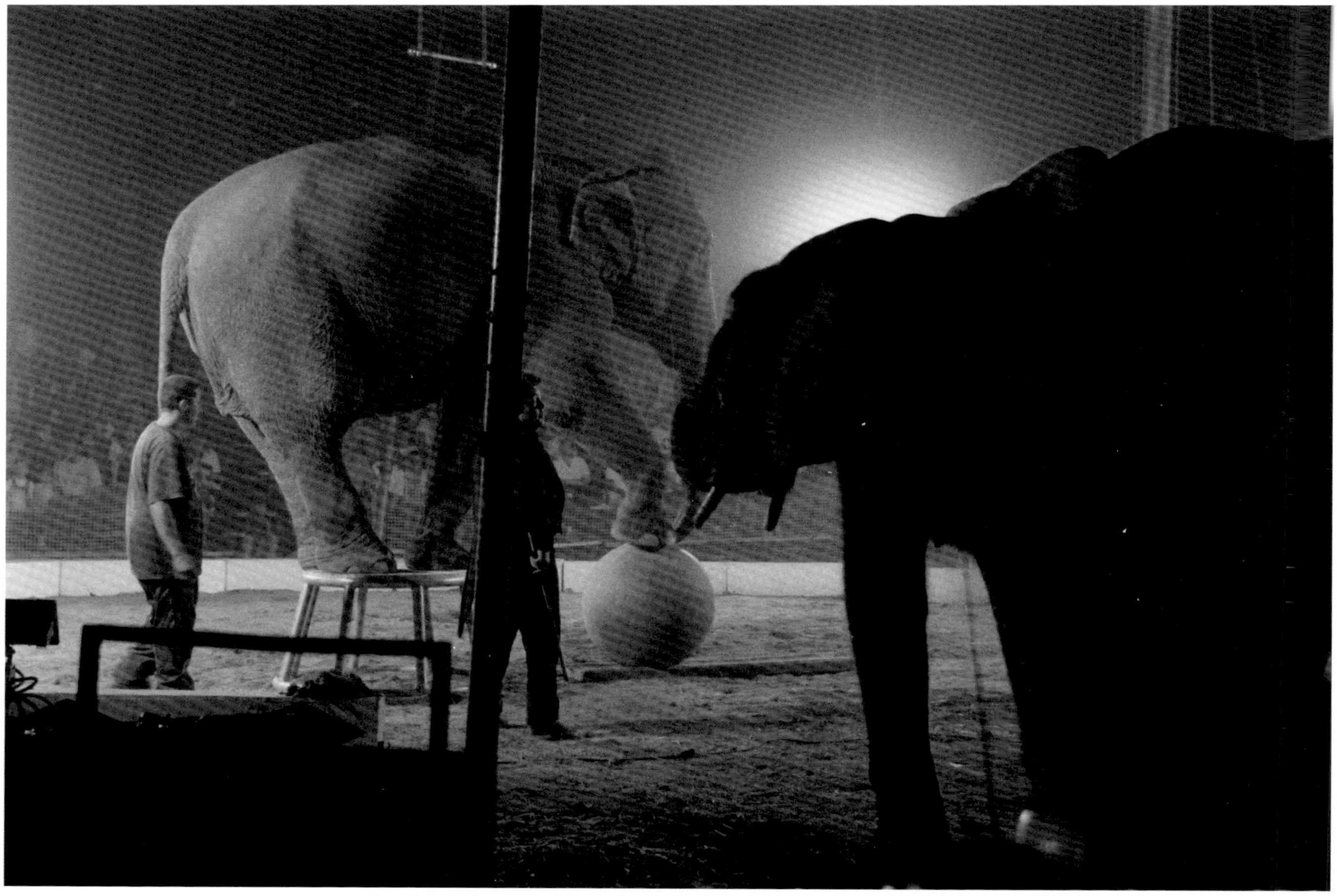

PLATE 239

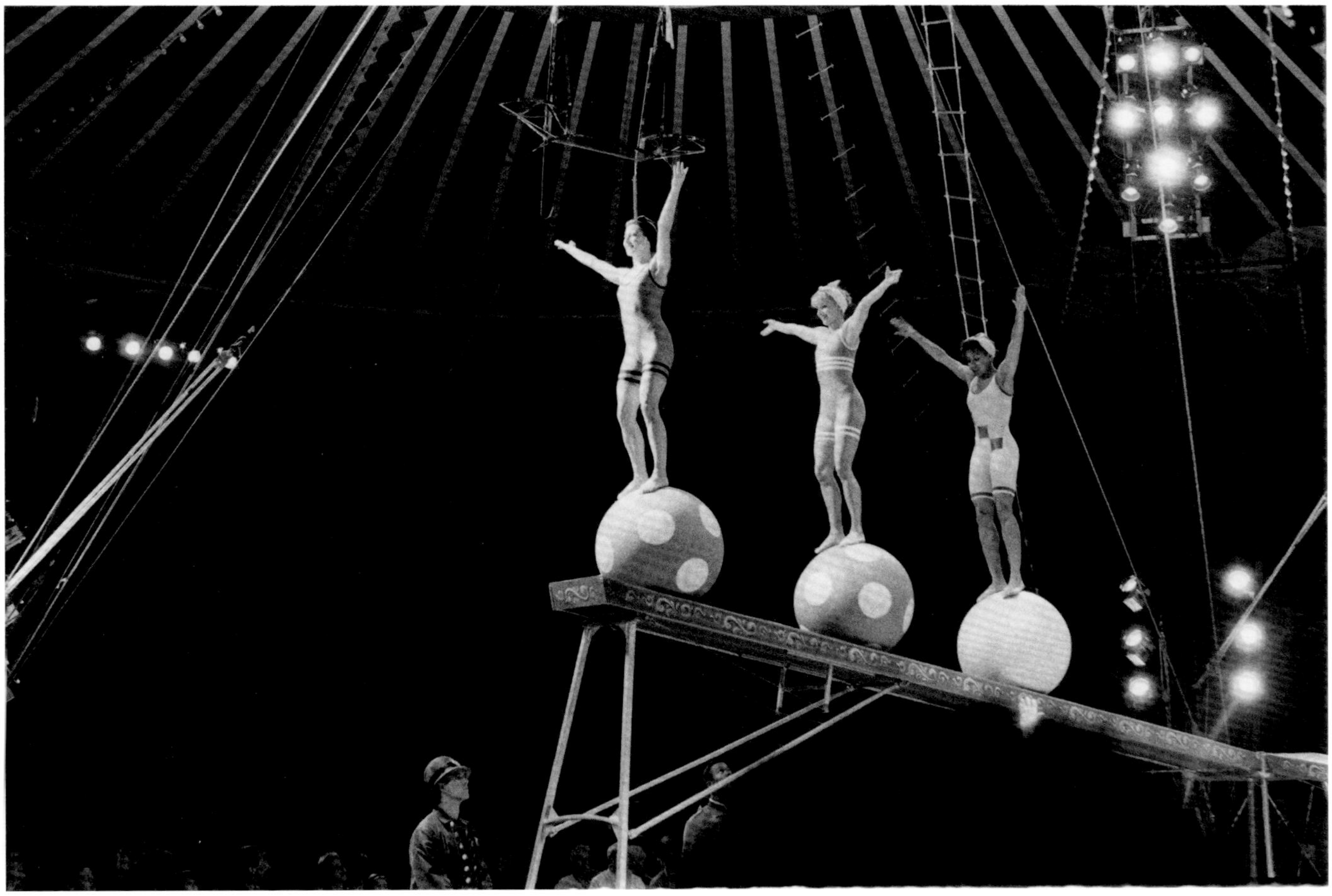

PLATE 240

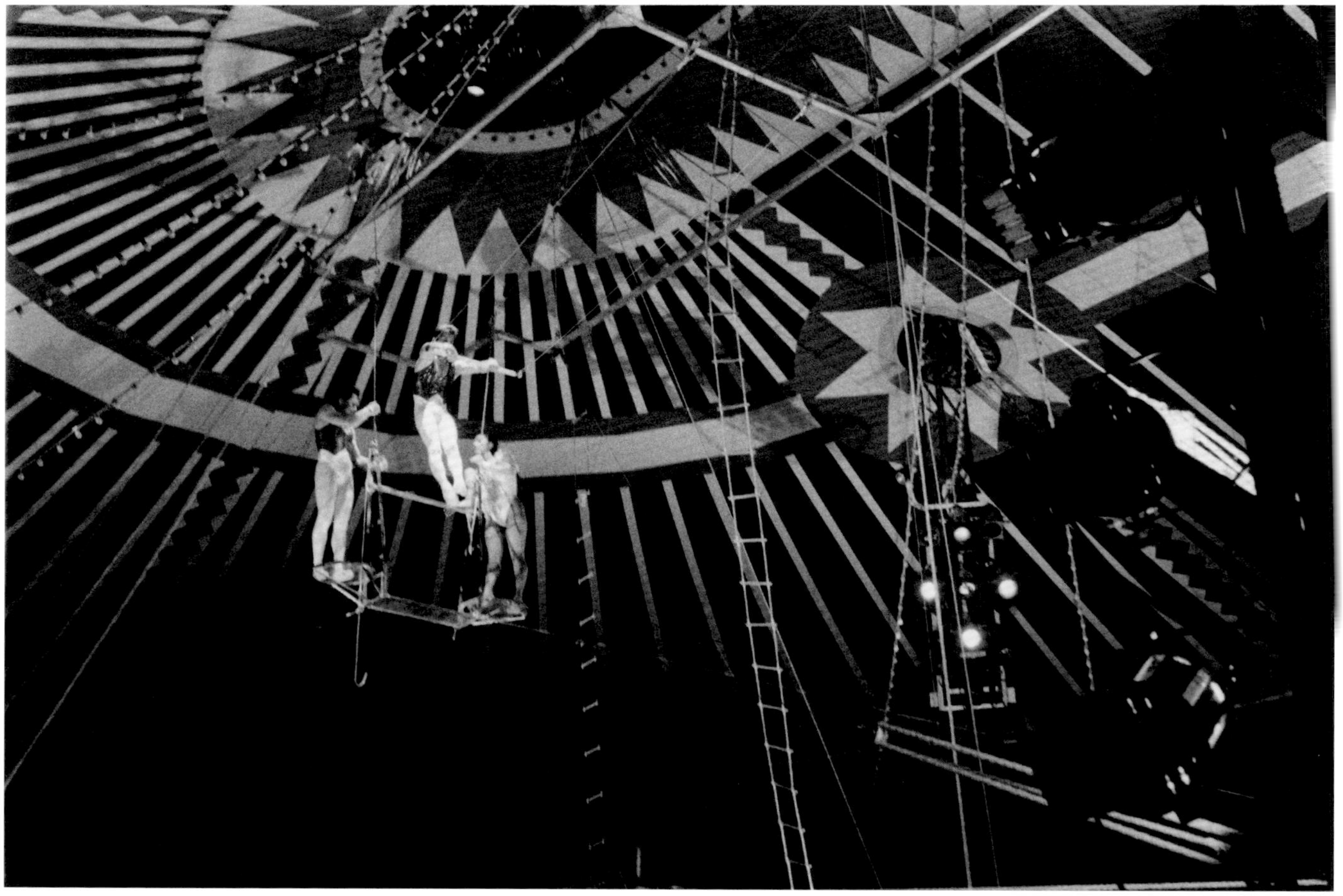

PLATE 241

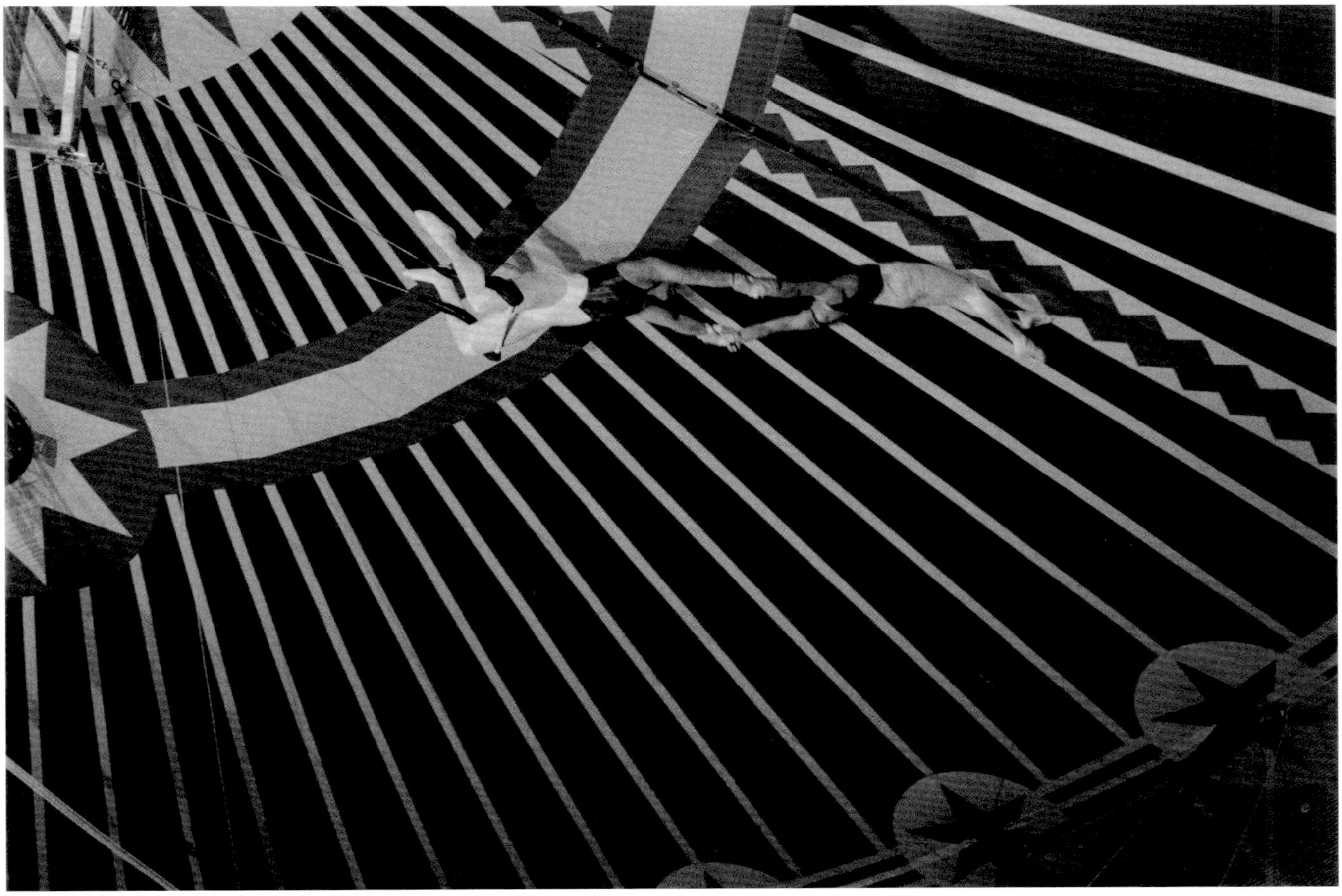

PLATE 242

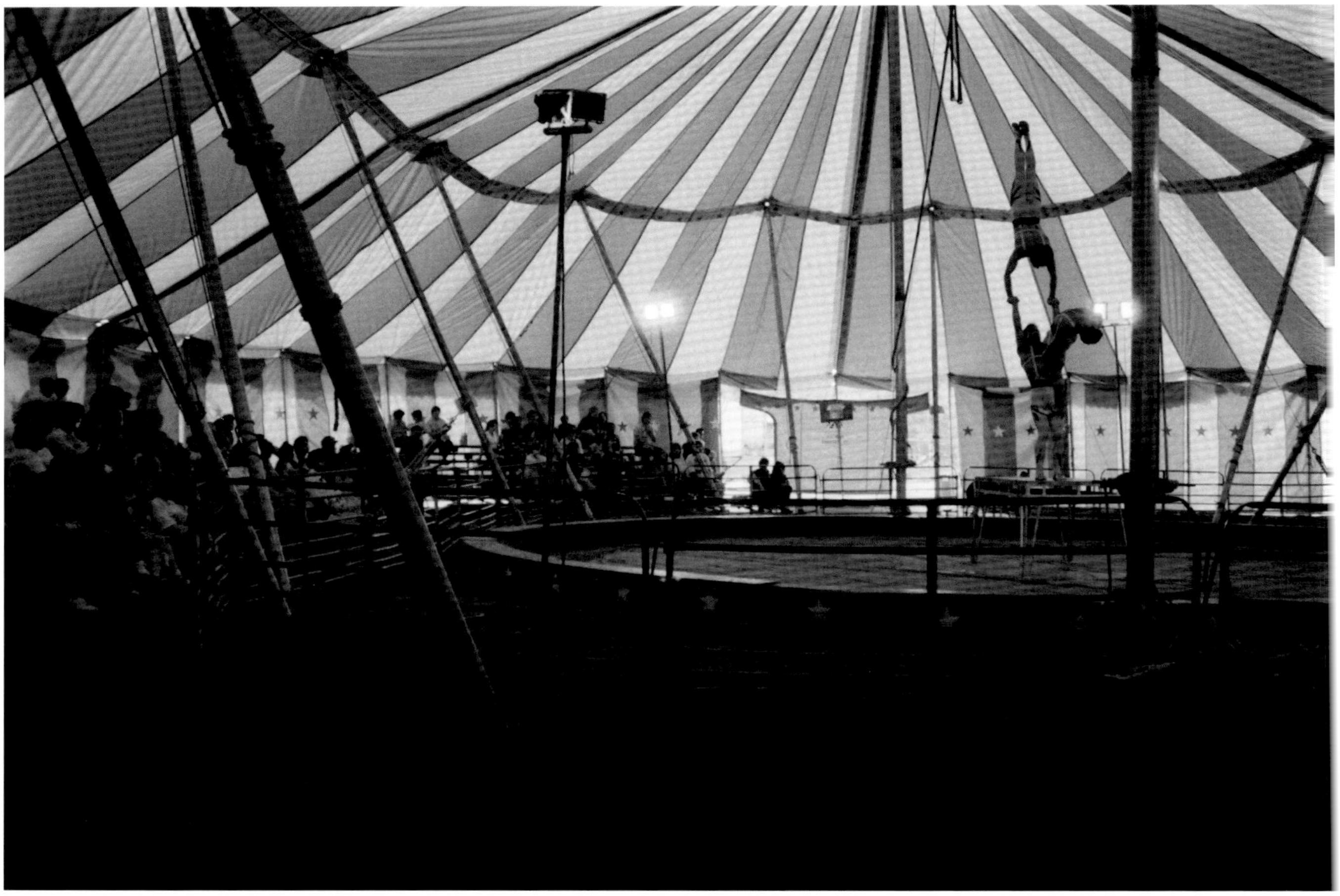

PLATE 243

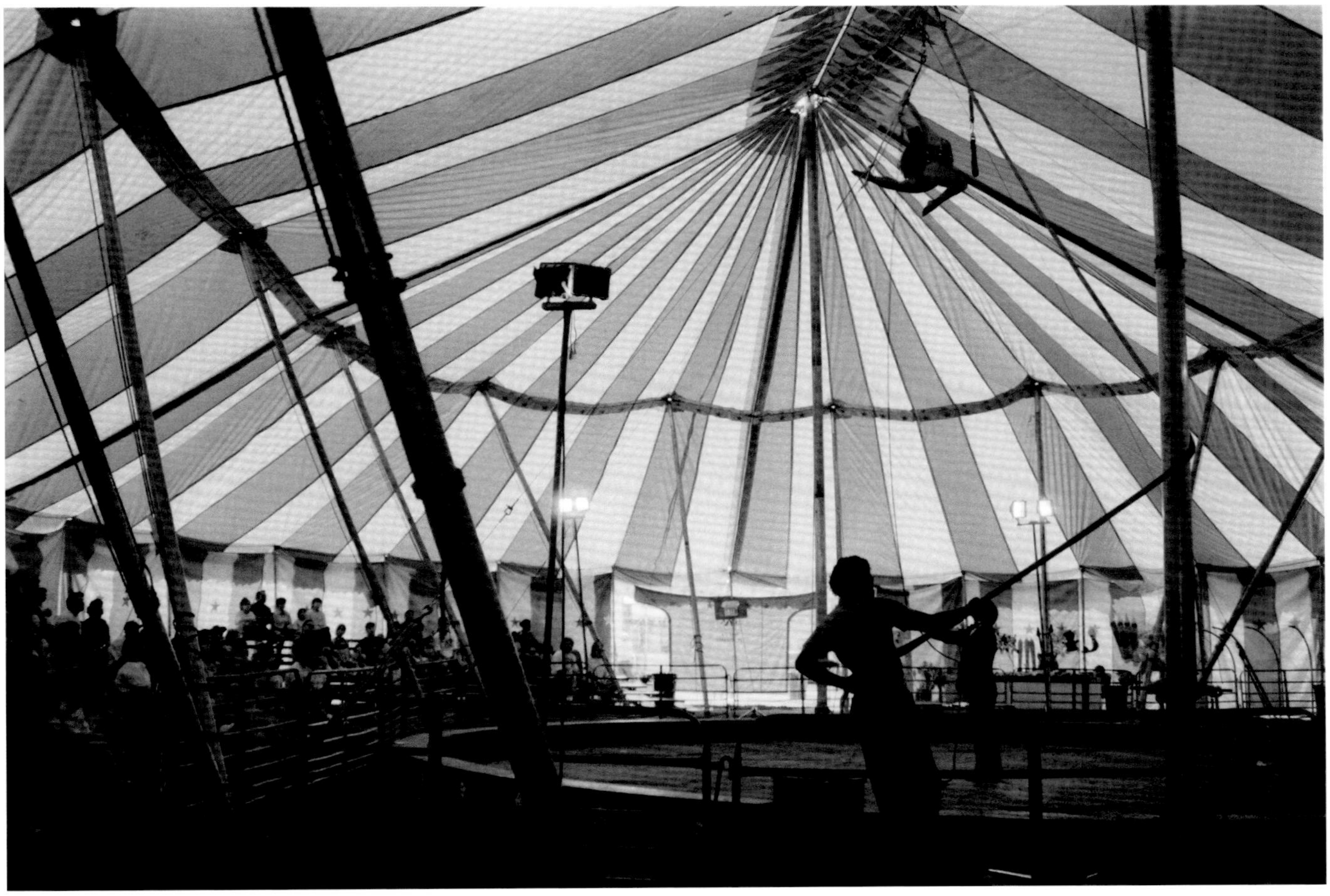

PLATE 244

★ ★ ★ ★ ★ ★ ★ ★ ★

When the trapeze artist flies, for a moment we all fly.

—Paul Binder, co-founder and artistic director, Big Apple Circus (1995)

★ ★ ★ ★ ★ ★ ★ ★ ★

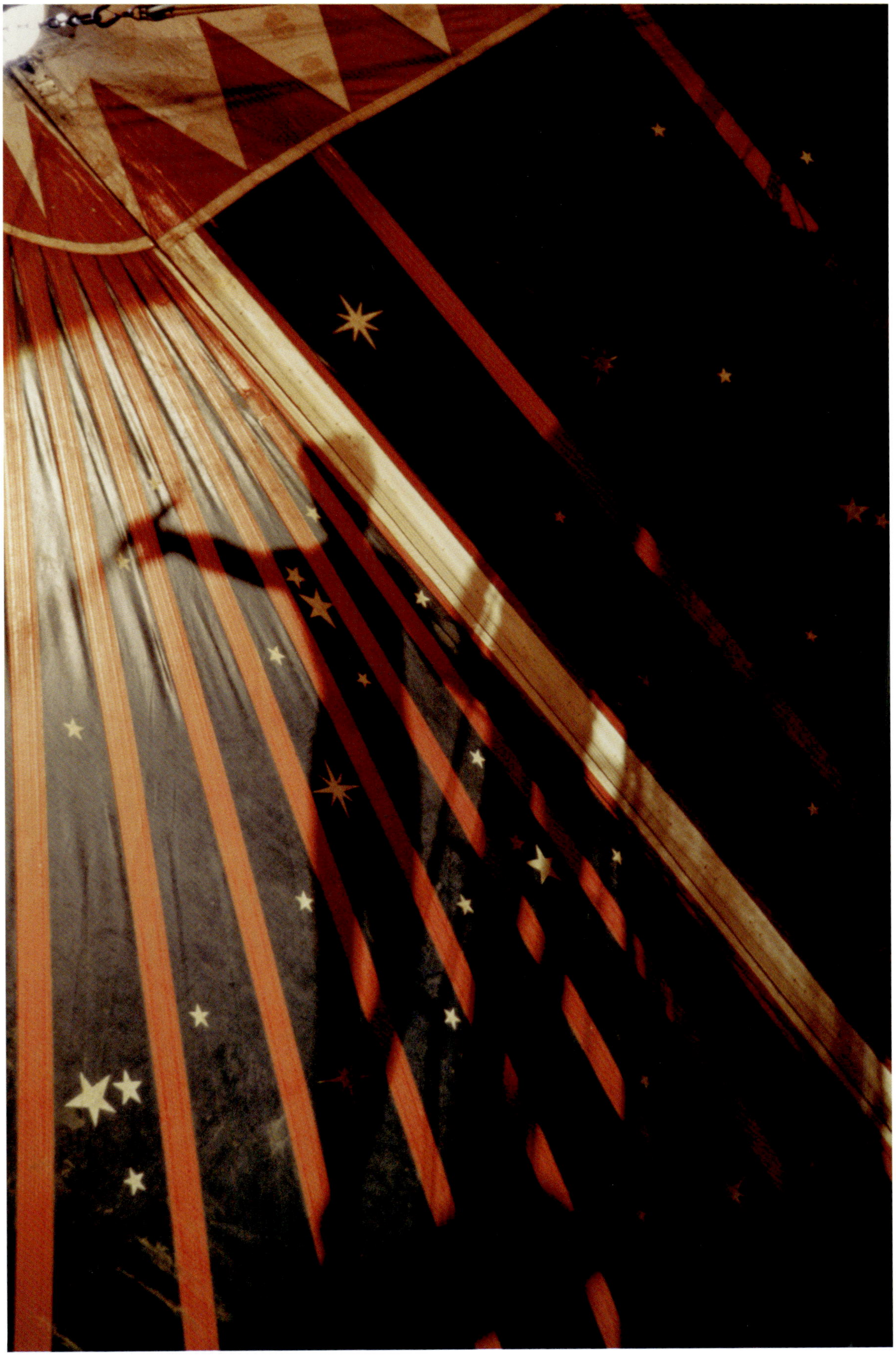

PLATE 245

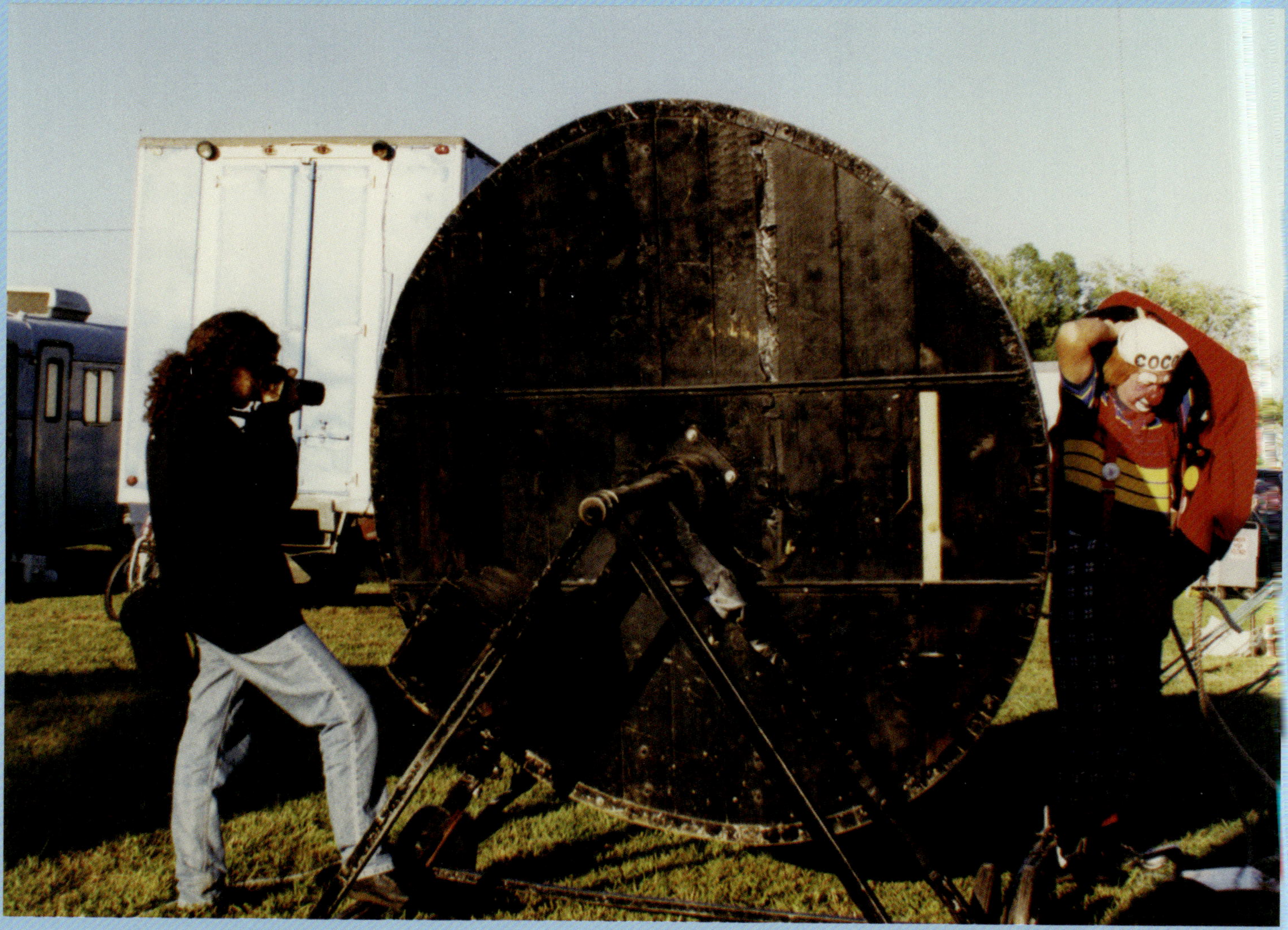

Running Away with the Circus A Photographer's Story

DAWN V. ROGALA

Y'know, people really do this for a living. They're out there living in trucks and trailers and washing their hair in buckets and putting on feathers and throwing triple somersaults in mid-air. . . . These guys are for real. They actually *do* this.

—Tim Tegge, Clyde Beatty-Cole Bros. Circus, 1995

I was on my way to a job interview in the spring of 1992 when I saw the Big Apple Circus tent set up in a parking lot. I'd never even been to a circus before. Skipping the interview, I walked up to a couple of guys standing by the **pretty fence*** that marked the boundary between public and private space on the circus lot. "Hi! Would it be possible for me to take some pictures?" I soon quit my job, bought an old RV, and spent the next six years on and off the road, traveling with big and small shows, photographing the daily life of the American circus (Figure 1). It was one of the best times of my life. And in the end, it was a record of a world rapidly vanishing from the American cultural landscape.

This book contains images and interview excerpts from the eleven full-time, tented American circuses with continuous travel schedules at the time of this project (1992–1998)—the last of this country's traveling circuses. This work documents a world that is rapidly vanishing—more than half of the shows that appear in this book are no longer in operation. I was working as a graphic designer at the time, but I was restless. One night, while out at a bar with folks from that first circus, someone asked me what I was going to do with all those pictures. What followed was a kind of out-of-body experience. I could hear myself answering, talking about a large-scale documentary project, and I remember thinking, "Hey, that sounds like a great idea. I could do that." I just had to figure out how.

With help from performers and staff from Big Apple Circus, I narrowed down a list of circuses from the trade magazine *Amusement Business* to a selection of a dozen full-time tent shows. (One show closed

FIGURE 1. Photographing Graham Polakovs (Coco the Clown) nearby props for the knife-throwing act, Walker Bros. Circus, 1995.

* Each initial use of circus terminology is **boldface**. There are numerous online listings of show lingo, including Wayne Keyser's comprehensive accounting of circus, carny, sideshow, and vaudeville lingo at www.goodmagic.com.

before I went on the road.) I wanted to experience the traditional American circus, the full-time, traveling tent show. The guidelines for selection were that the show needed to be held under a tent all season, the season needed to be at least eight months long, and the circus needed to move several times a week. (Big Apple Circus was the only exception to this last rule.) This is the traditional American circus—the full-time, traveling tent show (also known as **mud show**). I wrote letters and visited each show's **winter quarters** (off-season base of operations) in the autumn months, and coordinated schedules and permissions to join each show on the road. Behind the scenes and unbeknownst to me, people spoke on my behalf to family and colleagues at other shows, paving the way for me.

I lived in an RV that looked like an old ice cream truck. I purchased it from a guy who repaired circus vehicles, and I think it topped out at ten miles per gallon of gas. I needed to be economical with my mileage. Circus travel schedules are restricted information to avoid **day and dating** (when one show arrives unannounced to capitalize on another show's advertising), but the shows worked with me to help plan visits to others traveling the same region, and I would visit all the circuses in one area before taking the long drive across country to join another group of shows. Short trips home to the East Coast helped me earn just enough money to go back on the road. I stayed with some shows in the spring at the beginning of the

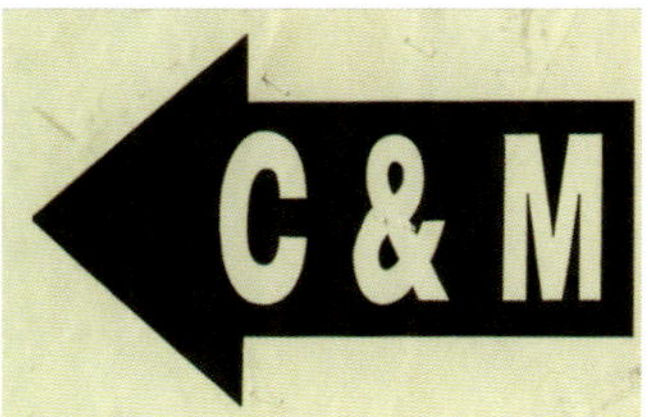

FIGURE 2. Route arrow, Culpepper & Merriweather Circus, 1996. **Route arrows** are posted by the **24-hour man**, a member of the **advance crew** who travels the route to the next lot, prepares driving directions, and places arrows along the route to help direct the convoy. Arrows are usually placed in multiples, and the orientation of the grouped arrows provides additional information (slow, turn ahead, etc.).

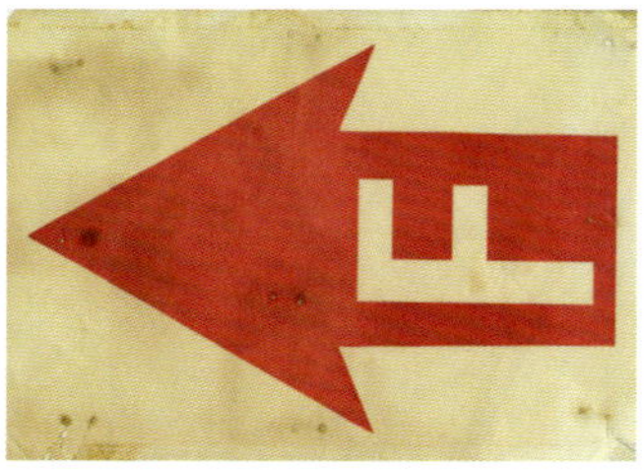

FIGURE 3. Route arrow, Franzen Brothers Circus, 1994.

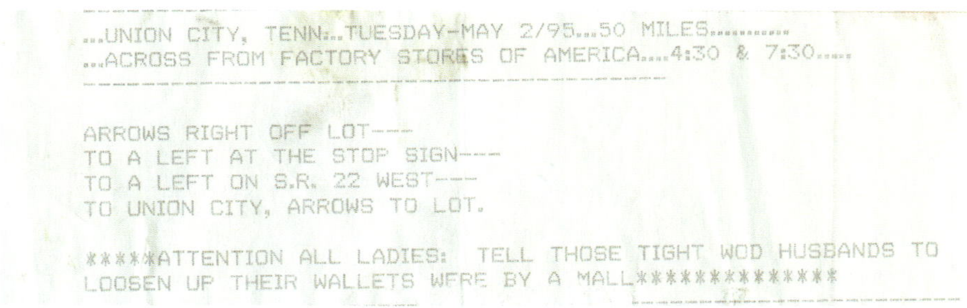
...UNION CITY, TENN...TUESDAY-MAY 2/95...50 MILES..........
...ACROSS FROM FACTORY STORES OF AMERICA....4:30 & 7:30.....

ARROWS RIGHT OFF LOT---
TO A LEFT AT THE STOP SIGN---
TO A LEFT ON S.R. 22 WEST---
TO UNION CITY, ARROWS TO LOT.

*****ATTENTION ALL LADIES: TELL THOSE TIGHT WOD HUSBANDS TO
LOOSEN UP THEIR WALLETS WERE BY A MALL**************

FIGURE 4. Route slip, Kelly Miller Circus, 1995. **Route slips** are placed on the windshield of each vehicle the morning of the jump and contain the most up-to-date information provided by the 24-hour man. Route slips may include alternative routes to avoid construction, or witty sayings, birthday announcements, and so on. This slip says, "Attention all ladies: Tell those tightwod [*sic*] husbands to loosen up their wallets. We're [setting up the circus] by a mall."

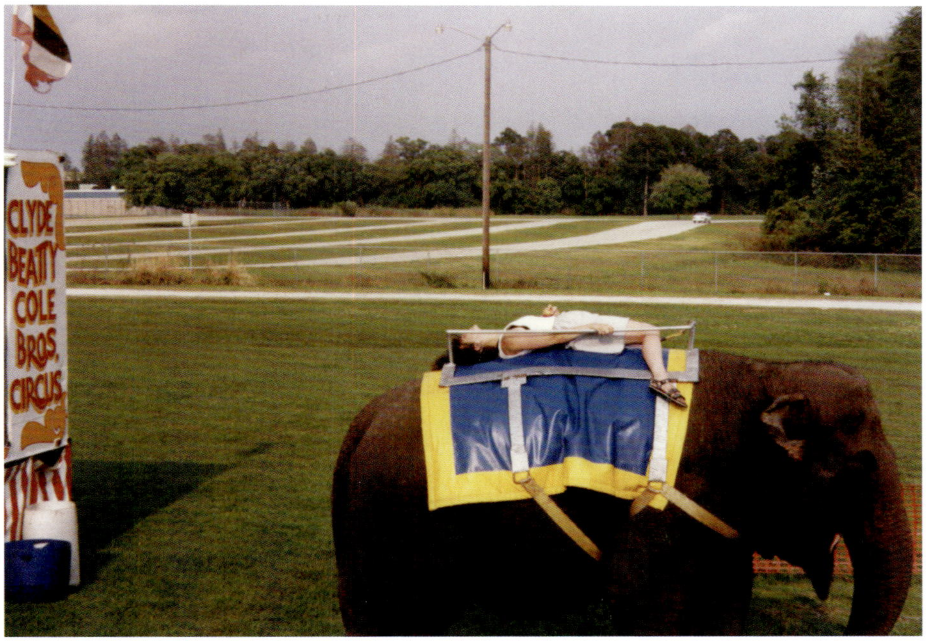

FIGURE 5. Goofing around on the **midway**, Clyde Beatty-Cole Bros. Circus, 1995. At another show on a muddy lot, I parked near the midway, and the route for the elephant ride made a circle around my RV.

season, some shows midseason, and some shows at the end of the season as the weather grew cold. I spent weeks with each circus. Up each morning before the rising sun to **jump** to a new town. Two shows each day; one show on jump days (Figures 2–4).

There were small shows where the concessions guy also did the dog act, assisted in the horse act, and helped with the tent during **tear down** (dismantling of the lot). Some shows were so large the convoy carried three truck cabs on a flatbed in case one broke down during the jump; nothing quite like stopping at a weigh station and presenting papers that say "Contents: Tigers"! By the end of my travels, I had crossed forty-two states with eleven different circuses, some for multiple seasons: Big Apple Circus (1992–1995), Carson & Barnes Circus (1995), Circus Vargas (1998), Clyde Beatty-Cole Bros. Circus (1995), Culpepper & Merriweather Circus (1996), Franzen Brothers Circus (1994, 1996), Kelly Miller Circus (1995), Roberts Bros. Circus (1994), Sterling & Reid Bros. Circus (1998), Vidbel's Olde Tyme Circus (1993), and Walker Bros. Circus (1995). (Figures 5, 6)

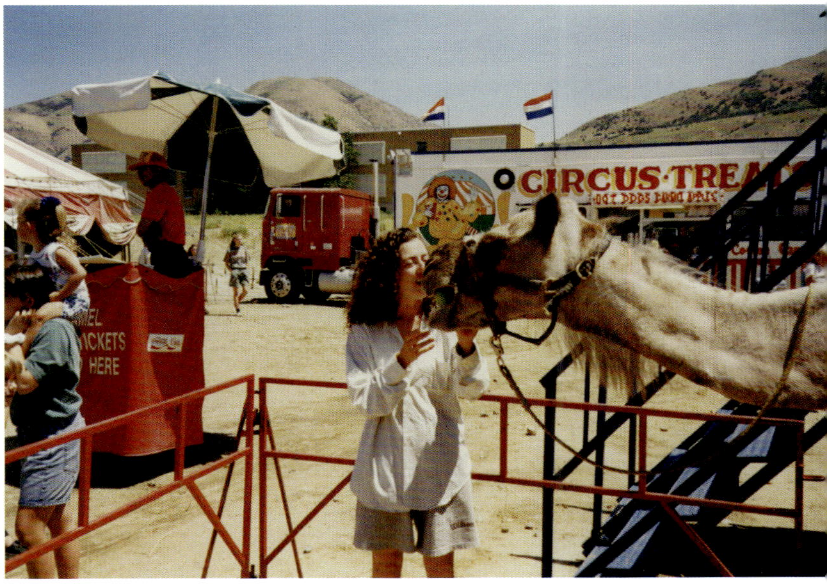

FIGURE 6. Getting to know the camels, Carson & Barnes Circus, 1995.

No matter the show, no matter the town, some rules stayed the same. Animals always got water first. Tip the water guy and you won't get *your* water last. Always thank the **24-hour man**, the advance crew member who assigns parking spots on lot. Always thank the cook. If the cookhouse isn't open, look for the **pie car** (a kind of circus corner store); I fell in love with breakfast burritos from the pie car at Carson & Barnes Circus. At Clyde Beatty-Cole Bros. Circus, I had to get photo release signatures from each **roustabout** (a workingman doing many different jobs). While everyone was gathered in a circle to raise the tent, I walked the **stake line**, photo release forms in hand. At the same show, my RV was part of the tiger compound. I learned how to **woofle** (a kind of tiger purr, also called a *chuff*). And I learned to jump out of the way when a tiger lifts its tail. Walker Bros. Circus had an elephant, Liz (Lizard was her nickname), who roamed free in the mornings. She walked around the lot, visiting each trailer and hanging out with the kids. One morning I saw her with her head in the concessions trailer. Unable to see the trainer, I mimicked the tone of voice he used, "Lizard! Get out of there. Put that [a bag of cotton candy] back!" She followed me around the lot while I took pictures.

I had no idea what I was doing, but I learned my craft on the road. I talked to everyone. My first day on each lot was pretty much wasted taking pictures because people expected me to, but there wasn't enough of a relationship to get anything good. I spent days at a time staring through a camera, trying to be invisible. I never posed anything. There is no cropping, no manipulation of the scene in my photographs. I tried to catch the moments of character—of strength and grace and goodness, of hardship and struggle—that were happening all around me. If I wasn't sure where to look first, I stopped moving. I would sit for hours in one spot, waiting for the moment. People got used to seeing me everywhere; they went about their lives. Some of my favorite photos are a set of close-quartered, intimate images of a family getting into costume at Walker Bros. Circus (see Plates 110–113.). I got those shots because the family trusted me enough to let me into their trailer, and they were relaxed and natural when I was there.

I built relationships; I tried to win over those who were reluctant to be photographed. I'd hang out with the mechanics who slept on the ground under the cabs of their trucks (they said the **sleepers** were too small) and play with their dogs while asking them about the towns we were headed to. Then one day they'd say, "Hey, how come you never take my picture?" It took time for people to trust me and to become comfortable with the constant gaze through my camera. Patience pays off.

I photographed with mostly black-and-white film, concentrating on details that might have gotten lost in color photographs, such as puffs of talcum powder as aerialists prepped their hands or feet, or when clowns set their makeup (see Plates 115, 119, and 211). The quality of light and air are well suited to black-and-white images. I remember an early morning **load in** for Kelly Miller Circus in western Kentucky; cold and gray with a heavy mist hanging over everything. I couldn't see anything. Heading back to my RV, I noticed a man emerging from the mist; a long side pole appeared across his shoulders. More figures appeared, and the mist came alive with a complex choreography of men and poles magically materializing. I stood in the wet grass and hoped the mist would stay long enough for me to get some pictures (see Plate 2).

Circuses can be dusty during **setup**, and shafts of sunlight cutting through the dust and dark inside a tent make it feel like a cathedral. I photographed setup from inside the Carson & Barnes Circus's five-ring tent. A line of elephants was made miniature in contrast to the massive walls of canvas, while the handlers yelled at me to wear a mask as protection against the dusty air. The tent poles cut long, meandering trails into the dirt as they slowly moved upright (see Plates 27–31).

One afternoon during my second season with Big Apple Circus, I found myself standing near the **back**

door, where acts enter and exit the tent. It was time for the **spec** (short for *spectacle*), a grand parade of performers and animals at the end of a show. You have no idea how big elephants are until you're wedged between half a dozen circus elephants and the side of a tent. I have never stood so still in my life. It seemed like forever. The trainer finally appeared and smiled at me before leading the elephants onward. Everyone had been watching. One clown, who had been hesitant to have his picture taken, walked over and threw open his arms to hug me. I remember thinking, "I must not be a **First of May** [newcomer] anymore."

Some days the circus was loud and bright and all I could see was color. On those days, I gave up the black-and-white film and surrendered to color photography and its vibrancy. Banners and flags. Sequins and feathers. Tent canvas and ropes were like giant sails and rigging at sea (see Plate 185). At some point, I stopped overthinking and let my eyes lead. If you spend enough time looking through a camera, your mind can wander while your eyes stay attentive. More than once, I would take a picture and suddenly shout, "Got it!," and when someone nearby would ask what I just photographed, I'd reply, "I have no idea." Trying to stay in the background can be difficult; using a flash, for example, disrupts everything. You have to give up the photos you expect to take in order to see the people and world around you. That's a trade worth making. Paul Binder, co-founder of Big Apple Circus, once said I was like wallpaper—familiar and everywhere you look. The best pictures are already there; you just have to find them.

Circus time moves differently from regular time. The show is the circus time clock. It dictates all schedules and activities. It is never late, and it never waits. When you are on a circus lot, time seems to move quickly or not at all. Relationships start faster and progress more quickly. Boys and girls look and act older than their years. While crew and office staff may stay with the same show year after year, the audience's desire for something new and different means that headline acts and other performing artists are always moving on to new circuses. I met one family of circus artists at three different shows (Kelly Miller Circus, Franzen Brothers Circus, and Sterling & Reid Bros. Circus) over three successive years. When my RV broke down, they put me up in one of their trailers. Their children grew up in my photographs (see Plates 180, 212, and 222–224).

People who work at the circus arrive with a dream: to fly through the spotlight high above the center ring, to tame a wild beast, to start over, to make enough money to get back on their feet. There is a strong sense of community among those who make the circus their home, but it is a hard life. You work eighteen hours a day, in the mud, in the sleet, with sore shoulders and backs and hands. It's hard work, and it can be dangerous. Sometimes no one shows up for the show. But sometimes they do, and the house is packed, the sky is clear, the kids are wide-eyed, and the sponsors are thrilled. One of those days can make up for a month of bad lots and bad crowds and a ton of self-doubt. If your dream is strong enough, you stay. Walking through the lot you can feel the palpable energy of a hundred different dreams.

Chance and hard work can bring good fortune when on the road. At Kelly Miller Circus a sudden reduction of work (and pay) left the ringmaster job vacant, giving the water boy his chance in the spotlight. At Big Apple Circus, one performer's journey started in the **house crew**, putting in bleachers and seating the public. He moved on to assisting the performers with props and stunts as a member of the **ring crew**. Then after practicing routines on his own and entertaining the audience in the stands before show time, he joined the company as a full-time acrobat and clown. I photographed Al over many years, in many phases of this transformation (see Plates 79, 82, and 121–123).

I traveled with the shows and lived on lot (Figures 7, 8). There is much interconnectedness among friends and relatives (by blood or marriage) within a single show or spread across several shows. You hear a lot

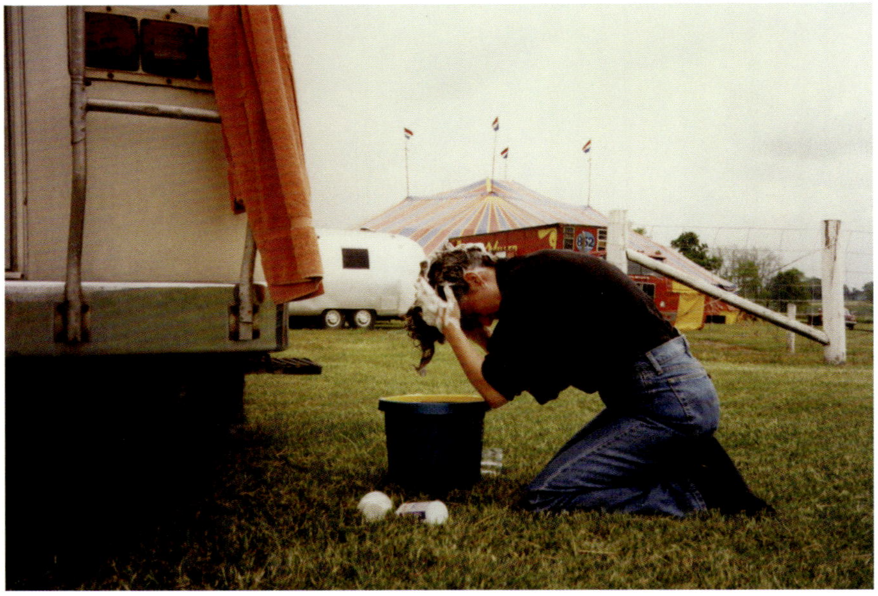

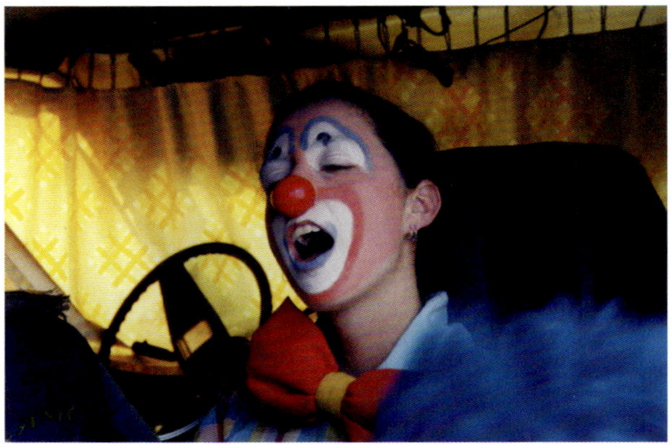

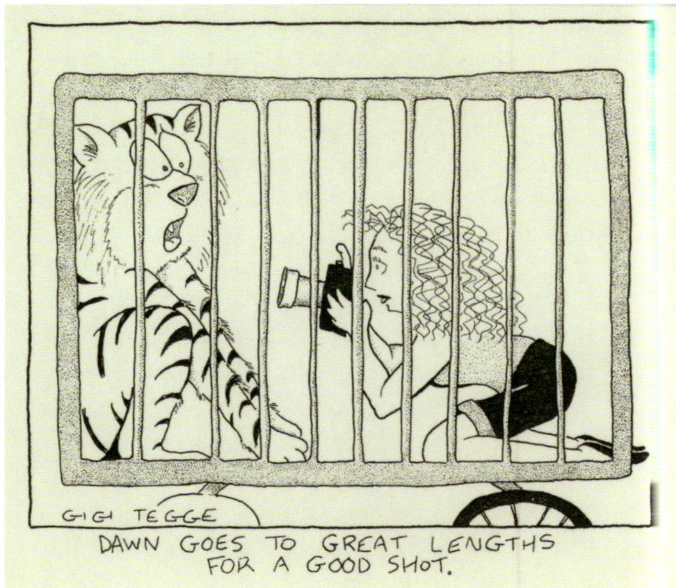

FIGURE 7. Washing my hair in a bucket, Kelly Miller Circus, 1995.

FIGURE 8. Getting ready to help with the clown act, Walker Bros. Circus, 1995. A veteran clown wanted me to understand that clowning is harder than it looks. I stood in the center ring in a summer heat wave in clown pants and a wig and shook a big box with balloons in it. My makeup melted and my plastic nose kept sliding off.

FIGURE 9. Start-of-season cartoon by clown Gigi Tegge, Clyde Beatty-Cole Bros. Circus, 1995. Every week Gigi would feature someone from the show in a cartoon posted by the **back door** of the tent. At this show, my RV was part of the tiger compound on each lot.

about people before you meet them. I delivered messages and packages from other circuses. I was invited to baptisms and birthday parties, razzed in cartoons, and treated to folklore, gossip, and history (Figure 9). I helped when they were short-handed at Franzen Brothers Circus and took **cherry pie** (extra jobs) at Sterling & Reid Bros. Circus when I needed cash. At Clyde Beatty-Cole Bros. Circus, I was given a **face name**—a pseudonym traditionally associated with circus veterans. (My face name is Soil. Band leader JP was working through the letter S that year and thought I seemed "earth mother-y.") Constantly in motion, most circuses have mail service, food service, churches, and entertainment. If they wanted to, a person could go for months without venturing beyond the circus lot. When I was off the road, performers and crew sent letters with tales of who got fired, who was dating whom, **blowdowns** in bad weather, the cost of tent repairs, and good and bad lots, sponsors, and audiences. Natalie fell from the high wire; Lauren broke her foot. Khris got hurt helping someone out of a car wreck just outside the grounds. Wayne was attacked by his tigers.

There is a lot of humanity condensed into a circus the size of a parking lot. There is an atmosphere of tolerance in that community. I am indebted to the many people who welcomed me—the owners, ringmasters, clowns, acrobats, trainers, workingmen, advance men, promoters, mechanics, and animal grooms—who trusted me to show the best of them, and who believed me when I said I wanted to learn about the circus world. The resulting archive of more than ten thousand images, interviews, and ephemera (see Appendix) is my attempt to capture what I learned and saw: the value of hard work, how to see strength in everyone, how to work and live together, how to look out for one another, how to withhold assumptions, how to get along. The circus remained a part of my life long after I stopped traveling with the shows. I spent years organizing and printing images, transcribing interviews, and working with text and image editors whose efforts laid the groundwork for this publication.

Almost twenty years after I came off the road, after I'd gone back to school to become an art conservator and joined the staff at the Smithsonian's Museum Conservation Institute, the Smithsonian Institution featured Circus Arts as part of its 2017 Folklife Festival. The festival explored the revival of circus arts in America and looked at circus history as part of our national identity. Some of my images appeared in festival publications from the Smithsonian Center for Folklife and Cultural Heritage, while the full archive of my negatives, images, and other materials was donated to the Archive Center and the Photographic History Collection at the Smithsonian's National Museum of American History. I am deeply grateful that this work has become a part of the Smithsonian at a museum where visitors and scholars explore American life and culture. These photographs join other circus-related artifacts throughout the Smithsonian's collections, as a record for future generations, a connection to a place that looks so different and yet feels so familiar. I welcome the opportunity to share life through the lens of the circus. It was an experience like no other. It should be like conscription; everyone should join the circus.

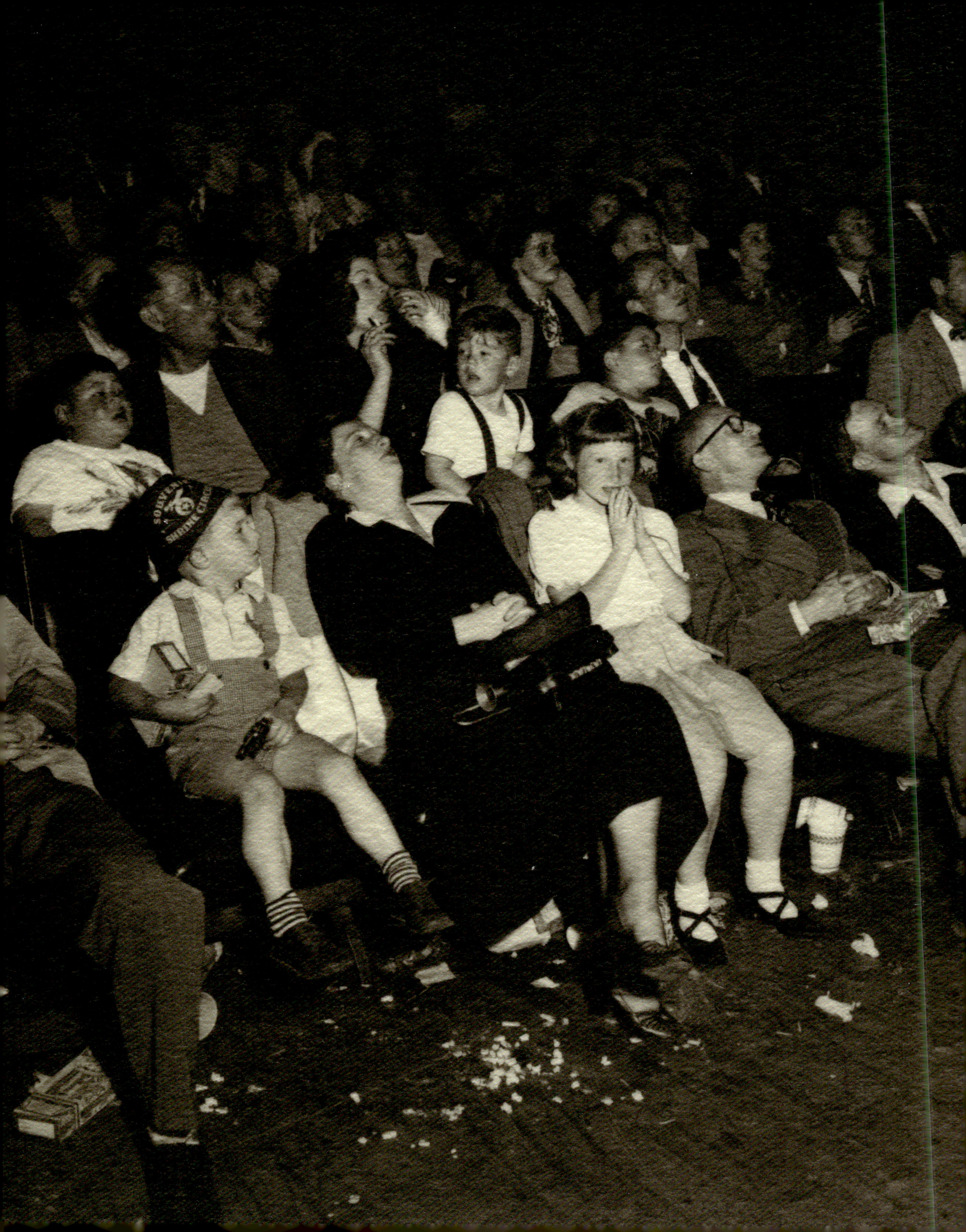

Step Right Up The History of Work Photography and Circus Photographs in Context

DAVID E. HABERSTICH

For an instant Adam's mind swam with visions of circuses. Circuses were boring, once they were set up. You could see better stuff on television any day. But the *setting up* . . . Of course they'd all go down there, and they'd help them put up the tents, and wash the elephants, and the circus people would be so impressed . . .

—*Good Omens: The Nice and Accurate Prophecies of Agnes Nutter, Witch* (Neil Gaiman and Terry Pratchett)

Dawn Rogala's extended documentary project of photographing small circuses encompasses all aspects of circus life, from setup to performance to teardown. She is fascinated by everything associated with the circus and its people, but nothing more so than the sheer physical labor that makes circuses possible. She is captivated by the grueling labor, including the hours of practice required to perfect performance arts, the erection of tents, and the creation of temporary villages inhabited by sometimes unusual people with unusual skills and jobs. She shares a vision with the fictional precocious child Adam of Neil Gaiman and Terry Pratchett's classic comic novel *Good Omens*. Adam is an unusual boy (even aside from his role as the Antichrist in this whimsical tale of forestalling the impending Apocalypse) because he dreams of impressing circus people with his *work*—not with his prowess as a performer. He finds the prospect of being a circus *spectator* "boring." Nor does he evince any interest in the glamor of performing under the big top. He is enthralled with the grittiness of circus *work.* He will set up tents and wash elephants to earn the approbation of professional circus workers. If he could have seen Rogala's lovely photograph of a trainer cuddling with his tigers (see Plate 92), he undoubtedly would have craved the acceptance of such fearsome beasts as well.

Rogala's unique circus archive is one of the most recent additions to the Archives Center holdings at the Smithsonian's National Museum of American History (NMAH), and a selection of display prints has been added to the museum's Photographic History Collection as well. In her extended study of traveling circuses

Detail of Figure 12

over a six-year period Rogala captured the lives of all types of circus employees—at work, waiting to make their entrances into the big top, and at leisure, as well as performing more mundane activities. She captures performers, to be sure, both rehearsing and entertaining their public, but also the workers behind the scenes doing demanding physical labor, their muscles straining to erect or dismantle tents in well-rehearsed, coordinated group efforts. Of course, setting up a circus can be a public performance as well, feeding the boyish imagination of Gaiman and Pratchett's character Adam. Years ago, watching the arrival, unloading, and setting up of a circus was itself a spectator sport, particularly in small towns. Each circus company is a business, employing all kinds of workers in time-honored roles, and Rogala's study of every one of these human cogs in the circus machine is exhaustive.

The circuses of the twentieth century were traveling shows that depended on modern forms of transportation for their existence, but there was little in the way of automation to aid in the rapid erection of the tents and other structures in the temporary encampments that constituted virtual villages. Specially designed tools and equipment facilitated much of the work, but it took hard-working muscle labor to accomplish it. The indefatigable Rogala essentially embedded herself in a number of these nomadic businesses to photograph them and their employees in all facets of circus life. She produced a multifaceted, deeply informative record of what turned out to be a gradually dying enterprise, a result of animal rights campaigns as well as changes in popular culture and entertainment. Rogala studied the life and culture of these unique environments intensively, learned how the businesses operated, how the employees fared at work and at play, and came to be regarded as a trusted observer and friend. She also collected poignant and distinctive ephemera that are included in her archive.

Rogala also conducted interviews with circus people to supplement her pictorial record and personal witness as an accepted observer and friend. The interviews reveal the dynamics of the circus life in its many facets, including the interdependence of its members and their joint efforts to make their shared business thrive. The insular nature of the business, as they relate, is demanding, yet offers a kind of freedom—an "all for one and one for all" spirit that provides comfort and incentive for an unusual lifestyle. The employees cannot go "home" at the end of a workday because their homes—usually trailers—are on the lot, perhaps a stone's throw from the big tent. They can get their daily eight hours of sleep, but it might be fragmented, not one continuous slumber.

One advantage of the circus life, as an acrobatics trainer explained, is a sense of control not often found in the larger world, where there are "too many people."[1] This control is closely related to an "incredible work ethic" and devotion to the job, as David LeBlanc explained. "It's not just the exposure of being next to an elephant. It's that [kids] see the elephant people *devoting their lives* to elephants."[2] Such circus work typically entails seven days a week on the job for the season, a point of both complaint and pride.

Rogala is part of a long line of dedicated documentary photographers who have photographed work and workers. Some photographers celebrated the hard physical labor that made business possible in the industrial age—long before much traditional "work" was transformed by computers—while others, such as Jacob Riis and Lewis Hine, famously sought to remedy the plight of laborers brutalized and exploited by industry and an unsympathetic culture.

I propose to place Rogala's output within an abbreviated and subjective, perhaps idiosyncratic, history of "work" photography. The Archives Center is particularly rich in documentation of American work and industry, in the form of both text documents and images. Therefore I'll highlight some Archives Center and Photographic History Collection holdings to make my points along the way.

Many of the earliest nineteenth-century photographs depict lower-class workers, whether taken from

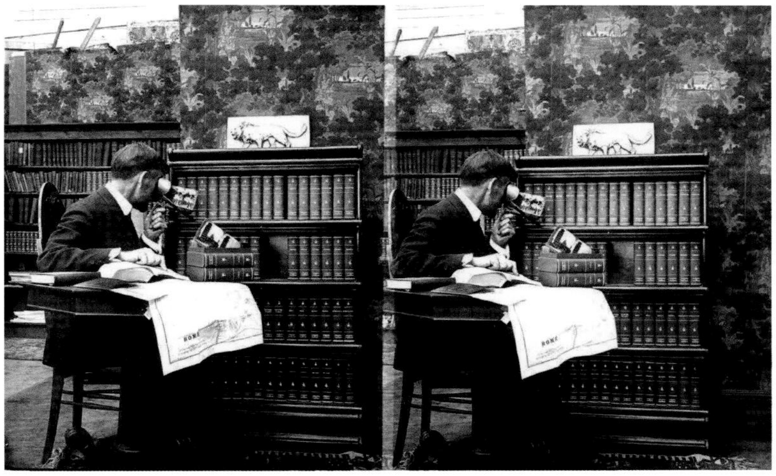

FIGURE 10. *Man Using Stereoscope and Underwood Travel System Map*, Underwood & Underwood, ca. 1900. Gelatin silver interpositive, Underwood & Underwood Glass Stereograph Collection, 1895–1921, Archives Center, NMAH, AC0143-0023714.

The genius of stereograph marketing was that cards could be purchased both individually and in sets, often packaged in boxes that mimicked library bindings, as in this view.

a sympathetic motive or for the images' "picturesque" value to a public that demanded authentic imagery outside of their normal experience or comfort zone. David Octavius Hill and Robert Adamson, among the first masters of photographic art and technology, documented the fishwives of 1840s Newhaven, Scotland, in terms of costume, equipment, and work culture, both as a social documentary project and to produce a body of self-consciously "artistic" imagery. As noted in the Metropolitan Museum of Art's "Timelines of Art History": "in the age of the Industrial Revolution and its attendant social problems, Hill and Adamson presented Newhaven as a model community bound by tradition, honest labor, and mutual support."[3]

Another motive for this type of documentation was perhaps the impulse to categorize and compartmentalize workers with the taxonomic zeal popular among photographers of a scientific or analytical bent, including William Henry Fox Talbot, the inventor of the photographic paper processes. Most quotidian professional photography in the nineteenth century focused on portraiture as a service to a paying clientele. Among the subjects that photographers chose to demonstrate their artistic skills and sensitivity in self-generated projects were the human face and form: "character studies" of interesting faces became popular, and some photographers produced "occupational" photographs—the work of Hill & Adamson being among the first examples. This genre of portraits certainly suggests photographers' preoccupation with classification. Itinerant photographers often set up temporary studios to which laborers might come for their portraits with the tools of their trade or with examples of their work. Since lengthy exposures made it difficult to photograph people at work, these portraits are records of the public dress and trades of the populace. Undaunted by the technical limitations of their equipment, Talbot and other photographers carefully posed static subjects and photographed them as if they were actively engaged in physical labor.

From the late 1890s until 1921, photographers for the stereograph publishers Underwood & Underwood documented scenery and architecture, as well as work and industry around the world. The three-dimensional photographs were packaged in sets and served as both educational resources and as "armchair travel" entertainment. Other American firms, such as Keystone View Company and H. C. White, manufactured similar stereographs. The Archives Center holds some twenty-eight thousand glass plate negatives and interpositives (positive copy images used to produce duplicate negatives) from the Underwood & Underwood archive (Figure 10). The variety of subjects is amazing, as publishers sought to depict all aspects of countries and cultures around the world in an encyclopedic manner—although often with a condescending and jingoistic spirit to their captions and comments.[4] These photographs, relying on the illusion of three dimensions, were intended to simulate the experience of direct observation. With travel photography, whether in the hands of the amateur or a professional publisher, photographers and their audiences were attempting to, as Susan Sontag wrote,

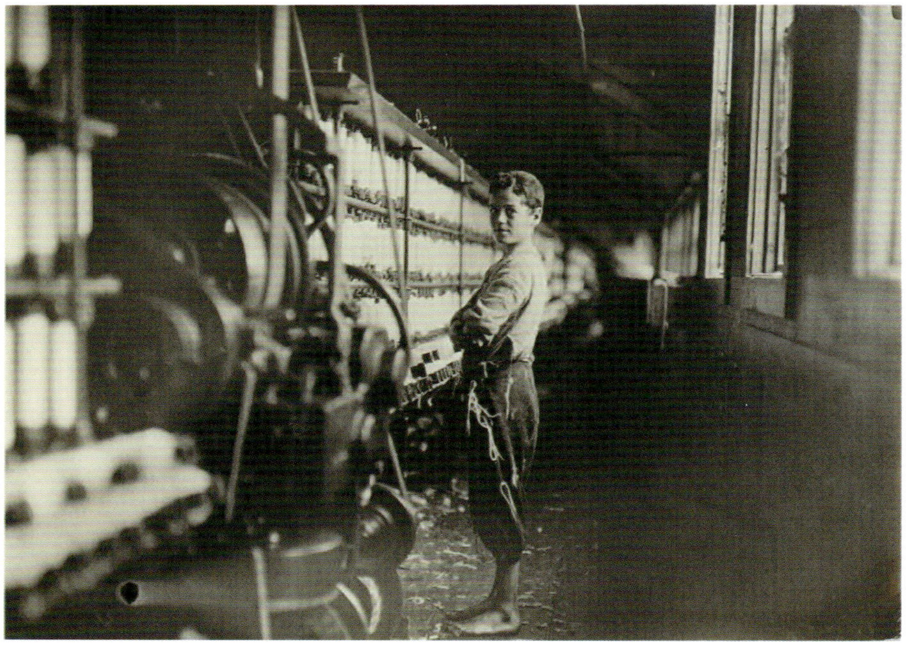

FIGURE 11. *Worker in Cotton Mill, Rhode Island,* Lewis Wickes Hine, 1909. Gelatin silver print. Photographic History Collection, catalog number PG.72.78.10.

Some of Hine's searing pictures of child labor were made surreptitiously or under false pretenses, without industrial managers' approval.

"collect the world."[5] A prominent feature of the carefully scripted, encyclopedic documentation produced by these stereograph publishers was the portrayal of the muscle labor that made the world work.

Jacob Riis, Lewis Hine (Figure 11), and many other socially conscious photographers are celebrated as the essential muckrakers who exposed the exploitation of workers—especially, and most shockingly, child laborers. The signal achievement of such photographers is that their imagery had a significant impact on reform movements, proving the power of social documentary photographic projects.

In the late nineteenth and early twentieth centuries, child labor was widely accepted, based on the argument that children could (and should) learn the value of hard work and productivity, which helped not only to "build character" but also to support their families (although their compensation was minimal). The necessary labor of children, both girls and boys, was for millennia an almost universal assumption of agrarian families, cultures, and economies. Depending on class and circumstance, many boys were also expected to learn the brutal skills of war. The Industrial Revolution was heralded by some as a social panacea, but there was initially resistance to what eventually became the twentieth-century ideal of a carefree childhood. As one mother told the National Child Labor Committee in 1907, "I am really tired of seeing so many big children ten years old playing in the streets." Child labor was justified on many grounds, but it was Hine's photographs that helped put an end to the practice, revealing poor and unsafe working conditions and the general exploitation of children at low wages. Some of Hine's sympathy for working children was inspired by his personal experience as an eighteen-year-old worker helping to support his own family.[6]

Child labor largely disappeared in the United States, but it still flourishes elsewhere in the world. The travel writer and novelist Paul Theroux seized on this topic as the central theme of his contemporary novel *A Dead Hand: A Crime in Calcutta*.[7] This fictional account of an American businesswoman posing as a benefactor for orphaned Indian children while secretly sending them to work as weavers in sweatshops is horrifying, suggesting that the underpaid workers—both children and adults—of India, China, and other locations around the world continue to be exploited by the dark side of American-style capitalism and still need an advocate, an equivalent of Riis or Hine, to visually document abusive practices in need of correction.

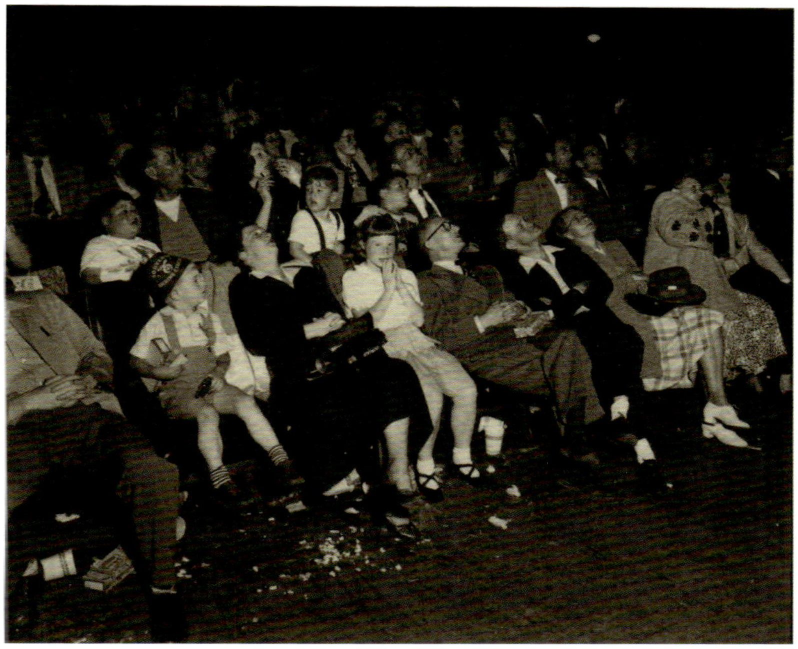

FIGURE 12. *Audience Watching Circus,* Glen Fishback, ca. 1940s. Gelatin silver print. Glen Fishback Papers and Photographs, ca. 1930–1976, Archives Center, NMAH, AC0714-0000001. Fishback's portfolio of candid circus imagery was not extensive, but he was especially interested in audience reactions, as seen in this image. He also delighted in posing his young daughter laughing with colorfully costumed clowns long before they became figures of creepiness.

It is interesting that allegations of the mistreatment of animals by circuses has been such a potent factor in the decline of these businesses, whereas there has been little serious criticism of children working in twentieth-century circuses, beyond the obvious observation that "show business," combined with the nomadic lifestyle of a circus caravan, is an unusual and challenging environment for a child. The exploitation of young and physically unusual performers by P. T. Barnum and other producers of early "museums" and carnivals (Barnum's Tom Thumb began working for the showman as a child), preceding the popularization of traveling circuses and carnivals, left its mark, however, culminating in Tod Browning's 1932 horror film *Freaks.* (The production is said to have abused the real-life sideshow performers who acted in the film.) While the modern-day circus or carnival spectator might be unaware of this history, the allure of circuses as live entertainment for paying customers arguably relies on their aura of multiple exoticism, spectacle, mystery—and occasional danger—and a distinctive combination of sights, sounds, and smells.

The grim expressions of Hine's child laborers contrast sharply with the happy faces of child circus performers seen in Rogala's photographs. The children in her photographs are members of circus families, not runaways taken in by greedy promoters. They are generally willing students in a family enterprise, all within a larger extended foster family, and they seem to be enjoying themselves in their circumstances—eager participants in a strange but exciting world.

Many photographers have captured the circus as spectacle, concentrating on the performers, both human and animal. Glen Fishback, a magazine and advertising photographer from the 1940s through the 1970s, recorded circus acts, performers, and audiences (Figure 12). He photographed clowns as symbols, as emblems of the circus, whereas Rogala shows us the behind-the-scenes work of the actors creating and sustaining their personas. Fishback gave us a sanitized view of circus performers as entertainers (especially clowns),[8] while Rogala shows us that for entertainers preparation involves meticulous work of one sort or another, including costuming, the application of makeup, and rehearsal.

The Dawn V. Rogala Circus Photographs and Papers, which includes all of Rogala's original negatives and the unique circus ephemera that she collected, came to the NMAH's Archives Center in 2017. The addition of Rogala's circus archive to the Archives

Center adds to the museum's documentation, presentation, and study of labor—a significant theme that the center has sought to emphasize through business records, ephemera generated by American businesses, and photographs. A recent exhibition from the Archives Center's collection featured early "work incentive" posters saluting the "work ethic" that has now pervaded American business and economics. An exhibition of these decidedly upbeat posters in 2018–2019, *Let's Get It Right: Work Incentive Posters of the 1920s*, emphasized the salutary and exemplary ideals of perseverance, hard work, and accuracy.[9] Such posters exhorted both white- and blue-collar workers to work hard and accurately, as if productivity were an end in itself. These advertisements for productivity embody what used to be called the "Protestant work ethic." Even Andrew Beyer, erstwhile horse-racing columnist for the *Washington Post* and author of self-help books for race-track devotees and avid gamblers, gloried in his own time-consuming research into the bewildering welter of statistics and past performance ratings of thoroughbreds in the *Daily Racing Form* as much as in the financial success that his enlightened gambling reportedly provided, and saw himself as the embodiment of the "Protestant work ethic," as if, whether he won or lost, feverish mental gymnastics and arcane calculations were their own reward.[10]

Athletes—whether human or animal—are workers also, and the sports pages of newspapers are filled with stunning photographs that record the sweat, strain, and talent of professionals and amateurs alike. Despite the anomalously big salaries of some athletes, in recent years some (especially football players) have become considered victims exploited by a ruthless industry. The

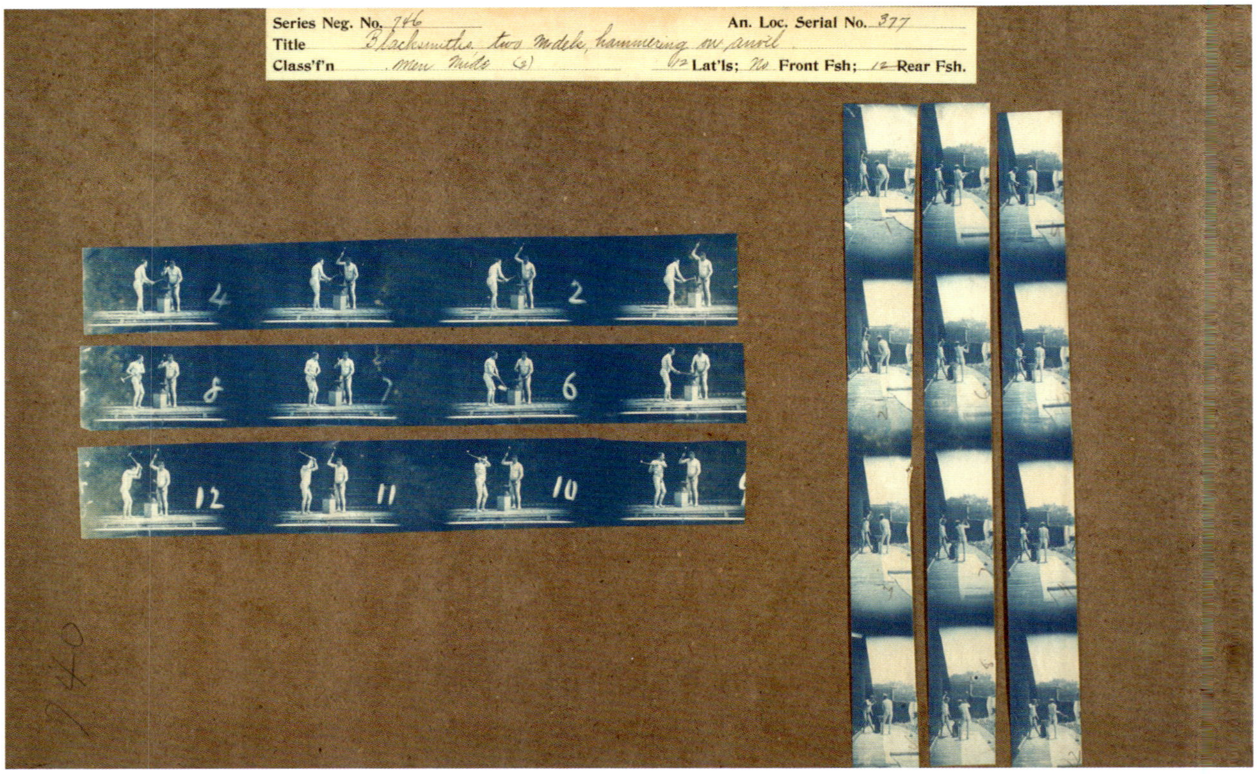

FIGURE 13. *Blacksmiths, Two Models, Hammering on Anvil*, Eadweard Muybridge, 1884–1886. Cyanotypes. Photographic History Collection, catalog number PG.003856.0296. Many collections contain photomechanical reproductions (collotypes) from Muybridge's monumental publication *Animal Locomotion*, but these cyanotype strips are unique.

collection of Eadweard Muybridge's historic photographs from his *Animal Locomotion* project in the museum's Photographic History Collection are important photographs within the context of work. Muybridge's famous analysis of physical movement began with the study of racehorses. Muybridge's curious sequences of men, women, and children (many in the nude) performing a variety of mundane or bizarre movements include several depictions of labor. Another photographic study of work movement is found in the motion analysis sequences and films of Frank and Lillian Gilbreth (Figure 13). The Gilbreths were advocates of scientific management, also known as Taylorism (named after engineer Fred W. Taylor), which sought to increase efficiency in the workplace through the study of human movement but often led to depersonalization and an almost machine-like level of specialization that could deprive workers of pride in their work. For good or ill, these photographic time-motion studies analyzing work movements owe a debt to Muybridge's pioneering images—in spirit and technique, if not in motive.

Many photographers have specialized in documenting work, especially hard physical labor, without eschewing the value of mental work. Some with activist or even socialist leanings have produced imagery that highlights the plight of underpaid and overworked laborers. Hine is perhaps the most well-known and influential labor photographer. Hine's early photographs portray the dangerous conditions of exploited workers; in later years, however, he depicted workers on the Empire State Building and Chrysler Building skyscraper projects as heroic figures engaged in the construction of a vibrant twentieth-century economy. At least one worker on these mammoth projects was directly inspired by Hine's work to take his own photographs while employed in the building of both skyscrapers: Charles Rivers, a machinist, and eventually a labor union organizer and civil rights and peace activist, smuggled his camera onto the work sites in his lunchbox, providing a laborer's-eye view of these buildings from precarious heights (Figure 14). Some of Rivers's

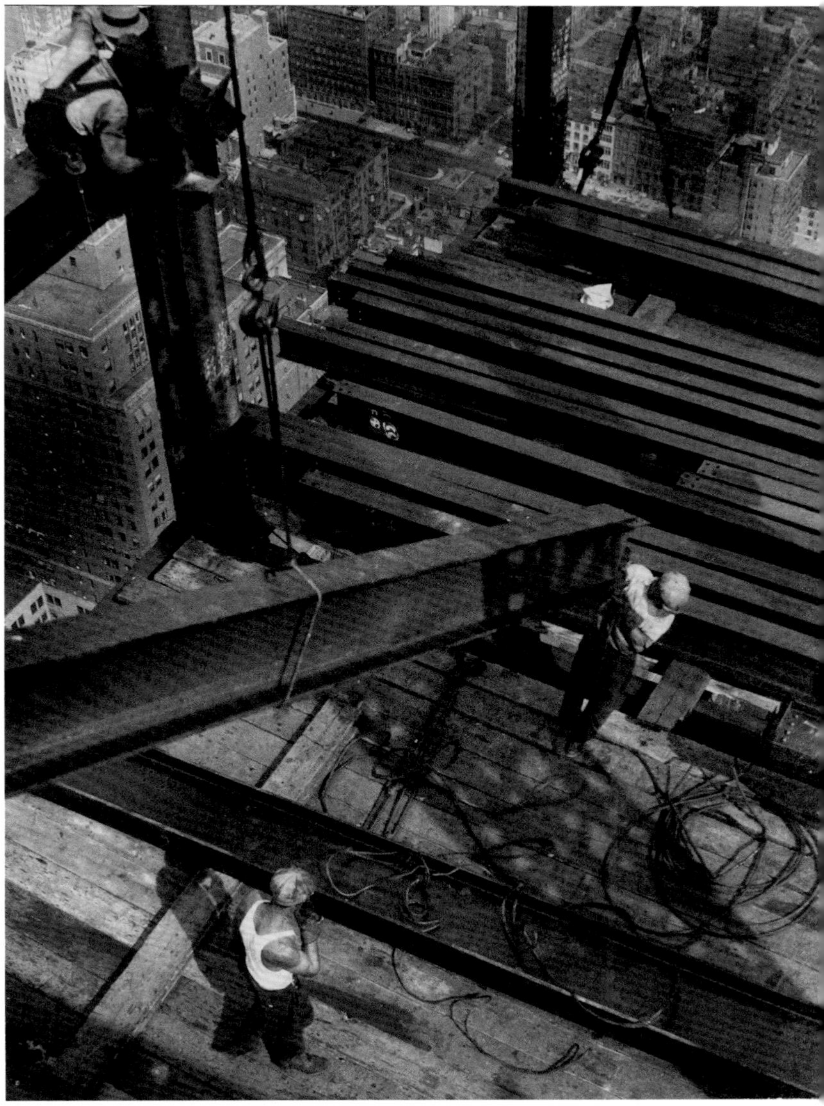

FIGURE 14. *Ironworkers Constructing the Empire State Building—New York*, Charles Rivers, 1930. Gelatin silver negative. Charles Rivers Photographs, Archives Center, NMAH, AC0360-0000001. Rivers was a Greek immigrant whose original name was either Constantinos Kapornaros or Kostandinos Kapernaros. He may have adopted a pseudonym due to his union activism.

negatives and prints are among the Archives Center's holdings.[11]

Leonard Nadel photographed Mexican migrant manual laborers (Figure 15)—"braceros" in a US government program—as well as their work in the fields and their lives in the camps. His archive has become one of the most popular in the Archives Center for research on hard labor and the exploitation of workers, especially Latinos. The comprehensive scope of his documentation includes the entire bracero experience, including bureaucratic paperwork, humiliating and dehumanizing inspections, and waits in long lines, as well as images of their living quarters, aspects of their daily routines, and Nadel's sympathetic view of their toil in lettuce fields.[12]

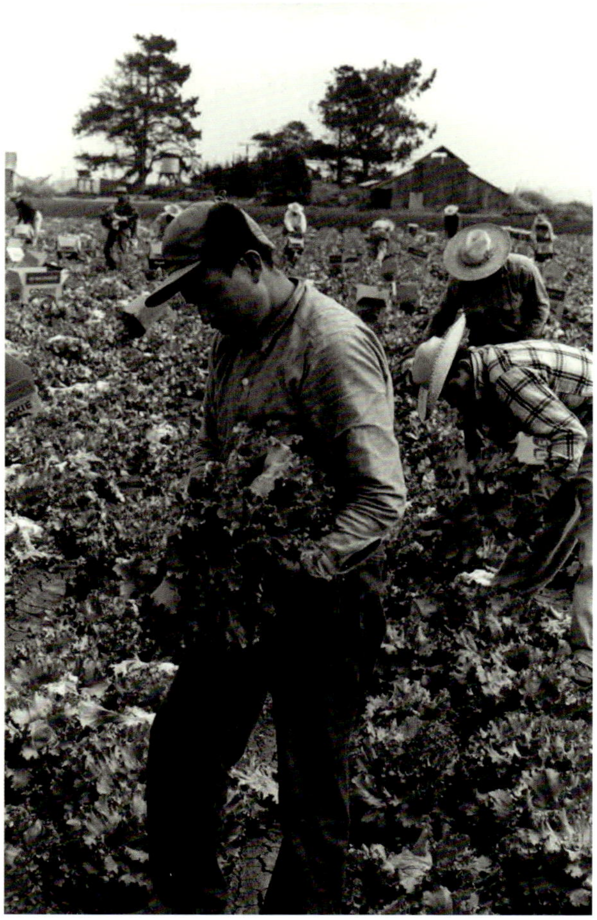

FIGURE 15. *Untitled (Mexican Workers),* Leonard Nadel, ca. 1956. Gelatin silver print. Leonard Nadel Collection, Bracero Program, Archives Center, NMAH, NAD-200401385620. Nadel photographed in California, Texas, and Mexico for the Ford Foundation's Fund for the republic from the late 1950s to the early 1960s, in support of a report by Dr. Ernesto Galarza titled *Strangers in Our Fields*.

Another government-sponsored program recorded in photographs was the Civilian Conservation Corps (CCC). The CCC was created in 1933 as part of the New Deal legislation initiated by President Franklin D. Roosevelt—a public work relief program for unemployed men designed to reduce high unemployment during the Great Depression. The CCC carried out a broad natural resource conservation program on national, state, and municipal lands from 1933 to 1942. The Archives Center acquired a collection of photographs from the National Association of Civilian Conservation Corps Alumni that documents government-sponsored CCC service projects at multiple sites.

The unheralded photographer Katherine Joseph photographed the International Ladies' Garment Workers Union in 1941, including both work in the factory and union activities (Figure 16). This documentation forms a little-known treasure trove of images depicting this important industry.[13]

Thanks to an active music program in the museum, especially in the field of jazz, the Archives Center has gradually assembled a rich aggregation of musical rehearsal and performance documentation by photographers such as Navroze Contractor, Francis Wolff, Bill Claxton, Chuck Stewart, Jeffrey Kliman, and Herman Leonard. These photographs convincingly demonstrate the physical work involved in traveling

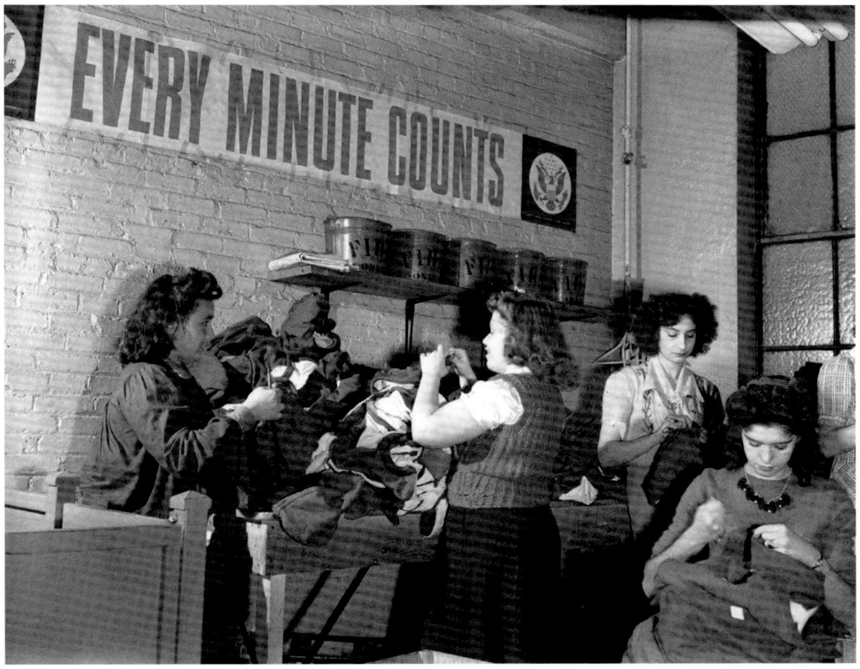

FIGURE 16. *International Ladies Garment Workers Union Workers Sewing Clothes,* Katherine Joseph, 1941. Gelatin silver negative. Katherine Joseph Papers, 1938–1944, Archives Center, NMAH, AC0944-0000010. Joseph's photographs celebrate what has been called "the golden age of organized labor."

and performance. Musicians glisten with sweat while employing the tools of their trade, even when playing "cool" jazz, and lie exhausted afterward. In one image, composer/bandleader Duke Ellington is seen slumped over his piano after struggling with an arrangement for his orchestra; perhaps it is "merely" mental work, but it takes a physical toll. The Dutch photographer Emile Waagenaar, himself a musician and aficionado of Cajun music, has made many trips to rural Louisiana and Mississippi to photograph authentic Cajun musicians,[14] and Jake Jacobson photographed musical instrument makers with the products of their painstaking expertise.[15]

Lesser-known photographers such as Alexander Alland[16] and Carlos de Wendler-Funaro, both represented in Archives Center collections, surveyed the exotic lifestyles of various American Gypsy groups, including stereotypical and culturally prescribed occupations, such as metalwork on one hand, and sedentary fortune-telling on the other. Both photographers depicted the celebrated "king" of New York's "Red Bandanna" Gypsy group, Steve Kaslov, hard at work in his metal shop (Figure 17).[17]

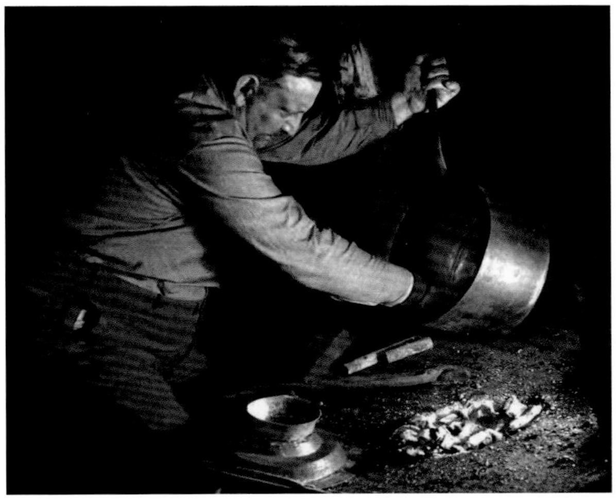

FIGURE 17. *Steve Kaslov / King of the Gypsies,* Alexander Alland, Sr., 1930s. Gelatin silver print. Alexander Alland, Sr., Photoprints, 1930–1943, Archives Center, NMAH, AC0204-0000002-01. Alland (original surname Landschaft) photographed many ethnic groups at home, in costumed celebrations, and at work for a book titled *American Counterpoint* (New York: The John Day Company, 1943).

Other Archives Center holdings include the business archives of many American companies, which

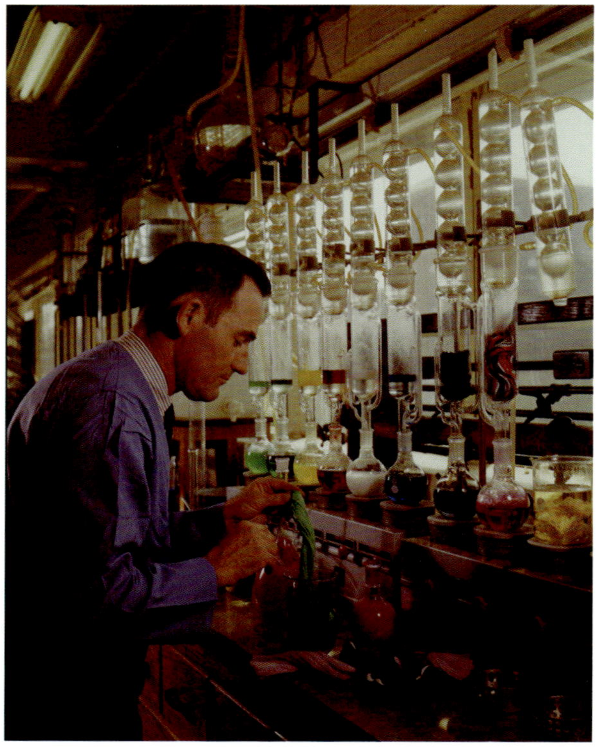

FIGURE 18. *Cone Mills Dye Lab*, Arthur d'Arazien, ca. 1950s. Ektachrome transparency, Arthur d'Arazien Industrial Photographs, 1930–2002, Archives Center, NMAH, AC0314-0000018.

usually include photographs. Many of these images were created for advertising and promotional purposes, but others record offices and shops, as well as the factories and employees who made the businesses hum with activity. The vast photographic component of the United Shoe Machinery Corporation portrays the human workers behind an automated enterprise—from men in the factory to female clerical workers in the offices.[18] The automated production methods that followed the Industrial Revolution spawned machines to perform and accelerate many tasks, but machines still required human attendants to keep them operating properly and efficiently. Many such machines provided little comfort to the "working class," for the labor involved could be just as backbreaking as earlier forms but with the addition of tedium, boredom, and a minimal sense of individual accomplishment.

Arthur d'Arazien, one of America's most renowned industrial photographers, earned fame through his spectacular color photographs of heavy industry—and the workers who operated the machinery (Figure 18). To capture these scenes, d'Arazien became a master of large-scale productions, which often required exhaustive, well-calculated multiple-flash techniques, time exposures, and other tricks of the photographer's trade, sometimes resembling the production of major cinematic extravaganzas. His work is celebratory, since it was usually commissioned by industries for annual reports, advertising purposes, and so on.[19]

David Plowden has spent his long career capturing scenes of industry and amassing an extensive catalog of images. Plowden's work has been published in scores of monographs on railroads, bridge architecture, and the steel industry. His work is the subject of many books of industrial photography, from majestic lake boats to small-town feed mills, featuring portraits of workers at their vocations. Plowden's subjects come from many occupations: farmers, mechanics, engineers, salespeople, shopkeepers, and ship captains. A Smithsonian exhibition early in Plowden's career highlighted machines, but he later concentrated on the workers who operated the machines.[20]

By contrast, some of the most poignant photographs of the early twentieth century document the effects of the *loss* of work and industry. Costa Sakellariou, for example, concentrated his photographic research on the "Rust Belt" of New York State, where those apparently idled and depressed by such loss seem to wander the streets aimlessly.[21] Negatives by a little-known African American photographer named Gilbert Dwoyid Olmstead depict the impoverished black working-class Hill District neighborhood in Pittsburgh around 1941, including a Labor Day strike by members of the Westinghouse UERMWA union of the AFL/CIO (Figure 19).

Unfortunately, Olmstead did not remain a photographer for long, despite encouragement from the Farm Security Administration's Roy Stryker, who assisted Olmstead in gaining acceptance to the Art Center School and in earning a fellowship through the

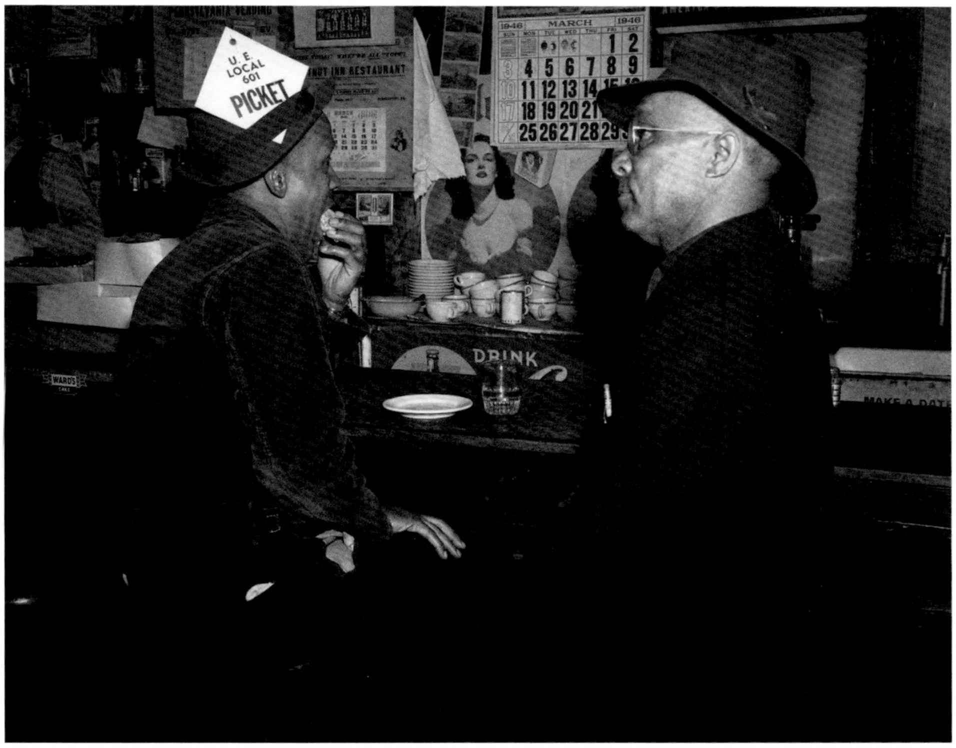

FIGURE 19. *Two African American Men at Restaurant Counter, One Wearing "Picket" Sign in Hat, Labor Day Series Involving Strike by UE-CIO,* G. Dwoyid Olmstead, 1946. Gelatin silver print. G. Dwoyid Olmstead Photonegatives, ca. 1941–1949, Archives Center, NMAH, AC0270-0000154. Olmstead primarily photographed adults and children coping with decrepit housing in Pittsburgh, but he also documented this major controversial strike against Westinghouse.

Julius Rosenwald Program for African American Visual Artists in 1946. The Rosenwald Program supported other African American photographers, including the renowned Gordon Parks. One of Parks's most iconic labor photographs depicts a charwoman (for a government agency in Washington) holding her mop and broom in a sardonic nod to Grant Wood's painting *American Gothic*.[22] This photograph is imbued with the legacy of race relations in America, the grim realities of slavery, and a bitter sense of bondage and enforced work. Even this free black woman of the twentieth century was tied to her work. In the picture book *Black: A Celebration of a Culture*, photographic historian Deborah Willis grouped a set of photographs into a category titled "Work" as an essential component of the black experience. The category is broadly conceived, including a variety of occupations such as nursing, military life, and small-business ownership and management, as well as an image of photographer Addison Scurlock. Scurlock was a respected professional working among the middle- and upper-middle-class residents of Washington's Shaw community. In a 1937 photograph by rival Robert H. McNeill he is shown photographing a large group with a tripod-mounted camera. Portraits of Scurlock and others in the professional sphere sit in sharp contrast to pictures showing hard agricultural labor and other signifiers of the history of slavery.[23]

The National Portrait Gallery's exhibition *The Sweat of Their Faces* (2017–2018) contained paintings and photographs of many "muscle" workers actively engaged in their work. A perceptive review by Elizabeth Bruenig noted the exhibition's obvious emphasis on the "working class" whose occupational and social mobility is often severely limited, and also observed the sense of loneliness and alienation pervading the portraits (Figures 20, 21).[24]

Contrast the grim images of workers with Addison Scurlock's portrayal of Howard University professor Kelly Miller, standing proudly in his sumptuous garden wearing bib overalls, a shirt with cuff links, and a spiffy bow tie (Figure 22). Clothing conventions were far more formal in the first half of the twentieth century, and it is not unusual to find photographs of manual laborers of this era wearing neckties. However, Miller was a

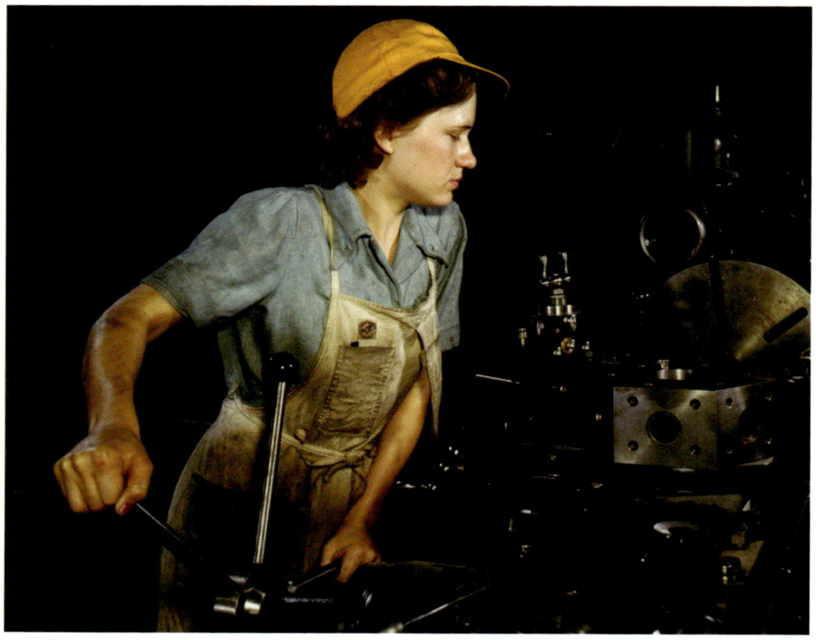

FIGURE 20. *Lathe Operator Machining Parts for Transport Planes at the Consolidated Aircraft Corporation Plant, Fort Worth, Texas,* Howard R. Hollem, 1942. Color transparency. Prints and Photographs Division, Library of Congress, Washington, DC.

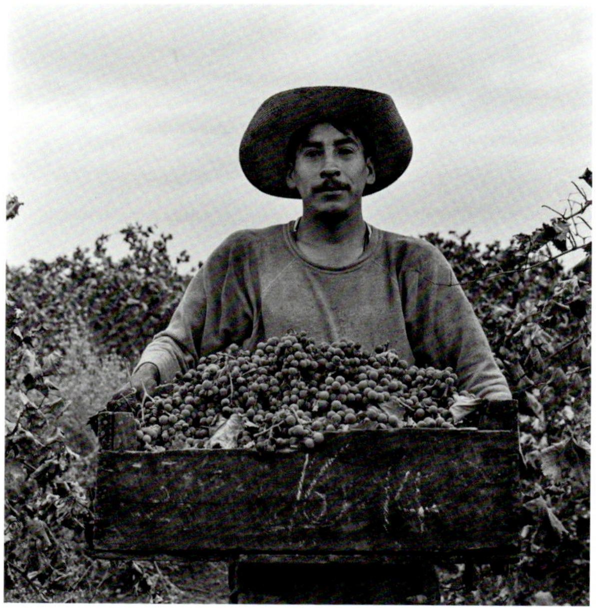

FIGURE 21. *Unidentified Migrant Worker Brought to the Valley for the Last Harvest,* from *Death of a Valley,* Pirkle Jones, 1956. Gelatin silver print. © Regents of the University of California. Courtesy Special Collections, University Library, University of California Santa Cruz: Ruth-Marion Baruch and Pirkle Jones Photographs and Papers.

professor, and gardening was his hobby, not his profession. He was one of the elite inhabitants of the segregated Shaw area of Washington. The Scurlock Studio was noted for its "dignified" portraits of African Americans, and this unusual al fresco portrait is no exception. Gardening has long been one of the acceptable avocations of the upper classes of America and Europe, offering opportunities for the gentry to intermittently engage in manual labor, producing "honest" sweat and dirty hands, albeit in a leisurely manner—a far different proposition from labor overseen by stern company foremen and distant bosses. Other Scurlock "work" photographs document black-owned businesses, and include students working in the darkrooms and studios of the Capitol School of Photography (an educational adjunct to the Scurlock Studio), biologist Ernest E. Just with his equipment in his Howard University laboratory, and students in Howard University classrooms and laboratories.[25]

I have emphasized Dawn Rogala's circus documentary project within the context of labor photography as a theme that I found meaningful and convenient, but also to indicate its significance within the collecting plans of my museum, my unit (the Archives Center), and my own curatorial collecting plan. The Archives Center maintains the Rogala Collection and hundreds

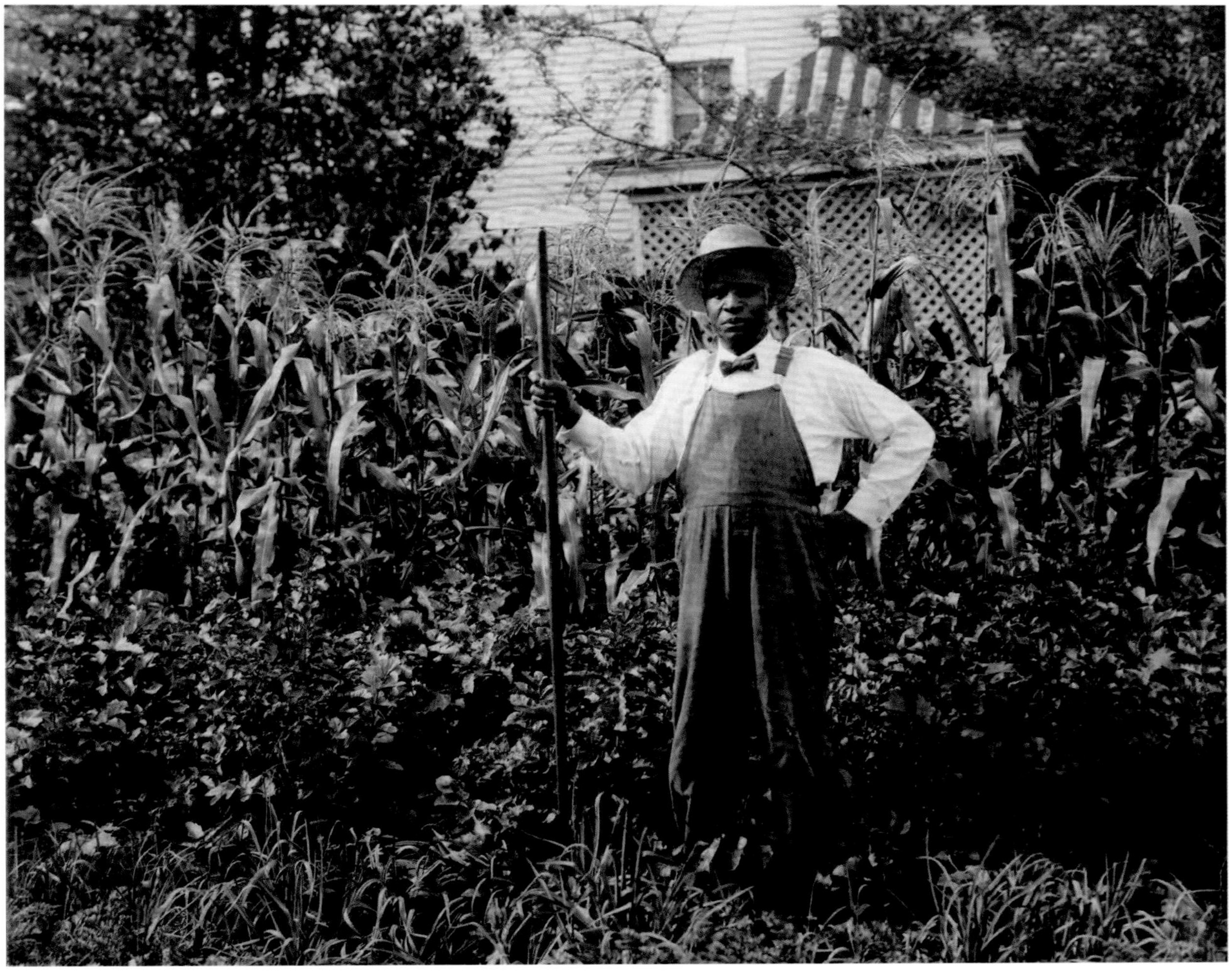

FIGURE 22. *Prof. Kelly Miller*, Addison N. Scurlock, 1909. Gelatin silver print. Scurlock Studio Records, Archives Center, NMAH, AC0618ns0227103-01pm. Kelly Miller (1863–1939) was a mathematician, sociologist, newspaper columnist, influential author, and longtime Howard University professor.

of other collections covering a wide range of topics, both specialized and general, for research. Collecting objects related to labor history is a significant aspect of the museum's mission, with one curatorial division called "Work and Industry." As this topic is a primary interest of the Archives Center as well, Rogala's documentation of the circus industry is of great significance. However, her circus photographs are not *merely* labor history or entertainment history. They are much richer and more multifaceted, not only creations of artistic self-expression but also vivid historical documents that record an unusual way of life during a brief period of time. From that standpoint, they have a clear significance for the study of social and cultural history. They are also very personal, as the photographer interacts with her subjects one-on-one. Each photograph in Rogala's archive contains multiple types of historical evidence, captured by her camera through her talent and unique sensibility. Her original negatives, prints, and related documents form a cohesive corpus that is now available for in-person, on-site study and interpretation, as well as through online visual access, and presentation in this book. The rich resources of our museum include artifacts from hundreds of years ago to some created just this year, ranging in size from locomotives and a Revolutionary War gunboat to smaller artifacts such as Judy Garland's ruby slippers. Our historical collections also include photographic documents and textual materials, in addition to "ephemera"—items intended to be discarded after a single use but retained instead for their underlying stories. Thus the Rogala archive of photographs, documents, and ephemera contributes to the museum's fundamental quest to collect, preserve, interpret, and present authentic materials of historical significance through exhibitions, publications, and media presentations.

NOTES

1 Dawn Rogala, interview with Lucio Nicolodi, Big Apple Circus, 1995.

2 Dawn Rogala, interview with David LeBlanc, director of operations and tent master, Big Apple Circus, 1995.

3 "[Newhaven Fishwives]," "Heilbrunn Timeline of Art History," The Metropolitan Museum of Art, March 20, 2019, https://www.metmuseum.org/toah/works-of-art/1997.382.19/.

4 "Guide to the Underwood & Underwood Glass Stereograph Collection," ca. 1895–1921, Smithsonian Institution, Smithsonian Online Virtual Archives, https://sova.si.edu/record/NMAH.AC.0143?s=0&n=10&t=C&q=Underwood&i=2. More Underwood & Underwood glass plates are in the Keystone-Mast Collection of the California Museum of Photography at the University of California, Riverside.

5 Susan Sontag, *On Photography* (New York: Farrar, Straus and Giroux, 1977).

6 Jessica Contrera, "His Photos Helped Abolish Child Labor," Retropolis, *Washington Post*, September 3, 2018, B1, B4.

7 Paul Theroux, *A Dead Hand: A Crime in Calcutta* (Boston: Mariner Books, 2010).

8 "Guide to Glen Fishback Papers and Photographs," ca. 1930–1976, Smithsonian Institution, Smithsonian Online Virtual Archives, https://sova.si.edu/record/NMAH.AC.0714?s=0&n=10&t=C&q=Glen+Fishback&i=0. Several of Fishback's circus images were reproduced in Noel Daniel, ed., *The Circus, 1870–1950* Cologne: Taschen Books, 2008), 53, 61, 62, 63, 315, 370, 388, 425, 546, and 588.

9 Kristen Page-Kirby, "Before Flextime and the 401(k): The Company Man of the 1920s Was Encouraged by Posters, a New Exhibit Shows," *Washington Post*, Weekend section, August 3, 2018, 22–23.

10 Andrew Beyer, *My $50,000 Year at the Races* (New York: Harcourt Brace Jovanovich, 1978), 150.

11 "Guide to the Charles Rivers Photographs, 1929–1963," Smithsonian Institution, Smithsonian Online Virtual

Archives, https://sova.si.edu/record/NMAH.AC.0360?s=0&n=10&t=C&q=Charles+Rivers&i=0. See also "Guide to the Charles Rivers Photographs and Scrapbooks," Tamiment Library and Robert F. Wagner Labor Archives, http://dlib.nyu.edu/findingaids/html/tamwag/tam_260/bioghist.html.

12 "Guide to the Leonard Nadel Photographs and Scrapbooks," 1950–2006, Smithsonian Institution, Smithsonian Online Virtual Archives, https://sova.si.edu/record/NMAH.AC.1313?s=0&n=10&t=C&q=Leonard+Nadel&i=0.

13 Suzanne Hertzberg, *Katherine Joseph: Photographing an Era of Social Significance*. (Washington, DC: Bergamot Books, 2016). Also see "Guide to the Katherine Joseph Papers," 1962–1962 and 1938–1944, https://sova.si.edu/record/NMAH.AC.0944?s=0&n=10&t=C&q=Katherine+Joseph&i=0.

14 Archives Center, *Guide to the Emile Waagenaar Photoprints of Cajun Musicians, 1980–2008*. Smithsonian Institution, Smithsonian Online Virtual Archives, https://sova.si.edu/record/NMAH.AC.1150?s=0&n=10&t=C&q=waagenaar&i=0.

15 "Jake Jacobson 'Heart and Hands' Color Iris Photoprints," 1996–2000, Smithsonian Institution, Smithsonian Online Virtual Archives, https://sova.si.edu/record/NMAH.AC.0866?s=0&n=10&t=C&q=Jake+Jacobson&i=0. *Heart & Hands: Musical Instrument Makers of America* was an exhibition of photographs by Jake Jacobson, circulated by the Smithsonian Institution Traveling Exhibition Service, from April 2000 to early 2004 to at least fourteen venues, after which the photographer donated them to the Archives Center.

16 "Alexander Alland, Sr., Photoprints," 1985–1986 and 1930–1943, Smithsonian Institution, Smithsonian Online Virtual Archives, https://sova.si.edu/record/NMAH.AC.0204?s=0&n=10&t=C&q=Alexander+Alland&i=0.

17 "Guide to the Carlos de Wendler-Funaro Gypsy Research Collection," ca. 1920–1975, Smithsonian Institution, Smithsonian Online Virtual Archives, https://sova.si.edu/record/NMAH.AC.0161?s=0&n=10&t=C&q=Carlos+de+Wendler&i=0.

18 "Guide to the United Shoe Machinery Corporation Records," 1898–1987. Smithsonian Institution, Smithsonian Online Virtual Archives, https://sova.si.edu/record/NMAH.AC.0277?s=0&n=10&t=C&q=United+Shoe&i=0.

19 See Arthur d'Arazien, *Big Picture: The Artistry of d'Arazien* (Kent, OH: Kent State University Press, 2002). "Guide to the Arthur d'Arazien Industrial Photographs," ca. 1930–2002, https://sova.si.edu/record/NMAH.AC.0314?s=0&n=10&t=C&q=Arthur+d%27Arazien&i=0. His prints are also in the NMAH Photographic History Collection, from a 1962 exhibition.

20 David Plowden, *The Hand of Man on America*, introduction by David Haberstich (Washington, DC: Smithsonian Institution Press, 1971). This publication accompanied one of Plowden's first exhibitions, at the Smithsonian Institution, in 1970.

21 "Costa Sakalleriou Photoprints," n.d., Smithsonian Institution, Smithsonian Online Virtual Archives, https://sova.si.edu/record/NMAH.AC.1456?s=0&n=10&t=C&q=Costa&i=0.

22 "Guide to the G. Dwoyid Olmstead Photonegatives," ca. 1941–1949, Smithsonian Institution, Smithsonian Online Virtual Archives, https://sova.si.edu/record/NMAH.AC.0270?s=0&n=10&t=C&q=G.+Dwoyid+Olmstead&i=0. Daniel Schulman, ed., *A Force for Change: African American Art and the Julius Rosenwald Fund* (Spertus Museum, Allentown Art Museum, Montclair Art Museum / Evanston: Northwestern University Press, 2009).

23 Deborah Willis, *Black: A Celebration of a Culture* (Irvington, NY: Hylas Publishing, 2004), 87–111.

24 Elizabeth Bruenig, "The Battered American Dream," *Washington Post*, July 17, 2018, A15.

25 "Scurlock Studio Records, Series 8: Scurlock Studio Business Records," 1907–1996, Smithsonian Institution, Smithsonian Online Virtual Archives, https://sova.si.edu/record/NMAH.AC.0618.S08?s=0&n=10&t=C&q=Scurlock+Studio&i=0.

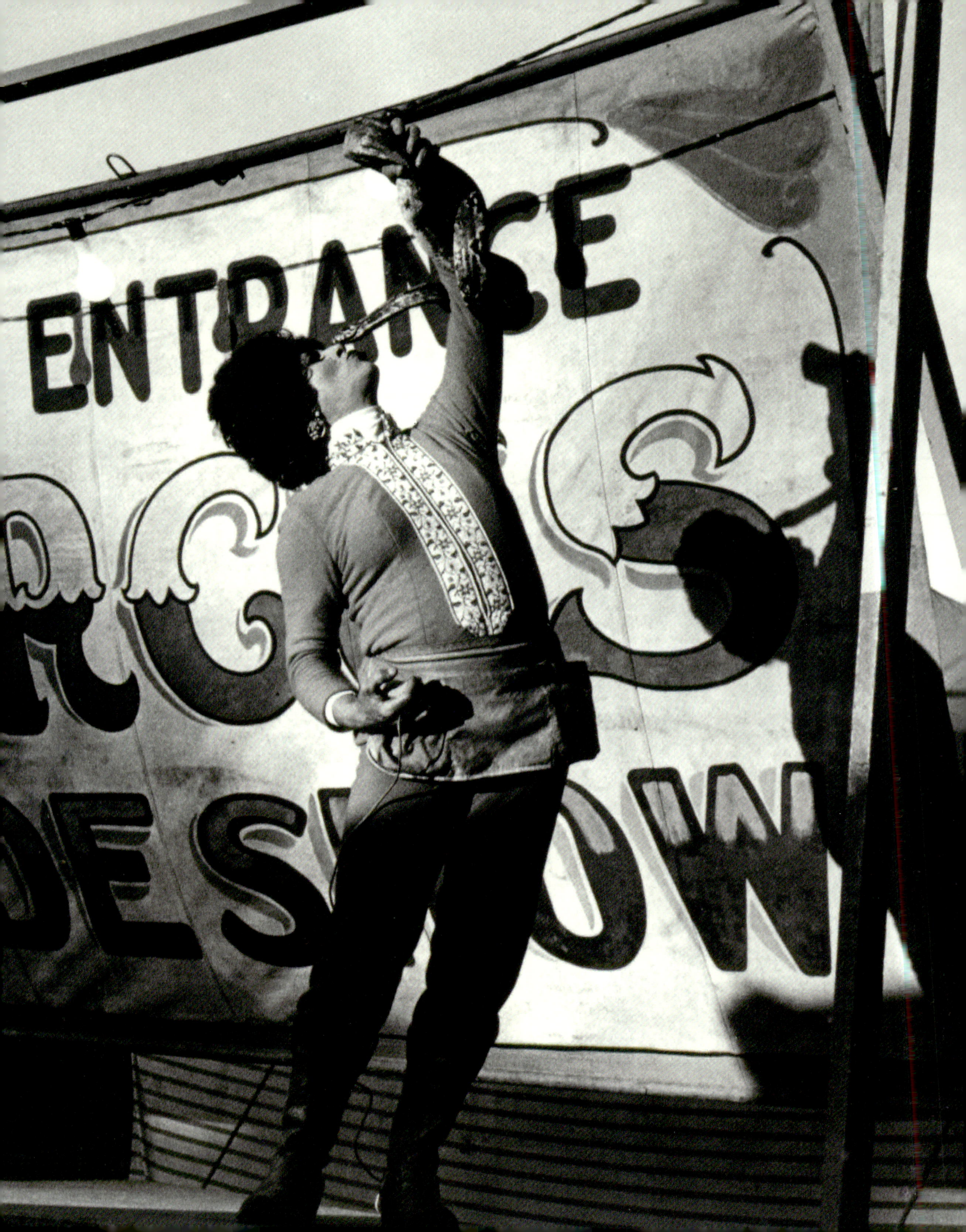
ENTRANCE

Ladies and Gentlemen Historical Parallels in Circus and Photography

SHANNON T. PERICH

Striking examples of the public's ongoing fascination with circus and photography from showman P. T. Barnum's era of the 1840s to Dawn Rogala's photographic project of the 1990s are found throughout the National Museum of American History (NMAH) Photographic History Collection. This record reveals the constant intersection of photography and circus, as rapid advances in technology captured more than a century of traveling shows across the American landscape. The public embraced photography across various technological and economic boundaries that tell the tale of the circus in different ways. When Rogala was compelled to photograph traveling circuses with her thirty-five millimeter and medium-format cameras in the 1990s, she did not know that this form of American entertainment was going to change dramatically and that traveling circuses would all but disappear within a decade of the completion of her project. Historians will be forever grateful for her wild idea, gumption, and persistence. The Smithsonian Institution is grateful for her donation of negatives, prints, and ephemera that capture the end of an era. Rogala's work joins the Smithsonian's early circus imagery, bookending a vital but now nearly extinct form of American entertainment. This essay is a photographic tour through the collection of circus imagery at NMAH, exploring how national identity and cultural history have informed the creation and use of circus photography.

The popular phrase "Yankee push" was used in P. T. Barnum's obituary (*New York Times*, April 8, 1891) to describe some of the showman's most striking achievements. "Yankee push" was seen as a powerful combination of energy, shrewdness, enthusiasm, self-reliance, pluck, and endurance. There is also a uniquely American gumption and boldness embodied in this phrase that is no longer in day-to-day use but might be revived to describe Dawn Rogala and the people depicted in her photographs. Rogala's small and relatively inexpensive cameras and film allowed her to be mobile, unobtrusive, and versatile. She could prowl behind the scenes and blend in to circus life. The portable technology gave her an opportunity to make some ten thousand negatives with relative ease. Her training as a graphic designer shaped her long-form documentary style and aesthetic, which combined action, narrative, and composition. Without knowing it, Rogala was following a tradition of documentary photographers and photojournalists who recorded and revealed aspects of American life. Rogala's images depict the rippling muscles of laborers pulling ropes (see Plates 34–37); the loving application of clown makeup (see Plates 122–123); well-worn shoes, refreshed with spray paint (see Plate 141); and picturesque scenes of elephants raising poles in the big top (see Plates 27–31). Her images focus on the reality of the labor and repetition of circus life, and are overtly influenced by her love of the circus and subtly informed by the fantasy and romance of the circus in American entertainment.

Rogala's circuses are not the slick, mass-audience productions of the late twentieth century. When Rogala photographed her first circus in 1992, Boyz II Men, Mariah Carey, and Pearl Jam were on the music charts.

Detail of Figure 35

The Mall of the Americas opened in Minnesota, and the video game company Nintendo opened their World of Nintendo stores to sell game consoles and cartridges. The circus, rooted in the tradition of nineteenth-century performance, was a struggling but still popular form of entertainment across the United States.

Circus acts arrived on American shores in the 1790s, but it was not until the 1830s that the circus became a favorite pastime for general audiences.[1] Photography, with patents in England and France in 1839, took a solid hold in popular culture over the course of the 1840s. Janet M. Davis, author of *The Circus Age: Culture and Society under the American Big Top,* suggests "The evolution of the circus during the nineteenth century is a cultural metonym [parallel] for national expansion and infrastructural development."[2] What we see happening in the circus, we see in the rest of American culture. Photography was evolving in the same environment, recording the very cultural and technological changes it was experiencing. In this way, the photographic record of the circus can be seen as a marker of the changing American culture. Railroads and an expanding highway system could take the same show to many towns, providing anticipated spectacular experiences announced in advance by circulated images by magazines, broadside posters, hype men, and newspaper stories.

The best-known name associated with circuses is perhaps P. T. Barnum (Figure 23). Barnum's flair for showmanship took hold of the American imagination, and his grandiose business plans succeeded in a burgeoning industrial economy that gave potential audiences more spending money and leisure time.[3] From the late 1700s and into early decades of the 1800s, the end of the first American Industrial Revolution saw the United States shift from an agrarian economy to one increasingly based on manufacturing. As the country began to build a national culture, the circus arts and photography needed mass appeal to generate cultural cachet and revenue. Both activities appealed to a growing middle class with a hunger for the spectacle and a desire for the newest forms of entertainment. In the beginning, photography and Barnum's unique brand of showmanship had a mutually beneficial relationship. The circus used photography as one method to attract audiences, and photography needed consumers to build its market. Photographers liked the circus because the images, which existed outside of most people's everyday experiences, made for good, saleable subject matter.

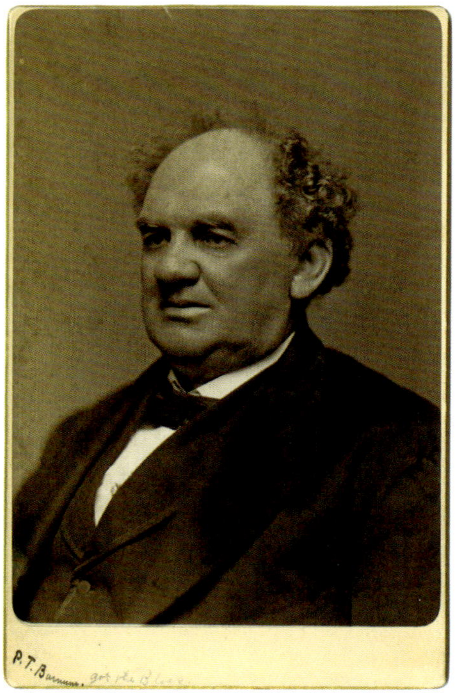

FIGURE 23. *P. T. Barnum*, George K. Warren, 1860s. Cabinet card. NMAH PHC catalog number 1995.0231.115. Warren's portrait of P. T. Barnum served as the image for the frontispiece in the 1878 edition of *Struggles and Triumphs; or Forty Years' Recollections of P. T. Barnum*. Barnum would use this image many times. Warren kept the glass plate negative and periodically made prints at Barnum's request.

THE CIRCUS IN EVERYDAY LIFE

The spectacle of the circus once loomed large in the American cultural narrative and imagination. It is a compelling subject that cuts across many aspects of photographic image making. In this set of images from the Photographic History Collection that accompany this essay we see the spectacle of the circus in advertising, in Halloween costumes, and as a subject for fine art.

The portrait of a clown taken by photographer William J. Nagel (Figure 24) may have been used to advertise Ansco Color Printon, a commercial printing process marketed to professional and amateur photographers. The image is a striking example of why clowns appear so often in color photography. In her essay, Rogala describes how she chose color film to capture the riot of circus color and excitement. The rough makeup of Nagel's clown seems not to upset the cheery child, dressed in his own vibrant and colorful patterns and textures. Ansco's Printon was a relatively limited-use color reversal process used from the mid-1940s into the 1960s. The unusual print was based on acetate film, rather than paper, which gave an extra sheen to the final image.[4] It is likely that the color saturation of this print has diminished a bit over time—as has the appearance of clowns in contemporary advertising.

The classic French clown Pierrot is known as a sad clown pining for the character Columbine after she spurns him for Harlequin. Margrethe Mather's platinum/palladium print from 1920 of Danish-born actor Otto Matiesen costumed as Pierrot (Figure 25) uses the sentimental, soft-focus style of pictorialism to emphasize the moody quality of the subject. By simultaneously employing a brutal minimalism, she further isolates the forlorn character.[5] In Rogala's photographs we see the ghost of Pierrot walking among trailers on an American circus lot (see Plate 55). Throughout the history of photography, especially when photographic imaging is less precious and less formal, many people have dressed in various forms of clown costumes,[6] not unlike the young boy in this 1950s snapshot (Figure 26).

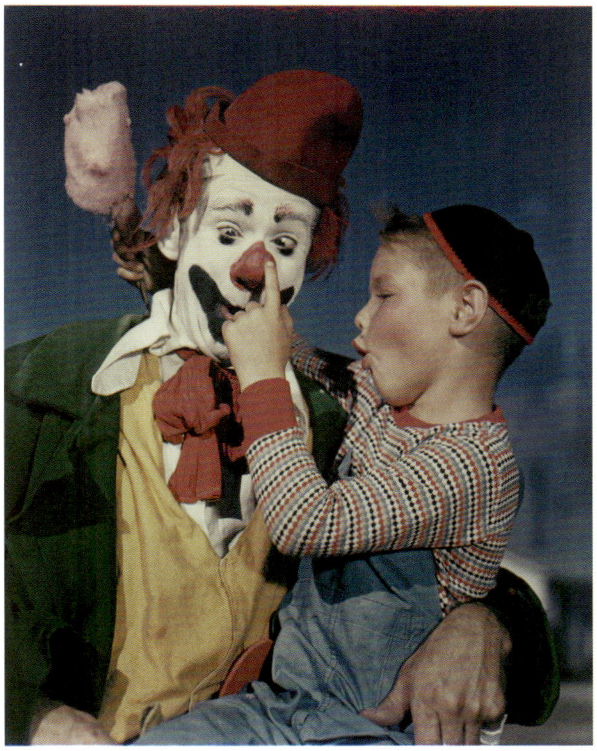

FIGURE 24. Untitled, William J. Nagel, 1940s. Ansco Printon print. NMAH PHC catalog number PG.004584E.

Clowns are not the only aspect of the circus that have been embraced outside the big top. Trapeze classes are available in many areas.[7] The author Alyssa Roenigk points out that the recent interest in learning to fly for fitness might be inspired by the musician Pink or by actor Reese Witherspoon, who starred in the 2011 film *Water for Elephants,* based on the novel of the same name and set in a 1930s traveling circus. Combining an appreciation for the strength, athleticism, and grace required in physical performance, a trapeze class also provides participants with the chance to feel like part of a circus when performing one of the more spectacular aspects of the show. Circus arts schools are now opening across the United States, but circus arts clubs have long histories at colleges and universities. Since 1947,

CLOCKWISE FROM TOP RIGHT:

FIGURE 25. *Pierrot*, Margrethe Mather, 1920. Platinum/palladium print. NMAH PHC catalog number PG.003622.

FIGURE 26. Boy in clown costume, unidentified photographer, November 1957. Gelatin silver print. NMAH PHC catalog number 1999.0281.047. The date of the photograph suggests that the child is wearing a Halloween costume.

FIGURE 27. *FSU Circus*, John Wesley Stipe, March 1970. Gelatin silver print. NMAH PHC catalog number 1995.0119.0273.

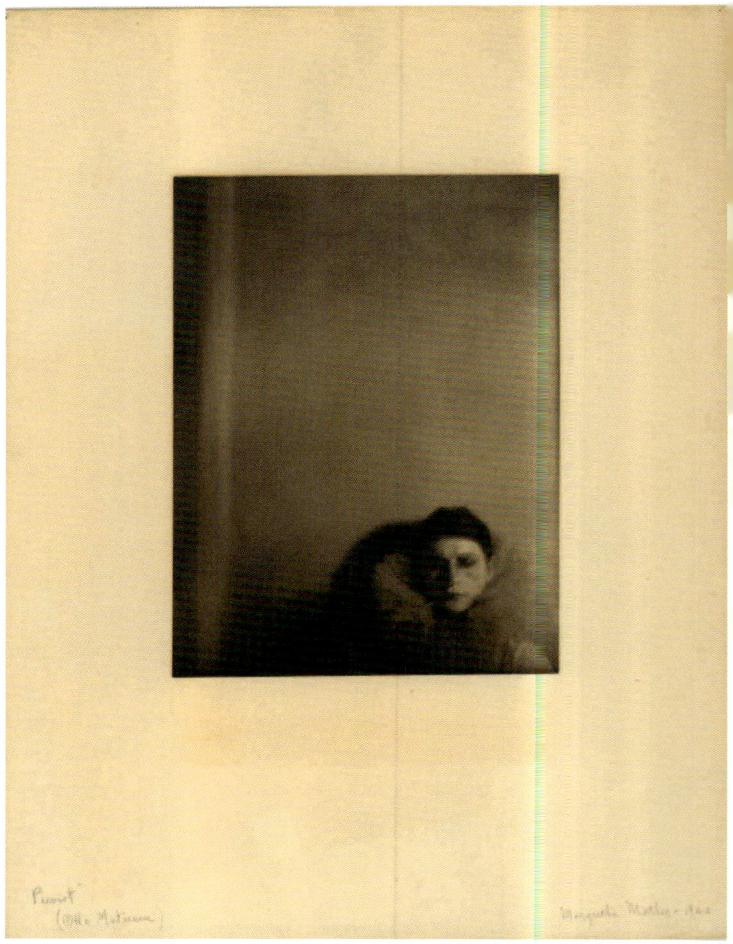

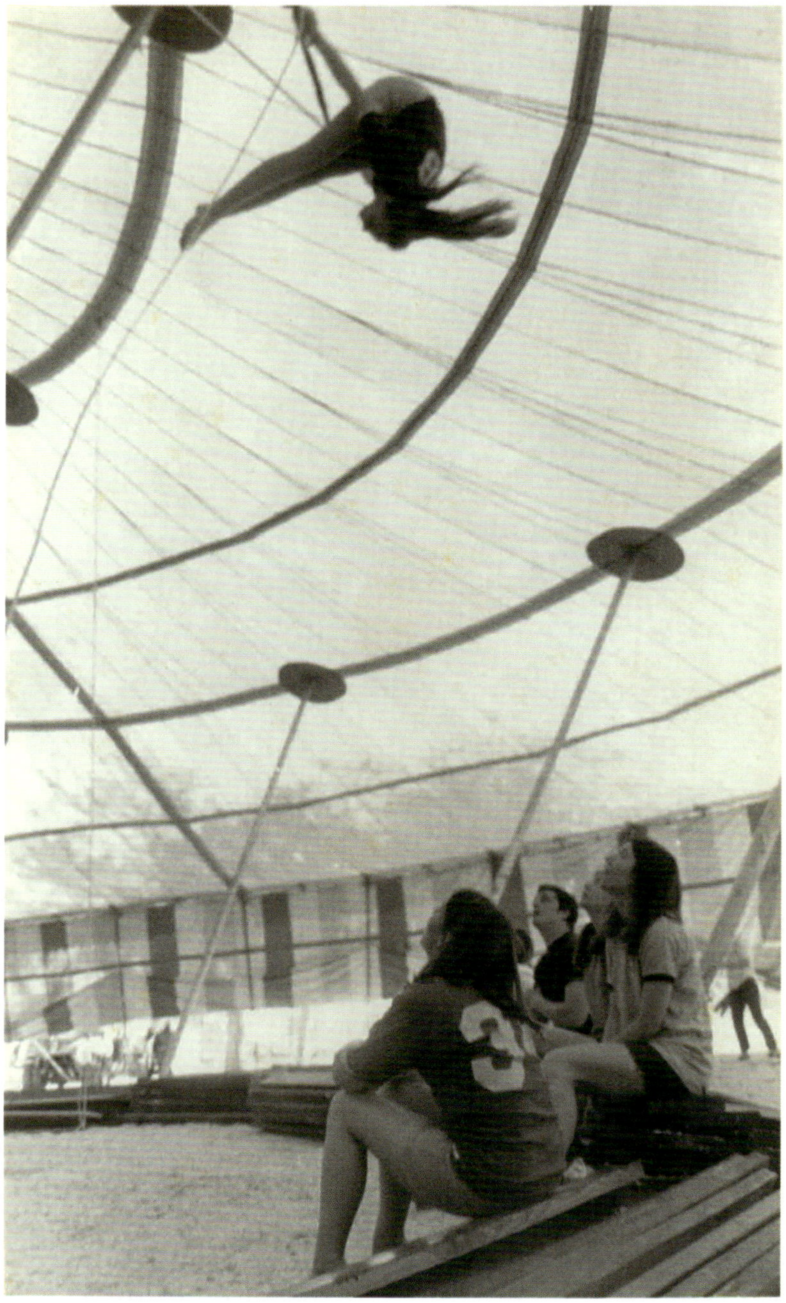

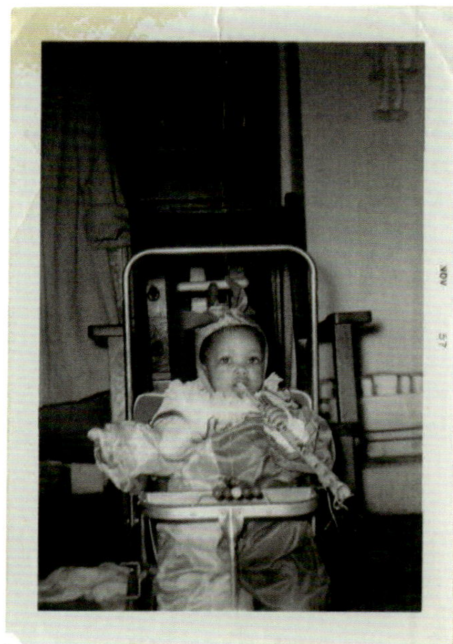

Florida State University has offered a coed, extracurricular activity group called the Flying High Circus.[8] This 1970 photograph (Figure 27), taken by *Florida Times-Union* photojournalist John Wesley Stipe, captures group members during trapeze practice.

Perhaps one of the best-known intersections of circus and photography is Richard Avedon's *Dovima with Elephants, Evening Dress by Dior, Cirque d'Hiver, Paris, August 1955* that appeared in *Harper's Bazaar* (Figure 28). The Phaidon book *Photographs That Changed the World* lists this image as one of the most influential photographs in history; in it Avedon contrasts the smooth, luscious fabric of an evening gown against the roughness of the elephants' skin, and juxtaposes human freedom with animals in chains. The model, Dovima, gestures with fearlessness and power, causing the much larger animal to shy from her. If only a beautiful evening gown could really subdue the circus of life and turn women into goddesses! In Rogala's photographs, women ride elephants too large to fit into the tent entrance (see Plates 146–148), yet the animals display power and grace, and the relationship between humans and animals is often gentler than as portrayed in Avedon's photograph (see Plate 59).

This small sampling of images begins to show how far the circus extends into our collective cultural experience as audiences, producers, and consumers to create meaningful narratives. Rogala's large body of photographs now at the Smithsonian Institution will help future researchers and historians understand, at least in part, how the widespread creative impulse to draw on ideas that represent the circus are understood broadly.[9] Those traveling circuses that went to rural and urban communities created shared experiences across the United States, forming a common cultural reference.

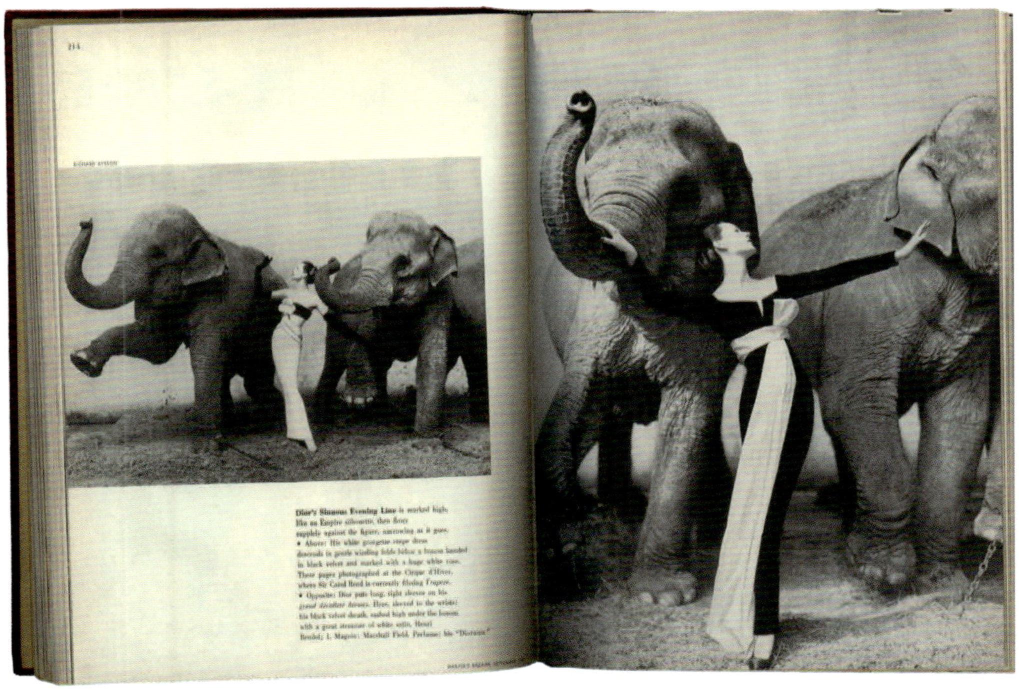

FIGURE 28. *Dovima with Elephants,* Richard Avedon, 1955. Spread from *Harper's Bazaar.* Smithsonian Library call number TT500.H3. These images appeared in the September 1955 issue of *Harper's Bazaar* among nearly a dozen photographs that accompanied "Carmel Snow's Paris Report." The image on the right-hand page would become one of Avedon's most iconic photographs. The version of this print held in the National Museum of American History's Photographic History Collection is from the photographer's first one-man show, held at the Smithsonian Institution in 1962. After the exhibition, Avedon donated all of the exhibition prints to the Smithsonian.

THE EMERGENCE OF CIRCUS IN PHOTOGRAPHY

The 2017 musical motion picture *The Greatest Showman*—featuring actor Hugh Jackman as P. T. Barnum—blended fact and fiction with much artistic license. The result was an award-winning soundtrack and a narrative that mixed Barnum's public persona with contemporary storytelling. Barnum's autobiography, *Struggles and Triumphs*, is also an entertaining—and less than accurate—representation of his life.[10] While much has been written about Barnum, it is the photographic legacy left in his wake that keeps his real-life cast of characters alive.

Barnum believed in the value of his contributions to American cultural life, but he knew that the social elite often disparaged popular forms of entertainment.[11] His notable efforts to combine audiences of high-minded moralists and those with broader tastes include the introduction of "moral dramas" and public performances by more sophisticated artists to bring the two groups together in the same performance spaces. Barnum turned Harriet Beecher Stowe's abolitionist novel *Uncle Tom's Cabin* into a play, and he produced an international concert tour for the Swedish opera star Jenny Lind.[12] The performances of *Uncle Tom's Cabin* were great successes. "I prided myself upon the fact that parents and children could attend the dramatic performances in the so-called, Lecture Room," a venue that expanded his ticket sales by allowing women and children to attend without worry of being offended or corrupted.[13] Jenny Lind's concert tour, with ninety-three performances held between September 11, 1850, and June 9, 1851,[14] was perhaps more personally significant to the showman. "The Jenny Lind enterprise was more audacious [and] more immediately remunerative," recounted Barnum, "and I remember it with a pride which I do not attempt to conceal."[15] Audience members paid up to $225 (about $7,200 in 2018 dollars) for tickets to a single performance by Lind, and the singer was mobbed at venues and hotels. One way fans could be close to Lind, as well as other favored performers, was to purchase a copy of her image. In the early 1850s, paper photography had not taken hold in the United States, and daguerreotypes were still popular. The only way to make multiple copies of a daguerreotype was to rephotograph it, as in this image of Lind (Figure 29).

While Lind's American success may have been Barnum's favorite achievement, it is the little person Charles S. Stratton—known by the stage name General Tom Thumb—who is best remembered by the public at large. Barnum and Stratton had a long run together. Tom Thumb began touring as a novelty act in 1843 at the age of five and soon became a cultural icon. More than ten thousand people attended the performer's funeral in 1883.[16] Stratton was small in stature but physically of ordinary proportions. By the standards of the day, this made his performances seem childlike and charming to audiences. Barnum employed other little people, as did his sometime-competitor and collaborator Colonel William K. Ellinger (Figure 30). Performers such as Colonel Small, and Commodore Foote and his sister Eliza Nestle—known as the "Fairy Queen"—would occasionally perform at circuses, as well as other venues, with Tom Thumb and other little people from other circuses.[17]

While some people of small stature were treated with a kind of dubious respect, others who did not conform to typical physical standards were relegated to traveling freak shows or sideshows that featured human oddities displayed to audiences on their way to the circus tent. Freak shows were not part of the circuses Rogala photographed. Though the treatment of these performers in the early days of the circus is an uncomfortable aspect of American history, they played an unwitting role in shaping circus appeal and increasing attendance numbers. Though Barnum may have created an extraordinary life for some of his employees, he and other promoters capitalized on an emerging cultural narrative of white superiority based on pseudoscientific ideas. Charles Darwin's *Origins of Species* was published in 1859, creating interest in finding a "missing link" in human evolution and enforcing cultural rationales that discriminated against people of

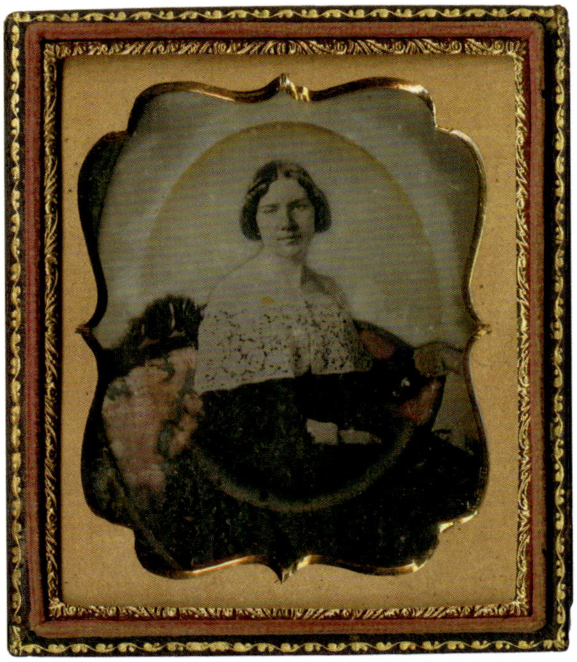

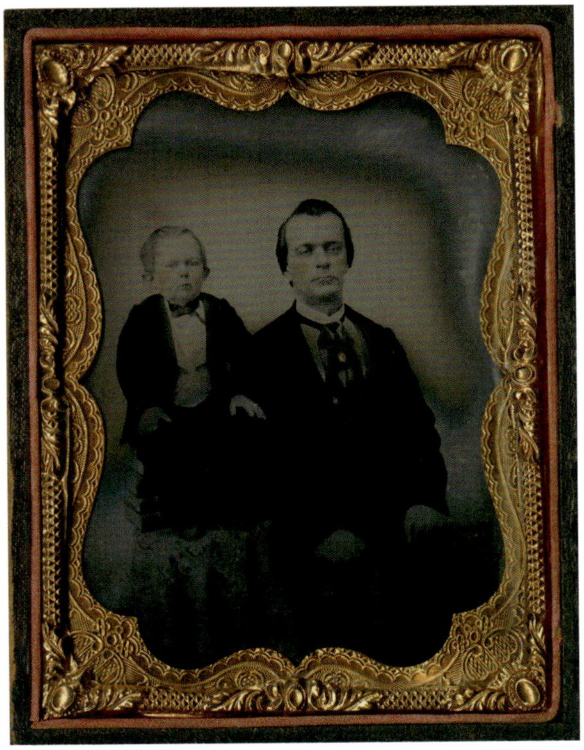

FIGURE 29. *Jenny Lind*, unidentified photographer, ca. 1850. Daguerreotype. NMAH PHC catalog number PG.76.05.1 This is a copy of a Southworth & Hawes daguerreotype depicting the "Swedish Nightingale" Jenny Lind. The tarnished circle in the center of the image is from a previous mat that was removed when an unknown owner chose to use the more decorative brass mat that now frames the image. A daguerreotype is a unique photographic image made in the camera on a highly polished silver surface of a copper plate. In most cases, the image is covered in glass and placed in a case. Note that here, the typically monochromatic image has been enlivened by the hand application of gold to Lind's necklace and red pigment to the couch.

FIGURE 30. *Commodore Foote and Colonel Ellinger*, unidentified photographer, late 1850s. Ambrotype. NMAH PHC catalog number PG.001563H. Ambrotypes are made when a glass plate negative is backed by a dark piece of paper, fabric, or even paint, which makes the image appear as a positive. Like daguerreotypes, they are most often cased with brass mats and protective glass.

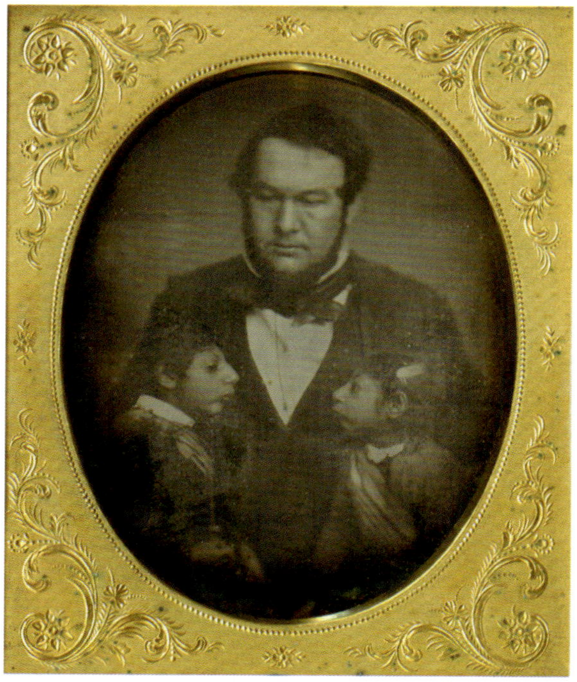

FIGURE 31. *Aztec Children with Unidentified Man*, unidentified photographer, 1857. Daguerreotype. NMAH PHC catalog number PG.000205.

color and gender in the guise of scientific and theological discussion. In his book *Staging Stigma: A Critical Examination of the American Freak Show,* Michael Chemers writes that the display of performers such as Tom Thumb was presented as "respectable and decent"—sometimes challenging prevailing prejudice by creating opportunities for those with disabilities to showcase their talents—but fueled by the values of conformity and commodity.[18] A daguerreotype in NMAH's Photographic History Collection from the early 1850s depicts "the Aztec children" (Figure 31), with the stage names Maximo and Bartola, who became part of Barnum's show after years of being exhibited to royal audiences and examined by scientists in the United States and Europe. The children were from El Salvador and were advertised as "the last of an ancient Mezo American race." Both children suffered from microcephaly and perhaps dwarfism.[19] Similar to the "respectable and decent" display of Tom Thumb, the daguerreotype of the children is composed with postures of dignity and artistic skill in lighting. The daguerreotype is a beautiful object, an image on a silver-coated copper plate encased with glittering brass, lush velvet, and tooled leather. The elegant material culture of the image and the object obscures the day-to-day existence and mistreatment of these children. The cased image might have been on display in a gallery, or in a home as proof of the owner's experience of having seen the abnormalities described in scientific and medical publications.

BRINGING THE CIRCUS HOME

By the mid-1850s, the one-of-a-kind daguerreotype gave way to techniques for producing multiple images. A newly discovered light-sensitive coating known as collodion—gun cotton dissolved in ether and mixed with silver nitrate—could be poured onto a variety of surfaces to produce images inexpensively. This single innovation created a new boom in photography. Flow collodion onto a thin sheet of iron, and it becomes an inexpensive tintype. Flow it onto a piece of glass and put it in a camera before it dries, and it becomes a glass plate negative from which many paper prints can be made and distributed. Underexpose the glass plate negative, put something dark behind it to highlight the positive image, place it in a case, and it becomes an ambrotype. Collodion made possible the very popular and highly collectible carte de visite.

The carte de visite (CdV) could be printed one image at a time, but specially designed cameras with multiple lenses and repeating back plate holders could quickly produce multiple images from a single plate. The glass plate negative was laid directly on top of thin albumen paper and exposed to sunlight. Once developed, the paper was cut into individual images, and each image was pasted onto a thin card (a bit larger than today's business card). Most CdVs were portraits. An 1850s CdV of Barnum performer Admiral Dot (Figure 32) made in photographer Mathew Brady's New York City studio is an example of how some images of circus performers were printed and distributed. CdVs were often placed into albums among portraits of family and friends, as well as celebrities. One album page from the Photographic History Collection displays Stratton (Tom Thumb) and his wife, Lavinia Warren, alongside members of the British royal family (Figure 33). The ability to purchase, collect, and organize portraits in albums allowed members of the public to incorporate the circus into their everyday lives.

Most early photographs of the circus are portraits of performers because early cameras were large and not easily taken out of studios, and long exposure times would create blurry images of performances in the dim tent. A large portion of circus portraits were of sideshow performers. Over time, advances in technology made it possible for photographers to capture a wider variety of circus activities, and advances in treating medical conditions and social attitudes have changed the ways we view people. The last widely produced collectable circus photographs appeared in the 1870s and were produced into the 1890s in the form of cabinet cards. Similar to cartes de visite, cabinet cards were larger photographs mounted to cards that could be displayed at home in frames as well as collected in albums.

Mademoiselle Aimee (Figure 34) may have traveled with the Bunnell Circus sideshows. A brochure found in the Beinecke Library at Yale tells a fantastical story about Aimee's immigration to Mexico and how her father began to tattoo her at the age of five, fearing she might be stolen. Her story includes a dramatic tale of traveling across the American West and joining the circus to earn an income.[20] The irony, of course, is that the feature that was to make her supposedly undesirable, the tattoos, is what drove audiences to see her and purchase her image. Over the course of the century, tattoo art and its history would become familiar and less exotic. Moral and ethical standards shifted. Carnivals and traveling circuses also saw a wider separation in that carnivals often centered on amusement rides. By the 1970s, freak shows reentered the public sphere alongside burlesque and striptease acts as forms of self-expression and self-agency.[21]

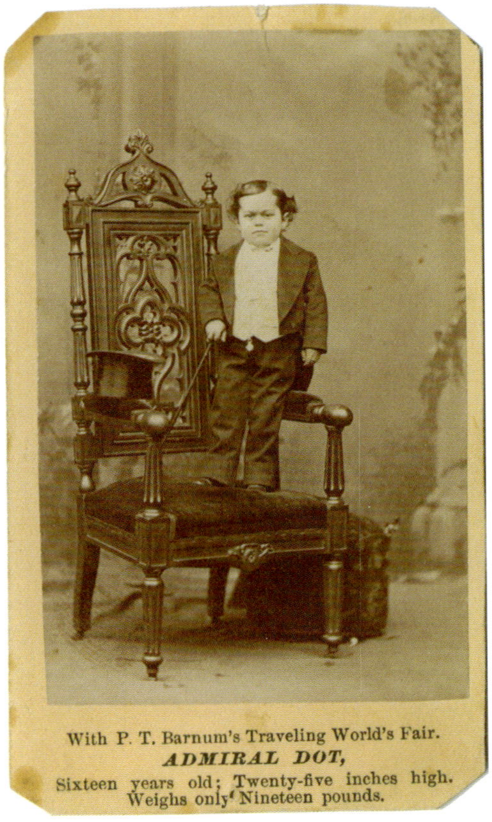

FIGURE 32. *Admiral Dot*, published by E. & H. T. Anthony, 1860s. Carte de visite. NMAH PHC catalog number 73.34.22.

Sally Bordwell photographed traveling carnivals in the American South, where she and writer Leslie Sussman met performers with acts that included a frog eater, a lizard woman, and other traditional gimmicks associated with the sideshows. Comparing Rogala's photograph of Bobby Fairchild with the Walker Bros. Circus (see Plate 218) to Bordwell's snake charmer (Figure 35), we see Rogala's depiction of an intimate human-animal relationship in a nonperformance setting rather than a relationship made exotic and sensational. In doing so, Rogala lifts the curtain, deflating a tingle of fear. The photographer Henry Horenstein, who has made a rich career of examining American communities and subcultures, recorded *The Little Cowboy, Fire Eater* (Figure 36) in 1997 in the context of performance art. This performer, who in Barnum's era might have had his stature and race dictate his act, can now present a circus act of his choosing.

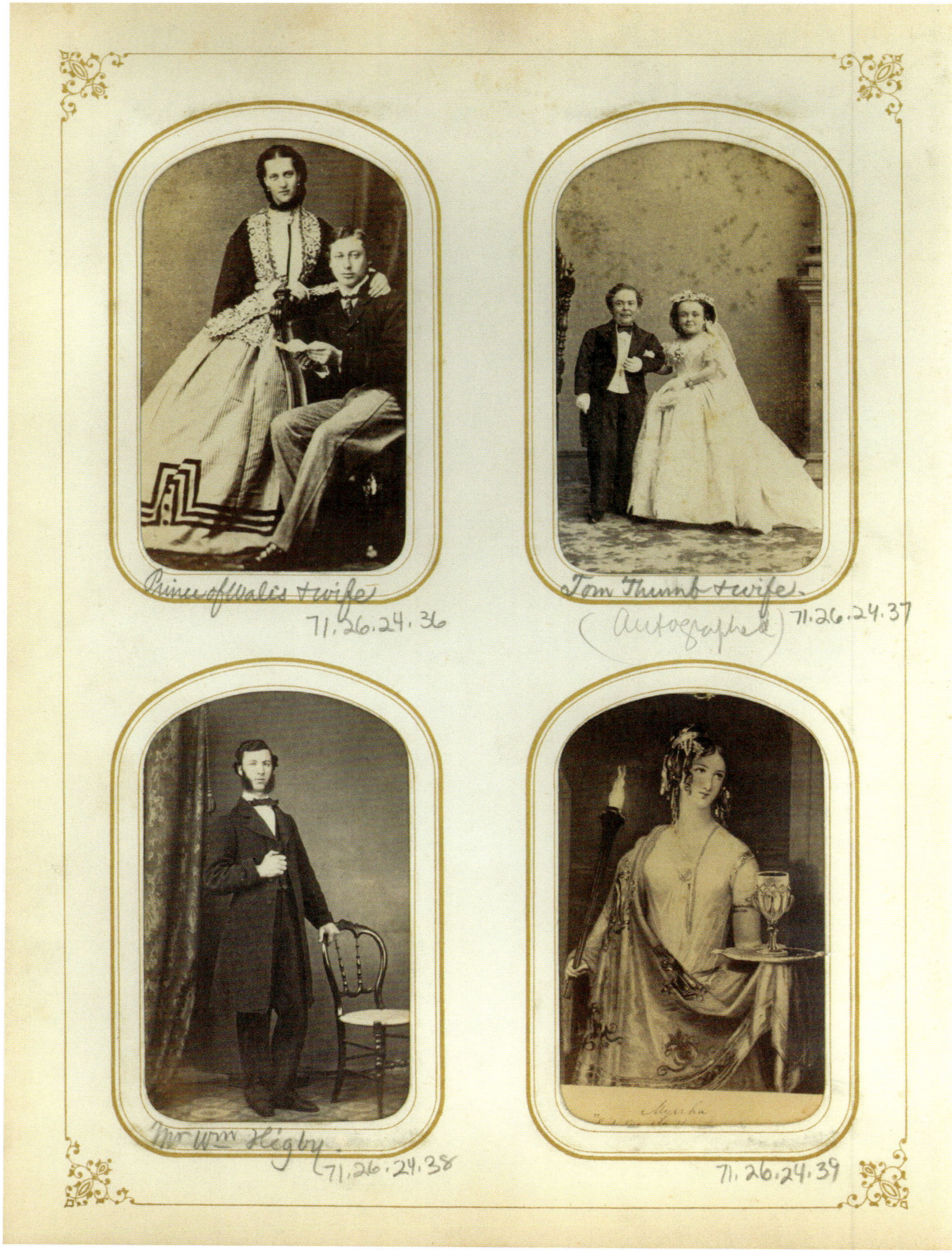

FIGURE 33. *Tom Thumb, Lavinia Warren, and Others*, 1860s. Carte de viste album page. NMAH PHC catalog number PG.71.26.24. In this album, the owners have placed the two iconic couples, the Prince of Wales and his wife and Tom Thumb and Lavinia Warren, with a young William Higby (who would go on to serve in both the Californian State Senate and the US Senate), and a copy of a painting depicting Mryyah, a Greek goddess and the mother of Adonis. The combination of these images suggests that the album owner was thinking about cultural and political power.

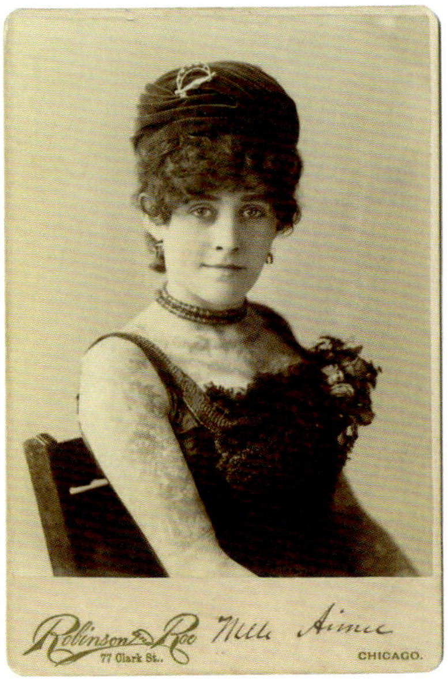

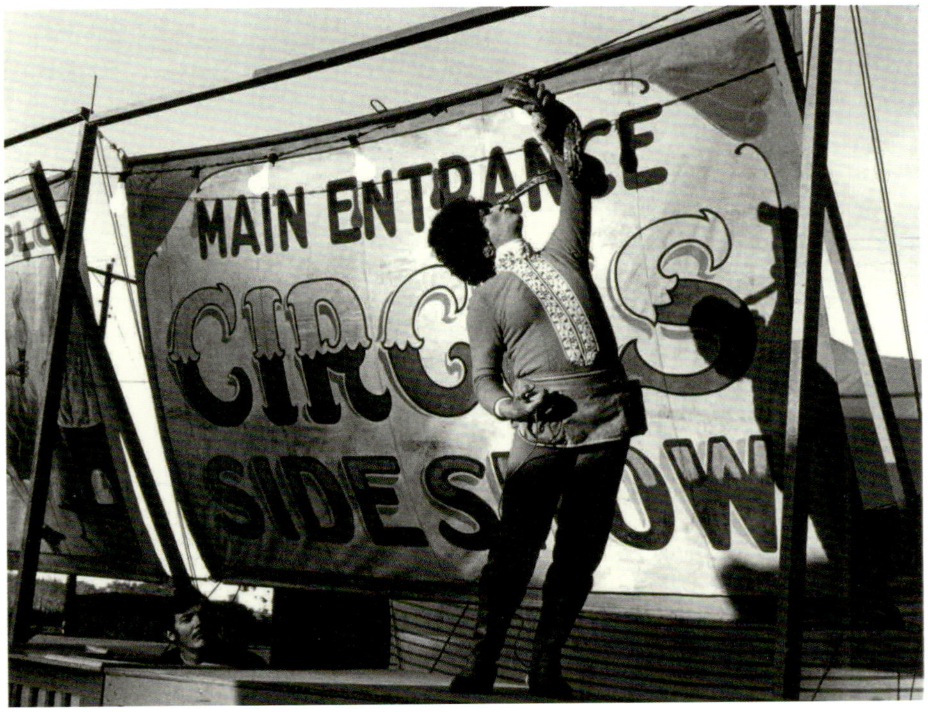

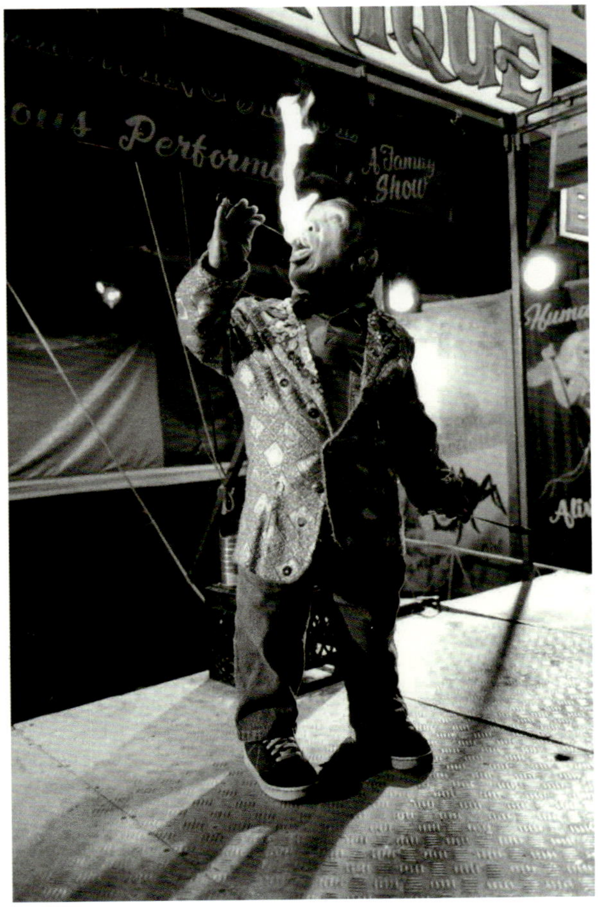

CLOCKWISE FROM TOP LEFT:

FIGURE 34. *Mlle Aimee*, Robinson & Roe, probably late 1880s. Cabinet card. NMAH PHC catalog number PG.74.25.04.

FIGURE 35. *Tony, the Snakecharmer*, Sally Bordwell, 1972. Gelatin silver print. NMAH PHC catalog number 2010.0250.057
In the early 1970s, photographer Sally Bordwell and writer Lesley Sussman traveled together through the American South documenting mobile carnivals. Through her photographs we can see a blend of the ride- and game-based carnivals with sideshows and circus-like attractions.

FIGURE 36. *Little Cowboy, Fire Eater*, Henry Horenstein, 1997. Gelatin-silver print. NMAH PHC catalog number 2011.0033.05.

TAKING THE CAMERA TO THE CIRCUS

Photographers such as Bordwell, Horenstein, and Rogala all benefited from the portability of modern camera equipment. In 1888, Kodak introduced the "You Push the Button, We Do the Rest" portable camera that initiated the era in which picture making was separated from film processing. The American circus was then in its golden era, strongly influenced by Barnum's showmanship and the subsequent iterations of Ringling Bros. and Barnum & Bailey Circus that would be billed as "The Greatest Show on Earth." Photography and the circus were becoming more spectacular, and more people were hungry for both. Millions of photographs were made possible by ever-smaller cameras and faster films that could capture action in low light. The popular Brownie camera was introduced in 1900 and marketed to women and children as an easy-to-use device. The increased ease of making photographs with cameras that were inexpensive and highly portable brought the camera to the circus in the hands of audience members. The circus was an exciting subject for amateur photographers, presenting a show under the big top with ringmasters in tuxedoes, tightrope walkers and trapeze artists, clowns, and animal tricks with elephants, tigers, dogs, and horses. And film was easily developed at the local drug store or even at home, allowing amateur photographers to print their own photographs.

In amateur circus-related images from the Photographic History Collection, we see a variety of processes, photographers' approaches, and ways in which the circus is shown as part of community life—if even for just one day. A photographic process that was often accomplished with ease at home was the cyanotype. Cyanotypes were images made from an iron-based photographic process that turns the paper blue, and required only paper, sun, and water. It was a quick and easy way of printing—as long as one didn't mind the azure-only hues. An album of cyanotype photographs from the 1890s (Figure 37) depicting scenes from around Washington, DC, includes two circus images. In this time period most circuses still traveled by train. In many cities, elephants would lead a parade from

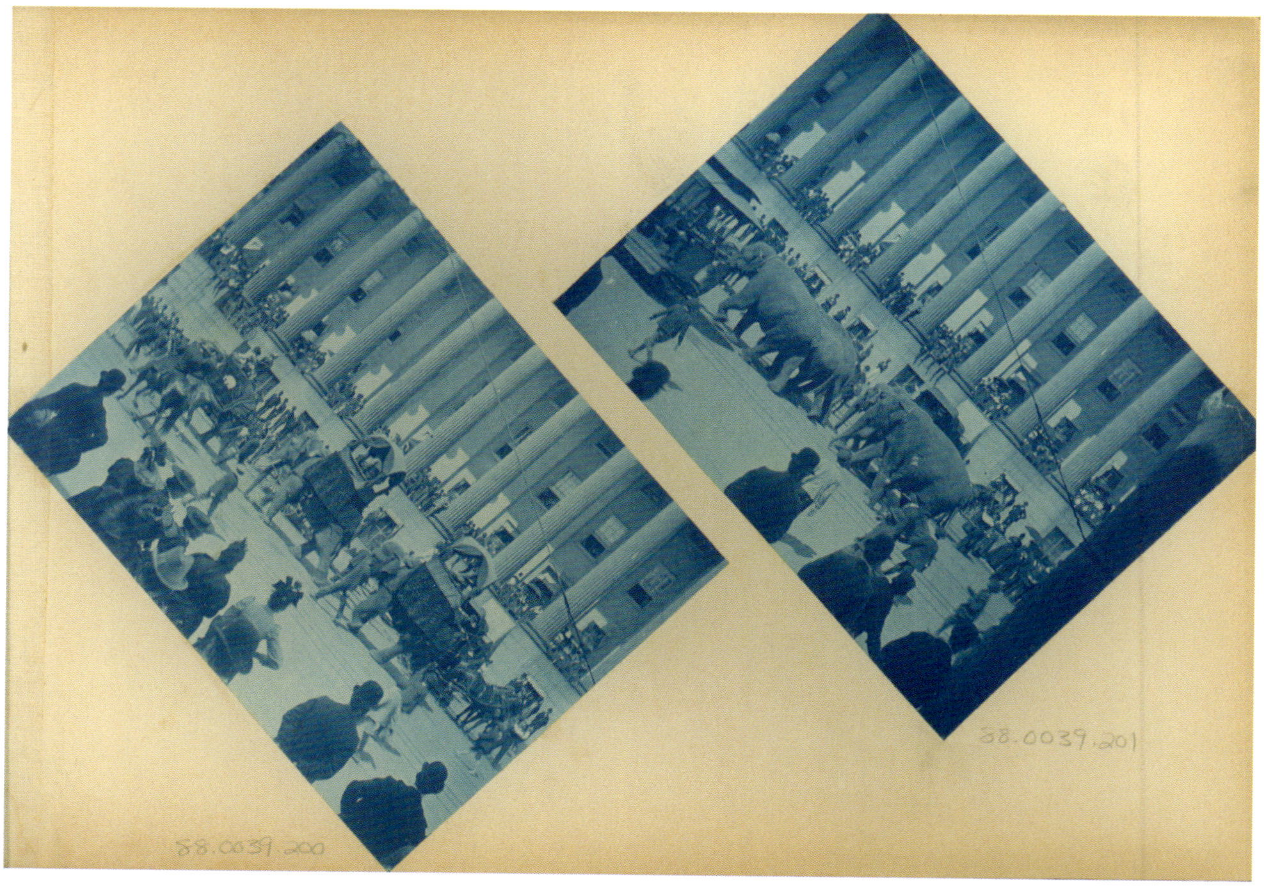

the train station to the circus grounds to announce the show's arrival. This led audiences to the venue and generated excitement and drew crowds as the parade passed by. In Rogala's archive, there is an image of an elephant posting the Big Apple Circus's taxes in a mailbox, as they usually played in Boston around tax day. Many elephants hold a unique place among circus animals as performers *and* as crew. Once at the circus grounds, some elephants help to raise the tents (see Plates 27–31). Rogala's archive holds many images of the relationships between elephants and people. (Rogala describes her elephant encounters in her essay in this volume.)

It wasn't just the elephants working behind the scenes. In 1909, travel writer Florence Albrecht and her husband, Emil, made a handwritten book, *Idle Record of an Idle Summer.* Created for their friend, the Philadelphia-based architect George Watson Hewitt, it details the couple's summer in Atlantic City, New Jersey. In her chapter for the month of May, Albrecht describes the circus coming to town. As an upper-class woman she did not attend the circus with the lower classes, yet she reveled in describing all the details of the parade, the circus preparations, and the impact it had on the city for the few days it was in town (Figure 38):

> Will it disturb you then to know that all those proud, white horses which by dozens and double dozens draw the huge red-and-gold "band-wagons," did prosaic service under plain, black, working harness before they donned these gorgeous trappings? That they hauled tents, poles, feed, pots and pans for the cooks, dishes for the mess tent, van-loads of drowsy animals, wagon-loads of paraphernalia for the performers from the train to the "grounds" and in a few hours will haul them all back again?[22]

Albrecht described camels as having "that supercilious look [that] is not assumed for, company manners' or parade."[23]

Camels were another favorite subject of circus goers with cameras. Between 1900 and about the start of World War I, photo postcards, actual photographs printed on photographic paper, with addresses and messages written on the back. This highly popular style of postcard was stamped and sent through the mail. One circus postcard mailed from Baraboo, Wisconsin, to Portland, Oregon, in August 1908 includes the handwritten note, "A camel can go eight days without a *drink*. How would you like to be a camel?" (Figure 39). Kodak's Autographic camera made negatives the same size as a postcard, and quick picture making

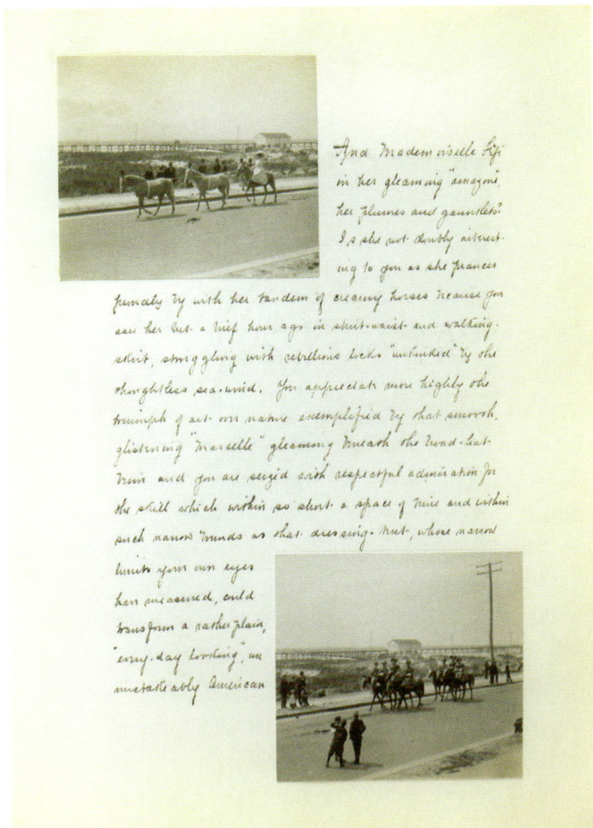

FIGURE 38. Page from *Idle Record of an Idle Summer*, Florence and Emil Albrecht, 1909. Platinum print. NMAH PHC catalog number PG.77.29.

(FACING) FIGURE 37. *Circus Elephants on Parade* likely Washington, DC, 1890s. Cyanotypes. NMAH PHC catalog number 88.0039.201. This page from a cyanotype album of scenes around Washington, DC, depicts the arrival of the circus in town.

FIGURE 39. "A Street Scene in Baraboo. A camel can go eight days without a *drink*. How would you like to be a camel?," unidentified photographer, 1908. Real photo postcard. NMAH PHC catalog number 2018.0166.0043. This postcard was sent to a Miss Emma A. Young. A handwritten note on the back states, "Received your postal, these are some of Ringling Bro's camels. If you have any postals, send them along. Yours without a struggle, L. P."

FIGURE 40. *Rice Brothers Circus, Alabama*, Walker Evans, 1936. Gelatin silver print. NMAH PHC catalog number, PG.069.143.10.

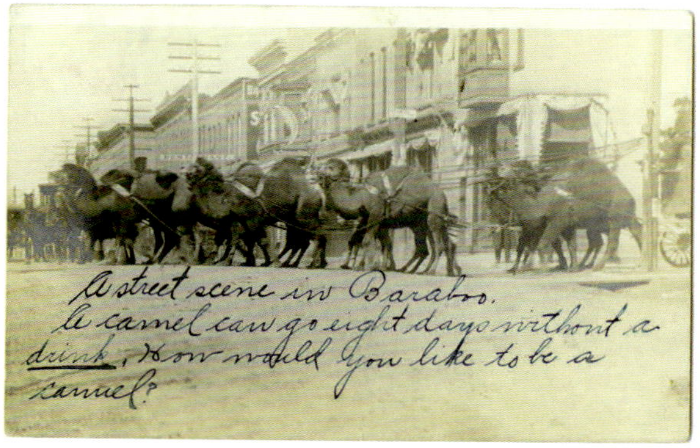

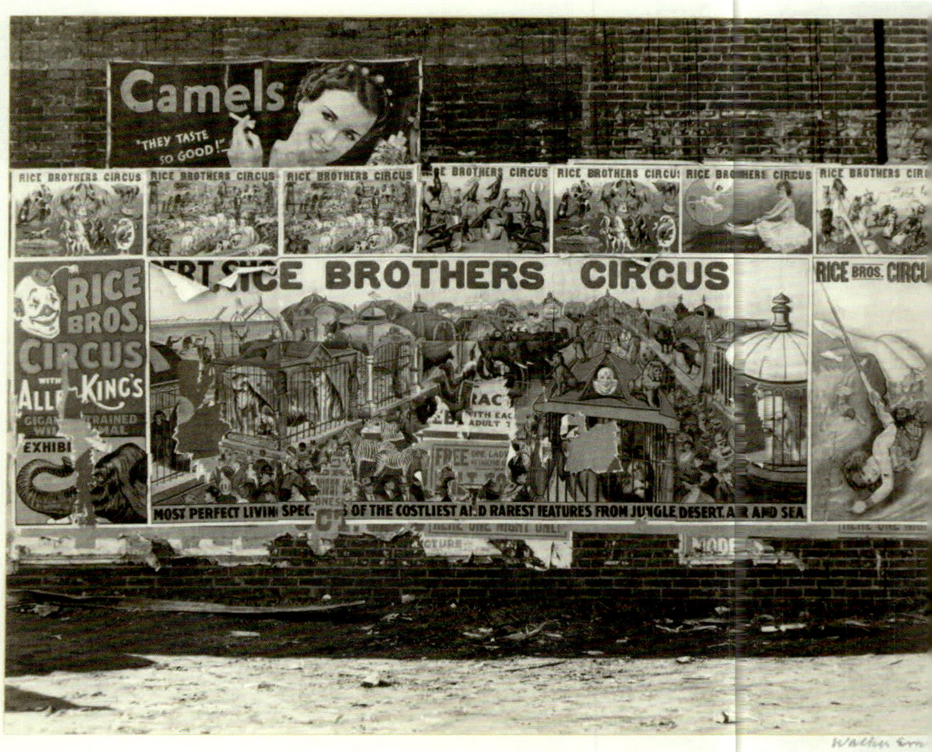

and printing meant that a local photographer could generate a small batch of postcards for a local market. The subjects of the postcards could be casual and personal, or more formal and professional. Like other small photographic formats and mass-manufactured postcards, real photo postcards were collectible. Today, with the aid of a postcard's postmarks, addresses, and handwritten titles and messages, we can map and track the routes of the circus and see the ways that individuals embraced and shared the circus experience.

While documenting American life in the mid-1930s for the Farm Security Administration, photographer Walker Evans recorded the trailers of the Ringling Brothers' winter quarters in Sarasota, Florida, and circus posters in Alabama.[24] In 1935, he recorded a group of posters advertising the Rice Brothers Circus (Figure 40) and the promise of a spectacular show that included performing seals, a rare sight in the Depression-era Deep South. The large, central image gives an overview of all there was to see and do, with smaller posters flanking the main image and forming a series of six vignettes across the top. The sheer scale of the advertising gives potential audiences the impression of a large and entertaining show. It is unclear how long those posters had been pasted to the wall before Evans recorded them. Large advertisements in this style were less frequent by the time Rogala traveled with the circus but were still in use by some of the larger shows (see Plate 190). The Federal Highway Act of 1956 created highways that bypassed many small towns at a time when the American circus faced added competition in a booming postwar economy in which music, movies, and television played a larger role in the amusement and entertainment businesses. In an article in *Billboard* in January 1959 , O. F. (Curley) Stewart—a circus manager for almost five decades—says there were once seventy-three "train circuses," most of which were no longer performing.[25]

By the mid-twentieth century, circus performances began to appear in convention centers and stadiums. In 1963, Harold "Doc" Edgerton photographed the acrobats of the Moscow Circus when the show performed at Boston Garden. A series of flashes created this single-frame image of multiple stages of the acrobat's trick to showcase the performer's physicality and studied movements (Figure 41). Edgerton's pioneering technique combined a camera flash with a shutter speed of roughly one-hundredth of second, allowing incremental exposures of the same movement.[26] Photographing with available light, Rogala's images convey as sense of motion and flight (see Plates 95 and 96) without a scientific breakdown of individual movement.

We are drawn to the circus by the spectacle, the performance, the animals, the clowns, and a world different from everyday life. The circus makes for exciting photographic content. Dawn Rogala embedded herself with eleven traveling circuses in the 1990s to give us a long-form photographic document of life at the circus. Her archive of materials resides at the National Museum of American History's Archive Center, and the museum's Photographic History Collection retains a print portfolio of eleven of her favorite images, printed to her specifications. Her photograph *Kiss, Carson & Barnes Circus, 1995*, is unlike any other circus image in the museum's collection (Figure 42). There is an ordinariness in the boredom of waiting; the clumps of stiff grass threaten delicate tights; the costumes hang limply on a portable rack; and a gracious privacy is given to the young couple. In this image we are voyeurs of an intimate moment in a life lived in persistently close quarters. Exploring Rogala's photographs gives us a greater appreciation for the individual and collaborative efforts of what it takes—physically, emotionally, and logistically—to put on a show.

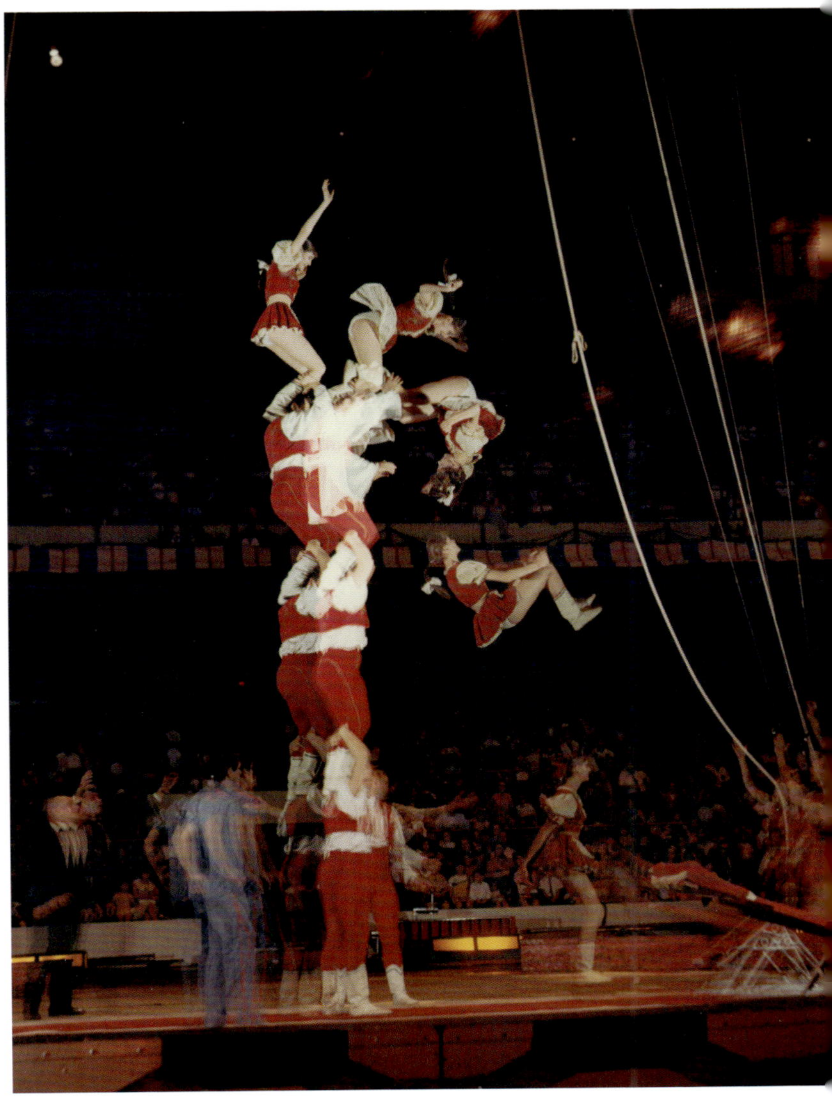

FIGURE 41. *Acrobats*, Harold Edgerton, 1963. Color photograph. NMAH PHC catalog number 68.65.03.

CONCLUSION

Dawn Rogala has captured the "Yankee push" that is a legacy of all the circuses that once traveled the country—and the few that still do so. The persistence and endurance required to put on the same show in town after town—the performances appearing fresh for each audience, even if the shoes, tent, and performers aren't—is part of the ephemeral spectacle recorded in Rogala's photographs. Her work encompasses the legacies of circus history and of those photographers who came before her. Her images are authentic representations of her joy and respect for the circus, even as it fades in our cultural memory. We should not view her images with nostalgia or sadness but rather see them as full of life and vigor. Her aptitude with an economical and portable imaging technology, combined with constant curiosity and openness, has created a substantial archive for us to investigate. As time passes, we will be grateful for the rich and deep archive of materials that Rogala has provided. David Haberstich's essay demonstrates how Rogala's project can be couched in the study of human labor outside of the specificity of her circus-based subject. The National Museum of American History, and the broader Smithsonian, welcomes photography specialists and researchers from many fields to find their own intersections in the Dawn V. Rogala Circus Photographs and Papers beyond the scope we have offered here.

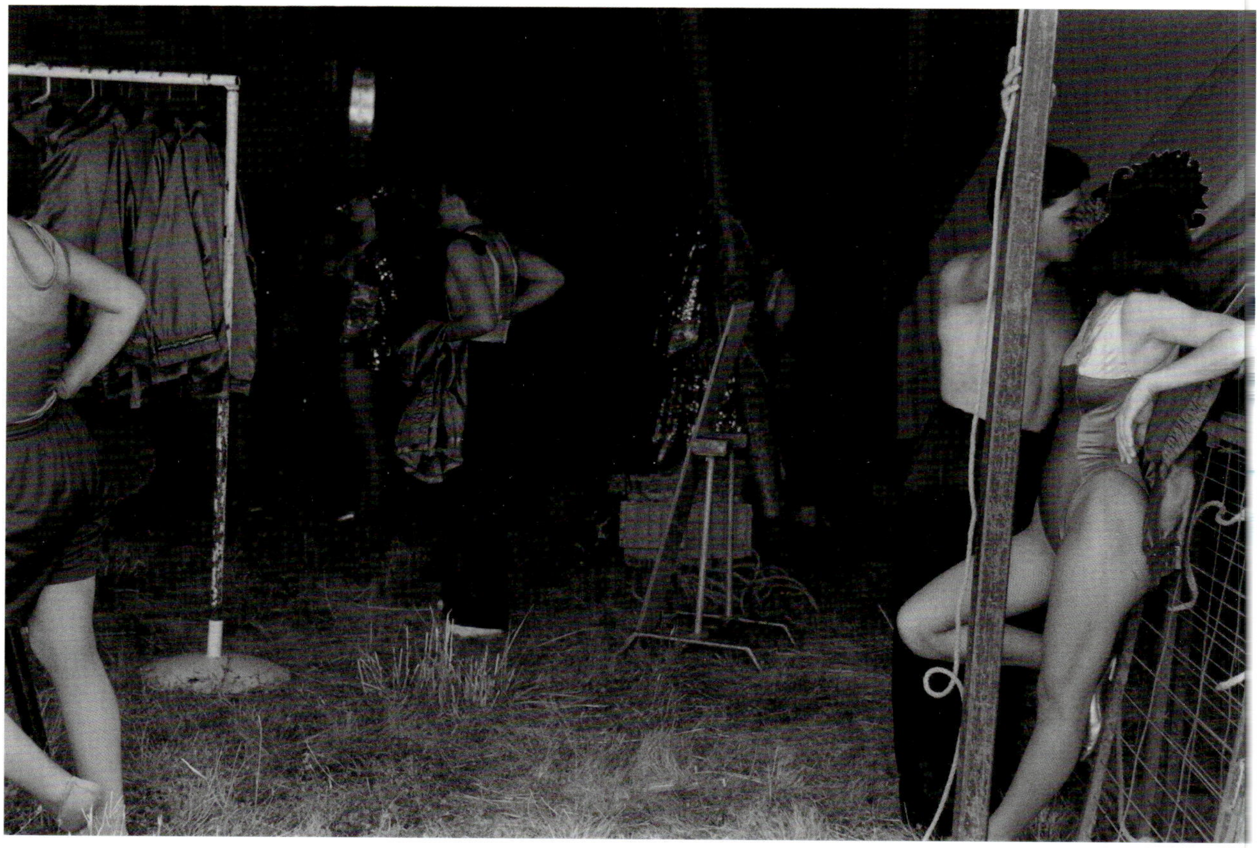

FIGURE 42. *Kiss, Carson & Barnes Circus, 1995*, Dawn Rogala, 1995. Gelatin silver print. NMAH PHC catalog number 2017.0202.0007.

NOTES

1 Mark Irwin, "A Spectrum of Spectators: Circus Audiences in Nineteenth-Century America," *Journal of Social History* 15, no. 2 (Winter 1981): 265.

2 Janet M. Davis. *The Circus Age: Culture and Society under the American Big Top* (Chapel Hill, NC: University of North Carolina Press, 2002), 12.

3 LeRoy Asby, *With Amusement for All: A History of American Popular Culture since 1830* (Lexington: University Press of Kentucky, 2012), 74.

4 Henry Wilhelm and Carol Browe, *The Permanence and Care of Color Photographs: Traditional and Digital Color Prints, Color Negative, Slides, and Motion Pictures* (Grinnell, IA: Preservation Publishing Company, 1993), 284.

5 Beth Gates Warren, *Margrethe Mater and Edward Weston: A Passionate Collaboration* (New York: W. W. Norton & Company, 2001), 26.

6 The author confesses to having worn a clown costume herself. As a young teen in the early 1980s after visiting France and seeing what looked to be moody and cultured posters of Pierrots, she had her mother sew her a Halloween costume. The costume was worn for many years after that while clowning in skits at various youth camps.

7 Alyssa Roenigk, "Trapeze Workouts Soaring in Popularity," April 27, 2011, ESPN Network, http://www.espn.com/espnw/training/workouts/article/6431754/trapeze-workouts-soaring-popularity.

8 "About Us." *The FSU Flying High Circus*, September 30, 2018, https://circus.fsu.edu/about-us.

9 Dawn V. Rogala Circus Photographs and Papers, 1992–1999, Archives Center, National Museum of American History, NMAH.AC.1427.

10 Phineas Taylor Barnum, *Struggles and Triumphs; or Forty Years of Recollections of P. T. Barnum* (Hartford, CT: J. B. Burr & Company, 1869).

11 Barnum, *Struggles and Triumphs*, 281–285.

12 Barnum, *Struggles and Triumphs,* 134.

13 Barnum, *Struggles and Triumphs,* 134.

14 Barnum, *Struggles and Triumphs,* 303.

15 Barnum, *Struggles and Triumphs,* 303.

16 Marc Hartzman, *American Sideshow: An Encyclopedia of History's Most Wondrous and Curiously* (New York: Tarcher-Perigree, 2006), 92.

17 *National Hall!* (Philadelphia PA: US Steam-Power book and Job Printing Office), "Civil War Playbills," Library Company, accession number (25)5761.F.99b (McAllister), September 30, 2018, https://digital.librarycompany.org/islandora/object/Islandora%3A8467.

18 Michael Chemers, *Staging Stigma: A Critical Examination of the Freak Show* (Basingstoke, UK: Palgrave Macmillan, 2008), 4–5.

19 Cassandra Grosh, Sarah Keck, and Isabel Vazquez, "The Life of the Aztec Children," *Digital Literature Review* 3 (2016): 7–18, http://bsuenglish.com/dlrOLD/past/issue3_aztec.pdf.

20 *Facts Relating to the Only Tattooed Lady: Being a Full and Complete Account of the Life Adventures of This Young Lady, the Only Tattoed [sic] Female in the World, Together with Many Extracts from the Metropolitan Press in Reference to Her, All Clearly Proving Her to Be One of the Most Remarkable and Rarest Curiosities Now on Exhibition* (New York: New York, Popular Press, ca. 1886), pamphlet digitized by Beinecke Library, Yale, September 30, 2018, https://brbl-dl.library.yale.edu/pdfgen/exportPDF.php?bibid=2108329&solrid=3445421.

21 Susan Meiselas's photographic project *Carnival Strippers* (1971–1978) must be mentioned as a photographic benchmark. This project to explore the on- and offstage lives of the women revealed complex struggles between choice, empowerment, and struggles for self-esteem and violence among the various men in their lives including audiences, show owners, and family.

22 Florence Albrecht and Emil Albrecht, "May," *The Idle Record of an Idle Summer* (handbound, 1909), 12, transcription by Andrea Hackman, ca. 2007, Photographic History Collection, National Museum of American History, Washington, DC, catalog number PG.77.29 p. 12.

23 Albrecht and Albrecht, "May," 10.

24 Walker Evans Collection, Photographic History Collection, National Museum of American History, Washington, DC, catalog number 69.143.

25 "Steward Recalls Old Railroad Shows," *Billboard*, January 19, 1959, 64.

26 Harold Edgerton, "History of the Strobe," transcript of talk delivered in Room 34-101 Massachusetts Institute for Technology, Boston, MA, for the Electrical Engineering and Computer History Lecture Series on November 27, 1984, https://infinitehistory.mit.edu/video/history-strobe%E2%80%94harold-%E2%80%98doc-edgerton-1984.

Appendix

Dawn V. Rogala Circus Photographs and Papers, 1992–1999

NATIONAL MUSEUM OF AMERICAN HISTORY ARCHIVES CENTER COLLECTION 1427

INTRODUCTION

Smithsonian museums and archives are rich sources of materials related to circuses, carnivals, and circus themes, including paintings, sculptures, and prints in art museums; toys in cultural history collections; and a trove of commercial and advertising imagery, photographs, text documents, and music (both published sheet music and original music manuscripts). In the Archives Center at the Smithsonian's National Museum of American History (NMAH), over a dozen collections include circus-related content. The Billings-Merriam Family Vaudeville Scrapbooks and the P. T. Barnum Collection of scrapbooks and children's books help frame early histories of the circus. The enormous Warshaw Collection of Business Americana has a "Circus" category containing trade cards, advertisements, and other items that help us understand how circus businesses were promoted. Sheet music in the Sam DeVincent Collection of Illustrated American Sheet Music (Series 11: Entertainment) contains songs and imagery both for and about circuses, as does the similar Donald J. Stubblebine Collection of Theater and Motion Picture Music and Ephemera. Photographs related to circus themes are found in the Scurlock Studio Records, which document twentieth-century African American life in Washington, DC. Photographs of circus and carnival bands are can be found in the Duncan P. Schiedt Photograph Collection. The Duke Ellington Collection, with its unique aggregate of original Ellington music manuscripts, includes compositions related to circuses. Even the Carolyn and Donald Grepke Paper Doll Collection includes circus figures, while the Mr. Wizard Papers has the script for a "Science in the Circus" television program. In each of these instances, a historical line might be drawn to some aspect of circus life, business, and history that can be found in the Dawn V. Rogala Collection.

Finding aids (collection guides) for NMAH Archives Center collections and other Smithsonian archival collections may be found in the Smithsonian Online Visual Archives (SOVA) at https://sova.si.edu, a comprehensive integrated platform for catalog database records throughout the Smithsonian provides information about individual items, frequently including images. Find the Collections Search Center in the Smithsonian Institution Research Information System at www.siris.si.edu, or go directly to collections.si.edu. You can locate images and descriptions of original photographs in both the Archives Center and the Photographic History Collection in the Collections Search Center. As an example, the finding aid for the Scurlock Studio Records in SOVA indicates the structure of this vast collection, with descriptions at the folder level to aid in on-site research requests. At the same time, catalog records with images for several thousand individual Scurlock photographs can be found in the Collections Search Center.

Cataloging and digitizing at the Smithsonian is iterative. By the time you read this, many of Dawn Rogala's photographs will be available in the Collections Search Center, and an enriched finding aid will be found in SOVA. The following images and preliminary finding aid will provide a sense of the riches of this collection.

KELLY MILLER 3 RING CIRCUS
AMERICA'S FINEST
FOUNDED IN 1938

P.O. Box 829 Hugo, OK 74743

OFFICIAL 1995 ROUTE CARD

No. 7

SEVENTH WEEK

Saturday	May 6	Leitchfield, KY 42755	60
Sunday	May 7	Elizabethtown, KY 42701	30
Monday	May 8	Campbellsville, KY 42718	42
Tuesday	May 9	Lebanon, KY 40033	20
Wednesday	May 10	Danville, KY 40422	30
Thursday	May 11	Nicholasville, KY 40356	30
Friday	May 12	Cynthiana, KY 41031	60

EIGHTH WEEK

Saturday	May 13	Alexandria, KY 41001	40
Sunday	May 14	Lebanon, OH 45036	54
Monday	May 15	Lebanon, OH 45036	00
Tuesday	May 16	Bellbrook, OH 45305	28
Wednesday	May 17	New Lebanon, OH 45345	25
Thursday	May 18	New Richmond, OH 45157	88
Friday	May 19	Cincinnati, OH 45242	51
	TOTAL MILEAGE		2,345

No Mail Saturdays, Sundays, Holidays or (☆) Above

THE WORLD'S LARGEST CIRCUS
CLYDE BEATTY-COLE BROS. CIRCUS

P.O. Box 127, DeLand, FL. 32721-0127

1995 **OFFICIAL ROUTE** No. 3

DATE		TOWN	STATE		MILES
		Previous Mileage			1826
		SIXTH WEEK			
April	17	Havelock	NC	28532	55
	18	Havelock	NC	28532	
	19	New Bern	NC	28562	15
	20	New Bern	NC	28562	
	21	Burlington	NC	27215	170
	22	Burlington	NC	27215	
	23	Burlington	NC	27215	
		SEVENTH WEEK			
April	24	Hickory	NC	28603	110
	25	Hickory	NC	28603	
	26	Salisbury	NC	28144	65
	27	Salisbury	NC	28144	
	28	Winston-Salem	NC	27102	40
	29	Winston-Salem	NC	27102	
	30	Winston-Salem	NC	27102	
		EIGHTH WEEK			
May	1	Danville	VA	24541	73
	2	Danville	VA	24541	
	3	Lynchburg	VA	24506	60
	4	Lynchburg	VA	24506	
	5-7	Winchester	VA	22601	185
		Total Miles		2599	

FIGURES 43 & 44. Route cards, Kelly Miller Circus and Clyde Beatty-Cole Bros. Circus, 1995.

FOR IMMEDIATE RELEASE

FOR MORE INFO:
LINDA HEATH
(714) 489-7826

THE INTERNATIONAL CAST OF CIRCUS VARGAS - 1994!

***FROM SPAIN - MIGUEL FERRARA,** TIGHT ROPE WALKER.

***FROM ARGENTINA - THE TABARES FAMILY,** ON THE FLYING TRAPEZE.

***FROM BULGARIA - THE ANGELS,** PROPELLING THEMSELVES THROUGH THE AIR FROM THE "RUSSIAN SWING," WHILE PERFORMING GYMNASTIC FEATS OF SKILL.

***FROM THE UNITED STATES - REBECCA PEREZ,** GRACEFUL AERIAL ACROBATICS ON THE SINGLE TRAPEZE.

***FROM GERMANY - MANNY VALDO,** A CIRCUS VARGAS CLOWN THAT RAISES TICKLING THE AUDIENCES FUNNY BONES TO NEW HEIGHTS.

***FROM KENYA - THE BANTU WARRIORS,** AMAZING SKILLS OF FIERY ACROBATICS AND TRIBAL DANCE.

*** FROM DENMARK - THE DUBSKY CANINES,** A CLUSTER OF COMEDIC CANINES CAVORTING AROUND AS SOCCER HOUNDS.

***FROM ENGLAND - TOMMY BAKER,** DASHING AND DEBONAIR THIS RINGMASTER IS SURE TO MAKE ALL THE LADIES SWOON.

***FROM THE PHILIPPINES - THE FAUSTO SCORPIONS,** THIS RISLEY ACT (FOOT JUGGLING) WILL DELIGHT YOU AS THEY PLAYFULLY TOSS THEMSELVES AND MEMBERS OF THE AUDIENCE IN TO THE AIR!

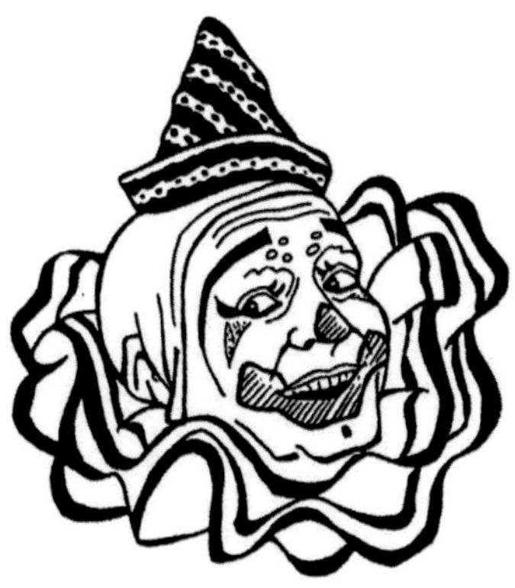

FIGURE 45. Performer list from a press release, Circus Vargas, 1994.

Wynne, AR
Sept. 21,'94

Greetings,

We entered Wynne, ARK following our arrows and some others both taking us toward town. Then there was this post with arrows like these showing, "turn here", a set pointing right, and the others a left turn. We knew that we were "day and dating" Walker Bros. Circus in Wynne but didn't know the loTS were that close. Walker to the right was about a quarter of a mile down the road. Our left turn arrows directed us to a driveway through a mobile home sales lot. Behind these units almost out of sight from the road was our lot. A cop came to the lot and I was told to get a license for the show. $250.00

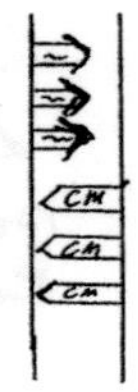

NOW IT'S (Oct. 2, Eagle Lake, TX. I'll finish this tonight or the season will end before you get the last route card)

The lot was $500 aand a health permit $25 plus booking fee $100 and newspaper ads $298. Sponsoring Walker was the Fire Dept. and Walker used phones. Some of our billing was down. It could have been pulled by Walker or the sponsor. It was a cold date for us. We flooded the area with 4000 free kids tickets and had free kids coupons with the newspaper ads. We go up a buck $8 for adults. Kids are the same $5 but with all the free tickets I only sold 32. As we were hid we put a truck at the light signal AND A lettered "CIRCUS" SIGN with a big arrow pointing to our show. A left turn would have sent them to Walker. When I opened I could see Walkers big top a quarter mile away. I took in $1857 and we took any circus ticket. Our concessions did OK but we didn't make the "nut". (A few days ago I took in $4746 on a cold date with free kids tickets) .... There was a lot of visiting between the two shows. I was able to ride around the other show but had no time to visit. They looked pretty good on the lot. Had two elephants but the show lacked the professionalism of ours. I hope you enjoyed reading about this rarity in the business.

As for me I'm feeling pretty good but have the 30th week blahs. Yesterday, (early 2 & 4 PM shows) I planned to finish this letter but after I finished eating and at six pm I laid down just for a few minutes. I woke up at midnight, cleaned the kitchen and back to bed. Season has been good. We left Col. with our best season ever. Then we hit Neb. and West Kan. and lost from one to two thousand dollars a day. Red figured it was an $18,000 loss. And what strange people. I guess they have been marrying cousins for the last hundred years. But our new Big Top ten feet longer and wider has been ordered and paid. Big Tops are custom made and all the cash is up front. It is the same with the new sleeper with showers for the working men. WE ORDERED. TENT $30.000 - GOOD FOR 4YRS.

FIGURE 46. Update memo to main office, Culpepper & Merriweather Circus, September 21, 1994.

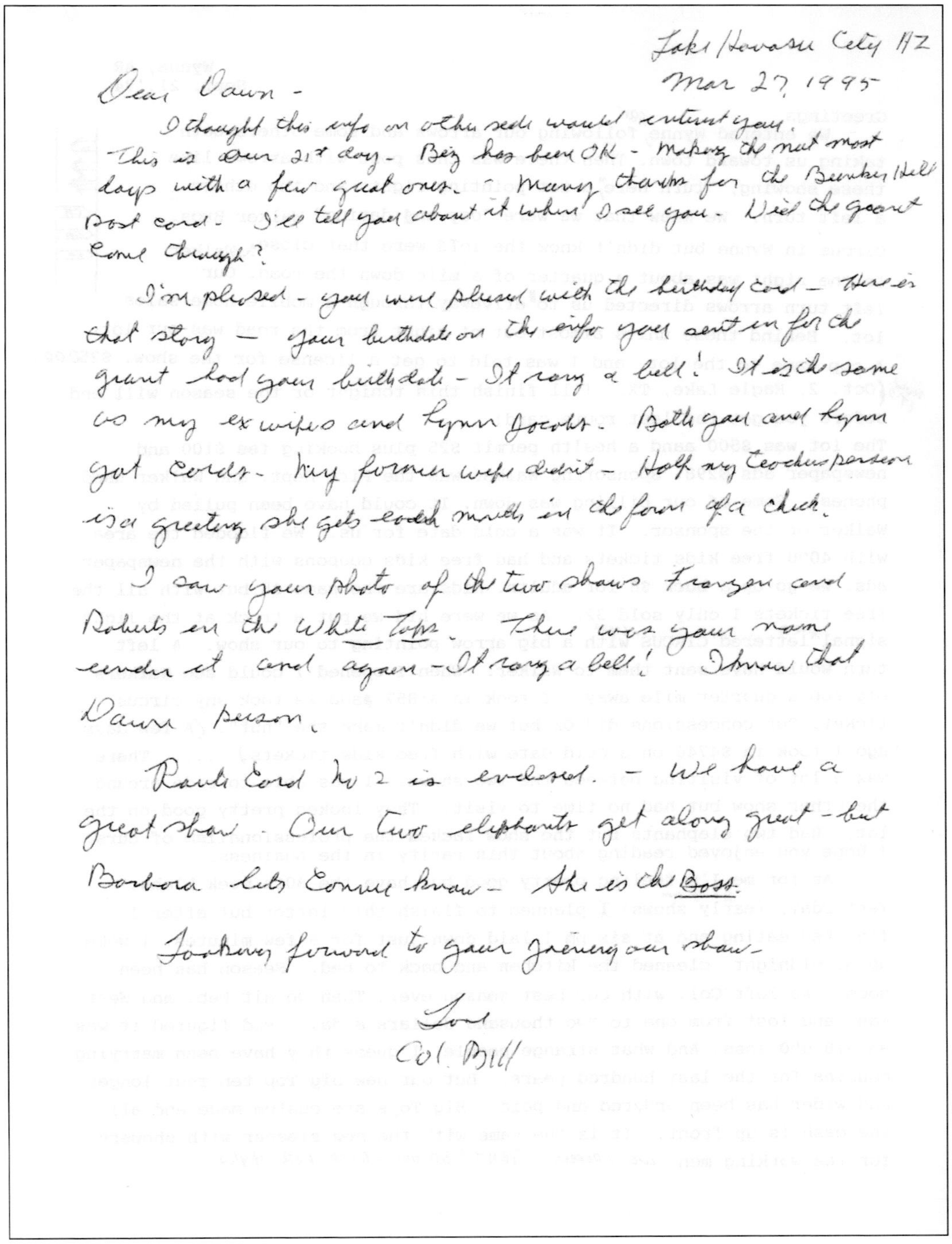

Lake Havasu City AZ
Mar 27, 1995

Dear Dawn -

I thought this info on other side would interest you. This is our 21st day - Biz has been OK - Making the nut most days with a few great ones. Many thanks for the Bunker Hill post card - I'll tell you about it when I see you. Did the grant come through?

I'm pleased - you were pleased with the birthday card - Here is that story - your birthdate on the info you sent in for the grant had your birthdate - It rang a bell! It is the same as my ex wife's and Lynn Jacobs. Both you and Lynn got cards - My former wife didn't - Half my Teamsters pension is a greeting she gets each month in the form of a check.

I saw your photo of the two shows Franzen and Roberts in the White Tops. There was your name under it and again - It rang a bell! I knew that Dawn person.

Route Card No 2 is enclosed. - We have a great show - Our two elephants get along great - but Barbara lets Connie know - She is the Boss.

Looking forward to your joining our show -

Love
Col. Bill

FIGURE 47. Note to Dawn from "Col. Bill," Culpepper & Merriweather Circus, May 27, 1995. This note was written on the back of the update memo in Figure 46.

DAY & DATE	CITY, VENUE, STATE	SHOWTIMES
MON. OCT. 5	KINGMAN, AZ Mohave County Fairgrounds	5:15 & 7:30
TUES. OCT. 6	PRESCOTT, AZ Fairgrounds	5:15 & 7:30
WED. OCT. 7	FLAGSTAFF, AZ Fort Tuthill Park Fairgrounds	5:15 & 7:30
THUR. OCT. 8	LAKE HAVASU CITY, AZ London Bridge Swap Meet Parking Lot	5:15 & 7:30
FRI. OCT. 9	OPEN	
SAT. OCT. 10	HEMET, CA Lot on Florida Ave. between Palm & Gilbert	1:00, 3:30 & 5:30
SUN. OCT. 11	HEMET, CA Lot on Florida Ave. between Palm & Gilbert	1:00, 3:30 & 5:30

— END OF SEASON —

SEPTEMBER

S	M	T	W	T	F	S
		1	2	3	4	5
6	7	8	9	10	11	12
13	14	15	16	17	18	19
20	21	22	23	24	25	26
27	28	29	30			

OCTOBER

S	M	T	W	T	F	S
				1	2	3
4	5	6	7	8	9	10
11	12	13	14	15	16	17
18	19	20	21	22	23	24
25	26	27	28	29	30	31

ROUTE SHEET

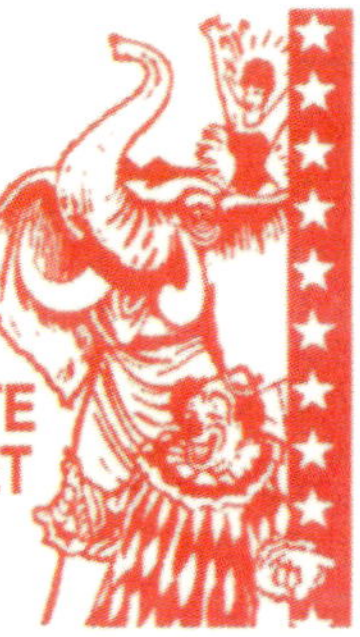

Sterling & Reid Bros. **CIRCUS**

WEEK 31

1998

To Our Circus Family:

Our 1998 tour of STERLING & REID BROS. CIRCUS started in Pasadena, Texas on March 14.

We played 21 states (9 of them twice)

44 - Two day stands 2 - Three day stands 1 - Four day stand
111 - One day stands

We had 3 days open for travel and drove a total of 17,442 miles. We lost one day in Missouri City, Texas due to a storm and changed lots for the next day. We lost one show in San Bernardino, California due to inspectors (our first day in California) and we lost one show and most of another show in West Salem, Wisconsin due to a blowdown.

The season was very successful financially, but most important, we didn't lose any of our circus family.

We look forward to seeing you all back with us in 1999 when we open January 16 in Albany, Georgia.

Enjoy your couple of months off.

Thank you!

Dick Garden & Niles Garden

Please call if you need anything during the winter.

A SPECIAL THANK YOU TO EVERYONE WHO HELPED REPAIR THE TENT... YOU'RE THE BEST!!!

FIGURE 48. End-of-season route card, Sterling & Reid Bros. Circus, 1998.

GUIDE TO THE DAWN V. ROGALA CIRCUS PHOTOGRAPHS AND PAPERS, 1992–1999, NMAH ARCHIVES CENTER COLLECTION 1427

NOTE TO USERS

This preliminary finding aid to the Rogala Collection can be used to identify the portions of the collection the researcher wishes to study. The Archives Center usually makes collection materials available by the box, so you can make your request with just the collection number and box numbers. If you wish to make an appointment to consult this or other collections in the Archives Center at the NMAH, please email archivescenter@si.edu or call 202-633-3270. You may consult an up-to-date version of this finding aid online at https://sova.si.edu/record/NMAH.AC.1427?s=0&n=10&t=C&q=Dawn+Rogala&i=0, since a more detailed version may be available, although box numbers will probably remain the same. Archives Center staff will require researchers to wear protective gloves when handling original photographs.

SUMMARY

Collection ID: NMAH.AC.1427
Creators: Rogala, Dawn V.
Dates: 1992–1999
Languages: English
Physical Description: 4 cubic feet
Repository: *Archives Center, National Museum of American History*

SCOPE AND CONTENTS

The collection, compiled and photographed by Dawn Rogala, documents daily life in traveling, tented circuses in America, including Big Apple Circus, Carson & Barnes Circus, Circus Vargas, Clyde Beatty-Cole Bros. Circus, Culpepper & Merriweather Circus, Franzen Brothers Circus, Kelly Miller Circus, Roberts Bros. Circus, Sterling & Reid Bros. Circus, Vidbel's Olde Tyme Circus, and Walker Bros. Circus. The collection consists of original photographic materials, such as color slides; color and black-and-white prints and negatives; and color transparencies, as well as low-resolution versions of the photographs and xerographic copies. It also includes Rogala's project files containing schedules, programs, notes, correspondence, pictures of her on the road, and so on, as well as transcriptions of interviews that Rogala conducted. In addition, there are publications such as magazines containing articles about circuses and circus life, programs, and brochures, as well as ephemera that Rogala collected during her days in the circuses.

ARRANGEMENT

1 series. The arrangement is largely the photographer's own, with minimal modifications, reflecting the way she worked.

Biographical / Historical Information

Now a paintings conservator and program manager for the Museum Conservation Institute at the Smithsonian Institution, Dawn Rogala photographed every tented, full-time American circus that traveled at least eight months of every year between the years 1992 and 1998. She photographed not only the performances but also the behind-the-scenes activities of setting up and breaking down, and activities such as animal care (especially elephants), costuming, makeup, and everyday life in the circuses during their time on the road. She received a BFA degree from Boston University, an MA from Buffalo State College, and a PhD from the University of Delaware. She is the author of *Hans Hofmann: The Artist's Materials* (Los Angeles: Getty Conservation Institute, 2016) as well as many professional papers. She is a Fellow of the American Institute for Conservation and the International Institute for Conservation.

Using the Collection

Preferred Citation: Dawn V. Rogala Circus Photographs and Papers, 1992–1999, Archives Center, National Museum of American History.

Conditions Governing Use

Reproduction restricted due to copyright or trademark. Photographer retains copyright during her lifetime.

Conditions Governing Access

Collection is open for research. Protective gloves must be worn while handling original photographs.

CONTAINER LIST

BOXES 1–3: Black-and-white negatives, color transparencies and negatives, contact sheets and contact proof prints; primarily 35mm, some medium format

Materials organized by circus, in individual archival binders. Binders include contact sheets, with various marking related to selection for printing. Some contact sheets include notes on back related to printing.

Box 1	Binder 1	Big Apple Circus, 1992–1994: color slides and transparencies; also color negatives and black-and-white prints
1	Binder 2	Big Apple Circus, 1992–1994: black-and-white negatives, primarily 35mm, with contact sheets and some enlargements
1	Binder 3	Big Apple Circus, 1995: color slides and transparencies
1	Binder 4	Big Apple Circus, 1995: black-and-white negatives, with contact sheets
Box 2	Binder 1	Carson & Barnes Circus, 1995: color slides, black-and-white negatives, contact sheets
2	Binder 2	Circus Vargas, 1998; Sterling & Reid Bros. Circus, 1998: black-and-white negatives and contact sheets, color slides
2	Binder 3	Clyde Beatty-Cole Bros. Circus, 1995: black-and-white negatives and contact sheets, color slides
2	Binder 4	Culpepper & Merriweather Circus, 1996: black-and-white negatives and contact sheets, color slides
Box 3	Binder 1	Franzen Brothers Circus, 1994, 1996: black-and-white negatives and contact sheets, color slides
3	Binder 2	Kelly Miller Circus, 1995: black-and-white negatives and contact sheets, color slides
3	Binder 3	Vidbel's Olde Tyme Circus, 1993; Roberts Bros. Circus, 1994: black-and-white negatives and contact sheets, color slides; some Roberts Bros. Circus images include Franzen Brothers Circus (from a shared lot)
3	Binder 4	Walker Bros. Circus, 1995: black-and-white negatives and contact sheets, color slides

BOX 4: Xerographic prints of color transparencies and black-and-white contact sheets from Boxes 1-3; includes notes on back of contact sheets

BOX 5: Low-resolution xerographic prints; selected images from each circus, arranged into bound collections according to circus

Box 5	Binder 1	Big Apple Circus, 1992–1994
5	Binder 2	Big Apple Circus, 1995
5	Binder 3	Franzen Brothers Circus, 1994, 1996
5	Binder 4	Vidbel's Old Tyme Circus, 1993; Roberts Bros. Circus, 1994
5	Binder 5	Carson & Barnes Circus, 1995
5	Binder 6	Clyde Beatty-Cole Bros. Circus, 1995
5	Binder 7	Kelly Miller Circus, 1995
5	Binder 8	Walker Bros. Circus, 1995
5	Binder 9	Culpepper & Merriweather Circus, 1996
5	Binder 10	Circus Vargas, 1998; Sterling & Reid Bros. Circus, 1998

BOX 6: Transcripts of interviews by Dawn Rogala		
Box 6	Folder 1	Selection of unedited interviews, includes notes and editor's questions, c. 2005
6	Folder 2	Selection of edited interviews, includes notes regarding thematic groups, c. 2005
INTERVIEWS WITH:		Angel, midway worker (snakes and other animals), Sterling and Reid Bros. Circus (1998)
		Paul Binder, co-founder and artistic director, Big Apple Circus (1995)
		Katherine Schumann Binder (10 years old), performing company member (and daughter of Paul Binder and Katja Schumann), Big Apple Circus (1995)
		Bill Brickle, ringmaster and animal trainer (dogs), Walker Bros. Circus (1995)
		Barbara Byrd, director and co-owner, daughter of D. R. Miller, Carson & Barnes Circus (1995)
		Al Calienes, performing company member, Big Apple Circus (1995)
		Martín Espana, performer and tent boss, Sterling and Reid Bros. Circus (1998)
		Doady Fornasari, performer (and ringmaster's father), Circus Vargas (1998)
		Jimmy James, performance director and ringmaster, Clyde Beatty-Cole Bros. Circus (1995)
		Jerry, "24-hour man," Carson & Barnes Circus (1995)
		Jim Judkins, vice-president (and owner of midway snakes), Carson & Barnes Circus (1995)
		J. R. Lara, house crew, Big Apple Circus (1995)
		David LeBlanc, director of operations and tent boss, Big Apple Circus (1995)
		Reginald "Reggie" Lindsey, Sr., exotic animal handler, Carson & Barnes Circus (1995)
		Barry Lubin, performing company member ("Grandma"), Big Apple Circus (1995)
		Eli Milcheva, performing company member, Big Apple Circus (1995)
		Jim Moran, assistant ring crew chief, Big Apple Circus (1995)
		John Moss, ringmaster, Carson & Barnes Circus (1995)
		Tuffy Nicholas, lot boss, Sterling & Reid Bros. Circus (1998)
		Lucio Nicolodi, acrobatics trainer, Big Apple Circus (1995)
		Denise Loyal Pickup, production office, Big Apple Circus (1995)
		Guy Pickup, assistant tent manager, Big Apple Circus (1995)
		Graham Polakovs, performer, Walker Bros. Circus (1995)
		Rambo, Mechanic, Carson & Barnes Circus (1995)
		Armando Rosales, bareback rider, with Peter Coolidge and Megan Murray (daughter of lot manager), midway and concessions and horses, Carson & Barnes Circus (1995)
		Tim and Gigi Tegge, performers, Clyde Beatty-Cole Bros. Circus (1995)
		Alice Walker, owner's mother, Walker Bros. Circus (1995)
		Laura Herriot Walker, performer and horse trainer, Carson & Barnes Circus (1995)
		Unidentified man, horse groom, Carson & Barnes Circus (1995)
		Unidentified man, Sterling & Reid Bros. Circus (1998)

BOX 7: Early organization of materials for book proposals

Box 7	Folder 1	Selection of xerographic prints with thematic groupings, c. 2005
7	Folder 2	Sample book layout, c. 2000

BOX 8: Miscellaneous ephemera: Publications, programs, documents, model releases, contracts, correspondence, advertising, route cards, notes, and memorabilia; arranged by circus

Box 8	Folder 1	Big Apple Circus
8	Folder 2	Carson & Barnes Circus
8	Folder 3	Circus Flora (not part of documentary group)
8	Folder 4	Circus Vargas
8	Folder 5	Cirque du Soleil (not part of documentary group)
8	Folder 6	Clyde Beatty-Cole Bros. Circus
8	Folder 7	Culpepper & Merriweather Circus
8	Folder 8	Franzen Brothers Circus
8	Folder 9	Kelly Miller Circus
8	Folder 10	Roberts Bros. Circus
8	Folder 11	Royal Hanneford Circus (not part of documentary group)
8	Folder 12	Sterling & Reid Bros. Circus
8	Folder 13	Vidbel's Olde Tyme Circus
8	Folder 14	Walker Bros. Circus
8	Folder 15	Miscellaneous circus publications

BOX 9: Miscellaneous materials related to travel: Publications, programs, documents, contracts, correspondence, advertising, memorabilia, ephemera, and snapshots

Box 9	Folder 1	Notes regarding circus contact information and selection of circuses for travel, notes regarding visits to circus winter quarters to obtain travel permission, example of model release used by other photographers, and miscellaneous (Polaroids of RV used for some travel, greeting cards, etc.)
9	Folder 2	Notes regarding personal expenses (film, travel) for project, final tally of rolls of film (color and black-and-white) used for each circus
9	Folder 3	Xerographic copies of page spreads from circus book used as reference during early preparation of book proposals, materials from early book proposals, and transcribed notes taken while on the road
9	Folder 4	Lists of images to print as 'thank you's for each show; lists are in a notebook that also includes notes from photography classes taken after travel was complete
9	Folder 5	Snapshots of Rogala during travels, 4″ × 6″ color prints and 35mm color negatives; letter regarding publication of an image in White Tops magazine (1994); announcements for SoHo Arts Festival exhibition (1996)

BOX 10: Photographic proof prints: Unmounted, various sizes, black-and-white and color, unsigned and uncaptioned; includes duplicates

Box 10	Folder 1	Black-and-white proof prints, 8" × 10" and 11" × 14", some on double-weight paper
10	Folder 2	Color proof prints, various sizes, some Cibachrome

BOX 11: Portable hard drive: High-resolution scans of all negatives and slides, and transcribed interviews (unedited and edited); digital image files include metadata

Acknowledgments

This book is part of a long-term project to preserve a piece of America's cultural heritage for future generations, and the scope of this endeavor reflects the collaborative efforts of many people and institutions. The creation of the Dawn V. Rogala Circus Photographs and Papers at the National Museum of American History (NMAH) Archives Center and the related print portfolio in the NMAH Photographic History Collection would not have been possible without the support of people at the Smithsonian Institution and beyond. We thank our colleagues throughout the Smithsonian, with special thanks going to those listed below. The exclusion of any names is an unintentional oversight and in no way lessens any individual's role in this project or our gratitude for his or her invaluable assistance.

National Museum of American History: Anthea Hartig, Elizabeth MacMillan Director; Catherine Eagleton, former Associate Director, Office of Curatorial Affairs; Robert Horton, Assistant Director for Collections and Archives, and Chair of the Archives Center; Laura Duff, Film and Media Manager; Sarah Oakman, Collections Specialist, Division of Work and Industry; Katherine Ott, Curator, Division of Medicine and Science; Helena Wright, Curator, Division of Work and Industry; Kira Leinwand, Smith College intern. National Museum of Natural History: James Di Loreto, Branch Chief, Office of Photography and Media; Kristen Quarles, Digital Collections Specialist. Smithsonian Center for Folklife and Cultural Heritage: James Deutsch, Curator; Robert Leopold, Deputy Director of Research and Collections; Sabrina Lyn Motley, Folklife Festival Director; Preston Scott, 2017 Folklife Festival Curator; Marissa Walker, 2017 Folklife Festival Coordinator. Smithsonian's Museum Conservation Institute: Robert Koestler, Director; Paula DePriest, Deputy Director; Jessica Johnson, Head of Conservation.

This publication would not exist without the support and hard work of many people. Our sincere thanks go to Ginger Minkiewicz, Director of the Smithsonian Institution Scholarly Press; to Julie Allred and Beth Mauldin at BW&A Books, and to the staff of Friesens Corporation; your talent and passion are reflected in this book. We also thank writer and editor Diana Stoll, who was an early believer in this project, and the peer reviewers and editors whose comments and suggestions helped bring the circus to life in these pages.

The images that appear in this publication are the result of unprecedented access to information and people, and years of work by many organizations and individuals. Dawn would like to thank the members of the Big Apple Circus (BAC), who were the first to put their faith in her, and to thank the staff, performers, and management of Carson & Barnes Circus (CB), Circus Vargas (CV), Clyde Beatty-Cole Bros. Circus (CBCB), Culpepper & Merriweather Circus (CM), Franzen Brothers Circus (FBC), Kelly Miller Circus (KM), Roberts Bros. Circus (RB), Sterling & Reid Bros. Circus (SR), Vidbel's Olde Tyme Circus (VC), and Walker Bros. Circus (WB). Dawn's thanks also go out to those named below—a fraction of the people who were instrumental in supporting this project and her work. She hopes they enjoy this book. BAC: Paul Binder and Katja Schumann, Lucio Nicolodi, Al Calienes, Doc, Shawn and Wes Hansen, Vanessa Thomas, Jeff Gordon, Carol and Dave LeBlanc, Guy Pickup and Denise Loyal Pickup, Willie and Edward in the cookhouse, Fred Smith, Tym, Andrew. CB: D. R. Miller, Barbara Byrd, Jim Judkins, Reggie (Reginald Lindsay, Sr.), Laura and Jason and Jennifer Herriott, Rambo (Rod Johnson Sr.), Okie Carr, Raymond L. Triggs, Jerry. CM: Red Johnson, Colonel Bill (Bill Burger), Heidi and Spider, Kelly and Alison and Casey, Lauren and Bobby Fairchild. KM: D. R. Miller and Barbara Byrd (again), Zippo and Skippy and Joe, David and Carol Rawls, Bill and Jody Rawls, Buddy and Jaime, Willy, Cindy and Roy Wells, Heidi and Chris and Ike the duck, and Analia, Damion, Alexandra, and Mario Galarreta. RB: Bill Schreiber, Ken Dennis, Bobby and Jeff and Doris Earl. VC: Alan Meredith. CV: Doady Fornasari, Roland Kaiser. SR: Tuffy Nicholas, the Galarreta family (again), Dick Garden, Tanya Herrmann, Brian Franzen. CBCB: Tim and Gigi Tegge, Jimmy James, Khristopher Glen Allen, Brian and Laura, Wizard (Bob), Catmandoo (John), Pops and Yoko and Charlie in the cookhouse, Fred Logan, Gene, Colleen, JP Cunningham and Charlie Harris, John W. Pugh. FB: Wayne Franzen, Ryan, the Galarretas (again), Natalie. WB: Johnny Walker, Catia Meluzzi, John Jr., Jerry and Alice Walker, Graham and Dave, Mike Donahoe and Tanya Herrmann (again), Lauren and Bobby Fairchild (again), Bill Brickle, Popcorn John, Curly, Jim, Jeremy, Kitty, and Antonette. And Dan and Andrew, who rode shotgun. Thank you all.

Plates by Show Name

Index

Page locators in **boldface type** indicate figures.

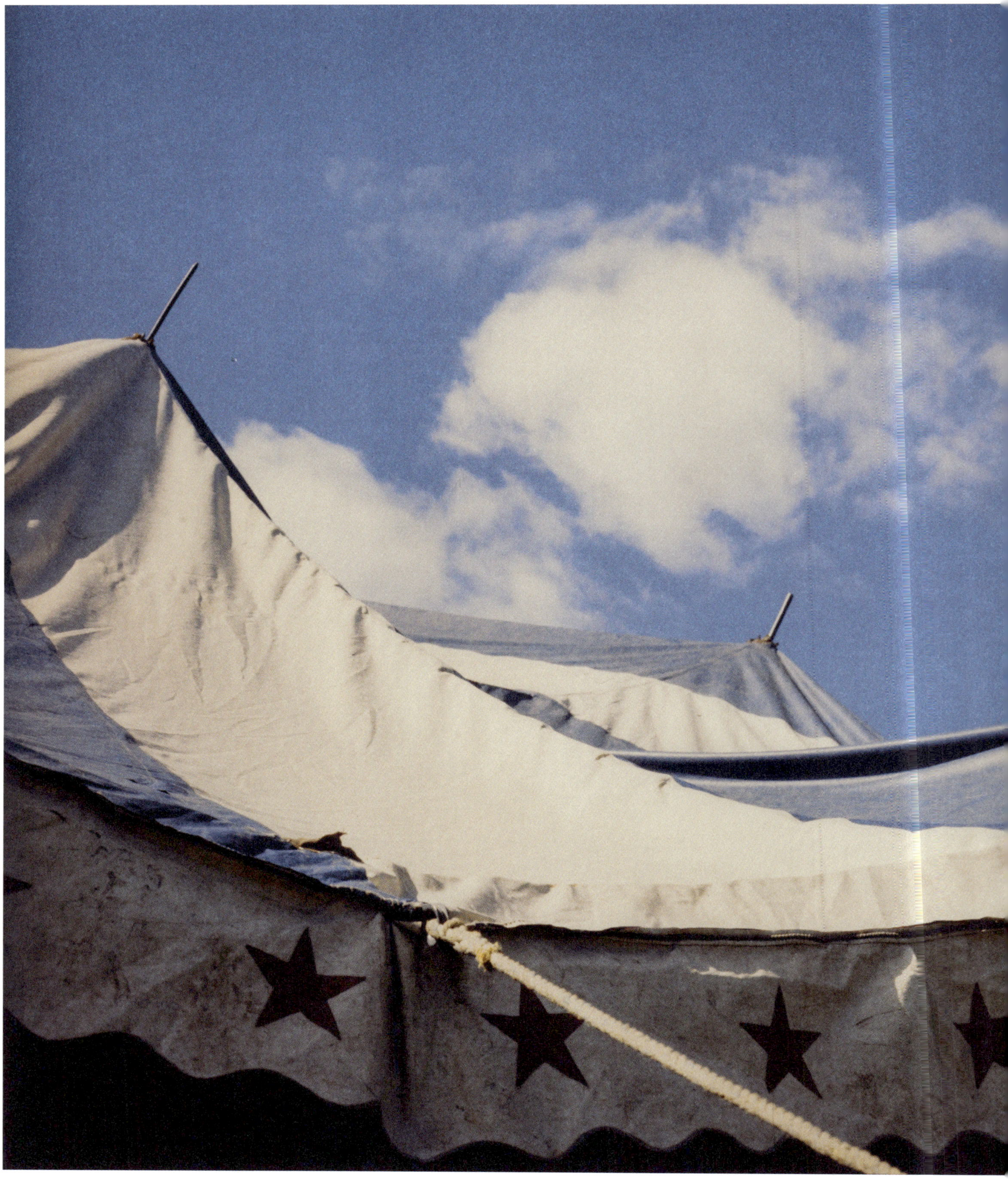